"Chris Bennett strikes again! In his latest tome, he examines the latest incontrovertible evidence of cannabis usage in the sacred Jewish rites at Arad and integrates those into his examination of this holy herb as foundational to various contemporary faiths. A provocative read, to be sure."

– Dr. Ethan Russo, author of *Cannabis and Cannabinoids: Pharmacology, Toxicology, and Therapeutic Potential*

"Chris Bennett's latest offering, *Cannabis: Lost Sacrament of the Ancient World,* is by far his most focused work to date. Building on the formidable research presented in his previous efforts, Cannabis goes even further in demonstrating that hashish, without a doubt, played an important role in the religious life of the ancient Hebrews. The final nail in the coffin of the Kaneh Bosm debate, Bennett's scholarly book challenges everything we thought we knew about both Judaism and ancient cannabis use."

– P.D. Newman, author of *Theurgy: Theory and Practice: The Mysteries of the Ascent to the Divine*

"Chris Bennett's *Cannabis: Lost Sacrament of the Ancient World* draws together scholarly and archaeological evidence for the use of cannabis in ancient magico-religious practices in a balanced, comprehensive and accessible manner. In particular Bennett explores the influence of cannabis, and cannabis occasioned altered states of consciousness, on the Judeo-Christian traditions, especially its role in facilitating a sense of communion with the divine. This book is essential reading for anyone interested in exploring the entheogenic roots of religions."

– Dr. Jack Hunter, author of *Spirits, Gods and Magic: An Introduction to the Anthropology of the Supernatural*

"Bennett gives us another tour de force of the deep history of Cannabis, spanning diverse societies of the Ancient Middle East. The scope of cannabis ritualization in the past elevates its current status as a perennial sacrament. Bennett totally revises the notion of what were the "Burning Times."

– Dr. Michael J. Winkelman, Editor of *Advances in Psychedelic Medicine*

"...One of the world's leading cannabis scholars and historians, Chris Bennett continues to expand on this body of knowledge in this, his fifth, book. *Cannabis: Lost Sacrament of the Ancients* ... a fascinating read and of great value to anyone who wants to know more about how intimately cannabis has travelled with and benefited humanity since time immeasurable."

– Stephen Gray, Editor/contributor, *Cannabis and Spirituality: An Explorer's Guide to an Ancient Plant Spirit Ally.*

"Chris Bennett has been easily the most important scholar of cannabis ... [he] has done the research to confidently argue, and maybe even prove that yes Virginia, the original tree of Life and the true Haoma/Soma of the Vedas and the Zoroasterae was Cannabis Sativa specifically."

– Yoseph Leib Ibn Mardachya, *Cannabis Chassidis: The Ancient and Emerging Torah of Drugs*

"Chris Bennett's latest book is an impressive, scholarly account of the little-known role of cannabis as a religious sacrament in the ancient Near East and Middle East. Marshaling an extensive array of archeological and literary sources, Bennett documents how the embrace of One Almighty God led to the displacement of cannabis, the polytheistic drug of choice, as a ceremonial substance in ancient Israel."

– Martin A. Lee, author of *Smoke Signals* and *Acid Dreams*

CANNABIS
Lost Sacrament of the Ancient World

CHRIS BENNETT
Author of *Liber 420*

"Chris Bennett ... explores the role of cannabis and consciousness in a groundbreaking original work."

Published by:
Trine Day LLC
PO Box 577
Walterville, OR 97489
1-800-556-2012
www.TrineDay.com
TrineDay@icloud.com

Library of Congress Control Number: 2023933384

Bennett, Chris.
–1st ed.
p. cm.

Cloth (ISBN-13) 978-1-63424-397-1
Epub (ISBN-13) 978-1-63424-399-5
Trade Paperback (ISBN-13) 9978-1-63424-398-8
1. Cannabis -- History. 2. Cannabis -- Religious aspects. 3. Drugs -- Religious aspects -- History 4. Hebrew Bible -- History. 5. Christianity -- History. 6. Gnosticism -- History. I. Bennett, Chris. II. Title

First Edition
10 9 8 7 6 5 4 3 2 1

Keneh Press is an imprint of TrineDay

Printed in the USA
Distribution to the Trade by:
Independent Publishers Group (IPG)
814 North Franklin Street
Chicago, Illinois 60610
312.337.0747
www.ipgbook.com

Publisher's Foreword

Well, they'll stone you when you're trying to be so good
They'll stone you just like they said they would
They'll stone you when you're trying to go home
And they'll stone you when you're there all alone
But I would not feel so all alone
Everybody must get stoned
...
Well, they'll stone you when you walk all alone
They'll stone you when you are walking home
They'll stone you and then say you are brave
They'll stone you when you are set down in your grave
But I would not feel so all alone
Everybody must get stoned
– Bob Dylan, *Rainy Day Women #12 & 35*

Marijuana, grass, weed, reefer, pot, ganja, boo, pakalolo ... are just a few of the slang terms for Cannabis. A plant that has a long, long relationship with mankind. One that has been hidden – mostly purposely – by entrenched power-brokers, especially recently, but the obfuscation truly began some millenniums ago.

Chris Bennett has been doing the heavy lifting on this subject for years, and for his trouble he has been pilloried by many and given accolades by a few. *It's never easy to plow new ground.*

TrineDay is proud and honored to publish his works.

I first came across marijuana in a matchbox from a friend in 1966 – a sign of the times – and then watched and participated in the creation of a counter-culture that has cannabis as one of its "sacraments." It took awhile, but I soon understood that my relationship with this plant was more than simply getting high (stoned) – there was something else there. What it was I had no idea, first I started looking at the medical values. I found that cannabis helped to keep the body's phlegm expectorant system functioning properly, which allows contaminants to leave the body. That seemed, and still seems, beneficial considering the polluted world we live in. Later I met Jack Herer and read his book, *The Emperor Wears No Clothes,* which helped to explain the prohibition that had made no sense to me. In the late sixties, I had been solicited by our local police to speak to other young folks about "pot," during the talk I made the comment that the laws against marijuana were more of a problem than the herb itself. *I wasn't asked again.*

I worked hard for legalization: organizing marches, writing letters, producing and speaking at hempfests, and testifying to government bodies.

Cannabis is wonderfully useful. It is one of the world's oldest cultivated plants. The Tamang people living high in the Himalayas use hemp for most everything: food, fodder, fiber and medicine. They weave ropes, cloth, baskets and even huge panels that are used for shelters.

Growing up, I was hauled off to church and Sunday school, and took the tales and lessons as they were told, and didn't think too much about the backstories. At 19, after reading *Lead Kindly Light* about Mohandas Gandhi, I became interested in vegetarianism, and remembering the prescribed sacrifice of two turtledoves after the birth of Jesus; I read deep in the Bible to try and understand how come we didn't sacrifice animals anymore. Coming across the "burning bush" and smoky tabernacles in the Bible caused me to wonder: *Could the Bible be talking about marijuana?*

Those thoughts became more than simply lingering questions after I came across Chris Bennett's book *Green Gold the Tree of Life: Marijuana in Magic and Religion,* and expanded with his *Sex, Drugs, Violence and the Bible*. Now with *Cannabis: Lost Sacrament Of The Ancient World* he definitely answers the questions ... and shows that he has been correct all along.

I'm one toke over the line, sweet Jesus
One toke over the line
Sitting downtown in a railway station
One toke over the line
Don't you know I'm just waiting for the train that goes home, sweet Mary
Hoping that the train is on time
Sitting downtown in a railway station
One toke over the line
– Brewer & Shipley, *One Toke Over the Line*

Onward to the Utmost of Futures,
Peace,
R.A. Kris Millegan
Publisher
TrineDay
April 20, 2023

Dedicated to Sula Benet (1903-1982)

Special thanks to my partner Celina, for her love and support throughout writing this book, Neil McQueen, as I could not present this case without the research we compiled for 'Sex, Drugs, Violence and the Bible (2001) Ariel Rozemberg and Ed Dodge author of "A History of the Goddess: from the Ice Age to the Bible" for research assistance and discussions and my publisher TrineDay for taking the risk on publishing my controversial books.

Contents

Dedication v
Acknowledgments v

Introduction 1
1) Cannabis Incense at Tel Arad… 9
2) The Wife of God 34
3) The Lost Word: Kaneh Bosm 73
4) Alternative Etymologies 104
5) Poly-Yahwism and Biblical Monotheism 114
6) Kaneh Bosm and The Holy Anointing Oil 127
7) Solomon and the Song of Songs 140
8) The Smoke of the Prophets… 177
9) The "Lost" Book Of The Law 189
10) The Babylonian Exile 221
11) The Persians 227
12) Ezra and the "Cup of Fire" 280
13) Drug Infused Wines and Strong Drink in the Ancient World 298
14) Taking Back Eden 327
15) Garden of Eden Redux 388
Conclusions 403

Appendix I: On Indications Of The Hachish-Vice In The Old Testament 423
Appendix II: Shemshemet, Cannabis in Ancient Egypt 436
Appendix III: "Cannabis is in the Bible?" 445
Appendix IV: Professor Zohar Amar on tel Arad and Kaneh Bosm... 448

Index 451

Bibliography 463

Introduction

Writing this book in Canada, where adults can freely purchase and consume cannabis, it's easy to forget that in much of the rest of the world, cannabis is illegal, in many areas with severe penalties. Having been a cannabis activist for over three decades, pushing for the legalization of hemp, then medical cannabis and finally recreational legalization, it was actually quite astonishing how quickly legal cannabis became normalized here. Adults of all ages enjoy cannabis and buy it in amounts that would see them jailed for years in some countries. Moreover, all the warnings of the naysayers against legalization, have been exposed for the mean spirited, unscientific, control trip that they were, and still are in many countries. That a plant so useful as cannabis, and which has been with us so long, should be outlawed, is the real crime.

Ironically, the prohibition of cannabis has in many ways increased the interest around the plant, and turned it into an international symbol of natural rights and freedoms. Like Adam and Eve who could not resist the temptation of the "forbidden fruit" in that first Garden, since the first Laws were enacted against the "Devil's Weed" by the Authorities in North America, people have ignored the warnings of dire consequence, and listened to the "Vipers" who offered it to them.

Generally, when people think about the history of cannabis' use, they don't go much further back than the Jazz Age, and the era of "Reefer Madness." This was a time when cannabis use was being popularized in the multi-racial Jazz scene. The social mixing of the races was seen as a threat to society from a country that had only emerged from slavery less than a century before, and the government spent tax dollars on racist propaganda which decried the use of "marihuana" and had it outlawed. However, this was far from the beginning of Humanity's relationship with this plant.

Few people realize the thousands of connections to this fabulous multi-use plant, reaches back tens of thousands of years. Cannabis played a pivotal role in the ancient world, that is only paralleled by the controversial role it plays today. This is my fifth book.[1] In some

1 Earlier works include: *Green Gold the Tree of Life: Marijuana in Magic and Religion*

ways this is a recap and compilation of much of that research, in light of some exciting new archaeological material that has arisen, and validates much of what I had been suggesting over the last three decades. For those who are familiar already with my work in this area, fear not, there is lots of new material here as well.

The role of cannabis in the ancient world was manifold: with its nutritious seeds, an important food; with its long, pliable strong stalks an important fiber, as well as an early medicine from its leaves and flowers, and then there are its psychoactive effects.... Due to its usefulness, Cannabis has a very long history of human cultivation. How long exactly, remains unknown.

There has also been interesting scientific speculation that the psychoactive properties of cannabis may have played a role as a catalyst in the time period of advancement for prehistoric humanity that is known as the "Great Leap Forward," which started about 65,000 to 50,000 years ago. It is suggested that cannabis may have enabled our prehistoric ancestors with novel new thought processes that aided in the development of tool making and other skills. Professor John McPartland and Dr. Geoffery Guy, in their fascinating paper, "The Evolution of Cannabis and Co-evolution with the Cannabis Receptor – A Hypothesis," postulate that a plant ligand, such as the cannabinoids of the hemp plant, which interact with the human body's endocannabinoid system, "may exert sufficient selection pressure to maintain the gene for a receptor in an animal. If the plant ligand improves the fitness of the receptor by serving as a 'proto-medicine' or a performance-enhancing substance, the ligand-receptor association could be evolutionarily conserved" (McPartland & Guy, 2004).

McPartland and Guy are suggesting a co-evolutionary relationship between "Man and Marijuana," and have indicated that somehow as we have cultivated cannabis – it may have cultivated us. Cannabis affects us through its similarity to certain chemicals that are natural in the human body and their receptor sites. Through the discovery and study of cannabinoids, science has unveiled the endocannabinoid system (ECS). "The ECS is critical for almost every aspect of our moment-to-moment functioning. The ECS regulates and controls many of our most critical bodily functions such as learning and memory, emotional processing, sleep, temperature control, pain

(1995) with Lynn and Judy Osburn; *Sex, Drugs, Violence and the Bible* (2001) with Neil McQueen; *Cannabis and the Soma Solution* (2010); and *Liber 420: Cannabis, Magickal Herbs and the Occult* (2018). I have also contributed chapters on the historical role of cannabis in spiritual practices in *Psychedelics Reimagined* (1999); *The Pot Book* (2010); *Entheogens and the Development of Culture* (2013); *Seeking the Sacred with Psychoactive Substances* (2014); *Cannabis and Spirituality* (2016); and *One Toke Closer to God* (2017).

control, inflammatory and immune responses, and eating. The ECS is currently at the center of renewed international research and drug development" (Grinspoon, 2021). McPartland and Guy explain how ingestion of this plant may have aided prehistoric humans:

> In a hunter-gatherer society, the ability of phytocannabinoids to improve smell, night vision, discern edge and enhance perception of color would improve evolutionary fitness of our species. Evolutionary fitness essentially mirrors reproductive success, and phytocannabinoids enhance the sensation of touch and the sense of rhythm, two sensual responses that may lead to increased replication rates.
>
> Some authors have proposed that cannabis was the catalyst that synergised the emergence of syntactic language in Neolithic humans (McKenna, 1992). Language, in turn, probably caused what anthropologists call "the great leap forward" in human behavior, when humans suddenly crafted better tools out of new materials (e.g. fishhooks from bone, spear handles from wood, rope from hemp), developed art (e.g. painting, pottery, musical instruments), began using boats, and evolved intricate social (and religious) organizations. This rather abrupt transformation occurred about 50,000 years ago… this recent burst of human evolution has been described as epigenetic (beyond our genes) – could it be due to the effect of plant ligands [i.e. plant based cannibinoids]? (McPartland & Guy, 2004).

It can be reasonably suggested that soon after agriculture started, if not at its very inception, the cultivation of cannabis began to spread widely, carrying its name and its cult with it. In his study on the botanical history of cannabis and man's relationship with the plant, Mark Merlin, Professor of Botany at University of Hawaii , put forth that "perhaps hemp was one of the original cultivated plants … [of] the progenitors of civilization" (Merlin, 1973). Merlin was not alone in this train of thought. In *The Dragons of Eden: Speculations on the Evolution of Human Intelligence,* the late Carl Sagan also speculated that early man may have begun the agricultural age by first planting hemp. Sagan, who was known to have a fondness for cannabis himself, used the pygmies from southwest Africa to demonstrate his hypothesis, the pygmies had been basically hunters and gatherers until they began planting hemp which they used for religious purposes (Sagan 1977).[2]

2 The pygmies themselves claim that at the beginning of time God gave them cannabis so they would be both "healthy and happy" (Hallet, 1975).

As Ethnobotanist Christian Rätsch explained:

> No other plant has been with humans as long as hemp. It is most certainly one of humanity's oldest cultural objects. Wherever it was known, it was considered a functional, healing, inebriating, and aphrodisiac plant. Through the centuries, myths have arisen about this mysterious plant and its divine powers. Entire generations have revered it as sacred.... The power of hemp has been praised in hymns and prayers (Rätsch 1997).

Professor Richard E. Schultes, of Harvard University, considered the father of modern ethnobotany, believed it was likely in the search for food, that humanity first discovered cannabis and its protein rich seeds, which have become a modern "super food" due to their richness in essential fatty acids:

> Early man experimented with all plant materials that he could chew and could not have avoided discovering the properties of cannabis (marijuana), for in his quest for seeds and oil, he certainly ate the sticky tops of the plant. Upon eating hemp, the euphoric, ecstatic and hallucinatory aspects may have introduced man to the other-worldly plane from which emerged religious beliefs, perhaps even the concept of deity. The plant became accepted as a special gift of the gods, a sacred medium for communion with the spiritual world and as such it has remained in some cultures to the present (Schultes, 1973).

Archaeological evidence attests to this ancient relationship as well. "In 1997 a hemp rope dating back to 26,900 BC was found in Czechoslovakia. It was the oldest evidence for hemp fiber" (Seydibeyoglu, et. al. 2017). Hemp fiber imprints found in pottery shards in Taiwan, just off the coast of mainland China, that were over 10,000 years old and remnants of cloth from 8,000 B.C. have been found at the site of the ancient settlement Çatal Höyük (in Anatolia, in modern day Turkey). Much older tools used for breaking hemp stalk into fibers, indicate humanity has been using cannabis for cloth "since 25,000 B.C. at least" according to prehistoric textiles expert Elizabeth Wayland-Barber (Barber, 1999).

Cannabis was also among our first medicines. A recent scientific study out of the USA led by Washington State University researcher Ed Hagen, has suggested that our prehistoric ancestors may have ingested cannabis as a means of killing of parasites, pointing to a similar practice among the primitive Aka of modern day central Africa. We do know that references to cannabis medicine appear in the world's oldest pharmacopeias, such as China's ancient *Pen Ts'ao,* in ancient Ayurvedic texts, in the medical papyrus of Egypt, in cuneiform medical recipes from Assyria, first on a list of medicinal plants in the Zoroastrian *Zend Avesta* and elsewhere.

Evidence of cannabis being burnt ritually is believed to date as far back as 3,500 BCE based on archaeological finds in the Ukraine and Romania. In *Incense and Poison Ordeals in the Ancient Orient,* Alan Godbey felt that in such immolation of psychoactive plants, we may find the genesis of the concept of "divine plants":

> As to the antiquity and genesis of such practices, it is to be recognized ... that they began when the primeval savage discovered that the smoke of his cavern fire sometimes produced queer physiological effects. First reverencing these moods of his fire, he was not long in discovering that they were manifested only when certain weeds or sticks were included in his stock of fuel. After finding out which ones were responsible, he took to praying to these kind gods for more beautiful visions of the unseen world, or for more fervid inspiration... So one group of "animate and divine plants" ... results from the most primitive empiricism, because of purely objective or concrete experiences... (Godbey, 1930)

Some researchers have suggested that humans' drive to alter their consciousness is as innate as the drives to fulfill sexual needs and hunger. Harvard psychiatrist and marijuana medical expert Dr. Lester Grinspoon held the "view that humans have a need – perhaps even a drive – to alter their state of consciousness from time to time." Likewise, well-known health and drug researcher Dr. Andrew Weil commented, "There is not a shred of hope from history or from cross-cultural studies to suggest that human beings can live without psychoactive substances."

Clearly, this plant has been with us longer than any religion or even language. Cannabis has served humanity for millennia as a food, fiber, oil, medicine and source of spiritual and mental relief, yet somehow we got separated from this, and this versatile plant and ancient sacrament was lost to us...

The focus in this volume will be the ancient Near and Mid East, and particularly the Hebrew Bible, as its influence has in many ways carried so much of that Bronze Age mentality into the modern day and kept it alive in our culture – for better or worse. The idea that there are indications of cannabis use in the Bible is something that I have been writing about for over three decades, and various Biblical Scholars have for over 170 years.

Most notable of these scholars was the Polish anthropologist and etymologist, Sula Benet[3] who suggested the Hebrew terms *kaneh,* and *kaneh bosm* identified cannabis. Benet, referred to five specific references in the "Hebrew Bible" (aka the "Old Testament"), Exodus 30:23, Song of Songs 4:14. Isaiah 43:24, Jeremiah 6:20, Ezekiel 27:19. However, when one reads these passages individually and compares them, they are left with a puzzle, as in Exodus 30:23, the reference is to an ingredient in the Holy Oil, which was used in the Holy of Holies, the inner chamber of the Temple in Jerusalem, whereas in Jeremiah 6:20, this same previously sacred substance is wholly rejected as an item of foreign influence and disdain. In this study, we will look at these references in the context of the story they tell, and it will reveal a whole new side of the Hebrew Bible and the history of its creation that few are familiar with.

The identity of *kaneh* and kaneh *bosm* have long been a topic of speculation. Benet's view was that when the Hebrew texts were translated into Greek for the *Septuagint,* a mistranslation took place, deeming it as the common marsh root "calamus." This mistranslation followed into the Latin, and then English translations of the Hebrew Bible. It should be noted that other botanical mistranslations from the Hebrew to Greek in the Hebrew Bible have been exposed.

However, among Jewish authorities, there are various views on what botanical species the terms *kaneh* and kaneh *bosm identify,* and suggestions range from cinnamon bark, sugarcane, lemon grass, ginger grass, camel grass, and others, with an increasing minority acknowledging the suggestion of cannabis.

Curiously, few of these suggestions have attempted to analyze the references to *kaneh* and *kaneh bosm* in context and explain the divisive statements they contain, and these really do help to identify the plant as we shall see. Regardless, it seemed like the subject would remain hypothetical and unresolvable until a fascinating archaeological study was released in 2020, by the *Journal of the Institute of Archaeology of Tel Aviv University,* "Cannabis and Frankincense at the Judahite Shrine of Arad."

The researchers noted at a shrine at an ancient Hebrew outpost in tel Arad, there had been two altars on which plant residues had been

3 Also known under the name Sara Benetowa.

burnt, one altar tested for frankincense, a well known Biblical herb, and the other altar showed that cannabis resins had been burnt upon it.

You can imagine my interest when the headlines about this study began to be released. The research, expectedly, caused a storm of controversy, with Biblical historians, religious authorities and other parties. In a *Haaretz* article on the findings, "Holy Smoke/Ancient Israelites Used Cannabis as Temple Offering, Study Finds" (2020) Ariel David raised the questions:

> So if the ancient Israelites were joining in on the party, why doesn't the Bible mention the use of cannabis as a substance used in rituals, just as it does numerous times for frankincense?
>
> One possibility is that cannabis does appear in the text but the name used for the plant is not recognized by researchers, Arie says, adding that hopefully the new study will open up that question for biblical scholars.
>
> Another answer may be that this particular custom was discontinued before the Bible was written, and whoever compiled and edited the holy text over the centuries had no knowledge of it or did not wish to preserve its memory. Researchers wildly disagree on when the earliest biblical texts were first put in writing, but many believe the process did not begin before the late seventh century B.C.E., during the reign of King Josiah in Jerusalem.

As we shall see, the references to *kaneh* and *kaneh bosm,* perfectly answer these questions, just as the discovery of cannabis on an altar at tel Arad, confirms the identity of this same term as cannabis. As we will also see on this journey of discovery, many of the cultures the ancient Hebrews came into contact with, such as the Scythians, Persians, Egyptians, Assyrians, Babylonians and Greeks, similarly used cannabis and influenced the Hebrews' use of this plant as well.

Importantly, we will also look in detail at how the identity of *kaneh bosm* came to be lost; how this relates to the composition of the Hebrew Bible and what the implications are of its discovery at this pivotal point in time for humanity.

Like the serpent before me, I bid you to ignore the warnings of political and religious authorities who would dissuade you from using this forbidden plant and discovering its secrets, and read on if you dare. "For God knows that when you eat of it your eyes will be opened, and you will be like God, knowing good and evil."

Chapter 1

Cannabis Incense at Tel Arad

Drugs in the Holy Land?

The idea that the Hebrew Bible/Old Testament/Tanakh prophets, may have been using psychoactive substances in order to attain a shamanic trance in which the revelations of Yahweh could be received, is as troubling for modern day believers, as Darwin's theory of Evolution was to their 19th century counterparts. Just as Darwin's theory of evolution challenged the myths of creation from the Books of Genesis, this entheogenic origin for the Jewish religion, indicates a scientifically and anthropologically based theory on the origins of the Bible itself through shamanism and psychoactive plants. Despite the dangers of treading on such hallowed ground as the origins of the Bible, carrying the forbidden apple of drugs, a number of authors and researchers have explored these themes.

Paul Johnson, noted in *A History of the Jews*: "Prophets practiced ecstasy states and may have used incense and narcotics to produce impressive effects.... The Israelite prophets ... acted as mediums. In a state of trance or frenzy they related their divine visions in a sing-song chant, at times a scream. These states could be induced by music... But the prophets also used, and sometimes abused, incense, narcotics and alcohol..." (Johnson, 1987). Maimonides, (1134-1204) a medieval Jewish philosopher, commented that "The object of incense was to animate the spirits of the priests," which would again indicate an entheogenic preparation. Such views, are less controversial than they would seem, as the authors and editors of the *Encyclopedia Britannica* have noted; "The ceremonial use of wine and incense [in contemporary ritual] is probably a relic of the time when the psychological effects of these substances were designed to bring the worshiper into closer contact with supernatural forces."

As the late Johns Hopkins University Professor Georg Luck, a classicist known for his studies of magical beliefs and practices in the Classical world, has noted "The idea that Moses himself and the priests who succeeded him relied on 'chemical aids' in order to touch with the Lord must be disturbing or repugnant to many. It seems to degrade religion – any religion – when one associates it with shamanic practices..." (Luck, 1985/2006). This author has personally interviewed scholars who have pioneered the role of entheogenic substances in the ancient world, such as Prof. Carl Ruck, Dr. David Hillman and Prof. Scott Littleton, and they found outright stonewalling of their research in some cases, although due to the increased interest in psychedelics these days, and growing evidence of their ancient use, the tide here is changing.

Luck experienced negative reactions, when his decades of research into magic rites in the ancient world, drew him to such a hypothesis. "As I was doing research on psychoactive substances used in magic and religion and magic in antiquity, I happened to come across chapter 30 in the Book of Exodus where Moses prescribes the composition of sacred incense and anointing oil. It occurred to me, judging from the ingredients, that... [these] substances might act as 'entheogens,' the incense more powerful than the oil. ..." (Luck, 1985/2006)

Professor Luck pointed to the alleged mild psychoactive effects of myrrh and particularly Frankincense, as has been suggested by a number of recent studies, (Drahl, 2008; Khan, 2012).

> The high value of frankincense is further reflected in the Bible, where its price is compared several times with that of gold and precious stones, and it is often described as a royal treasure.... Frankincense was also highly esteemed throughout Assyria, Babylonia, Persia, Greece and the demand reached

> its peak when Romans burned it in temples, at funerals and in domestic contexts for appeasing the gods.... [T]he high price of frankincense was due to the efforts required for its import from the remote production areas over long distances, to regions where it was in demand (Luck, 1985/2006).

As with cannabis in the ancient world, Frankincense was a prized exotic substance and preserved generally for ritual use, or by royalty. Frankincense resin is a yellowish to red oleogum-resin produced by several types of *Boswellia* trees and contains *Trahydrocannabinole,* which is similar in molecular structure to *Tetrahydrocannabinol, the* psychoactive component of cannabis. And it has been suggested that even in modern church rituals, the mild mood elevating effects of this may help to create a religious state of mind in parishioners close enough to inhale its effects. However, this alleged effect has been hard to reproduce in any notable way under clinic conditions. Luck noted this, explaining that "No two kinds of frankincense... have exactly the same effect. There are many varieties, coming from different regions along the ancient incense route, and some of the more potent ones may not be available any more. The blends used in churches today, seem rather mild, if they can be called psychoactive at all" (Luck, 1985/2006).

Regardless of the potential psycho-activity of Frankincense, what Luck and Johnson seem to be unaware of, was both the etymological and now archaeological evidence for cannabis in just this context. First, let's look at the archaeological evidence.....

Cannabis History Uncovered in the Desert Sands of Arad

In June of 2020, in the midst of a world seized and distracted by a pandemic, and the twitter account of an American President gone mad, some revelatory headlines passed through the world's news agencies. Considering the implications of these headlines regarding the origins of some of the world's oldest and largest religions, they fell short of the sort of impact they might have held in less intense times.

The *Journal of the Institute of Archaeology of Tel Aviv University,* Volume 47, May 28, 2020 – Issue 1, published the paper "Cannabis and Frankincense at the Judahite Shrine of Arad," by Eran Arie, Baruch Rosen & Dvory Namdar. The article was based around the analysis of unidentified dark material preserved on the upper surfaces of two altars that were used at a 2,800 year old Jewish temple site. The temple in question was located in a larger fortress complex in Jerusalem, known as the 'fortress mound' of tel Arad, which had guarded the Judahite kingdom's southern border. The initial excavations of the site took place between 1962–1967 by the Institute of Archaeology of the Hebrew University of Jerusalem, however, the research indicating the role of cannabis at Arad, relied on technologies of analysis that have only come into their role in archaeology more recently.

This academic paper did not go completely unnoticed and led to some pretty potent headlines:

- *Newsweek* – **Cannabis Discovered in Shrine From Biblical Israeli Kingdom May Have Been Used in Hallucinogenic Cult Rituals**

- *BBC* – **"Cannabis burned during worship" by ancient Israelites – study**

- *Popular Archeology* – **New research reveals Cannabis and Frankincense at the Judahite Shrine of Biblical Arad**

- *The Times* (UK) – **Judean worshipers were high on cannabis, archaeologists reveal**

- *Haaretz* – **Ancient Israelites Used Cannabis as Temple Offering, Study Finds: Analysis of altar residue shows worshipers burned pot at a Judahite desert shrine – and may have done the same at the First Temple in Jerusalem**

As the *Newsweek* article described:

"We can assume that the fragrance of the frankincense gave a special ambience to the cult in the shrine, while the cannabis burning brought at least some of the priests and worshipers to a religious state of consciousness, or ecstasy," Arie said. "It is logical to assume that this was an important part of the ceremonies that took place in this shrine."

The tel Arad archaeological site

"The new evidence from Arad shows for the first time that the official cult of Judah – at least during the 8th century B.C. – involved hallucinogenic ingredients. We can assume that the religious altered state of consciousness in this shrine was an important part of the ceremonies that took place here."

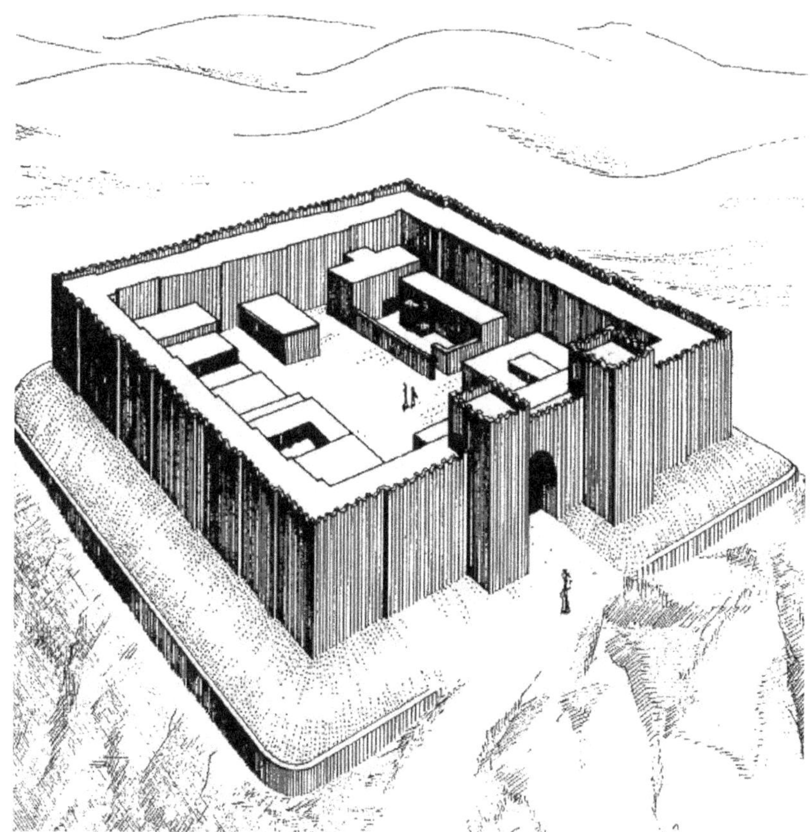

A reconstruction of the Arad fortress from "The Fortress Mound at Tel Arad an Interim Report"(2002) by Ze'ev Herzog, *Journal of the Institute of Archaeology of Tel Aviv University*. The temple is in the top right, the inner Holy of Holies where the shrines were located would have been in the enclosed room, in the far back right corner.

The Temple at Arad

Arad is marked as a Jewish archaeological site, not just through its location, but rather due to archaeological finds of numerous inscriptions on pottery shards known as "ostraca', dating back to the 6th or 7th century BCE, when the kingdom fell to the Assyrians, or just before they fell again to the Babylonians a century later. Most of these unscripted clay shards detail administration activities, however one ostraca, housed and displayed at the Israel Museum reads "the house of YHWH," i.e. a place of worship dedicated to the Hebrew God, likely in reference to the shrine located within the fortress.

Iron Age temples in the region were commonly built on an east-west axis and generally held a courtyard, a main prayer hall and a small, raised inner room: the holy of holies. Due to its similar structure, the temple site in the Arad fortress is seen by researchers as a sort of miniature Holy of Holies, the inner chamber of the Temple of Jerusalem, where the High Priest conferred with God.

An artist's depiction of the inner chamber of Holy of Holies in Jerusalem.

From Biblical descriptions, we know that fumigation with incense was an integral part of the rituals performed within the Holy of Holies, an artists depiction of a High Priest, burning incense before the ark of the covenant within the Holy of Holies.

The High Priest burning incense on the altar in the Holy of Holies in Jerusalem.

The Holy of Holies; illustration from the 1890 *Holman Bible*

The well preserved inner room, or "Holy of Holies" at the Arad temple, held two small altars upon which the resins of frankincense and cannabis were found.

The "cella'" inner chamber of the Temple at Arad, as reconstructed at the Israel Museum from the original archaeological finds. The larger altar on the left held residues of frankincense and the smaller altar on the right cannabis resins. (Image from "Cannabis and Frankincense at the Judahite Shrine of Arad," 2020) "Tel Arad is the first locale where incense from Iron Age Judah has been successfully examined. Two different incense components and two different fuel beds were defined on two altars from an 8th century BCE shrine. The results show that the larger altar contained frankincense that was mixed with animal fat for evaporation. On the other altar, cannabis substance was mixed with animal dung to enable its mild heating."

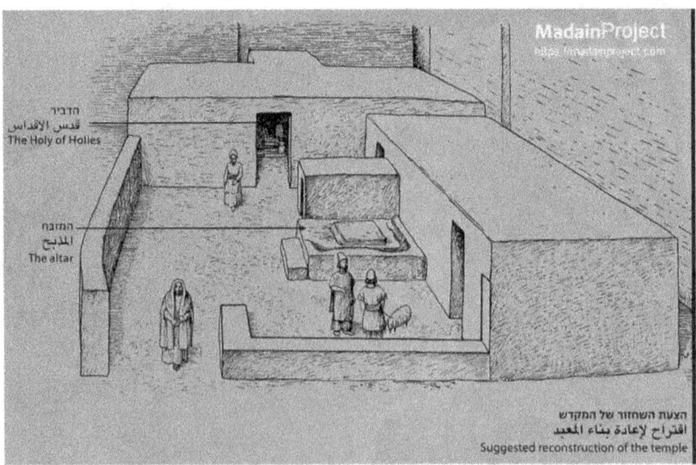

A Reconstruction of the Arad temple site, with the Holy of Holies in an enclosed space in the back. Illustration from the Mandain Project.

As the authors of the original study noted:

> Based on the finds unearthed here and in comparison with other Near Eastern temples it was concluded that the cella was the heart of the shrine; it was therefore termed "Holy of Holies" or *debir*. The Arad shrine was compared to the First Temple in Jerusalem ... and it seems that the two indeed share similar architectural characteristics (e.g., the east–west axis and the division of the architectural spaces). This may allude to similarity in cultic rituals performed in these structures.

As a *Haaretz* article on the Arad discovery noted:

> The citadel was excavated in the 1960s and the discovery of the shrine was a major coup for Israeli archaeologists, because its layout was a scaled-down version of the biblical descriptions (1 Kings 6) of the Temple supposedly built by King Solomon in Jerusalem.
>
> Today, the Muslim holy places atop the Temple Mount make that site inaccessible to archaeologists, so Arad, as well as other similar shrines across the Levant, have functioned as sort of proxies for scholars to study and understand the structure and functioning of the first incarnation of the Temple, of which almost no extra-biblical evidence is known. (David, 2020).

Within the Holy of Holies at Arad, archaeologists discovered a standing stone, with possible indications of a second, that is believed to be a "*massebah*" a ritual object that would have represented the deity within the shrine, alongside the two limestone altars that contained the residues of frankincense and cannabis. Interestingly, the altars had been placed on their sides and purposely buried under a plaster floor when the temple had been decommissioned from use around 700 BCE

The 'massebah', standing stone found at the Arad temple site.

The altars had residues from the resins of material burnt upon them, which due to their deliberate burial and the dryness of the desert, were considerably well preserved. These residues were submitted for analysis at two unrelated laboratories that both used similar established extraction methods. As the original paper on this discovery noted:

> On the smaller altar, residues of cannabinoids such as Δ9-tetrahydrocannabinol (THC), cannabidiol (CBD) and cannabinol (CBN) were detected, along with an assortment of terpenes and terpenoids, suggesting that cannabis inflorescences had been burnt on it. Organic residues attributed to animal dung were also found, suggesting that the cannabis resin had been mixed with dung to enable mild heating. The larger altar contained an assemblage of indicative triterpenes such as boswellic acid and norursatriene, which derives from frankincense. The additional presence of animal fat – in related compounds such as testosterone, androstene and cholesterol – suggests that resin was mixed with it to facilitate evaporation. These well-preserved residues shed new light on the use of 8th century Arad altars and on incense offerings in Judah during the Iron Age.

The authors believe the evidence suggests "that the use of cannabis on the Arad altar had a deliberate psychoactive role. Cannabis odors are not appealing, and do not justify bringing the inflorescences from afar. The frequent use of hallucinogenic materials for cultic purposes in the Ancient Near East and beyond is well known and goes back as early as prehistoric periods.... These psychoactive ingredients were destined to stimulate ecstasy as part of cultic ceremonies. As shown in this study, 8th century Judah may now be added to the places where these rituals took place."

This image provided by archaeologist Caroline Tully offers a perspective on how exactly confined the enclosed temple space was and the size of the altars. (Prior to seeing this image with a person for perspective, I had assumed the site was about four times this size.)

In this respect, it should be noted that the size of the inner

"Holy of Holies" in Arad was about the size of a typical walk in closet, and the altars about knee high. The perfect size for a fumigation ritual, what in modern times might be seen as a "hot box" situation where a car, closet or other small space holds the smoke of cannabis in place.

Other evidence of Ritual Drug Use in the Ancient Near East

The indications are that hallucinogenic incenses were long known in the region, and a variety of substances likely came into use. The 2014 paper "Tracking Down Cult: Production, Function and Content of Chalices in Iron Age Philistia," (which was co-authored by Dvory Namdar, one of the co-authors on the paper analyzing the altars from Arad) identified hallucinogenic properties in this context in their chemical analysis of artifacts believed to have been used for burning incenses:

Philistine chalice, used for burning psychoactive incense.

> The significant lipids identified show that the Philistine chalices were used for heating incense and evaporating psycho-active compounds. As opposed to their relatively free-style construction patterns their use seems to have been uniform, related to ritual contexts. The "mother" compound – *trimyristin* – is highly abundant in plants that are known to cause hallucinogenic effects when inhaled or digested.... We therefore suggest that the chalices were used as incense burners, in which an oily bed was liquefied in order to help evaporate the hallucinogenic substances (Gadot, Finkelstein, Iserlis, Maeir, Nahshoni,Namdar, 2014).

An interesting find of cannabis was recovered from a Carthaginian ship. The Carthaginians descended specifically from the Phoenicians and were more closely related to Canaanites than Israelis or other occupants of Palestine.

> "Leaves of cannabis" have been found in an underwater archaeological excavation of a Carthaginian warship from 241 BC which are on display in Sicily. Dr. Phillip Seff reported that aboard the find of an ancient Carthaginian vessel "There was so much of this plant material that a bagful was easily obtained, more than enough for laboratory analysis. The results confirmed that the material was most probably Cannabis sativa..."

> What can one conclude from abundant supplies of marijuana aboard a fighting ship? In the quantities that were found, it seems to have been a regular ration. Since most of the plant material was stems, which provide mild doses of the drug, it may have been used as a medication to reduce fatigue. Or the soldiers may have been encouraged to use the marijuana to become euphoric, to reach what is today known as a "high" to intensify their courage and fearlessness. The soldiers may have chewed on the stems and infused the weed into a tea. (Seff, 1996)

Daniel Morneau also notes,"That the Punic sailors drank wine on board came as no surprise, and the presence of amphorae with the resinous lining associated with wine-carrying proves it. But the totally unexpected discovery of a bundle of cannabis sticks indicates the sailors indulged in a mild form of marijuana tea as well" (Morneau, 1986). The Times (UK) reported of the find:

> The Marsala Punic Ship was uncovered in Marsala harbour by a dredger in 1969, and restored by a team of underwater archaeologists from the British School... They concluded that the warship had been sunk stern-first after being rammed by the Romans. The crew had apparently abandoned ship, taking their weapons with them, but left evidence of their diet including deer, goat, horse, ox, pig and sheep as well as olives, nuts and fruit.
>
> There were also traces of cannabis, which the crew may have chewed as a stimulant before going into battle or simply to keep awake. (Owen, 2004).

That the material was mostly cannabis stalks, along with wine and amphora also opens up the possibility that the cannabis may have been infused into wine which was a widespread technique of cannabis ingestion.

The April 20th issue of the respected journal, *Science*, Vol 360, Issue 6386, contained the story, "Cannabis, opium use part of ancient Near Eastern cultures":

> For as long as there has been civilization, there have been mind-altering drugs. Alcohol was distilled at least 10,000 years ago in the Fertile Crescent, about the same time that agriculture took hold there. Elsewhere, for example in Mesoamerica, other psychoactive drugs were an important part of culture. But the ancient Near East had seemed curiously drug-free – until recently.

> Now, new techniques for analyzing residues in excavated jars and identifying tiny amounts of plant material suggest that ancient Near Easterners indulged in a range of psychoactive substances. Recent advances in identifying traces of organic fats, waxes, and resins invisible to the eye have allowed scientists to pinpoint the presence of various substances with a degree of accuracy unthinkable a decade or two ago (Lawler, 2018).

However, as the *Science* article notes: "Some senior researchers are still dubious, pointing out that ancient texts are mostly silent on such substances. Others consider the topic 'unworthy of scholarly attention'" (Lawler, 2018).

Archaeologist David Collard, who discovered evidence of ritual opium use in Cyprus, dating further back than the first millennium BCE, has noted that "The archaeology of the ancient Near East is traditionally conservative." More recently the paper "Opium trade and use during the Late Bronze Age: Organic residue analysis of ceramic vessels from the burials of Tel Yehud, Israel" (2022) identified the likely ritual use of the poppy in the Holy Land. "Organic residue analysis was conducted on various vessels from burials at Tel Yehud, Israel. The analyses led to new reliable evidence for the presence of opioid alkaloids and their decomposition products. This research revitalizes a decades-old discussion on the presence and function of the opium trade across a cultural region of utmost significance in the Ancient Near East" (Linares, Jakoel, Be'eri, Lipschits, Neumann, & Gadot, 2022).

> The first known mention of the opium poppy in antiquity is found on Sumerian clay tablets written in Cuneiform script c. 3000 BCE.... The tablets were found at Nippur and describe the cultivation of the opium poppy.... The Sumerians named opium 'Gil,' (happiness), which is a term still applied to opium in certain world cultures today.... The Assyrians, like the Sumerians, collected poppy juice early in the morning by scraping the poppy capsule with an iron scoop and placed these collections in clay vessels.... The ancient Egyptians cultivated their own opium poppies in Thebes called opium *thebaicum* and *thebaine*. This opium was generally restricted to priests, magicians and warriors, and was associated with religious cultism.... Evidence of the poppy harvest is known from the New Kingdom period in Egypt and the LBA in the Levant. It is possible that various jewels, such as gold earrings and pendants discovered in tombs, symbolize the poppy capsules...

> On the island of Crete a ceramic figurine of a female deity with her hands raised and a crown wrapped around her head was found. The crown is adorned with three poppy-shaped grooves.… The goddess's face is seen in a state of intoxication, suggesting that opium was used as a hallucinogen during a ritual. A gold seal ring found in Burial Circle A in Mycenae, attributed to the 16th–15th centuries BCE, shows the goddess holding the three poppy capsules (Linares, Jakoel, Be'eri, Lipschits, Neumann, & Gadot, 2022).

Poppy Goddess of Crete

As the *Haaretz* article on the find "Bong Age? Israeli Archaeologists Find Opium in Bronze Age Ceramics" noted "Residue analysis of 3,300-year-old vessels from Canaanite tombs at Tel Yehud sheds light on ancient drug trade between Cyprus and the Levant"

The *Haaretz* article states that Linares, the head researcher on the paper about the opium vessels, feels that the fact these vessels "once held opium points to the importance to the ancient Canaanites of the substance in the mortuary rituals – and perhaps other aspects of life." As the *Haaretz* article further explains, "the opium may have been intended for use both by the dearly departed to ease their passage into the next world, and also by the living, who may have actually consumed it at the funeral or during commemoration ceremonies to achieve an ecstatic state and commune with the dead (or think they were communing with the dead)" referring to the speculations of co-author on the paper Be'eri.

Interestingly, opium residues were also recovered at a burial site in Megiddo, and this may give some indications how it was used in mortuary rituals. In "Transformations in Death: The Archaeology of Funerary Practices and Personhood in the Bronze Age Levant" Melissa S. Cradic has noted a number of lamps found in a tomb at a Northern Israeli site, "importantly, residue analysis from one lamp unexpectedly yielded morphine-derived compounds":

> The enclosed space of the tomb chamber may have facilitated morphine consumption through fumigation. The presence of such a powerful and disorienting psychotropic substance inside the tomb carries important implications concerning the ritualistic, symbolic, and sensorial aspects of the funerary sequence during close encounters with the dead. In the wider region, the presence of opium has been documented during the Bronze Age in Egypt, and it is also known from residues of opium alkaloids in Cypriot Base Ring juglets to a limited degree.... Two Base Ring juglets were found inside [the] Tomb..., possibly providing additional indirect evidence of the presence of opium in this funerary context.
>
> Although the use of psychedelic drugs in funerary contexts is not currently known in the second millennium B.C.E. Levant, the presence of mind-altering drugs in other sacred spaces in the Levant and globally has a long history that contextualizes the presence of opium in the mortuary realm. A ceramic storage jar from the temple courtyard at Late Bronze Age Kamid el-Loz, for example, contained ten liters of Viper's Bugloss (*Echium linné*), a powerful hallucinogen.... Beyond the Levant, botanically derived psychoactive drugs have been found in diverse mortuary contexts spanning several millennia and continents (Cradic, 2017).

Bronze Age vessels in which opium residue was detected. Credit: Clara Amit / Israel Antiquities.

Interestingly, Cradic suggests a similar form of use for opium, as is indicated by the findings of tel Arad for cannabis, the suffumigation of it as an incense in a small, confined space.

Many researchers have suggested that Hebrew references to Gall, (as with the "wine to drink, mixed with gall" given to Jesus on the cross) were an adoption of the suggested Sumerian name for the opium poppy noted by the authors "Gil." But both of these designations have been hotly disputed. As it stands, there is no confirmed word for the opium poppy in either Akkadian or Sumerian texts, there have been suggestions in the past, but those are now widely rejected, as Barbara Böck has noted "It seems that *Papaver somniferum* is absent from the cuneiform record or the plant is hidden behind one of the many plant names that cannot be identified" (Böck, 2021). Similar statements have been made about cannabis and the linguistic identifications challenged. However, as with the archeology of Arad, this new evidence has also confirmed the ritual use of opium in the Holy Land.

Similarly, there have been etymological, or linguistic claims about evidence of cannabis, interpreted from ancient texts, including the Bible. However these have been generally dismissed or overlooked by the wider academic community. As with the evidence of ritual opium use at Tel Yehud, the archaeology out of Arad now provides physical proof of cannabis' ritual role in the ancient Near East and these claims should now be harder to ignore.

The Implication of Tel Arad

Eran Arie, curator for archaeology of the Iron Age and Persian Period at the Israel Museum in Jerusalem, which now houses the ancient artifacts from the shrine in Arad and a co-author of the paper on the altars from Arad, stated in an interview with *Haaretz* on the evidence of ritual cannabis use at the site: "This may reflect the cultic activities in Jerusalem, in Judah and possibly in the broader region," he says. "If the shrine at Arad was built according to the plan of the Temple in Jerusalem, then why shouldn't the religious practices be the same?" Co-author Dvory Namdar, a chemist and archaeologist from the Volcanic Agricultural Research Center, also see this use as likely indicating a mainstream practice which had been officially sanctioned and financed by the monarchy of that time.

The authors of the paper are not alone in this respect. Yifat Thareani, an archaeologist from Hebrew Union College in Jerusalem, who read the paper with great interest, is in agreement with the authors' view that cannabis likely played a role throughout the region. "We don't have remains from the First Temple so we can only assume what kind of cultic activity went on there," she says. "But there are enough indications from Arad to give us a sense, or in this case a smell, of how the rituals in Jerusalem were performed." (Quoted in *Haaretz*)

Although the Arad site indicates the ritual use of cannabis, as the authors of the paper have noted, this is not the only evidence of cannabis use in the "Holy Land":

> The species also has a number of medicinal properties, from which the best known is its pain relieving ability, especially pain associated with childbirth. In Africa, the Sotho smoked the leaves and other parts of the plant for this reason.... In Morocco, midwives used the smoke of cannabis to induce abortion in pregnant women wishing to terminate their pregnancy.... In the archaeological record, in a cave dated to the 4th century CE in Jerusalem, remains of a 14-year-old girl who died during labor were found, with the skeleton of a 40-week fetus trapped in her pelvis. A juglet with black material in it was retrieved near the skeletons. The analysis of the dark material revealed the presence of Δ6-THC, an acid catalytic by-product of Δ1-THC and cannabidiol (CBD). Zias et al. (1993) concluded that the purpose of feeding the cannabis to the girl (by inhalation) was to increase the force of uterine contractions and to reduce birth pain.

In this case, there were indications of both burnt, and topical use of cannabis. Besides evidence cannabis was burnt for medical purposes at Bet Shemesh, a balm of cannabis had been rubbed on the girl's pelvis. This indicates a record of about 1200 years of known use of cannabis in the region, extending into the first centuries after Christ. In both this 4th century CE find from Bet Shemesh Jerusalem, and the 8th century BCE find in Arad, it is also interesting to note that a refined resin product was in use, not raw leaves or flowers.

As the authors of the paper on the Arad altars have noted:

> [P]ollen analysis carried out on samples taken from both altars by Dafna Langutt (Tel Aviv University) concluded that no plant material was preserved on the Arad altars. In fact, no cannabis seeds or pollen remains are known from archaeological contexts in the Ancient Near East, as opposed to northeast China or southeast Russia, where all parts of the cannabis plant and seed were found at different archaeological sites and

contexts and were dated as early as 2000 BCE.... Therefore, we suggest that cannabis female inflorescences may have been imported from distant origins and were transported as dried resin (commonly known as hashish).

A later reconstruction of the shrine at the original archaeological site in Arad, Jerusalem.

The larger temple site, at Arad, with the Holy of Holies top center.

HASHISH AND THE TEMPLE OF ARAD

As the authors of the original paper have noted "The very high price of frankincense, and presumably that of cannabis, reinforces the assumption that the fort of Arad was an official institution, owned by the Kingdom of Judah. Being part of the kingdom administration, the residents of the fort could have had the resources to obtain such precious materials."

Indeed, the precious spice road, bringing in exotic goods to the region, is believed to have passed through Arad, and this is a likely avenue that both the cannabis and frankincense took in reaching the ancient Israelites as there are no indications that it was grown in the region at that time, but rather came as a finished and refined product.

The researchers identified other chemicals in their analysis, and this indicated that both the cannabis and frankincense had been mixed with other ingredients, likely to help them burn better. In the case of frankincense animal fat was used, and with the cannabis resins, animal dung, a common fuel in the iron age, was combined.

As noted in an article on the discovery in *Haaretz,* 'Holy Smoke | Ancient Israelites Used Cannabis as Temple Offering, Study Finds', there are indications that there was clear reasons for these combinations:

> The fat would have helped achieve the high temperature of around 260 degrees Celsius at which frankincense releases its aroma, while the dung would have burned the cannabis at a lower temperature, below 150 degrees Celsius, which is necessary to activate the drug's psychoactive compounds. Fire it higher and all you get is soot.
>
> "To induce a high you need the right temperature, and they clearly knew this well, just as they knew which fuel to use for each substance," Namdar explains.
>
> This indicates that the ancient worshipers at Arad were getting deliberately stoned and were not burning cannabis just for aromatic purposes – an idea that is also supported by what was probably the drug's very high cost (David, 2020).

The identification frankincense at Arad marks the first time the resin has been identified in an archaeological dig in the Levant, although this is not surprising as the Bible and other ancient sources describe the ritual burning of frankincense resin (see Leviticus 2:1-2).

Eran Arie explains that "If they just wanted to make the temple smell nice, they could have burned some sage, which grows in the area of Jerusalem... Importing cannabis and frankincense was a big investment that could not be made by some isolated group of nomads, it required backing from a powerful state entity." It is believed that both the frankincense and cannabis traveled from afar, along ancient spice routes, as a refined product, likely dried resin, Arie suggests a hashish like product. Likewise with the frankincense, collected from Boswellia trees and this came via traders from southern Arabia.

Over and above being a temple site, Arad was positioned as both a major military fortress at the border of the kingdom as well as a stronghold that protected the spice road caravan trade that passed through the region, bringing precious goods to the kingdom. "Frankincense comes from Arabia. Therefore, the presence of frankincense at Arad indicates the participation of Judah in the south Arabian trade even before the patronage and encouragement of the Assyrian empire. Arad provides the earliest evidence for frankincense in a clear cultic context. Frankincense is mentioned as a component of the incense that was burned in the Temple of Jerusalem for its pleasant aroma" (David, 2020). Unfortunately the potential psycho-activity of the frankincense at Arad was not explored in the paper on the altar residues.

Aromatherapy expert Susanne Fischer-Rizzi noted: "We once called all herbs burnt as incense 'frankincense'" (Fischer-Rizzi 1990). "The article now known as frankincense is the resin called thus, a common, inodorous article, little better than common white rosin. The article once so highly valued ... must have been some other drug more precious than pine or spruce resin." Today the word frankincense has come to specify the gum resin from the North African tree Boswellia and Fischer-Rizzi, points out that this modern source also contains psychoactive properties, and is still used in churches to instill a chemically induced feeling of religious awe:

> In the last few years, scientists have grown interested in frankincense. They were intrigued by reports that inhaling certain fragrances became addictive for some people, such as altar boys. Some members of the Academy of science in Leipzig, Germany, found in 1981 that when frankincense is burned, another chemical is produced, *trahydrocannabinole*. This psychoactive substance expands the subconscious.
>
> The Australian scientist Dr. Michael Stoddard found something else in frankincense. It seems that frankincense, according to Stoddard, awakens sexual, ecstatic energy sources within people. Traditional religious rituals tap and re-channel these energies (Fischer-Rizzi 1990).

The Cancelation of Tel Arad

The fortress at tel Arad survived until about 586 B.C.E., and the end of the First Temple era. The shrine itself was only in use from around 760 B.C.E. to 715 B.C.E. As Ariel David noted on this ancient decommission of the site in his well written article on the find in *Haaretz*:

> Scholars have long debated why the temple at Arad was decommissioned and its ritual objects, like the two altars, carefully buried. Some believe this was a way to protect the holy place ahead of the invasion of Judah by the Assyrians around 701 B.C.E., triggered by a failed region-wide revolt spearheaded by the Judahite King Hezekiah. However, the shrine's closure seems to precede the Assyrian onslaught by a few years, Arie notes, meaning that it is more likely connected to the religious reforms that were carried out by Hezekiah in the early days of his reign, just around 715 B.C.E.
>
> According to the Biblical account, which finds some support in the archaeological record, Hezekiah attempted to centralize the cult of Yahweh at the Temple in Jerusalem and ordered the destruction of competing holy sites throughout his kingdom. Acting on his orders, the Israelites "tore down the high places and altars throughout Judah, Benjamin, Ephraim, and Manasseh, until they were all destroyed" (2 Chronicles 31:1) (David, 2020).

Ancient Prohibition at Arad?

Interestingly, this is a history that may have been intentionally suppressed, as the authors of the paper on the Arad altars have noted:

> The excavator of Arad assumed that the two altars (and the entire shrine) were deliberately buried for ritual reasons…. The motivation for this cultic interment is debated. Many scholars followed the excavator and assume that it was part of a cultic reform in Judah under King Hezekiah…. Other scholars suggest that the abolishment of the shrine came out of a desire to protect it from the danger of damage prior to the Assyrian occupation … it was only after the Assyrian destruction that the altars were interred by the Judahites to preserve their sanctity. Our results cannot side with any of these theories, but the very good preservation of the organic material on the altars does indeed reinforce the assumption that they were intentionally interred.

The shrine in Arad during the original excavation, the altars had been turned on their sides and the whole shrine purposely buried around the 7th century BCE. (Photo-original article)

According to Ze'ev Herzog in "The Fortress Mound at tel Arad an Interim Report" (2002) the evidence for this desacralizing is:

- A metal object, possibly for holding the burning coals, was removed from the head of the sacrificial altar;
- The standing stone (הבצמ) was laid on its side;
- The incense altars were buried below the floor of the debir ("holy of holies");
- No remains of cultic paraphernalia or votive offerings were found, implying that they were removed.

Curiously, Herzog left out mention that female pillar figurines associated with Asherah, were also discovered from the tel Arad temple. As noted by archaeologist Dr. Elizabeth Bloch-Smith in 'Judean Pillar Figurines, 8th century BCE': "While most figurines derive from household contexts, examples also come from tombs, the Arad temple, and public buildings."

One reason that suppression of the site has been suggested is that Arad holds evidence of polytheistic cultic activities and that besides the two altars at the site, there are indications originally there were two standing stones, and this reconstruction brought about the conclusion that two deities were worshiped at the shrine, and this has suggested to some researchers, a divine couple. Ziony Zevit, an American scholar of biblical literature and Northwest Semitic languages, and a professor at the American Jewish University, explained in *The Religions of Ancient Israel: A Synthesis of Parallactic Approaches:* "Evidence for the worship of more than one deity, usually in the form of redundant or paired appurtenances such as altars, stands, and steles, is indicated at the temple of Arad XI (ninth century) ... Dan (eighth century) ... Hazor XI (tenth century) ... Lachish (end of tenth century) ... Megiddo (end of tenth century).... My own interpretational preference for the phenomenon of "twoness" ... is to consider it a reflection of the worship of YHWH and Asherah, lord and lady of the Israelite pantheon" (Zevit, 2001). [Emphasis added].

This is interesting in light of the clear evidence that shall be discussed, that for large periods of Israeli history, the region was polytheistic, and Yahweh was coupled with a Goddess, Asherah. Interestingly, even prior to the study of the altars, tel Arad had long been viewed by many scholars as a site indicating the combined worship of Yahweh and the Goddess as Asherah. This has been seized upon by religiously biased historians and archaeologists in response to claims that the ritual use of cannabis in Arad, were indications of what took place within the Holy of Holies in the temple of Jerusalem. The evidence of ritual cannabis use at Arad, is seen here instead as further evidence of polytheistic heresy, and a reason for the original sites ' cancellation and burial.

Hezekiah's reforms referred to above in regard to the shrine at Arad, were directly related to stomping out these longstanding polytheistic practices involving Asherah and replacing them with the worship of Yahweh alone. As *2 Kings* 18:3-6 records:

> Hezekiah did what the LORD said was right.... He broke the memorial stones and cut down the Asherah poles. At that time the Israelites burned incense to the bronze snake made by Moses. This bronze snake was called "Nehushtan." Heze-

> kiah broke this bronze snake into pieces. Hezekiah trusted in the LORD, the God of Israel. There was no one like Hezekiah among all the kings of Judah before him or after him. He was very faithful to the LORD and did not stop following him.

In relation to the serpent referred to in this passage, it is worth noting that Asherah is referred to as the "lady of the serpent" in second-millennium B.C.E. inscriptions. The Hebrew Bible's narrative is clear, these monotheistic renovations were directed against the worship of the Goddess, and this was also what they taught led to the fall of their kingdom. "All this took place because the Israelites had sinned against the Lord their God.... They set up sacred stones and Asherah poles on every high hill and under every spreading tree. At every high place they burned incense ... they ... made for themselves two idols cast in the shape of calves...." (2 Kings 17:7-17). The solution to avoiding such punishment had been made clear "Break down their altars, smash their sacred stones and cut down their Ashera poles. Do not worship any other god, for the Lord, whose name is Jealous, is a jealous God" (Exodus 34:13-14). And again: "By this, then, will Jacob's [figuratively speaking of Israel] guilt be atoned for, and this will be the full fruit of the removal of his sin: When he makes all the altar stones to be like limestone crushed to pieces, no Asherah poles or incense altars will be left standing" (Isaiah 27:9).

Hezekiah's reforms here were far from successful, and we see the worship of Asherah and other deities still firmly in place, when his grandson Josiah pursued a somewhat more successful path of Yahweh alone reforms decades later.

Both the archaeological record and the words of the Bible itself indicate that the worship of a Mother-Goddess was an early integral part of the religion of ancient Israel for centuries. Throughout the region, finds of countless goddess figurines, ritual objects, alongside other iconography, offer indisputable evidence that goddess worship was practiced throughout ancient Israel.

As Dvora Lederman Daniely, a lecturer and researcher at the David Yellin College of Education in Jerusalem noted recently in the article "Who's Afraid of the Goddess of Ancient Israel?" published in *The Ancient Near East Today* (June, 2022):

> Many studies on Asherah in the Bible have concluded that Asherah was a popular and beloved Mother-Goddess in the religion of Israel. Asherah was regarded as a benevolent, divine kingship (also known as the "Queen of Heaven") who bestows abundance

> and protection to the people. The human queens were in charge of Asherah's worship and hosted her priests. The worship of Asherah, as the Book of Kings itself disapprovingly attests, was conducted within the Holy Temple itself alongside the worship of Yahweh – "And the carved image of Asherah that he had made he set in the house of which the Lord said to David and to Solomon his son, 'In this house, and in Jerusalem, which I have chosen out of all the tribes of Israel, I will put my name forever'" (2 Kings 21).
>
> Although biblical authors cast worship of this divine spouse as idolatry leading up to sin, this characterization was contrary to the prevalent cultic religion in the early days of Israel. This portrayal was intended to preserve the appearance of monotheism. It suited the spirit of religious reform that prevailed in the days of the seventh century king Josiah that abolished all divinities other than Yahweh. This monotheistic outlook took central place in the edited version of the Bible. Essentially, biblical editors presented a new, more stringent cult, in which monotheism was present from the beginning of time, when in fact it was not (Daniely, 2022).

The worship of Asherah was popular with the people, but opposed by a faction of kings and prophets in Jerusalem who were devoted exclusively to Yahweh at the First temple in Jerusalem. Most people didn't actually worship at the temple, it was reserved for elites and royals. It was these same people who composed the The Hebrew Bible. The general population worshiped in small community shrines, or at a site like that at tel Arad. During periods when they held power, this Royal cabal sought to abolish the worship of other deities, particularly Asherah. From the Hebrew Bible narrative we see that for centuries the statue of Asherah was repeatedly removed and reinstalled in the temple of Solomon who himself burnt incense to her. Despite this violent opposition, the murder of her priests and priestesses, and the destruction of her cultic sites and icons, her statue stood in the temple for 236 years, nearly two-thirds of the time that the temple stood in Jerusalem.

As we shall see in the next chapter, the cancelation of the Arad temple, and the ritual use of cannabis, alongside so much of the Hebrew Bible's sexual morality, is wound up with the suppression of the divine feminine by a cabal of Patriarchal minded Jewish elite. Despite what the Bible teaches us Asherah's worship was once both prominent and well accepted in the region. Moreover, throughout the ancient Near East "the worship of the goddess played a much more important role in this popular religion than that of the gods" (Patai 1990).

Chapter 2

The Wife of God

I first wrote about Asherah in the 1990s, at that time it seemed so radical and unbelievable, fringe academia at best, that the God of the Bible, for most of what would be considered the Hebrew Bible period, had a wife. It had been some time since I had delved into the topic prior to the discovery of cannabis resins at Arad, but the acceptance of this unavoidable reality, due to increasing archaeological evidence of Goddess worship in ancient Israel, seems to have now won the day. It is generally now accepted by the majority of historians and archaeologists that Yahweh was initially not a monotheistic figure, and like other deities of the Near East headed a pantheon and was coupled with a Goddess.

Throughout the many centuries that this popular goddess was worshiped, her mythology combined and overlapped with that of other Near Eastern goddesses (Astarte, Anath, Astargatis, etc.) making it hard at times to see a historical distinction between them. Anat and Astarte were considered to be the daughters of Asherah. The renowned Judaic scholar Raphael Patai was amongst the first to note that together this trinity represented the different aspects of the Triple Goddess, i.e.: Virgin-Maiden-Crone, but he is far from alone in this view. Both in the texts of the Hebrew Bible and "in Canaan there is a tendency for the distinctive functions of the three goddesses to fuse together" (Gray 1969). "It can be assumed that the three goddesses mentioned represent different developments of the motif of the feminine generative power as something divine and important for the continuation of life and the community" (Rinngren 1973). All three of these goddesses were worshiped by the ancient Semites at different times throughout the Biblical period. However Asherah is clearly the most prominent in the Hebrew Bible narrative. Anat is mentioned only once, Astarte just a few times, whereas the term Asherah appears over 40 times. Combined with this is a trove of artifacts from the Kingdom period that attest to her popularity in that era.

Complicating things, there are various regional names of the Asherah, such as Elat and Athirat in Canaan, along with titles like Qodesh (Holy One). As well, regionally Asherah's origins have been connected with other ancient goddesses, such as Ishtar, Ishara, Cybelle, the Egyptian Hathor and others. "[W]e have to keep in mind that in polytheistic cultures the prevalent tendency often was to identify one god with another, or call one god by the name of another, as we know from many examples in the Egyptian, Babylonian, Hittite or Canaanite religions..." (Patai 1990). Raphael Patai, believed that this factor led to some confusion in the Biblical narrative, and at times this caused Asherah to appear under alternative names such as Ashtoreth, the Goddess introduced to Solomon by his foreign wives in the Hebrew Bible narrative (1 Kings 11:33). "There can be little doubt that it was the worship of Asherah, already popular among the Hebrews for several generations, which was introduced by Solomon into Jerusalem as part of the cult of the royal household, for his Sidonian wife" (Patai 1990). Despite these name variations, and overlapping Goddesses "the one variety of worship in which the Israelites engaged more frequently than any other was the cult of the Goddess Asherah, symbolized and represented by her carved wooden images [Asherah poles]" (Patai 1990).

Raphael Patai, in his groundbreaking book, *The Hebrew Goddess* (1967) did much to sort out these differences and establish the paramount role that Ashera, and other Goddesses played in ancient Semitic culture, particularly among the Hebrews, where at times they were worshiped right along side Yahweh, with Asherah being referred to as his consort. "Recently discovered tenth-century B.C.E. inscriptions from Judea invoke the blessing of Yahweh and his Asherah testifying to their combined cult" (Gaddon 1989). As we shall see further, the temple at tel Arad testifies to this relationship as well. In much later Hebrew Bible times, during the age of Prophets like Jeremiah, the Hebrew priesthood became particularly incensed with the worshipers of the Goddess, as her cult successfully competed

for popularity (particularly with women and homosexuals) against the cult of Yahweh. The "canceling" of the temple at Arad, and burial of the altars there beneath a plaster floor, is a physical remnant of the religious prohibition of her cult and its lost sacrament.

As William G. Dever, the American archaeologist, Hebrew Bible scholar, and historian, noted in his 1984 article, "Asherah, Consort of Yahweh? New Evidence from Kuntillet Ajrfid,'" the silence regarding Asherah as the consort of Yahweh in the existing Hebrew Bible narrative, "may now be understood as the result of a near-total suppression of the cult by 8th-6th century reformers" (Dever, 1984). Ellen White, Ph.D. (Hebrew Bible, University of St. Michael's College), formerly the senior editor at the Biblical Archaeology Society, likewise explains, in her article "Asherah and the Asherim: Goddess or Cult Symbol?" despite the denial that causes some to view "the idea that Yahweh had a wife disturbing, it was common in the ancient world to believe that gods married and even bore children. This popular connection between Yahweh and Asherah, and the eventual purging of Asherah from the Israelite cult, is likely a reflection of the emergence of monotheism from the Israelites' previous polytheistic worldview" (White, 2021).

Most references to "asherah" appear as a symbol of the goddess in the Biblical narrative, and one that is clearly rejected and prohibited. The Israelites are repeatedly commanded by god to chop down the asherahim, break it into bits, and burn it. Scholars say this was either a "living tree, or a wooden pole" (Dever, 2013). However half a dozen times Asherah appears as a personal name, such as when the Goddess is coupled with the Canaanite god, Baal. Patai, Dever and other scholars see a direct attempt to bury the Goddess Asherah, by the original authors and editors of the Hebrew Bible texts. Certainly they do not match the archaeological record, which fully attest to her prominence and popularity with the Israelite people.

Let Me Tell You About Your Mother…

Raphael Patai, the respected Hungarian-Jewish ethnographer, historian, Orientalist and anthropologist, has done much to resurrect the historical role of this ancient Semitic Goddess, since the 1960s. His book *The Hebrew Goddess* (1967) went a long way in documenting her relationship with Yahweh in pre-reformation Jerusalem

Similarly, William Dever's book *Did God Have a Wife?* (2005) compiled archaeological evidence, such as inscriptions and the numerous clay female figures found throughout Israel and known as 'pillar-base figurines', due to their sturdy bases, as clear indication of the popularity of Goddess worship in the region throughout the Biblical age of kings. Dever explains that Asherah's position was as the goddess and consort of Yahweh, and she was recognized as the "Queen of Heaven." Dever specifically points to the shrine of tel Arad and the indications there of polytheistic practices, two altars, standing stones, as well as figurines of the goddess recovered at the site, as evidence of the combined worship of Yahweh and Asherah. "The only goddess whose name is well attested in the Hebrew Bible (or in ancient Israel generally) is Asherah" (Dever, 2005)

Dever is a revisionist, who sees the Hebrew Bible texts as put together by a handful of male elites after the fall of Jerusalem, and in no way representative of the history and beliefs of the past they purport to record. The Hebrew Bible narrative handed down to us, is more like this cabal's patriarchal wet dream as to how things should have been in their minds. Monotheism was not the original state and from about 1200-600 BCE Israel was polytheistic. This is what archaeology clearly shows and this is the standard mainstream view among academics now.

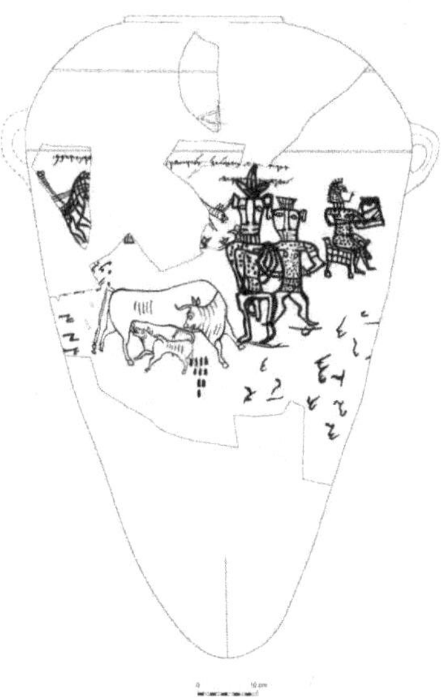

8th century BCE Kuntillet Ajrud jar with painting and inscription "Yahweh of Samaria and his Asherah" and "Yahweh of Teman and his Asherah." (https://upload.wikimedia.org/wikipedia/commons/c/ca/Ajrud.jpg)

Dever has played a prominent role in the Near Eastern archeology that has been uncovering the prominent role of Asherah in ancient Israel and Judah, through finds of Hebrew inscriptions which refer to her by name in conjunction with Yahweh, as well as ritual objects and amulets.

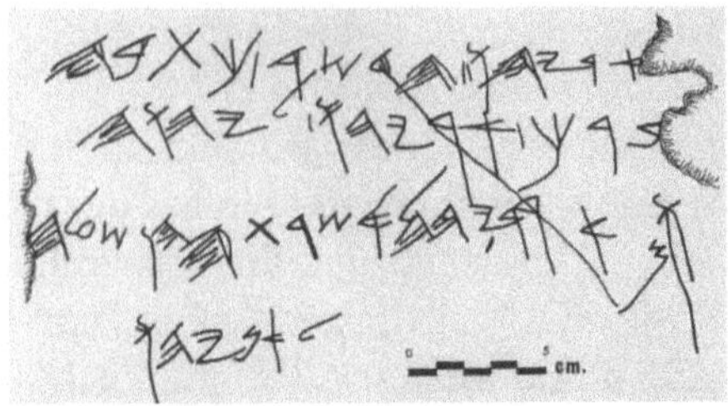

Khirbet el Qom inscription (750-700 BCE: "Uriyahu, the prosperous, his epitaph Blessed be Uriyahu, by Yahweh and from his enemies, by his Asherah, save him." (Written) by Oniyahu.

This four-tiered cult stand, from the 10th-11th century B.C.E., found at Taanach is thought to represent Yahweh and Asherah, with each deity being depicted on alternating tiers. It is widely recognized that the bottom and upper middle tiers depict a goddess, probably Asherah. The identity of the deity represented by the empty lower middle tier is not as clear. Numbers of researchers believe that it is an early representation of Yahweh, who was not supposed to be depicted pictorially or as a graven image, but this leaves the problem of identifying a deity who is not there. On tier two, which is dedicated to Asherah, is the image of a living tree, often thought to be how the asherim as a cult symbol was expressed. Photo: © The Israel Museum, Jerusalem/Israel Antiquities Authority (photograph by Avraham Hay).

> The Taanach stand, almost two feet high is capped by a shallow basin to contain the incense…. The identity and relationship of the deities on this complex tableau is controversial. Holladay suggests that the first and third tiers represent two aspects of Asherah, the second and forth Yahweh. One of the principle epithets of the Canaanite goddess was "Lion Lady." In Israelite culture, the tree was her most important iconic form. Holladay views the empty space on the second tier as the aniconic representation of Yahweh, the bull calf with the sun disc as his iconic form and the Temple of Solomon his house…
>
> If we accept Holladay's reading,[1] the imagery on the Taanach stand reveals a syncretic cult in transition, the combined

1 John S. Holladay, *Religion in Israel and Judah Under the Monarchy: An Explicitly Archaeological Approach* (1987)

cult of a God and goddess, not that of a god and his consort. Her symbols are the aniconic tree and the fully anthropomorphic form of the nude female. Yahweh is present in both his invisible form and in his manifestation as bull calf.

On the third register a pair of heraldically arranged goats nibble from a stylized tree flanked by two lions who look much like those on the bottom tier. In the center of the upper register, a calf with a sun disk on its head stands between a pair of volutes that represent columns like those described at the entrance of Solomon's temple (Gadon 1989).

Numerous female clay "pillar figures," believed by many historians to represent the Goddess Asherah, have been found throughout the area, attesting to the popularity of the Goddess with the ancient Hebrews. A number of such pillar figurines were found at the Arad Temple site.

As Caroline Tully, who has written about these figurines explains "Archaeologists term them 'Judean Pillar Figurines' and biblical scholars call them 'Asherahs,' after the presumed goddess who is mentioned forty times in the Hebrew Bible. They date from between the 9th century BCE to the early 6th: the Iron Age II up to the Babylonian Period" (Tully, 2011). Almost all of them have been found broken at the neck, and this has caused some to see evidence of purposeful destruction, such as through the reforms indicated in the Hebrew Bible narrative, and that which took place at tel Arad – a time period which fits with their disappearance. Others have suggested such breakage is typical of artifacts in general, and others yet, that they contained prayers or messages and the object had to be broken to deliver the message. In the case of acting as a ritual envelope, this does "not… contradict the idea of Judean Pillar Figurines also representing a goddess who intercedes with a more remote god because if to break is to send, then figurines are still fulfilling the mediating/communicating role. The figurines could very well represent Asherah as a messenger and/or mediator; a more approachable, sympathetic divine figure, a bit like Mary is thought to be in Christian belief" (Tully, 2011).

As noted by Elizabeth Bloch-Smith an Adjunct Professor of Biblical Studies at the Princeton Theological Seminary in the article "Judean Pillar Figurines, 8th century BCE" :

> Approximately 1000 examples of Judean Pillar Figurines (JPF) are known. These female figurines, standing roughly six inches tall, have a pillar-shaped body (no legs indicated), either hollow or solid, with prominent breasts encircled or supported by the arms. Heads are either mold-made with distinctive features and short curly hair or simply pinched to form indented eyes and a protruding nose. Vestiges of paint on some figures indicate colored facial features and adornment with bracelets or necklaces.
>
> Surprisingly, these figurines are a predominantly Judean phenomenon, with the greatest numbers from Jerusalem (405), and sites along Judah's borders to the north (Tell en-Nasbeh, 143 examples), to the south (Tel Beer Sheva, 43 examples), and along the western border with Philistia (Tell Beit Mirsim with 37, Bet Shemesh with 30, and Lachish with 29). While most figurines derive from household contexts, examples also come from tombs, the Arad temple, and public buildings. Early examples date to the late tenth or ninth century BCE but the figurines greatest popularity and distribution dates to the eighth century BCE. Few seventh century BCE examples survive.
>
> **Judean Pillar Figurines and the Bible**
>
> With no distinctive markings these figurines defy certain identification. Few toys or objects of amusement were manufactured in this period so the figurines presumably represent a deity or a magical object rather than a simple plaything such as a doll. Who or what does the figurine represent?
>
> The prominent breasts suggest a connection to lactation and by extension to infants' welfare. The distinctive pillar-shaped body resembles a wooden pole or tree trunk, the symbol of the fertility goddess Asherah or her attributes. Accordingly, the figurines are interpreted as either fertility goddesses, most frequently Asherah or Astarte, or as sympathetic

> magical items to promote fertility in general and lactation and infant survival more specifically.
>
> While female figurines are known from all periods, the sudden appearance of these figurines in the late tenth or ninth century and their widespread distribution in the eighth century are surprising. Why would Israelites in the ninth and especially the eighth century BCE manufacture a figurine depicting a female goddess or a talisman? And why might the practice taper off and cease in the seventh or early sixth century? (Bloch-Smith, 2008).

A time period that fits completely with the disappearance of the Arad temple, where the combined worship of Yahweh and Asherah is indicated by the two altars, standing stones and female pillar figures, as well as other indications, which had all been "canceled" by 7th century religious reforms.

In *The Origins of Yahwism*, Jürgen van Oorschot and Markus Witte refer to Arad specifically in this context:

> The potential variety and the lack of exclusivity in cultic matters is illustrated by the later sanctuary (late 8th c. B.C.E.) in the Arad fortress .... There, pillar figurines of goddesses, which were typical for Judah and belong to the realm of local production and piety, were found on the surrounding deposit benches of the sacrificial altar in the courtyard. These clay figurines originated during the second half of the 8th c. and found great appeal during the 7th c. They display a goddess who is not identifiable by name (Asherah?) in a bell shaped skirt who supports her breasts. In the niche of the temple there stood a standing stone (or perhaps two of them) and two incense altars. The standing stone(s) and the pillar indicate that multiple deities in different forms (as a standing stone, anthropomorphically as a goddess supporting her breasts, and also zoommorphically) were represented at the temple of Arad, which must be regarded as a local temple of YHWH during that time. In any case, the figurines speak against the generalized conclusions about the anionic character of the religion of Judah during the monarchic period (Oorschot & Witte, 2017).

However, the Biblical descriptions do offer some indications of Asherah's popularity with the wives of kings and women in general throughout the Biblical narrative, and this is indicated by archaeological finds as well. Dever suggests that one of Asherah's primary functions was the role of a protector of pregnant women. He bases this assertion on cultic sites of Dan, Kuntillet' Arjud, Schechem, and particularly Arad as well figurines and pictorial representations of the Goddess, along with other artifacts retrieved from these sites.

In this respect, we should note again the use of medical cannabis as an aid in child birth from the later 4th century CE archaeological find in Bet Shemesh, noted in the previous chapter, as well as more ancient references from Egypt, indicate a long standing knowledge of cannabis effectiveness in this area of women's medicine in the ancient world. The *Eber's Papyrus,* circa 1550 BC, one of the oldest and most important medical papyri of ancient Egypt, prescribes cannabis and honey "to cool the uterus and eliminate its heat" during childbirth. This use was likely widespread in the ancient world. In *Women and Cannabis Medicine, Science, and Sociology* (2002) the authors affirm that "archaeological, and written records substantiate that the plant was often used to treat female ailments, such as dysmenorrhea, ease labor, alleviate morning sickness/ hypermesis gravid arum, and/or facilitate childbirth in places such as: Ancient Egypt, Judea, and Assyria..." (Russo, et. al. 2002).

A History of Jewish Gynaecological Texts in the Middle Ages, records a medieval Hebrew medicament for pregnancy that contained cannabis called the "Head Shield," which included cannabis alongside nard, saffron, frankincense, cassia and other exotic ingredients came down through the medieval Rabbis Sheshet, and Yehudah Harizi. It is unknown if this was based on earlier medical recipes. (Barkai, 1998).

From the Israel Museum publications:
The Israel Museum, Publisher: Harry N. Abrams, Inc., 2005

This figurine may represent Asherah, the "one of the womb." According to myth, Asherah gave birth to the twin gods Shahar and Shalem, (who represent dawn and dusk). Other symbols of Asherah on the amulet including the sacred tree with goats nibbling on it, appear on the goddess' thigh. The figurine was probably an amulet for women in childbirth. It is likely a necklace such as this, that was condemned by the prophet Hosea, when he demands that Israel remove the "adulterous look from her face and the unfaithfulness from between her breasts." Hosea 2:2). This unfaithfulness was a symbol of Asherah worn at the end of a necklace by the female Hebrew worshipers of the goddess. A galling sight to the god whose name is Jealous.

To the polytheistic Hebrews fertility was fostered by sacred sexuality, a theme that will come to light more when we discuss Solomon's "Song of Songs." Sacred sexuality was the domain of Asherah. In fact many of the traditional sexual taboos of the Hebrew Bible, likely came about in reaction to the cultic activities of the worshipers of Asherah.

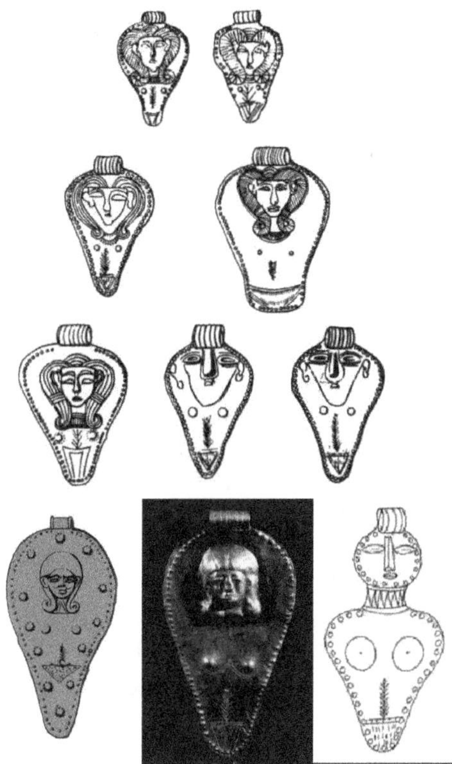

Near Eastern Goddess pendants, indicating the belief that human sexuality fostered the fertility of nature, with the sacred tree of the Goddess, growing from her vagina, from 'Western Asiatic Tree-Goddesses' (Irit Ziffer, Israel Museum, 2011).

In *Sex and Love in the Bible* (1959) William Cole explained:

> The Canaanite [and Near Eastern] pantheon ... included goddesses, such as Ashera, consort of El and Baal, She ... was a nature deity, symbolizing sexuality and fertility. In some passages in the Hebrew Bible there are references to an *asherah* as a wooden pillar, an object of cultic devotion.... All of ... [the] gods and goddesses worshiped by Israel's neighbors near and far were intimately and organically related to nature and the various forces and powers encountered there. For the most part they appeared in male/female pairs and were pictured in the myths and legends creating the world by copulation. They had special responsibility for fecundity and fertility of all sorts of conditions. Their worship apparently required a kind of imitative magic in which male and female devotees yoked their bodies sexually and spilled their seed upon the field they desired to yield bounteous crops. Orgies involving the use of intoxicants and indiscriminate sexual activity played an important part in these cults, and many Israelites gladly became apostates to these weird and wondrous religions. The inexperience of the nomadic Hebrews in the task of agriculture in their new homeland made them easy converts to the local Baals who promised good harvests. The exotic character of the cult with its mystic roots extending far back into antiquity, together with the highly sensual pleasures afforded in the worship, combined to make it an attractive type of religious experience. Any such temple in modern society would encounter no difficulty in attracting large numbers of devotees... (Cole 1959).

It has been suggested that the orgiastic worship of Baal and Asherah\Anath in this context, began with the introduction of the date palm – a dioecious tree with sexes in separate trees, requiring fertilization by man's intervention, or by that of cherub nature daemons (wind, birds, bees etc.), thus making the relationship analogous to human sexuality in the mind of primitive people (Smith 1927). This is also particularly true in association with cannabis, which as we have documented played a major role in the Canaanite cult, and like the date palm is dioecious, having two very distinct sexes. Cannabis can be more easily interpreted as the sacred tree on the Asherah pendants above, than the date palm.

In reference to cannabis in this respect it should also be noted that hemp is an annual crop and would require continued fertilization each year for the seeds of the next generation, unlike the date palm, which grows larger, year after year, resulting in continually standing groves. Thus hemp is a far more likely candidate for the crop which continually required, in the minds of the ancient Near Eastern fertility cult, orgiastic rites of sympathetic magic. It is also known that "number of traditions developed around the hemp harvest that involved rituals based on intoxication from the volatile resins and oils"(Emboden 1972). The addition of sexual license developing at such pagan rituals does not take a lot of imagination. As the anthropologist Sula Benet noted:

> Since the plant was associated with religious ritual and the power of healing, magical practices were connected with its cultivation.... The odor of ... hemp is stimulating enough to produce euphoria and a desire for sociability and gaiety and harvesting of hemp has always been accompanied by social festivities, dancing, and sometimes even erotic playfulness (Benet 1975).

One of Asherah's titles was Qodesh or Qudshu, "holiness," and this name can be seen in the name of the male and female cult prostitutes that served for Asherah in temples like that found in Arad. According to the Bible, this was the case in the main temple in Jerusalem as well.

When Prostitution Was Divine Service

> The profession of harlot carried no stigma in Sumerian times, or in Babylonian ... temples were staffed by priests, servants, and artisans, and by a number of highly respectable priestesses and nuns, often from the best families, as well as sacred prostitutes who acted as congenial intermediaries between worshiper and deity. The exact purpose of sacred prostitution is obscure; it may well have had its origin in fertility rituals. But by historical times, the sacred prostitutes' earnings accounted for a substantial part of the temples' income (Tannahill 1980).

This was a widespread cultural trait throughout ancient western Asia. The sanctuary of Aphrodite at Old Paphos on Cyprus "was one of the most celebrated shrines in the ancient world" (Frazer 1922). "Foreign as the notion is to the modern religious consciousness, the worship of Ishtar and Tammuz was a fertility cult in which union with the hierodule [temple prostitute] consecrated to the service of the goddess was thought to have magical functions and powers. Such hierodules could be either male or female ... the singular kadesh in I Kings 14:24 is to be taken as a collective, meaning 'hierodules as a professional caste' who were 'in the land,'" (Dynes, Percy, Johansson, and Donaldson, 1990).

This popularity was for a very good reason, this being that in some regions all women were obliged to go to the temple and there partake of the ceremony of fertility by acting as a prostitute and donating the money made to the temple funds. Likewise, at the temple of Ishtar in Mylitta in ancient Babylon the wages earned by the devotees were dedicated to the Goddess. As Sir James George Frazer says the rite was seen as a "solemn religious duty performed in the service of that Great Mother Goddess of Western Asia...."(Frazer 1922). Indeed, up until recent centuries in India, which has been discussed for its profound similarities to the ancient Near eastern cults, "many girls were dedicated to the temple where they carried out this social and religious duty, which is the gift of love. They received a careful education, including music, dancing, and erotic techniques" (Danielou 1992). Further, the male "client" who had ritualized sex, and paid for it with donations to the temple, was performing a sacred act of worship.

It was not only women who inhabited these temples of the Goddess for the purpose of practicing cult prostitution. Men who had been made into eunuchs also lived there in the service of the Great Mother, distributing her love in homo-erotic rites.

> In the Old Testament the word *qedesim* means the male practitioner of temple prostitution, while the feminine ones are described as *qedesot*, temple prostitutes ... the institution ... had an important part to play in the fertility cult. The Old Testament prophets direct harsh criticism against the custom, for example Amos 2.7: "son and father both go into the same prostitute"; Hos. 4.14: "men go aside with harlots, and sacrifice with cult prostitutes"; Jer 2.20: "under every green tree you bowed down as a harlot." Classic authors such as Herodotus, Strabo, and Lucian also attest that sacral prostitution was a custom in the whole north-west Semitic area in their time (Ringgren 1973).

Cult prostitution existed from the earliest times: "Time after the time the prophets denounced Israelite women for following Canaanite practices; at first, apparently, with the priests approval – since their habit of dedicating to God the fees thus earned is expressly forbidden in *Deuteronomy* xxiii. 18." (Graves and Patai 1963) In Monarchic times the Hebrew Bible condemnations against prostitution are only directed against that of a cultic nature, and has nothing to do with the morality of the issue. "That there was little or no prejudice against purely secular prostitution in Israel seems relatively clear ... Judah lay with Tamar, thinking she was a harlot (Genesis 38). Rahab, the whore of Jericho, was singled out for remembrance and praise. Jephtah, the judge of Israel, was the son of a harlot, who despite evil treatment from his half brothers who were of legitimate birth (Judges 11), rose to prominence in Israel and was used by Yahweh" (Cole 1959). Further, even the active condemnation of cultic prostitution was only periodical, and as often as not the temple prostitutes are present in the kingdom. In later times the male cult prostitute even penetrated onto the grounds of the Temple of Jerusalem itself!

We come full force into what anthropologists call ethnocentricity, or cultural bias when we deal with the ancient and common practice of cult prostitution. The very term prostitute is misleading, although money certainly did change hands at these temples. Like the opinions of the Yahwists of old, which so strongly impressed the morality of our modern era, our cultural experience of prostitution is a world away from the fertility rights practiced in the Fertile Crescent. It is difficult for us to imagine a world in which sex wasn't felt to be such a rarefied and private act and it is important to convey how different these people's conceptions of their actions were from our own.

Cult sex at the temple was the duty of every member of the culture and as such carried no stigma with it. Our own cultural bias can be seen amongst many of the scholars of ancient western Asian societies who rarely touch on the subject of the ancient fertility rites, and when they have it has generally been in reference to their 'heinous' nature. As in the difficulty in obtaining scholarly information about the use of hallucinatory and psycho-active plants in ancient cultures, in trying to discover more about these central and obviously important fertility rituals, over and over again one finds but the scantiest references to them in books on the ancient Near East.

These ancient fertility cults remain as foreign and steeped in mystery to us, as they did to the early Yahwehist who condemned their practice. As the feminist historian Riane Eisler explained:

> Because we have been taught to think of sex as sinful, dirty, titillating or even prurient, the possibility that sex could be

> sacred, may seem shocking. Even stranger in a world where female genitals are sometimes described as "cunts" (one of the most obscene swear words in the English language), is the idea that women's bodies – and particularly women's vaginas – could be sacred (Eisler 1995).

In light of the derogatory connotations to the word "cunt" referred to in Riane Eisler's comments, it is interesting to note that the Canaanite priestesses were known by the name *khnt*, being the most likely source from where we get the modern day swear-word for the female genitalia, the "cunt."

> In traditions that go back to the dawn of civilization, the female vulva was revered as the magical portal of life, possessed of the power of both physical regeneration and spiritual illumination and transformation.... Far from being seen as a "dirty cunt," woman's pubic triangle was the sacred manifestation of creative sexual power. And far from being of a lower, base or carnal order, it was a primary symbol of the powerful figure known in later Western history as the Great Goddess: the divine source of life, pleasure and Love (Eisler 1995).

The ancients saw in the sexual relationship of man and woman, the very secrets of creation itself, and in taking part in that relationship as a part of their religious worship, they felt that they themselves were taking part in the divine drama on a cosmic scale. "Through their bodies, these temple prostitutes, associated with such goddesses as Hathor, Ishtar, Anath, Astarte, and Asherah, offered access to the divine, a pathway to wholeness and unity with the One" (Hutchison 1990). "Thus, in the Sumerian narrative of Gilgamesh, hailed by scholars as the first Western epic, we read that a woman (whom translators alternately call a 'love-priestess' of the Goddess, a 'temple-whore,' or a 'temple courtesan') transforms the wild Enkidu from a beast to a human being by having sex with him – thereby helping him 'become wise like a god'" (Eisler 1995). "Hesiod said the sensual magic of the sacred whores or Horae 'mellowed the behavior of men.' Ishtar, the Great Whore of Babylon, announced, 'A prostitute compassionate am I'" (Walker 1983).

> In these temples, men were cleansed not sullied, morality was restored not desecrated, sexuality was not perverted but divine... The original whore was a priestess, the conduit to the divine, the one through whose body one entered the sacred arena and was restored. Warriors, soldiers, soiled by combat

> within the world of men, came to the Holy prostitute ... in order to be cleansed and reunited with the gods.... As the body was the means, so inevitably pleasure was an accompaniment, but the essential attribute of sexuality, in this context, was prayer(Metzger 1985).

There are many references to this practice within the house of Israel throughout the writings of the prophets. Hosea is very open about it: "the men themselves consort with harlots and sacrifice with shrine prostitutes" (*Hosea* 4:14). He even makes a reference to the celebration of the New Moon Festival, for which Yahweh will "devour them in their fields" (*Hosea* 5:7). Here again we see the Israelites participating in the pagan fertility rituals out in the fields under the new moon mimicking the sexual union of the gods and goddesses, to bring fruitfulness to the land and to themselves.

The Qedeshim

The Hebrew hostility towards homosexuals was particularly directed at a class of gender-variant shaman-priests who followed the goddess Ashera, challenging the more patriarchal priests of Yahweh for popularity with the ancient Semites. The Hebrew Bible refers quite clearly to these ancient priestly transvestites, who were known as the *qedeshim*, "holy ones," and alternatively as *kelabim*, or dogs. "The epithet 'dog' is not necessarily a term of abuse, but merely descriptive of their manner of copulation" (Allegro 1970).

Qadesh is the singular and *qedeshim*, the plural and the terms are also translated with a K instead of a Q. The Hebrew here translates as "holy one," however, Biblical translators have rendered it "sodomite" in the past (as in the King James Version). Many modern bibles translate it as "male cult prostitute." As we read in *1 Kings* 14:23-24, of the "disobedient" Israelites: "They ... set up for themselves high places, sacred stones and Asherah poles on every high hill and under every spreading tree. There were even male shrine prostitutes in the land.... Evidently, male cult prostitutes were a common phenomenon throughout the years of the monarchy, with some kings supporting them and other kings exterminating them. They went hand in hand with the phallic symbols of pillars and Asherim [Asherah poles], the worship on the high places, the exaltation of fertility and sexuality" (Cole 1959).

The Encyclopedia of Homosexuality (Dynes, Percy, Johansson, and Donaldson, 1990) states of the term under "Kadesh," (Qedeshim here translated with a "K" instead of the more common "Q"):

...It is a key term for understanding the Old Testament references to homosexuality. It occurs as a common noun at least six times (Deuteronomy 23:18, I Kings 14:24, 15: 12 and 22:46, 11 Kings 23:7, Job 36:14). It can also be restored on the basis of textual criticism in 11 Kings 23:24 (= Septuagint of 11 Chronicles 35:19) and in Hosea 11:12. They all ostensibly designate foreigners (non-lsraelites) who served as sacral prostitutes (hierodules) in the Kingdom of Judah and specifically within the precincts of the first Temple (ca. 950-622 B.C.). That these men had sexual relations with other males and not with women is proven by Hosea 4:14, which castigates the males exclusively for "spending their manhood" in drunken orgies with hierodules, while their wives remained at home, alone and unsatisfied, and by the reading of Isaiah 65:3 in the Qumran manuscript: "And they (m. pl.) sucked their phalli upon the stones." Their involvement in the Ishtar-Tammuz cult – an obvious rival of the monotheistic Jahweh religion-is responsible for the Biblical equation of homosexuality with idolatry and paganism and the exclusion of the individual engaging in homosexual activity from the "congregation of Israel," which persists in the fundamentalist condemnation of all homosexual expression to this day.

...To understand that the condemnation of the kadesh was a cultic prohibition and the self-definition of a religious community, not a moral judgment on other acts taking place outside the sphere of the sacral, it is necessary to see the kadesh or male hierodule (with the kedesha as his female counterpart) in his historical and cultural setting, as a part of Northwest Semitic religion on the territory of the Kingdom of Judah down to the reforms of King Josiah (622 B.C.). The commandments forbidding male homosexual activity on pain of death in the Holiness Code (Leviticus 18:22 and 20:13) were added only in the Persian period (first half of the fifth pre-Christian century specifically). Critical scholarship generally dates the Holiness Code to the beginning of that period, but Martin Noth in his major commentary *Leviticus* (Philadelphia, 1965) ascribes this part of Leviticus to a time slightly after 520 B.C., when the new and reformed Jewish religion set about throwing off all the associations believed responsible for the catastrophe of 586 B.C., the destruction of the first Temple and the exile of the population of Judah to Babylon. The proof of the later ori-

> gin of the verses indicated above is the prophetic reading ("haphyariih") for the portion of the Torah including Leviticus 18, namely Ezekiel 22: 10-1 1, a comparison of which shows that Ezekiel was alluding to a text which in the final years of the First Commonwealth began with Leviticus 18:7 and ended with 18:20, as if to say "You have committed every sexual sin in the book." While there are those who maintain that the Levitical references condemn all male homosexual acts, the character of the Holiness Code suggests that it had the sacral aspect of the sexual liaison in mind (Dynes, Percy, Johansson, and Donaldson, 1990).

The *qedeshim* dressed in multi-colored caftans, and may have worn veils over their faces. They maintained the Temple grounds and sacred groves as well as creating ritual objects, such as pots and weavings. Besides their ritual homosexuality, to the horror of the ancient priests of Yahweh, the *qedeshim* employed self-wounding and flagellation in a sacred dance, in order to reach altered states of consciousness. They also utilized cannabis, in the form of ointments and incense, as means of achieving shamanistic ecstasy, and there are indications that this was practiced by some of the regional counterparts, such as the transvestite *kurgarrus* who served Ishtar and the Gallus of Cybelle, who shall be discussed. "The *qedeshim* were condemned by the Israelites on four accounts. First, they were mostly Canaanites, although biblical passages suggest that a number of Jewish men and women may have forsaken Judaism to become *qedeshim* and *qedeshtu* [feminine]. Second, they worshiped the Goddess and her male consort rather than Yahweh, or Jehovah. Third, they were effeminate, dressing in feminine attire and behaving in a gender-variant manner. Fourth, they engaged in cultic eroticism and, more specifically, in same-sex eroticism" (Conner 1993).

Having sex with either the male or female cult prostitutes of Asherah was believed to bring the ancient worshiper into intimate contact with the goddess herself. It is believed by some scholars that the *qedeshim* may have used anal-intercourse as a means of achieving shamanistic trance. Conner states that this "practice will be familiar to students of Indian tantra. Gay male practitioners of tantra employ anal intercourse to stimulate the kundalini, the serpentine Goddess of Wisdom, in the body of the receptive partner"(Conner 1993). Conner quotes Samuel Terrien on the *qedeshim*, "The function of the male prostitutes ... was related to an ecstatic ... divination technique." A statement echoed by W.L. Moran who commented that the *qedeshim* "may well have obtained his oracular function through sophisticated techniques of sexual trance." It has been suggested that the use of intoxicants also played a role in such rites, and this is indicated in ancient literature as well, as shall be noted. We see a similar connection with the use of cannabis and other psychoactive substances in Indian Tantric rites, which are thought to go back to much more ancient times.

Homosexuality was a very common trait in shamans of tribal peoples, worldwide, who believed that these people, who had characteristics of both sexes, were somehow also living in two worlds, and could travel between the two. The messages "channeled" by these ancient diviners was taken as authoritative advice by the chieftains and the tribe. In this sense, the Shamans acted as the conscience or mind of the whole group.

The Goddess Cybelle's original Phrygian priests, known as *Gallus,* or *Galli,* assumed women's clothing after a sacrificial castration, the gender transfer being a form of worship of the Goddess by identification. "We know that the Phrygian tribes ... during the 1st millennium BCE were weavers of hemp (and possibly imbibers of intoxicating hemp preparations)" (Merlin, 1973). References to some Galli being awakened to this form of worship, after ingesting a certain kind of "herb growing along the banks of the Maeander River" (Conner 1993), as well as acknowledged use of mysterious sacraments amongst the cult, indicate clearly that they were practicing the common trait of mystery religions of the time – ingestion of entheogenic sacraments. Referring to the visionary dream which was said to awaken the Gallus to their new identification with the Goddess, Randy P. Conner commented; "It is possible to see the ... drinking or eating of special substances as a fated occurrence that triggered the awareness of one's destiny. Such experiences were said to cause an individual to experience sophrene, to 'recover one's senses'" Conner 1993).

Recent archaeological finds have established that Cybelle was worshiped among the Thracian tribes, who were known for using cannabis to attain mystic states, especially amongst their own transvestite shamans. Interestingly, certain male functionaries of Cybelle and Attis' cult were known as *cannophori,* which has usually been translated as "reed-bearers," but linguistically, with "*canno,*" this may have implications of "cannabis-bearers" instead. As William Bell noted more than a century and a half ago of this: "The Latin name of cannabis, perhaps *rectius cannevas,* as the Italian name is *cannevacchio* (our English canvass was made from it) would connect it with ... the cannephoroi ..." (Bell, 1852). Archaeological evidence shows the Phrygian culture from which the religion arose used hemp (Abel 1980).

Likewise, with Inanna the ancient Mesopotamian goddess of love, war, and fertility, who overlaps with Ishtar over time, and possibly also in origins. Ancient Babylonian records refer to large amounts of cannabis being delivered to the temple of Eanna, in Uruk which was dedicated to her. As with these other Goddesses, she had her own cultic prostitutes, both male and female. A branch of transvestite priestesses known as *gala* served in Inanna's temple. Male-born individuals who became *gala* sometimes adopted female names and their songs were composed in the Sumerian *eme-sal* dialect, which, in literary texts, is normally reserved for the speech of female characters.

Similar cannabis-using transvestite worshipers of the Goddess, known as *Enaries,* could be found amongst the Scythians, who were closely related to the Thracians, referred to above, and who possibly picked the cultic practice up from contact with the *Galli,* or alternatively carried it on from an even earlier identical source. It has been recorded that the Scythians believed that the feminine characteristics of the shamans was punishment from the Great Goddess for desecrating her shrine at Ashkelon in Israel.

The *Enaries* uttered prophecies in high pitched voices while twisting fibers in their fingers, a technique which they held was taught to them by the goddess Aphrodite. Most archaeologists agree that Aphrodite originated as Ishtar.

Interestingly, as we have been discussing Goddesses and cannabis, a Scythian tomb found by the Russian archaeologist Sergei Rudenko that held the implements for fumigating with cannabis, in the form of a tent bowl and brazier with rocks, that held the carbonized remains of burnt cannabis and its seeds, also held a carpet, possibly used around the poles of the tent to hold in the smoke from the cannabis burning brazier. The rug had a border frieze with a repeated composition of a horseman approaching the Great Goddess Tabiti-Hestia, the patroness of fire and beasts, who

A Scythian rug, found with a brazier and tent poles used for cannabis suffumigation had the repeated design of a horseman approaching the "Great Goddess."

holds the "Tree of Life" in one hand and raises the other hand in welcome (one is reminded of the Grail legend in the depiction).

Although the Scythians had a pantheon of deities, Herodotus recorded Zeus, Apollo, Heracles and others, the Goddess Hestia was their chief deity. The Great Goddess alone is the only deity who figures in Scythian art. As the Mythologist Barbara Walker has noted:

> The only deity shown in Scythian art was the Great goddess whom the Greeks called Artemis, or Hestia or Gaea (The Earth) ... Scythians were governed by priestess-queens, usually buried alone in richly furnished Kurgans (queen graves).... The moon-sickle used in mythical castrations of god was a Scythian weapon. A long handled form therefore came to be called a scythe, and was assigned to the Grim Reaper, who was originally Rhea Kronia in the guise of Mother Time, or Death – the Earth who devoured her own children. Scythian women apparently used such weapons in battle as well as religious ceremonies and agriculture" (Walker, 1986).

Walker's comments regarding the use of the scythe and agriculture, can be particularly applied to the Scythians favorite and most versatile crop, cannabis hemp, as the long handled scythe with its curved blade, is particularly well designed for harvesting hemp, enabling the harvester to cut the hemp along the soil line thus preserving its long fiberous stalks.

One thing that differentiated the sites of the tombs of Royal Scythian Queens, with that of the kings, is the complete lack of human sacrifices. A 1995 episode of *The National Geographic Explorer,* "The Frozen Siberian Tombs," profiled a dig centered around a recently discovered Kurgan, and the program televised such things as an over 2,000 year old hemp shirt, weaved as fine as silk; A beautifully embroidered and decorated bag, used for holding marijuana; And an exotic Persian rug, testifying to wide ancient trade routes. In the case of the Scythians, we are not only dealing with male to female transvestism, but also female to male, and it is now believed that some Scythian tombs thought to have been those of male warriors, may in fact have been females, in traditionally male attire. Scythian women in general had a reputation for fighting in battle alongside their men.

As we shall see in the next chapter, there are indications that the use of cannabis may have come to the Holy land via Scythian traders.

Despite the Biblical fundamentalist's view that homosexuality is an abhorrent sin, and its practitioners are sick individuals who "have a far greater incidence of mental breakdown, form notoriously unstable relationships, and have exceedingly high suicide rates," this has not inherently always been the case. The mental breakdowns, suicides, and unstable relationships that have been attributed to homosexuals in past decades, have little to do with the collective mental state of those who choose to tread "gaily" down the path of life, and far more to do with local cultural pressures from a rejecting society that has been strongly influenced by Judaic-Christian homophobic views. "Homosexuals in many societies are not incompetent, but they may be such if the culture asks adjustment of them that would strain any man's vitality. Wherever homosexuality has been given an honorable place in any society, those to whom it is congenial have filled adequately the honorable role society assigns them"(Benedict 1934). In other cultures, such as certain tribes of North American Indians, as well as other indigenous peoples, and especially during the classic period of Greece, where Platonic love was accepted without prejudice, gay people have adjusted fully into the culture, rising to positions of prominence and even taking roles of leadership, as they have been able to again in recent years with the lessening of societal pressures against them.

Discussing the "Aftermath and Parallels" of the suppression of the Qedeshim, the Editors of *The Encyclopedia of Homosexuality* (Dynes, Percy, Johansson, and Donaldson, 1990) wrote that "The taboo on homosexuality in Western civilization is thus a legacy of the religious rivalries and conflicts in Ancient Israel, and of the formation of the Jewish community after the Babylonian captivity as a client-ethnos of the Persian monarchy."

As the Christian author Dr. Robert Greenblatt, explained in *Search the Scriptures: A Physician Examines Medicine in the Bible* (1963):

> In the original Hebrew, *kadesh* [*qedesh*], literally "holy one," is the word which in translation was writ as "sodomite" – not exactly a complimentary substitute. In the Christian liturgy the resounding passage, "Holy, holy, holy, is the Lord of hosts: The whole earth is full of his glory" (Isaiah 6:3), is a quite familiar one. In Hebrew the word for Holy is *kadosh*. This passage is recited solemnly beginning in the words, "*Kadosh, kadosh, kadosh*" – Holy, holy, holy. It is not difficult to surmise how the word *kadesh* evolved to describe someone set apart for holy purpose. In later years, the term was used to refer to "devotees of the fertility cult." Without this historic background, the association of the word *kadosh* (holy) with *kadesh* (sodomite) would appear wholly ludicrous. The reforming zeal of king Jo-

> siah ultimately prevailed and these abodes of immorality and heresy were destroyed (2 Kings 23:19) (Greenbatt, 1963).

The Christian doctor here reveals his religious bias, as the pogrom enlisted by Josiah and his grandfather Hezekiah before him, that labeled the *qedeshim* as immoral and heretical were hardly reforms, they were a new aggression against long-standing traditions. The "Sin" of homosexuality, came as part and parcel of the suppression of Goddess worship, along with the power of women and the disappearance of ritual cannabis use, and all part of the same religious-based pogrom that led to the cancelation of the temple site at tel Arad.

The Biblical fundamentalist, who tries to claim religious morality as a basis for scientific analysis, referring to homosexuality as an "unnatural act," and evidence of "deviant behavior," has no logical basis for these claims, making them solely from a theological standpoint. In the natural world, homosexual behavior has been observed in a number of species such as dogs, cats as well as more complex life forms such as apes, and especially dolphins, (the males of which have a slit that other males can penetrate). Recent scientific studies on the brain patterns of homosexuals, have shown that their minds often operate in a gender specific way that is opposite to that of their bodies. Such research has been seen as indicative that some people are "naturally" pre-inclined for homosexual behavior. This is an important difference in regards to the acceptance of these traits, between the polytheistic and matriarchal cultures that proceeded the patriarchal monotheism depicted in the Hebrew Bible

The Cult of Asherah

As Francesca Tronetti, a professor of Religious History at Cherry Hill Seminary, has explained in her article "The Queen of Heaven: Depictions of Asherah in Ancient Israel" (2020) of the copious archaeological evidence indicating Asherah worship in the ancient Levant:

> These findings are evidence for a widespread cult of Asherah and connect her worship, specifically to a woman's cult. Evidence for the existence of this cult can also be found in the Jewish Bible, though it is primarily through negative polemic. The symbol for the Goddess Asherah often found at these sites was a wooden pole or a tree that represented the "tree of life." This "tree of life" originated in the ancient Near East sometime

> in the 3rd millennium BCE. By the 13th century BCE, it had become the symbol of the goddess in ancient Israel.
>
> We can surmise that the asherah was more than a Canaanite import based upon analysis of the inscriptions and the biblical evidence. The asherah appears to have been an accepted religious cultic symbol in ancient Israel during the pre-exilic period. Biblical texts indicate that as time progressed, the asherah cult became partially or fully integrated into the worship of YHWH. Deuteronomic history rarely criticizes the goddess; it focuses its attention on the cultic symbol of the asherah. Biblical texts indicate that asherah worship continued during the period of Judges (1200-1000) and lasted to a few decades before the fall of the southern kingdom of Judah (587/586) (Tronetti, 2020).

Some see evidence for the worship of Asherah as dating as far back as 5,500 BCE, which would make Asherah's worship long pre date that of the Bible's first texts, or even the concept of Yahweh. A *Haaretz* article "7,500-year-old Burial in Eilat Contains Earliest Asherah" suggests that a "Juniper tree trunk in a grave in Eilat" is "the earliest 'Asherah' discovered so far in the Near East ... dated by radiocarbon analysis to 4540 B.C.E. It is the oldest 'Ashera' found anywhere" (Greenboim Rich, 2022).

In light of this ancient date, it is worth noting that Sula Benet, the woman who first identified kaneh bosm as cannabis, connected the ritual use of cannabis worship to the Goddess cults that preceded the rise of Yahweh and Patriarchal monotheism. "Taking into account the matriarchal element of Semitic culture, one is led to believe that Asia Minor was the original point of expansion for both the society based on the matriarchal circle and the mass use of hashish" (Benet, 1936).

The Goddess of Plants

The Matriarchal Circle, refers to the age of the Goddess, and what Benet is identifying is her belief that it was amongst the Near Eastern worshipers of the goddess that the cultic use of cannabis may have originated.

The Matriarchal theory holds that as humanity made the transition from a nomadic hunter-gatherer, into a pastoral agriculturist, much of the earlier focus on animal totems (humanity's oldest religious symbols which were used to symbolically attract game), later became focused on the image of the Great Goddess, Mother Earth and the proper worship of her so that the earth would bear its fruits. As the developing mind of humanity struggled to comprehend the patterns of order in the seemingly chaotic world around them, they perceived that all new life was given birth by the feminine. "In the presence of birth, they were doubtful not merely about the father's identity but about his existence. Sex relations occurred without pregnancy; why should not pregnancy occur without sex relations? Woman alone was the visible life bestower" (Ashe 1976).

> In paleolithic times it was natural for a woman to be pregnant, and there was no particular reason to wonder how it came about.... Man's role in procreation was not one that could be easily deduced from the pattern of everyday paleolithic life, when intercourse was frequent and pregnancy commonplace, when the only calendar was the moon, and nine months in relation to life expectancy almost as long as two years today.... there is nothing in all the long millennia of the paleolithic era to prove that ... [man] knew about ... [his role in procreation] (Tannahill 1982).

As Erich Neumann wrote in *The Great Mother: An Analysis of the Archetype*:

> In the early situation of human culture, the group psyche was dominant. A relation of participation mystique prevailed between the individual and his group and its environment, particularly the world of plants and animals.... For many good reasons, the basic matriarchal view saw no relation between the sexual act and the bearing of children. Pregnancy and sexuality were disassociated both in the inner and outward experience of woman. This may be readily understood when we consider that these early societies were characterized by a promiscuous sex life that began far before sexual maturity... In the primordial phase therefore, the woman always conceived by an extrahuman, transpersonal power... (Neumann 1955\1974).

This primeval concept of the female as the sole creatrix of life gave rise to the cult of the Great Mother and thus many of the most ancient surviving religious artifacts are images of the female form. Her millennia of worship and veneration lasted well into Biblical times. "Evidence that worship of divinity in its feminine aspect had a place of importance in Canaan and Syria is given by the numerous small female statuettes with sexual characteristics emphasized which have been found by archaeologists ... it is clear that the worship of the goddess fits in well with the Canaanite fertility cult, and the number of these figurines attest to the high measure of popularity which she enjoyed" (Ringgren 1973). This is the cultural environment within which the origins of the Bible were rooted. The Patriarchal monotheism of the Bible was virtually unknown.

In the majority of hunter-gatherer societies Women generally balanced the males, supply of game with their collected harvest from the surrounding wilderness. It is believed that women, who acted as the gatherers in the early nomadic clan, were the first to recognize how the plants they collected propagated themselves, and this led to the development of agriculture. "Since the cultivation of plants was first undertaken by women, their importance in the social structure greatly increased, which, in turn, gave rise to a cult of Mother Earth, as well as to a mythology of the moon conceived as female" (Patai 1967). Agriculture, and an abundant harvest, led to more settled communities, and in light of this, it is not at all surprising to find that most of the earliest civilizations were both matriarchally structured and agriculturally based, i.e., Mohenjo-Daro, where evidence of ancient cannabis cloth has been recovered dating back to 9,000 BCE

Cannabis's relationship with things feminine likely goes back to its primordial discovery in the hunter-gatherer period of pre-history. Current archaeological evidence places the use of hemp fibers as far back as 25,000 years ago.

These early agriculturally based communities had a relationship and knowledge of the natural world around them that was likely comparable to that of the few un-Christianized aboriginal communities that have managed to survive down to our modern day – groups that have such an intense knowledge of the properties of the plants around them that it astounds many an academically trained botanist and chemist. As Anthropologist Richard Rudgley has commented on the early matriarchal situation;

> While animal proteins are highly prized, the bulk of the staples are usually the result of female labor. This division of labor may suggest that in prehistoric times women's role vis-a-vis plants were not limited to the culinary or even medical spheres, but extended into the discovery of psychoactive plants (this has a distant echo in the female dominated European witchcraft tradition ...). Gatherers have an extremely detailed knowledge of their land and its natural resources, and having considered the technical and in-

> tellectual achievements of hunter-gatherer communities past and present we should not be surprised that they were able to identify, collect and process a variety of species… (Rudgley 1993).

In sync with the developing social power and magic of the females, were many of the attributes acquired by the goddesses who represented her, particularly her association with magical plants. As Erich Neumann explained in *The Great Mother*:

> As goddess of the food-giving plants, herbs, and fruits, she numinously transforms these basic elements into intoxications and poisons. It is quite evident that the preparation and storage of food taught woman the process of fermentation and the manufacture of intoxicants, and that, as a gatherer and later preparer of herbs, plants, and fruits, she was the inventor and guardian of the first healing potions, medicines, and poisons…. The goddess is therefore not only the queen of the ennobled fruit of the soil but also of the spirit matter of transformation that is embodied in … wine [and other intoxicants]…
>
> In the pile dwellings of the Stone Age we already find evidence of the growing of poppies, the typical plant of the Cretan Goddess, of Demeter, Ceres and Spes…. The efficacy of the poppy as a magic potion … is a secret of the woman… (Neumann 1955\1974).

With her primordial association with the magical poppy, it is not so surprising to find the Goddess connected with other sacred plants as well. As noted the development of agriculture first took place during what is known as the matriarchal period of human culture when the image of the mother Goddess was the most widespread and common motif. Carl Sagan has suggested that cannabis was humanity's first agricultural crop (1977). Likewise the entheogen and aphrodisiac researcher Christian Rätsch has noted; "No other plant has been with humans as long as hemp. It is most certainly one of humanity's oldest cultural objects" (Rätsch 1997). With the views of such eminent scholars in mind along with the historically known popularity of the goddess at this same time, it only seems conclusive that there had to have been a deep rooted relationship between the ancient hemp crop and the Great Mother worshiped by the people who originally planted it. A hypothesis which is strengthened immensely with a look through the historical record.

Sula Benet explained:

> Let us look at the factors which could have contributed to the start of mass use of hashish in the matriarchal circle. One important factor is that in preparing fiber from plants and during the harvest the strong odor intoxicates the workers. According to ancient customs still surviving in modern times, all work involving hemp is done in mass. Since antiquity the hemp harvest has been considered a holiday, especially for the young people. In many countries the harvest is a sort of reunion to which guests come with or without masks and give all sorts of presents to the workers. Here we see an obvious link with the masculine secret societies in the matriarchal circle in which there is mass use of hashish (Benet/Benetowa, 1936).

Benet takes us back to a time period from which one of the most prevailing artifacts recovered has been various artifacts relating to the worship of the Great Goddess. A theory postulated by some anthropologists, that is fostered by these artifacts, suggests that in Palaeolithic, Mesolithic eras and/or Neolithic Europe and Western Asia and North Africa, a singular, monotheistic female deity was worshiped prior to the development of the polytheistic pagan religions of the Bronze Age and Iron Age.

Variations of the Great Goddess figurines that have been recovered from various archaeological sites.

Asherah's origins are believed to have developed out of early incarnations of the Goddess and her cult. Considering the length of time here, it's not surprising to find that the various regional offshoots of the Goddess took on a variety of new names and mythologies. However there are still commonalities that help to identify their shared origins.

Seated Mother Goddess of Çatal Höyük: (the head is a restoration), Museum of Anatolian Civilizations. Remains of Hemp cloth have been recovered from this same ancient site.

Prior to the rise of the Israelites and their God in the region, it is believed that Asherah was worshiped as Athirat, by the Canaanites who inhabited the region prior to the Israelite dominance of the area. One of Athirat's titles was "*Elat*" meaning "the Goddess," the feminine form of "*El*" (God). William Dever refers to a Canaanite clay jar shard that reads "A lamb, a gift for my lady, Elat" as Dever notes "Elat, is the feminine form of El, so you have the male and the female deity El and Elat ... there are two name in the Hebrew Bible for God, one is Yahweh, [translated as "Lord"] the National Hebrew deity, the other name is El, the name of the old Canaanite high God and it appears not only in this singular, but in the plural 'the gods'" [i.e. Elohim] (Dever, 2013). Here Dever sees more evidence of the Goddess and the earlier cosmology hidden by the final authors and editors of the Hebrew Bible texts.

As Caroline Tully, who holds a PhD. in archeology and has written about cult objects associated with Asherah, has noted "We know that in mythology Athirat interceded with El on behalf of petitioners, both gods and humans. Asherah may have interceded in the same way with Yahweh when he took over from El as chief god of the Israelites":

> "Athirat" ... was a queen mother and consort to El, the chief god of Ugarit. Athirat also appeared in other cultures such as Mesopotamia and South Arabia where she was similarly associated with the chief male deity. In Ugaritic myth Athirat was ... considered to be the mother of both gods and kings, and her function as the queen mother was to assign gods and mortals their roles in life. Athirat was also renowned as a successful intercessor with El – often only she could persuade El about something when everyone else had failed. Both gods and humans sought the ear of El through her. Athirat may also have been a deity petitioned particularly by women: she is described as holding a spindle, the typical tool of the housewife and her name may even be related to the Ugaritic word for woman, "att" ... Most scholars agree that Canaanite Athirat is equivalent to the biblical Asherah (Tully, 2011).

In relation to Athirat's spindles, its worth noting that "in the temple of the Lord ... women did weaving for Asherah" (2 Kings 23:7). Both forms of the Goddess also seem to have held a role in funerary cults, and in respect to weaving and funerary cults, and in respect to the findings of Arad, there have been claims that it was at one time a religious requirement in Mishnic times that the dead be buried in hemp shirts.

In her article "Asherah and Textiles" Jeannette H. Boertien noted "In Ugaritic texts Asherah ... is described ... with a spindle in her hand, dropping the spindle from her hand (= spinning)." Boertien refers to two archaeological sites that indicate the weaving of ritual garments and cloths, that may be associated with Asherah or one of her regional counterparts, where hemp cloth was found in this context:

> Fragments of textile were also found. Most were carbonized threads retrieved from the holes of some loom weights. In a room directly south of the benched room a small fragment of fabric, measuring 52 x 32 mm, was still lying in situ between 38 loom weights. These finds were analyzed by Dr. W.D. Cook of the Manchester Department of Textiles using a Scanning Electron Microscope.... The fabric turned out to be a very fine hemp cloth, a textile rarely encountered in the Middle East.... Deir 'Alla is the only known site in the Levant where hemp fiber has been identified in an archaeological context. The find of a fragment of finely woven hemp cloth ... is very exceptional, as hemp cloth has never before been reported from Iron Age levels in the Levant. Beside wool, linen is the most commonly used plant fiber. The presence of cloth made of the fiber hemp in the same complex in which a cult room with a religious inscription is found raises the question whether this special kind of cloth could have had a cultic use (Boertien 2007).

Similarly, the Hebrew male cult prostitutes, the *qedeshim* and their female counterparts, wove clothes for the Ashera which stood in the temple, from within the *qedeshim*'s chambers, also on the Temple grounds.

This aspect of weaving and spindles, seems to have been somewhat of a common factor with Goddesses associated with Asherah, who are believed to have come from a shared older origin, but took on their own regional names and myths over time. Professor of Northwest Semitic Languages at Yale University, Marvin Pope referred to an ancient hymn to Ishtar in this context: "The expert singers sit before her on the ground, those who play the lyre, the harp and the clappers ... the kurgarrus <who carry> the spindle ... and the whip, ease her mind with (incense of) 'sweet reeds.'" Pope compares these "sweet reeds" to references to the Bible that "The 'sweet reed' ... with which the goddess' inwards are soothed, is presumably the same 'aromatic cane' of Exodus 30:23 and the 'sweet cane' of Jer 6:20; Isa 43:24; Ezek 27:19 and simply 'cane' in Canticles 4:14" (Pope 1977). Interestingly, these same references to "cane" are the references that we will be looking at in the next chapters, as Sula Benet identified them in 1936 as references to cannabis. In the case of Ishtar, the use of cannabis seems likely as this is indicated in ancient Assyrian inscriptions as well. More interestingly, as we shall see, is that Ishtar is directly connected to cannabis in Assyrian and Babylonian texts.

The *Kurgarrus* who carried the spindles, were the transvestite worshipers of Ishtar, and they were the Mesopotamian counterparts of the *Qedeshim* who served Asherah and did ritual weaving for her in the temple precincts.

Assyriologist Erica Reiner reveals a connection between the goddesses Ishara and Ishtar and cannabis that is not mentioned in more than a couple of books on the ancient Near East in reference to the: "herb called *Sim.Ishara* 'aromatic of the Goddess Ishtar,' which is equated with the Akkadian *qunnabu*, 'cannabis', [which] may indeed conjure up an aphrodisiac through the association with Ishara, goddess of love, and also calls to mind the plant called *ki.na Ishtar*" (Reiner, 1995). This is also the view of Barbara Böck, of the Institute of Languages and Cultures of the Mediterranean and Near East, who stated that "A small cuneiform tablet which states '*qunnubu* is the aromatic plant of the goddess Ishkhara' [*sic*-Isharra] is notable because it has been interpreted that *Cannabis sativa* might have been used as an aphrodisiac" (Böck, 2022).

It should be noted that throughout the centuries in literature referring to cannabis, including medical journals, the aphrodisiac potential of the plant is acknowledged (Mikuriya, M.D. 1973, Grinspoon, M.D., & Bakalar 1993). In *The Encyclopedia of Erotic Wisdom*, which contains a number of entries regarding different preparations and utilizations of hemp, Rufus C. Camphausen notes that, "It is well known among the users of hashish and marijuana that THC, the main active ingredient of cannabis, is – among other things – a strong aphrodisiac, a fact even recognized by the *Encyclopedia Britannica*" (Camphausen 1991). In fact, so renowned is cannabis for its aphrodisiacal properties, that in his extensive book on aphrodisiacs, *Plants of Love,* Christian Rätsch writes "No matter which culture, no matter what time: hemp has been repeatedly deemed the aphrodisiac" (Rätsch 1997).

A 2002 edition of the *Compte Rendu, Rencontre Assyriologique Internationale,* a journal from the Rencontre Assyriologique Internationale (RAI) [which is the annual Assyriological Conference], (Parpola & Whiting ed. 2002) has a paper on hashish and opium, and it is noted that *"A Neo-Assyrian tablet reveals qunnubu to us as 'the aromatic of the love goddess Išhara' :.. ŠIM Iš - ha - ra qu - nu - bu - 'The herb of Ishara (is)."* The paper also noted the use of cannabis in ritual aromatic oils and delivery of large quantities of cannabis to Eanna, the temple of Inanna, the ancient Sumerian goddess of love, sensuality, fertility, procreation, and also of war. Inanna later became identified by the Akkadians and Assyrians as the goddess Ishtar, and further with the Hittite Sauska, the Phoenician Astarte and the Greek Aphrodite, among many others.

The Herb of Ishara

In *Studies on Neo-Assyrian Texts II: "Deeds and documents" from the British Museum* (1983) Frederick Mario Fales, translates the following ancient cuneiform verse (No. 12. BM103205. Copy: p. 252) regarding Ishara and *qunubu* cannabis

The salve of Ishara
is cannabis;
The salve of Ishara
is cannabis:
From the mouth of Qisirayyu
I hear so

As Fales explains "the connection between the salve of the plant *qunubu* and the name of this goddess might be sought in the aspect of the latter as deity of love. On *qunubu* ... as cannabis ... another [Assyrian] attestation of the plant [is translated]... (She) said: 'what is required for the ritual?' Quality oil, wax, quality salves (and particularly) salve of myrrh and salve of cannabis..." (Fales, 1983).

As Gavin White has also noted:

> ...[T]he multifaceted goddess Ishara. She does not appear to be a native Mesopotamian deity, but was worshiped by many people throughout the ancient Near East, which has led to a confusing array of attributions – she is known as a great goddess to the Hurrians, the wife of Dagon among the West Semites, and to the Akkadians she was a goddess of love with close affinities to Ishtar, whose sacred plant cannabis (qunnabu) was known as the aromatic of Ishara ... from her widespread worship she is also known as the queen of the inhabited world (White, 2008).

Ishara may represent a possible origin point for the use of cannabis in these ancient Goddess cults. It has been suggested that her name may come from an Indo-European root that means "rope" or "bind" likely in references to her role in oath keeping agreements, a role she shares with the Semitic Asherah. She was worshiped by the Hittites and they had the oldest attested Indo-European language. "Ishara" is affirmed as a loanword in the 19th century BC Assyrian Kültepe texts, and as such this would be among the earliest evidence of a written word of any Indo-European language.

Variations of "Ishara" appear as "Ašḫara" (in a treaty of Naram-Suen of Akkad with Hita of Elam) and "Ušḫara" (in Ugarite texts). In the archaeological site at Alalah, her name appeared with the Akkadogram IŠTAR plus a phonetic complement "-ra," as IŠTAR-"ra." All phonetically similar to Asherah and Ishtar.

The connection to Ishtar here is interesting, as this Goddess' cult, like that of Asherah's was known for its shamanic priestesses. As the British Archaeologist Diana Stein has noted "Inspired prophecy is a Mesopotamian phenomenon that is linked, in particular, to the ecstatic cult of Ishtar. The cult of Ishtar is described as an esoteric mystery cult that promises transcendental salvation and eternal life to its initiates. Altered states of consciousness, visions, and inspired prophecies were achieved by means of various ecstatic techniques..." (Stein, 2009). We can see here that cannabis and likely other entheogenic substances were a part of this technique.

Volkert Haas, a German Assyrologist and Hittitologist stated in *Geschichte der hethitischen Religion* (1994) that: "the nature of Išḫara is closely related with that of the goddess Ištar [*sic*-Ishtar]. At the end of the 2nd millennium BC Išḫara is hard to distinguish from Ištar anymore. For instance in a cuneiform lexical list 'the star of Išḫara' is similar with 'Ištar, the mistress of the Lands.' In the beginning of the 1st mil. her aspect as goddess of sexuality is completed with goddess of war. Then epithets like 'Išḫara, Mistress of Mankind' show that henceforth she is melded with Ištar."

Considering the Indo-European (IE) ritual use of cannabis in funerary rites is indicated as far back as 3,500 BCE in Romania and the Ukraine regions, and is known to have spread throughout the ancient world with IE culture in the Mid-East, China and India, combined with the known goddess worship of cannabis using IE groups like the Scythians, Ishara worship by Indo-European speaking Hittites, does seem a likely ancient avenue of ritual cannabis use into the region.

However, this Indo-European etymology of the name Ishara has been called into question, since the goddess appears from as early as the mid-3rd millennium as one of the chief goddesses of Ebla. Although her worship by the IE language Hittites assures that cannabis could still have been adopted by her cult. Ebla is interesting for its own evidence of ritual drug use.

Drug infused rituals at Ebla?

It has been claimed that the earliest known medical recipes come from the third millennium BCE city of Ebla, which was in Syria, and some also see indications of ritual drug use as well. Before the Syrian civil war, archaeologists digging in Ebla collected samples from a site that was described as a "kitchen," although there were no indications of the plant and animal remains that would usually be associated with food preparation. However as noted in the April 20th, 2018, issue of *Science*, in the story, "Cannabis, opium use part of ancient Near Eastern cultures":

> The researchers found traces of wild plants often used for medicine, such as poppy for opium to dull pain, heliotrope to fight viral infections, and chamomile to reduce inflammation. Given that the space contained eight hearths and pots that could hold 40 to 70 liters, the drugs could have been made in large quantities.... Some of these extracts, such as opium, can induce hallucinations, although it's unclear whether the potions were used in ritual or medicine. The kitchen's location near the heart of the palace suggests its products were used for ceremonial occasions, and cuneiform tablets from the building mention special priests associated with ritual beverages.... The distinction between medicine and mind-altering drug may have been lost on ancient peoples (Lawler, 1918).

Cannabis coming in via IE trade routes to the Hittites, would likely only have been added to the domain of an already existing Goddess who was associated with sacred plants. Thus regardless of her origins, Ishara still seems like an early possible avenue for the ritual use of cannabis to have been introduced in the Near East, as well as account for the plant's association with other Near Eastern Goddesses, such as Asherah and Ishtar, both of whose origins are likely tied back with the earlier Ishara.

However, many sources see an older relationship between Ishtar and Inanna, another goddess that holds ties with cannabis. Like Ishtar, who she is conflated with, Inanna was an ancient Mesopotamian goddess of love, war, and fertility. She is also associated with beauty, sex, divine justice, and political power. As with other similar near Eastern Goddesses, Inanna also seems to have had strong ties with the ritual use of cannabis. Inanna had a famous cultic temple in Eanna, and as noted "later Neo-Babylonian text records the delivery of large quantities of *qunnabu* [cannabis] to the great temple of Eanna" (Stein, 2009).

Cannabis also "appears as one of two ingredients in a sacrifice for another goddess, namely Tašmetu, divine spouse of the god Nabu" (Böck, 2022). Tašmetu's main position was that of wife to Nabu, divine scribe of destinies. Nabu functions as a god of wisdom, because knowledge and learning were often transmitted via writing and thus by association, Tašmetu also became bound with wisdom, and is deemed a wise goddess in a fragmentary prayer (CTN 4, 166). Like Ishara, Ishtar and Asherah, Tašmetu has a link with sexual attractiveness, which may stem from a shared aspect with the goddess Nanaya, a Mesopotamian goddess of love, who is closely associated with Inanna.

In first-millennium Assyria, Tašmetu was Nabu's consort but in Babylonia this role was taken by the goddess Nanaya (Inanna/Ištar). "Tašmetu is mentioned in association with both sexual attractiveness and wisdom in first-millennium prayers. In another prayer (CTN 4, 168) she is described as the 'queen and lady of the fates' (obv. ii 53). The same prayer also describes Tašmetu as a 'goddess of sex appeal and sensuality' (rrev. i 25) and 'mistress of the lovers in the inhabited world' (rev. ii 19). Tašmetu's associations with both sex and wisdom may stem from a shared aspect with Nabu's other consort Nanaya/Ištar" (Horry, 2013).

Ishtar may have also received a cannabis infused drink offering under the epithet *Beltu*. As noted in *Dictionary of Deities and Demons in the Bible* (1999):

> The name of the Babylonian goddess Beltu (var. Belit, Belti) is the feminine form of Bel ("Lord") and means "Lady." She is identified either with Ishtar or Ṣarpanitu [Wife of Marduk, and a goddess of childbirth]. Her mention in the Hebrew Bible is conjectural ... *biltî* in Isa. 10.4 into *bēltî*, "my Lady." ... Since the name Beltu is not really a name but an epithet ("Lady"), the identification with a specific deity is beset with problems. Used in genetical constructions such as Belet-Akkadi or Belet-ekaliim, the term "Lady" is an element in the name (or epithet) of numerous Babylonian and Assyrian ... goddesses.... The goddess to have been designated most frequently by this epithet, both in Sumerian ... and Akkadian ... is no doubt Ishtar.

In a *Sourcebook for Ancient Mesopotamian Medicine* (2014) JoAnn Scurlock records a recipe that requires 3 shekels of *qunnabu* [cannabis] to be mixed with other aromatic plants "a total of 26 shekels of aromatics in a mortar. You wash raisins in date beer. You take (them) out and mix these aromatics into them. You pour white (beer) onto it and then it is sealed for three days. On the fourth (!) day, you open (it) and pour out a libation to Beltu (before use)."

This is notable in relation to references to Ishtar in 18th century BCE tablets from the Palace of Mari, which was located in modern day Syria. These texts refer to a ritual dedicated to the Ishtar and refer to a drink given to ecstatic seers, who spoke on behalf of the Goddess."Presumably this drink contained psychoactive substances, perhaps mixed with wine, as Mari was a key center in the wine trade" (Stein, et. al., 2022). (This passage is also interesting in relation to references in *Jeremiah* 44, that shall be discussed in a later chapter, which condemn both the burning of incense to the "Queen of Heaven" as well as "pouring out drink offerings" to her.)

n. Mari Ishtar Temple

An engraving from the Ishtar temple at Mari, possibly depicting Ishtar with a plant and a drinking vessel, From (Stein, 2017)

Asherah and Cannabis

Asherah shares many traits with these other near Eastern Goddesses, and many scholars believe this is due to a much more ancient common origin. In light of the findings in Arad, it is interesting that Asherah has similarly been connected to cannabis. The first time I read about this was in a chapter on cannabis by the Botanist William Emboden which stated that "There is a classic Greek term, *cannabeizen,* which means to smoke Cannabis. *Cannabeizen* frequently took the form of inhaling vapors from an incense burner in which these resins were mixed with other resins, such as myrrh, balsam, frankincense, and perfumes; this is the manner of the shamanistic Ashera priestesses of pre-reformation Jerusalem, who anointed their skins with the mixture as well as burned it" (Emboden 1972).

Over the years I've spent a bit of time, trying to understand the basis and source for Emboden's claim, and recently found that this information came from the poet, novelist, and historical author Robert Graves, who wrote in an article in the 1970 edition of *The Atlantic*:

> Taking cannabis is indeed an ancient enough practice; cannabeizein, "to smoke pot," appears in the ordinary Classical Greek dictionary. Presumably its fumes were absorbed through the pores of the skin when the cannabis itself was smoked over a low fire – the pot taker crouching over it clad only in a poncho. This at least seems to have been how the Ashera priestesses of the pre-Reformation Temple at Jerusalem impregnated their skins with the holy incense, which was mixed with other perfumes (Graves, 1970).

Unfortunately, Graves gave no indication for the origins of this claim and I cannot find anything regarding this, beyond his statement. However, what is interesting is that Graves had a very close relationship with Rapahel Patai, author of *The Hebrew Goddess* (1967) who was discussed earlier. In fact in the early 1960s the two wrote a book together, *The Hebrew Myths* (1964). I can find nothing indicating Patai ever wrote about such a connection, but interestingly enough, he does seem to be acquainted with the anthropologist and etymologist discussed in the next chapter, Sula Benet. Benet theorized that the Hebrew term *kaneh bosem*, was actually a reference to cannabis. This new archeology from tel Arad, vindicates her claim, and takes it from being a 'theory' into the realm of historical fact. Moreover what these references to cannabis tell, is the story of a plant, once burnt in the Holy of Holies in Jerusalem, that fell out of favor due to its association with the cult of Asherah, the Queen of Heaven, and one time wife of the Biblical God!

More recently, Father Angelo Bellon op of Amici Domenicani*, suggested that the use of cannabis in the tel Arad temple, was likely connected to Asherah:

> ...we know that even after the Jewish occupation some signs of Canaanite divinities remained here and there, in particular of Asherah, who together with Anat and Astarte, were the Canaanite ideas of fertility. The Old Testament mentions superstitious practices, referring to the aforementioned Canaanite goddess, practices that were opposed by the civil and religious authorities. It can be understood how the priests of pagan

> gods, who according to St. Paul are demons (1 Cor 10:20), needed certain practices to stimulate concentration in order to get in touch with occult forces.... But this mentality and similar rituals are despised by Holy Scripture (Bellon, 2021).[2]

As well Steve Wiggins, a Biblical scholar and author of *A Reassessment of Asherah: With Further Considerations of the Goddess* (2007) has noted of my own research connecting Asherah and the Hebrew Bible with cannabis via kaneh bosm:

> Biblical scholars, on their own, are unlikely to explore such "outsiders'" claims, like those who find references to cannabis in the Bible, do. Clearly cannabis was known in the ancient world and people then didn't have our modern filters of "the war on drugs," or, as Bennett makes clear, prohibition, to tell them drugs were bad. In fact, traditional cultures around the world believed natural hallucinogens were sacred, or at least gateways to sacred experiences. Bennett presents an overarching revisionist view of the Hebrew Bible (including the Apocrypha). There are many parts where my scholarly spidey-sense was tingling – one of the first things you learn in the academy is that connections have to be tested and retested and run by other scholars for their approval before they can be deemed valid – but overall it's clear a lot of research went into this.
>
> The academic heart that still beats in this weary chest says, "but wait, too many connections are made and it all fits into too tidy a package." ... And yes, Asherah is part of this tidy package too. There are some very interesting ideas here. While scholars argue about J, E, D, and P and their possible non-existence, others have already moved on to some interesting conclusions based on a fiery cup*[3] and its contents. I was ousted from the academy for being too liberal in a conservative environment. I have watched how the academy behaves for at least thirty years now. It seems to me that we should pay attention to what those outside, who have larger followings than those in ivory towers do, are saying. (Wiggens, 2021)

---

2 Bellon belongs to the Order of Dominican Priests. He completed his studies in the Order's own academic institutions (Studium Generale of Chieri, the Theological Faculty of Bologna and the Pontifical University of San Tommaso). He has been teaching moral theology for several years, especially in the Theological Faculty of Northern Italy

3 See Chapter 12

Chapter Three

The Lost Word: *Kaneh Bosm*

A May 31, 2020 *Haaretz* article, "Ancient Israelites Used Cannabis as Temple Offering" asks:

> So if the ancient Israelites were joining in on the party, why doesn't the Bible mention the use of cannabis as a substance used in rituals, just as it does numerous times for frankincense? ...One possibility is that cannabis does appear in the text but the name used for the plant is not recognized by researchers, Arie says, adding that hopefully the new study will open up that question for biblical scholars.

I suspect that this is an indirect reference to Sula Benet's theory on *kaneh bosm*.

A question is also raised as to whether this was religiously condoned use or heresy? Some researchers have suggested the evidence of tel Arad indicates the practices of the Holy of Holies at the main temple, other sources see this as proof of the sort of pagan activities taking place at the "high places" which were condemned in the Hebrew Bible narrative, particularly in regards to the cult of Asherah.

Religiously biased commentators, who hold a lot of sway on opinions of what various artifacts uncovered from the desert sands of the Holy Land, constitute, have been quick to note that the temple site in Arad, also betrays evidence of heretical polytheistic practices.

Another question is raised in that the original research paper on the Arad altars noted that there is little evidence that the frankincense and cannabis resins burnt on the altars at Arad were even produced in the Holy Land, and suggest they were imported into the region. If that is the case, where would they have come from?

The answers to all of these questions can be found in the Hebrew references to *kaneh bosm*, just as the proof of *kaneh bosm* as cannabis can be found in tel Arad.

Tel Arad was of particular interest to me, as for more than three decades, I have been suggesting that there are indications of the ritual use of cannabis in the Biblical narrative. However, this theory was based purely on etymological evidence regarding Hebrew terms, *kaneh* and *kaneh bosm,* that a little known Polish Anthropologist and linguist, Sula Benet, first suggested in a 1936 paper, were references to cannabis. What is most interesting, is how closely what we know about the finds of cannabis resins at the shrine in Arad, parallels the story told by the *kaneh* and *kaneh bosm* references identified by Sula Benet.

Sula Benet and *Kaneh Bosm*

In her essays "Tracing One Word Through Different Languages" (1936) and "Early Diffusions and Folk Uses of Hemp" (1975), Benet demonstrated that the Hebrew terms "*kaneh*" and "*kaneh bosm*" identified cannabis:

> Both in the original Hebrew text of the Old Testament and in the Aramaic translation, the word *kaneh* or *keneh* is used either alone or linked to the adjective *bosm* in Hebrew and *busma* in Aramaic, meaning aromatic. It is *cana* in Sanskrit, *qunnabu* in Assyrian, *kenab* in Persian, kannab in Arabic and *kanbun* in Chaldean. In Exodus 30: 23, God directed Moses to make a holy oil composed of "myrrh, sweet cinnamon, *kaneh bosm* and kassia." In many ancient languages, including Hebrew, the root *kan* has a double meaning – both hemp and reed. In many translations of the Bible's original Hebrew, we find *kaneh bosm* variously and erroneously translated as "calamus" and "aromatic reed," a vague term. Calamus, [*Calamus aromaticus* is a fragrant marsh plant]. The error occurred in the oldest Greek translation of the Hebrew Bible, Septuagint, in the third century B.C., where the terms *kaneh, kaneh bosm* were incorrectly translated as "calamus." And in the many translations that followed, including Martin Luther's, the same error was repeated…
>
> In Exodus 30:23 *kaneh bosm* is translated as "sweet calamus." In Isaiah 43:24 *kaneh* is translated as "sweet cane," although the word "sweet" appears nowhere in the original. In Jeremiah 6:20 *kaneh* is translated as "sweet cane." In Ezekiel 27: 19 *kaneh* is translated as "calamus." In Song of Songs 4:14 *kaneh* is translated "calamus."
>
> In the course of time, the two words *kaneh* and *bosm* were fused into one, *kanabos* or *kannabus,* known to us from Mishnah, the body of traditional Hebrew law. The word bears an unmistakable similarity to the Scythian "cannabis." Is it too far-fetched to assume that the Semitic word *kanbosm* and the Scythian word *cannabis* mean the same thing? (Benet, 1975).

Brian Du Toit, a South African anthropology educator and University of Florida President's scholar, further clarifies this situation:

> There exists a number of historically related words, differing to some degree in the characters employed, but quite clearly derived from the same stem. Sanskrit uses *Cana,* Hebrew Kaneh and Aramaic *Keneh.* Persian employs *Kenab,* Arabic *Kannab,* Assyrian *Qunnabu,* Chaldean *Kanbun,* and Scythian *Cannabis.* Benet (1975) suggests that, in time, Hebrew and Aramaic linked their root forms with the word meaning 'aromatic', namely, *bosm* and *busma,* respectively. The result are terms which look much like other Middle East terms, namely *kanabos* in Hebrew and *kannabus* in Aramaic (Du Toit, 1996).

As Benet has explained, the Hebrew word *kaneh-bosm* was mistranslated into Greek as calamus at the time the Septuagint was being composed. Calamus is a common marsh plant found throughout much of the Mid East with little monetary worth that does not have the qualities or value ascribed to kaneh-bosm.

It should also be noted, the identification of *kaneh bosm* with calamus, does not discount the use of a psychoactive substance in the Holy anointing oil. Prof. Carl Ruck, a proponent of Benet's etymological theory, has noted "It is ironic that calamus 'sweet flag,' the substitute for the alleged cannabis, is itself a known hallucinogen for which TMA-2 is derived" (Ruck et. al., 2001).

Meyler's Side Effects of Herbal Medicines also notes this: "Acorus calamus has been used as a hallucinogen since ancient times and it has several uses in folk medicine. It may have been one of the constituents of the Holy Oil that God commanded Moses to make (Exodus 30) and is mentioned by ancient writers on medicine, such as Hippocrates, Theophrastus, Dioscorides, and Celsus" (Aronson, 2008).

Although *kaneh* is described as an item coming in through trade caravans in *Ezekiel* 27:19, and from a "foreign land" in *Jeremiah* 6:20, *Bible Flowers and Flower Lore* (1851) reports that "roots and preparations" from calamus "are still obtained from the East , and principally from the Levant." This is a longstanding and common view, as noted under "CALAMITIS (from calamus, a reed)" in *Dictionarium Medicum Universale* (1749) "This little reed grows in several parts of the Levant, from whence it is brought" (Barrow, 1749).

Ancient sources also refer to its production in the countries surrounding Israel, so the idea that the plant would have stopped growing at imagined borders, is preposterous to say the least. Calamus: "An aromatic reed (*kalamos euödes; calamus odoratus*) was, in fact, to be found in Arabia, according to Theophrastus and Pliny, both of whom knew it to grow in Syria, too; in particular, it grew by the dried-out lake in the Lebanese valley in which sweet rushes (Arabic *idhkhir*) were also to be found (Theophrastus, *Plants*, ix, 7: if.; Pliny, *Natural History*, xn, 104 ff.). It grew in south Arabia, too, according to Agatharchides" (Crone, 2015).

Because of this issue and other reasons, alternate sources have suggested the Biblical *kaneh* was not calamus, but rather "lemon grass" or "ginger grass," the *Andropogon schoenanthus* imported from India. However, there is little evidence for this claim, in comparison for the identification of cannabis. As noted in *The Perfume Handbook*, "the calamus of the ancients ... was a different plant from that known as calamus today. It grew, according to the classical authors, in Arabia, the best coming from north Arabia, and Syria as well as in Egypt, and was probably the plant now known as Lemon Grass" (Groom, 2013).

The Ultimate Bible Dictionary adds "Ginger Grass" to this list, stating under "Calamus: The Latin for cane, Hebrew *Kaneh*, mentioned (Ex. 30:23) "It was probably that which is now known in India by the name of 'lemon grass' or 'ginger grass,' the *Andropogon schoenanthus*" (Easton, 2012).

The *Encyclopedia Judaica* (2007) viewed *kaneh bosm* as a reference to both Lemon grass (*Cymbopogon*), and Schoenus, a predominately austral genus of sedges, commonly known as bogrushes, or veldrushes, adding to the candidates, based on the reference to calamus in the writings of Theophrastus (371-237 BCE). Apparently both grew locally, which would discount them as an item of trade: "An interesting problem is posed by the statement of Theophrastus about calamus and schoenus, apparently two species of keneh-bosem – (*Cymbopogon*) growing in a valley not far from the Lebanon, probably the Ḥuleh area. The English naturalist H.B. Tristram, who explored Ereẓ Israel in the second half of the 19th century, wrote that the second species grew then in the vicinity of Lake Kinneret" (Skolnik, 2007).

In *Duke's Handbook of Medicinal Plants of the Bible*, James Duke as well lists a variety of candidates for *kaneh bosm*:

> Admitting that it is hopeless to speculate about which of the possible species (*Cymbopogon citratus, Cymbopogon martinii*, or *Cymbopogon schoenanthus*) [Lemon Grass] was intended by the biblical writers, Zohary [Michael Zohary, a pioneering Israeli botanist] led his discussion with ginger grass.... In my first Bible book, I followed Moldenke's [an American botanist/taxonomist] suggestion it could be *Andropogon schoenanthus* [Camel Grass]

> or *Andropogon muricatus* (which is apparently *Vetiveria*) and they leaned towards the vetiver. After reading Zohary, I am more inclined to side with him. No one seems to push *Acorus calamus.*... It seems less likely to have been imported than the *Cymbopogon* or *Vetiveria,* to either of which the alternate translation of "sweet [smelling] cane" seems more appropriate (Duke, 2007).

Aryeh Kaplan in *The Living Torah,* quotes four opinions as to the identity of *keneh bosem*: calamus (Septuagint, Rambam Peirush HaMishnayos, et. al.), *Cympopogan* (Rambam Mishneh Torah), Cannabis ("some"), and Cinnamon (Radak, Abarbanel): "Fragrant cane Keneh bosem in Hebrew. Ancient sources identify this with the sweet calamus (Septuagint; Rambam on Kerithoth 1:1; Saadia; Ibn Janach). This is the sweetflag or flagroot, *Acoras calamus* which grows in Europe. It appears that a similar species grew in the Holy Land, in the Hula region in ancient times (Theophrastus, *History of Plants* 9:7). Other sources apparently indicate that it was the Indian plant, Cympopogan martini, which has the form of red straw (Yad, Kley HaMikdash 1:3). On the basis of cognate pronunciation and Septuagint readings, some identify *Keneh bosem* with the English and Greek cannabis, the hemp plant. There are, however, some authorities who identify the 'sweet cane' with cinnamon bark (*Radak, Sherashim*). Some say that *kinman* is the wood, and *keneh bosem* is the bark (Abarbanel)" (Kaplan, 1981).

Exodus כי תשא

ראש מר־דרור חמש מאות וקנמן־בשם מחציתו חמשים
24 ומאתים וקנה־בשם חמשים ומאתים׃ וקדה חמש
25 מאות בשקל הקדש ושמן זית הין׃ ועשית אתו שמן
משחת־קדש רקח מרקחת מעשה רקח שמן משחת־
26 קדש יהיה׃ ומשחת בו את־אהל מועד ואת ארון העדת׃
27 ואת־השלחן ואת־כל־כליו ואת־המנרה ואת־כליה ואת
28 מזבח הקטרת׃ ואת־מזבח העלה ואת־כל־כליו ואת־
29 הכיר ואת־כנו׃ וקדשת אתם והיו קדש קדשים כל־
הנגע בהם יקדש׃

fragrant cane. *Keneh bosem* in Hebrew. Ancient sources identify this with the sweet calamus (Septuagint; Rambam on Kerithoth 1:1; Saadia, Ibn Janach). This is the sweetflag or flagroot, *Acoras calamus* which grows in Europe. It appears that a similar species grew in the Holy Land, in the Hula region in ancient times (Theophrastus, *History of Plants* 9:7). Other sources apparently indicate that it was the Indian plant, *Cympopogan martini*, which has the form of red straw (*Yad, Kley HaMikdash* 1:3). On the basis of cognate pronunciation and Septuagint readings, some identify *Keneh bosem* with the English and Greek cannabis, the hemp plant.

There are, however, some authorities who identify the "sweet cane" with cinnamon bark (Radak, *Sherashim*). Some say that *kinman* is the wood, and *keneh bosem* is the bark (Abarbanel).

30:24 **cassia** (Radak, *Sherashim; Peshita;* Vulgate). *Kidah* in Hebrew; *ketzia* in Aramaic (*Targum;* Rambam on *Kelayim* 1:8). Cassia is the common name for the bark of the tree *Cinnamomum cassia* or *Cassia lignea* belonging to the laurel family, which grows in China. (*Pachad Yitzchak,* s.v. *Ketoreth;* cf. Pliny 12:43; Theophrastus, *History of Plants* 9:7; Diodorus Siculus 3:46; Herodatus 3:110)

There are some, however, who identify the "cassia" of the ancients, and hence *kidah* here, with costus, known as *kosh't* in the Talmud (*Yad, Kley HaMikdash* 1:3; Saadia; Ibn Janach. cf. Rashi). Costus is the root of the annual herb, *Saussurea lappa,* which grows on the mountain slopes of Kashmir, and is used for incense and perfume.

The Septuagint translates *kidah* here as *iris,* possibly *Costus speciosus.* Others suggest that it is kitio or morylon, a plant very much like cassia, coming from Meuzel on the African coast (cf. Dioscorides, *De Materia Medica* 1:13).

— **gallon.** *Hin* in Hebrew. Actually 0.97 gallon, or 3.6 liter.

30:25 **blended compound.** The anointing oil was made by soaking the aromatic substances in water until the essential essences are extracted. The oil is then placed over the water, and the water slowly cooked away, allowing the essences to mix with the oil (*Yad, Kley HaMikdash* 1:1; from *Kerithoth* 5a). According to another opinion, the oil was cooked with the aromatic herbs, and then filtered out (*Ibid.*).

A page from Rabbi Kaplan's *The Living Torah*, referring to kaneh bosm, and listing cannabis as a candidate "on the basis of cognate pronunciation."

Dr. J. Alan Branch, a Professor of Christian Ethics at Midwestern Baptist Theological Seminary, recently wrote an article rejecting Sula Benet's hypothesis, and made a rather novel generalization about the term kaneh bosm. "Benet's bizarre assertion is not substantiated by the definitive Hebrew lexicon, The Hebrew and Aramaic Lexicon of the Old Testament, which says the term qanēh-bōśem [kaneh bosm] is referring to a type of balsam oil. Balsam simply refers to aromatic resins derived from certain plants, and not cannabis (Branch, 2022).[1] As the recipe given in Exodus 30:23 is elsewhere quite specific on both measurements and ingredients, and includes already a distinct variety of aromatic plants to be prepared in Olive oil, this suggestion seems particularly doubtful, and is not found among the Hebrew sources we have cited here. Although writing his article, in 2022, Professor Branch seems to be sadly unaware of the discovery of cannabis resins on an altar in tel Arad, two years prior.[2]

When the discoveries of cannabis resins at tel Arad were made public, one who was quick to respond was Professor Zohar Amar, of the Department of Land of Israel Studies at the religious-Zionist Bar-Ilan University. His specialty is in identifying the plants of the ancient Levant,and he is highly respected in his field. His article "The Israelites did not smoke cannabis in the Temple," appeared in the *Makor Rishon,* an Israeli weekly newspaper, on June 12th, 2020 is translated and reprinted in full, in Appendix 4. In his article, Amar opens with the statement: "*The Israelites did not smoke cannabis in the temple and cannabis is not 'kaneh bosm'. There is no evidence of its use in the temple in Jerusalem. Quite the opposite: Judaism abhors intoxicating its believers*" (Amar, 2020).

Lots to unpack there, and I will get into his reasons for the dismissal of kaneh bosm in more detail. But obviously, we can only speculate in

1 We have included Professor Branch's complete article "Cannabis is in the Bible?": Debunking an Interpretative Myth" as Appendix 3

2 A Christianity.com article by Ann de Zande, "What Does the Bible Say about Smoking Weed?," echoed Branch's comments.

"Even though the Bible never mentions cannabis, and despite centuries of credible Hebrew scholarship, a myth to the opposite persists. It began with twentieth-century Polish anthropologist Sula Benet (1903-1982), who studied Polish and Judaic customs.... One of those ingredients is the Hebrew word, qanēh-bōśem, translated as "aromatic or fragrant cane." Hebrew lexicon experts translate the term to mean balsam, but Benet switched the ingredient from balsam to cannabis with no hard evidence to back her assertion…

"Misinformation and myths rely on the new, exciting, potent, and intriguing. The problem can be compounded by academics overreaching to provide new ideas. Academic research looks for new concepts or discoveries. If a scholar or researcher provides an intriguing but inaccurate new insight, sometimes the idea gains notoriety, as seen in Benet's translation.

"Despite Benet's theory being shown false and disregarded, the myth that the Bible talks about cannabis persists today" (de Zande, 2023).

Similarly, Dr. Claude Mariottini, an Emeritus Professor of Old Testament at Northern Baptist Seminary, published an article dismissing claims of Biblical cannabis use titled "Marijuana and Archaeology", in 2006, When he was reminded of this in 2020, in regards to the new evidence from tel Arad, he wrote "There is no doubt that, according to recent archaeological discoveries, the use of cannabis is dated back to antiquity. However, I am not willing to promote the use of cannabis…" and then subsequently pulled the earlier article from his website with no comment.

regards to the main temple in Jerusalem, as no archaeological remains of the site have been examined. We have been over the connections that have been made about practices between tel Arad and the main temple already in Chapter 1, and one could argue the inscription found there, referring to it as a "House of Yahweh," clearly mark that connection.

In regard to Judaism and intoxication, we have the example of Purim day,when a festive meal called the *Se'udat Purim* is held. There is a longstanding custom of drinking wine at the feast. On Passover, the four cups of wine are for joy and for sanctification, "Rava said: It is one's duty[*levasumei*], to make oneself fragrant [with wine]on Purim until one cannot tell the difference between '*arur Haman*' (cursed be Haman) and '*barukh Mordekhai*' (blessed be Mordecai)" (Babylonian Talmud). This does indeed sound like intoxication, and the festivities of these events are well known. In regards to cannabis incense however, that they would have considered this as a mere recreational intoxication, seems doubtful.

Amar indicates that the basis of the claim that *kaneh bosm* is cannabis is purely phonetic, and the similarity in sound to our own term "cannabis." However this similarity is more direct with contemporary names for cannabis in the surrounding region, such as *qunnabu* in Assyrian, *kenab* in Persian, *kannab* in Arabic and *kanbun* in Chaldean. As well as the later Mishnic term for cannabis *kanabos* or *kannabus*. Here the similarities go far beyond the merely phonetic, and we see comparable use of those indicated for *kaneh* and *kaneh bosm* in place as well. Assyrian references refer to the use of cannabis specifically in ointments, incenses and for the sacred rites.

This is important, as Professor Amar disqualifies cannabis as *kaneh bosm*, as he claims that cannabis "and its products are not defined as perfumes and are not mentioned in the use of scent and incenses in cultures of the ancient world" (Amar, 2020). This is of course preposterous. Cannabis appears in ointments like that described in Exodus, such as the "salve of Ishara" discussed in Chapter 2. Moreover, ancient references to *qunnabu* refer to it directly and specifically in the preparation of perfumes, ointments, incense and beverages, as an offering at temples and the sacred rites, all of which will be explored fully later in this chapter.

I would also suggest, Amar made the mistake of only looking at the context of the first reference to *kaneh bosm*, inExodus30:23: "*Kaneh bosem* was used as one of the components of the anointing oil in which the holy vessels and the priests were anointed (Exodus 30:23-25) and is not at all related to the incense ingredients that were burnt in the temple" (Amar, 2020). Here, he seems to be unaware of the context of both Isaiah 43:23-24, and Jeremiah 6:20,where *kaneh* appears arguably as an incense and alongside frankincense, as with the two altars at tel Arad.

Amar, bolsters his claim with the comment that cannabis "does not appear in this context in any of the ancient identification traditions or in the authorized studies that deal with the identification of biblical plants" (Amar, 2020). True enough, and that is worth noting, as none of these studies, predicted the discovery of cannabis resins at an ancient Hebrew sacred site,in the same way that the linguistic theory of *kaneh bosm* does.

Professor Amar closes his article with the statement: "Due to the idolatrous-themed activity and the desire to have one central worship in Jerusalem, the activity of the temple at Tel Arad was cancelled, probably as part of Hezekiah's religious reform (2 Kings 18:4). This points to the opposite conclusion: the Israeli faith rejected the use of cannabis or any narcotic substance for the purpose of the work" (Amar, 2020).

This is not wholly in dispute with what I have written in this book. As noted in Chapters 1 and 2, tel Arad, was known for the combined worship of Asherah and Yahweh, and this likely was a reason behind the cancellation of the site by Hezekiah. However, this is also further confirmation of *kaneh* as cannabis, as Jeremiah 6:20 sees the rejection of both cannabis and frankincense, and this reference as we shall show in Chapter 9, is tied to Jeremiah 44, where former citizens of Jerusalem are blamed by Jeremiah for the fall of Jerusalem, due to "burning incense to the Queen of Heaven." Although in this regard, it is important to remember here, we are dealing with centuries of time, and many changes happened throughout the history of the ancient Hebrews, which archaeology shows, were polytheistic in the Kingdom period. The linguistic references to *kaneh* and *kaneh bosm*, tell the tale of a plant which was once a part of sacred worship in the temple, that was later rejected as the kingdom moved from polytheism into monotheism. Amar's religious bias is evident here, as he projects later Jewish monotheism, onto the polytheistic past of Israel and Judah, a situation that will be explained more fully on the pages of this book.

What this shows, is the lack of an actual firm identification, of the Biblical kaneh. Candidates include calamus, schoenus, bark of cinnamon, vetiver, ginger grass, camel grass, lemon grass, and cannabis. However, the evidence sits much more firmly with cannabis than any of these other candidates as we shall see, and the evidence for this goes far beyond the similarity in the cognate pronunciation noted by Kaplan.

Both the *Septuagint* and the later Latin *Vulgate* are known for their mistranslation of Hebrew words into Greek (Gordon, 2006; Henslow, 2009). Most notable is the *Septuagint* mistranslation of the Hebrew term "*almah*" meaning "young woman," which was translated into the

Greek as "parthenos – "virgin." This single example had a monumental effect on later Christian cosmology and theology as it resulted in the later belief that the Messiah must be born of a virgin. Moreover, in relation to our study, the mistranslation of Hebrew botanical names is also believed to have occurred:

> The fast-growing plant referred to in the biblical Book of Jonah is most often translated into English as "gourd." However, this is a mistranslation that dates to the appended Septuagint, the Greek translation of the Hebrew Bible, in which the Hebrew word *qiqayon* (castor, *Ricinus communis*, Euphorbiaceae) was transformed into the somewhat similar-sounding Greek word *kolokynthi* (colocynth, *Citrullus colocynthis*). In translation of the Greek into Latin, *kolokynthi* became the similar-sounding *cucurbita* (gourd). This is reflected in early iconography, the plant most often depicted being a long-fruited *Lagenaria siceraria* (bottle or calabash gourd), a fast-growing climber. (Janick & Paris, 2006).

I would suggest that a further potential direct use of the term *kaneh* in reference to cannabis occurs in Genesis 41:22, and this passage, which refers to grains, also disallows an interpretation of calamus, as calamus is not known for edible seeds or grains: "In my [Joseph] dreams I ... saw seven heads of grain, full and good, growing on a single stalk [kaneh]." The highly nutritious seeds of cannabis have been referred to as grains, and 7 heads, or large kola buds, on a marijuana plant, would be a sign of abundance. Calamus has a single stalk and head. The hemp seed's use as a food and oil source can be traced back to the very beginnings of civilization and Hebrew references to the use of it for food are known

The German botanist, Immanuel Löw, referred to a sixth century BCE Persian name for a preparation of cannabis seed, *Sahdanag* (Löw, 1925; reprinted 1967). *Sahdanag*, translated as "Royal Grain"; or "King's Grain" demonstrates the high regard the ancient Persians held for the nutritious oil rich seeds that came from the same plant which provided them also with a means of religious revelation by means of the drink *bangha*, which we will discuss in a later chapter. This fits well with the "*kaneh*" "grain" noted in Joseph's dream (Genesis 41:22). *Sahdanag* was generally prepared in the form of a heart shaped cookie, possibly indicating that the ancient Persians recognized the seed's close relationship with health and vitality (Löw, 1925; reprinted 1967). Sometime after the Persian Empire took control of the ancient world, the Jews adopted this Persian preparation of hemp seed and retained its name of *Sahdanag*.

In *Hebraic Literature: Translations from the Talmud, Midrashim and Kabbala,* Maurice Henry Harris records that in the *Nedarim,* fol. 49. col. 1, "Rav Yehudah [(220-299 CE)] says it is good to eat ... the essence of hemp seed in Babylonian broth; but it is not lawful to mention this in the presence of an illiterate man, because he might derive a benefit from the knowledge not meant for him" (Harris, et al., 2004). [This "benefit" may have been acquired from brewing seeds with the THC rich calyx covering the seed, being intact when it was prepared.]

Immanuel Löw also suggests that the formerly unidentified Hebrew word, tzli'q, (Tzaddi, Lamed, Yod, Quoph), makes reference to a Jewish meal of roasted hemp seeds that was popular into medieval times and was sold by Jews in European markets. (The first part of the name tzli'q simply means roasted, the final letter, Quoph, an abbreviation of *kaneh,* which begins with that letter – Löw's reference to this may also indicate independent support for Benet's interpretation of the term kaneh as cannabis) (Löw, 1925; reprinted 1967).

Benet suggested the use of kaneh in reference to cloth as another example "Another piece of evidence regarding the use of the word *kaneh* in the sense of hemp rather than reed [or calamus] is the religious requirement that the dead be buried in kaneh shirts. Centuries later linen was substituted for hemp (Klein 1908)" (Benet, 1975). Calamus is not a fiber plant.

Benet cited Siegfried Klein's *Tod und Begräbnis in Palästina zur Zeit der Tannaiten* (H. Itzkowski, 1908), and unfortunately, that reference is less clear on this matter. Although Klein does identify hemp cloth, he does not use the older term kaneh, as Benet claimed, he used the later *Mishnah* term *kanabos,* which does indeed identify cannabis, and which Benet saw as a development of the earlier term *kaneh bosm.* However other sources would argue the *kanabos* of *Mishnah,* marks the adoption of the Greek *kannabis,* during the Hellenistic period. From what I have seen, I think *shesh,* which will be discussed in the next chapter is a more likely term for hemp cloth during the earlier period, and later in during Mishnic times, this was identified as *kanabos.*

Sula Benet, noted that *kanabos,* for "cannabis" appears in the *Mishnah,* the oldest authoritative post biblical collection and codification of Jewish oral laws, systematically compiled over a period of about two centuries and given final form early in the 3rd century CE. Benet asserts that *kanabos* derived from *kaneh bosm.* "In the course of time, the two words '*kaneh*' and '*bosm*' were fused into one, '*kanabos*' or '*kannabus,*' known to us from Mishnah, the body of traditional Hebrew law" (Benet, 1975).

Klein's reference to hemp cloth refers to "the various types of clothing for the dead mentioned by the Talmud," and identifies a Persian word, *sadra,* which identifies a "coarse garment." Klein notes that the 10th century scholar Rashi explains that it is "(probably κάνναβις) [Greek 'Cannabis']" (Klein, 1908). Klein here referring to the term used by Rashi *qnbws,* also translated *kanabos,* which Klein equated with the Greek *kannabis.* Similarly, Nahum Ben-Yehuda, in "Cannabis – Chanvre – Hemp in Rashi's Commentary to the Talmud," noted that "Rashi mentions hemp in his exegesis to the Talmud and have interpreted them as reflecting contemporary material culture" (Ben-Yehuda, 2011).

Similarly, Rav Pappah, (300-375 CE) a Babylonian rabbi, informs us in his time the practice was to bury the dead in inexpensive shrouds made of coarse cloth, known as "Ṣadra bar zuza" – "A garment (shroud) made of qnbws, [kanabos-cannabis] which costs only a dinar" (Ketubbot 8b).[3]

In regards to *kaneh* and *kaneh bosm,* Rav Pappah 4th century and Rashi's tenth century CE use of the same term, *kanabos,* tends to be unconvincingly discounted as being a counterpart of the earlier Hebrew *kaneh bosm,* and is instead claimed as the later Hebrew version of the Greek, "kanabis" (cannabis) that was adopted during the Hellenistic period. This may have been a valid argument prior to the discovery of cannabis resins at the shrine in tel Arad. However, the case for a Greek origin of the *Mishnah kanabos* loses ground now that we have direct evidence for cannabis use during the composition period of the Hebrew Bible. To suggest that the Mishnah term *kanabos* was derived from the Greek *kannabis,* would now require the discovery of an alternative ancient Hebrew name for cannabis, unrelated to *kaneh bosm,* that was replaced by the Greek term, to be believable. Such a move would have garnered discussion from the Rabbis.

The *Ben Yehudas Pocket Dictionary,* written by Eliezer Ben Yehuda, the father of modern Hebrew, defines the Hebrew word "*kanabos*" as hemp.

3 Comparatively, *A Biblical and Theological Dictionary* records: "SACK CLOTH a cloth made of hemp worn in mourning on occasion of death great calamity and trouble 2 Sam iii 21 1 Kings xx 31 xxi 27 Esther iv In time of joy or on hearing good news they who were wearing sackcloth tore it off Ps xxx 11 See Isa xx 2 Zech xiii 4" (Green, 1840).

Regardless of the controversy regarding the identification of the origins of the *Mishnah* term *kanabos*, with *kaneh bosm* or Greek *kannabis*, cannabis was seen as a suitable cloth for ritual attire well into the 16th century. Chapter 9 of the *Shulchan Aruch*, Code of Jewish Law, records that prayer shawls could be made from wool, silk, flax or hemp. Recently Rabbi Yosef Glassman, summarized "the Talmud does discuss the growing of fields of cannabis, the Shulchan Aruch, Code of Jewish Law, mentions using cannabis for Shabbat wicks, and many sources talk about cannabis as a staple in Jewish clothing, since it doesn't absorb spiritual impurity ... and it ... was found to have been used in ancient Israel as an anesthetic, even during childbirth."

As with finds of cannabis resins in ancient Israel, there is also notable archaeological evidence for hemp cloth. Hemp fiber has been found in the Levant at the 800 BCE archaeological site of Deir 'Alla, in a context which implies ritual use, (Boertien 2007). Hemp fiber has also been recovered from the later Talmudic period "Hemp in ancient rope and fabric from the Christmas Cave in Israel: Talmudic background and DNA sequence identification" (Murphy, et. al., 2011).

This, and the new archaeological evidence from the 8th century BCE temple site in tel Arad, have reignited the debate regarding *kaneh bosm* as cannabis. I think when one sees how seamlessly this etymological evidence fits with tel Arad, most would agree that it clearly settles that debate.

Prior to the discoveries at tel Arad, only limited academic support had emerged for Benet's theory on the identification of *kaneh* with cannabis. Notably, in 1980 the respected anthropologist Weston La Barre (1980) referred to the Biblical references in an essay on cannabis, concurring with Benet's earlier hypothesis. In that same year respected British Journal *New Scientist* also ran a story that referred to the Hebrew Old Testament references: "Linguistic evidence indicates that in the original Hebrew and Aramaic texts of the Old Testament the 'holy oil' which God directed Moses to make (Exodus 30:23) was composed of myrrh, cinnamon, cannabis and cassia" (Malyon & Henman 1980). Further, online, the Internet's informative *Navigating the Bible*, used by countless theological students, also refers to the Exodus 30:23 reference as possibly designating cannabis.

Noted cannabinoid researcher and historian, Dr. Ethan Russo, has stated: "I firmly believe that *kaneh bosm* in the Hebrew was cannabis, so I am absolutely convinced it was there ... it's mentioned in *Exodus* that *kaneh bosm* was part of the Holy Anointing Oil, also used as an incense and it really makes sense" Making this statement before the discovery of burnt cannabis resins on the altar in Arad, Russo referred to another archaeological find of cannabis residues in the region: "I think it is absolutely clear that cannabis was in the Holy Land, we have archaeological proof dated to the 4th century [AD] there was this carbonized fragment of cannabis that was found in a cave at Bet Shemesh in Israel" (Russo, 2003).

Professor of Classical Mythology at Boston University, Carl Ruck, who is also a linguist, has summarized:

> Cannabis is called *kaneh bosem* in Hebrew, which is now recognized as the Scythian word that Herodotus wrote as *kannabis* (or cannabis). The translators of the bible translate this usually as "fragrant cane," i.e., an aromatic grass. Once the word is correctly translated, the use of cannabis in the bible is clear. Large amounts of it were compounded into the ointment for the ordination of the priest. This ointment ... was also used to fumigate the holy enclosed space. The ointment (absorbed through the skin) and the fragrance of the vessels (both absorbed by handling and inhaled as perfume) and the smoke of the incense in the confined space would have been a very effective means of administering the psychoactive properties of the plant. Since it was only the High Priest who entered the Tabernacle, it was an experience reserved for him... (Ruck, 2009).

I queried Ruck shortly after the initial paper on the altars at tel Arad was published, and he gave this statement:

> The discovery of cannabis residue on an ancient altar in Israel is presented with amazement by the archaeologists although one wonders where they have been for the last century. The *kaneh-bosem* of *Exodus* was identified as cannabis by Sula Benet nearly a century ago and has been the subject of numerous works since. Similar archaeological evidence is confirming the use of other drugs in Classical Greco-Roman and Judeo-Christian antiquity and is presented by scholars who apparently come upon their discoveries *in vacuo*.

More recently, Peter Margolis, who holds degrees in Jewish Studies from the Hebrew University in Jerusalem, visited this topic in "Lessons of Eish Zarah: The Ritual use of Kaneh-Bosm." Noting Sula Benet's etymological research, the recent archaeological evidence from tel Arad and other evidence, Margolis wrote, "combination of historical, anthropological, archaeological, and etymological studies strongly suggest that one of the ingredients of the Hebrews' incense was cannabis" (Margolis, 2021).

As Israel has become a leading figure in medical cannabis and research, and with the discovery of tel Arad, Jewish religious views seem to be coming more open to the possibility that *kaneh bosm* is cannabis. Rabbi Baruch HaLevi, the spiritual leader of Congregation Shirat Hayam, one of the fastest growing congregations in the Greater Boston area, was recently quoted in *Jewish Boston*: "It is not a stretch to say that *kaneh bosem* in Shemot and the other mentions in *Tanach* is what we call cannabis."

THE ORIGINS OF *KANEH BOSM*

Benet's etymological research regarding the Hebrew terms *kaneh bosem* and *kaneh* was based in part upon tracing the modern word "cannabis" back through history to show the similarities between the cognitive pronunciation of "cannabis" and "*kaneh bosem*" and comparing the term to the names used for cannabis by contemporary kingdoms, such as the Assyrian and Babylonians terms for the plant "*qunubu*." Sula Benet believed that the term cannabis "is derived from Semitic languages and both its name and forms of its use were borrowed by the Scythians from the peoples of the Near East" (Benet, 1975).

Source: William Walter Smith, *The Students' Illustrated Historical Geography of the Holy Land* (Philadelphia, PA: The Sunday School Times Company, 1911)

Independent support for Benet's view of the Semitic origins of the term kaneh can be found in the controversial work *The Word: The Dictionary That Reveals the Hebrew Source of English*, by Isaac E. Mozeson. In reference to Hebrew kaneh, Mozeson follows a similar view to Benet's that the "so-called IE root *kanna* ... is admitted to be 'of Semitic origin' ... the IE word *kannabis* (hemp – a late IE word borrowed from an unknown source)" (Mozeson, 1989).

> ... *Kanboos* is an early post biblical term for hemp. ... The word Hemp is traced to Greek *kannabis* and Persian *kannab*. ... The ultimate etymon is conceded by Webster's to be "a very early borrowing from a non-IE, possibly Semitic language."
>
> In seeking related words ... consider Aramaic ... *Kenabh* ... and [Hebrew] *Kaneh* ... (Mozeson, 1989).

This author's view differs in this respect, and I would suggest the term "*kaneh bosem*," (also rendered *q'neh bosem* and keneh bosm) is the Hebrew transliteration of an earlier Indo-European term for the plant "*kanna*" combined with the Hebrew term for fragrance "*bosem*." The Indo-European term "kanna," was spread around the ancient world by nomadic Scythian tribes, and has left traces through the vernacular "*an*" seen in various modern terms for cannabis in Indo-European family languages, such as the Indian *bhang*, the Persian *bhanga*, the Greek *kannabis*, the French *chanvre*, the Dutch *canvas* and the German *hanf*. This is also the view of Prof. Carl Ruck who has commented that "*kaneh bosem* in Hebrew ... is now recognized as the Scythian word that Herodotus wrote as *kannabis* (or cannabis)" (Ruck, 2009). Anthropologist Weston La Barre noted in regard to this as well:

> [T]he word would seem very old in Indo-European, rather than multiply borrowed. ... [I]f as the anthropologist Sula Benet proposes, the cannabis terms are borrowed from a Semitic language, then there is the problem of a seemingly pan-Indo-European term diffused from ancient northern Eurasia. And cannabis, of course grows wild in north central Eurasia, whence the Indo-Europeans came. That the terms [in IE languages for cannabis] are manifest dialectic equivalents would constitute the solidest possible evidence for the antiquity of the word, since the undivided Neolithic Indo-Europeans began to migrate (spreading prehistorically all the way from Ireland to Ceylon) and to break up dialectically in the early Bronze Age (La Barre, 1980).

In some cases, as Sula Benet noted, kaneh does indicate "reed", and this may have a Semitic origin. It is possible that when the cannabis arrived on the caravan as *kanna*, or close variations of the Indo-European root word, it was adapted and combined with an existing semitic word. We can see this sort of adoption with the generic "grass" in our modern usage, and the term "hashish" as well is generally thought to come from a word that meant "herb," and used here in regards to cannabis as "the herb."

The Indo-European root for cannabis is *kanna* and its appearance in the Hebrew language shows that cannabis came to the Near East from foreign sources and, as an item of trade, likely via the Scythians. As an item of trade it retained the same name it arrived with. Indeed, in the Jeremiah 6:20 and Ezekiel 27:19 references to *kaneh* referred to by Benet, cannabis is identified as coming on a caravan from a foreign land. Certain researchers, who claim the designation of "calamus" as *kaneh bosem* stands correct, have failed to note that the plant *kaneh* is clearly described as an item of trade from a foreign land in both the Ezekiel and Jeremiah and these references disallow the *Septuagint* identification with calamus, as calamus is indigenous to the area in question and can commonly be found throughout the Middle East (Bennett & McQueen, 2001).

Besides the linguistic evidence for the Hebrew *kaneh*, being an adoption of the Indo-European "kanna," the archaeological evidence clearly indicates that the cannabis used in rituals at tel Arad, also arrived as an item of trade, as did the frankincense that was burned on the altar beside it. This concurs specifically with Jeremiah 6:20 references to both frankincense and kaneh, as coming from a "distant land."

It is likely that cannabis arrived in the ancient Near East via Scythian traders. A number of artifacts attest to the Scythians' activity in the region, and other IE groups were deeply involved in the trade routes as well. The city now known as *Beit She'an* was originally called *Bethshan* but was later renamed *Scythopolis* by the Greeks during the Hellenistic period, since many Scythians had settled there during the great invasion of Palestine in the seventh-century B.C., during the reforms of Josiah.

The Scythians were but a small part of a larger Indo-European cultural complex that used cannabis in funerary rituals. The term Scythian itself, is broadly used here to identify a wide range of interacting Indo European tribes who shared both language and cultural traits, that extend back deep in history.

John Allegro's Claims on Cannabis and *Kaneh Bosm*

There is no doubt that Allegro was at one time a respected archaeologist, scholar and philologist, but that all went out the window when he wrote *The Sacred Mushroom and the Cross* (1970). Let me give you an example of some of Allegro's philological work, in regards to a word that I have spent considerable time studying the origins of, "Cannabis."

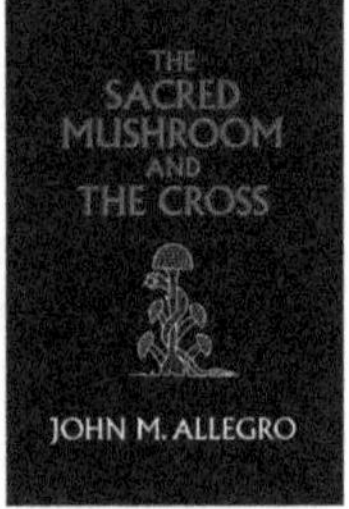

Allegro made etymological arguments suggesting that the Greek term "*Kannabis*" somehow referred to a mushroom top, and "red hashish" belladonna or nightshade! This caused him to miss the actual indications of cannabis use in the Hebrew Bible narrative, now confirmed by archaeological evidence. Here is a quote from Allegro on cannabis:

> The herb which gave them their name, *khaslzish*, "Hashish," means in Arabic no more than 'dried herbage'. If used of a particular drug it properly requires some qualification, like "Red Hashish," meaning Belladonna, Deadly Nightshade. The word Hashish alone has become attached to one particular form, *Cannabis sativa*, or Hemp, and the enervating drug made from its resin. But it is difficult to believe that the "pot"-smokers of today, the weary dotards who wander listlessly round our cities and universities, are the spiritual successors of those drug-crazed enthusiasts who, regardless of their safety, stormed castles and stole as assassins into the strongholds of their enemies. If their "Hashish" correctly interprets Cannabis then the latter must represent some more potent drug.
>
> The Greek word *Kannabis* may now be traced to the Sumerian element GAN, "mushroom top," followed by the word which we saw earlier was part of the name of the New Testament Barnabas, and meant "red, speckled with white," denoting, in other words, the color of the *Amanita muscaria*. As well as the transfer of its name to the less powerful "Hashish," it underwent a jumbling of its form to produce the Greek *Panakës*, a mysterious plant also called *Asciepion* (elsewhere used of the mushroom), which required atonement to the earth of various cereals when pulled up. It seems, therefore probable that the original Cannabis was the sacred fungus, and that the drug which stimulated the medieval Assassins to self – immolation was the same that brought the Zealots to their awful end on Masada a millennium earlier. Indeed, we may now seriously consider the possibility that the Assassin movement was but a resurgence of a cultic practice that was part of Islam from the beginning, and had its real origin thousands of years before that. It seems to be a pattern of religious movements based on the sacred fungus that long periods of relative calm and stagnation are interspersed with flashes of violent extremism which die away again after persecution, only to reemerge in much later generations. In this, history is reflecting the action of the drug itself on its partakers. After hectic bouts of uncontrolled activity, the fungus-eater will collapse in a stupor from which only a resurgence of the stimulatory poison in his brain will arouse him (Allegro, 1970).

Allegro never smoked marijuana, but his own observations of what he referred to as "the 'pot'-smokers of today, the weary dotards who wander listlessly round our cities and universities," caused him to discount any possible use of cannabis as a means of achieving spiritual ecstasy. In *The Sacred Mushroom and the Cross,* Allegro translated the *Kaneh-Bosm* reference in Exodus as aromatic cane when mentioning the holy unction of the Hebrew Bible, even commenting how the anointing oil would have added to a "kind of intoxicating belief in self-omniscience," but failed to make the rightful connection with cannabis.

> [T]he traditional Israelite anointing oil: myrrh, aromatic cane, cinnamon, and cassia, all representing the powerful semen of the god. Under certain enclosed conditions, a mixture of these substances rubbed on the skin could produce the kind of intoxicating belief in self-omniscience referred to.... Furthermore, the atmosphere of the oracular chamber would be charged with reek of sacred incense consisting of "sweet spices. stacte, and onycha, and galbanum, sweet spices with pure frankincense..." (Exod. 30: 34). giving the kind of overpowering hypnotic effect referred to by an early ... writer when he speaks of "the frenzy of a lying soothsayer" as a "mere intoxication produced by the reeking fumes of sacrifice."
>
> That these ingredients formed only part of the sacred incense formula is well known. Josephus says there were thirteen elements, and the Talmud names eleven, plus salt, and a secret "herb" which was added to make the smoke rise in a vertical column before spreading outwards at the top. With the characteristic shape of the mushroom in mind, we can hazard a fair guess now at this secret ingredient (Allegro, 1970).

It is well known that hashish smoke rises in this exact way, and there are no indications of psychoactive mushrooms in the temple incense by any stretch. Sadly, Allegro's legacy is a mistaken hypothesis about mushrooms as the sacrament of a desert people. Allegro missed the etymological clues for cannabis, the use of which has now been confirmed by archaeological evidence out of tel Arad, documenting its use in a Jewish temple site from 800 BCE. Moreover, the general consensus is that the root word for "Cannabis" originated in a Proto-Indo-European word *kanap* and from there spread through various later Indo-European family languages. No respected linguist or etymologist supports Allegro's preposterous assertions on the term "Cannabis."

THE IE ROOTS OF *KANEH* AND CANNABIS' RITUAL USE

The Indo-European language is the mother tongue of many modern dialects. Ancient Sanskrit, Greek, Latin, Hittite, Old Irish, Gothic, Old Bulgarian, Old Prussian, and many of the languages of Iran, Afghanistan, Pakistan, Bangladesh, and India have their common roots in Indo-European languages. In our own time, surviving Indo-European languages with over 100 million speakers include English, Hindi-Urdu, Spanish, Bengali, French, Russian, Portuguese, German, and Punjabi (there are others but they are declining and in danger of extinction).

Even before Indo European itself was a language, the proto-Indo-Europeans, were ritually using cannabis – a technique of worship that continued for thousands of years and spread throughout the ancient world, leading to its continued use in various religions.

The Proto-Indo-Europeans were a prehistoric ethnolinguistic group of Eurasians who spoke Proto-Indo-European (PIE), the ancestor of the Indo-European languages according to linguistic reconstruction.

The Indo-European name for cannabis, *kanna,* is derived from the proto-Indo-European language, Finno-Ugric, *kannap*. The Assyrian *qunubu* and Hebrew kaneh, *kaneh bosm,* are likewise the cognate adoption of the IE root word *kanna.*

Knowledge of the Indo-Europeans comes chiefly from that linguistic reconstruction, along with material evidence from archaeology and archaeogenetics. The Proto-Indo-Europeans likely lived during the late Neolithic, roughly the 4th millennium BCE. Mainstream scholarship places them in the Pontic-Caspian steppe zone in Eastern Europe (present day Ukraine and southern Russia). It is in these same regions we find the earliest evidence of the ritual use of cannabis, and dating back to this same period. This was a technique of religious ecstasy still found at Indo-European sites thousands of years later at diverse locations, Western and Eastern Europe, Persia, India and even stretching into central China with IE groups who settled there.

In 2016 a slew of news articles have come out with Headlines like "Founders of Western Civilization Were Prehistoric Dope Dealers" (*New Scientist*); "Was Marijuana the Original Cash Crop?" (*Men's Journal*); "Surprising 5,000-Year-Old Cannabis Trade: Eurasian Steppe Nomads Were Earliest Pot Dealers" (*Ancient Origins*); all stemming from a multi-authored academic paper, "Cannabis in Eurasia: origin of human use and Bronze Age trans-continental connections" (Tengwen, Wagner, Demske, Leipe, Tarasov, 2016) that was published in the journal *Vegetation History and Archaeobotany* and which detailed the paramount role cannabis played in the trade, tradition, and spread of Indo-European Culture. Archeology has shown how the Proto-Indo-European Yamnaya culture brought cannabis into Europe and the Near East. Ritual use of cannabis in funerary rites in the region inhabited by the Yamnaya goes back at least 5,500 years, as evidenced through a find of skeletal remains and burnt cannabis seeds recovered at a burial mound at modern day Gurbăneşti, Romania. (Rosetti, 1959).

The authors of *The Encyclopedia of Indo-European Culture* note that "Hemp has not only been recovered from sites in Romania but also from a Yamma burial at Gurbanesti (Maldova) where traces were found in a 'censer' (a shallow footed bowl believed to have been used in the burning of some aromatic substance). It has been found in a similar context from an early bronze age burial in the north Caucasus.... Ceramics were more elaborate than those of the Yamma culture and included, especially in female burials, low footed vessels interpreted as 'censers,' presumed to be used in rituals involving some narcotic substance such as hemp" (Mallory, et al., 1997).

The late British archaeologist Andrew Sherratt, notes of this "It seems, therefore, that the practice of burning cannabis as a narcotic is a tradition which goes back in this area some five or six thousand years and was the focus of the social and religious rituals of the pastoral peoples of central Eurasia in prehistoric and early historic times" (Sherratt, 1995). When we add the evidence for the Near East ritual use of cannabis, we can begin to understand how widespread this practice was in the ancient world.

Although there is archaeological evidence that cannabis was prepared into a drink at some of these IE sites, the earliest and most widespread evidence indicates it was burnt in Braziers of heated rocks, in enclosed places at the sites of tombs in a rite for the dead. Generally a tipi-like structure held in the fumes.

Nomadic Scythians had a portable set-up for their ritual use that consisted of a small bronze brazier and a tent to capture the fumes. Herodotus wrote of their ritual use of cannabis, but this was largely considered mythical until the Russian archaeologist Sergei Rudenko recovered the implements used at a Scythian burial site in Siberia in the 1940s. Since that time several other Scythian burial sites with evidence of ritual cannabis use have been discovered at various locations.

An article published in *Science Advances*, Vol. 5, No. 6, (2019) "The Origins of Cannabis Smoking: Chemical Residue Evidence from the First Millennium BCE in the Pamirs" discussed ten wooden braziers that had been used for burning cannabis which had been recovered from eight tombs at the ancient Jirzankal Cemetery in what is now western China. As the authors noted from the collected evidence, "We can start to piece together an image of funerary rites

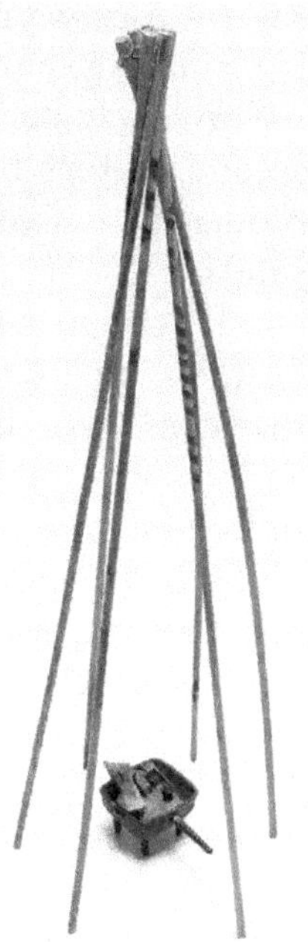

Right: Six sticks of a smoking tent frame and brazier, a cloth would have been placed over the frame and then when the cannabis was placed upon the heated rocks on the brazier, the user would place their head inside the tent and inhale the captured fumes. Photograph: Terebenin Vladimir/© State Hermitage Museum, St Petersburg. Cannabis has also been recovered in a similar context at Indo-European sites in China. **Below:** A Cannabis burning Brazier recovered from an Indo European site on the Pamir Plateau in Western China.

that included flames, rhythmic music, and hallucinogen smoke, all intended to guide people into an altered state of mind." Yimin Yang, an archaeologist at the University of Chinese Academy of Sciences and a co-author of the study, further clarified in the media that cannabis was "being used during funeral rituals, possibly to communicate with nature or spirits or deceased people, accompanied by music."

As well, in recent years there have been discoveries of a cannabis burial shroud, made from female cannabis plants at the Jiayi Cemetery (ca. 800-400 BCE) in Turpan and dried stems, flowers, and branches were preserved in burials in the Yanghai tombs (ca. 500 BCE).

DNA of human remains at some of these sites, as well as artifacts indicates an Indo-European origin for the people and practices, which can be seen reflected in the similar rites of the Scythians and likely originated with the Proto-Indo-Europeans as can be seen through the etymology of the word cannabis, and evidence recovered in Ukraine and Romania which indicates similar funerary rites extending back to 3,500 BCE, noted above.

As Melissa S. Cradic has noted in "Sensing the Dead in Household Burials of the Second Millennium BCE," this sort of use of entheogenic plants is considerably ancient and widespread: "Globally, the presence of psychoactive substances in mortuary contexts has a long and rich history. For example, burnt cannabis seeds have been found in third millennium burials in Eastern Europe and the Caucasus. Intoxicating preparations of wormwood and cannabis occurred in Bronze Age burial mounds in Russia, and beer with hallucinogenic additives was attested in Spain during both the third millennium and second century BCE. From second millennium BCE Iberia opium residues in vessels and opium poppy seeds inside burials showed a similar use…" (Cradic, 2022).

The region in China these particular finds are from, the Pamir Plateau, was an essential channel of cultural communication and trade that connected ancient China, Central Asia, with southwest Asia and was a key point of the ancient Silk Road The Scythian and other Indo-European groups often acted as couriers. It was through such routes that cannabis arrived in the Near East, and indicates how the Hebrews and Assyrians adopted their own variants of the IE term *kanna* as *kaneh bosm* and *qunubu* as well as the ritual use of the plant.

In later ritual magic, burning cannabis in this sort of context would be referred to as *Capnomancy*. As Ernest Bosc De Veze, who wrote *A Treatise on Hashish*, noted in *Petite Encyclopedie Synthetique des Sciences Occultes*, in reference to "capnomancy ... for divination ... the smoke obtained from psychic plants such as verbena, hashish or Indian hemp ... [are] used" (Bosc, 1904). In cases like this, not only was there the psychoactive effect of the smoke used, but the smoke provided the partially material basis in which the invoked entity or vision might be viewed. Such use is indicated in one of the foundational documents of Western Magic, the 13th century Latin work *Picatrix*.

Picatrix describes the use of cannabis resins in a incense to invoke the servant of the moon in a pillar of smoke above it, and the 10th century Arabic work from which it was largely copied, the *Ghayat AlHakim*, describes cannabis used in incense mixtures for temples in India. This ritual fumigation (or rather "suffumigation" through direct inhalation) required the magician, shaman or priest to stand or sit over the burning fumes of the preparation and inhale the smoke in an enclosed space, and from some of the ingredients and amounts used of these substances, we can be sure a ritual intoxications was received.

The technique of ritual suffumigation of cannabis resins in an enclosed space, as indicated in tel Arad, likely followed with the adoption of the name *kaneh bosm*, as IE cultures are well known to have fumigated with cannabis in funerary rites for thousands of years before the time period we are dealing with in the Near East situation. Similar ritual use is indicated in Assyrian references and iconography as well, along with the IE cognate word for cannabis, *qunubu*.

THE RITUAL USE OF CANNABIS IN ANCIENT BABYLON AND ASSYRIA

The references to *kaneh bosm,* fill in many blanks in regards to the finds of cannabis resins on an altar in Arad, as do their counterparts in the contemporary Assyrian references to *qunubu,* where it was also used in the '"Sacred Rites":

> In the second quarter of the first millennium BCE, the "word *qunnabu (qunapy, qunubu, qunbu)* begins to turn up as for a source of oil, fiber and medicine" (Barber 1989). In our own time, numerous scholars have come to acknowledge *qunubu* as an early reference to cannabis. As Prof. of Botany Richard Evens Schultes and father of LSD Dr Albert Hoffmann have noted "It is said that the Assyrians used hemp as incense in the seventh and eighth century before Christ and called it "*Qunubu*"(Schultes & Hoffmann 1979).

A 2002 edition of the *Compte Rendu, Rencontre Assyriologique Internationale,* a journal from the Rencontre Assyriologique Internationale (RAI) the annual Assyriological Conference, in a paper on hashish and opium noted "*Qunnabu* or *qunnubu* has emerged as the best candidate for identifying cannabis." The respected journal gives us some insights into the methods and extent of its use: "... A Neo-Assyrian recipe for making perfume speaks of steeped cannabis; a smoking pool is mentioned immediately in front of it. The context is unfortunately destroyed ... cannabis together with other aromatics. Oil and wash was used in an unspecified ritual process.... Not insignificant quantities of this plant are delivered to the large temples – Eanna and Ebabbar." Eanna was an ancient Sumerian temple in Uruk. Considered "the residence of Inanna" and Anu, is mentioned several times in the Epic of Gilgamesh. Ebabbar, was the temple of the sun-god Shamash, the chief deity of the pantheon. These were the main temple sites of the region. The Journal also notes that "In recipes, hemp is often combined with myrrh," which may prove to be significant in reference to myrrhed wine and other Biblical references.[4] The paper from the *Compte Rendu, Rencontre Assyriologique Internationale,* also refers to a ritual drink, thought to be entheogenic, but of unknown contents. However, as noted in Chapter 2 there is a

4 Dr. David Hillman, who holds combined degrees in Classics and Bacteriology, has also suggested that ancient myrrh was often doctored with cannabis resins: "The [ancient] Arabs ... will take the rub, basically the hashish ... they adulterate it with myrrh, so you end up with these combinations of plants that actually end up together ... myrrh and cannabis, you see them associated ... often" (Hillman, 2015).

surviving recipe for infused beer that contained cannabis and other aromatics, and was poured out in a drink offering to Ishtar, under the epithet of *Beltu* (Lady).

In *Science and Secrets of Early Medicine*, Jurgen Thorwald records: "Quunabu – such was the Assyrian name for Indian hemp. This is basically the same word as it was later known by cannabis (Cannabis India), and hemp is cognate with it ... it was often employed in Mesopotamia to relieve the pain of bronchitis, bladder trouble, rheumatism, and as a remedy for insomnia" (Thorwald, 1963). Likewise, as noted in the 1907 German edition of *Mitteilungen zur Geschichte der Medizin und der Naturwissenschaften* (Notes on the History of Medicine and Science) in reference to "the Indo-European plant names" that appear in Assyrian texts, "the plant *qunubu* – hemp corresponds exactly to the form of the name cannabis, as well."

Note, there are no claims that *qunubu* was an adoption of the Greek term *kannabis,* as is the case for the later term *Kanabos* of the *Mishnah.* Considering the cognate similarity between *qunubu* and *kaneh bosem,* there is no real reason to see the Mishnic *kanabos,* as a Greek adoption, but rather the phonetic continuation of these earlier Near Eastern terms. Indeed, a case could be made for an adoption of the Greek *kannabis* from these Near Eastern terms, rather than directly through the Scythian language.

More recently, Barbara Böck, of the Institute of Languages and Cultures of the Mediterranean and Near East, explained in her essay "Mind Altering Plants in Babylonian Medical Sources" in *The Routledge Companion to Ecstatic Experience in the Ancient World*:

> A plausible candidate for *Cannabis sativa* in Akkadian[5] is the plant term *qunnabu* or *qunubu.* The name is a *Wanderwort* that has entered as loanword not only Akkadian but many other languages and cultures. Interestingly, the name *qunnabu* is attested relatively late in the ancient Mesopotamian record, namely from the eighth century BCE onwards. This late appearance fits well with the fact that wandering words spread usually through trade connections, and it occurs in cuneiform documents at a time the Assyrian and Babylonian empires reached their greatest territorial expansion and thus expanded commercial contacts. The origin of the Cannabis plant is thought to be Central Asia.... The Persian term is *qinnap,* re-

5 An East Semitic language, now extinct, that was spoken in ancient Mesopotamia (Akkad, Assyria, Isin, Larsa and Babylonia) from the third millennium BC until its gradual replacement by Akkadian-influenced Old Aramaic among Mesopotamians by the 8th century BC.s

> ferring to both the plant and ropes made of hemp … and in all likelihood, it is the Persian name from which the Akkadian got its name. Interestingly, Persian *qinnab* and *qunnab* are often associated with the adjective Hindi "Indian," pointing to the travel route that the plant took. The form with the final "s" comes from the original Greek *qunbus,* common Greek *kannabis,* which becomes Latin *Cannabis* … Akkadian *qunnabu* is almost exclusively attested as one ingredient among many in incense blends and perfume mixtures used in the religious cult… (Böck, 2022).

Like the Hittites the Persians spoke an IE dialect, and they also traded with the Scythians, or "*Saka,*" as they were known in that region. In both the Assyrian and Hebrew references Q and K are used by translators of both *Kaneh bosm* and *Qunubu,* for the first letter, and the two words are linguistically connected by the same earlier Indo-European root word for cannabis, "*kanna.*" As well, it is known that cannabis came into India via the same Aryan groups who brought the Vedic religion with them. The ritual use of Cannabis has continued since ancient times in India, to this day.[6]

Recipes for cannabis, *qunubu,* incense, regarded as copies of much older versions, were found in the cuneiform library of the legendary Assyrian king Ashurbanipal, (b. 685-ca. 627 BCE, reigned 669-ca. 631 BCE). Ashurbanipal was a scholar trained in the scribal arts and kept a private library in his palace in Nineveh. He took it upon himself to update and re-edit the medicinal texts of the past and methodically arrange them for better study and access. Ashurbanipal himself is credited with some of these chemical recipes. Cannabis was not only sifted for incense like modern hashish, but the active properties were also extracted into oils. "Translating 'Letters and Contracts, no.162' (Keiser, 1921), *qu-un-na-pu* is noted among a list of spices (Scheil, 1921)(p. 13), and would be translated from French (EBR), '(*qunnapu*): oil of hemp; hashish'" (Russo, 2005).

An ancient Babylonian inscription reads: "The glorious gods smell the incense, noble food of heaven; pure wine, which no hand has touched do they enjoy." According to Donald Alexander Mackenzie, in Babylonian religious rites, "inspiration was derived by burning incense, which, if we follow evidence obtained elsewhere, induced a prophetic trance. The gods were also invoked by incense" (Macken-

6 There is a strong case for the plant being a key ingredient in the Vedic ritual sacrament Soma, as well as its Persian counterpart Haoma that I have discussed at length in my book *Cannabis and the Soma Solution* (Bennett, 2010)

zie, 1915). "Cannabis as an incense was burned in the temples of Assyria and Babylon 'because its aroma was pleasing to the Gods'"(Benet 1975). A view that was shared by even earlier researchers:

> The Chaldean Magus [Mesopotamian holy men of the Chaldean kingdom, circa 400-500 BC] used artificial means, intoxicating drugs for instance, in order to attain to [a] state of excitement ... acts of purification and mysterious rituals increased the power of the incantations.... Among these mysterious rituals must be counted the use of enchanted potions which undoubtedly contained drugs that were medically effective (Lenormant 1874).

Records from the time of Ashurbanipal's father Esarhaddon, (reigned 681-669 BC) give clear evidence of the importance of such substances in Mesopotamian rites, as cannabis, '*qunubu*' is listed as one of the main ingredients of the pivotal 'Sacred Rites'. This use is contemporary to that indicated in the Bible, and it should be noted both father and son appear in the Hebrew Bible narrative (Esarhaddon – II Kings 19:37, Isaiah 37:38, and Ezra 4:2: Ashurbanipal - *Ezra* 4:10).

In a letter written in 680 BCE to the mother of the Esarhaddon, reference is made to *qu-nu-bu*, In response to Esarhaddon's mother's question as to "What is used in the sacred rites," a high priest named Neralsharrani responded that "the main items ... for the rites are fine oil, water, honey, odorous plants (and) hemp [*qunubu*]." Cannabis was clearly an important ritual implement from early on in Mesopotamia. Professor George Hackman referred to 4000 year-old inscriptions indicating cannabis in Temple Documents of the Third Dynasty of Ur From Umma. The inscription is described as a "Memoranda of three regular offerings of hemp" (Hackman, 1937).

In *The Cults of Uruk and Babylon*, Marc Linssen notes another cultic use of cannabis, "some of the known aromatics, such as ... *qunnabu* ... are mentioned in the ... Kettledrum ritual text TU 44, IV, 5ff... In the list of ingredients for this rite ten shekel *qunnabu*- aromatics" (Linssen, 2004). The Kettledrum was an object of divine inspiration, and their consecration often accompanied the ceremonies in opening a new temple, even their reskinning was ritualized, as the drum itself was a divine messenger. The sacrificing of a bull raised for this sacred purpose was called for the drum skin, and a priest would whisper incantations in its ear through a reed, which included the words "Great Bull that treadest the celestial herbage" (Hooke 1963). Conceivably the Bull was in a subdued state for both its receiving of incantations and ritual slaughter, and this may have been related to the requirement of cannabis for the ritual. One is reminded of the Biblical account of the Babylonian king Nebuchadnezzar eating "grass as doth an oxen" for seven years, in order to humble himself (Daniel 4:32). Possibly influenced by a common origin, Zoroastrian mythology recounts how the ailing Bull of Creation was eased of its pain with cannabis by the God of Light, Ahura-Mazda, "Ohrmazd gave the healing Cannabis, which is what one calls 'banj', to the 'Gav' [Bull] to eat" (*Bundahishn* 4:20).

Esarhaddon monument, detail, depicting both the king and the sacred bull

However, the references from Ashurbanipal and Esarhaddon certainly indicate its use by Kings in the sacred rites, and not just bovine! In a 1903 essay, "Indications of the Hachish-Vice in the Old Testament," Dr. C. Creighton put forth the idea that the Biblical tale of Nebuchadnezzar eating grass "as doth an Ox" (Daniel 4:33) gave indication of cannabis use. He stated that "in the case of Daniel's apologue of Nebuchadnezzar's fall, it arises from the eating of 'grass', the Semitic word having both a generic and a colloquial meaning (*hachish*), as well as from the introduction of the subjective perceptions of *hachish* intoxication as gigantic or grotesque objects" (Creighton 1903).

Kettledrums were an important ritual object, and imbued with the same sort of sacredness we see in the Exodus descriptions for the tools of the Inner Temple and Tent of the Meeting. From the ancient inscription, it would seem this cannabis fumigation ritual was a guarded secret of the Priests involved, we will see similar prohibitions around *kaneh bosm* later:

> You will make a libation of first quality beer, wine and milk. With censer and torch you will consecrate (the kettledrum). You will lead the Kettledrum before the gods.... The ritual

> procedure you perform, only the novice may see (it); an outsider, someone who is not responsible for the rites may not see (it) (because if this happens) his days will be short. The one who is competent may show the tablet only) to one who is (also) competent; he who is not competent may not see (it). Taboo of Anu, Enlil and Ea, the great gods.

This gives us an indication of some of the deities involved, notably Ea, whose mythology has been seen as potentially influencing that of Yaweh, and who has his own Eden-like Garden stories, as well

In detail from an ancient stele, king Esarhaddon stands before an elaborate curtained incense chamber with an altar base similar to that found in tel Arad. The tent was used to hold the smoke of cannabis incense, which the king would inhale by placing his head inside of it; a common means of marijuana inhalation in the ancient world, and an act of worship. In relation to this practice which like the word *qunubu*, is indicative of a Scythian influence, Brotteaux referring to ancient Assyrian use of cannabis, noted that "They called it '*Quounoubo*' and employed it in the manner of the Scythians."(Brotteaux, 1934)

as a connection to the flood mythology, as well as Shamash, the sun-god and chief of the pantheon. As noted earlier, Goddesses such as Inanna, Ishtar, and Ishara have been connected not only in their combined origins, but also with the ritual use of *qunubu* (Reiner, 1995; White, 2008) in the same way and context as Asherah can be with cannabis. These common connections help to identify the extremely ancient nature of this practice to a time period prior to their splitting off into their various regional personalities and rituals.

Apparently cannabis was used not only as an incense, but in topical lotions as well, for both medicinal purposes such as skin conditions and dressing wounds, and also for spiritual purposes. As Dr. Ethan Russo noted; "cannabis was used with the plant El in petroleum to anoint swelling ... [and] was also employed as a simple poultice" (Russo 2005). More interestingly, records of topical ointments used in the treatment of "Hand of Ghost" an ancient malady now thought to be epilepsy, included cannabis as a key ingredient. A prescription for the disease was "Cannabis, styrax, oak, Ricinus, Oenanthe, linseed, kelp (?), myrrh, wax of honey, lidrusa-plant, sweet oil, together thou shalt mix, anoint him therewith with oil."

The following passage regarding the topical application of cannabis is very interesting when compared alongside the use of the cannabis infused "Holy Oil" for similar purposes amongst ancient Hebrew figures, that will be discussed later. "An Assyrian medical tablet from the Louvre collection (AO 7760)(Labat, 1950)(3,10,16) was transliterated as follows..., *'ana min sam mastabbariru sam a-zal-la sam tarmus.'* Translating the French [EBR], we obtain, 'So that god of man and man should be in good rapport:---with hellebore, cannabis and lupine you will rub him.' (Russo 2005). However this last reference relies on another Assyrian term for its identification of cannabis, *azallu,* and there is a more general acceptance of the identification of *qunubu* as cannabis amongst researchers than with *azallu,* (Reiner, 1995). Although this term as well has its supporters, with some suggesting that *azallu* represents the earlier name for cannabis, which only later came to be popularly known as *qunnubu,* in the 8th century BCE:

> ...In a review, Farber (Farber, 1981) pointed out that there is no unequivocal proof of cannabis being the identity of *azallu.* Other dictionaries have conservatively labeled it as "a medicinal plant" (Black, George & Postgate, 2000; Oppenheim et al., 1968), but, as we have seen, many of the great Assyriologists of the age accepted Thompson's assignation, and it is certain that no other known plant in nature aside from cannabis re-

> motely conforms to Thompson's description of its attributes. We have a plant that was considered psychoactive, was used in fabric, was administered as a fumigant, insecticide, orally, cutaneously, and as an enema. It was pounded and strained as hashish, and its seed, stem, leaf and flower were all utilized. An alternative identification beyond cannabis strains credulity (Russo, 2005).

The indications of medicinal, intoxicating and fibrous qualities associated with *azallu* has had more than a few researchers regard this as a reference indicating Hemp.

"*Cannabis sativa,* Indian hemp, is the *azallû* of the Assyrians according to M.R.C. Thompson; its virtue is in combating "depression of the spirits," anxiety, sorrows, which accords well with its action; its name reconciles with the Syriac verbal root which signifies to spin or weave, a term which also accords with the usage that one makes with hemp in the rope industry" (Contenau, 1940).

Ritual use of cannabis fiber in ancient Mesopotamia has also been noted: "*hu-sab A.ZAL-LA'* to be knotted on a white thread and hung on the neck." *Azalla* has also been seen as indicating that beverages were prepared from cannabis as well. "Cannabis was cited as a drink for unknown purposes (Thompson, 1949)(p. 221)(Thompson, 1923)(41,2,7). Similarly, (Oppenheim et al., 1968)(p.524) noted a potion of cannabis, '*A.ZAL.LA isattima*' in (K. 13418)(97,2,4) (Thompson, 1923)" (Russo, 2005).

There are other early Mesopotamian names besides *azallu* that unlike *qunubu* do not have any etymological indications of an Indo-European origin, and if they are indeed references to cannabis, this combined with their identification of going back as far as the third millennium, may mark an original indigenous cultic and medicinal use of cannabis. This could possibly be separate in origin to that of the traditions we have been discussing, or alternatively, interactions between these cultures date back to remote periods of time greater than what we have been dealing with in this study (which from what we have learned so far, is a very realistic possibility). As well, that cannabis may have held multiple names over these time periods, is more than a likelihood, as even today, cannabis is likely only second to "sex" for the amount of names which it can be recognized under.

As the British Archaeologist Diana Stein has summarized in relation to ancient Near Eastern references: "Cannabis has many variants, and it is possible that these were known by a variety of different names, some cryptic and others descriptive or allegorical (as is the case today: marijuana, hashish, hemp, grass, weed, dope, pot, skunk, kit, bhang, etc.). The use of cannabis for incense during the first millennium BCE certainly suggests that its properties as an intoxicant were already known. The burning of incense tends to be a milder relic of earlier forms of consumption" (Stein, 2009).

The case for *qunubu* as cannabis, however, is built on much more solid ground than these other words:

> *Qunnabu*, the probable Assyrian word for cannabis, is attested in texts of the first millennium BCE. It occurs in a Neo-Assyrian recipe for perfume, and a contemporary letter refers to its use in ritual contexts. A later Neo-Babylonian text records the delivery of large quantities of *qunnabu* to the great temple of Eanna and Ebabbar, and there are recipes in which hemp is an ingredient of aromatic oil used for cultic purposes. So cannabis was available in Mesopotamia during the sixth century BCE at the time when the Hebrew Bible was compiled in Babylon (Stein, 2009).

With the similar way that the Assyrian *qunnabu* is used as *kaneh bosm*, *i.e.* as a ritual incense and salve, it seems that the Assyrian sacred rites likely influenced those of the ancient Hebrews, in this regard.

Chapter 4

Alternative Etymologies

For more than a century various researchers have been trying to bring attention to potential cannabis references within the Hebrew Bible. There have been a variety of suggestions regarding references to cannabis in scripture, and although the most convincing linguistic evidence for cannabis in the Bible, is Benet's identification of *kaneh bosm*, these are worth consideration and discussion as well. These include:

> 1) Dr. C. Creighton's 1903 essay, 'Indications of the Hachish-Vice in the Old Testament' which suggested Hebrew words for '*honey wood*' and '*honeycomb*' were hidden terms for a hashish confection.
>
> 2) Cannabis scientist Dr. Raphael Mechoulam's suggestion of the Hebrew term *pannag*.
>
> 3) 19th century Biblical scholar John Kitto's suggestion of *shesh* for fiber cannabis and *eshisha* for a resin product produced from the fiber plant.

Dr Creighton's "Honey wood"

A British physician, Dr. C. Creighton, concluded in 1903 that several references to cannabis can be found in the Hebrew Bible. His examples were the "*honeycomb*" referred to in the Song of Songs, 5:1, and the "*honeywood*" in I Samuel 14: 25-45. Creighton felt that in the Hebrew Bible "there are some half-dozen passages where cryptic references to *hachish* may be discovered.... But that word, which is the key to the meaning, has been knowingly mistranslated in the Vulgate and in the modern version, having been rendered by a variant also by the LXX [Septuagint] in one of the passages, and confessed as unintelligible in the other by the use of a marginal Hebrew word in Greek letters" (Creighton 1903).

> *Hachish*, which is the disreputable intoxicant drug of the East ... is of unknown antiquity. It is known that the fiber of hemp-

> plant, *Cannabis sativa*, was used for cordage in ancient times; and it is therefore probable that the resinous exudation, "honey" or "dew," which is found upon its flowering tops on some soils, or in certain climates (*Cannabis Indica*), was known for its stimulant or intoxicant properties from an equally early date ... we may assume it to have been traditional among the Semites from remote antiquity. There are reasons, in the nature of the case, why there should be no clear history. All vices are veiled from view; they are *sub rosa*; and that is true especially of the vices of the East. Where they are alluded to at all, it is in cryptic, subtle ... and allegorical terms. Therefore if we are to discover them, we must be prepared to look below the surface of the text (Creighton 1903).

Creighton pointed to accounts like Nebuchadnezzar eating "grass as an ox" (Daniel 4:25), King Saul's madness, Ezekiel's Vision and other biblical events could be accounted for through the ingestion of cannabis. However, although interesting speculation, with no corroborative linguistic evidence, Creighton's suggestion has garnered little attention. A copy of Creighton's full essay has been included as an appendix.

MECHOULAM AND *PANNAGH*

Dr. Raphael Mechoulam, is widely regarded for his localization and discovery of the molecule THC, and he has been studying the science and history of cannabis for decades. Mechoulam was aware of Sula Benet's research, but suggested a different etymology and word. "Benet's supposition is not unreasonable in view of the close etymological similarity between *kaneh-bosem* and the semitic forms of the word.... It seems to me more probable, however, that *pannagh*, an unidentified product exported through, Judea to Tyre, and mentioned by the prophet Ezekiel, was in fact cannabis" (Mechoulam, 1986)

Mechoulam and associates at the Hebrew University in Jerusalem have suggested the following etymology for cannabis: Greek *cannabis* < Arabic *kunnab* < Syriac *qunnappa* < Hebrew *pannag* (= bhanga in Sanskrit and *bang* in Persian). Mechoulam explains that in Hebrew, only the consonants form the basis of a word and the letters p and b are frequently interchangeable. In his view, this makes it probable that *pannagh,* which was seen as indicating a preparation of cannabis rather than a whole plant product, was the plant mentioned by the prophet Ezekiel as being an item of trade on an incoming caravan (27:17)[1].

1 It should also be noted that one of the references to *kaneh*, as cannabis, sug-

Mechoulam's suggestion of "*pannagh*" may have some support through its similarity to the Egyptian *Nepenthe,* an infused wine many researchers have suggested contains cannabis and which we will look at later in a discussion of infused wines and 'strong drink'. Interestingly it has been suggested that "Scythians took cannabis into Egypt via Palestine..."(Feinberg and Keenan, 2005).

In *A Glossary of Colloquial Anglo-Indian Words and Phrases,* Yule and Crooke note an interesting connection between a Coptic (Greek-Egyptian) term and the nepenthe; "Bhang is usually derived from Skt. *Bhanga,* 'breaking,' but [Sir Richard] Burton derives both it and the Ar. *Banj* from the old Coptic *Nibanj,* 'meaning a preparation of hemp; and here it is easy to recognize the Homeric *Nepenthe*'" (Yule, et al., 1903/1996). As Abram Smythe Palmer also notes in *Folk-etymology*: "Nepenthe, the drug which Helen brought from Egypt, is without doubt the Coptic *nibendj,* which is the plural of *bendj,* or *benj,* hemp, *'bang,'* used as an intoxicant" (Palmer, 1882). When one returns to the contemporary Avestan term for cannabis, *b'aŋ'ha,* the similarity in this context, *ne- b'aŋ'ha,* brings us to an even closer to the cognate pronunciation "*nepenthe*." There is a lot of debate about the ingredients in nepenthe, so it serves as a questionable source for etymology.[2]

One can also note a similarity to the Indian term *'panga,'* which refers to a paste made from pounded cannabis leaves mixed with water (Watt, 1908).[3] Interestingly, both *pannagh* and *panga* can be seen as a processed form of cannabis.

However, the reference to *pannagh* in Ezekiel, is the sole appearance of the term in the Hebrew Bible, so there is not a lot to go in regard to its further identification with ancient Israel, and it seems doubtful that it would have identified the precious substance that was burned in the Holy of Holies at tel Arad.

JOHN KITTO ON *SHESH* AND *ESHISHA*

In different publications of *A Cyclopaedia of Biblical Literature,* beginning in 1845 and continuing for decades after, scholar John Kitto put forth two, potentially related, etymologies for both "hemp" and "*hashish,*" through Hebrew terms *Shesh,* which originates in reference

gested by Sula Benet, in *Ezekiel*, occurs in a reference to its arrival via trade caravan routes. "Greeks from Uzal came to trade for your merchandise. Wrought iron, cassia, and fragrant cane (*kaneh*) were bartered for your wares" (Ezekiel 27:19).

2 We will discuss nepenthe later in the book when we look at infused wines.

3 However, Watts may have misinterpreted panga from bhang as I do not see this term elsewhere.

to some sort of "fiber plant," and the possibly related word, *Eshishah*, (*E-shesh-ah*) which holds connotations of "syrup" or "unguent."

Shesh

The Hebrew word *shesh,* occurs twenty-eight times under another meaning in Exodus, once in Genesis, once in Proverbs and three times in Ezekiel. Although often translated as "White linen," considerable doubts have long been entertained respecting the true meaning of the word. A number of sources have suggested this was a specific reference to hemp cloth. The term *shesh* also refers to the number six, and some have seen this as identifying the number of stitches in the cloth (a six-ply linen thread).

As with finds of cannabis resins in ancient Israel, there is also notable archaeological evidence for hemp cloth. Hemp fiber has been found in the Levant at the 800 BCE archaeological site of Deir 'Alla, in a context which implies ritual use, (Boertien 2007). Hemp fiber has also been recovered from the later Talmudic period "Hemp in ancient rope and fabric from the Christmas Cave in Israel: Talmudic background and DNA sequence identification" (Murphy, et. al., 2011).

As John Kitto explained of the term:

> "SHESH... also SHESHI, translated *fine linen* in the Authorized Version, occurs twenty eight times in Exodus, once in Genesis, once in Proverbs, and three times in Ezekiel. Considerable doubts have, however, always been entertained respecting the true meaning of the word; some have thought it signified *fine wool,* others *silk*; the Arabs have translated it by words referring to colors in the passages of Ezekiel and of Proverbs. Some of the Rabbis state that it is the same word as that which denotes the number six, and that it refers to the number of threads of which the yarn was composed.... This interpretation, however, has satisfied but few...
>
> Shesh ... must ... be taken into consideration. In several passages where we find the word used, we do not obtain any information respecting the plant; but it is clear it was spun by women (Exod. xxx. 25), was used as an article of clothing, also for hangings, and even for the sails of ships, as in Ezekiel xxvii. 7. It is evident from these facts that it must have been a plant known as cultivated in Egypt at the earliest period, and which, or its fiber, the Israelites were able to obtain even when in the desert. As cotton does not appear to have been known

> at this very early period, we must seek for *shesh* among the other fiber yielding plants, such as flax and hemp. Both these are suited to the purpose, and were procurable in those countries at the times specified. Lexicographers do not give us much assistance in determining the point, from the little certainty in their inferences....
>
> Hemp is a plant which in the present day is extensively distributed, being cultivated in Europe, and extending through Persia to the southernmost parts of India. There is no doubt, therefore, that it might easily have been cultivated in Egypt. We are, indeed, unable at present to prove that it was cultivated in Egypt at an early period, and used for making garments, but there is nothing improbable in its having been so. Indeed, as it was known to various Asiatic nations, it could hardly have been unknown to the Egyptians. Hemp might thus have been used at an early period, along with flax and wool, for making cloth for garments and for hangings, and would be much valued until cotton and the finer kinds of linen came to be known.... There is no doubt ... that it might easily have been cultivated in Egypt."
>
> ...Indeed, as it was known to various Asiatic nations, it could hardly have been unknown to the Egyptians, and the similarity of the word h*asheesh* to the Arabic *shesh* would lead to a belief that they were acquainted with it... (Kitto, 1885)

Support for Kitto can be found in numerous sources, particularly in the 19th century but continuing on till the 20th as well. In the 1901 edition of *The Popular and Critical Bible Encyclopedia and Scriptural Dictionary,* Samuel Fallows, and his co-authors reiterated much of what Kitto said, and concluded, as did John McClintock in *The Strong Biblical Cyclopedia* (1867). In *The Plants of the Bible,* John Hutton Balfour shared the general 19th century view on the subject: "SHESH ... The material of which this fine linen was wrought is considered by many to have been the produce of the hemp plant. This is rendered probable also by the similarity between *shesh* and the Arabic word *haschesch* which is applied to hemp. Hemp consists of the fibers of *Cannabis sativa* (Balfour, 1885).

Closer to our own time, in *The Bible Dictionary,* Rand Williams writing under the heading of "Linen" notes that: "Some think [Hebrew] BUTZ, in Latin *byssus,* denotes cotton cloth, and SHESH that made of hemp" (Williams, 2015). However, this seems to be a minority view, and few modern authorities seem to address hemp as a possibility for *shesh* and express the more common general view, that the term shesh simply means fine linen, and address no specific plant. In the *Institute Of Biblical Studies: The Book Of Genesis,* Terry Puett shares the now common view that the "Hebrew word שֵׁשׁ (*shesh*) is an Egyptian loanword that describes the fine linen robes that Egyptian royalty wore" (Puett, 2016). Not much of an attempt to identify the source of this fiber is currently being made.

Microscopic analysis of Predynastic Egyptian textiles were performed by W.W. Midgley in the first quarter of the twentieth century. Midgley proposed that the fiber from a number of Predynastic, and some Dynastic sites could be identified with "hemp"\(Midgley, 1937). Midgley wrote that "Hemp ... is found in the Badarian, Predynastic, and Pan – grave clothes, and I find it in the Dynastic fabrics from the Badarian sites also" (Midgley, 1937). However, Midgley's findings have been called into question, due to the now outdated methods of analysis employed.[4]

There are also other Archaeological claims of evidence of ancient hemp fragments. In *The City of Akhenaten,* Thomas Peet referred to "a three-ply hemp cord" (Peet, 1923). In *Ancient Egyptian Materials & Industries,* Alfred Lucas refers to "a large mat from El-Amârna [City of Akhenaten] was of palm fiber tied with hemp cords" (Lucas, 1937). This was mentioned more recently in *An Ancient Egyptian Herbal,* Lise Manniche reported hemp fibers recovered from the tomb of Akhenaten (Amenophis IV), dated ca. 1350 BCE (Manniche, 1989). However here again, there are uncertainties surrounding this identification.

ESHISHA

In the Hebrew term *eshisha,* Kitto saw a counterpart to *shesh,* indicating a syrup or resin product. The word has been translated in various ways, leading to confusion regarding its origin and identity. Moreover, Kitto suggested *eshisha* as the likely root for the later Arabic term *hashish,* which most modern researchers suggest is derived from a general Arabic term, meaning "dried herb."

4 As Midgley's finds conflicted with the finding of other researchers who suggested flax and other fibers this has resulted in continuing uncertainty in the literature about the types of vegetable fibers used in Predynastic textiles. Midgley's analyses were carried out before the introduction of modern techniques of microscopy such as phase contrast, differential interference contrast (DIC) and electron microscopy, thus his identification of the fibers is now seen as inconclusive.

The word *shesh* ... appears to us to have a very great resemblance, with the exception of the aspirate, to the Arabic name of a plant, which, it is curious, was also one of those earliest cultivated for its fiber, namely hemp. Of this plant, one of the Arabic names is ... *husheesh,* or the herb par excellence, the term being sometimes applied to the powdered leaves only, with which an intoxicating electuary is prepared. This name has long been known, and is thought by some to have given origin to our word assassin, or *hassasin.* Makrizi treats of the hemp in his account of the ancient pleasure grounds in the vicinity of Cairo, "famous above all for the sale of the *hasheesha,* which is still greedily consumed by the dregs of the people, and from the consumption of which sprung the excesses, which led to the name of 'assassin' being given to the Saracens in the holy wars." (Kitto,1856).

ESHISHAH, *eshishah,* once translated "flagon" only: in three passages "flagon of *wine*" and once "flagon" with grapes joined to it in the original, as noticed in the margin (Hosea iii. 1). The *Sept.* renders it in four different ways, viz ... "a cake from the frying-pan... (2 Sam. vi. 19); in another part, which narrates the same fact ... "a sweet cake of fine flour and honey" (1 Chron. xvi. 3) ... "a cake made with raisins" (Hos. iii. 1), raisins here corresponding to "grapes" in the Hebrew; and by one copy ..."sweet cakes" (Cant. ii. 5) ; but in others "unguents" [!-emphasis added]. In the Targum to the Hebrew... *tzappikhith.* in Exod. xvi. 31, the Chaldee term is ... [Hebrew] *ethiilian,* "a cake," rendered in our version by "wafers." *Eshishah* has been supposed to be connected with [Hebrew] ... ash, "fire" and to denote some sort of "sweet cake" prepared with fire; but the second part of the word has not been hitherto explained.

Perhaps the following extract from Olearius (1637) may throw light on the kind of preparations denoted by *shemarin* [preserves or jellies] and *eshishah*: "The Persians are permitted to make a sirrup of sweet wine, which they boyl till it be reduc'd to a sixth part, and be grown as thick as oyl. They call this drug *duschab* [*debhash*], and when they would take of it, they dissolve it with water.... Sometimes they boyl the *duschab* so long that they reduce it into a paste, for the convenience of travelers, who cut it with a knife, and dissolve it in water.' At Tabris they make a certain conserve of it, which they call *halva* ... mixing therewith beaten almonds, flour, &c. They put this mixture into a long and narrow bag, and having set it under the press, they make of it a paste, which grows so hard that a man must have a hatchet to cut it. They make also a kind of conserve of it, much like a pudding, which they call *zutzuch,* thrusting through the middle of it a small cotton thread to keep the paste together.... Amongst the presents received by the ambassadors there is enumerated 'a bottle of *scherab* [syrup] or Persian wine" ... This *zutzuch* is but a harsh corruption of the Hebrew *eshishah,* and is by others called *hashish* and *achicha.* Even this substance, in course of time, was converted into a medium of intoxication by means of drugs. Hemp is cultivated and used as a narcotic over all Arabia. The flowers, when mixed with tobacco, are called *hashish.* The higher classes eat it (hemp) in a jelly or paste called *majoon* mixed with honey, or other sweet drugs ... De Sacy and Lane derive the name of the Eastern sect of "Assassins" (*Hashshusheen*), "hemp- eaters," from their practice of using *shahdanaj* [Persian – cannabis] to fit them for their dreadful work. El-ldreesee, indeed, applies the term *Hasheesheeyeh* to the "Assassins"(Kitto, 1845/1854).

Another interesting possible derivative of *shesh* is the Hebrew word for lily - שושנה / שושן *shoshana.*[5] Ibn Ezra connects *shoshana* to *shesh* in his analysis of *Shir HaShirim* 2:2: "It is a white flower of sweet but narcotic perfume, and it receives its name because the flower has, in every case, six [*shesh*] petals, within which are six long filaments." The Midrash refers to it having an abundance of sap, but the species identified remains unknown. An entry in the *Jewish Encyclopedia* from Rabbi Emil Hirsch, and Rabbi Immanuel Löw, notes that the "identifications of the 'lily-of-the-valleys' (*ib.* ii. 1) and the 'royal lily' of the Syriac translation of Ecclus. (Sirach) xxxix. 14 and the Mishnah (Kil. v. 8; 'Tiḳḳunim,' iii. 78, l. 2) are uncertain, although the latter has been regarded plausibly as a species of *Fritillaria.*"

Despite differences on whether the term *shesh* specifically identified "hemp" or "fine linen," the general view has maintained that the term was an Egyptian loan word, that would have been picked up in the pre sojourn residence of Egypt, prior to the Exodus. The name of cannabis in Egypt, is *shemshemet,* which would be a big jump phonetically to the Hebrew *shesh,* but is not without possibility.

Up until recent times, many Egyptologists failed to acknowledge much of a role for cannabis in ancient Egypt beyond that of a source of fiber for ropes, but recent research identifying a plant in the

5 A common women's name in Hebrew, and the root of the English name Susan.

Egyptian texts with fibrous and medicinal properties, as well as edible seeds, under the name *shemshemet,* or sm-sm-t, are now generally regarded as identifying cannabis. In ancient Egypt the healing herb *shemshemet* was believed to have been a creation of the Sun God Ra. Besides this linguistic source, pollen analysis of ancient soil layers and deep tissue samples from Egyptian mummies, have indicated that in Egypt, like much of the rest of the ancient world, cannabis held an important role.

In fact from about 3000 BC onward there is evidence of cannabis pollen in Egypt. According to the Codex of Ancient Egyptian Plant Remains, (1997) pollen has been identified at Egyptian sites dating from the Predynastic period (c.3500-3100 BCE); the 12th Dynasty (c.1991-1786 BCE) includes not only pollen, but also a hemp "fiber (ball)"; from the 19th Dynasty (c.1293-1185 BCE) found on the Mummy of Ramses II; and the Ptolemaic period (323-30 BCE) (Vartavan & Asensi, 1997).

In the 2004 paper, "Pollen analysis of the contents of excavated vessels – direct archaeobotanical evidence of beverages," Manfred Rosch refers to vessels collected from a site in Saruma/Al-Kom Al-Ahmar in Middle Egypt on the Nile:

> At this place the Institute of Egyptology of the University of Tubingen is excavating a graveyard which was used from the 6th Dynasty until the Roman period.... Here some wine amphorae were excavated, from the bottom of which we obtained samples of organic material for pollen analytical investigations.... The useful plants, Cerealia and Humulus/Cannabis were present (Rosch, 2004).

However it should be noted that the samples isolated in the "black organic residues inside containing pollen" found at the bottom of the amphora, may just indicate what was growing in the area, and represent things caught in the air, so at this point not conclusive evidence of an Egyptian cannabis infused wine. "Bearing in mind the low pollen concentration and the composition with a high amount of airborne pollen, we suppose that a large part of the pollen content reflects contamination of the amphora during its filling or opening." It does however show that the Egyptians were growing cannabis in the region at that time.

As it has been suggested that this term *shesh* has an Egyptian origin, it would be interesting to find a suggested root that helped further its identification. In regard to cannabis, the suggested Egyptian name is *shemshemet.* No clear connection has been suggested between the two terms that I am aware of. However, as the Israelites are said to have come out of Egypt, a look at Egyptian references for another possible source of influence, seems prudent and a paper on this has been included in the appendix.

Regardless of these other potential etymologies, when one sees both the similarity in name and in mode of ritual use, as shall be explored in the coming chapters, it becomes clear that the Hebrew *kaneh bosm,* is but the semitic counterpart of the Assyrian *qunnabu* and that both identify "cannabis."

Chapter 5

Poly-Yahwism and Biblical Monotheism

Who among the gods is like you, O LORD? (Exodus 15:11)

Yahweh, who came to be the National God of Israel, is of unknown and complicated origins. As the story of how he became the one supreme god of Israel is wrapped up with the cancellation of the Holy of Holies at tel Arad, as well as the *kaneh bosm* references we will be discussing in the next chapters. For this to make sense a bit of an understanding of how Israel was taken from polytheism to monotheism is required.

The focus of this book is not a complete breakdown of biblical monotheism, so this is an intentionally brief overview of some of the main points. I only delve into this here, as the story of the rise and fall of the ritual use of cannabis, is wound up with the rise of monotheism and the fall of polytheism. There are many well written scholarly works, which describe the polytheistic nature of the ancient Near East and Israel, and how one deity rose to prominence out of the many in great detail. For those who seek a deeper understanding of the current scholarship on this, there are numbers of detailed books such as Mark Smith's *The Origins of Biblical Monotheism: Israel's Polytheistic Background and the Ugaritic Texts* (2001) or *Gods, Goddesses, and Images of God in Ancient Israel* (Keel & Uehlinger, 1998).

Yahweh[1] is the same god we now generally know as Jehovah (though there is no Hebrew letter J) or more simply as "The Lord." For the ancient Hebrews of 300 BCE forward it was forbidden to speak the name Yahweh out loud, and Adonai, "the Lord," came to be used as a substitution.

The vowels used in the pronunciation of Yahweh are unknown and no clear etymology of the name exists in Hebrew, or any known language. The worship of Yahweh is thought to have come from foreign sources into Israel. Even in the Bible, Abraham brought the God

1 Sometimes presented YHWH as ancient Hebrew did not have vowels.

of his fathers with him out of Ur, so from even the fundamental perspective, Yahweh was an import, not an indigenous god.

The oldest reference to the name of Yahweh, is about 3,500 years old, a challenge for the Biblical creationist, who places the origins of the world itself at about 6,000 years ago. Regardless of his origins, it was Yahweh alone, that arose out of the plethora of Gods and Goddesses of the ancient Near East, to be worshiped as the One supreme God of the Jewish people. Considering there are an estimated 2.5 billion people who pray to and believe in Yahweh, and the other ancient Gods and Goddesses of the Levant are only remembered in the history books, this has been a very successful campaign.

Although the ideas we will be discussing may seem radical to people who only know the Bible through their faith, these actually represent very mainstream views among Biblical Historians and are taught at secular universities in colleges.

Yahweh's Origins

Like other ancient deities, it is believed that Yahweh originated as an answer to explain natural phenomena. Ancient people around the globe attributed natural phenomena to supernatural forces. We see this with the worship of sun gods like Shamesh, ocean god like Neptune and his counterpart Poseidon, grain goddesses, fertility goddesses, rain gods etc., etc. In the case of Yahweh, the general view is his worship and identity arose to explain volcanoes and storms. Throughout the Hebrew Bible, Yahweh's appearance coincides with volcanic-like phenomena. When Yahweh descends from Mt. Sinai to reveal the Torah to Moses and his people, the mountain bursts forth with fire, spewing lava and billowing clouds of smoke accompanied by both earthquakes and thunderstorms (Exodus 19:16-19). Psalm 18:18 describes Yahweh as billowing with smoke and fire "smoke rose from his nostrils; consuming fire came from his mouth, burning coals blazed out of it."

Like the other gods of his day, Yahweh required copious animal sacrifices, ones which would make a modern Vodou ritual seem like a friendly weenie roast in comparison. Another reason that the Hebrews burned copious amounts of fragrant incense in and around their places of worship was the unbearable stench from the massive animal sacrifices. These sacrifices were a daily occurrence and constituted a large part of ancient Hebrew worship. In fact, many of the laws and instruction recorded in the books of Moses are concerned with rules for proper sacrifice; which from the descriptions given, must have been a very gruesome sight indeed:

> This is what you are to do to consecrate ... priests. Take a young bull and two rams.... Bring the Bull to the Tent of Meeting.... Slaughter it in the Lord's presence at the entrance to the Tent.... Take some of the bull's blood and put it on the horns of the altar ... pour out the rest of it at the base of the altar. Then take all the fat around the inner parts, the covering of the liver, and both kidneys with the fat on them, and burn them on the altar.... Take one of the rams.... Slaughter it and take the blood and sprinkle it against the altar on all sides. Cut the ram into pieces.... Then burn the entire ram on the altar. It is a burnt offering to the lord, a pleasing aroma, an offering made to the Lord by fire (Exodus 29:1-20).

This was typical of Near Eastern worship, and by no means something particular to the worshipers of Yahweh alone. Again like the other deities of the ancient Near East, Yahweh was part of a pantheon of deities, and the decline and disappearance of this polytheism, or more distinctly Poly-Yahwism, as Yahweh came to head a pantheon, is wound up with the eventual disappearance of cannabis from Hebrew worship.

The leading theory on how the worship of Yahweh came to the Israelites is known as The Kenite Hypothesis (also known as The Midianite Hypothesis) which has Yahweh originate with a foreign group of miners and blacksmith, who brought the worship of Yahweh to Canaan. Once in Canaan Yahweh was adopted into an existing pantheon there, and Yahweh became one of the 70 sons of Canaanite high god El, many of whose attributes he would later come to take for himself.

The Kenite Hypothesis

The Kenite hypothesis was first proposed in 1872 by the Dutch historian of religion, Cornelis P. Tiele, in an attempt to explain the origin of the Yahwist religion. Since then, many scholars have built upon Tiele's theory, and archaeological evidence has emerged which has supported it.

The Kenites were members of a nomadic tribe of metalworkers and coppersmiths, often described as a sect of the Midianites, although some see distinctions between the two. Jethro, the father in-law of Moses, is described as both a Kenite and Midianite. Jethro is further identified as a priest of Yahweh and a tribal leader. It was only after meeting Jethro that Moses would later reveal to the Hebrews that Yahweh was their own God whom they had forgotten. Moreover, it was while working for Jethro that Moses had his first meeting with Yahweh through the burning bush. When Jethro inaugurated the Tent of the Meeting, he proclaimed "Yahweh is greater than all other gods" (Exodus, 18:11).

The Kenite theory is seen as bolstered by what are considered the first inscribed references to the name of Yahweh, in an inscription referring to a semi-nomadic semitic group known in Egyptian writings as the *Shasu*. It is believed the root behind the name *Shasu,* indicates a "wandering" or nomadic people and refers primarily to a group of nomadic people who were located primarily in Syria-Palestine, and it is believed they may have also settled in regions of Canaan. The name Shasu is found in a variety of New Kingdom references including in administrative and military documents from the reigns of Thutmosis III, Amenhotep II, Thutmosis IV, Amenhotep III, Akhenaten,[2] Seti I, Ramses II, Merneptah, and Rameses III.

The Egyptian Pharaoh Amenhotep III, who is believed to have reigned around 1386 to 1349 BC, had a temple built in honor of the god Amun-Ra. The temple held a series of columns which listed various enemies the pharaoh had vanquished, with each listed alongside a depiction of the captive which depicted their ethnicity, and the indications in the image of the Shasu, portray semitic features, rather than the African ones more widely engraved. Most interestingly is the engraving that accompanied the image, "the land of the Shasu (nomads) of Yahweh."

A reconstruction of the "Land of the Shasu of Yahweh" inscription at the temple of Soleb. Photo Credit: https://flic.kr/p/dULpbp

2 Akhenaten is interesting here, for his role as the first monotheist, indicating the possibility of an influence. See Moses and Monotheism (1939) Sigmund Freud.

A 13th-century BCE topographical list composed at the time of Rameses II in West Amāra mentions the "Shasu of Seir" this is interesting in combination with the other engraving referencing Yahweh, as Deuteronomy 33:2, Judges 5:4 both state this is where Yahweh came from.

> When you, LORD, went out from Seir, when you marched from the land of Edom, the earth shook, the heavens poured, the clouds poured down water (Judges 5:4).
>
> (Moses) said: "The Lord came from Sinai and shone forth from Seir to them; He appeared from Mount Paran and came with some of the holy myriads; from His right hand was a fiery Law for them" (Deuteronomy 33:2-3).

Seir refers to a mountainous region stretching between the Dead Sea and the Gulf of Aqaba in the northwestern region of Edom. As noted earlier, fourteenth and thirteenth centuries B.C.E. Egyptian texts refer to "Yhw [Yahu] in the Land of the shasu," while a twelfth century B.C.E. papyrus Anastasi VI links the Shasu tribes with Seir and Edom. In her article "Who Were the Kenites" Marlene Mondriaan notes of this: "The latter region was in the 'South', a territory frequented by the Kenites. It is therefore possible that a connection existed between the Shasu tribes and the Kenites and thus, by implication, linked the Kenites and Yhw" (Mondriaan, 2011). Mark S. Smith, Professor of Bible and Ancient Near Eastern Studies at New York University, has gone further and suggested that the Shasu could be added to the Midianite-Kenite combination, or at least came into deep contact with them. Egyptian records indicate conflicts with the Shasu over lands with copper resources, indicating they were metal workers and miners like the Kenite/Midianites. As a result of this connection the Midianite-Kenites adapted Shasu Yahwism to suit their own communities and sanctuary spaces, and conceivably, if we are to consider Moses as a historical figure,[3] through Jethro, the Father in Law of Moses, this worship was adopted by the Israelites.

Alternatively Yahweh was imported into the land of Canaan by Shasu who had settled there, and Yahweh was adopted into the already existing pantheon of Canaanite gods. This introduction would have come as a shock to the various already existing Canaanite pantheon cults, and no doubt created conflict. A Semitic tribe forced out of Egypt like the Shasu, is clearly a scenario which conceivably may have influenced the *Exodus* migration myth. (There is little to no evidence for the mass exodus as described in the Biblical account).

3 There is a lot of debate about this, I'm not confident in a historical Moses.

Archaeological finds at Kuntillet 'Ajrud in the Sinai peninsula, which is believed to have been a shrine in the late 9th and early 8th centuries BCE, has inscriptions that make reference to "Yahweh of Teman" and "Yahweh of Samaria" along with dedications to El, Baal, and Asherah, indicating Yahweh as part of this wider pantheon and that he was worshiped in Edom (Teman) and in Israel (Samaria) early on, alongside these other deities.

El

Translations from the Hebrew record "El" as the more generic "God," and both could be applied to any male deity. The religious view is that the names Ēl and Ĕlōhîm, when used in the Hebrew Bible, refer to Yahweh alone, who in the earlier period is seen as more powerful than other Gods, while later, he becomes the sole God of the Universe. However, many historical scholars, basing their views on sources outside of the Hebrew Bible, see an altogether separate God, in the name El, and one whose identity morphed with that of Yahweh.

Supporting the latter view, El appears in Ugaritic texts dating back to the second millennium, and this is seen as the same deity worshiped in Canaan as El. In Canaan, under the Hebrew influence, El's imagery was increasingly adopted by the newcomer Yahweh's cult, to the point the two became indistinguishable. This view has become increasingly popular with the discovery and translation of Ugaritic mythological texts. In *El in the Ugaritic Texts,* Professor Marvin Pope explains; "The Ugaritic mythological texts have completely dispelled any doubt as to the existence of El as the proper name of a specific deity. The long mooted question whether the Semites in general or any considerable section of them originally, or at least anciently, worshiped a god name El is now answered in the affirmative..." (Pope, 1955).

El, the Canaanite creator deity, Megiddo, Stratum VII, Late Bronze II, 1400-1200 BC, bronze with gold-leaf image from the Oriental Institute Museum, University of Chicago.

Originally the Supreme god of the Canaanite pantheon, sometime after the adoption of Yahweh, El became conflated with the new God, who acquired many of his attributes in this transition, and even El's wife Asherah. Through various Ugaritic texts, we know he was the King and Father of the other Gods and Goddesses in the pantheon, and was coupled with Asherah as their mother. His sons included: Baal (Storm and War God); Yam (God of the Sea); Mot (God of the Underworld). Mot was appeased with child sacrifice, so came to be particularly despised, although Biblical condemnations seemed particularly focused on Baal, and this may be due to the two sharing so many attributes.

In her paper "Asherah and the God of the Early Israelites" Professor Johanna H. Stuckey explains the likely situation here:

> ....[I]n Canaan, the early Israelites, originally pastoral semi-nomads, were slowly becoming settled agrarians. As such they would have needed to worship deities who promoted their farming activities: a heterosexual couple one of whose concerns was the land's fertility. In that worship they would be like the cultures surrounding them. What would be more natural, then, than their adopting and adapting deities from the agrarian peoples among whom they were settling? So they identified their main god with Canaanite El and, as consort for their own god, took over El's female counterpart Asherah (Stuckey, 2004).

We can see the merging of other deities in the history of the ancient world, and the syncretistic relationship which saw the merging of El and Yahweh can be compared to the two Egyptian gods, Amun and Re, who were combined into the singular supreme deity Amun-Re.

Baal

Baal was worshiped throughout the Middle East, but, especially among the Canaanites, who considered him a fertility deity and one of the most important gods in the pantheon. In Phoenician Baal was called *Baal Shamen*, "Lord of the Heavens," as thunder and storms were a sign of his presence.

Baal, as a storm and war god, shared these attributes with Yahweh, and this was likely a source of conflict early on between their sub-cults. In Ugaritic and Hebrew, Baal's epithet as the storm god was "He Who Rides on the Clouds."" Comparatively, Psalm 68:4 has been translated as describing Yahweh as "him who rides on the clouds." Baal was coupled with his sister, Anath, a goddess of war, and as with the later adoption of El's wife Asherah as the wife of Yahweh, in later times in Egypt, and possibly elsewhere, Yahweh was coupled with Anath as well.

Confusing matters, Baal means "Lord," and was used as a generic title for a number of regional gods. Some scholars suggest that in earlier times "*Baal*" was even applied to Yahweh. Existing Biblical references to Baal are generally viewed as referring to *Baal Hadad,* who was worshiped by the Canaanites.

Baal, God of Fertility and Storms, Megiddo, Strata IX-VII, Late Bronze Age, 1550-1200 BC, bronze –Oriental Institute Museum, University of Chicago-DSC07738.JPG

The title *ba'al* was used at times as an equivalent of the Hebrew *adon* "Lord" and *adonai* "My Lord," both of which are still used as epithets of the Lord of Israel, Yahweh. We can see the term *ba'al* used in the names of figures depicted clearly as worshipers of Yahweh in the Hebrew Bible, the judge Gideon was also known as *Jeruba'al,* Israel's first king Saul's son is named *Eshba'al,* and David's son *Beeliada,* as well as others.

As noted in Brad E. Kelle's *Hosea 2: Metaphor and Rhetoric in Historical Perspective all inscriptions from 8th century BCE Kuntilet Arjud* "offer blessings in the names of El and Baal" and other fragments "also contain the names of Yahweh and Baal" (Kelle, 2005). Kelle's notes that "many scholars" see the sexual imagery of Hosea 2, as being a metaphor for the Israelites "apostasy," and they were either choosing the worship of Baal over that of Yahweh, or combining the two.

As noted in the early period, it appears that the name "*Baa*l" was used by the Hebrews to refer to their God without concern, but as a competitive struggle between the cults of Baal and Yahweh developed, the name *Baal* became detestable. Hosea 2:16 indicates the cult of Yahweh's anger at the obvious conflations which saw the two gods often combined by the Israelites "No Longer will you call me Baal."

Polytheistic Israel

This sort of polytheistic pantheon was actually a stepping stone towards later monotheism, as it represents a coalition of gods and goddesses, likely brought together from unifying various tribes who worshiped them prior to their incorporation. In the view of many scholars, initially Yahweh was adopted into the Canaanite pantheon as one of the 70 sons of El.

In his book *Origins of Biblical Monotheism* (2001), Mark Smith, suggests that evidence of Yahweh as more of a bit player, can be determined from Psalm 82, which "presents Yahweh in an explicit divine council scene does not cast him as its head (who is left decidedly mute or undescribed, probably the reason why it survived the later collapsing of the different tiers)" (Smith, 2001).

> God (*Elohim*) stands in the divine assembly/assembly of El (*Adat El*), Among the divinities (*Elohim*) He pronounces judgment. (Psalm 82:1).
>
> Psalm 82:6 refers to the "Sons of the Most High (*Elyon*)." Smith suggests that "*Elyon*" here is "a title of *El* at an early point in biblical tradition (cf. *El Elyon* mentioned three times in Genesis 14:18-20). The term *Elohim* is a "Plural form usually translated in English Bibles as the singular 'God', because in Jewish thought there is only one supreme, true god" (Jones, 1982).

We see this in other passages in the Psalms as well

> Ascribe to Yahweh, sons of Gods (*bênê 'Ēlîm*), Ascribe to Yahweh, glory and strength (Psalm 29:1).
>
> For who in the skies compares to Yahweh, who can be likened to Yahweh among the sons of Gods (*bênê 'Ēlîm*) (Psalm 89:6).

A final occurrence of this can be found in Daniel 11:36:

> And the king will do according to his pleasure; and he will exalt himself and magnify himself over every god (*ēl*), and against the God of Gods (*El Elîm*) he will speak outrageous things, and will prosper until the indignation is accomplished: for that which is decided will be done.

As Mark Smith explains in *The Origins of Biblical Monotheism*: "If this supposition is correct, these passages preserve a tradition that casts the god of Israel in the role not of the presiding god of the pantheon but as one of his sons. Each of these sons has a different nation as his ancient patrimony (or family inheritance) and therefore serves as its ruler" (Smith, 2001). Thus we see names like Baal and Yahweh incorporated into various place names, such as *Baal-gad, Baal-hermon, Belmarkos,* or in the case of the newer adopted God Yaweh, this name is incorporated into the second syllable of *Judah,* as is the name of the supreme deity El, into the last syllable of *Israel.*

Many scholars have noted that in the stories of Abraham, Isaac and Jacob, El was their god. Abraham does not know the name of Yahweh which is introduced much later in the story of Moses, and came through an introduction by his Midianite/Kenite Father-in-Law, Jethro. Exodus 6:2-3 reads "God also told Moses, 'I am the LORD (*Yahweh*). I appeared to Abraham, to Isaac, and to Jacob as God Almighty (*El Shaddai*), but by My name the LORD (*Yahweh*) I did not make Myself known to them." Everywhere in the Hebrew Bible where the name "God" appears, is actually a translation of a word with *El,* as a component, and "Lord" is a translation of *Yahweh.* God Almighty here is an incorrect translation of *El Shaddai,* which is more correctly translated as "God of the Mountain" a known attribute of the Canaanite El. Exodus 6:3, shows the efforts to merge these two deities.

The "House of God" Jacob builds is called *Beth El,* i.e. "The House of El." Jacob's name is changed to *Israel,* "El Perseveres" in two conflicting accounts: Genesis 32:22-28 where he gets the title after he wrestles with God, and the other Genesis 35:9-10 where El himself dubs Jacob "*Israel*" on his return from Paddan Aram.

Yahweh is often identified in the Hebrew texts with the Canaanite *El Elyon* however, this was after a long process of conflation with El that came through religious syncretism which likely took place over a few generations. Over time, El (Hebrew: לא) became a generic name for "God," and was applied in epithets to a number of deities, as opposed to the name of just the supreme Canaanite God. Through this titles such as *El Shaddai* over time came to be applied to Yahweh alone. As well, Baal's qualities of a storm god became increasingly assimilated into Yahweh's own identification with storms and fire.

Initially, the call for Yahweh alone worship, was not the denial that other gods existed, but rather their rejection. It was much later that the concept that there was only one god emerged. Thus the earlier supporters and some of the prophets of the Yahweh faction are widely regarded as being monolatrists rather than true monotheists. This means they did not deny the existence of other deities, but that for them, it was Yahweh alone who should be worshiped.

The Hebrew Bible was created by the merging of various texts and traditions, particularly the reluctant marriage of the traditions of the

"Yahwist Text," said to embody the beliefs of the 9th century kingdom of Southern Judah, and the "Elohihist Text," a compilation of the beliefs and myths of the eighth century BCE kingdom of Northern Israel. Throughout much of Kings and Chronicles these two kingdoms are in almost constant battle, sometimes allying with different powers in the region. In their last war, Judah allied with Assyria while Israel allied with another power named Aram. This last war led to the destruction of Israel by an Assyrian force in 723 B.C. under Hezekiah, and then later Josiah would see the Babylonians take over in Judah resulting in their period of Exile.

An Assyrian influence on Judah, may account for the similar use of cannabis in the Yahwist Exodus 30:23 account as well as explain its presence within the Holy of Holies at tel Arad. This could also explain its cancellation, as Hezekiah had been on a mission to remove Assyrian religious influences from the Holy Land.

As noted, in the later translations of the Yahweh text, *Yahweh* is always rendered in English as "Lord." Mixed with this was the Elohist Text, which uses the plural *Elohim* to describe the deity and this word is translated as the singular "God" in most modern Bibles, although as noted above Elohim is an intensive Hebrew plural of the Canaanite singular deity name El, and in actuality it means "the goddesses and the gods."

After the fall of the Elohist kingdom in the north around 700 BC, the remnants of their sacred scriptures were taken to the southern kingdom of the Yahwist's. The Yahwist point of view by an editor, apparently of the seventh century BC, merged the texts. Making things even more complicated, both the Elohist and Yahwist texts were restructured in the sixth century BCE to fit with the later "Deuteronomist Text." These were in turn edited and revised around the fifth century BCE by a later group whose handiwork is known as the "Priestly Texts." Modern translators of the Bible have carried on this tradition by often unconsciously making their translations fit in with their belief system, (i.e. translating the plural *Elohim* as the singular God), as did their earlier counterparts. Although, it shouldn't be supposed that these re-writers and editors of the older Hebraic traditions were always forgers and falsifiers in our modern conception of the word. The ancients in general had no idea of literary ethics as we understand them, and writing of a religious character usually resulted from a calling of the inner spirit, which to people of this long ago time was identical to a calling from the gods.

This merging of texts has created many contradictions in the Hebrew Bible narrative. Notable examples of this can be distinguished between Genesis 1, where "God" is translated from *Elohim,* a pronounced plural, while in Genesis 2, the singular name *Yahweh,* the "Lord," is used, (sometimes in conjunction with Elohim, making a singular Lord-God). A close reading reveals that the Elohim of Genesis 1, is more androgynous than the later solely male deity, Yahweh-Elohim (Lord God) of Genesis 2, which was written much later and then inserted at the front of the Hebrew Bible. In Genesis 1:27, Elohim states; "So God created man in his own image, in the image of God he created him: male and female he created them." Alternatively in Genesis 2, Man is created first, then later Eve is created from the rib of Adam after the Lord notices the first man's loneliness and decides to create him a mate. In 1863 a Bishop John Colenso, noted other points of contention between the two differing cosmologies;

> 1. In the first the earth emerges from the water and is therefore saturated with moisture in the second, the "whole face of the ground" requires it to be moistened.
>
> 2. In the first, the birds and the beasts are created before man. In the second, man is created before the birds and the beasts.
>
> 3. In the first, "all fowls that fly" are created out of the waters. In the second, "the fowls of the air" are made out of the ground.
>
> 4. In the first man is created in the image of God. In the second, man is made of the dust of the ground; he is placed by himself in the garden, charged with a solemn command, and threatened with a curse if he breaks it; then the beasts are made, and the man gives names to them, and lastly, after all this, the woman is made out of one of his ribs, but merely as a helpmate for man.

The fact is , that the second account of Creation together with the story of the fall, is manifestly composed by a different writer altogether from him who wrote the first.

> This is suggested at once by the circumstance that, throughout the first narrative, the Creator is always spoken of by the name Elohim (God), whereas, throughout the second account, as well as the story of the Fall, he is always called Jehovah Elohim (Lord God), except when the writer seems to abstain, for some reason, from placing the name Jehovah in the mouth of the serpent.
>
> This accounts naturally for the above contradictions. It would appear that for some reason, the production of two

> pens have been here united, without any reference to the inconsistencies (Colenso 1863).'

***

The next time the argument over teaching creation versus evolution comes up at a school board meeting or elsewhere, these contradictions need only be pointed out. The modern-day Biblical defenders can first decide whether they mean the version of creation in Genesis one or in Genesis two!

We will take a deeper look at the Genesis 2 account of Creation, which was actually composed quite late in the compilation, and placed at the front, for its reversal of so much the early Hebrew Polytheism held dear, in the concluding chapters.

This merging of texts took place in stages. Particularly during the reign of Hezekiah's grandson Josiah, after the Fall of Israel to Assyria, and the alleged discover of Deuteronomy, "The Second Book of the Law," during renovation at the Temple of Solomon. A "discovery" which saw drastic changes directed towards instilling and enforcing monotheism. Not only theological views led to monotheism, there were political reasons as well. A kingdom divided by cults, was a kingdom divided, and Monotheism was a means of unified rule. These factors will be explored more thoroughly later.

After the Fall of Jerusalem to the Babylonians, yet another group of editors, known as the Priestly group, are thought to have emerged. The Priestly Editors further worked the texts during the Exile, bringing us into the era of time where other gods were not only to be not worshiped, but also said to have no existence, and the concept of Yahwehist monotheism as we know it today, was more fully established. This new monotheistic theology came into Israel when the exiled Jews returned to their homeland. Monotheistic Judaism had to be taught and enforced on the people who had remained in Israel through the Exile, with foreigners the Babylonians had placed there and with whom they had intermarried. The cultural upheaval and trauma in this period, along with the loss of continuity of tradition here, can only be compared to what happened to the First Nations people of what is now the Americas.

The story of the Bible, is in many ways, the story of the theological evolution of monotheism, and the story of cannabis in the Bible, is in many ways related to the cultural evolution of the development of religion itself and its origins in plant-based shamanic ecstasy. These two tales, as we shall see, are intertwined.

Chapter 6

Kaneh Bosm and The Holy Anointing Oil

Sula Benet chose 5 specific references to demonstrate that the terms *kaneh* and *kaneh bosm*, identified cannabis: Exodus 30:23; Song of Songs 4:14; Isaiah 43:24; Ezekiel 27:19 and Jeremiah 6:20. Unfortunately she only went into a limited description of the context of these references, and focused mostly on the Exodus account. When I first came across them, and looked them up, not having much of a background in the Bible at the time, I was puzzled. Read individually, they do not add up and make sense, or even clearly indicate cannabis. Moreover, the reference in Exodus is clearly positive, whereas the account in Jeremiah is clearly negative.

This left me with the task of trying to understand these references in the context of the Hebrew Bible narrative – which took years. I have written about these references in earlier books trying to explain them, however, this question seemed destined to remain a debatable theory. That is, until the discoveries of cannabis resins on the altar in Arad. Curiously, historians discussing the tel Arad altars, rarely mention the *kaneh* and *kaneh bosm* references, and when they do, they don't seem to be aware of the context of them, beyond the initial reference in Exodus 30:23.

When the references to *kaneh* are looked at in the context of the Biblical narrative, they fit seamlessly with the evidence found at tel Arad. The *kaneh* references indicate a sacred plant which had once been used within the confines of the Tent of the Meeting (Exodus 30:23) and later the Holy of Holies in Jerusalem (Isaiah 43:24), that later came to be rejected (Jeremiah 6:20). The debate about tel Arad, has been whether the ritual evidence of cannabis use indicated heretical pagan practices, or mirrored the activities of the Holy of Holies in Jerusalem. In a sense, it can be seen as both. In both cases, the indication is a plant that was once considered holy, which came to be rejected through its association with Asherah in later times.

The Holy Oil in the Tent of the Meeting

The first of the references to *kaneh bosm* occurs in the story of Moses, who, it should be remembered, initially met the angel of the Lord from "flames of fire within a bush." Moses is a complicated figure historically, and outside of the accounts recorded in the Torah and adopted into the Bible, which would have been written down centuries after his alleged life, there is little to go on for evidence of his existence. It seems clear from a variety of ancient references, that many Hebrew people were unaware of his existence for centuries after his supposed lifetime. There is a lot of debate about this, more faith-based researchers see a single man and an authentic account of his life, whereas scholars are divided in Moses being composed from a collection of accounts and stories, a sort of composite figure, and still others as a much later complete fabrication.

As the noted American anthropologist Weston La Barre stated "Moses is a ... legendary figure, of whom consistency may not be expected. The foundling-child of the waters is a widespread myth, and one moreover of clear if complex symbolism: in the alleged life-history of Moses are many motifs of the 'myth of the birth of the hero' as well as the usual 'family romance' of royal parents and adoption ..." (La Barre 1970). The assimilation of mythologies in building up the character of Moses can be seen right from its very beginnings, with Moses being placed in a basket of reeds and set adrift, an obvious adaptation of the much more ancient story of the secret birth of Sargon, the ancient Ruler of Agade (2371-2230 B.C.E), which is seen as a likely source for the later Biblical tale (Gray 1969):

> My mother, an enitum, conceived me; in secret she bore me,
> She set me in a basket of rushes, with bitumen she sealed my lid,
> She cast me into the river, which rose not over me,
> The river bore me up and carried me to Akki, the drawer of water.
> Akki, the drawer of water lifted me out as he dipped his bucket.
> Akki, the drawer of water, took me as his son and reared me,
> Akki, the drawer of water, appointed me as his gardener.
> While I was a gardener, Ishtar granted me her love,
> And for four and ... years I exercised kingship,
> the black-headed people I ruled, I governed.

In *Sex, Drugs, Violence and the Bible* (Bennett & McQueen, 2001) we took the existence of Moses quite literally, intrigued by Freud's suggestion in *Moses and Monotheism* (1939).[1] Sigmund Freud hy-

1 The Father of Psychiatry's final work, composed from his deathbed

pothesized that the Semites had picked up the conception of the worship of one god in Egypt under the influence of heretic Pharaoh Akhenaten. The evidence of the *Shasu* of Yahweh in Egypt, does open up the possibility of a potential monotheistic influence at that early date, but the archaeological record, along with the annals of other ancient kingdoms, make it very unlikely that the sort of Exodus of Moses and the Israelites as described in the Hebrew Bible ever took place.

However, when I later revisited this material in *Cannabis and the Soma Solution* (2010) it became clear that the ancient Hebrews did not become fully monotheistic until after the Babylonian Exile. Monotheism came through the influence of the Persians who returned them to Israel. Much of the supposedly earlier material in the Hebrew Bible, was either composed then or adapted to fit with a new monotheistic history. The general view among religious scholars is that the Book of Exodus was compiled as late as 600 BCE and finalized by 400 BCE. This would place it close to a thousand years after Moses and the Exodus is portrayed as occurring.[2]

We will touch on these sorts of elements in the back story here and there, as its relevant to the references we are discussing, but the intention of this study is on the particular cannabis references identified and establishing their context, not the historicity of Biblical figures. Moreover, it is not important to establish Moses' own historicity in regard to the first of the references of *kaneh bosm*, as the Exodus reference occurs in a recipe with a list of directions for the invocation and worship of the deity, Yahweh, that were to be followed by the priestly caste and particularly the High Priest.

Exodus 30:23 describes cannabis in a list of ingredients in the "Holy Anointing Oil."

> Then the Lord said to Moses, Take the following fine spices: 500 shekels of liquid myrrh, half as much of fragrant cinnamon, 250 shekels of fragrant cane [kaneh-bosm], 500 shekels of cassia – all according to the sanctuary shekel – and a hin of olive oil. Make these into a sacred anointing oil, a fragrant blend, the work of a perfumer. It will be the sacred anointing oil. Then use it to anoint the Tent of the Meeting, the ark of the Testimony, the table and all its articles, the lampstand and its accessories, the altar of incense, the altar of burnt offering and all its utensils, and the basin with its stand. You shall con-

2 Although, it should be noted that many scholars don't see this as precluding the view that Moses and the Exodus may have been pre-existing motifs in Israelite thought, and the narrative based on an existing oral tradition. The age of this theorized oral tradition, however, cannot reasonably be determined with any veracity, nor even its existence confirmed.

> secrate them so they will be most holy, and whatever touches them will be holy.
>
> Anoint Aaron and his sons and consecrate them so they may serve me as priests Say to the Israelites, "This is to be my sacred anointing oil for the generations to come. Do not pour it on men's bodies and do not make any oil with the same formula. It is sacred, and you are to consider it sacred. Whoever makes perfume like it and whoever puts it on anyone other than a priest must be cut off from his people" (Exodus 30:22-33).

As one shekel equals approximately 9.8 grams, this would mean that the THC of 2.450 kilograms, or close to 5 and half pounds of flowering cannabis tops were extracted into a hin, about 6.5 liters of oil (1.6 gallons). The entheogenic effects of such a solution, even when applied topically, would undoubtedly have been intense. Health Canada has done scientific tests that show transdermal absorption of THC can take place. The skin is the biggest organ of the body, so of course considerably more cannabis is needed to be effective this way, much more than when ingested or smoked. The people who used the Holy Oil literally drenched themselves in it. Based upon a 25mg/g oil Health Canada found skin penetration of THC (33%). "The high concentration of THC outside the skin encourages penetration, which is a function of the difference between outside and inside (where the concentration is essentially zero)" (James Geiwitz, Ph.D, 2001). I talked to Dr. Geiwitz personally and he told me that he felt this offered strong evidence for the potential psychoactive effects of the Holy Oil.

It should also be noted, that in relation to the Assyrian Sacred Rites, ingredients required included specifically "quality salves (and particularly) salve of myrrh and salve of cannabis [*qunubu*]" (Fales, 1983). As well, as noted earlier, it has been suggested that cannabis, under the name *azalu,* was prepared in an ointment with "hellebore, cannabis and lupine" in order that "god of man and man should be in good rapport."

More recently, Dr. Gary Wenk, a Professor of Psychology & Neuroscience & Molecular Virology, Immunology and Medical Genetics at the Ohio State University and Medical Center, has noted:

> The act of anointing for religious purposes is incredibly ancient.... Extracts of the cannabis plant were often included in these ancient anointing oils.... The plant is mentioned several times as "kaneh-bosm," in the Hebrew Bible, for example per

> Yahweh's instruction to Moses in Exodus 30:23.... [A]nointing oils containing cannabis extracts would have had psychoactive and healing actions' (Wenk, 2022).

As Sula Benet explained:

> The sacred character of hemp in biblical times is evident from Exodus 30:22-23, where Moses was instructed by God to anoint the meeting tent and all its furnishings with specially prepared oil, containing hemp. Anointing set sacred things apart from secular. The anointment of sacred objects was an ancient tradition in Israel: holy oil was not to be used for secular purposes.... Above all, the anointing oil was used for the installation rites of all Hebrew kings and priests. (Benet 1975)

Only those who had been "dedicated by the anointing oil of ... God" (Leviticus 21:12) were permitted to act as priests. In the "holy" state produced by the anointing oil the priests were forbidden to leave the sanctuary precincts (Leviticus 21:12), and the above passage from Exodus, makes quite clear the sacredness of this ointment, the use of which the priests jealously guarded.

These rules were made so that other tribal members would not find out the secret behind the priesthood's new found shamanistic revelations. Or even worse, take it upon themselves to make a similar preparation. Widespread free use of the entheogen, would likely lead to Moses and his fellow Levites losing their authority over their ancient tribal counterparts. Secrets revealed equals power lost, is a rule of thumb that is common to shamans and magicians worldwide, and as shall be seen, the ancient Hebrew shamans guarded their secrets as fiercely as any.

The punishment for those that transgressed these prohibitions, was the same as that of Adam and Eve for eating the forbidden fruit – Banishment. Those who broke this strong tribal taboo risked the penalty of being "cut off from their people" a virtual death-sentence in the savage ancient world.

As Prof. Luck also noted: "The words spoken by the Lord to Moses ... 'where I shall meet with you,' should be taken in the strictest literal sense. God will appear to the priest who uses the substance in the proper way. But the sanctions against any frivolous, casual use is formidable.... By its nature, an 'entheogen' is surrounded by taboos, because it gives access to the deity, and the tremendous power it transmutes must be controlled" (Luck, 1985/2006).

Moreover, this Holy Oil was to be used specifically in the Tent of the Meeting, where the Lord would "speak" to Moses. From what can be understood by the descriptions in Exodus, Moses and later High Priests, would cover themselves with this ointment and also place some on the altar of incense before burning it. "Besides its role in anointing, the holy oil of the Hebrews was burned as incense, and its use was reserved to the priestly class" (Russo, 2007). The Exodus account describes Moses as seeking the Lord's advice, from a pillar of smoke emanating from the altar of incense, in the enclosed chamber of the tent of the meeting. This is reminiscent of the cannabis burning tents of the Scythians and even more so the Assyrian accounts.

> The burning of specific psychoactive plants in tents may have spread from the Indo-European nomadic cults, the prime example of which are the Scythians ... [participating] in the enclosed inhalations of Cannabis vapors ... the enclosure in tents or closed rooms is similar to the common practice in modern Cannabis culture referred to as "hot-boxing" (Dannaway, 2009).

In Jewish tradition, the pillar of smoke that arose before Moses in the "Tent of the Meeting," is referred to as the "Shekinah" and is identified as the physical evidence of the Lord's presence. None of the other Hebrews in the Exodus account either see or hear the Lord, they only know that Moses is talking to the Lord when the smoke is pouring forth from the Tent of the Meeting.

As noted earlier, in cases like this, not only were there the psychoactive effects of the smoke, but the smoke provided the partially material basis in which the invoked entity or vision might be viewed. "The magician ... burned aromatic substances and anointed his/her body with perfumed ointments. The whole set-up for an epiphany was there: now all that was necessary was for the deity to appear" (Brashear, 1991). As Professor Luck explained "[T]he smoke itself was the epiphany. The smoke was inhaled by the magician and his client, and the vision came in trance. The smell of psychoactive substances ... acts on the human brain in a very quick, very predictable way":

> [T]he inhalation of the sacred incense could create a powerful vision of the deity in the priest. Other factors were probably involved too, the smell of the holy oil with which the priest, the altar, and other sacred objects within the temple were anointed, the golden surface of the altar that reflected the shine of lamps.... The shiny surfaces, reflecting the sacral lamps near-

> by, could help induce trance in the priest as he was breathing smoke. (Luck, 1985/2006)

Classical elements of shamanism can be found in the description of Moses' encounter with God within the smoke filled "Tent of the Meeting." Even if we do not consider Moses himself as a historical figure, it seems likely that the events described, indicated the ritual activities performed within the Temple grounds. The pouring of holy oil onto the altar of incense to "speak" with the Lord in the pillar of smoke, is in sync with the burning of cannabis and frankincense in the "House of the Lord" at tel Arad.

This is a powerful revelation for our time: The main holy books of Western Culture, and much of the Middle East and other areas of the world, find their roots in shamanic exploits that included psycho-active plants.

Samuel and Saul: The Age of Kings

At the time of the prophet Samuel, the use of the shamanic Hebrew anointing oil was extended from just priests, to include Kings as well. Although cannabis is not mentioned directly by name in Samuel, the description of events that take place after Samuel anoints Israel's first king, Saul, make clear the psycho-active nature of the ointment used. Samuel "took a flask of oil and poured it on Saul's head" (1 Samuel 10:1). After the anointing Samuel tells Saul: "The Spirit of the Lord will come upon you in power ... and you will be changed into a different person"(1 Samuel 10:6), a statement indicating that the magical (psycho-active) power of the ointment will shortly take effect. Samuel tells Saul that when this happens, he will come across a band of prophets (*Nebiim*) Coming down from a mountaintop, "with harp, tambourine, flute, and lyre before them prophesying" (1 Samuel 10:5), and that Saul will join them.

> [After Saul's anointing] As Samuel foretold, the spirit of Yahweh came mightily upon the new king and he "prophesied among them." The verb "to prophecy"in this context [nebiim] meant not to foretell the future but to behave ecstatically, to babble incoherently under the influence of the Spirit. This bizarre conduct associated with prophesying is apparent when in a second burst of such activity, Saul stripped off his clothing and lay naked all day and night, causing the people to ask, "Is Saul among the prophets?"(1 Samuel 19:24)(Cole 1959).

Note the musical instruments listed; earlier Paul Johnson's *A History of the Jews* was quoted: "Prophets practiced ecstasy states and may have used incense and narcotics to produce impressive effects.... The Israelite prophets ... acted as mediums. In a state of trance or frenzy they related their divine visions in a sing-song chant, at times a scream. These states could be induced by music.... But the prophets also used, and sometimes abused, incense, narcotics and alcohol..." (Johnson, 1987).

Saul Prophesies Before Samuel by James Tissot (1836-1902)

I would suggest that all of these were used in combination, and that we can witness similar effects from cannabis still, in modern music. Cannabis has been a catalyst in a variety of musical genres, Jazz, Greek Rembetika, Rock and Roll, Reggae and notably for our discussion, Hip Hop or rap music. The combination of Cannabis and music can help facilitate a right brain trance. In the altered state produced by cannabis and other drugs, when rhythmic music is played, words can begin to flow out in accordance with the beat and melody. Similarly in ancient temples, the combination of psychoactive incenses and likely other drug infusions, were combined with the set and setting of the temple, the candle light flickered, and gave the statues movement through their shadows, the tambourines and drums, provided a rhythm and melody that the seers swayed to, and eventually verses started to come forth, in the same way, that Rap artists sharing a "blunt" and listening to a beat, might themselves start *rhyming*, only in the ancient world scenario, this was not recorded as top ten hits, but rather written down by scribes as divinely delivered messages.

As psychologist Julian Jaynes has noted, much of the religious texts of the ancient world were written in verse. "Tacitus, for example, visited the oracle of Apollo at Claros about AD 100 and described how the entranced priest listened to his decision-seeking petitioners; he then '... swallows a draught of water from a mysterious spring – though ignorant generally of writing and of meters – delivers his response in set verse'" (Jaynes, 1976). Note in this case as well, something is taken for inspiration. Likewise, the earliest Biblical literature is written in verse, prose was a much later development in Biblical writing.

It is interesting to note that David, who would replace Saul and his line as King of Israel, was known as Israel's "singer of songs." David's inspiration from God was recognized through his profound ability for poetic prose, and furthers this ability was closely associated with the holy cannabis anointing oil – "The oracle of David son of Jesse, the oracle of the man exalted by the Most High, the man anointed by the God of Jacob, Israel's singer of songs: 'The Spirit of the Lord spoke through me: his word was on my tongue'" (2 Samuel 23:1-2).

In his brilliant work, *The Origin of Consciousness in the Breakdown of the Bicameral Mind* (1976) Julian Jaynes explains: "The function of meter in poetry is to drive the electrical activity of the brain, and most certainly to relax the normal emotional inhibitions of both chanter and listener" (Jaynes 1976). In view of this, and Jayne's theory of the origins of consciousness, it is not surprising to find that the "first poets were gods," or more appropriately – the voices of gods; "The god-side of our ancient mentality, at least in a certain period of history, usually or perhaps always spoke in verse" (Jaynes 1976). Indeed, in this grouping we can include the early epics of Greece; the Indian *Vedas*; and as well the Oracle of Delphi. Further, although the ancient writings of both Mesopotamia and Egypt have left us with little conception of their verbal pronunciations, most can still be seen to have been written in verse. Likewise, the "Hebrew Prophets ... when relaying the hallucinated utterance of Yahweh, were all poets, though their scribes did not in every case preserve such speech in verse" (Jaynes 1976). Or more importantly, the final, uninspired editors certainly did not.

> Poetry then was divine knowledge ... poetry was the sound and tenor of authorization.... The association of rhythmical or repetitively patterned utterances, with supernatural knowledge endures well into the later conscious period. Among the early Arabic people the word for poet was sha'ir, "the knower," or a

> person endowed with knowledge by the spirits; his metered speech in recitation was the mark of its divine origin. The poet and divine seer have a long tradition of association in the ancient world, and several Indo-European languages have a common term for them. Rhyme and alliteration ... were always the linguistic province of gods and their prophets (Jaynes 1976).

Like Homer's *Odysseus,* the foundational words of the Torah are believed to have been first composed with metrical verse. As Yoseph Needelman-Ruiz, author of *Cannabis Chassidis: The Ancient and Emerging Torah of Drugs* (2012) has noted of this:

> Traditionally, the rhythmic tics and musical notations in the Torah are the longest and most fundamental parts of the Oral Tradition that settle the Hebrew Torah into a continuous expositional tradition. Mystically, the assumption was always that the music came first, the vowels followed, and only then came the letters and words that made the sounds audible, and made the devotional reading into an ecstatic field of Sharing. This was always the main way the Torah was given over, since the beginning of scrolling. (Personal correspondence with Needelman-Ruiz, 2022)

Jaynes comments further that in the ancient world, poetry was song, and the rhythmic patterning of music facilitates activity in the right side of the brain, which delivers it back out as "measured-verse" or "dactylic hexameters." "Speech ... is a function of the left cerebral hemisphere. But song ... is primarily a function of the right cerebral hemisphere... [A] buildup of excitation in those areas on the right hemisphere serving instrumental music should spread to those adjacent serving divine auditory hallucinations – or vice versa ... hence this close association between instrumental music and poetry, and both with the voices of the gods" (Jaynes 1976). It is in the right side of the brain that Jaynes sees the "god-side" of man, and his research has led him to believe that this side of man's brain, in some miraculous way, preceded the left half into consciousness and this is how all the "highly patterned legend, which so clearly can be taken as a metaphor of the huge transilience towards consciousness" (Jaynes 1976), was written by seemingly unconscious and primitive men.

Jaynes' theory about music, poetry and consciousness establishes itself by the fact that music is prevalent in shamanistic ceremonies worldwide,(even surviving down into the traditional music of modern religious ceremony, but in this case it is merely as the reciting of a left hemispheric memory alone, rather than a tool for shamanistic revelation). "[T]he invention of music may have been as a neural excitant to the hallucinations of gods for decision-making in the absence of consciousness" (Jaynes 1976). Considering the numerous references to musical instruments of many kinds, "lyres, tambourines, sistrums and cymbals," etc., as well as their association with the *naabi,* in the books of Samuel, and that David himself was a lyre playing poet, Jaynes' theories are of the utmost relevance. In the more reflective time of King David, through the "enthusiasm" initiated by the entheogenic anointing oil and music, David's "genius" came forth and his "muse" gave him the "spirit" to speak on behalf of a Lord. This would come to be a standard practice, as the Prophet Amos recorded centuries later:

> They chant to the tune of the lyre,
> Like David they improvise song.
> They drink wine from bowls,
> Choicest oils they smear (Amos 6:5-7).

In the Biblical references to the dancing and singing prophets that Saul encounters after being anointed, one is clearly reminded of the ecstatic worshipers of the Thracian-Greek god Dionysus, and his lyre playing hero-counterpart Orpheus. Indeed, we find that, "Prophetic activity associated with music ... dancing and leaping was evidently a religious phenomenon of Canaanite origin.... Historical and archaeological studies of Asia Minor and Syria have shown that orgiastic cults of this type flourished in ancient times. The devotees of Bacchus, of Dionysus, of Syrian Baals, participated in wild rites involving the use of fermented beverages and frequently culminating in the letting of blood and/or sexual activity" (Cole 1959).

One of Dionysus' alternative names was Adonis, which is derived from the Semitic Adonai, the Lord, a title which is often applied to Yahweh. Likewise, in the Book of Samuel, the Hebrew term, for "to make *nab*i" (prophet), corresponds in meaning to the Greek term "to be bachant," (In reference to another of Dionysus' names, Bacchus) a connection made on the basis of the ecstatic and frenzied nature of the prophets from both cults (Jeanmaire 1951). In the centuries just prior to Christ, Dionysus held a cult center in Jerusalem, as well as in most of the other major cities in the ancient middle east, but the God's influence on the developing Hebrew cult likely goes back to much earlier times. This is a connection that we shall return to later in relation to infused wines amongst the ancient Hebrews in Chapter 13.

The authors of the Hebrew Bible use three different Hebrew words which have been translated into the English word "prophet": *hozeh, roeh,* and *nabi.*

Hozeh has been translated as "to see" in the sense of a deep perception, but it has also been used in reference to musicians. It has also been used to describe a counselor or an advisor to a king. A little less supernatural, and more about wisdom and insight.

Roeh also means "to see" or "to perceive," but with more supernatural overtones, one who has visions for instance.

Nabi, is more ecstatic, a literal translation would be "to bubble up" as in one who is stirred up in spirit. *Nabi* is the most frequently used of the three.

Saul must have been either temporarily, mentally disabled by the psychedelic experience of his anointing and the time spent amongst the ecstatic *nabi,* or reluctant to fulfill his appointment as the new king – for when the tribes of Israel are gathered to be shown their new leader, Saul is nowhere to be found. This causes Samuel to consult the Lord on Saul's whereabouts, and the Lord reveals that Saul, "has hidden himself among the baggage" (1 Samuel 10:22).

Clearly from the description of Saul's anointing we are dealing with the effects of much more than a mere placebo. However the effects seem much more intense that one could expect from just cannabis, and one is left to wonder if perhaps other ingredients, such as mandrake, which appears with *kaneh* in the next verses we shall look at regarding cannabis, in Solomon's Song of Songs.

This ritual anointing continued with the renegade who usurped Saul's reign, and whose own bloodline would be instituted in place of Saul's:

> And Samuel took the horn of oil (semen) and anointed (mashach [messiah]) him in the midst of his brothers. And the Spirit of the Yahweh came upon David from the day forward (1 Samuel 16.13).
>
> I have exalted a young man from among the people. I have found David my servant; with my sacred oil I have anointed him. My hand will sustain him ... and through my name his horn will be exalted (Psalm 89:19-24).
>
> ... my horn shalt thou exalt like the horn of an unicorn. I shall be anointed with fresh oil (Psalm 92:10).
>
> Here I will make a horn grow for David and set up a lamp for my anointed one (Psalms 132).

And when the first of David's descendants replaced him:

> Zadok the priest took the horn of oil from the sacred tent and anointed Solomon (1 Kings 1:39).

Those who see an indication of virility in these references, may not be too far off, and it may well have been intentional. Throughout the ancient world the use of anointing oils seems to have been often intertwined with a fertility ritual known as the Sacred Marriage, or *Hieros Gamos*. Regardless of this controversial suggestion, through the rite of anointing, the king and his kingdom believed they attained the assurance of the continued fecundity of the land. A similar relationship is inferred from Solomon's coronation and anointing. In the Psalms we read of the King's role as the bestower of fertility through the rite of the Sacred Marriage: "Endow your king with justice, O God.... He will endure as long as the sun.... He will be like ... showers watering the earth.... Let corn abound throughout the land; on the tops of the hills may it sway. Let its fruit flourish like Lebanon; let it thrive like the grass of the field. May his name endure forever" (Psalm 72:1-17). The Sacred Marriage was a pagan ritual which held paramount importance in the ancient world, and through the evidence of the Songs and Solomon's own reign, we will see that it was apparently practiced in the Temple of Jerusalem itself. Moreover, that the sexual symbolism contained within it, is much more direct and obvious than the above verses.

Chapter Seven

Solomon and the Song of Songs

The next reference to *kaneh* occurs in Song of Songs 4:14, a love poem, and in this author's opinion the most beautiful piece of prose in the Bible. Tradition places King Solomon himself as its author. This attribution in the Biblical narrative places Solomon as a poet king, as was his father David before him (listed as author of 73 Psalms in the titles of the Psalms). According to what is written in the Bible the Israelites reached their zenith of glory under Solomon's reign.[1]

Described as a more cosmopolitan ruler than the tribal figure David had been, he is depicted as being far more influenced by foreign culture. Although, in this respect, it is important to remember the Books of Kings and Chronicles were written well after the reigns of the kings involved and are based on a later Yahweh monotheistic, perspective on the past.

At this point in the Biblical narrative, the ancient Hebrews have successfully subdued the Canaanites, whose lands they conquered, and have stabilized their borders. They hold command and control of the overland trade routes putting them in a position where they can begin to amass vast wealth. The glory days of the Israelites were inaugurated, and although short-lived, they left an indelible mark upon the Hebrew people which has lasted down to the present, as well as having had a profound shaping influence upon the course of later world history.

According to Kings, as the Lord doesn't have a temple of his own, the Israelites were making offerings on the high places, and in doing this they were committing a grave sin. In light of this it is curious to note that it is here on the high place of Gibeah that Yahweh first appears to Solomon while he is making one of these supposedly improper sacrifices. (The same high place upon which Saul was anointed King over Israel). The very high places which are here, apparently, le-

1 However, it should be noted that some question his existence, as there is little to no confirmed archaeological evidence for Solomon's kingdom, or of his father's before him. The general view among historians currently is that there likely was a Solomon, but the glories of his kingdom are a later embellishment. David's reign is much more questioned by historians.

gitimate places of worship, are to be a major bone of contention to the later kings of the divided kingdom of Northern Israel and Southern Judah, but obviously at this period in history there wasn't anything unlawful about them; until much later, when the Yahwhist instilled their god, as the one god alone to be worshiped. Archaeological evidence attests to the polytheistic nature of the area in this time period, as already noted.

The building of Israel's first temple is something that clearly establishes Solomon above all other Hebrew Kings. The temple is constructed using mostly foreign expertise imported from the neighboring city of Tyre. It is a lavish production and no expense is spared. Like most of the great buildings of the ancient world, Solomon's Temple was also said to have been built out of the sweat of forced labor. All "the people left from the Amorites, Hittites, Perizittes Hivites and Jebusites ... that is their descendents living in the land, whom the Israelites could not exterminate – these Solomon conscripted for his slave labor force" (1 Kings 9:21). Imitating the kingdoms around him, Solomon not only orders the new Temple of Yahweh built by his massive slave force, but his own palace, the supporting terraces, as well as walls around the cities of Jerusalem, Hazor, Megiddo and Gezer. The building of the Temple marks the completion of the Israelites transition from their nomadic shepherding roots.

The narrative records that Solomon had built the temple for Yahweh at the Lord's request. However, it is here in the temple that the idolatrous worship so despised by the later editors of the Hebrew Bible expresses its strongest relationship with the Jewish people. As Professor Bernhard Anderson explains in *Understanding the Old Testament*: "[T]he Temple – designed by Phoenician (that is Canaanite) architects – represented the invasion of Canaanite culture right into the center of Israel's life and worship. Any conservative Israelite who cherished the faith of his fathers must have been shocked by Solomon's bold imitation of foreign way" (Anderson 1975).

However, there is no indication that the people were in fact "shocked" by the temple, so the faith of their fathers' was clearly different than that depicted in the Hebrew Bible. The temple stood for centuries with this imagery intact.

Considering the obviously pagan fertility rites being practiced in the Temple, it is interesting to note that the site picked for its construction was the same threshing floor purchased by David near the end of his reign (2 Chronicles 3:1). Some have seen the purchasing of a threshing floor for the building of the temple, as evidence that the promotion of agricultural fertility was closely associated with the worship of Yahweh, showing that at the time of David, Yahweh was a Semitic Tammuz or Baal and his proper worship was closely affiliated with the fertility of both the land and king. Throughout the ancient world, kings acted as a sort of human counterpart of the fertility god, and it seems likely a variety of this relationship existed amongst the Hebrews. Dr. Hugh Schonfield has suggested that there was a connection between the name of David, and that of *Dad*, (also *Adad, Dod*), the counterpart of Tammuz in Palestine. David was portrayed as a shepherd, as was Tammuz, and there "was a shrine of Adonis-Tammuz in David's city of Bethlehem (the place of Bread)" (Schonfield 1966). With David's purchase of a threshing-floor in order to build an Altar for the Lord (2 Samuel 24 18-25; I Chronicles 21 22-30) along with sacrifices during the harvest and in order to restore waning fertility in both David and the Land (2 Samuel 21:9),[2] Yahweh could be seen as a Semitic Tammuz – as his proper worship was closely affiliated with the fertility of both the land and king.

Tammuz, Sumerian Dumuzi, in the Mesopotamian religion Tammuz was a god of fertility, who embodied the powers for new life in nature in the spring. Terracotta Ancient Sumerian depiction of the marriage of Dumuzid and Inanna (Image Wikki Commons).

The Israelites kept the inner sanctuary of the temple, the "Holy of Holies," a secret from outsiders. Only the high priests and kings could cross its threshold. The text describes in great detail the construction and the layout of this inner sanctuary and we learn that within the

2 Other indications of fertility cult practices are indicated. A Biblical account of human sacrifice ordered by David at the end of his reign to end a three year drought: "All seven of them fell together; they were put to death during the first days of harvest, just as the barley harvest was beginning."(2 Samuel 21:9) has been seen as an attempt to restore fecundity to both David, who had stopped sleeping with his concubines, and the land which was equally dry and barren. One can see the roots of the Grail myth here as well as connections to the fertility cults that dominated much of the Near East at this time.

temple of Solomon there was, harboring over the ark of the covenant, two cherubim. They are described in detail from their size to their positioning, and were made all in one piece of beaten gold facing each other with wings outstretched over the ark, their wing-tips touching. Likewise in the desert tabernacle, the Tent of the Meeting, the statues of the cherubim are described as being present. Like the anomaly of the Brazen Serpent made by Moses, the Lord's order to make the cherubim is a very surprising command coming from the same jealous god who was recorded as commanding that "You shall not make for yourself an idol in the form of anything in heaven above or on earth beneath or in the waters below. You shall not bow down to them or worship them…" (Exodus 20:4-5).

The cherubim bring to mind the Eden mythology, as they were placed to guard the way of the Tree of Life and entrance to Eden. Interestingly other contents of Solomon's Temple also "imitate the expulsion from Eden" (Bloom 1990). Apparently, from the time of Moses, to that of the later reformer Hezekiah, the Bronze serpent Moses made, and that "the Israelites had been burning incense to" (2 Kings 18:4), was present within the confines of the Temple. As well, as noted, the Hebrew Bible contains numerous references to the image of the Mother Goddess Asherah, (the proto-type of the later mortalized Eve – "Mother of All Living"), being contained within the confines of the Temple throughout most of the Hebraic monarchic period.

Considering the supposedly monotheistic nature of Judaic worship, these contents would seem rather curious. This is particularly true of the Biblical cherubim, who were depicted as both male and female. Although the descriptions given of the first Temple cherubim is vague, by the time of the building of the Second Temple, the two brazen idols were clearly depicted in a sexual embrace – ritual statuary that was only revealed to the initiated, and believed to depict the deepest secrets of the Hebraic faith.[3] The ancient Jewish Philosopher Philo (20 BCE-50 CE) felt that the cherubim represented the male and female aspects of God, (an idea that would profoundly influence the later development of the *Kabbalah*). In light of Philo's speculation, it is interesting to note the comments of Biblical scholar, Samuel Terrien, who wrote that the Temple cherubim "may have been … related both to the … *Magna Mater* [the Great Mother] and to the ritual of cultic male prostitution" (Terrien, 1970).

Like the sexual symbolism of the cherubim indicating Hebraic ties to the fertility cults of the ancient Near East, we find similar

3 https://belover.medium.com/angels-had-sex-in-the-jewish-temple-aa3dd76e7565

cultic imagery associated with one of the most sacred symbols of the Hebrew Religion, the Ark of the Covenant, Hugo Gressman (1920) suggested that originally there must have been two images in the Ark, one representing Yahweh and the other his wife Anatyahu or Astarte, although here Asherah seems much more likely for reasons already discussed, but based on archaeological evidence that was not known in Gressman's time.

Similarly Julian Morgenstien (1940) conjectured that the two sacred stones in the Ark originally "represented Yahweh and, in all likelihood, His female companion." Other sources see that the ark itself represented the divine female genitalia, which held the phallic stone representative of Yahweh, in a similar manner to the yonic images which act as stands for upright lingams in India (Sellon 1865). These comments clearly bring to mind the phallic and yonic images that were also used in the worship of Baal and Asherah or Anath, and are of further relevance when we consider that amongst the sins of King Solomon (who is supposedly the wisest of men) was the transgression of worshiping foreign Gods, and especially Goddesses. "When Solomon grew old his wives swayed his heart to other gods; and his heart was not wholly with Yahweh his God as his father David's had been. Solomon became a follower of Ashtoreth, the goddess of the Sidonians…" (I Kings XI: 4-5). In reference to Solomon's worship of the Goddess, Harry Thomas Frank notes in *An Archaeological Companion to the Bible* that "Asherah" who is "seemingly interchangeable with Ashtaroth in, the Hebrew Scriptures, is by far the most widely known fertility goddess in the Old Testament" (Frank, 1972).

In light of this it is not so surprising to find that recent scholarship has suggested Solomon's Song of Songs, considered by many to be the most beautiful piece of poetry in the whole Hebrew Bible, was originally derived from Semitic hymns in honor of the sacred marriage ritual between a God and Goddess. The Sacred Marriage, also known as the *Hieros Gamos,* had already existed for millennia before the time of Solomon, under numerous variations throughout the ancient world. "Kings and queens, pharaonic couples (sometimes brother and sister), or priest and priestess – such personages would join in sexual union once a year in order to ensure general fertility and the well-being of 'their' people" (Camphausen 1991).

The Song of Songs is often portrayed as the pious song of the love of a people for their god, when in actuality it testifies to the practice of erotic fertility rites amongst the Hebrews. It is generally believed that the Songs were composed from a mosaic of cultic liturgies and hymns from ancient Palestine which were artificially synthesized into

An Erotic terracotta plaque from the Old Babylonian Period (c. 1830 BC) from the Archaeology Wing in the Israel Museum at Jerusalem. This sort of imagery has often been interpreted as evidence of the *Hieros Gamos*, or Sacred Marriage ritual in which the king would take on the role of Tammuz and engage in sexual intercourse with the priestess of Inanna/Ishtar. (Image: Yoav Dothan, Public Domain).

a single narrative and placed with the authorship of Solomon. The text itself is called a "ritual song" (*Zarir*) at 2:12, and this same word is used to describe the fertility rite liturgies of Tammuz and Ishtar. Fertility cults of the Near East, including ancient Palestine, involved the ritual courtship and consummation of a goddess with a god to insure fertility.

In some cases these ritual songs were reenacted by participants, whether priest and priestess, King and Consort, and they were sung in hopes of inspiring the deities to make love, ensuring the fertility of the land and herds. There are abundant clues that the Songs were stitched together from earlier fertility rite hymns. The title "beloved" (5:9) was that applied to *Dad* aka Tammuz the god who was partnered with Ishtar. Likewise, the title "Shepard King" was that of fertility god Tammuz.

The Hieros Gamos and the Song Of Songs

As Professor of Northwest Semitic Languages at Yale University, Marvin Pope explained in his excellent review of the Biblical Sacred Marriage hymn, *SONG OF SONGS: A New Translation With Introduction and Commentary*:

> The view that the Song of Songs derives from pagan fertility worship was developed in the present century and, in spite of resistance, has continued to gain ground with the accelerating recovery and progress in interpretation of documents of religious literature of the civilizations of the near East, especially

> Mesopotamia, and more recently the Ugaritic mythological and religious texts. Already in 1906, Wilhelm Erbt ... suggested that the Song of Songs is a collection of paschal poems of Canaanitish origin, describing the love of the sun-god Tammuz, called Dod or Shelem, and the moon-goddess Ishtar under the name Shalmith.... The cultic interpretation of the Song of Songs received new impetus from a catalog of Akkadian hymn titles edited near the end of the First World War by E. Ebeling (1923)(Pope 1977).

The ancients worshiped the Goddess as a nude female image, the earth they lived on and the nature around them. The fertile rays of the sun on the earth, was thought of as God's fertilization of the Great Mother-Earth, as were showers of rain, and morning dew. Remnants of this belief can be found in the etymological origins of certain Hebrew words. The word *zirmah*, which means "a gushing of fluid (semen):--issue" (Strong 1979) besides having similarities to the word for "seed" of man, animal and vegetation, *zera*, is also directly related to the Hebrew word *zerem*, meaning "flood ... shower, storm" (Strong 1979).

Despite the supposed monotheistic nature of the Hebrew Bible, Solomon's Song, is full of both erotic and vegetative imagery, and this testifies to the pagan origins of the poem attributed to the wisest of the Biblical patriarchs. As the feminist mythologist Barbra Walker has written: "The fragment of love-liturgy now called Solomon's Song has been an embarrassment to theologians ... the 18th century scholar Herder was persecuted and hounded from one pastorate to another for daring to suggest that Solomon's love poem should be accepted at face value, as a piece of erotica" (Walker 1983):

> When the metaphors of this poem are unraveled, they prove to be ... frankly sexual. The *hortus conclusus* or "enclosed garden" is the internal genitalia of the virgin bride, where her spouse "enters paradise" – from Hebrew *pardes*, "garden." Solomon says, "A garden enclosed is my sister, my spouse; a spring shut up, a fountain sealed." He proposes to unseal her, unlock her door, and "drink of spiced wine of the juice of the pomegranate" (Song of Solomon 8:2).This metaphor is explained by the contemporary image of the pomegranate, rimmon, as a female-genital symbol. Spiced wine meant the secretion of the Goddess...
>
> Solomon's bride said invitingly, "Let my beloved come into his garden, and eat his pleasant fruits." Solomon answered,

> "Open to me, my sister, my love, my dove, my undefiled: for my head is filled with dew, and my locks with the drops of the night. I have put off my garment; how shall I put it on?" The king's dew filled "head" was the common symbol of the penis, in royal wedding hymns of Sumer and Akkad. A king's union with the Goddess Inanna, Queen of the Universe, was so described: "The king goes with head lifted to the holy lap, he goes with lifted head to the holy lap of Inanna." Every king's divine bride was Inanna "the queen, the vulva of heaven and earth" (Walker 1983).

Perhaps the most blatant of all the ancient fertility songs, and highly descriptive of the correlation between sex and fertility in the minds of the ancient worshipers, is the hymn *Plow My Vulva*; "My vulva is a well-watered field – Who will plow it?" The answer comes; "O Lordly Lady, the king will plow it for you, Dumuzi, the king, will plow it for you." Even more explicit is the description given in the following Sumerian hymn celebrating the union between Innana and Dumuzi (Tammuz):

He caressed my loins with his fair hands,
The shepherd Dumuzi poured milk and cream into me,
He stroked my pubic hair,
He irrigated my womb.
He laid his hands upon my holy vulva,
He nourished my black boat with his cream,
He ripened my narrow boat with his milk,
He caressed me on the bed.
Now I'll caress my priest on that bed,
I'll make love to the faithful shepherd Dumuzi.

Not to be outdone by its Mesopotamian predecessors, Song of Songs 5:4-6, amply demonstrates the explicit nature of the sexual imagery contained in this ancient piece of Biblical erotica;

My love thrust his hand into the hole,
and my inwards seethed for him.
I rose to open for my love,
and my hands dripped myrrh,
My fingers liquid myrrh,
On the hands of the bolt.
I opened to my love...

Thirteenth Century B.C. standing stones at Hazor. Note the "hand" carved into the phallic stone. (Image from Israel Exploration Society/Hazor Expedition).

The reference to hand in the above passage likely refers symbolically to another appendage on the body of man. "The use of ... 'hand' as a euphemism for phallus was recognized in the last century by some commentators on Isaiah 57:8-10 where the term is twice used in that sense.... Whether the word 'hand' in the present passage refers to the *membrum virile* depends on the nature of the hole into which it is inserted" (Pope 1977). Marvin Pope explains: "It is no accident that tombstones and memorial stelae are sometimes distinctly phallic in form ... and the term *yad*, 'hand', in Ugaritic and Hebrew is applied to the phallus and in Hebrew to a memorial stela (I Sam 15:12; II Sam 18:18; Isa 56:5)"(Pope 1977).

"For Love is Stronger than Death"[4]

When faced with the death of nature each winter and its rebirth in spring, the ancient Canaanites saw an imitation of their own lives and mortality. Since through sexuality their own lines continued, so through imitative magic and the proper worship of the God and Goddess, fertility was transferred to nature each spring and the fecundity of both their lines and the land was ensured.

In their orgiastic excess in the fields and funerary grounds, the ancient practitioners believed their erotic worship bought Life's continuing victory over Death. "It is no accident that tombstones and memorial stelae are sometimes distinctly phallic in form" (Pope 1977). Riane Eisler has noted of such rites:

> For if plants could be born again and again from the earth (the womb of vegetation) one could believe, even though it was not given to humans to witness that process, that the Goddess – who recycled days and nights, barley and wheat, and spring

4 Songs 8:6

> and fall – would also recycle human life. And one could also believe that through erotic rites of alignment with the mysterious power of sex through which the Goddess performed her miraculous work of birth and rebirth, we humans could not only find protection and solace in our inevitable pain, sorrow and death but also augment our chances, generation after generation, for a joyful and bountiful life (Eisler 1995).

Similar erotic imagery is repeated in verse 7 of Solomon's Song, in which the concept of human fertility in the Love drama was closely intertwined with the fertility of the land around them – the lush growth of vegetation is clothed and combined with the physical attributes of human sexuality. A beautiful celebration of Life and Love in all respects:

Leap, leap, O Shulamite!
leap, leap, and let us gaze on you…
Your curvy thighs like ornaments
Crafted by artists' hands.
Your vulva a rounded crater;
May it never lack punch!
Your belly a mound of wheat
Hedged with lotuses…
Let your breasts be like grape clusters,
The scent of your vulva like apples,
Your palate like the best wine
Flowing (for my love) smoothly…
Come, my love,
Let us hie to the fields,
Let us lie in the cypress,
Let us get to the vineyards.
We will see if the vine sprouts,
If the blossoms bud…
There will I give you my love…[5]

The Song of Songs, like the Tammuz-Ishtar hymns from which it derived, is testimony to the linking of ritualized human sexual behavior and the fertility of the land. The very roots of this belief system can be seen in Song of Songs 8:6, "For Love is strong as Death." In his brilliant commentary on the Songs, Pope suggests that the Songs, and the fertility rite from which they were derived, may originally have been connected with funerary feasts "which in the Near East were

5 As translated by (Pope, 1977)

love feasts celebrated with wine, women and song" (Pope 1977). Apparently, these wakes would often become drunken orgies and as the mourners grief turned to ecstasy, love overcame death as the orgiastic excess of the participants ensured both the continued fecundity of the land, as well as their own lines. In tune with this are the revelries of Baal Peor, which are clearly defined as funeral feasts in Psalms 106:28: "They yoked themselves to Baal Peor, And ate the sacrifices of the dead.... Ugaritic tablets also detail the events of the *marzeah* feast, a repast in which ... dead kings were summoned to wine and dine with the living..." (Noegel & Wheeler, 2010).

> These sacrifices of the dead characterized by sacral sexual intercourse are identified by the rabbis as *marzehim.... Midrashic* commentaries related the *marzeah* to the Mayumas festival ... a celebration which featured wife swapping. Mayumas festivals were observed along the Mediterranean ... with such licentiousness that the Roman rulers felt constrained to ban them. Rabbi Hanan apparently alluded to such rites in his comment that "it was done in the cities of the sea what was done in the generation of the flood." ... From the various strands of evidence, we gather that the marzeah was a religious institution which included families and owned houses for meetings and vineyards for supply of wine, that the groups met periodically to celebrate seven-day feasts with rich food and drink and sometimes with sexual orgies (Pope 1977).

Depiction off of a cup showing El receiving offerings of wine. This was found with an Akkadian text describing the marzeah feast found at Ras Shamra (13th BC) in which El gets so intoxicated he sees an apparition and ends up "wallowing in his excrement and vomit" (Pope 1994).[6]

6 Image -Monsieur Claude F.-A.,Schaeffer Le culte d'El à Ras Shamra (Ugarit) et le veau d'or (supplément à la séance du 25 février)

It is believed that the word *marzeah* means to unite, or possibly a cultic union. In relation to this word and the *Mayumas* festival to which it was so closely connected, it is interesting to note the similarity to the Hindu Tantric term *maithuna* – sexual union (the last of the sacred five M's of the Left handed path) which take place in ceremonies similar to those described above. "The Tantric tradition of India, especially the left handed erotic rites, are of particular interest for the appreciation of ... the parallels alleged to have persisted in Western funeral feasts into Christian times" (Pope 1977). Interestingly, *bhanga*, a cannabis beverage, has been used in this Tantric ritual since ancient times. In their orgiastic excess in the fields and funerary grounds, the ancient practitioners believed their erotic worship bought Life's continuing victory over Death.

In light of sexual rites in relation to funerary practices, it is interesting to note Marvin H. Pope's comparison of the Songs' "Black I am and beautiful" (1:5), in relation to the imagery associated with the Hindu Black Goddess Kali, stating that the "Tantric hymns to the Goddess offer some of the most provocative parallels to the Songs" (Pope 1977). These similarities are so profound, that some scholars believe they could in fact indicate a similar origin for both the Tantric and Biblical hymns. As Raphael Patai has also noted "Unquestionably, the verse 'I am black and beautiful, O daughters of Jerusalem' (Songs 1:5) is strongly reminiscent of certain Hindu hymns celebrating the swart beauty of Kali, and especially the lines "Dark art Thou like the blue-black cloud Whose face is beauteous as that of *Samkarshana* [i.e., Shiva]" (Patai 1990).

Kali from an 1895 illustration

Kali, who is generally depicted with a girdle of human arms and a necklace of skulls, could be seen as the Hindu counterpart of the ferocious and sensuous Canaanite goddess, Anath, described in the Canaanite Baal Epic with "attached heads to her back, Girded hands to her waist." Referring to the similarities between the mythology of Anath and "the mythology and iconography of the Indian goddess

Durga [Kali]," Mircea Eliade wrote that "Carnage and cannibalism are characteristic features of archaic fertility goddesses. From this point of view, the myth of Anath can be classed among the elements common to the ancient agricultural civilization that extended from the Eastern Mediterranean to the plain of the Ganges" (Eliade 1978). In relation to the drug induced orgiastic rites that we have attributed to the ancient Canaanite fertility cult, it is interesting to again note that cannabis was likely used before recorded history by Tantric cults in complicated sex rites dedicated to Kali.

Left: Anath seated or on a war chariot 2nd Millennium B.C. **Right:** Bronze figurine of Anat wearing with arm raised (originally holding an axe or club), dated to 1400–1200 BCE, found in Syria.

In line with the orgiastic Baal and Asherah\Anath worship which was said to have taken place on "the high places," Shiva is especially revered on mountain tops, and his "feminine aspect [*Parvati*] is the 'Lady of the Mountain'"(Danielou 1992). Shiva's popular title as *Bh-upati*, "Lord of the Earth," is comparable to Baal's epithet of *Beelzebul*, "Lord of the Land," and the Hindu deity can be seen as an Indian form of Baal, although any original connections between the two gods are lost in the shadowy time of prehistory. Alaine Danielou, an expert on Shaivism, has noted that: "The struggle of the new Hebrew mono-theism against the Baal cult reflects the deep penetration of Shivaite concepts in the Semetic world" (Danielou 1992).

Shiva's strong connections with hemp as an agricultural crop are clearly demonstrated in his ancient mythology involving the plant as well as the strict observances which his devotees still pay when sowing and harvesting the sacred crop. Shiva is the "Lord of Bhang." Reminiscent of the phallic Baal stones referred to in Biblical passages, is Shiva's *lingam*, represented by an oblong stone, and which up until modern times has been consecrated by pouring bhang over it, a religious sacrifice of unknowable antiquity. The Indian ritual use of hemp obviously developed out of similar, if not identical fertility rites as those practiced in Canaan and throughout the Mediterranean cultural complex.

Like their Near Eastern counterparts, the Tantric worshipers of Kali and her consort Shiva are known to practice their Tantric sex ceremonies in graveyards, (often involving the initiatory cannabis drink '*bhang*'). Kali's worship can be traced back before recorded history; the similarities between her and ancient Mesopotamian Goddesses of Love and War, like Ishtar and Anath, indicate that they may all have evolved out of a singular preceding archetypal goddess. Such cultural connections would also account for the noted and profound similarities between the Near Eastern terms for cannabis, *kaneh* and the earliest Sanskrit name *canna*, as well as the similar cultic use. "In India it is still possible to relive and understand the rites and beliefs of the ... Middle East in ancient times" (Danielou 1992).

By the time of Solomon, the earlier pagan fertility rites and their massive orgies, such as those described at Baal Peor (Numbers 25), became slightly more refined and the sexual congress may have been more focused on the King and the High Priestess, although there were still likely some occasions that this erotic activity broke out into bouts of ritual promiscuity among the people. In the Sacred Marriage, the king became the god Tammuz and was "married: to the Goddess Inanna\Ishtar whose part was enacted by a priestess. It would seem from the references to David's last concubine, the Shulamite, in the *Songs*, along with Solomon's brother Adonijah's attempt to gain her as his wife (1 Kings 2), that the Shulamite was a high priestess of some sort and she played the goddess in the Hebraic counterpart of the ritual fertility drama.

As early as 1906 Wilhelm Erbt regarded the Songs as a collection of spring songs which originated in Canaan and described the love of the sun god Tammuz, also known as *Shekem*, and his consort the moon goddess Ishtar, under the feminine form of the name *Shelem*. This line of thought was followed by T.J. Meek, who in 1924 proposed that the name Solomon is derived from the divine name *Shelem*, equated with Tammuz, and the "*Shulamite*" an epithet of Ishtar in Jerusalem.

In 1963 W.F. Albright also saw the references to the Shulamite as indications that the Hebraic Sacred Marriage was derived directly from the Canaanite fertility cult. Although in Albright's view Solomon and his bride appeared as the Canaanite counterparts of Tammuz and Ishtar; *i.e.*- Baal and his sister-lover Anath, (the daughter of Ashera, also known as the Virgin). "We may safely suppose that the Canaanite prototype of *Shulamanitu-Shulammith* is the goddess Anath, whose sanguinary play is so vividly portrayed in the Anath episode of the Baal Epic" (Albright 1963).

Baal, was another figure with pivotal influence on the development of Yahweh's characteristics, despite the hostility that existed between their cults in the Hebrew Bible narrative. Amongst the developing god Yahweh's assumption of many of the aspects of his predecessor Baal, may have been the Jewish god's romantic association with Anath. Although Asherah was indicated as Yahweh's wife in inscriptions from the 10th to 8th century BCE, in later times in Egypt at least, Anath was seen as coupled with Yahweh. "In the fifth century B.C. a Jewish colony in Elephantine, Egypt, did apparently believe that Yahweh had a partner Anath" (Anderson 1975).

As John Day explained of this situation in his essay "Asherah in the Hebrew Bible and Northwest Semitic Literature": "It is understandable that in certain circles Yahweh should have Asherah as a consort, since Asherah was originally El's consort and we know that El and Yahweh were equated in ancient Israel. Similarly, the fact that Yahweh has Anat as a consort at Elephantine presumably goes back to an equation of Yahweh with Baal, since Anat was Baal's consort originally" (Day, 1986).

Also important to note here is that polytheism was completely still in play amongst the Jewish community at Elephantine in the 4th century BCE, and they were in correspondence with high officials in Jerusalem, who seemed to have no issues with the polytheism there. The Elephantine papyri pre-date all extant manuscripts of the Hebrew Bible, and thus give scholars a very important glimpse at how Judaism was practiced in Egypt, and likely other areas during the fifth century BCE.

The name "Anath" appears infrequently in the Biblical narrative, occurring only in place names such as *Beth-Anath*, and *Anathoth* (Joshua 15:59; 19:38; Judges 1:33; Joshua 21:18; 1 Kings 2:26; Isaiah 10:30; Jeremiah 1:1) and the personal names *Shamgar ben Anath* (son of Anath) (Judges 3:31; 5:6), *Anthothijah* (1 Chronicles 8:24), and *Anathoth* (1 Chronicles 7:8; Nehemiah 10:19). When compared to the frequent references to Asherah in the Bible, along with the considerable archaeological evidence for both Asherah's worship and inscriptions coupling her with Yahweh in the time period we are dealing with that has accumulated since Albright's reference, this would make Asherah a much more likely candidate for the bride in the Songs. However, it is also important to keep in mind, we are dealing with polytheism here, and all sorts of Gods and Goddesses were part of the pantheon and played a part in the ritual life of the people, and in this respect the role of Anath in the Canaanite cosmology, and her relationship with her brother/lover Baal, can not be ruled out as a source of inspiration for the Biblical Love poem.

The Mesopotamian version of the Sacred Marriage is believed to have taken place in a chamber at the top of the huge temple complex in which was kept only a bed. The legs of the bed were animal shaped, either lions claws or bull's hooves, further linking the ritual that was to take place to the fecundity of the land and animals around them. On the evening of the Sacred Marriage the king as Tammuz went into a priestess who played the Goddess Inanna and on the hallowed bed, "Sexual intercourse between the incarnate god and goddess then took part in the sacred chamber of the temple" (Saggs 1962). "The core of the ritual was an act of sexual congress between king and goddess-figure.... The sexual union was intended to promote the fertility of the land" (Frymer-Kensky 1992).

As we have seen, the temple of Inanna in Uruk, *Eanna,* was recorded to have received copious amounts of *qunnabu* (cannabis). The idea that here as well, we might find indications of the ritual use of cannabis in the Sacred Marriage, does seem probable. In *The First Great Powers: Babylon and Assyria* (2019) Arthur Cotterell explains "In a temple set within a beautiful garden at Uruk the ruler impersonated Dumuzi, an early king and husband of Inanna, while the high priestess took on the role of the goddess herself. One text has the king of Uruk boast how he 'lay on the splendid bed of Inanna, strewn with pure plants.... The day did not dawn, the night did not pass. For fifteen hours I lay with Inanna'" (Cotterell, 2019). Assyriologist Erica Reiner believed the "Bed of Ishtar" (Inanna) indicated an aphrodisiac plant and compared it to the aromatic of Ishara, *qunnabu,* "cannabis,"noting that this calls to mind the plant named "*ki.na Istar,* in Akkadian *suhsi Istar,* or *majal Istar,* both meaning bed of Istar" (Reiner, 1995). The Akkadian *ki.na* here holding a phonetic similarity to the Indo-European root *kanna.*

Rediscovered Mesopotamian hymns and songs also give ample evidence that the union between the king and the goddess-figure was sexual. In the *Shulgi hymn* we read that "by his fair hands my loins were pressed ... he [ruffled] the hair of my lap" and "he laid his hands on my pure vulva." And again in the *Iddin-Dagan hymn*, "When holy Inanna has stretched out on the bed.... She makes love to him [the king] on her bed." It is obvious from the closing words of the Song of Songs, that an identical sexual motif and act as that described in the Mesopotamian Sacred Marriage hymns, lay at the core of the ancient ritual drama that it was composed for:

> Come away, my lover,
> and be like a gazelle
> or like a young stag
> on the spice-laden mountains
> –Song of Songs 8:14.

The ritual of the Sacred Marriage in Mesopotamia has been dated as far back as the fourth millennium B.C. Throughout the Fertile Crescent the Great Mother and her counterpart were worshiped in sexual rites in the temples and high places. In T.J. Meek's view, from its beginnings the Song of Songs was a religious composition that was originally connected to the cult of Tammuz\Adonis and Astarte\Ishtar, rather than the followers of Yahweh. However, because of its popularity, it had been adapted over time to become less offensive, and harmonized with Yahweh's cultus:

> Even a casual perusal of the ... [Tammuz-Ishtar] hymns ... must convince the most skeptical ... that the similarity between them and the songs in the book of Canticles [another name for the Song of Songs] is so close that both belong together. The structure of the songs is the same (two lovers representing god and goddess wooing each other and alternating in the praise of each other's charms); the general theme is the same (love); many of the phrases are quite identical; the figures are introduced in similar fashion; the lines breath the same delight in love; and the intent of all is manifestly to bring about the awakening of life in nature. Both are liturgies of the fertility cult. The only difference is that one group has come from Babylonia and the other from Palestine, where numerous influences tended to obscure and efface its original character (Meek 1924).

Later Hebrew Bible writings condemn the worshipers of Tammuz, indicating the popularity of the cult in the ancient world and even among the Israelites. The vegetation god Tammuz, personified the spring sun believed to die and descend to Hades each winter and with the aid of his mourning worshipers, annually made to return to life each spring, when his followers held a celebration and burned incense proclaiming "On the day which Tammuz rises up, when the flute of lapis lazuli and the ring of carnelian rise up with him, when male and female mourners rise up with him, may the dead also rise and inhale the incense" (Ringgren 1973). A similar seasonal descent\return mythology concerning Baal and Anath has also been noted, and this also was reenacted in a ritual drama. Comparative to the "incense" in the Tammuz hymn, are the "weeds" in an ancient poem about Baal; "Be it told to Puissant Baal: Summon weeds into thy house, Herbs into the midst of thy palace.... Puissant Baal rejoice. He summoned weeds into the house, Herbs into the midst of his palace" (Pritchard 1958).

Patai, pointed out that the title "Rider of Clouds," an epithet of Yahweh, was originally attributed to Baal, in both cases the epithet was associated with the copious incense used in their worship. The incense and plant imagery of rebirth from the Baal and Tammuz hymns described above, appears to be repeated much later in Isaiah 26:19; "your dead will live; their bodies will rise. You who dwell in the dust, wake up and shout for joy. Your dew is the dew of herbs; the earth will give birth to her dead." In this passage, we not only see the potency of the Lord's dew, but also its association with herbs, here *owrah*, a word meaning "bright-plant," and possibly referring to an entheogen. This term is incorporated into the tree like sacred candle stick, the *menorah*. The association of a potent "herb" with heavenly "dew," is one that is also evident in the Sacred Marriage, and the Song of Songs.

In relation to the fertility aspect of Baal\Tammuz and the references to incense it is of interest to note that the Songs tells us that Solomon had a vineyard in Baal Hamon (8:11). In no other place in the Bible does this place-name occur. Professor Helmer Ringgren reports that a *Ba'al Hamano* was worshiped in Carthage, Phoenicia and Palmyra and "the name has been interpreted as 'the lord of the altar of incense' ... In Latin inscriptions he is called *frugifer*, 'the fruit-bearer,' and *deus frugum*, 'the god of fruits,' which points in the direction of a vegetation god" (Ringgren 1973).

In the cases of both Tammuz and Baal, the burning of the incense and herbs referred to, revolves around the rebirth of the God and relates to the fertility rites of the Spring festival, which involved the ritual dramatization of the Sacred Marriage. In the time of Solomon it is indicated that the Hebrew kings took on a similar role to that of the other Near Eastern kings who played the part of the Baal or Tammuz, so it is not at all surprising to find references to the burning of incense being associated with both Solomon and the Sacred Marriage in the *Songs*:

Who is this coming up from the steppe,
Like a column of smoke,
Redolent with myrrh and incense,
All the peddler's powders?
Behold Solomon's bed,
Sixty heroes around it...
– Song of Songs 3:6

The German researcher Hartmut Schmokel, like other scholars, suggested that in the *Song of Songs*, a syncretized form of Yahweh was cloaked in the habiliments of the returning Tammuz, who was festally received each spring. The sixty warriors who accompanied Solomon's bed and carriage in the above verse, were seen by Schmokel as relating to the sacred number of Ishtar, (appearing also in the 6:8 reference to the sixty Queens), and were present to protect Tammuz in his return from the Netherworld. "The sword bearers surround the throne on which the chosen representative of Tammuz sits in splendor; smoke rises from the brazier before him and the choir assembled in the sanctuary sings an introit. This is the beginning of the third and final scene of the cult-drama of the Song of Songs as understood by Schmokel" (Pope 1977).

The ancient hymn "Descent of the Goddess Ishtar into the Lower World" makes it clear both anointing oils and incenses played a paramount role in the Near Eastern ritual drama.

For Tammuz, the beloved of her [Ishtar's] youth...
anoint with good oil, dress him in a bright red garment!
...On the day on which Tammuz rises up,
...when male and female mourners rise with him,
may the dead also rise and inhale the incense.

In light of these connections it is not so surprising to note that in 1924, W.H. Schoff wrote an article which suggested that the anointing oils and incense contained in the descriptions of the Temple and Tabernacle, originated from the cult of Tammuz:

> The transfer of the features of the Tammuz cult to the worship of Yahweh, Schoff suggested, occurred in the following way. When Jerusalem was captured by David, the worship of Tammuz and Astarte continued and Solomon for political reasons installed it in the Temple. Its influence can be seen in the description of the Temple structure, vessels, and ceremonies... Spices peculiar to the Tammuz cult were used in the sacred

> oil and incense, Exodus 30. A strong party, including many Judeans, was devoted to these divinities and their interests had to be considered and conciliated, especially in view of the prophetic opposition. At the spring festival the king and queen represented the god and goddess in a sacred marriage.... Yahweh was gradually substituted for Tammuz and the Daughter of Jerusalem for Astarte, but the ritual remained essentially the same.... The Canticles, originally a Tammuz liturgy, were preserved among other sacred scriptures in the temple archives "Because they referred in some way to the service and ceremonies of the temple" [(Schoff, 1924)] (Pope 1977).

Anointed in Marriage

The royal priestess, acting as the surrogate of the goddess, prepared the chosen bridegroom for the *Hieros Gamos,* or Sacred Marriage, by anointing him with oil, which some sources have suggested represented the semen of the fertility god that the male participant was imitating, whether that Baal, Tammuz, Adonis, Attis or another regional deity. Professor John Allegro referred to anointing with "various saps and resins as representing the divine semen."

John Allegro, the controversial English archaeologist and Dead Sea Scrolls scholar, made the claim "Since all life derives from the divine seed, it follows that the most powerful healing drugs would be pure, unadulterated semen of the god. Some plants were thought to have sap or resin approximating to this, their 'purity' or 'sanctity' in this regard being measured by their power as drugs to kill or cure or intoxicate" (Allegro 1970).

> The semen of the fertility god could be seen spurting as rain from heaven during an orgasmic thunderstorm; in concentrated form it appeared in certain powerful plants like the Mandrake, or Holy Plant ... or in aromatic gums and resins that formed part of the traditional unctions of the priests and kings. Such functionaries thus became "holy," that is, separated to the god's for service, being smeared, or "anointed" with his divine Substance. They were therefore called the "anointed ones," that is "messiahs," or "Christs," more specifically in the Old Testament, "those anointed with Jehovah/Yahweh" (1 Samuel 26:11, Psalms 2:2). (Allegro 1980).[7]

7 In *The People of the Dead Sea Scrolls,* Florentino García Martínez and Julio C. Trebolle Barrera relates an example related to this subject and Allegro, which they say contributed to

Unfortunately, in this regard, as noted earlier, Allegro failed to recognize the role of cannabis in regard to *kaneh bosm*, due to his own apparent cultural bias. However, despite Allegro's confusion of the sacred mushroom with cannabis, the connection between divine semen and the precious ointment is made more intriguing by context and also by the Hebrew word for ointment, and the sacred oil, semen. The priestly traditions describe the oil used as the *semen hammišṇâ*, "the anointing oil," or šemen mišḥat-qodes "sacred anointing oil." However, the English term "semen," is generally believed to have come through late Middle English: from Latin, literally "seed," from *serere* "to sow." As noted earlier, the Hebrew name for semen, *zera* also means "seed," and is phonetically similar to *serere*. Besides having similarities to the word for "seed" of man, animal and vegetation, *zera*, is also directly related to the Hebrew words "*zerem*," meaning "flood ... shower, storm and the word *zirmah*, means "a gushing of fluid (semen):--issue" (Strong 1979).

Despite the limited use of anointing oil in the Hebrew kingdom, as well as in the surrounding empires, the use of the sacred incense went far beyond the Spring Festivals, and was a year-round event: "the cloud filled the temple of the Lord [that Solomon built]. And the priests could not perform their service because of the cloud" (1 Kings 8:10). Like the references to this cloud in the story of Moses and the Tent of the Meeting, the cloud of incense smoke "was the palpable sign of God's presence in Solomon's temple" (Patai 1967).

The Sacred Incense of the *Songs*

Apparently, Solomon did not limit his use of incense to the temple of Yahweh, or the Lord's worship. "Solomon loved Yahweh: he followed the precepts of David his father, except that he offered sacrifice and incense on the high places" (I Kings 3:3). Here we can see references to Solomon's worship of the Goddess who was conventionally worshiped on mountains and hilltops. The Hebrew Bible

the secrecy and delays of the publication of the Dead Sea Scrolls and their translations. Allegro, who was on the team of translators, saw an 11 line fragment that had been assigned to a colleague, and "thought that it was an extraordinarily important text, the publication of which had been kept secret because it could be used as the basis for a gnostic interpretation of Christian initiation by means of anointing with sperm" (Barrera & Martinez, 1979). Allegro published his own curious translation of the text in the appendix of his 1979 book, *The Dead Sea Scrolls and the Christian Myth*, a much better work than his career killing *The Sacred Mushroom and the Cross*. Its a pity it had not come out first, as the damage done by Allegro's mushroom book, assured it garnered little attention. Accusations, by the early Catholic Church Fathers against both Jewish and Christian Gnostic sects were indeed directed against this sort of act, as we have detailed in *Sex, Drugs, Violence and the Bible* (2001, Bennett & McQueen). Thus, similar interpretations as Allegro's may have well been found in the ancient world.

itself testifies to this, telling us that Solomon's "foreign wives led him astray" and that through them the Hebraic king had begun "following Ashtoreth, the goddess of the Sidonians" (1 Kings 11:3-5). This Goddess is usually associated with Astarte, but in reference to this Patai suggested that this was actually Asherah under the regional name of the Elath of Sidon. "Asherah was associated with several cities where she was worshiped in her local manifestations. She was the 'Asherah of Tyre' and the 'Elath [Goddess] of Sidon'" (Patai, 1990).:

> Among the deities whom Solomon worshiped was "the Goddess of the Sidonians" who ... was none other than Asherah. However, the historian recording this calls her "Ashtoreth, Goddess of the Sidonoans." Also, the prophet Ahijah the Shilonite, an uncompromising Yahwist, who flourished towards the end of Solomon's reign ... reproaches the Israelites with once worshiping "Ashtoreth, the Goddess of the Sidonians," and another time with serving Asherah. However, such confusion ... is not confined to the Biblical authors who equally detested both of them; it is found ... in the Amarna letters written in the 14th century B.C.E. by people who should have known better because they believed in the two goddesses and worshiped them. But we have to keep in mind in polytheistic cultures the prevalent tendency often was to identify one god with another, substitute one god for another, combine one god with another, or call one god by the name of another, as we see from many examples in the Egyptian, Babylonian, Hittite or Canaanite religions. In any case, there can be little doubt that it was the worship of Asherah, already popular among the Hebrews for several generations, which was introduced by Solomon into Jerusalem as part of the cult of the royal household, for his Sidonian wife (Patai 1990).

While both Biblical references and archaeological finds attest that "the worship of Asherah was thus a central feature of popular Hebrew religion in the pre-monarchic period, and her statues stood in many a local sanctuary, it remained for King Solomon to introducer her worship into his capital city of Jerusalem" (Patai, 1990).

Like the *Qedeshim* of Asherah Astarte\Ishtar's worshipers included male transvestites, (which can be identified with the male cult prostitutes in the Hebrew Bible and who at times penetrated into the Temple itself), known as *kurgarrus* who performed music for the goddess' pleasure, as well as fumigating her with incense of fragrant cane, i.e.: *qunubu*.

> The expert singers sit before her on the ground, those who play the lyre, the harp and the clappers ... the kurgarrus [who carry] the spindle ... and the whip, ease her mind with (incense of) sweet reeds.

Pope compares these "sweet reeds" to the same references in the Bible that we have been focusing on: "The 'sweet reed' ... with which the goddess' inwards are soothed, is presumably the same 'aromatic cane' of Exod 30:23 and the 'sweet cane' of Jer 6:20; Isa 43:24; Ezek 27:19 and simply 'cane' in Canticles 4:14" (Pope 1977).

Unfortunately, Pope seems to be unaware, or chose not to mention it, that these same references to "cane" are the ones that Sula Benet first identified in 1936 as references to cannabis under the name *kaneh*. As we have seen, *qunubu* was one of the main ingredients in the Near Eastern Sacred rite, (Waterman 1930) and we now know of direct references to the use of both a cannabis infused beverage and ointments that were dedicated to Ishtar from ancient inscriptions. We can be relatively sure that the reference to how the fumes of the incense "ease her mind," identify the entheogenic properties of cannabis smoke. The fragrant procession described in the ancient pagan hymn, clearly "recalls the columns of smoke and clouds of myrrh and frankincense which accompany Solomon's litter as it rises from the desert or steppe-land surrounded by the sixty skilled swordsmen, like the *kurgarrus* who accompany Inanna/Ishtar" (Pope 1977).

I do find Pope's use of these specific reference here intriguing, and in the context used, I find it difficult to believe the respected Professor was unaware of Sula Benet's use of these same citations.

The description of the carriages and processions which accompanied "Solomon's bed," and its Mesopotamian counterparts, once again brings to mind some amazing parallels with still existent rituals practiced in India. This time we look at the "Festival of Chariots," as performed by the Jagannath cult in Puri, a ritual that is of pre-Vedic origins. In this ancient and still partially performed rite, massive elaborately decorated chariots (representing the world in motion) are drawn carrying the veiled figures of Jagannath, "the Lord of the Universe" his brother Balabhadra and his sister Subhadra. It is believed by some, that one of these veiled figures is a giant *Lingam*, although this is unknown as the Jagannath Mandir in Puri is off limits to outsiders.

As noted Ethnobotanist Jonathan Ott has described:

> The Jagannath Mandir was the last temple to maintain classical [Indian] dance, up until the mid-1950s – now it is strictly a

> theatrical art.... The British ... suppressed this aspect of liturgy as rude, calling the *devadasis* or *maharis* [the ritual wives of the god] *nuatch-girls* or prostitutes [they performed naked, judging by the sculpture on the natamandapas or natamandiras, "dance platforms or temples," for the public, and among their duties was *maithuna-type* ritual sex with the Brahmins in the temple, with which Cannabis use seems to be associated, to please Indra and bring on the monsoon]. As a result the practice, once widespread throughout India ... all but disappeared, except in Puri, and the other styles were preserved only in villages by gotipuas, boys dressed as girls, only to be revived as classical art in our time... (Ott 1996).

In the Jagannath festival of Puri, we see the massive chariots and their entourage, analogous to the procession which accompanied Solomon's bed, and Ishtar's in the Mesopotamian counterpart. Temple prostitutes played the role of "the wives of the god-king," and had sex with the king (or priest) in order to bring on the seasonal rains. A similar role was taken on by the Shulamite in the Songs, and the priestess who enacts the part of Ishtar in the Sumerian counterpart of the ritual drama. Other similarities occur throughout, such as the role of transvestites in all three ritual-dramas, and the use of cannabis in their cultic rituals. Anthropologist Frederique Marglin, who noted the use of cannabis by the Jagannath cult, referred to the many similarities between the Indian and Mesopotamian fertility dramas and commented that in both cases, in the performance of the sexual act it is "not procreation" that is sought, "but the assurance of abundant crops and endorsement of the kings ability to rule... The sacrifice of one's reproductive capacity is symbolically akin to death. The paradox of general fertility brought about by sexual activity of persons who have sacrificed their own fecundity ... [and is a] symbolic expression of the widespread sacrificial theme of renewed life through death" (Marglin 1986).

> For Love is strong as Death
> – Song of Songs 8:6.

In light of Pope's connection of the fragrant incense used by the cult of Ishtar with the Biblical references to *kaneh* (cannabis), and the copious incense referred to in the Songs, it is interesting to note that the next direct Biblical account of cannabis by the name *kaneh* appears in Solomon's Songs, (the poetic imagery of this verse brings to the initiate's mind the sweet seductive scent of blonde Lebanese hashish):

> Come with me from Lebanon, my bride,
> Come with me from Lebanon.
> Descend from the crest of Amana, from the top of Senir,
> The summit of Hermon [High Places] ...
> How delightful is your love, my sister, my bride!
> How much more pleasing is your love than wine,
> And the fragrance of your ointment than any spice!...
> The fragrance of your garments is like that of Lebanon...
> Your plants are an orchard of pomegranates,
> With choice fruits, with henna and nard,
> Nard and saffron, kaneh [cannabis] and cinnamon,
> with every kind of incense tree ...
>
> – Song of Songs 4:8-14

In the Songs, we see cannabis not only as incense, but also in relation to the sacred anointing oil in the above verse in the form of the fragrant "ointment." The comparison between the fragrance of the oil, with that of the wine also occurs in Songs 1:2-4 "...for your love is more delightful than wine. Pleasing is the fragrance of your precious ointments; your name is like precious ointment poured out.... We shall inhale thy love rather than wine."

LOVE APPLES

It should also be noted that references to the powerful visionary drug mandrake, (also referred to in *Genesis* 30:14-16) occurs in the Song of Songs (7:14): "The mandrakes send out their fragrance."

This indicates the possibility that at this time mandrake was being used in conjunction with hemp in the Holy anointing oil, as it was in 19th century astral traveling salves, as well as medieval magical ointments. Such would account for some of the more ecstatic behavior associated with the anointing oil, such as the frenzied behavior of Saul a generation earlier.

Ethnobotanist Christian Rätsch claims that its probable that "the oldest written mentions of the mandrake occur in the cuneiform tablets of the Assyrians.... An Ugaritic cuneiform text from Ras Shamra (fifteenth to fourteenth century B.C.E.) appears to refer to a ritual text, '[P]lant mandragoras in the ground' ... Mesopotamian cuneiform texts make frequent mention of a wine known as cow's eye,[8] which was purportedly a wine mixed with mandrake" (Rätsch, 2005).

Rätsch also refers to the use of the plant in ancient Egypt, where "mandrake fruits were used as gifts of love during courtship and probably were eaten as aphrodisiacs. The love plant appears to have been associated with Hathor the goddess of love" (Rätsch, 2005). Interestingly this goddess has a well known association with Asherah and numerous Canaanite amulets depict her wearing a bouffant wig identical with that of the Egyptian Hathor. One of the potsherd inscriptions of blessings discussed earlier of "Yahweh and his Asherah" from 8th century BCE Kuntillet Ajrud, appears with a cow feeding its calf, which is also seen as a symbol associated with Hathor.

Left: Canaanite amulet depicting Asherah with a Hathor Wig. **Right:** (Egyptian statue of Hathor) In *Reinstating the Divine Woman in Judaism*, Jenny Kien explains "In the 14-12th century BCE, Asherah became popular in Egypt, where she was known as Qudsu (Qadesh) or holiness, and this epithet spread to Phoenicia. Qudsu became so strongly associated with the Egyptian goddess Hathor that no description of Ashera-Qudsu is complete without mentioning Hathor" (Kien, 2000).

8 A name that is suggested as having come through the effects of the root upon the pupil.

> The Egyptians recognized Hathor in the Asherah known as the Ba'alat (Mistress) of byblos. The north Canaanite port of Byblos was one of Egypt's major trading partners, and Egyptian influence was so strong there that the Ba'alat of Byblos took on Egyptian form. Hathor's cow ears and typical hairstyle - the wig with the "Hathor curls" (two slender spirals or thick curls extending down to the shoulders or breasts) – were now incorporated into Canaanite depictions of Asherah" (Kien, 2000).

In relation to mandragoras this connection is interesting. Rätsch refers to a "mandrake beer that was consecrated to her." As the German ethnobotanist explains, this mandrake beer played "an important role" in a "myth describing the destruction of the human race and the creation of heaven":

> The sun god Ra was angry with humans because they had contrived to attack him. In his anger, he created the terrible lion-headed goddess Sekmet (an early form of Hathor) to punish the race of humans. She raged among the people for an entire day and was not yet finished when the sun set, for she wanted to utterly extinguish humanity. But Ra did not want this, and he thought of a trick to end the goddess's deadly rampage. He had mandrake fruits brought to him from Elephantine, an island in the Nile ...; according to other versions and/ or translations, ... "red ocher" was brought as well.... At the same time, he ordered the production of a huge amount of barley beer (seven thousand jugs). He mixed the mandrakes (and the ... red ocher) into this and had the fields covered in the blood-red beer (the "sleeping drink"). The following sunrise, when the goddess saw the beer, she first perceived her reflection and thus recognized herself. Because of its red color, she thought the beer was human blood, and she eagerly drank it to the last drop. "Her countenance became gentle as a result, and she drank; this did her heart well. Drunken did she return, without having recognized the people"...
>
> Out of thankfulness, humans never again rose up against Ra. Sakmet transformed herself into the cow Hathor and carried Ra into the heavens.
>
> In commemoration of these dramatic events, which took place at the beginning of time, Ra established the Hathor festival (literally, "festival of drunkenness"), during which young maidens consecrated to the goddess would make a beer known

> as sdr.t (= "sleeping drink" [?]) using a similar recipe. The Hathor festivals were ecstatic orgies with obscene performances, sacrificial activities, and wild music.... Later, Hathor was celebrated as the inventor of beer and the "mistress of drunkenness without end..." (Rätsch, 2005).

Othmar Keel, Professor of Old Testament and Biblical Studies at the University of Freibourg, Germany, points out the similarity between Egyptian love poems with references to mandrakes and the Songs: "The plant occurs frequently in Egyptian pictures from the New Kingdom (1540-1075 B.C.).... The ancient Egyptian love song also describes the effect of the love apple. The man sings: 'If only I were her Nubian maid, her attendant in secret! She would let me bring her love apples [i.e., mandrakes]; when it was in her hand, she would smell it, and she would show me the hue of her whole body' [*Cairo Love Songs*, Group B, no. 21]. The woman's skin is described in another love song: 'Your skin is the skin of the mandrake, which induces loving'" (*The Song of Songs, Continental Commentaries*, 1994).

Another of the Egyptian love songs mentions mandrakes in an interesting parallel to the blossoming of love we have seen: "If only my sister were mine every day, like the greenery of a wreath! ... The reeds are dried, the safflower has blossomed, the *mrbbflowers* are (in) a cluster(?), the lapis-lazuli plants and the mandragoras have come forth.... [The blo]ssoms from Hatti have ripened, the bsbs-tree blossomed ... the willow tree greened. She would be with me every day, like (the) greenery of a wreath, all the blossoms are flourishing in the meadow ... entirely"[9]

In *The Complete Gods and Goddesses of Ancient Egypt,* Richard H. Wilkinson, notes that "the Greeks identified Hathor with Aphrodite" (Wikinson, 2003). In this regard it is worth noting that when the ancient Greeks referred to Egyptian gods by the names of their own deities, through a practice called *interpretatio graeca,* they sometimes called Hathor, Aphrodite. Aphrodite is also connected with other ancient Near Eastern Goddesses.

Pope noted that the "association of mandrakes with fertility and with the love-goddess is of particular interest. Hesychius... [a Greek grammarian] noted that *mandagoritis* was an epithet of Aphrodite" (Pope, 1977). As Rätsch has also noted of this:

> The Cypriot cult of Aphrodite developed directly out of the Oriental cult of the love goddess Ishtar, Astarte, Asherot, et

9 Cairo Love Songs, Group B, no. 21E, translated by Michael Fox, *The Song of Songs and the Ancient Egyptian Love Songs*, p. 38.

> cetera. J Rendel Harris proposed the theory that the Greek cult of Aphrodite could be traced back to the Greek assimilation of the Oriental conceptions about the mandrake (Harris 1917). Aphrodite was also known as Mandragoritis ("she of the Mandragora"...). The Mandragora thus had an intimate connection to the love goddess and was sacred to her.... In the late ancient Mysteries of the Great Goddess, Aphrodite was identified with Hecate.... Thus the "mandrake of Hecate" was nothing other than the sacred plant of the love goddess (Rätsch, 2005).

The idea that behind the figure of Aphrodite there stands the more ancient Semitic goddess of love, Ishtar-Astarte was recognized in ancient times, Herodotus (1.105, 131) and Philo of Byblos (Eus. Prep. evang. 1.812) both referred to this connection. We have discussed the blending and overlapping of various regional goddesses, in some cases going back to their common origins, in others later adaptations and Asherah, as well, can be tied in with these other Goddesses. As William Dever has noted: "Canaanite-Israelite Asherah appears later as Greek Aphrodite ... goddesses of beauty, love, and sexual pleasure. The similarities are unequivocal: Asherah and Aphrodite are both connected to the sea, and doves are symbols of both. Aphrodite's lover Adonis clearly preserves the earlier Phoenician-Hebrew word *adon*, 'Lord'" (Dever, 2008).

In a love poem dedicated to Ishtar translated in *Babylonian and Assyrian Literature* (1901) we read:

> The Mandrakes ripened golden, glows around:
> The fruit of Love is fragrant on the ground.
> Amid the Dud'im plant he now reclines,
> And to his welcome fate himself resigns
> The lovely queen beside him now doth lay
> And leads his soul along the blissful way.

Besides known narcotic effects, mandrake like cannabis, has a long held reputation as an aphrodisiac. According to Rätsch, who has written extensively on both psychoactive plants and alleged aphrodisiacs:

> In ancient times, the primary ritual significance of the mandrake was in erotic cults. Because of the poor quality of the sources that have come down to us, however, only rudimentary information about these practices is available. The most important source about the use of mandrake in the Orient is the Old Testament, where the fruits (love apples) are mentioned

> numerous times under the Old Testament Hebrew name duda' im, and namely as an aphrodisiac... (Rätsch, 2005)

Referring to mandrakes or love apples, as they were otherwise known, W.E. Budge commented that, "These are mentioned in the Bible ... and there is no doubt that ancients used decoctions of the plant both as aphrodisiacs and as narcotics" (Budge 1930). In the Genesis 30:14-15 account, it is in exchange for sex, that mandrakes are given.

The Hebrew name of the plant דּודאָים, *dudaïm'* shares the same root as דוד/*dod* – the Hebrew word for love or lover, and this is seen as a connection between the two. Pope notes reference to a cognate term in the Baal and Anat *hieros gamos* hymns, clearly indicating the use of mandrakes in the Ugaritic love poems, and with yet another Near Eastern Goddess.

Interestingly, the "Syriac version of Hermes Trismegistos contained a story in which King Solomon had a mandrake in his signet ring whose miraculous qualities enabled women to give safe birth without pain" (Riddle, 2010). As well, we will discuss in a later chapter, mandrake and its fruits, or "love-apples" have been seen as the Biblical Tree of Knowledge in Eden, from at least the 2nd Century CE. In that account, both aphrodisiacal and psychoactive effects might be interpreted: "Eve's act of eating the mandrake caused her and Adam to conceive, but her persuasion of Adam to eat it in the first place caused him to have understanding (reason)" (Riddle, 2010).

However, despite this strong connection to love poems and sexuality in the ancient literature, no medical reason behind the aphrodisiacal reputation of the mandrake has ever been discovered. In reference to the Genesis account, the Christian Doctor Robert Greenblatt suggested "What helped Rachel to conceive was not the fertilizing but the tranquillizing properties of the mandrake; the mandrake soothed her anxieties" (Greenblatt, 1963).

Although I think Greenblatt is correct here, it is worth noting Prof. Pope's observations on the scent of mandrakes in regard to the Songs:

> The odor of mandrakes is reportedly pungent and distinctive and was presumably pleasant or exciting. While Occidental aesthetics may regard the scent as fetid rather than fragrant, it is well known that odors which may be offensive to some can be highly provocative to others. The belief that the plant has potency as an aphrodisiac could influence one's reaction to the

> odor. Just where the mandrakes were located with relation to the lovers, whether in the field, or at the door with other delectables, or by their couch is not clear (Pope, 1977).

> The mandrakes are breathing their fragrance,
> at our door is most luscious fruitage,
> Now ripe or ripened aforetime,
> which I, for thee, dearest, have treasured.
> –Song of Songs 7:14

As Pope explains it, mandrake and cannabis, with their shared reputation as entheogens and aphrodisiacs, seemed to have traveled the road together somewhat through history, to the point that a name for cannabis came to be applied to mandrake. "Among the modern Palestinian names for the mandrake ... [is] *banj* which appears suspiciously similar to the Indian term bhang which in northern India is applied by Hindu votaries of Tantrism to ... *Cannabis Indica,* used as an aphrodisiac in the 'left handed' rites which are climaxed with ... *maithuna,* sexual union. The hemp is prepared as a dessert in the shape of molasses, or as a beverage with sweet sherbet" (Pope, 1977).

Considering Pope's comparison of the *Songs* with the hymns of Kali, the connection here with the use of cannabis is interesting. Kali's cannabis mantra is, "Om, Hrim Ambrosia, that springeth forth from ambrosia, Thou shalt showerest ambrosia, draw ambrosia for me again and again. Bring Kalika within my control. Give success; Svaha" (Avalon, 1913). In Tantric rites, cannabis retained its ancient Vedic epithet of '*Vijaya*' (Victory). As Arthur Avalon (aka, Sir John Woodroffe) explained: "Vijaya, (victory) used in ceremonies to Kali: That is the narcotic Bhang (hemp) ... used in all ceremonies" (Avalon, 1913).

As Robert Anton Wilson, noted in his ground-breaking study *Sex & Drugs*: "the cannabis drugs are especially likely to cause [the] ... kind of concentration ... in which one may ... become totally identified with the sex organs and lose all other awareness entirely" (Wilson 1973). A perfect frame of mind for the orgiastic type of worship inferred by the Hebrew Bible narrative. A number of books have been written specifically regarding cannabis' role in sex, and more recently, A Stanford University study published in *The Journal of Sexual Medicine,* released a paper "Association Between Marijuana Use and Sexual Frequency in the United States: A Population-Based Study" (2017) that concluded "The results of 28,176 women (average age = 29.9 years) and 22,943 men (average age = 29.5) were analyzed ... marijuana users had significantly higher sexual frequency compared with never users.... An overall trend for men ... and women ... was identified showing that higher marijuana use was associated with increased coital frequency" (Sun & Eisenberg, 2017).

Methods of Employment

How the mandrakes and cannabis would have been used from the Songs is unknown. References to ointments in the Songs indicate that they were likely in use here "How much more pleasing is your love than wine, and the fragrance of your ointment than any spice!" (Song of Songs 4:10); As our indications of incense in association with cannabis: "with henna and nard, nard and saffron, kaneh [cannabis] and cinnamon, with every kind of incense tree..." (Song of Songs 4:14).

Dr. Creighton suggested Song of Songs 5:1 made reference to ingested cannabis: "I am come into my garden, my sister, my spouse; I have gathered my myrrh with my spice: *I have eaten my honeycomb with my honey*; I have drunk my wine with my milk." As Creighton explained:

> In the Hebrew text, the phrase in italics reads: "I have eaten my wood (*yagar*) with my honey (*debash*)." St. Jerome, in the Vulgate, translated the Hebrew word meaning "wood" by favum, or honey-comb – *comedi favum cum melle meo*; which is not only a bold license, but a platitude to boot, inasmuch as there is neither wit nor point in making one to eat the honeycomb with the honey. The LXX adopted a similar license, but avoided the platitude, by translating thus: ... "I have eaten *my bread* with my honey" ... the word *yagar*, which the Vulgate translated *favum* for the occasion, is used in some fifty or sixty other places of O.T. always in the sense of wood, forest, planted field, herbage, or the like. The meaning of Cant.[10] 5:1, is clear enough in its aphrodisiac context: "I have eaten *my hemp* with my honey" (Creighton, 1903).

In relation, one of the references to the Hebrew term *eshisha*, which the 19th century Biblical scholar Kitto suggested served as a root word for the Arabic *hashish*, occurs in Song of Songs 2:5, here translated as "raisin cake": "Strengthen me with raisin cakes [*eshisha*], refresh me with apples, for I am weak with love." These same cakes would come to be detested "they turn to other gods and love the

10 Song of Songs

sacred raisin cakes [*eshisha*]" (Hosea 3:1). This later rejection does make one ponder whether raisins were intended in the Hebrew *eshisha* or something with more of a ritual effect.

Some of the above references to similar rites clearly indicate a sacred beverage was infused with the plant. Perhaps sacred infusions were part of the ritual sacred weddings? This is intriguing given that Ishtar had her own cannabis infused aromatic beer, and lotions as well. Moreover, as we have seen, mandrakes appear in Ishtar's love liturgy and we also have Hathor's mandrake beer. In reference to the Assyrian sacred rites, a paper on opium and hashish from the *Compte Rendu, Rencontre Assyriologique Internationale,* also refers to a ritual drink, thought to be entheogenic, but of unknown contents. It is conceivable that references to "spiced wine" in the Song of Songs refers to a similar infusion. As we shall see later in our discussion of the prophet Ezra, there are numerous indications that the ancient Hebrews, like their neighboring kingdoms, had beverages infused with cannabis, opium, mandrake and likely other psychoactive ingredients.

A Fertility Rite

The Sacred Marriage was a pagan ritual which held paramount importance in the ancient world, and it was believed to endure the fertility of the land. Clearly, both the use of entheogenic substances and ritual sex played paramount roles in this ritual drama. Through the evidence of the Songs and Solomon's own reign, we can see that this sacred ritual would have been practiced in the Temple of Jerusalem itself. As with tel Arad and its two altars, indicating the combined worship of Yahweh and Asherah, we can be confident that the temple Solomon built paid reverence to the Goddess as well. The references to both cannabis and mandrake in the Songs, show these same practices at play in the Hebrew variation of the *Hieros Gamos*

Through this rite, the king and his kingdom believed they attained the assurance of the continued fecundity of the land. A similar relationship is inferred from Solomon's coronation and anointing. In the Psalms we read of the King's role as the bestower of fertility through the rite of the Sacred Marriage: "Endow your king with justice, O God.... He will endure as long as the sun.... He will be like ... showers watering the earth.... Let corn abound throughout the land; on the tops of the hills may it sway. Let its fruit flourish like Lebanon; let it thrive like the grass of the field. May his name endure forever" (Psalm 72:1-17).

The fecundity was endured through imitative magic via the procreative act. As Patai explained in *The Hebrew Goddess*:

> Ritual license as a regularly (in many places annually) recurring feature of temple worship is well attested from all over the ancient Near East. It was ... standard practice of the cultic veneration of the divine powers of life and fertility. As Nelson Glueck recently observed: "The excitement of pagan worship and participation in feasts of sacrificial offerings apparently often led male and female worshipers to join together in feverish consummation of fertility rites."
>
> The mythical counterpart of this orgiastic ritual was, in ancient Israel as well as among other ancient Near Eastern peoples, the great cosmogonical and cosmological myth cycle, according to which the annual period of vegetative fertility was preceded by a union of the male and female elements of nature. To ensure that this great cosmological copulation take place in the proper measure and with the requisite intensity, man himself, it was felt, had to perform the sacred sex act, thereby both indicating to the elements of nature what was expected of them and inducing them to do the same through the compulsive force of a religio-magical act. (Patai 1990)

Moreover, this was a standard form of religious worship throughout the Mid East, as William Cole explained in *Sex and Love in the Bible*:

> All of ... [the] gods and goddesses worshiped by Israel's neighbors near and far were intimately and organically related to nature and the various forces and powers encountered there. For the most part they appeared in male/female pairs and were pictured in the myths and legends creating the world by copulation. They had special responsibility for fecundity and fertility of all sorts of conditions. Their worship apparently required a kind of imitative magic in which male and female devotees yoked their bodies sexually and spilled their seed upon the field they desired to yield bounteous crops. Orgies involving the use of intoxicants and indiscriminate sexual activity played an important part in these cults, and many Israelites gladly became apostates to these weird and wondrous religions. The inexperience of the nomadic Hebrews in the task of agriculture in their new homeland made them easy

> converts to the local Baals who promised good harvests. The exotic character of the cult with its mystic roots extending far back into antiquity, together with the highly sensual pleasures afforded in the worship, combined to make it an attractive type of religious experience. Any such temple in modern society would encounter no difficulty in attracting large numbers of devotees. (Cole 1959)

It has been suggested that such ritual sexual pairing in this context, began with the introduction of the date palm – a dioecious tree with sexes in separate trees, requiring fertilization by man's intervention, or by that of cherub nature daemons (wind, birds, bees etc.), thus making the relationship analogous to human sexuality in the mind of primitive people (Smith 1927). Cannabis, as we have seen, played a major ritual role in the ancient Near East, and like the date palm is dioecious, having two very distinct sexes. In reference to cannabis in this respect it should also be noted that hemp is an annual crop and would require continued fertilization each year for the seeds of the next generation, unlike the date palm, which grows larger, year after year, resulting in continually standing groves. Thus hemp is a far more likely candidate for the crop which continually required, in the minds of the ancient Near Eastern fertility cult, orgiastic rites of sympathetic magic. It is also known that a "number of traditions developed around the hemp harvest that involved rituals based on intoxication from the volatile resins and oils" (Emboden 1972). The addition of sexual license developing at such pagan rituals does not take a lot of imagination. As Sula Benet also noted:

> Since the plant was associated with religious ritual and the power of healing, magical practices were connected with its cultivation.... The odor of ... hemp is stimulating enough to produce euphoria and a desire for sociability and gaiety and harvesting of hemp has always been accompanied by social festivities, dancing, and sometimes even erotic playfulness (Benet 1975).

It is in the orgiastic and drug induced ecstasies of the "high places," practiced through the Tantric-like fertility rites found throughout the ancient Near East, that we find the paganistic roots of the Sacred Marriage described in the *Hebrew Bible*'s Song of Songs. Further evidence that Solomon adopted aspects of the already existing Canaanite fertility cult can be seen in Psalm 110:4, where Solomon acts the part of a priest by blessing the assemblage at the consecration of the Temple, and is referred to as "a priest of the order of Melchizedek for ever." "Melchizedek was a priest of El 'Elyon ('God most High') in Salem, i.e. Jerusalem, and it is clear that he represents Canaanite religion" (Ringgren 1973). A later Gnostic tractate the *Pistis Sophia*, describes Melchizedek as the "hand" of the goddess herself.

THE WISEST OF MEN

Despite Solomon's connection with the fertility rituals practiced throughout the ancient world, and his supposedly sinful worship of gods besides Yahweh, he is referred to in the Bible as the wisest of men. Yahweh himself bestowed this gift upon Solomon at the high place of Gibeah after granting the king the fulfillment of one wish. For this wish Solomon chose wisdom, and was told by the Lord "I will give you a wise and discerning heart, so that there will never have been anyone like you, nor will there ever be" (1 Kings 3:12).

Interestingly, Solomon's relationship with cannabis extends beyond the reference in the Songs, and can be seen in later literature that developed around the king's alleged magical abilities and knowledge. *The Testament of Solomon*, thought to date from sometime between the first and third century AD, is one of the oldest magical texts concerning the ancient Jewish king. This text is a pseudepigraphic catalog of demons summoned by King Solomon, and how they can be countered by invoking angels and other magical techniques. *The Testament of Solomon* refers to a story where the magician-king forces a demon to spin hemp! "So I commanded her to spin the hemp for the ropes used in the building of the house of God; and accordingly, when I had sealed and bound her, she was so overcome and brought to naught as to stand night and day spinning the hemp" (*The Testament of Solomon*, 100-300 AD). Sula Benet, referring to the 1912 work of Georg Salzberger, *Salomons Tempelbau und Thron*, wrote "King Solomon, ... friend of King Hiram of Tyre ..., ordered hemp cords among other materials for building his temple and throne" (Benet, 1975).

Solomon's reputation for magic persisted through the centuries and we can see this in medieval European magical traditions where grimoires like, *Clavicula Salomonis*, "The Key of Solomon" (14th-15th century) and the 17th-century *Clavicula Salomonis Regis*, "The Lesser Key of Solomon" both of which represents a typical example of Renaissance magic, carried his name. Most interesting of such magical manuscripts, is the 16th century *Sepher Raziel: Liber Salo-*

monis, which refers to cannabis specifically, in an anointing oil used to see spirits:

> The third herbe is Canabus [cannabis]& it is long in shafte & clothes be made of it. The vertue of the Juse [juice]of it is to anoynt thee with it & with the juse of arthemesy & ordyne thee before a mirrour of stele [steel]& clepe thou spiritts & thou shallt see them & thou shalt haue might of binding & of loosing deuills [devils]& other things. (*Sepher Raziel: Liber Salomonis,* 1564).

Indeed, cannabis seems to have been used here, in a similar way that it was used in the Holy of Holies, but instead of seeing *spirits* and *devils* in a blackened mirror, the "angel of the lord" was seen and consulted in a pillar of smoke. And it is such a scenario as this we will be turning to, with a look at the reference to *kaneh* in Isaiah.

Chapter 8

The Smoke of the Prophets ...

Clearly, the indications from the Song of Songs, and the account of Solomon, indicate that polytheism was a standard form of religion in Jerusalem at that time. Archaeological evidence attests to this state as well. Both the books of Kings and Chronicles indicate the prevalence of the worship of Asherah, through the *ashiram* or asherah poles, along with Baal and other deities in the Holy land, and even within the confines of the temple itself.

Polytheism, like monotheism, comes with its own set of problems. One of these is the vying for favor with the Royalty and the people that supported the temples. Also important to note is that there was virtually no separation between church and state at that time, so political influence and control came into play as well. These factors can be seen in the account of the Biblical prophet Isaiah, who was said to have lived during the reign of the King Hezekiah (722-701 BCE) whose monotheistic reforms are believed to have been behind the cancellation of the tel Arad temple site.

Interestingly, the account of *kaneh* as cannabis in Isaiah, may give us some indication about the core issues of the conflict that led to a campaign of Yahweh-alone worship. This is a complicated issue, and there are multiple compounded factors at play here. Some of it was purely political. The Jewish kingdom, surrounded by larger encroaching empires, did indeed have a need to consolidate for political reasons of protecting its existence. However, other reasons had to do with temple life, and where the various votive offerings went. We have already seen the popularity of cannabis at the various temples throughout the ancient Near East, and discussed the expense this imported and sought after rare spice would have acquired. We can only imagine the competition between cults for a sacred incense and entheogenic substance, that aided one to hear the voices of the gods!

It should be noted that although the traditional view is that the 66 chapters of Isaiah, were composed by the prophet himself, in two periods sometime between 740 BCE and 686 BCE set about 15 years apart, the current academic view is that more than one hand is at work in the books attributed to the prophet. The general historical view is that parts of the Chapters of 1-39 include works from Isaiah, but are also interspersed with later insertions from Deuteronomists writing at the time of Josiah, close to a century later, who will be discussed in the next chapter, in order to further justify the radical changes in religious practices and life that were instilled then. The remaining chapters (40-66) were composed during the Babylonian Exile, around two hundred years after the alleged life of the historical Isaiah.

Just as Moses received his answers in a billowing cloud of cannabis resin-infused smoke, we can see from the reference to *kaneh* in Isaiah, that when the cannabis was lacking, the scryed answers were more difficult to bring forth. Moreover, the Lord complains he has been shortchanged of his offering of cannabis explicitly. When the prophet seeks advice, the Lord angrily responds:

> "...You have not brought me sheep for burnt offerings nor honored me with your sacrifices. I have not burdened you with grain offerings, nor wearied you with demands for frankincense. You have not bought me any fragrant cane (cannabis [*kaneh*]) with your silver, or lavished on me the fat of your sacrifices. But you have burdened me with your sins and wearied me with your iniquities" (Isaiah 43:23-24).

An earlier account from Isaiah, although not identifying cannabis by name, gives clear indications that at times the Lord's hunger for his favorite smoke was being appeased and cannabis was being used as a shamanic incense inside the precincts of the temple at Jerusalem, in elaborate shamanic ceremonies:

> And the posts of the door moved at the voice of him that cried, and the temple was filled with smoke.
>
> Then said I, "Woe is me, for I am undone; because I am a man of unclean lips, and I dwell in the midst of a people of unclean lips; for mine eyes have seen the King, the Lord of hosts."
>
> Then flew one of the seraphims unto me, having a live coal in his hand, which he had taken with the tongs from off the altar, And he laid it upon my mouth and said, "Lo, this hath touched thy lips; and thine iniquity is taken away, and thy sin purged" (Isaiah 6:4-7).

These two accounts in Isaiah, 43:23-24 and 6:4-7, are clearly connected. In Isaiah 43:24 God complains that he was not brought any cannabis (*kaneh*) "but thou hast made me to serve with thy

Isaiah taking a hit from a coal off the altar, by Matthaeus Merian, (1630)

sins, thou hast wearied me with thine iniquities" and after his lips touch the tongs and a coal of incense from the altar, these are both cleansed: "this hath touched thy lips; and thine iniquity is taken away, and thy sin purged" (Isaiah 6:7). A redemptive act, comparable to the consumption of the later Eucharist, in the way it relieves one of the burdens of sin and iniquity, and this also which clearly connects the two verses. In one verse Sins and Iniquities are lifted through the use of *kaneh,* in the other God complains of being burdened by them, without an offering of kaneh.[1] As well we see both kaneh (cannabis) and frankincense here together, both of which were recovered from the altars at tel Arad. There is a clear connection here. Both kaneh and frankincense will be found together again in the Jeremiah 6:20 reference, and as noted this was the case with the Song of Songs 4:14 as well.

Also of interest here is the use of the term *seraphim,* as this clearly has connotations of serpents. A number of Hebrew Bible passages associate śērāphîm with serpents. In response to the Israelites' rebellion in the wilderness the Lord sent "venomous [śērāphîm] snakes among them" (Numbers 21:6). After the people confessed their sin, the Lord ordered Moses "to make a snake [śārāph] and put it up on a pole" (Numbers 8). In this last verse the term śārāph refers back to

1 This connection follows through into the original Hebrew as well. Isaiah 6:7 and 43:24 "sin" חַטָּאת chatta'ah Strong #2403 ; Isaiah 6:7 "Iniquity" עֲוֺנֶ֑ךָ 'ă·wō·ne·ḵā , Isaiah 43:24 plural "iniquities" בַּעֲוֺנֹתֶֽיךָ׃ ba·'ă·wō·nō·ṯe·ḵā Strong #5771 in both cases.

the full phrase "venomous [śeraphîm] snakes." In Deuteronomy 8:15 the wilderness is described as a "thirsty and waterless land, with its venomous snakes [*nāchāš śārāph*, literally, "*seraph* snake"] and scorpions." Seraphim has also been translated as "fiery serpent" due to the verb śārāph, which means "to burn completely." The noun śārāph would then mean "the burning/fiery one." In relation, it has been suggested that the name of the priesthood instilled by Moses to man the Temple, the Levites, is related to the name Leviathan, a serpent like figure from Hebrew Bible mythology. Biblical reforms from Hezekiah included removing the bronze serpent from the temple, as the people burned incense to it.

Later accounts in Isaiah, indicate that the use of the *kaneh-bosm* anointing oil, also enabled him to speak on the Lord's behalf. "The Spirit of the Sovereign Lord is on me, because the Lord has anointed me..." (Isaiah 61:1)

So, from these passages, we can see that cannabis was an integral part of temple worship at the time of Isaiah, and the Lord's anger burned when he was not given his due offering of it. Such a shortage was due to the stiff competition for this precious commodity, by the cults of other gods and goddesses. At this time Israel is clearly polytheistic and Yahweh although at the top of the pantheon, competed for worshipers with other deities; Asherah was particularly popular. Yahweh's grievance about not receiving enough cannabis is likely related to this precious commodity being used up by other cults, particularly Asherah's. This is important to note, as this passage was written by the Deuteronomists, and indicates that they still favored cannabis as an integral part of their ritual worship. The rejection of it, as we shall see, comes from Jeremiah, whose works are wound up with the later "priestly editors," after yet further reforms.

Isaiah laments for the day when the people will "turn their eyes to the Holy One of Israel. They will not look to the altars, the work of their hands, and they will have no regard for the Asherah poles and the incense altars their fingers have made" (Isaiah 17:7-8). Yahweh, the God "whose name is jealous" through Isaiah, condemns "a people who continually provoke me to my very face, offering sacrifices in gardens and burning incense on altars of brick" (Isaiah 65:3).

Isaiah 27.9 has the patriarch Jacob, representing his descendants and describes what the Jews must do to atone for their sins of worshiping Asherah and burning incense to her: "Therefore, in this will the transgression of Jacob be atoned for, and this all the fruit of the removal of his sin, in his making all the stones of the altar like pulverized limestone, and they will not raise asherahs and incense altars."

The condemnations of the prophet Isaiah give us a clearer picture of the happenings in the southern kingdom, and the rebellious nature of its incorrigible inhabitants;

Come, you sons of sorceress,
Spawn of whoring adulteress,
At whom you are gibing,
At whom are you gaping.
Poking out your tongue?
You rebel rabble,
Progeny of deceit,
Inflaming yourselves at the oaks,
Under every green tree;
Butchering babes in the valleys
Beneath the clefts of the cliffs.
On the valley banks is your part;
To them you pour libations,
Offer up your grain gifts.
On a high and lofty hill you set your couch,
And go up to sacrifice.
Behind the door you set the (phallic) symbol,
Without me you strip and mount,
You spread your bed,
And make alliance with them.
You love their couch,
on the hand you gaze.
You go to the King (Molek) with oil,
Multiply your perfumes.
You send emissaries afar,
You descend to the netherworld.
With your great strength, you are weary,
But never say Enough,
You find life in your hand,
And you do not weaken.
–Isaiah 57:3-10

The "hand" here is likely a reference to the phallus. The condemnations of the Lord through the prophet Isaiah would seem to once again tie these rites with the Tantric-like fertility rites indicated by the earlier Song of Songs.

All day long I have held out my hands
to an obstinate people,

who walk in ways not good...
offering sacrifices in gardens
and burning incense on altars of brick;
who sit among the graves
and spend their nights keeping secret vigil;
who eat the flesh of pigs
and whose pots hold broth of unclean meat;
who say, 'Keep away; don't come near me,
for I am too sacred for you!'
Such people are a smoke in my nostrils,
a fire that keeps burning all day.
–Isaiah 65:2-6

In the aforementioned passages from Isaiah, we see both the holy anointing oil (57:9) and the incense (65:3) being used in association with the pagan fertility rites. In the eyes of the Yahwehist prophet, the use of these substances is only evil when it is combined with the adulterous practice of worshiping other gods. Moreover, Isaiah 43:23-24, makes it abundantly clear, the Lord is angered when he does not receive his due of these substances.

Up to this point, the prophets have been verily quiet on the subject of Asherah worship, and besides Isaiah 17:7-9 and 27.9 as well as Micah 5:14 ("I will uproot from among you your Asherah poles, when I demolish your cities") there has been little to no reference to the cultic representation of the goddess. Phillip Johnston, a lecturer and supervisor at the Cambridge Faculty of Divinity has noted "the notable paucity of such texts indicates that the prophetic movement did not especially target Asherah worship, still less single it out for condemnation. For them it was simply one minor element of pervasive idolatry" (Johnston, 2003). However, her cult clearly did create a competition for cannabis and other offerings, as well as other forms of temple support, and we can be sure this created a bone of contention.

This situation continued under a number of royal households, with Queens such as the infamous Jezebel worshiping Asherah in both the temple and the palace. Asherah poles, both male and female temple prostitutes, are all described as present on the temple grounds. It was not until the time of King Hezekiah, who came to power during the time of Isaiah, that any form of monotheistic worship of Yahweh alone was successfully attempted. In the eyes of the Yahwehist narrator, Hezekiah (Strengthened of Jah) who ruled the southern kingdom from (715-687), only came second in his service to the Lord, to that of his even more aggressively reforming grandson Josiah.

> [Hezekiah] did what was right in the eyes of the LORD ... He removed the high places, smashed the sacred stones and cut down the Asherah poles. He broke into pieces the bronze snake Moses had made, for up to that time the Israelites had been burning incense to it. (It was called Nehushtan). Hezekiah trusted in the LORD, the God of Israel. There was no one like him among all the kings of Judah, either before him or after him (2 Kings 18 3-5).

After ridding the land of the high places and Asherahs, the next step taken by King Hezekiah is a very radical and surprising one: "He broke into pieces the bronze snake Moses had made, for up to that time the Israelites had been burning incense to it." This is the first reference to this brazen serpent forged by Moses since the Exodus, created after his involvement with the Midianite "sons of the snake." From the account here it had been worshiped by the Israelites continuously in the interceding centuries. Here in the Temple of Jerusalem itself, with the image of the serpent, the Ashera, the Cherubim, and the Menorah-representing the Tree of Life, we can clearly see the images of the fabled Garden of Eden that had been so demonized in the Genesis tale, continuing as regular aspects of Hebrew cultic worship! Obviously these figures all played an important role in the ritual dramas practiced in the Hebrew kingdom since the time of Solomon.

Hezekiah, also desecrated the holy places he destroyed: "Then they demolished the pillar of Baal, and destroyed the temple of Baal, and made it a latrine to this day" (2 Kings 10:27). Interestingly, archaeological evidence of this particular reform has been recovered. As noted in the Newsweek article "Toilet Found in 3,000-Year-Old Shrine Verifies Bible Stories Against Idol Worship" by Kastalia Medrano:

> Archaeologists have discovered a symbolic toilet from the eighth century B.C. in Jerusalem that could be a clue to religious reforms in the Kingdom of Judah. Religious reforms, in this case, is a euphemism for quite literally defecating on the holy places one wishes to drive out of business.
>
> The stone toilet sits in Tel Lachish, a sprawling Iron Age city and the Kingdom of Judah's most important one after the capitol, Jerusalem. It was found in what the archaeologists believe to be a gate-shrine within Israel's largest ancient city gate. The ruler at that time, King Hezekiah, enacted campaigns of religious worship and reform that made their way into the Hebrew Bible on multiple occasions.

In one corner of the shrine sits a stone seat with a hole in the center. The archaeologists believe that not only is it definitely a toilet, it's a toilet that was installed for the express purpose of literally desecrating the shrine. Hezekiah, it seems, was just following instructions against idol worship in the scriptures. (Medrano, 2017)

Hezekiah's holy latrine

Hezekiah's reforms also included reestablishing the holiday of the Passover which hadn't been celebrated as the law was said to have required, for some centuries. Hezekiah's reforms may have been done in part, under a sort of religio-political motivation, as an attempt to consolidate his kingdom in defense of the strong Assyrian presence and influences taking place. As pastor and Old Testament (Hebrew Bible) scholar Bernhard Anderson explained:

> As in the case of other religious revivals in Israel. Hezekiah's religious reforms had certain political implications. When he ascended the throne, Judah was growing restive under the Assyrian yoke. Ahaz's appeasement policy, symbolized by the installation of an Assyrian altar in the Temple, had proved unpopular, especially among those who had to dig down in their pockets to pay heavy taxes for Assyrian tribute. Hezekiah's purification of worship, including no doubt the removal of Assyrian cult objects from the Temple, was a stimulus to Judaean nationalism, for he was virtually declaring independence from Assyrian domina-

> tion and throwing his weight behind the revolutionary spirit of the day. And he got away with this nationalistic policy for the time being, because ... the Assyrian king was busy waging war in the mountains of northern Mesopotamia (Anderson 1975).

We should consider these reforms in regard to the cancelation of the temple at tel Arad. The use of cannabis aka *kaneh bosm*, may well have been seen at the time to have been derived from Assyrian practices (considering the very similar ritual applications) even those indicated by Exodus 30:23. Tel Arad's "disuse" is within the suggested time frame, although the temple may not have been canceled until the even more severe reforms carried out by Hezekiah's grandson, Josiah.

Hezekiah not only reformed his own people, he was also successful in battle, overcoming the Philistines "as far as Gaza" (2 Kings 18:8). So enthralled was Hezekiah with his own military success, that he went so far as to stop paying tribute to the Assyrians. A grave mistake in foreign policy, as the Assyrian forces would soon be returning from their foreign conquest. The Assyrians received tribute from many petty kingdoms of the region, a deal was that either they paid or suffered the wrath of their military, as did Judah from the result of Hezekiah's deferred payment: "Sennacherib king of Assyria attacked all the fortified cities of Judah and captured them" (2 Kings 18:13).

We learn more of Jerusalem's siege in an account which describes the Judahites rebellion against their Assyrian overlords, both through withholding tribute and joining an anti-Assyrian coalition led by the Egyptians. An alliance that angered the Lord who the Bible has speak through the prophet Isaiah stating: "Woe to the obstinate children ... to those who carry out plans that are not mine, forming an alliance, but not by my Spirit, heaping sin upon sin; who go down to Egypt without consulting me, who look for help to Pharaoh's protection, to Egypt's shade for refuge" (Isaiah 30:1-2). Sentiments that were echoed by the Assyrian king through a field commander, who sends word to Hezekiah, that the Assyrians forces had marched upon Jerusalem on the Lord's own orders:

> On what are you basing this confidence of yours? You say you have strategy and military strength – but you speak only empty words ... you are depending on Egypt, that splintered reed of a staff, which pierces a man's hand and wounds him if he leans on it! And if you say to me, "We are depending on the Lord our God" – isn't he the one whose high places and altars

> Hezekiah removed, saying to Judah and Jerusalem, "You must worship here before the altar?
>
> "... Furthermore, have I come to attack and destroy this land without the Lord? The Lord himself told me to march against this country and destroy it" (Isaiah 36:5-10).

Here we see the beginnings of an expression of the universality of Yahweh. He is now not only the God of his chosen people, but also God over the Assyrians, even though they don't worship him. That the Assyrians acknowledge and obey the God of the Israelites as their own is of course nonsense from a historical point of view. Asshur was the high god of the Assyrian pantheon and they were never subject to Yahweh. The composer of the text, by pointing out that even the Assyrians were obedient to Yahweh, is emphasizing the opposite extent to which the Israelites had departed from their covenant with the Lord by their adulterous practices. To the point that even the foreign Assyrians were to be preferred and given the guidance of the Lord to strike against his own Chosen People!

We know there is a historical basis for all this, as Sennacherib, who led the Assyrians, left an inscribed clay prism, which gloated about having Hezekiah trapped "like a caged bird," held prisoner, along with his people, in Jerusalem. Sennacherib demands that Hezekiah pay a tribute of three hundred talents of silver and thirty talents of gold which he gets from the royal treasury and the temple of Yahweh by stripping the gold off the doors and doorposts.

Hezekiah acknowledges his defeat and agrees to terms which saw him released back to his own kingdom. The rest of his reign was relatively calm, and upon his death, his son, Manasseh, "Causing to Forget," came to power, and undid all the Yahweh alone reforms of his father. During Manasseh's reign, it is related that the prophetic authors aren't ministering, thus the "idolatrous" king Manasseh, goes about unchallenged as he rebuilt the high places, erected an Asherah pole and reconstructed the altar to Baal. During his lengthy forty five year reign (687-642) he also built altars to the Assyrian starry hosts, whom he bowed down to, practiced sorcery divination and consulted spiritists and mediums. Things returned to how they had long been in the kingdom...

Manasseh, can also be found in one of the more obvious inconsistencies in the Hebrew Bible narration, and which make obvious the fact that multiple authors worked on the texts. The contradiction can be found between the books of Kings and Chronicles account of the reign of Manasseh. According to the Chronicles the Assyrians invade Judah, capture Manasseh and "put a hook in his nose, bound him with bronze shackles and took him to Babylon"(2 Chronicles 33:11). While a captive, Manasseh prays to Yahweh and humbles himself. The Lord takes pity on him and he is released by the Assyrians. Upon his return to Judah, Manasseh then carries out a massive reform. He removes all the foreign idols and altars and restores the altar to Yahweh, then practices perfect monotheism for the rest of his life. "The people however continued to use the high places, but only to the Lord their God" (2 Chronicles 33:17) and accordingly Manasseh rested with his fathers after a forty-five year reign .

Conversely, this whole episode from the Assyrian invasion to the repentance of Manasseh is not even mentioned in the book of Kings. To that author of Kings, Manasseh is the villain who is ultimately responsible for the destruction of the kingdom. Yet in the book of Kings Manasseh reigns for forty-five years without suffering any taste of the Lord's anger. Moreover he dies peacefully in his own palace and is buried in his gardens, to be succeeded by his son Amon. The author doesn't even try to rationalize this lack of action by Yahweh, but instead records the wrath of the Lord on the people as a whole for the singular sins of the king;

> Manasseh king of Judah has committed these detestable sins. He has done more evil than the Amorites who preceded him and has led Judah into sin with his idols. Therefore this is what the Lord, the God of Israel says: I am going to bring such disaster on Jerusalem and Judah that the ears of everyone who hears it will tingle.... I will wipe out Jerusalem as one wipes out a dish, wiping it and turning it upside-down. I will forsake the remnant of my inheritance and hand them over to their enemies. (2 Kings 21:12-14).

These condemnations are echoed by the prophet Jeremiah who has Yahweh proclaim against his own Chosen People: "I will make them abhorrent to all the kingdoms of the earth because of what Manasseh son of Hezekiah king of Judah did in Jerusalem" (Jeremiah 15:4). Interestingly, it is here with the Prophet Jeremiah, a firm Yahwehist alone reformer, where *kaneh* clearly falls out of favor, and through Jeremiah, Yahweh rejects offerings of kaneh, cannabis.

Manasseh's son Amon also did evil in the eyes of the Lord, following in his fathers footsteps. He reigned for only two years, (642-640), before he was assassinated by his officials. Then "the people of the land killed all who plotted against King Amon, and they made Josiah his son king in his place" (2 Kings 21:24). Josiah would sacrifice the priests of the high places, and then burn their bones upon their altars! Curiously, his reforms were justified by the alleged discovery of a book supposedly written by Moses, creator of the brazen serpent destroyed in Hezekiah's reforms, a book that had been hidden in the Temple built by the polytheistic king Solomon. A book that seemed to address the concerns of Yahwehist prophets such as Isaiah, Micah and especially Jeremiah, who was very active and influential during Josiah's reign.

Chapter Nine

The "Lost" Book Of The Law

In this chapter, we will see the *kaneh* (cannabis) offerings of previous generations wholly rejected by Yahweh through the words of Jeremiah. This prophet was particularly incensed at the "Queen of Heaven," in what is generally seen as a reference to Asherah, and blames the fall of Jerusalem on her cult's continual burning of incense and pouring out drink offerings to her. Jeremiah's time as a prophet coincides with the reign of the most ambitious of Yahweh alone worshiping Kings, Josiah, the grandson of Hezekiah. Although a number of scholars have suggested that the tel Arad temple was canceled during Hezekiah's reign, others have suggested this coincides with Josiah's reforms, which were directed at removing all remnants of the High Places, the incense altars, all competing deities, and any temple outside of the main temple in Jerusalem.

Josiah became king when he was just eight years old. It was during his reign that one of the greatest frauds in history was perpetrated. The repercussions from what was an early case of perjury went vastly beyond the scope of those who committed the crime and are still with us today, as it has had a profoundly formative influence on history. The narrative of 2 Kings recalls that in the eighteenth year of his reign, Josiah ordered some renovations to the temple of Yahweh. He tells one Shaphan the scribe to go to Hilkiah the high priest and carry out these repairs. During the course of this work a startling discovery is made: "Hilkiah the high priest said to Shaphan the secretary, 'I have found the Book of the Law in the temple of the Lord'" (2 Kings 22:8). This lost "Book of the Law" is none other than the book of Deuteronomy, that allegedly had been written by Moses some six hundred years earlier. "This sacred text was not surprisingly, completely responsive to the prophetic tradition of Hosea, Amos, Isaiah, Micah, and especially Jeremiah, who was alive and at work when this new book was 'discovered'" (Spong 1991).

That this fifth book of Moses is mysteriously unearthed from the temple is extremely curious, as the temple wasn't constructed until the reign of Solomon and no mention of it had heretofore ever been made. To ascribe this book's authorship to Moses raises some problems. It is known that the culture of the Hebrews was an oral tradition not to be committed to the written word until approximately the time of David. Up to this time, most religious writing appeared as poetry or song, very little prose is known. In fact, by the style of writing in Deuteronomy, Biblical scholars have placed the text at a much later date of composition. "This new literary style, found in the Deuteronomic literature and the prose sections of Jeremiah, seems to have been characteristic of the late seventh and early sixth centuries B.C."(Anderson 1975). The very time of the alleged "discovery." Anderson suggests that the Book of the Law was written by an anonymous author in the seventh century who put his own words in the mouth of Moses; although he also felt that the work was "not a complete literary fiction .... [and] is essentially a revival of Mosaic teachings as it was understood in the seventh century B.C." (Anderson 1975).

Other scholars have been far more hard-hitting in their comments upon this so-called discovery suggesting that it was a forgery created by a Jerusalem lawyer and produced by a priest of the temple, an act committed by the Hebrew priesthood in hope of eradicating the competing cults and their deities, which were getting more sacrifices from the people than was the Temple of Yahweh.

As the authors of the exhaustive *The Columbia History of the World* explained of this event:

> Sometime about 630, when Assyria was losing her grip, a lawyer in Jerusalem produced a new code as a program for future reforms, including the prohibition of the worship of gods other than Yahweh, and relief of the poor. He drew on older "Yahweh alone" traditions, common usage, and ancient taboos, but his work was organized by his own thought, replete with his own invention, and cast with his own style. He represented it as "the law of Yahweh" and – probably – as the work of Moses, and he arranged to have it "found" by the high priest in the Jerusalem temple in 621. It was taken to king Josiah, authenticated by a prophetess, and accepted. Most of it is now preserved, with minor interpolations, in chapters 12-26 and 28 of Deuteronomy. (Garraty & Gay, 1981)

The high priest Hilkiah (*Portion of Jah*), the scribe Shaphan (*Conceal*) and the cabal they founded, play a pivotal role in the conspiracy about to unfold. Considering Deuteronomy's nature and focus on strict patriarchal monotheistic forms of worship, it is interesting to note that the book was taken for verification "neither to a prophet or to a priest, but to a prophetess to learn the judgment of their god" (Campbell 1964). The prophetess Huldah, whose name aptly comes from the feminine word for "weasel," seals the doom of her sisters for millennia afterwards by verifying the newly "discovered" book as authentic. Thus the strictures of the sharp-toothed Book of Deuteronomy were passed into the realm of Divine Edict as the words of Moses, a figure of mythical status who was believed to have lived more than six hundred years earlier and who was used to justify the book's recently composed strict monotheistic codes. In the *Talmud* it is stated that Huldah was a relative of the prophet Jeremiah, (both depicted as descendants of Joshua, who accompanied Moses). Jeremiah's role in the monotheistic take-over that is about to befall Jerusalem, cannot be understated.

The prophet Jeremiah (*Jah will rise*) is worthy of careful consideration not only for the drama and color with which he ministered his prophetic role, but also for the blood ties that bound him in with the families that had perpetrated the great counterfeit of ancient Judaic history: the "Book of the Law." Jeremiah was the son of Hilkiah, this is the same name of the high priest who "discovered" the Book of the Law. His allegiance with the sons of Shaphan, Hilkaiah's cohort, also run through his writings with a striking frequency and reveal the influence they were still exerting for the propagation of their monotheistic worldview.

As archaeological evidence shows, and the Hebrew Bible writings themselves indicate, up "...until the eighteenth year of the reign of King Josiah of Judah neither kings nor people had paid attention whatsoever to the law of Moses which, indeed, they had not even known. They had been devoted to the normal deities of the nuclear Near East, with all the usual cults..."(Campbell 1964). Until the "discovery" of the Book of the Law, the "Hebrew people worshiped in the old ways, practicing their cult in open places on peaks and hills and mountains, and even caves below" (Gadon 1989). Clearly, monotheistic Judaism was a new event, and an attempt at a combined religious and political movement to consolidate the Hebrew people under one rule. In some ways an understandable political view in light of the encroaching Assyrians. This act was also directed at ensuring all temple offerings were allocated to the main temple in Jerusalem.

Considering the harsh reforms that are to be initiated by the Book of the Laws discovery, it is extremely curious to note that the last great Judaic reformer was Josiah's grandfather, Hezekiah, and he was said to have destroyed the brazen serpent made by Moses (2 Kings 18:4). Yet this same Moses, the maker of a graven image, is reputedly the author of the book that brings the harshest monotheistic religious reforms in Hebrew history and the ancient narrator of Kings never even tries to account for this blatant contradiction. The contents of the book of Deuteronomy clearly betray its more recent authorship.

The four major stages of Josiah's cultic reforms were:

> (1) The destruction and removal of all other cult objects pertaining to the "other gods" worshiped in the region and burning them in the Kidron Valley.
>
> (2) The murder and suppression of the competing priesthoods who were installed by the previous kings of Judah to serve the astral deities, and who had served at shrines all over the kingdom.
>
> (3) The burning and destruction of the images of the Asherah and scattering their dust in unclean places (i.e., burial ground)
>
> (4) The centralization and confinement of worship to the temple of Yahweh in Jerusalem alone.

There are a number of laws in Deuteronomy that testify to its new theology. The most extraordinary of these changes is the centralization of worship: "you are to seek the place the Lord your God will choose from among all your tribes to put his name there for his dwelling. To that place you must go; there bring your burnt offerings and sacrifices, your tithes and special gifts" (Deuteronomy 12:5-6). The tribes of Israel are being directed to use the temple in Jerusalem alone for their principle sacrifices, other generations old places of worship are to be destroyed. They are no longer to make burnt offerings or sacrifices anywhere in Israel except for the Temple in Jerusalem. All tithes also are to be brought from throughout the kingdom to the main Temple.

All this was directed by the Jerusalem priesthood, who had their own motivation to see competing temples destroyed and banned, and a "Yahweh alone" a religio/politico monopoly instilled in their place. As Joseph Gutmann explained in *No Graven Images: Studies in Art and the Hebrew Bible*: "Josiah ... apparently at the insistence of the Jerusalem priesthood, on whom he may have depended for support and who no doubt lost prestige – and tithes when many sacrifices were diverted to the numerous "high places," insisted on the centrality of worship. To accomplish this end, an unwavering affirmation of Yahweh's exclusiveness and the centrality of the Yahweh cult was necessary; all attempts to decentralize the cult and to worship other gods had, of course, to be eliminated" (Gutmann, 1971).

Prior to the Deuteronomic reforms, the priests of Yahweh's temple had to angrily and jealously sit by and watch the wealth of the kingdom dispersed throughout the many different temples of numerous deities which were spread throughout Judah. Thus the lament in Isaiah 43:23-24 about the lack of kaneh (cannabis) offerings.

There is more : "You must not eat in your towns the tithe of your grain and new wine and oil, or the firstborn of your herds and flocks..." (Deuteronomy 12:17). This of course adds up to a profound amount of booty. It is all to be brought conveniently to the temple in Jerusalem. Jerusalem had, not long before, undergone a siege from the Assyrians while under the reign of Hezekiah. Thus it is no surprise that those living within the city walls should want to lay up as much food as possible. Especially when one considers the political situation that Israel was facing. At this time, Assyria, the undisputed superpower in the region for the past several centuries, had gone into decline and the Babylonians (Chaldeans) from the south of Mesopotamia had come into power. Nabopolassar (626-605 B.C.) was expanding the Babylonian empire and threatening all the small nations of the Fertile Crescent, and these invasions play a decisive part in the drama about to unfold.

As noted the forgery of the Book of the Law may have been done with good reason, likely in an attempt to politically consolidate the fragmented populace of the Southern Kingdom into a united force with similar goals and beliefs, in front of an ever-changing onslaught of invading kingdoms. It is believed that around this same time period, many of the books of the Hebrew Bible were edited and added to. As Bishop John Shelby Spong explained: "By the time the Deuteronomists had finished their work they had colored the books of Joshua, Judges,1 and 2 Samuel and 1 and 2 Kings. They had supplied their nation with a philosophy of history, and they had touched up the books of the prophets. They had taught the Jewish people to see the past through their eyes" (Spong 1991).

Most notable of the many effects rendered by the book's supposed "discovery" were Josiah's murderous purge of the cults of the high places. The book of Deuteronomy is explicit in its instructions of how best to deal with all the religious worship going on in Judah, other than the centralized worship of Yahweh in the temple in Jerusalem: "Destroy completely all the places on the high mountains and on the hills and under every spreading tree where the nations you are dispossessing worship their gods. Break down their altars, smash their sacred stones and burn their Asherah poles in the fire, cut down the idols of their gods and wipe out their names from those places" (Deuteronomy 12:2-3).

Johanna H. Stuckey, a University Professor Emerita at York University, suggests that it is only in the works of the Deuteronomists, that we see a concerted effort to remove Asherah from places of worship, and prior to this she was a recognized sect of Yahweh's cult:

> The Hebrew Scriptures regularly pair Asherah's name, especially "the asherahs," with Baal's, so that some scholars have wondered whether Asherah had ousted Astarte as Baal's consort. In 1963 Yamashita noted that most of the references to Asherah in the Hebrew Bible, including those pairing Asherah with Baal, were associated with only one source (1963:123-137). Later, Olyan argued very convincingly that the biblical attacks on Asherah were "restricted to the Deuteronomistic History" and to texts exhibiting Deuteronomistic influence. For instance, the numerous pairings of Baal with Asherah's "cult symbol," called "the asherah," are part of a reformist, monotheistic "anti-asherah polemic" aimed at discrediting "the asherah" by associating it with "Baal and Astarte" (Olyan 1988 ...). This polemic was necessary because Asherah "had some role in the cult of Yahweh ... not only in popular Yahwism, but in the official cult as well (Olyan 1988:74)(Stuckey, 2004).

As the authors of 2 Kings record, when Josiah discovers the new laws he is horrified. "Great is the Lord's anger that burns against us because our fathers have not obeyed the words of this book; they have not acted in accordance with all that is written there concerning us" (2 Kings 22:13). The Israelites weren't able to obey the strict edicts, as the book (written by a maker of brazen images) had never even been read before, as it had been reputedly entombed somewhere in the depths of a temple (built by a polytheistic king).

King Josiah took immediate action obeying completely the severe dictates of the law and went about the land removing the altars of the various gods and goddesses being worshiped by the Israelites. The text goes into some detail concerning the violence unleashed by the king, beginning with reforms in the Temple of Jerusalem itself, the home of much pagan worship and where ironically the "new" book was found. It is from the description of Josiah's reform that we receive a clearer idea of what the actual religion of the Judaic peoples was like:

> And the king commanded Hilkiah high priest ... to bring forth out of the Temple of the Lord all the vessels that were made for Baal and for Ashera, and for all the hosts of heaven. He burned

> them outside Jerusalem in the fields ... and took the ashes to Beth-El. He did away with the pagan priests appointed by the kings of Judah to burn incense on the high places of the towns of Judah and on those around Jerusalem--those who burned incense to Baal, to the sun and the moon, to the constellations of the starry hosts. He took the Asherah pole from the temple of the Lord to the Kidron Valley outside Jerusalem and burned it there. He ground it to powder and scattered the dust over the graves of the common people. He also tore down the quarters of the male shrine-prostitutes which were in the temple of the Lord and where woman did weaving for Asherah.
>
> Josiah brought all the priests from the towns of Judah and desecrated the high places, from Geba to Beersheba, where the priests had burned incense. He broke down the shrines at the ... Gate of Joshua ...
>
> He pulled down the altars the kings of Judah had erected on the roof near the upper room of Ahaz, and the altars Manasseh had built in the two courts of the temple of the Lord. ... The king also desecrated the high places that were east of Jerusalem on the south of the hill of Corruption – the ones Solomon the king of Israel had built for Ashtoreth the vile goddess of the Sidonians, for Chemosh the vile god of Moab, and for Molech the detestable god of ... Ammon. Josiah smashed the sacred stones and cut down the Ashera poles and covered the site with human bones.
>
> Even at the altar of Beth-El, the high places made by Jeroboam ... who caused Israel to sin – even that altar and high place he demolished. He burned the high place and ground it to powder, and burned the Asherah pole also. Then Josiah looked around when he saw the tombs that were on the hill side, he had the bones removed from them and burned on the altar to defile it ...
>
> Just as he had done in Beth-El, Josiah removed and defiled all the shrines at the high places that the kings of Israel had built in the towns of Samaria that had provoked the Lord to anger. Josiah slaughtered all the priests of those high places on the altars and burned human bones on them (2 Kings 23:4-20).

The bloodthirsty reforms carried out by Josiah were taken throughout the land and right into the temple in Jerusalem. The description of all the various cults that were being practiced in the central sanctuary in Jerusalem reveals the full extent that the Israelites had become syncretistic with Canaanite and Near Eastern religion. We learn that not only were there male and female shrine prostitutes in Israel, but they were even living and practicing in the temple of the Lord itself! Further we learn that the adulterous religious sites made by Solomon and other Kings had still been standing throughout the many intervening centuries.

Also of interest is the condemnation of the burning of "incense," Josiah "did away with all the pagan priests appointed by the kings of Judah to burn incense on the high places around Jerusalem" (2 Kings 23:5). Here for the first time the death penalty is exacted for the burning of incense. That these were "pagan" priests indicates that they were practicing Canaanite religion. 2 Kings says of Josiah's actions: "This he did to fulfill the requirements of the law written in the book that Hilkiah the priest had discovered in the temple of the Lord" (2 Kings 23:24). The Hebrew Bible is very pleased with the king for this appalling display of righteous violence. In fact Josiah has gone down in history as one of the few good kings of Israel. "Neither before nor after Josiah was there a king like him who turned to the Lord as he did – with all his heart and with all his soul and with all his strength, in accordance with all the Law of Moses" (2 Kings 23:25). Upon his return to Jerusalem he commanded the surviving people: "Celebrate the Passover to the Lord your God, as it is written in this Book of the Covenant" (2 Kings 23:21). A request, which after witnessing the results of Josiah's homicidal purging, the Hebrew populace were only too eager to comply with.

The festival of Passover itself was not new, this had been the date of a longstanding agricultural festival; tying it with the Exodus of Moses, however, was new. Indeed, most archaeologists and many biblical historians see little evidence of the Mosaic past prior to these events. The adoption of these agricultural festivals, which would surely have been bound up with polytheistic beliefs and practices, is comparable to the later adoption of December 25th, originally celebrated for the sun god Sol, and Mithras, as Christmas and the birthdate of Jesus sometime around the 4th century, after Christianity had become a State Religion in a similar bid for consolidation and power.

Josiah's reforms were only possible because the Assyrians were losing control of their provinces. The changes made by Josiah as he carried out the commands of the newly found Book of the Law included removing Assyrian altars, idols and practices from the temple as well as throughout Judah. During the height of Assyrian power this move would have prompted the immediate retribution of the Assyrian military. We saw this with Hezekiah. As we shall see, there may have been a view present, that saw the use of cannabis, as deriving from an Assyrian influence, as we can see indicated by the very similar ritual use of *qunnabu* and *kaneh bosm* incenses and salves, as well as the linguistic connections. Dr. Raphael Mechoulam has suggested that it was at this juncture a ban on cannabis was instilled:

> While most Scythians were only temporary visitors to the Middle East, the Assyrians were one of the major military powers in the area for hundreds of years and their influence was powerful. As mentioned above, the Assyrians employed cannabis, apparently quite extensively. The contacts between the Jews and the Assyrians were prolonged and wide. During certain historical periods the trade of Judea depended on Assyria; the cultural-religious impact of the Nineveh court and temples penetrated not only the royal and priestly class in Jerusalem but also the lower classes. Gradually in the 7th century B.C. even the Assyrian cult of heavenly constellations was adopted; the ancient forms of augury were revived; in the Temple itself an image of the Assyrian"queen of heaven" was erected; within the Temple young women offered their bodies in honor of the deity. During the reigns of the Assyrian kings Esarhaddon (681-669 B.C.) and Ashurbanipal (669-626 B.C.), the Jewish King Manasseh, who was their vassal, fought beside them in their wars with Egypt and probably also in Transjordan in order to secure the commercial roads for drugs and spices. The influence of the kings of Nineveh ("the bloody city, full of lies and robbery") in Judea was immense. It can be assumed that under these conditions Assyrian medicine and drugs were known and used, at least among the ruling class.
>
> After the death of Ashurbanipal the decadent and hedonistic kingdom of Assyria swiftly disappeared from history. The Jewish King Josiah (628 B.Cn.) is known to have taken advantage of the Assyrian decay to remove vigorously all pagan influence from Jewish life and religious customs. Hashish, presumably a symbol of Assyrian moralaxity, would have been banned. This is, of course, an assumption but it fits the historical background, the insular character of the Jews at the time, and the needs of the independent Judaean state. It explains the strange absence of the word cannabis in the Bible (Mechoulam, 1986).

As noted in Chapter 4, Mechoulam doubted the etymology of *kaneh bosm,* and instead suggested the term *pannagh,* which appears only once in the Hebrew Bible, in a later reference from Ezekiel, and arriving in a caravan. The references to *kaneh* and *kaneh bosm* from Yahwist and Deuteronomist writers, do not actually portray it in a negative light. It was clearly listed as an important ritual commodity in the Exodus, Isaiah and Songs references. As we shall see, this rejection came shortly after this through the prophet Jeremiah, who did however list its foreign source as an indication of something of disdain, but more pointedly, its association with the "Queen of Heaven."

Interestingly, descriptions in the *Babylonian Talmud: Tractate Horayoth*, Folio 12, indicate that the anointing oil was hidden away in the days of Josiah, with the Ark of the Covenant and as a result his son, Jehoahaz was anointed with balsam oil, not with the Holy anointing oil: "... At the time when the Holy Ark was hidden away there were also hidden the anointing oil ... And who hid them? It was Josiah, King of Judah, who hid them; because, having observed that it was written in the Torah, The Lord will bring thee and thy king ... [unto a nation that thou hast not known], he gave orders that they shall be hidden away, as it is said, And he said unto the Levites that taught all Israel, that were holy unto the Lord, "Put the Holy Ark into the house which Solomon the son of David, King of Israel, did build; there shall no more be a burden upon your shoulders."

As it was supposedly the worship of foreign gods that caused Yahweh to destroy so much of the kingdom, and Josiah's reforms purged the land of these rites, it is curious the narrative next comes up with the following statement: "Never the less the Lord did not turn away from the heat of his fierce anger, which burned against Judah because of all that Manasseh had done to provoke him to anger. So the Lord said. 'I will remove Judah also from my presence as I removed Israel, and I will reject Jerusalem, the city I chose, and this temple, about which I said 'There will my name be'"(2 Kings 23:27). What we see here, is the retrospective Yahwehist author, trying to make historical reality fit with the supposed actions of a Lord, who should have logically rewarded the severe reforms in his favor.

There is further irony for the Yahwehist writer to deal with when the righteous King Josiah is inexplicably killed in battle by Pharaoh Neco. Old Yahweh does not inspire much confidence in his sense of justice if his most devoted king does not receive the benefits of his obedience but instead meets such an ignominious end. As a result of the loss of Josiah's patriarchal leadership, within a scant forty years Judah would once again have "as many gods as you have towns." Such Pagan activities causes the prophet Jeremiah, who begins to play a pivotal role at this time, to condemn the Israelites by pointing out that:

"the altars you have set up to burn incense to that shameful god Baal are as many as the streets of Jerusalem" (Jeremiah 11:13). Clearly, this was the preferred form of worship, and the Deuteronomic code was forced upon a pagan people, in much the same way as the Bible has been forced upon the aboriginal peoples of today's world. Apparently Josiah's "defeat seems to have been taken as proof of the error of his ways; the later prophecies of Jeremiah and Ezekiel show polytheism back in practice" (Bickerman & Smith, 1976). The burning of "incense" and worshiping the Queen of heaven continued as well.

The words of Jeremiah, who was writing around this time, clearly show that Yahweh's taste for the holy herb had declined. The dour Prophet went as far as to claim the burning of incense to the Queen of Heaven was the reason the Lord brought the wrath of the Babylonians upon Jerusalem:

> Hear, O earth! I am bringing disaster on this people, the fruit of their own schemes, because they have paid no attention to My word and have rejected My instruction. What use to Me is frankincense from Sheba or sweet [smelling] cane [kaneh-cannabis] from a distant land? Your burnt offerings are not acceptable; your sacrifices do not please Me (Jeremiah 6:19-20).

Clearly it is in the harsh reforms of Josiah and the words of the Lord through Jeremiah that the ritual use of cannabis fell out of favor with the Israelite priesthood, and the modern monotheistic form of Judaic worship had its forced inception. Apparently, the use of cannabis had become so associated with the pagan worship practiced throughout Jerusalem that despite its earlier popularity with the Hebrews, its sacramental use was now seen as unreformable and the burning of *kaneh*, for prophetic trances, had become associated with pagan worship.

Jeremiah seems to have been at first a full supporter of the edicts of the newly discovered Deuteronomic code, even walking the streets preaching for its acceptance (Jeremiah 11:1-13), and exalting Josiah for his fanatical reforms (Jeremiah 22:15-16). But in later times, he came to reject it, seeing that it failed in its purpose of bringing the people to true repentance, "but yielded only a defiant nationalism and an external piety" (Anderson 1975). Believing, like all religious fanatics, that only he knew the way, Jeremiah separated himself somewhat from the Deuteronomic conspirators, proclaiming, likely in reference to the forgery of Deuteronomy itself; "How can you say, 'We are wise, and the law of Yahweh is with us'? But, behold, the false pen of the scribes has made it a lie" (Jeremiah 8:8). Jeremiah 14:14, indicates no prophet but Jeremiah should be heeded: "The prophets are prophesying lies in my name; I did not send them. They are prophesying to you a lying vision, worthless divination, and the deceit of their own minds." Sentiments repeated in Jeremiah 8:10: "... [F]rom prophet to priest everyone deals falsely"; "... [E]lders and dignitaries are the head, and prophets who teach lies are the tail; for those who led this people led them astray" (Jeremiah 6:13); "See, therefore, I am against the prophets, says the Lord, who steal my words from one another, who use their own tongues and say 'Says the Lord," against those who prophesy lying dreams" (Jeremiah 23:30-32).

Jeremiah himself was much less of an ecstatic, shamanic prophet, and much more of a diviner. Unlike other prophets, it would seem that Jeremiah had the peculiar habit of divining meanings from otherwise ordinary events, and interpreting them as messages from the Lord: A boiled over cauldron, signifies trouble brewing from the northern Babylonians; Watching a potter at work, Jeremiah deciphered that Israel was like potters clay in the hands of Yahweh, if the shape failed to take hold, it could be destroyed and reworked; After buying a linen waist-cloth and leaving it on some rocks, upon rediscovering it Jeremiah concluded that Yahweh would spoil the adulterous pride of the people, although at one time he had clung to them like a garment.[1]

Another one of the characteristics that distinguish the sullen prophet Jeremiah, from all other biblical prophets "is the large number of confessions and references to his personal feelings" (Eliade 1978). He "complains about his lot, cries out for vindication, and even hurls defiance at God ... shadowed by doubt ... self pity, and despair" (Anderson 1975). No one felt more sorry for Jeremiah than himself, as can be seen by his constant complaints to the Lord; "Alas, my mother that you gave me birth, a man with whom the whole land strives and contends! ... everyone curses me ... I sat alone, because thy hand was upon me and you filled me with indignation" (Jeremiah 15:10-17); "O lord, you deceived me, and I was deceived ... I am ridiculed all day long; everyone mocks me ... the word of the Lord has brought me insult and reproach all day long.... Cursed be the day I was born!" (Jeremiah 20:7-14). Indeed, morose Jeremiah's resentment could be seen to have led him to mistake his own harsh judgment of others, for the judgment of the Lord himself! A hypothesis demonstrated in the words of the dour prophet himself, who angrily goes so far as to ques-

1 Imagine if someone were to proclaim in today's world that they were interpreting similar revelations from otherwise ordinary events. They would likely find that they were having as much trouble, as did lonely Jeremiah in attracting interested and devout followers while preaching his dour message of punishment and destruction.

tion even the Lord's own judgment; "Why is it that the wicked live so prosperously? Why do scoundrels enjoy peace?"(Jeremiah 12:1). Indeed, why?

Jeremiah also confesses to being driven to such a point of frustration, that "I smote upon my thigh"(Jeremiah 31:19). As it has long been noted that "thigh" is a Biblical euphemism for genitals, it is interesting to note that there is a longstanding tradition that Jeremiah, who never married, was notoriously known for his own self stimulation! "The prophet Jeremiah laments his having been made a *sahuq,* a compulsive masturbator, repeatedly abused by all of his oppressors. He even styles himself a contemptible *sahuq* (jerk-off) to his own people…" (Edwardes 1967).

The Doom of Jerusalem

Jehoahaz, (*Jehova-seized* 609 B.C.) Josiah's son, is anointed king "by the people of the land" but he reigns for only three months. He then does evil in the Lord's sight, i.e. returning to the traditional Semitic-pagan religion, that existed prior to his father's radical reforms and their exhalation of the monotheistic cult of Yahweh. Reference indicating the widespread nature of such activities can be found in the condemnations and warnings of Jeremiah: "The towns of Judah and the people of Jerusalem will go and cry out to the gods to whom they burn incense.… You have as many gods as you have towns, O Judah; and the altars you have set up to burn incense to that shameful god Baal are as many as the streets of Jerusalem" (Jeremiah 11:12-13). "The covenant has been broken!" wails Jeremiah, "I brought on them all the curses of the covenant I had commanded them to follow but that they did not keep" (Jeremiah 11:8).

Jeremiah also gives us much detail concerning the continuing cult of Asherah, (or her daughter counterparts Astarte, or Anath, as the text is unclear on this point) who by this time is generally referred to as the Queen of Heaven. It is through the writings of Jeremiah that we can see just how interwoven with Hebrew culture the worship of the Goddess was. The judgmental prophet's first references to it give us a clear indication that the Queen of Heaven was being worshiped in sexual rites: "Indeed on every high hill and under every spreading tree you lay down as a prostitute" (Jeremiah 2:20). Jeremiah describes the lust of Judah in lurid tones, and like Hosea, Isaiah, and other prophets refers to the pagan worship of the Judahites, in the terms of a husband to his adulterous wife. Many indication of Asherah worship we have discussed can also be see in these passages from Hosea 2; Asherah pendants; ritual prostitution; weaved garments; offerings of incenses and oils not making it to Yahweh etc:

> Rebuke your mother, rebuke her, for she is not my wife, and I am not her husband.
>
> Let her remove the adulterous look from her face and the unfaithfulness from between her breasts.
>
> Otherwise I will strip her naked and make her as bare as on the day she was born; I will make her like a desert, turn her into a parched land, and slay her with thirst.
>
> I will not show my love to her children, because they are the children of adultery.
>
> Their mother has been unfaithful and has conceived them in disgrace. She said, "I will go after my lovers, who give me my food and my water, my wool and my linen, my olive oil and my drink."
>
> Therefore I will block her path with thornbushes; I will wall her in so that she cannot find her way.
>
> She will chase after her lovers but not catch them; she will look for them but not find them. Then she will say, "I will go back to my husband as at first, for then I was better off than now."
>
> She has not acknowledged that I was the one who gave her the grain, the new wine and oil, who lavished on her the silver and gold – which they used for Baal.
>
> Therefore I will take away my grain when it ripens, and my new wine when it is ready.
>
> I will take back my wool and my linen, intended to cover her naked body."
>
> So now I will expose her lewdness before the eyes of her lovers; no one will take her out of my hands.
>
> I will stop all her celebrations: her yearly festivals, her New Moons, her Sabbath days – all her appointed festivals.
>
> I will ruin her vines and her fig trees, which she said were her pay from her lovers;
>
> I will make them a thicket, and wild animals will devour them.
>
> I will punish her for the days she burned incense to the Baals; she decked herself with rings and jewelry, and went after her lovers, but me she forgot, declares the Lord. (Hosea 2: 1-13)

Calling the kingdom of Judah a she-camel and a wild donkey in heat, the angry prophet Jeremiah states: "Any males that pursue her need not tire themselves, at mating time they will find her" (Jeremiah 2:24). Jeremiah's further rantings against the kingdom give clear indication why there is little reverence for women in his life: "I will pull your skirts over your face that your shame may be seen – your adulteries and your lustful neighings, your shameless prostitution." (Jeremiah 13:26-27).

Jeremiah expresses in some detail the rites of the goddess. He describes how the whole family took part in the worship: "Do you not know what they are doing in the towns of Judah and in the streets of Jerusalem. The children gather wood, the fathers light the fire and the women knead the dough and make cakes of bread for the Queen of Heaven" (Jeremiah 7:17).

The reference to "cakes" here is interesting, as Kitto's suggestion of a cannabis resin product, or syrup, *eshisha,* noted in Chapter 4, occurs in reference to "sweet cakes." *Eshisha* appears in The Song of Songs, which we looked at for its evidence of the Sacred Marriage between Asherah and Yahweh, as well as in Hosea, where they are condemned in a likely reference to their use in the Asherah cult, "they turn to other gods and love the sacred raisin cakes [*eshisha*]" (*Hosea* 3:1). In Charles Ellicott's *An Old Testament Commentary for English Readers,* these are described as "the luscious sacrificial cakes used in idolatrous worship: a term generally descriptive of the licentious accompaniments of the Ashtoreth worship" (Ellicott, 1884). *The Cambridge Bible for Schools and Colleges* (1882) noted:

> The cakes here mentioned ... must have been of a superior kind; they bear a different name, [eshisha] and appear from Isaiah 16:7 ... to have been considered as luxuries. They formed part of David's royal bounty on the removal of the ark to Jerusalem (2 Samuel 6:19), or more correctly of the sacrificial feast implied by the context. This latter point is interesting as it suggests that Baal-worship was closely related to the festivities of the vintage (Prof. Robertson Smith, *The Old Testament in the Jewish Church,* p. 434). Hosea too seems to refer to these cakes in connection with the sacrificial feasts, not without a touch of sarcasm (Perowne, 1882).

The reference to *eshisha,* in the context of 2 *Samuel* 6:19, is comparable to the use of the shewbread in the temple, and this is what John Perowne is indicating above.[2] Perhaps like *kaneh,* which was

2 In relation to these cakes, it is worth noting that in his *De Occulta Philosophia* (1651) Agrippa refers to how "Rabbi Israel made certain cakes, writ upon with certain divine and angelical names, and so consecrated, which they that did eat with faith, hope, and charitie [charity], did presently break forth with a spirit of prophecie [prophecy]. We read in the same

used in the Holy of Holies, and then later condemned for its association with pagan worship, we can see a similar situation with the formerly celebrated and then condemned *eshisha*? And within this a connection between the shewbread of the main temple and the cakes offered to the Queen of Heaven?

Jeremiah clearly marks Asherah as the main culprit of blame for the doom of Jerusalem: "The sin of Judah is written with an iron stylus, engraved with a diamond point on the tablets of their hearts and on the horns of their altars. Even their children remember their altars and Asherah poles by the green trees and on the high hills. My mountain in the land and your wealth and all your treasures, I will give away as plunder, together with your high places, because of sin throughout your country" (Jeremiah 17:1-3). Altars, which we now know through the findings at tel Arad, where upon cannabis was once burned to Asherah.

However, it is only after the fall of Judah and the destruction of the temple in Jerusalem that the true depths of the theological struggle between the polytheistic worshipers of Asherah, the Queen of Heaven, and the monotheistic worshipers of the Yahweh alone cabal are revealed, as we shall see.

It is over this issue that Jeremiah has Yahweh reject completely the cannabis offerings of previous generations. "What use to me is frankincense that comes from Sheba, or sweet cane [kaneh - cannabis] from a distant land? Your burnt offerings are not acceptable, nor your sacrifices pleasing to me" (Jeremiah 6:20). Clearly, up until this time, hemp had been an integral and popular part of mainstream Judaic worship, as practiced by the people of the land. Jeremiah's prohibitions against it in the name of the Lord were seen by the populace as the empty words of a pseudo-prophet. Important to note here, Frankincense and cannabis are specifically identified in this passage, and these are the exact items that were found on the two altars at the canceled Holy of Holies in the tel Arad temple. We have noted that both kaneh and frankincense appear together in the Isaiah 43:24 and Song of Songs 4:14 references as well. I would argue, these references particularly secure and prove Sula Benet's etymological theories that the Hebrew *kaneh bosm* and *kaneh* references identified cannabis. The appearance of *kaneh* alongside frankincense in these references shows

---

place that Rabbi Johena the son of Jochahad, did after that manner enlighten a certain rude countryman, called Eleazar, being altogether illiterate, that being compassed about with a sudden brightness, did unexpectedly preach such high mysteries of the Law to an assembly of wise men, that he did even astonish all that were near him" (Agrippa, 1651). A description that indicates more than sigils on cakes were in use, although the ingredients of said cakes are not included.

that kaneh is "cannabis" as this is the combination recovered in the temple at tel Arad. The indications of the combined worship of Yahweh and Asherah taking place in tel Arad is also further confirmation for Robert Graves claim of ritual cannabis use by the cult of Asherah, as are these condemnations of *kane*h and frankincense in Jeremiah 6:20.

Ezekiel

Ezekiel begins his own prophetic mission around this time, and it is in his account we find our final reference to *kaneh* as cannabis. The final Biblical reference to *kaneh* appears in Ezekiel 27, in a passage called "A Lament for Tyre." Judah and the kingdom of Tyre had fallen into disfavor with Yahweh, and cannabis appears as just one of many of the wares received by Tyre, the merchant of peoples on many coasts: "Because of your many products and your great wealth of goods, Damascus traded with you wine from Helbon, wool from Zahar, and casks of wine from Izal for your wares. Wrought iron, cassia, and sweet cane [*kaneh*] were exchanged for your merchandise"(Ezekiel 27:18-19). As with Jeremiah 6:20, this indicates that cannabis came to the Israelites as an item of trade, this was also the view in regard to the source of the cannabis and frankincense recovered from the tel Arad temple.

Isaiah 43:23-24 indicated that the Lord had been shortchanged in regard to his due offerings of cannabis, and comparatively, Ezekiel has the Lord likewise complain about his incenses and oils being offered to other deities.

> "You ... took the fine jewelry of gold and silver I had given you, and you made male idols with which to prostitute yourself. You took your embroidered garments to cover them, and you set My oil and incense before them. Also My food which I gave you – the pastry of fine flour, oil, and honey which I fed you – you set it before them as sweet incense; and so it was," says the Lord GOD (Ezekiel 16-19).

"Embroidered garments," is a likely reference to the sacred weaving done in the temple by the worshipers of Asherah. In *Ezekiel and the World of Deuteronomy*, Jason Gile notes that "Many scholars have identified Ezekiel's image of jealousy [(Ezekiel 8:5)] with Asherah, particularly the 'statue of Asherah' set up by Manasseh in the Jerusalem temple (2 Kgs 2:17)" (Gile, 2021). Indications in Ezekiel, Isaiah, and even Jeremiah as well as Hosea are that, still at this time, monotheism was not in place. Even those prophets themselves were not monotheists in the sense that they believed there was only one god, but rather they acknowledged the existence of these other deities, while preaching that it was Yahweh alone who should receive offerings and be worshiped by the Hebrews, his "Chosen People."

Again like Isaiah, there are indications that although complaining about not receiving the Lord's due of the sacrament, there was occasion where they were provided. Although unlike Isaiah's inhalation of an incense coal from the altar held in tongs to his lips, Ezekiel seems to have ingested an entheogenic preparation.

The ingestion here occurs just before Ezekiel's famous apocalyptic vision which took place in Babylon, shortly after the period we have been discussing, during the Exile. Ezekiel 3 describes this shamanistic scenario perfectly, as well as describing the ingestion of the unknown entheogen to initiate the shamanistic flight. The ancient prophet tells us that the Lord told him:

> Son of man, eat what is before you, eat this scroll; then go and speak to the house of Israel." So I opened my mouth and he gave me the scroll to eat.... So I ate it, and it tasted as sweet as honey in my mouth.... Then the Spirit lifted me up, and I heard behind me a loud rumbling sound – May the glory of the Lord be praised in his dwelling-place! – the sound of the wings of the living creatures brushing against each other and the sound of the wheels beside them, a loud rumbling sound. The Spirit then lifted me up and took me away... (Ezekiel 3:4-14).

The account in Ezekiel is among those suggested by Dr. C. Creighton in 1903, as evidence of hashish use in the Hebrew Bible. Creighton believed that cannabis dipped in honey was a "secret vice" of the Hebrew Temple and Palace, and was evidence of a polluting foreign influence:

> ... [I]n the first chapter of Ezekiel a phantasmagoria of composite creatures, of wheels, and of brilliant play of colors, which is strongly suggestive of the subjective visual perceptions of hachish, and is unintelligible from any other point of view, human or divine. This is the chapter of Ezekiel that gave so much trouble to the ancient canonists, and is said to have made them hesitate about including the book. Ezekiel was included in the Canon, but with the instruction that no one in

> the Synagogue was to attempt to comment upon Chapter I, or, according to another version, that the opening chapter was not to be read by or to persons under a certain age. The subjective sensations stimulated by hachish are those of sight and hearing. It would be easy to quote examples of fantastic composite form, and of wondrous colors, which have been seen by experimenters (Creighton, 1903).

Referring to Creighton's research, Harvard Medical School Professor, Dr. Lester Grinspoon commented that the account in *Ezekiel* "does sound like a description of an intense cannabis intoxication – an almost psychedelic experience" (Grinspoon 1971).

Interestingly, the whole scenario of ingesting a scroll for the purpose of prophecy plays out almost identically in the New Testament's Book of Revelation 10:10 as well. Likewise a clear influence on the Book of Revelation's "Tree of Life" (22:2) can also be noted in Ezekiel:

> And by the edge of the river, on this side and on that, will come up every tree used for food, whose leaves will ever be green and its fruit will not come to an end: it will have new fruit every month, because its waters come out from the holy place: the fruit will be for food and the leaf will make well those who are ill (Ezekiel 47:12).

Although the above verse reference refers to a variety of "trees," it seems that in Ezekiel there was also concern for one particular plant as well, as can be seen in this quote often referred to by Rastafarians and other cannabis using Biblical influenced groups: "And I will raise up for them a plant of renown, and they shall be no more consumed with hunger in the land, neither bear the shame of the heathen any more" (Ezekiel 34:29).

As Ezekiel's vision occurred in Babylon during the Exile, it is not surprising that the beasts he saw in his vision bear a marked resemblance to those depicted in surviving Babylonian art, and these are connected with Assyrian "Tree of Life" images that may have influenced Ezekiel's reference to a sacred tree. This may also play a role in the Eden mythology as well, as it is believed that the story of Adam and Eve was contrived around this same time. As the 19th century scholar and archaeologist Austen Henry Layard noted, the four creatures most often depicted in sculptures accompanying that of the sacred Assyrian Tree of Life, were "a man, a lion, an ox, and an eagle" (Layard 1856). Babylon was the origin and heart of the initiation mysteries that took place all over the ancient world, thus it became a symbol of idolatrous worship in the Bible. As part of their complicated rituals, these initiation rites used props to create sounds which represented things such as large wings flapping rapidly, accompanied by fierce animal noises in the background. These shamanistic rites were performed in elaborately decorated, smoke filled temples by participants wearing masks and costumes that represented both real and imaginary beasts. A scenario that fits well with the account described in Ezekiel 3. As well, we can be sure that as with the Assyrian Sacred Rites, entheogens were likely liberally employed in such rituals.

Are the costumes of still-performed North American Indian rites with winged dancers, indications that ancient depictions of eagle-headed deities were devotees wearing similar costumes?

An ancient Babylonian inscription reads: "The glorious gods smell the incense, noble food of heaven; pure wine, which no hand has touched do they enjoy." In *Myths of Babylonia and Assyria,* Donald Mackenzie suggested that in Babylonian religious rites, "inspiration was derived by burning incense, which, if we follow evidence obtained elsewhere, induced a prophetic trance. The gods were also invoked by incense" (Mackenzie, 1915). A view that was shared by even earlier researchers: "The Chaldean Magus [Mesopotamian holy men of the Chaldean kingdom, circa 400-500 BC] used artificial means, intoxicating drugs for instance, in order to attain to [a] state of excitement acts of purification and mysterious rituals increased the power of the incantations. Among these mysterious rituals must be counted the use of enchanted potions which undoubtedly contained drugs that were medically effective" (Lenormant 1874). Considering what these 19th and early 20th century scholars saw as obvious, it is indeed puzzling how the majority of today's researchers on these topics have been woefully able to ignore these elements of ancient religious practices, despite the mounting evidence now in place.

In light of the sacred tree references, it is worth noting that as with Asherah in the Holy Land, Ishtar was associated both with cannabis and sacred tree imagery in Babylon. We noted the connections between Ishtar, Asherah and other goddesses in their origins in Chapter 2, so this is not surprising. The Feminist scholar Buffie Johnson noted that not only is the "Mother Goddess, strongly connected with the Tree of Life, [she] is in a sense the tree itself. At the same time she is outside the tree, vivifying it to bud and flower" (Johnson 1981). Thus a Babylonian Prayer to the goddess Ishtar proclaimed;

> Who dost make the green herb to spring up, mistress of mankind!
> Who has created everything, who dost guide aright all creatures!
> Mother Ishtar, whose powers no god can approach!

Curiously, no surviving texts give a clear indication as to what plant is depicted in the Babylonian and Assyrian Tree of Life images, or their context beyond an association with the sacred rites. But as we shall see later when we return to a discussion of these images and their relation to the Eden mythology, there is much to indicate a connection both to cannabis and to the archetypical ancient Near Eastern Goddess. We do know certainly through references to *qunnabu* that cannabis was used in the identical Assyrian sacred rites, which were also depicted in imagery with sacred trees, and eagle headed figures like that described in Ezekiel, and that *qunnabu* was used in a salve dedicated to Ishtar, and a beer prepared for her that was infused with cannabis, as we have noted earlier.

An Eagle headed figure stands beside the 'tree of life'

During his shamanistic flight Ezekiel was taken in spirit back to Jerusalem, to be Yahweh's witness to the idolatries that had been taking place there. The prophet is shown the "idol that provokes jealousy," this has been generally viewed as an Asherah image placed near the altar. As well, Yahweh's anger burns at seeing "men of the ancients of the house of Israel" worshiping other deities in the confines of the House of the Lord in Jerusalem "with every man his censer in his hand; and a thick cloud of incense went up" (Ezekiel 8:11). "Then he brought me [in a vision] to the entrance of the north gate of Yahweh: and behold, there sat women weeping for Tammuz. Then he said to me, "Have you seen this, O son of man? You will see still greater abominations than these" (Ezekiel 8:14). Ezekiel is then shown twenty-five men, with their backs towards the temple bowing down to the sun in the East, further identifying the Semitic acknowledgment of the sun as a visible symbol of the Lord. Ezekiel then condemns a pagan rite performed in the Temple, where the participants were "putting the branch to their nose" (Ezekiel 8:17). This is another likely reference to the inhaling of the smoke from burning the branches of cannabis.

The cult of Tammuz may have been introduced to the Kingdom of Judah during the reign of King Manasseh, who allied himself with the Assyrians after his father, the reformer Hezekiah died. However, some of these elements may have already been long in place. We saw the obvious influence of the love poems of Tammuz and Ishtar on Solomon's Song of Songs already. As well, as we noted earlier, Dr. Hugh Schonfield suggested that there was a connection between the name of Solomon's father David, and that of *Dad*, (also *Adad*), the counterpart of Tammuz in Palestine. Both were shepherds, and there were indications of fertility worship during David's reign (2 Samuel 24 18-25; I Chronicles 21 22-30 and 2 Samuel 21:9). As well, there "was a shrine of Adonis-Tammuz in David's city of Bethlehem (the place of Bread)" (Schonfield 1966). Adonis is the Semitic name of Tammuz, and it has been also associated with Dionysus, and Adonai, the name that would be used in place of 'Yahweh'. Adonis is taken from the Phoenician *adon,* which means "lord." This very same root word is the basis of the Hebrew word *Adonai,* which also means "Lord." It is technically not a proper name, but a title. It became used in place of the proper name for God Yahweh, due to the latter being forbidden to be spoken aloud. Interestingly, as shall be discussed later, these roots may have contributed to a later conflation between Dionysus and Yahweh as well.

It is for such idolatry and pagan practices that Ezekiel is told that the Lord's anger burned against Jerusalem and its fall was imminent. The Babylonian siege of Jerusalem lasts for two years, and over this time all the food runs out. Even the measures taken by Josiah to centralize the kingdom around the royal city of Jerusalem, and stock it against this eventuality, do not prevent the famine. Jeremiah's Book of Lamentations describes the onset of cannibalism in the intensity of the famine that beset the people: "With their own hands compassionate women have cooked their own children who became their food when my people were destroyed" (Lamentations 4:10).

In a grimly humorous account, Yahweh commands his prophet Ezekiel, who begins to be quite active at this point, to do some ritualized performance art in order to demonstrate to his fellow citizens what is about to befall them. Ezekiel is first told to make a clay table with the image of Jerusalem on it, and with toy props "lay siege to it: Erect siege works against it, build a ramp up to it, set up camps against it and put battering-rams around it" (Ezekiel 4:2). After he is finished with his toy battlefield, Ezekiel is further enticed by his daemon Yahweh, to place an iron pan between his face and the city, to show how the inhabitants are going to be cut off from outsiders. But when Ezekiel is commanded to enact how the people of Jerusalem will be forced to eat unclean food, by preparing and eating a cooked meal, "using human excrement for fuel" (Ezekiel 4:12), the prophet is pushed beyond his limit, and exclaims "Not so, Sovereign Lord!," forcing Yahweh to compensate by replacing human excrement with more palatable cow dung!

In regards to Ezekiel, in rabbinic tradition, he was considered as Jeremiah's son, as he is described as the son of "Buzi," a Jewish name that indicates "Despised" and by which Jeremiah was nicknamed for all his doom-saying by his countrymen. Ezekiel's first vision was said to have occurred about 30 years after the alleged discovery of Deuteronomy in the Temple during the reign of King Josiah. Ancient Jewish sources claim, Ezekiel did not compose the books attributed to him, but instead his prophecies were collected and put into writing by the Men of the Great Assembly, generally identified with Ezra and the group of scribes and lawmakers that accompanied him on his return to the Holy Land after the Exile. Although it is believed Ezekiel was active as a prophet while in Israel, it was while he was in Exile in Babylon that much of the texts that were attributed to him were depicted as taking place.

Jeremiah expresses the reason for this disaster overtaking the kingdom in terms of Deuteronomic morality: "The Babylonians who are attacking this city will come in and set it on fire: and they will burn it down, along with the houses where the people provoked me to anger by burning incense on the roofs to Baal, and by pouring out drink offerings to other gods" (Jeremiah 32:29). This passage also indicates the extent that Josiah's reform had failed in its attempt to rid the land of all traces of competing worship, all of which returned almost immediately after his unkingly demise. By the reign of Zedekiah the Judahites had fully reverted to the practices of their ancestors. Jeremiah's prophecies are vindicated as he had described the coming siege in detail: "I will make them eat the flesh of their sons and daughters, and they will eat one another's flesh during the stress of the siege imposed on them" (Jeremiah 19:9). Although, it is important to remember vindication here is based on texts that were composed a considerable amount of time after the events in question, and were likely added to by later Biblical editors.

The general view among Hebrew Bible scholars is that Jeremiah was a historical figure, and that much of the texts attributed to him were either written by him and/or his scribe Baruch. Views among historians range from the belief that the narratives and poetic portions of Jeremiah are contemporary with the Prophet's life, to the view that the work of the original prophet is beyond identification or recovery as so much has been added by later Priestly editors. The Hebrew Bible makes it clear, he was not popular with the people to whom he preached! And with good reason, as he gloated at their demise: "So give their children over to famine; hand them over to the power of the sword. Let their wives be made childless and widows; let their men be put to death, their young men slain by the sword in battle" (Jeremiah 18:20-21).

This vindictive nature of Jeremiah's preaching called his primary allegiance into question. Jeremiah's constant haranguing as to the guilt of the Judahites, and gleeful warnings of the coming victory of the Babylonians over the southern kingdom were taken as treasonous by many of the people of Jerusalem and the councilors of the king. Thus Jeremiah is accused of such treachery by the majority of the people and the king's officials. But, likely with the hopes of an allegiance with the new power, the Babylonians, enough members of the population, and officials stood by Jeremiah, so that "he was not handed over to the people to be put to death" (Jeremiah 26:24).

The final wrath of the Babylonians is unleashed on the Judahites. The Babylonians invade with a full military force and in time they show even less mercy. They overrun Judah and besiege Jerusalem. They strip the temple of all precious metals before burning it to the ground. The royal palaces are likewise burned along with all the important buildings in Jerusalem. The walls surrounding the city are also destroyed, a focused act of demolition which made the city virtually indefensible.

King Nebuchadnezzar himself is depicted as on site when the latest king of Judah, Jehoiachin surrenders to the Babylonians. The temple is pillaged, and the royal palace stripped of all valuables. The king, and his family, all the Judahite nobility, the military officers and fighting men, artisans and craftsmen, numbering seventeen thousand in total are all taken captive to Babylon. After Jehoichan's removal to Babylon, Nebuchadnezzar puts Mattaniah on the throne and he changes his name to Zedekiah (*Right of Jah,* 597-587 B.C.). Zedekiah soon made the mistake of rebelling against the might of the Babylonians and Jerusalem was again immediately besieged, and in the eyes of the Yahwist prophets, this was due to the kingdom's continued adulterous worship.

The remainder of the population that was left behind after the first Babylonian conquest was carried away to Babylon, leaving behind only the poorest of its residents there. Through the Babylonian conquest, the kingdom of Judah and perhaps more importantly the line of king David, comes to an end. The ruling class are exiled to Babylon, and foreigners are placed in Israel and Judah by the now reigning Babylonians.

> These are the Lord's people, and yet they have to leave his land. "I [Yahweh] had concern for my holy name, which the house of Israel profaned" (Ezekiel 36:21).

Jeremiah vs the Queen of Heaven

After the fall of Jerusalem and the beginning of the Exile a very curious occurrence takes place. First the Babylonians release Jeremiah and give him free reign to come or go as he pleases (Jeremiah 40:4). Then the Babylonian commander says to the newly released Jeremiah: "Go back to Gedaliah son of Ahikam, the son of Shaphan, whom the king of Babylon has appointed over the towns of Judah, and live with him among the people, or go anywhere else you please" (Jeremiah 40:5). Here at this pivotal point in the history of the Kingdom, it is the Deuteronomic cabal that is given power, giving more weight to the accusation that Jeremiah was a traitor and conspirator with the Babylonians. Obviously the denunciations of Jeremiah for treachery against the state were more than just slanderous attempts at discrediting him. Once again Jeremiah and the families of the priest and scribe that penned the Book of Deuteronomy are in alliance, this time openly supported by the Babylonians. King Nebuchadnezzar was familiar with the preaching of Jeremiah which was aligned so seamlessly to the Babylonian foreign policy. Jeremiah and the royal and priestly officials who supported each other are all amply rewarded for their part in the campaign against their own people, the Judahites.

For Jeremiah's recognized service to the Babylonians in advising the successive kings of Judah to bow down to them and admit defeat, the Babylonians released him from prison where King Zedekiah had him placed for his seeming treachery, leaving him free to go wherever he chose. After the fall of Jerusalem a remnant of the people had gone to Egypt to resettle, so Jeremiah decided to follow behind to act as a prophet of Yahweh for these Israelite immigrants, whether they liked it or not! Jeremiah begins his ministry in Egypt by blaming the displaced Judahites and their ancestors for the fall of Jerusalem, and then continues with further condemnations against them for continuing on with the adulterous practices of their ancestors, it is made clear, that the burning of incense to the Queen of Heaven, was a core aspect of these adulterous practices:

> This is what the LORD Almighty, the God of Israel says: "You saw the great disaster I brought on Jerusalem and on all the towns of Judah. Today they lie deserted and in ruins because of the evil they have done. They provoked me to anger by burning incense and by worshiping other gods.... Again and again I sent my servants the prophets, who said, "Do not do the detestable things I hate!" But they did not listen or pay attention; they did not turn from their wickedness or stop burning incense to other gods. Therefore my fierce anger was poured out; it raged against the towns of Judah and the streets of Jerusalem and made them the desolate ruins they are today."
>
> "...Why provoke me to anger [again] ... burning incense to other gods in Egypt, where you have come to live? You will destroy yourselves and make yourselves an object of cursing and reproach among all the nations of the earth. Have you forgotten the wickedness committed by your fathers and by the kings and queens of Judah and the wickedness committed by you and your wives in the land of Judah and the streets of Jerusalem? Up to this day they have not humbled themselves or shown reverence, nor have they followed my law and decrees I set before you and your fathers."
>
> Therefore, this is what the Lord Almighty, the God of Israel says: "I am determined to bring disaster on you and destroy all Judah. I will take away the remnant of Judah who were

> determined to go to Egypt to settle there. They will all perish in Egypt.... I will punish those who live in Egypt with sword famine and plague, as I punished Jerusalem. None of the remnant of Judah who have gone to live in Egypt will escape or survive to return to the land of Judah..."
>
> Then all the men which knew that their wives had burned incense unto other gods, and all the women that stood by, a great multitude, even all the people that dwelt in the land of Egypt, in Pathros, answered Jeremiah, saying, "As for the word that thou hast spoken unto us in the name of the Lord, we will not hearken unto thee. But we will certainly do whatsoever thing goeth forth out of our own mouth, to burn incense unto the queen of heaven, and to pour drink offerings unto her, as we have done, we, and our fathers, our kings, and our princes, in the city of Judah, and in the streets of Jerusalem: for then we had plenty of victuals, and were well, and saw no evil. But since we left off to burn incense to the queen of heaven, and poured out drink offerings to her, we have wanted all things, and have been consumed by sword and by famine."
>
> The women added "When we burned incense to the queen of heaven, and poured out drink offerings unto her, did we make her cakes to worship her, and pour our drink offerings to her, without our men?"
>
> Then Jeremiah said unto all the people, to the men, and to the women, and to all the people which had given him that answer saying, The incense that ye burned in the cities of Judah, and in the streets of Jerusalem, ye, and your fathers, your kings, and your princes, and the people of the land, did not the Lord remember them, and came it not into his mind? So that the Lord could no longer bear, because of the evil of your doings, and because of the abominations which ye have committed; therefore is your land a desolation, and astonishment, and a curse, without an inhabitant, as at this day. Because ye have burned incense and because ye have sinned against the Lord, and have not obeyed the voice of the Lord, not walked in his law, nor in his statutes, not in his testimonies; therefore this evil has happened to you, as at this day (Jeremiah 44:1-23).

From the description given in the words of the angry prophet himself, we can see that Jeremiah was viewed with disdain by the populace. They likely saw him as a traitor for siding with the Babylonians, who themselves liked the prophet enough not to kill him, even rewarding with release from prison and right of free access. The "reforms" Jeremiah represented as a member of the cabal which formed around the forged Book of Deuteronomy, were clearly unpopular and had to be forced upon the people by threat of death for non-compliance. As we have seen, even with such Draconian edicts, these counterfeit decrees failed to last a lifetime after Josiah's initial actions to institute them.

In this telling passage, we learn so much about the Biblical roots of prohibition. Jeremiah's reference to the previous kings and princes, who burned incense to the Queen of Heaven can be seen as referring to King Solomon, his son, Rehoboam, and most of the other Biblical Kings and apparently, from the Bible's own records, most of the populace. The evidence at tel Arad make it clear as to what form of incense was used, as does the sweet smelling kaneh reference in Jeremiah.

It is also likely that the pouring out of drink offerings referred to a cannabis infusion, as we know such preparations were poured out to Ishtar. As noted in Chapter 2, *The Sourcebook for Ancient Mesopotamian Medicine* (2014) recorded a recipe that requires three shekels of *qunnabu* [cannabis] to be mixed with other aromatic plants in a beer libation dedicated to be poured out to Ishtar, under the title *Beltu,* meaning "Lady." This ritual act could easily have been followed by the cults of other related Goddesses.

Interestingly, in the words of Jeremiah we find absolutely no reference to the holy anointing oils and incenses, as he himself apparently did not use them. This was due to its content of *kaneh,* which he himself, speaking for the Lord, condemns by name. "What do I care about frankincense from Sheba or sweet smelling cane [kaneh] from a distant land? Your burnt offerings are not acceptable; your sacrifices do not please me" (Jeremiah 6:20). Clearly, up until this time, cannabis had been an integral and popular part of mainstream Judaic worship, as practiced by the people of the land. Jeremiah's prohibitions against it in the name of the Lord were seen by the populace as the empty words of a pseudo-prophet and the lies and decrees of a traitor to his people.

We see the beginnings of what led to Jeremiah's complete cannabis prohibition in the words of Yahweh, through earlier prophets like Isaiah, who condemn not cannabis itself, but its use in pagan worship instead of being dedicated to him: "You have not brought any kaneh for me, or lavished on me the fat of your sacrifices" (Isaiah 43:23). Here it is the lack of cannabis offerings that is condemned through the prophet. According to Isaiah, Yahweh is angry because kaneh was used in the worship of other gods, and the anger of the prophets who spoke in his name, can be seen as jealousy over watching their beloved cannabis going to other temples instead of their own. Sentiments that are echoed in the book of Ezekiel, where Yahweh, speaking in the first person, condemns the Israelites who "offered my oil and incense before" other gods in orgiastic rites. Such anger over dissuaded sacrifices of tithes and other offerings resulted in the "discovery," or rather creation, of Deuteronomy. By the time of Jeremiah, the use of cannabis had become associated so fully with "idolatrous worship" that it had fallen completely out of use amongst the Hebrew Priestly caste. The words of the Lord through Jeremiah, are the words of the dour old prophet himself; and his condemnations against cannabis incense, the prohibitions of a corrupt regime that would likely have completely lost its hold over the people, without the Babylonian's conquest of Jerusalem.

Clearly, the goddess had been worshiped throughout the history of the Hebrews, along with Yahweh. The refusal by the Jews of Egypt to give up the worship of the Queen of Heaven, was not in any way a rejection of Yahweh, who they continued to worship alongside her. Because of her historical association with Yahweh in inscriptions, and frequent mention of her iconography in the Hebrew Bible, many scholars see the 'Queen of Heaven' as a direct reference to Asherah. Jeremiah's specific condemnations against both Frankincense and *Kaneh*, help to secure the identification of cannabis as *kaneh* per Sula Benet's etymological theory, as these are the very items recovered off the two altars at the canceled temple in tel Arad, which has its own association with the combined worship of Yahweh and Asherah. The people who Jeremiah are rallying against as well, make it very clear, these were long standing practices that had been in place for generations prior.

However, I should acknowledge other goddesses have been suggested as the "Queen of Heaven" worshiped by the Hebrews in Egypt encountered by Jeremiah. Ishtar, who is often equated with Astarte, has been suggested due to her association with Tammuz, who according to Ezekiel, was worshiped within the Jewish temple prior to the fall of Jerusalem. As well, historically we know from ancient inscriptions that read "Anat-Yahu," that "in the fifth century B.C. a Jewish colony in Elephantine, Egypt, did apparently believe that Yahweh had a partner Anath" (Anderson 1975). Anath is generally paired with Yahweh's constant rival Baal, however Asherah was paired with Canaanite El, before Ugaritic inscriptions depicted her as the wife of Yahweh. As we have seen, Yahweh assimilated aspects of both Baal and El. The syncretism of Yahweh's cult has been the key to its lasting success. That Yahweh may at this time have been paired with Anat, in some regions and time periods, is clearly possible, and in Elephantine it certainly was the case. Also important to remember in this regard, is that some scholars hold the view that these three goddesses, Anat, Asherah and Ishtar/Astarte represented a single triple goddess.

The Elephantine papyri are interesting, as they depict Jewish polytheism still clearly in play in the 5th century BCE. As well, they contain correspondence with the religious authorities in Jerusalem, who seemed to hold no issue with this polytheism. In discussions of how to perform Passover, no mention of Moses or the existing mythology of the holiday are in place in the correspondence. As Mircea Eliade noted: "Without religious elites, and more especially without the prophets, Judaism would not have become anything very different from the religion of the Jewish colony in Elephantine, which preserved the popular Palestinian religious viewpoint down to the fifth century B.C. ... History had allowed these Hebrews of the Diaspora to retain, side by side with Yahweh ... other divinities ... and even the goddess Anath.... This is one more confirmation of the importance of history in the development of Judaic religious experience and its maintenance under high tensions" (Eliade 1954).

The Egyptian remnant of Judahites, did not in fact deny Yahweh but acknowledged him alongside the goddess. What was rejected was Jeremiah's own political religious view of state-monotheism, a new theological viewpoint that had risen after the alleged "discovery" of the Book of the Law, Deuteronomy, which was established through the fall of Jerusalem. The Yahwists' rigid insistence upon not only Yahweh's supremacy, but also Yahweh as the only god was a very late development. As Tikva Simone Frymer-Kensky, who was a Professor at the University of Chicago Divinity School, has noted "Ancient customs and symbols, long part of Israel's heritage, eventually did not fit the increasingly radical monotheistic sensibility. They were condemned as 'foreign' and ultimately eradicated. The bronze serpent is one such symbol, the asherah is another" (Frymer-Kensky 1992). Cannabis still another....

That Rehoboam should plant an Asherah pole which remained standing until the reform of Hezekiah in the eighth century testifies to the centrality of the worship of Asherah in Hebrew culture. Likewise that Jehu's reforms removed all traces of Baal worship but didn't disturb the rites of Asherah, not even to mention them, further testifies to the irreproachability of the cult of Asherah. Again even the purges of Elijah the great, involved only the massacre of the priests of Baal.

There is no mention of the deaths of the worshipers or ministers of Asherah in the slaughter. Thus, the "complex of altar, tree, hill, and megalith that characterized this worship was an ancient and integral part of Israel's religious life, and the 'reforms' of Hezekiah and Josiah that destroyed this complex were a radical innovation rather than a return to some pristine purity" (Frymer-Kensky 1992).

Further, if we were to look at the Hebrew Bible's historical record itself, we would find that the people were correct in their statements concerning the prosperity of the kingdom coinciding with the supposedly pagan worship that Jeremiah so harshly condemned. High points in the kingdom occurred under idolatrous kings such as Solomon, Ahab, Manasseh, and Jereboam II. The only two kings after David who appear in the Lord's favor, Hezekiah and Josiah, both had unpopular reigns, and their actions throughout can be seen as contributing greatly to the kingdom's eventual demise. Hezekiah was forced to bow down to the Babylonians and the Assyrians, and Josiah particularly comes to an ignominious end by receiving the arrow of an Egyptian Pharaoh.

However, through their reforms, along with the influence of Jeremiah, and the prophets of Yahweh that rallied against the "adulterous" fertility worship practiced throughout the land, they were eventually suppressed. The fertility worship, the religion of the people of the land, was seen as "prostitution" by the Yahwist dictators, but in actuality "represents one of the most widespread forms of cosmic religiosity. Specifically characteristic of agriculturists, cosmic religiosity continued the most elementary dialectic of the sacred ... the belief that the divine is incarnated, or manifests itself, in cosmic objects and rhythms" (Eliade 1978).

> The prophets finally succeeded in emptying nature of any divine presence. Whole sectors of the natural world--the 'high places', stones, springs, trees, certain crops, certain flowers--will be denounced as unclean because they were polluted by the cult of the Canaanite divinities of fertility. The preeminently clean and holy region is the desert alone, for it is there that Israel remained faithful to its God (Eliade 1978).

The prophets also marked the disappearance of the *qedeshim,* the hierodule "cult-prostitutes," who as we have discussed, at times occupied the Temple of Jerusalem itself. "They seem to have been eliminated finally only after the Fall of the Temple and the Babylonian exile. Cultic sexual activity became synonymous with abandoning the worship of the true god and turning to the worship of false gods.... The terms used to identify the cult priestesses became insults used as invectives against the Goddess worshipers" (Gadon 1989).

> The disappearance of cultic sexual activity was of primary importance to the establishment of the ancient Hebrew faith. As long as the temple priestesses were the bearers of the mysterious, life-enhancing powers of creativity and procreativity, these powers could not be claimed by the creator-god. The Hebrew god took unto himself the sacred life-giving powers of the Goddess (Gadon 1989).

As with Yahweh's absorption of aspects of Baal and El, he took on the aspect of the Goddess he was earlier paired with as his wife, Asherah. Syncretism, as already noted, was the key aspect of Yahweh's longevity.

Chapter Ten

The Babylonian Exile

Babylon's conquest of Jerusalem, particularly the destruction of the temple, was in many ways a reset button for the religion. The resulting "Exile" also had some profound effects upon the people, especially those who were subjected to captivity. Besides producing some of the more memorable poetry of the Psalms, the time spent in the great Chaldean capital of Babylon contributed enormously to the Israelites continually evolving theology, and colored the books of prophets like Ezekiel and Daniel, as well as others. It was through the Exile that the Hebrews were exposed to the culture of the greatest city up to that point in history, and after such exposure things would never be the same for them again.

The Israelites were a displaced people in the city of Babylon and as such didn't possess land to farm, so they became merchants. The trade that passed through Babylon as the center of the Chaldean empire provided an opportunity for gathering wealth, and it is here that the Jewish people gained a strong and lasting association as merchants. Thus it was for the prosperity they experienced that many of the exiles chose to remain in the great Babylonian cities, even after their later liberation.

The priestly theocracy, the increased urbanization of the Israelites, the Jewish apocalyptic literature, and the pointed formation of messianic expectation all resulted from this period of the exile. With the ending of political power, and the line of Hebrew kings, the role of the priesthood became increasingly important. No longer having a nation to call their own, the Israelites turned to their priesthood for their sense of national identity. "It was in this period that traditional Judaism appeared, the new Law was elaborated and imposed in all its force, and the priestly projection of Hebrew origins became rampant" (La Barre 1970). Clearly, the leading focus in this final group of Biblical re-writers and compilers known as the Priestly editors, were the views held by Jeremiah. Having seen first hand how his father and other figures re-invented Judaic history through the Book of the Law, Jeremiah took this further, and established the priestly theocracy as the new foundation of the faith. As the editors of the *Dartmouth Bible* stated, the aim of these Priestly editors was "to translate into reality the blueprint for a theocratic state." As Bishop John Shelby Spong explained of these revisions:

> Synagogues were built under the leadership of the priestly group in the exile to indoctrinate the coming generation, who would not remember Jerusalem, including in time those who had never known Jerusalem. The details of worship, the rules of worship, the observance of worship became all important and resulted in the creation of much of the Book of Exodus, almost all the Book of Leviticus, and major portions of the Book of Numbers. The Yahwist-Elohist-Deuteronomic version of the Hebrew sacred story was thoroughly edited by the priestly writers to include the ancient priestly traditions and to affirm the sanctity throughout all of Jewish history of the traditions now being required of faithful Jews (Spong 1991).

It was the fifth century BCE priestly writers who gave us the definition of "Kosher" foods. "A history of every ritual observed in Jewish worship entered the sacred story" (Spong 1991), *i.e.,* former agricultural festivals such as Passover were incorporated into a mythic past about the Exodus, in much the same way Christmas replaced earlier solstice celebrations of paganism. "The Priestly Code also invented exorbitant tithes and inserted them into older documents, now including cattle and sheep in addition to the proper measure of corn and oil and wine – almost a blasphemy in terms of the older religion" (La Barre 1970).

All the chronologies in the Hebrew Bible were in fact composed by the Priestly writers, who wanted to have a seeming historical basis for their religious authority. But in the re-recording of historical fact, the saga was appended with new fictional material to justify Yahweh's workings through history, as well as the addition of non-existent persons, and supposedly ancient prophecies that predicted what were by then historic events. Indeed, the Priestly editors rewrote the history of a scattered and dismayed people in a bid for both power and control that was more successful than they ever could have imagined. Moreover, the effects of this theological and political coup can still be felt in the modern day.

With the fall of the kings and rise of the new priestly class, which took place in the Babylonian exile, it is interesting to note that it is at this juncture in history that the Levites begin garnering a pronounced decline in Yahweh's favor. The Hebrew Bible makes it clear this was due to allowing the pagan practices of the pre-exilic period. The Lord warned the Levites through the prophet Malachi (Messenger), telling them "Because of you I will cut off your seed, and spread on your faces the dung from your festival sacrifices ... you have turned from the way and by your teaching have caused many to stumble; you have violated the covenant with Levi.... So I have caused you to be despised and humiliated before all the people" (Malachi 2:3-9).

Ezekiel's writings also refer to Yahweh's condemnation of the "Levites who went far from me when Israel went astray and who wandered from me after their idols must bear the consequence of their sin ... because they served them in the presence of their idols and made the house of Israel fall into sin, therefore I have sworn with uplifted hand that they must bear the consequence of their sin" (Ezekiel 44:10-12). These were the same Levites, who for centuries had been burning the incense to the brazen serpent that was said to have been made by their sect's founder Moses, and who acted as shaman initiators, the seraphim, or fiery serpents in the temple in the story of Isaiah. These were the same Levite, sons of snakes who tended the temple throughout the whole monarchic period, at times, alongside both male and female cult prostitutes. Nowhere can this sudden disfavor of the Levites be more clearly seen than in the rise of the priestly caste, through the edicts of Deuteronomy. It was a new religious renovation, or even a religio-political coup.

Those Levites who remained were limited to the role of the priests' servants: "They are not to come near to serve me as priests or come near any of my holy things or my holy offerings; they must bear the shame of their detestable practices. Yet I will put them in charge of the duties of the temple and all the work that is to be done in it" (Ezekiel 44:13-14).

The Book of Leviticus also did not reach its present form till the Persian Period, from 538-332 BCE. The entire composition of the book of Leviticus is Priestly literature. Considering what we have seen in regards to *kaneh* from the Priestly caste, Leviticus 10:1-2 is very interesting: "Aaron's sons Nadab and Abihu took their censers, put fire in them and added incense; and they offered strange fire before Yahweh, contrary to his command. So fire came out from the presence of the Yahweh and consumed them, and they died before the Yahweh." It seems that it was here, with the Priestly writers and particularly Jeremiah, that an intentional suppression of the earlier ritual use of cannabis was iinflicted.

The Slave-Prophet; The Book of Daniel

The Book of Daniel (*Judge of God*) is written in the tradition of the great prophets, and portrays events that take place during the Babylonian Exile, depicting historic figures such as Nebuchadnezzar and other foreign kings. But, in scholarly circles, the Book of Daniel is believed to be of a much later composition than that of the stories which it depicts, and is actually considered by some to be the last book added to the Hebrew Bible. It is usually read as a miraculous foretelling of future events, records of Daniel's prophetic visions of invasions and conquerors. In actuality the Book of Daniel as it reads in the Hebrew Bible has been dated at 165 B.C. and these 'prophecies' were written in hindsight.

The "Daniel" the book is supposedly authored by was a traditional and pious Israelite referred to in the writings of Ezekiel, alongside other legendary figures such as Noah and Job. However, this is believed to be in reference to *Dan'el*, who was a heroic figure from the Canaanite Ras Shamra texts. That Ezekiel wrote of *Dan'el* in favorable terms reveals his resonance with these facets of Northern kingdom culture. "The reference to Dan'el as he was spelt in the Ras Shamra legend of Aqht, indicates Ezekiel's familiarity with the literary tradition of Canaan" (Gray 1969). The author of the Book of Daniel chose this name to write under to give his writings the respect and authority associated with this name. "In the late post-exilic period, when prophecy was believed to have ceased, it was common to release writings under the name of some figure of ancient Jewish tradition" (Anderson 1975).

Curiously Josephus tells us that Daniel was a eunuch which as we know from the laws of Moses would have precluded him from worship in the temple (Josephus; *Antiquities* 10:10:2). The Hebrew Bible portrays Daniel as an ascetic vegetarian, who along with three of his countrymen were trained in the language and culture of the Babylonians, and worked in the service of king Nebuchadnezzar, his successor, and then later the Persian kings, who overcame the Babylonians.

After, showing evidence of wisdom and understanding that was "ten times better than all the magicians and enchanters in his whole kingdom," Daniel was appointed by the ancient Babylonian king Nebuchadnezzar as his head dream interpreter and astrologer, a job Daniel was paid for with offerings of incense. That Daniel accepted offerings of incense shows his unfamiliarity with the reforms of Jeremiah, (if Daniel existed at all, he would have been in exile through the peak of Jeremiah's career).

The famous account of Nebuchadnezzar eating "grass as doth an oxen" for seven years, in order to humble himself, was foretold in a dream interpreted by Daniel, who tells the king that his descent and sojourn into the wilderness, will last "until you acknowledge that the Most High is sovereign over the kingdoms of men and gives them to anyone he wishes" (Daniel 4:25). Interestingly, here we see the tradition that began with the fall of Samaria (in which the Assyrians were working on behalf of the Lord), that all victors and rulers, despite their religious creed, were placed as such by Yahweh's divine will and edict. A curious way of interpreting their own continued defeat and subjugation, as further evidence of their own God's interaction with history. (With this line of religious thought, the southern prophet Isaiah would refer to the Persian king Cyrus as "the anointed of Yahweh").

Dr. Creighton, who saw references to cannabis in the Biblical term "honey-wood," also felt the tale of Nebuchadnezzar eating grass, gave indication of cannabis use. He stated that "in the case of Daniel's apologue of Nebuchadnezzar's fall, it arises from the eating of 'grass', the Semitic word having both a generic and a colloquial meaning (hachish), as well as from the introduction of the subjective perceptions of hachish intoxication as gigantic or grotesque objects" (Creighton 1903).

In relation to Nebuchadnezzar eating grass, as noted earlier in the *P'sachim*, "Rav Yehudah says it is good to eat ... the essence of hemp seed in Babylonian broth; but it is not lawful to mention this in the presence of an illiterate man, because he might derive a benefit from the knowledge not meant for him. Nedarim, fol. 49, col. 1" (Harris, et al., 2004). In many ancient references that mention cannabis "seed" it is likely meant "seeded bud" or seeds with the THC calyx enveloping them still intact. This passage is interesting in its reference to both the "benefit" from the broth and its origin in "Babylon."

Nebuchadnezzar eats grass, "as doth an oxen" for seven years, which brings back to mind the ox of creation, depicted with Esarhaddon. He tells us at the end of his seven year sojourn; "I raised my eyes towards heaven, and my sanity was restored. Then I praised the Most High: I honored and glorified him who lives for ever.... I was restored to my throne and became even greater than before. Now I, Nebuchadnezzar, praise and exalt and glorify the King of heaven"(Daniel 5:34-37). Here the author of Daniel would have us believe that the famous Babylonian king had accepted the divine rule of Yahweh, the god of a people he easily conquered. A fact that the historical records blatantly contradict, and again gives us ample evidence of the vast theological transition within Hebrew thought, in that Yahweh, the God of a limited and tribal "chosen people," through their defeat, had become the cosmic, Most High, ruler of all humanity and the universe in general.

Upon the fall of the Babylonians to Persian forces, the later Persian kings who now ruled the ancient city, Cyrus and Darius, are said to have retained Daniel in the position of dream interpreter and councilor. Both Darius and Cyrus are known historically to have been followers of the teachings of the Persian shaman Zoroaster and his monotheistic-like god Ahura Mazda – a deity who shares many traits with Yahweh. Like other ancient cultures, as we shall see, the Zoroastrians utilized cannabis in rituals.

That Daniel mentions King Darius is particularly interesting, as Darius, both in tradition and in the view of some scholars, is said to have been the son of King Vishtaspa, In some ancient inscriptions and sources, *Hystaspes,* a Greek name, is viewed as identical with Vishtaspa (the Avestan name for *Hystapes*), an early patron of Zoroaster. Also interesting is that Vishtaspa was said to have taken on the faith of Zoroastrianism, after an intense initiation with bhanga, becoming Zoroaster's first convert. A situation we will look at more closely in the next chapter with a look at the Persian Empire, the Zoroastrian influence on the ancient Hebrews, and their return to their homeland…

Chapter 11

The Persians

Although the references to *kaneh* and *kaneh bosm*, came to an end in the Hebrew Bible, this does not seem to be the case for the story of cannabis and the Biblical Jews. Although, going forward here, the evidence indicates infused wines as the mode of consumption. The evidence for the use of such mixtures is very intriguing. This is particularly true in regards to the story of Ezra, who by tradition is said to have collected and placed the various books that make up the Hebrew Bible in their current order.

As this influence likely came through Ezra's Persian overlords, and the Persian religion of Zoroastrianism had such a profound effect on the Hebrew religion from here forward, a look at both the Persians and the use of cannabis in Zoroastrianism is relevant to this discussion.

The Persian Empire rose to power and replaced the Babylonians. At the height of their glory they stretched from the Greek Ionian Islands to the Punjab and the Indus valley in India. The Persians differed from the Egyptian, Assyrian and Babylonian Empires that had preceded them in a number of ways, particularly in regard to being more liberally minded and compassionate than the previous Empires. As well, when they expanded the Persians instilled a system of viable roads, and then policed them. This fostered an increased trade across the huge continental expanse of the Persian empire – trade which was encouraged and thrived. Part of this cultural exchange was also cosmological.

The Persians practiced the religion of Zoroaster. This religion was a departure from the practices of Sumer that had so influenced the entire Fertile Crescent. Zoroastrianism is often suggested as the world's oldest monotheistic religion, or at least one of the earliest, however it contains both monotheistic and dualistic elements. Good and Evil were strictly delineated from each other. *Ahuramazda* being the supreme god of the Zoroastrians and *Angra Mainyu*, his evil arch rival. The later Christian views of Satan and Hell are based more on Zoroastrian views than Jewish. Zoroastrianism is responsible for the introduction of many other ideas that were to have a profoundly formative effect upon both Judaism and later Christianity.

The testimony of the Bible also sheds light on the more benevolent policies of the Persians. The Israelite captives who had been taken from the pillaged Jerusalem by the victorious Babylonians were all returned to their homelands by Cyrus, who was praised lavishly in the writings of Second Isaiah for his benevolent acts of restoration:

> This is what the Lord says to his anointed, to Cyrus, whose right hand I take hold of to subdue nations before him and to strip the kings of their armor, and to open doors before him so that gates will not be shut: I will go before you and level mountains; I will break down gates of bronze and cut through bars of iron. I will give you treasures of darkness, riches stored in secret places, so that you may know that I am the Lord, God of Israel, who summons you by name. For the sake of Jacob my servant, of Israel my chosen, I summon you by name and bestow on you a title of honor, though you do not acknowledge me. I am the Lord, and there is no other; apart from me there is no God. I will strengthen you, though you have not acknowledged me.... I will raise up Cyrus in my righteousness (Isaiah 45:1-13).

Upon returning the Israelite exiles to their former homeland, Cyrus appointed a Hebrew governor over them, his former cupbearer Nehemiah. Cyrus also permitted the reconstruction of the temple and the re-establishment of the sacrifices to Yahweh. The Bible's book of Ezra even presents letters of Cyrus testifying to his support of this venture. Thus the exile of the Israelites lasted for only half a century. The Babylonians had conquered Jerusalem and destroyed the temple in 586 B.C. and the exiles were returned by Cyrus in 538 B.C. But the Israelites were changed forever.

It is significant that Cyrus is referred to as the Lord's anointed. This makes Cyrus the *messiah*, the "anointed one," a title formerly given to the Hebrew priests and kings who had been anointed with the cannabis holy oil. The ritual use of cannabis in ancient Persia is well attested. Here again, as with earlier cultures the Hebrews came into contact with, perhaps the use of the identical sacrament acted as some sort of a catalyst for a symbiosis between the two religions?

There are some interesting parallels to the fate of *kaneh bosm*, to be made with Zoroastrian history of cannabis and the religious reforms around an entheogen known as *haoma*, and the histories which took both religions into Monotheism.

Haoma and Zoroastrianism

Zoroaster was a religious reformer who took the multi-pantheon Ancient Iranian religion, and raised one deity from that to be the sole deity, Ahura Mazda. However, since considerable power was handed over to his arch enemy Angra Mainyu, a figure that is comparable to the later Christian concepts of Satan, some see Zoroastrianism as Dualistic rather than Monotheistic.

The religion most comparable to the pre-Zoroastrian situation, would be Hinduism in India. Indeed, due to similar myths, god names, and the use of a sacred beverage, made from a plant-based sacrament known as *Haoma* in Persia and *Soma* in India, as well as in the language of the Persian *Avesta* and the Vedic Indian *Rig Veda,* a general view is that these two regions emerged from the same earlier source.

All though there are many suggestions as to what plant was originally used for this ancient entheogenic sacrament, my view, which is laid out in more detail in *Cannabis and the Soma Solution* (2010) than there is room for here, is that the origins and identity of Haoma, and thus Soma, can be made on a combination of archaeological and linguistic evidence in a similar way to what we have seen with cannabis and *kaneh bosm,* and likewise it was cannabis based. Both the ritual use of cannabis and *haoma/soma* can be traced back to Indo-European cultures. The ritual consumption of Haoma and Soma still continues to this day, but it has generally been acknowledged that the modern counterpart of these sacred beverages differs from the ancient in content, and at one time the preparation held a powerful psychoactive effect. Whereas today, it's more of a mild stimulant, an effect produced by the currently used Ephedra, which was likely a part of the ancient drink as well.

The physical attributes of Haoma give clear indications of cannabis as described in the Avesta:

> Haoma is golden-green (*Yasna* 9.16 et al)
>
> Haoma is tall (Yasna 10.21, *Vendidad* 19.19)
>
> Haoma has roots, stems and branches (*Yasna* 10.5)
>
> Haoma has a pliant stem, asu (*Yasna* 9.16)
>
> Haoma is fragrant (*Yasna* 10.4)
>
> Haoma grows on the mountains, 'swiftly spreading', 'apart on many paths' (*Yasna* 9.26, 10.3-4 et al) 'to the gorges and abysses' (*Yasna* 10-11) and 'on the ranges' (*Yasna* 10.12)
>
> Haoma can be pressed (*Yasna* 9.1, 9.2)

In the 10th Mandala of the *Rig Veda* there are also clear descriptions of the plant and references to the rocks pressing the soma as being turned green in the process and also the reference to soma as "the purple tree" in what seems to be a clear description of the color of ripened Cannabis indica:

> *Rig Veda* 10.94 – (Wilson's 1928 translation)
>
> Let these (stones) speak.… Ye solid, quick moving stones, you utter the noise of praise … full of the Soma juice.
>
> They roar like a hundred, like a thousand men; they cry aloud with green-tinted faces; obtaining the sacrifice, the pious stones … partake of the sacrificial food…
>
> They speak, they received into their mouth the sweet (Soma juice) … chewing the branch of the purple tree, the voracious bulls have bellowed.
>
> Splitting, but unsplit, you, O stones … enjoying the Soma, flowing green (with Soma), they made heaven and earth resound with their clamor.
>
> The stones proclaim it with their clamor at the issue of the Soma-juice … like cultivators sowing the seed, they devouring the Soma, mix it, and do not hurt it.
>
> … Proclaim the praise of (the stone), which has effused (the Soma-juice); let the honored stones revolve. [Emphasis added].

The preparation of Soma, pulverized with rocks, is similar to the preparation of the Indian cannabis beverage *bhang*. As noted by the respected Indologist scholar Alain Danielou (1907-1994) of the connection:

> This ancient sacred drink was likely to resemble a drink what today is called bhang, made from the crushed leaves of Indian Hemp. Every Shaivite has to consume bhang at least once a year. The drink, which intensifies perceptivity, induces visions and above all leads to extreme mental concentration. It is widely used by Yogis. Details concerning its preparation are to be found as early as the Vedic period. The description of the way soma was prepared and its immediate use without fermentation, can only apply to bhang and is identical to the method employed today (Danielou 1992).

Likewise, the noted historian and Indologist Professor. A.L. Basham, recorded in his *The Wonder That Was India: A Survey of the Culture of the Indian Sub-Continent before the coming of the Muslims*: "The drink prepared from the plant ... was made with great ceremony in the course of the sacrifice, when the herb was pressed between stones, mixed with milk, strained, and drunk on the same day.... The effects of soma ... are rather like those attributed to such drugs as hashish. Soma may well have been hemp, which grows wild in parts of India, Central Asia and South Russia, and from which modern Indians produce a narcotic drink called 'bhang'" (Basham 1961).

We also find this identification with a number of Indian scholars as well. Braja Lal Mukherjee was the first amongst a number of Vedic researchers who suggested *bhang* (hemp) as a candidate for Soma in his 1921 essay, "The Soma Plant." Other Indian researchers who have made this distinction include Joges Candra Ray (1939); Chandra Chakraberty, (1944); Vikramasiṃha, (1967); Indian botanist B.G.L. Swamy (1976); Ramachandran and Mativāṇan̲, (1991); Dr. N.R. Waradpande (1995); and Indra Deva & Shrirama, (1999).

The Russian archaeologist Victor Sarianidi (1929-2013) claimed to have found archaeological evidence in the Afghanistan desert, related to the production of this sacred beverage, stating it was generally composed of cannabis and ephedra, but in some cases opium poppy was also used. Although there is controversy around Sarianidi's archaeological claims, I think the Russian Archaeologist was correct in his designation of soma as a preparation of cannabis and ephedra and his claims are slowly becoming mainstream enough to be cited in texts like *The Persian Empire: A Historical Encyclopedia* in its description for "Haoma": "The ingredients of the sacred Haoma juice were most probably ephedra mixed with poppy and cannabis" (Kia, 2016).

Sarianidi based his claims on archaeological discoveries from the Bactria Margiana Archaeological Complex (BMAC) in Afghanistan, a region thought to be the birthplace of the Zoroastrian religion. Sarianidi found three large temple sites, and suggested that a large portion of the temple grounds were dedicated to the preparation of a sacred beverage that contained cannabis and ephedra, and in later cases opium was also found.

Sarianidi claimed evidence of residues of these plants in gypsum sediments of ancient pots, as well as impressions of seeds he identified as cannabis seeds. Unfortunately, working on a low budget, the items that were tested were left exposed in the sun after the Russian scientists' analysis, Western scientists were unable to reproduce them, and this has resulted in a dispute over the Russian results, where they are generally still accepted in Russia, but dismissed by Western Scientists. The debate continues....

Artifacts found by Sarianidi which he saw as tools for the preparation of soma, are indeed comparable to implements still used in the preparation of bhang.

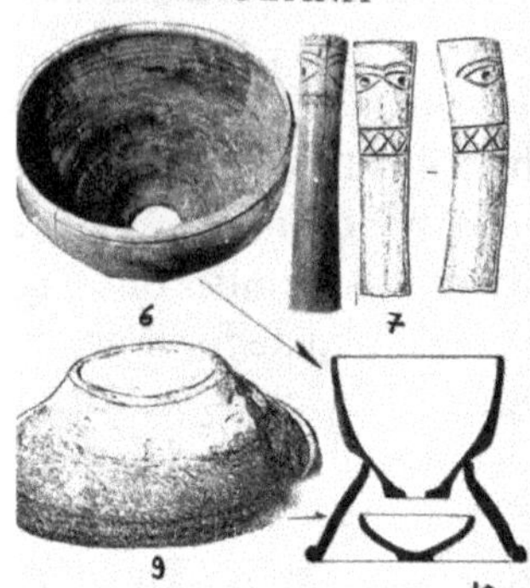

Left: Soma/Haoma strainer found at BMAC, the bone cups with eyes were for drinking an elixir. Residues of opium were claimed by Sarianidi and his team. **Right:** Detail from 18th century painting 'Fakirs prepare bhang', note the straining device.

However, despite the controversy that plagues Sarianidi's team's claims, other archaeological and linguistic evidence that corroborates Sarianidi's research have since emerged. In Chapter 3 we discussed the Indo-European evidence for cannabis, which included braziers, used for burning it in rituals discovered with IE groups who had settled in China. Not only evidence of burnt cannabis in braziers were found, but also processed female cannabis flowers were also recovered in tombs, as well as ephedra.

Evidence from artifacts recovered from both these Chinese sites and BMAC in Afghanistan indicate there were trade routes between these locations. As we have noted the etymological origins of cannabis in IE languages, an explanation is needed for the origins of the term *haoma,* and it seems it is likely with the groups in China that the term first originated.

It would seem that it was here, at this meeting place of cultures in China, that the *Haoma/Soma* cult may have first originated under the name *hu-ma,* or other Chinese variations, which have been translated as "Scythian cannabis," or "fire cannabis." Cannabis has its own Indo-European name *kanna,* and this is derived from the proto-Indo-European language, Finno-Ugric, *kannap*. However, the name

Haoma may have been developed from the Chinese term. As has long been noted, there are Chinese words indicating an Indo-European origin, thus it would not be surprising if the "linguistic may ... have been two-way ... European words for silk ... are related to the oldest reconstructable Chinese words for silk, *s'e(g)" (Barber, 1999) thus the same situation could take us from *hu ma* to *haoma*.

In relation, it should be noted that along with the finds of cannabis flowers and braziers already discussed, bundles of ephedra twigs were found with the bodies of the Indo-European mummies at these same regional Chinese sites. This may be another important piece of evidence when trying to understand the identity of the ancient *soma/haoma* plant, as ephedra is used to this day as haoma and soma, in rites in both Persia and India, and were part of Sarianidi's finding in BMAC. Like the Haoma beverage which contained both Ephedra and cannabis, allied forms of the Chinese term "*huang-ma*" and other variations such as "*hu-ma*," "*ho-ma*" can and have been applied to both plants. S. Mahdihassan, who has given this etymology a lot of thought and study, has noted in 'The Seven Theories Identifying the Soma Plant':

> ... [T]his much may be said that the name soma is really Sau–Ma, and its original is Chinese as Hau-Ma, which means fire-ed-Hemp. The plant which was first discovered in china had yellow stalks which resembled the fibers of hemp in shape and in color. It may be boted [sic] that the hemp fibers are yellowish or orange colored and there was no word for orange hence it was compared to the color of fire. Thus soma or better sau-Ma would suggest a herb like hemp-fibers. It has therefore been mistaken for the hemp plant itself, which is also the Bhang plant (Mahdihassan, 1989).

One thing that comes to mind in this is that S. Mahdihassan assumes fire-hemp, identifies the color of the plant, and on that makes a connection to the color of ephedra's flowers. However we now know the Indo-European groups in China were burning cannabis, as were the Scythians and this could well identify that, and this has been the view of other researchers on the meaning of the term *hu-ma*. We also know in this same time period Taoist adepts were burning cannabis in incense censers and traveling to the "Land of the Immortals" likely influenced by the use they were witnessing among the Indo-European settlers, who used it in funerary rituals. Moreover the name *Hua-ma* favors this interpretation as in modern Chinese, Ephedra is actually a reversal of this term, *Ma Huang* (a situation that may address the ying yang like relationship between the two plants' varying effects!). Mahdihassan tries to address this situation in another article with its long explanatory title "Ephedra as Soma Meaning Hemp Fibers With Soma Later Misidentified As The Hemp Plant Itself" (1989).

> The two medicinal plants, Cannabis and Ephedra, are given very allied names in Chinese; Cannabis = Huang-Ma and Ephedra = Ma Huang. These names are mirror images of each other and as such next to being identical. The similarity of these names assumes that Ephedra, Ma-Huang, was discovered later than Hemp, Huang-Ma, and that Ephedra was given the name of Hemp itself. This is so because at that early stage Ephedra had no name of its own so that the designation of Hemp was transferred onto Ephedra... (Mahdihassan, 1982).

Mahdihassan notes that in later times cannabis became known under the more generally used name of *Ho-Ma*. Writing sometime prior to the discovery of the archaeological find of remnants from both cannabis and Ephedra at the Haoma temple in Margiana, as well as amongst the IE tribes in China, and recognizing the modern use of Ephedra in Haoma preparations, Mahdihassan concludes;

> Aryan ascetics must have ... come into contact with those of China with the results that the Chinese name, Ho-ma, for Ephedra, as also its energizing properties, were communicated to their Aryan compatriots. As a result, Ho-Ma, as Hao-Ma is found in Avesta while Ho-ma became So-Ma in Sanskrit; it is known that 'H' mutates into 'S'. This in brief is the etymology of the names Homa and Soma. It is natural to expect that the plant would be known first... and later the name of the plant Soma would be transferred on to the juice which is also called Soma (Mahdihassan 1982).

Mahdihassan was very close, but contrarily, the later Margiana find "shows that Haoma's preparation was a temple activity, along with extracting of juices from poppy, hemp and ephedra. It is clear that the whole consumable was called 'hom' and that the word did not correspond to the name of a specific ingredient. Among the effects of the ephedra itself was to speed up the metabolism and raise the blood pressure" (Mirfendereski, 2005). Mixed with cannabis and/or opium it must have held considerable mind bending effects. Thus, it seems likely that the name *hu ma*, which originated as a term for "cannabis" and served as the later basis in reversal for the name of ephedra, came into BMAC under the collective name Haoma, and was thus ritually prepared under this name, and variations of this etymology, ended up as Soma in India as well.

Cannabis was believed to have been couriered along the ancient route between the IE tribes in China, with their counterparts in BMAC, by IE Scythian traders. Interestingly one of the names of the Scythians from this area and time, was the Haomavarga, the "Haoma gatherers," and they were criticized by Zoroastrian writers for burning haoma as well as drinking it. In relation, it is important to note that both braziers and ritual vessels have been found at Scythian sites, that showed evidence of cannabis residues. This includes golden goblets that tested positive for both cannabis and opium, that the Russian archaeologist Anton Gas has suggested were used for the ritual consumption of *haoma*.

Zoroaster, as noted, took the polytheistic religion of the generation prior, through a number of innovative reforms, creating something closer to Monotheism, or Dualism. A major part of these reforms included drastic changes to the Haoma ritual, which from ancient accounts was a rather orgiastic event.

Zoroaster's Reforms of the Haoma Ritual

Zoroastrian mythology has it that the prophet Zoroaster was conceived after his body came down to earth through heavenly rain, which brought forth plants that were consumed by cows belonging to the people selected to become his parents. The cows gave milk which was pressed with Haoma and drunk by the prophet's parents, who later conceived him while making love for the first time (*Yasna* 9.13).

As an adult, *Yasna* has it, the God Haoma appeared before Zoroaster "at the time of pressing" in the form of a "beautiful man" (this is the only anthropomorphic reference) who prompts him to gather and press Haoma plants.

> At the proper time, at the Haoma-pressing Hour,
> Haoma went up to Zarathustra,
> who was purifying the fire and chanting the Gathas.
> Zarathustra asked him:
> Who are you,
> the most beautiful I have ever seen
> in the entire bony existence,
> with your sunny immortal life? (*Yasna* 9.1).

Thus he answered me,
the Orderly death-averting Haoma:
I am, O Zarathustra,
the Orderly death-averting Haoma.
Ask me hither, Spitamid[1],
press me forth to drink.
Praise me for strength,
like the future Revitalizers too will praise me (*Yasna* 9.2).

In light of this auspicious introduction it is curious to note that since the 19th century the view has been that Zoroaster condemned the Haoma ritual. The view that Zoroaster rallied against the Haoma cult is based on the following two verses. A thorough analysis of them, and the discussion they have engendered amongst religious scholars offers some very interesting insights into the matter:

> When, O Mazda, will the nobles understand the message? When will thou smite the filthiness of this intoxicant, through which the Karapans[2] evilly deceive, and the wicked lords of the lands with purpose fell? (*Yasna* 48.10).

> The "glutton" and the "poets" deposit their guiding thoughts here in this cord work
> Their "miracle-works," by daily pouring when they are ready to be help for the one possessed by the Lie
> And when the cow has been mistreated to (the point of) being killed (by him) who "purifies" the haoma (Dûraosha -death averter is used) by "burning" (*Yasna* 32:14).

Identification of cannabis is indicated in *Yasna* 32.14 reference to its fibrous qualities "The 'glutton' and the 'poets' deposit their guiding thoughts here in this cord work." This is also interesting in regard to the ritual weaving done in the cults of Cybelle, Asherah and Scythian groups that have been mentioned. Zoroaster is indicated specifically in opposition to the Scythian groups, as we shall see.

Dr. Ali Jafarey, who believes the original Haoma recorded in the *Yashts* was a cannabis-based preparation which Zoroaster prohibited, wrote of these verses: "Zarathustra condemns '*Dûraosha*' (Y.2.14). This word is definitely an epithet of Haoma alone and of no other object in the *Avesta*. Paradoxically, Zarathustra is shown by the composer/narrator of the *Hom Yasht* to be praising it by using this very word

1 *Spitamid* – brilliant, white, an epithet for Zoroaster.

2 *Karapan* – a class of priests opposed to Zoroaster and representing the pre Zoroastrian religion.

'*Dûraosha.*' How could he have a double standard?!?! The word literally means "far-from-death" and also "far-from-intellect." In another *Gathic* stanza, Y.48.10 Zarathustra calls it "*mûthrem mada ...*" literally "intoxicating urine" (Y.48:10)" (Jafarey , 2000).

> Two terms, mada (intoxicant) and duraosha (death repeller), used for the haoma drink in the Younger Avesta, are found in a manner that shows complete rejection of the substance and as well as the cult connected to it. Haoma stands condemned in the Gathas (32:14;48.10) (Jafarey, 2000).

This view has prevailed with a number of scholars as well as historians of the Zoroastrian faith. Daryoush Jahanian notes that "The text of the Gathas clearly indicates that in the rituals of the pre-Zoroastrian faith it [Haoma] was consumed by the princes (*Kavis*) and priests (*Karapans*), and caused them to behave irrationally. Zarathustra has derided and condemned the Haoma ritual by mentioning its epithets as invincible (!), and wisdom wasting (*Dura Osham*) (Y.32.14) and intoxicant (*Madahya*) (Y.48.10)" (Daryoush, 2005). This has been a longstanding view "It is therefore the haoma cult that Zarathustra is fighting" (Nyberg,1938).

This has been a difficult issue for many orthodox Zoroastrians to reconcile with their current religious practice, as a form of the Haoma ritual has continued down to the present day. Jafarey's claims that the pre-Zoroastrian version of the Haoma contained cannabis, has caused Jafarey to be viewed as a very controversial figure amongst fellow members of his faith.

The issue of Zoroaster's alleged condemnation of Haoma, in addition to other verses where Zoroaster sings the praises of Haoma, such as those below, have indeed been a cause of considerable confusion:

Thus said Zarathustra:

> Homage to Haoma! Good (is) Haoma,
> well set up (is) Haoma, set up straight,
> good, healing according to the established rules,
> of good shape, giving good invigoration,
> an obstruction-smasher,
> golden-colored with pliable twigs,
> the best when they drink (him)
> and the best flight-maker for the breath-soul. (*Yasna* .9.16)

> I call down, O golden one, your intoxication
> and your might and your obstruction-smashing power,
> your talent, your healing,
> your furthering, your increasing,
> your strength in the whole body,
> your all-adorned wisdom.
> (I call) down (all) that so that I may go forth
> among the living beings commanding at will,
> overcoming hostilities, conquering the Lie! (*Yasna* 9.17).

R.C. Zaehner noted in *Dawn and Twilight of Zoroastrianism* "It seems contrary to the evidence of the history of religion that a cult which has been fervently denounced by the founder of a religion should have been adopted ... by that founder's earliest disciples" (Zaehner, 1961). As Zoroastrian scholar Mary Boyce, Professor of Iranian Studies at the University of London, also noted:

> In this case the assumption of fervent denunciation was based on a Gathic verse Y.48.10: "When, O'Mazda ... wilt thou smite the filth (*muthra-*) of this intoxicant (*mada-*), with which out of enmity, the pagan priests ... deceive..." The term *mada-* is, however of wide application, and can be used of anything which exhilarates the spirits; and in view of the honored place enjoyed by haoma in Zoroastrianism it seems that the *mada* condemned here by the prophet must be something else perhaps a debilitating drug such as opium or hemp, which enslaves those who take it in chains of addiction. The words he uses are very strong (for *muthra* literally means either excrement or urine), and evidently expressed the harshest condemnation. The only other piece of positive evidence adduced from the Gathas for the prophet's condemnation of the *haoma* cult comes from an obscure verse Y.32.14, where amid a puzzling account of evil-doing the term *duraosa* occurs. This is a word of disputed meaning, which is known only as an epithet of *haoma*; but since translations of the Gathic passages in which it occurs differ widely, no sound deductions can be drawn from its implications there. As for negative evidence, there is the fact there is no explicit reference to haoma in the *Gathas*. Considering the character of these hymns, this is a weak argument to rely on (Boyce, 1982).

Now, Boyce here seems to suggest that the condemnation were against substances like cannabis and opium, and *Yasna* 32:14 uses the epithet *Dûraosha* to identify them, an epithet that elsewhere is only used in reference to haoma, but in this case it is not haoma, which she sees as something that would not have had the negative connotations she associates with cannabis and opium. However, this may well be more of an indication of Boyce's own personal bias about drugs, as current evidence makes an extremely plausible case for both cannabis and opium being used in the original preparations of haoma.

However, Mircea Eliade felt that recent "research has shown that the *haoma* ritual ... was not condemned by Mazdaism [Zoroastrianism], not even in the Gathas.... It seems ... that Zarathustra primarily opposed the excess of orgiastic rites, which involved countless blood sacrifices and immoderate absorption of *haoma*" (Eliade, 1978). "The violent hallucinations it [Haoma] engendered were probably intensified by the sight of blood" (Messadié & Romano, 1996). It has been suggested that Zoroaster "made modifications ... in the rituals..." (Boyce, 1990). Modifying her earlier view, Boyce explained:

> It seems very possible that Zoroaster ... did this because he regarded haoma as potentially dangerous in its potency to people (cf. his probable denunciation of it, as mada-, in Y. 48.10). An extract from it was drunk by warriors to stimulate their battle lust, and (on Vedic evidence) it was prominent in the cult of warlike Indra, to Zoroaster a daêva [demon].... If then he restricted its use in his own act of worship to yielding a libation to the Waters, it must be supposed that, as his religion spread, priestly converts in ever increasing numbers were reluctant to abandon the old rite, believed to give the celebrant an increase in awareness and power, and so this came to be reinstated as a preliminary to the one he had established (Boyce, 1990).

This brings us to some very interesting points; first it should be noted that Boyce had varied opinions on *Yasna* 48.10, in the above reference she seems more willing to accept the insulting reference of *mada* "intoxicating urine" and this as a possible reference to "a dehibilitating drug such as opium or hemp" both of which have been likely identified at the site of a pre-Zoroastrian Haoma Temple in BMAC. In relation to this it is interesting to return to the work of Dr. Ali Jafarey who believed that "the pre-Gathic Haoma was most probably '*bhang*' and that the post-Gathic priests, wanting to retain their pre-Gathic rituals, substituted it with 'Ephedra,' the present plant used in the Haoma ritual. I repeat, the present Haoma twigs used is not the original pre-Gathic plant. It is a substitute and devoid of the harms the original had" (Jafarey , 2000). A look at the other verse which has been identified as evidence of Zoroaster's prohibition of the cannabis in the Haoma offers evidence that collaborates with Jafarey's controversial solution to the debate:

> ...when the cow has been mistreated to (the point of) being killed (by him) who "purifies" the haoma by burning (*Yasna* 32:14).

Some have seen this reference as a condemnation of cattle sacrifice, but as this continued unfettered throughout the period, and even Zoroaster took part in such rites, this must not have been too much of a concern for the Persian reformer. Obviously there was more than this at issue in the *Yasna* 32.14 reference.

> In the prevailing religious tradition, Zarathustra probably found that the practice of sacrificing cattle, combined with the consumption of haoma (intoxicating drinks), led to orgiastic excess. Zarathustra in his reforms, did not, as some scholars would have it, abolish all animal sacrifice but simply the orgiastic and intoxicating rites that accompanied it. The haoma sacrifice, too, [after Zoroaster's reforms] was to be thought of as a symbolic offering. It may have [originally] consisted of unfermented drink or an intoxicating beverage or a plant (Hoiberg, et al., 2000).

Henrik Nyberg saw the *Yasna* 32.14 as evidence of a new cult in which the "haoma ... 'is brought to flames,'" instead of consumed as a consecrated beverage, and this new cult vied for power with Zoroaster (Nyberg, 1938). Similarly, the respected religious scholar R.C. Zaehner, saw the reference in *Yasna* 32.14 as not condemning cattle sacrifice, but likewise "a sacrament involving the immolation of the Haoma plant" (Zaehner, 1961). Zaehner notes that the sacrifice of the Bull was not at issue for the Persian reformer, as in *Yasna* 29.7 Zoroaster himself refers to the "sacred formula of the oblation of fat," indicating a ritual involving the fat of an animal which had been immolated.

> What Zoroaster actually condemns is not the Haoma ritual as such but some peculiar combination in which the plant appears to have been burnt.... He did not object to the haoma

> rite as such, but to the daeva-worshipers method of performing it (Zaehner, 1961).

This view has been shared by other sources as well, "Zoroaster ... condemns certain barbarian heretics who 'burn' the Haoma rather than drink it" (Bey, 2004). In *Incense and Poison Ordeals in the Ancient Orient* Allen Godbey expands on this theme, giving even clearer indications as to what was being burnt:

> Zarathustra ... was protesting without avail against the ancient Aryan intoxicant haoma or soma. The Sanskrit literature makes this religious narcotic all but omnipotent, and invokes it as a god, a great warrior conquering all enemies of man, a cure for every ill. Among the Iranic peoples this haoma seems to have been bhang, or Indian hemp, for Herodotus (iv. 75) tells us that the Iranic Scythians ... burned Indian hemp in their religious exercises, until bystanders were intoxicated with their fumes. In India the soma was the juice of a certain milkweed in some districts, but others insist that the bruised green leaves of hemp provide the orthodox soma (Godbey, 1930).

So it was the burning of Haoma that was at issue, which if it were cannabis, as has been suggested by literary, archaeological and other historical evidence, would make much more sense. Likewise Gérald Messadié and Marc Romano in reference to "sacrifices and the ritual consumption of haoma" have noted that as this was the long standing practice to which Zoroaster would have been exposed from the early stages of his life onwards. "In his youth Zoroaster may have participated in the ecstatic hemp ceremonies of Scythian shamans" (Messadie & Romano, 1996). In a rejection of these cultic activities the "Zoroastrian cult banned the use of intoxicants and haoma (soma), probably the old Persian name for hashish" (Bowles, 1977).

The Scythians, as discussed in Chapter 3, burned cannabis and inhaled its fumes, as well as prepared the Haoma beverage from it. Their transvestite priests prophesied while weaving from spindles, similar to the "cord work" condemned by Zoroaster. Just as the *Qedeshim* came to be rejected in Judaism, we see a similar rejection of homosexual acts in Zoroastrianism.

From the descriptions of their religious practices it is clear they were practicing the older pre-Zoroastrian form of Persian polytheistic nature worship. As Victor Sarianidi notes: "In the Avesta one finds numerous references to the fact the settled Zoroastrians had constant contacts with the nomadic Scythians who are mentioned under the name of *Saka* in the ancient Persian inscriptions…. The Scythian element played an important role in Zoroastrianism and … it … emerged in direct contact with the Scythian environment" (Sarianidi, 1998).

It seems clear that it was this older practice of burning Haoma, as had been done by the Scythians and their ancestors for millennia, which the "new" Zoroastrian religion was rallying against, rather than a new competing cult that was burning Haoma, as Nyberg suggested. Godbey's comments about the Scythian's burning hemp/Haoma in relation to those of Zaehner's and *Yasna* 32.14 give clear indications that this was the core issue for Zoroaster's reforms.

Thus Zoroaster's reforms are on par with those of the earlier Hebrew reformer Moses, who similarly rallied against the influences of the polytheistic Canaanite fertility cult in the Golden Calf incident and the orgiastic rites taking place. Gone from Zoroastrian worship were the Old Gods and orgiastic rites, all future Haoma sacrifice would come via the placebo sacrament void of its former entheogenic effects, and offered ritualistically to Zoroaster's one supreme God, Ahura Mazda:

> Let them go away from here,
> old gods and deceptive females!
> …here in this home, in which Ahura Mazdâ is sacrificed to,
> which (is that) of Haoma, conveyor of/through Order.(*Yasna* 10.1).

In this transference, Indra, a revered deity of the old pantheon, and the former celebrated recipient of haoma offerings, becomes in Zoroastrianism the leader of "false gods" (which refers to virtually all gods other than Ahura Mazda, Zoroaster's supreme deity). "Indra was undoubtedly associated with Haoma … in this religion against which Zarathustra rebelled – Indra is invoked by the Mitanni Aryans in 1380 B.C. – but he was dethroned and made a demon by Zarathustra" (Parpola, 1995). In the *Vendidad,* Indra is identified as one of the six chief demons; thus, in the eyes of Zoroaster and his new faith, Indra is the opponent of order, truth, and righteousness.

> From what has been stated, it clearly emerges that the appearance of Zarathustra in the ancient Arian milieu, that is widely similar to the Vedic-Indian, brought with it a complete upheaval. Zarathustra arises as a representative of a new religion contrary to the ancient Aryan religion. Not only that he

> condemned bloody sacrifices and haoma intoxication, but rather with him we seek the ancient names of deities in vain. They were replaced by spiritual entities, the so-called *Amesa Spentas*, the "holy immortals." After the results of the latest research, it can certainly no longer be doubted that the Amesa Spentas represent a spiritualising reinterpretation of the gods of the Indo-Iranian society (Widengren, 1965).

Although some figures from the earlier pantheon remained on as the *Amesa Spentas*, many more of the other long standing Aryan deities, such as Indra the original Lord of haoma, were transformed into demons through the words of Zoroaster and the cult which formed around his teachings. Meanwhile in India, in this time period, Indra was still held as supreme deity, and offerings of soma were still dedicated to him. Indra would however see a similar fall from grace, coinciding with the loss of the original soma identity, a few centuries later, as I have discussed in detail in *Cannabis and the Soma Solution* (2010).

The difficulty of many Zoroastrians in accepting the evidence of the reality of Zoroaster's reforms of the Haoma ritual, in light of its continued use, is on par with that of Christians who have a hard time reconciling the conflicting texts of the Hebrew Bible and New Testament, with the wrathful, jealous Jehovah of the Old, and the forgiving father of the New. In the case of the Bible, it is clearly due to the texts being composed by different authors, from different times, with different religious beliefs and practices. As Dr. Ali Jafarey explains, "The same holds true about the *Avesta*, 'the Sacred Books of the Zoroastrians'" (Jafarey, 2000).

Like many ancient myths and religious texts, it is likely that the accounts in the *Avesta* were passed down as an oral tradition, a reason for them being in verse, long before they were written down, which likely first took place "during the Achaemenian period (550-330 BCE) when the Iranians learned how to read and write" (Jafarey, 2000).

In 321 BCE the collection suffered a disaster from Alexander's invasion of Iran, which put an end to the Achaemenian Empire, and devastated the royal treasuries in which the *Avesta* was reportedly kept. During the Parthian period (250 B.C.-224 CE) an effort began to collect what remained in scattered records and the memories of the priest class. This considerable task was completed and the collection was collated, augmented, and canonized centuries later during the reign of the Sasanian King Chosroes I in about 560 CE. There was a Pahlavi translation and commentary created for every Avestan text and it was these Pahlavi renderings which the later priests counted on for expounding the religion. As the original language of *Avesta* became less and less utilized, it eventually became a mystical divine dialect that was not only unknown to the common people, but even the Sasanian and post-Sasanian priests.

> The collapse of the theocratic Sasanian Empire in 651 CE left the Zoroastrian church without its dominating royal support, and the whole system, including the Avestan and Pahlavi scriptures, began to fall apart. Nevertheless much of the collection survived as late as the 10th century CE, a period during which many of the Pahlavi scriptures were written – also revised to suit the times – in a rather salvage operation. It is estimated that between one third to one fourth of the entire collection has been salvaged. The extant Avesta, mostly religious, has been re-shaped, somewhat casually, sometimes after the 10th century, to make a little more than six books. (Jafarey, 2000)

Jafarey suggests that the *Gathas*, the texts attributed directly to Zoroaster "miraculously suffered no loss. We have the entire divine message of Zarathustra – fresh and inspiring – in the very words of the Teacher, a feature none of the ancient religions can boast of... The ... *Gathas* ... [are] the only doctrinal documents and ... the remaining parts of the extant *Avesta* and Pahlavi writings ... have their ethical, historical, geographical, and anthropological values. They are, nevertheless, of significant help in better understanding the *Staota Yesnya* from philological and sometimes philosophical points of view. And they are a part and parcel of the rich Iranian Heritage" (Jafarey, 2000).

> The ... post-Gathic period, clearly shows that Zarathustra ... [the author] of the *Gathas*, did not recite any "*Yasna* Liturgy" to perform the haoma ceremony. He only sang his Gathas, the only liturgy, before a fire-altar. It also shows the way the traditional priests brought in their age-old haoma cult into the Good Religion. This time it was not "bhang" or another strong intoxicant but a very mild substitute, ephedra. The *Yasht* mentions this mildness:"'Indeed all other intoxicants (*maidhyâongho*) are accompanied by wrath of the bloody standard but the intoxicant (*madho*) of Haoma has the right calm following it. Its intoxication gives lightness." It is acknowledged as an intoxicating drink and is compared with other intoxicants. The

> substitute "Ephedra" was soothing, indeed. Haoma was re-introduced to continue to be "central to the [expanded] Yasna liturgy" (Jafarey, 2000).

As Jafarey tried to explain to his detractors "No one is <<attacking the ritual use of Haoma.>> It has already been attacked and well attacked. Zarathustra was/is the first, foremost, and best to attack the ritual and/or any other use of the *haoma dûraosha*, the wisdom wasting drink" (Jafarey, 2000).

> It is true that haoma was an integral part of the Daevayasna rituals. It is true that since the composition of the Later Avesta, particularly the *Haoma Yasht* (*Yasna* 9-11), haoma (the substitute) has been <<central to the Yasna liturgy.>> It is true that in the Gathas, the original Haoma, bhang or any other instant intoxicant, stands rejected and condemned. It is equally true that the Sublime Songs, with their simple and sublime rituals, cannot accommodate the elaborate Haoma ceremony in any form (Jafarey, 2000).

Dr. Jehan Bagli sees the Haoma sacrifice as "one of the most controversial and debated" rituals of the Zoroastrian religion.

> The *Haoma* plant has a checkered history associated with it. Although the original identity of the plant has been obliterated through the antiquity, the plant is generally regarded as one of *ephedra* species. It is clearly evident from the Haoma yasht that the consecration of *Haoma* is a pre-Zarathustrian ritual. However history has evolved it as a central sacrament in the Zarathustrian traditional ritual. The twigs of *haoma* plant are ceremonially consecrated for use in the preparation of *parahaoma*. It is the enactment of straining of the crushed *haoma* and the pomegranate twigs with consecrated water that constitutes the ritual of *parahaoma*. (Bagli, 2005)

Thus, we can see that certain members of the Zoroastrian religion acknowledge that the Haoma was at one time a psychoactive sacrament, but was later replaced with the current placebo, void of the entheogenic properties of its former counterpart. As Prof. Victor Sarianidi explained:

> The linguists long ago noticed that in the ancient parts of the Avesta it is said that in the beginning the Prophet rejected this

> narcotic beverage but then it was included in his religious doctrine as one of its main cults. Some authors qualify this fact as a "restoration of the 'pre-Zoroastrian' ritual" ... Indeed, judging by the Margiana temples, this ritual beverage played almost the primary role in the religious ideas of Iranian paganism and if the Prophet had denied its role, he would have risked losing his followers. It seems that this was the compelling reason that made Zoroaster change his first decision and include this beverage as one of the main ritual ceremonies of his doctrine.
>
> ...Zoroaster was the product of the pagan community that was represented by that part of Iranian paganism which is best studied on the basis of the ... material of Margiana and Bactria.... The temples of Margiana and Bactria substantiate that the main cults that were practiced in this area were: (1) fire worship, (2) the libation of hallucinogenic drinks of the soma-haoma type, (3) and probably, the worship of water. In other words, the same cults that later became the main elements of the origin of Zoroastrianism (Sarianidi, 1998).

Patrick McGovern, a Professor of Anthropology and Scientific Director of the Biomolecular Archaeology Laboratory for Cuisine, Fermented Beverages, and Health at the University of Pennsylvania Museum in Philadelphia, referring to the work of Sarianidi at the Bactria Margiana Archaeological Complex has suggested in *Uncorking the Past: The Quest for Wine, Beer, and Other Alcoholic Beverages* (2009) that soma/haoma was likely a wine or mead-like infusion of cannabis. McGovern based his view on later Zoroastrian accounts, such as the *Book of Arda Wiraz*, which has cannabis (*bhanga*, or *mang*) mixed into wine. "From a chemical standpoint, the advantage of using an alcoholic beverage is that it dissolves the plant alkaloids" (McGovern, 2009).

> When I first considered wine as the most likely vehicle for haoma, it was under the assumption that the Margiana sites were within the sphere of the wine culture that is so well attested to in the Fergana Valley, even deeper in Central Asia.... The archaeological and botanical evidence from the ... excavations provide new clues for identifying haoma, at least in prehistoric Central Asia. If we accept Sarianidi's premise that a special beverage was being prepared ... with the reading that wine and a hallucinogen were mixed together in the Arda Wiraz story, then the evidence of ephedra, hemp and poppy pollen in

> the pottery vessels ... begins to make sense ... these plants... have been well known since antiquity as medicinal and narcotic agents in Central Asia.... With more archaeological and chemical investigation, we should be able to re-create the ancient haoma/soma or central Asian grog, which was probably much stronger than modern versions (McGovern, 2009).

In relation, it is interesting to note that the Vedic God most associated with Soma, Indra, also received offerings of wine. Michael Witzel, Professor of Sanskrit at Harvard University and the editor of the Harvard Oriental Series has noted: "When Alexander [the Great] came across the vines in the eastern Hindu Kush, he immediately concluded that this area must have been that of Dionysus. Indeed, the inhabitants of Nuristan and Kashmir (both before Islam) and of the modern pagan Kalash Land (north-western Pakistan) still grow vines and press grapes there each fall. The new wine is still dedicated to Indra" (Witzel, 2012). As Dr. Richard Stoneman, a professor of classics and ancient history, describes of the Greek connection in T*he Greek Experience of India: From Alexander to the Indo-Greeks*: "It is sometimes argued that this Dionysus is a form of Indra as first king, culture-hero of the Aryans, warrior-leader and bringer of agriculture. Martha Carter produces some compelling evidence that Alexander's expedition may have wandered into the Indrakun festival in the Kafir lands, in November or January, which involved a dancer dressed as a horned goat, behaving lewdly, while wine was pressed and drunk" (Stoneman, 2019).

Both Mircea Eliade, and Erwin Rohde, one of the great German classical scholars of the 19th century, suggested a role for cannabis in the formation period of Dionysus cult. More recently Professor of classics, Carl Ruck, has suggested that "Since the wine of Dionysus is a mediation between the god's wild herbal ancestors and the civilized phenomenon of his cultivated and manufactured manifestation in the product fermented from the juice of the grape, it is most probable that this was the way in which the Greeks incorporated hemp into their pharmacopoeia" (Ruck, 2007). (As we will discuss later Dionysus, as well, has his own overlap into the Jewish conceptions of their god).

Such infusions were known in ancient Greece, and these as well are generally believed to have contained cannabis, under the names "*thalassaegle*," "*potammaugis*" and "*gelotophyllis*" which were recorded by Democritus (*circa* 460 BCE.) and later referred to by Pliny. "The *gelotophyllis* of Pliny ... a plant drunk in wine among the Bactrians, which produced immoderate laughter, may very well be identical with hemp, which still grows wild in the country around the Caspian and Aral Seas" (Houtsma, et al., 1936/1993). Pliny (23-79 CE) quotes the following description from Democritus:

> The *Thalassaegall* he speaks of as being found on the banks of the river Indus, from which circumstance it is also known as *potamaugis*. Taken in drink it produces delirium, which presents to the fancy visions of a most extraordinary nature. The *theangelis*, he says, grows upon Mount Libanus in Syria, upon the chain of mountains called Dicte in Crete, and at Babylon and Susa in Persia. An infusion of it imparts powers of divination to the Magi. The *geolotophyllis*, is a plant found in Bactriana , and on the banks of the Borysthenes. Taken internally with myrrh and wine all sorts of visionary forms present themselves, excite the most immoderate laughter.

Interestingly, Bactria, mentioned in the quote from Pliny, is part of the Bactria Margiana Archaeological Complex (BMAC), a site where as we have seen, the Russian archaeologist Victor Sarianidi has claimed to have found ancient temples where there was evidence of cannabis, ephedra and opium in the preparation of haoma.
We certainly know from later ancient references in Zoroastrian texts, that cannabis-infused wines were in fact consumed for visionary purposes, even visiting the land of the dead.

Banging on About *Bhanga*!

Part of the reason for the confusion regarding Zoroaster's relationship with Haoma has to do with the fact that another plant name begins to take precedent in the Magi literature at the time of Zoroaster's prohibitions, *banga,*[3] a term that is still in use to this day in both Persia and India (*bhang*), and is generally used to describe cannabis and its products, although this has not always been the case. As with the identification of Haoma and Soma, there is debate surrounding the identity of the plant designated by *banga,* and its Pahlavi counterpart *mang*.

There is considerable confusion regarding *bhang* and *mang,* in both its method of use and identity. In 1938 the renowned Swedish Orientalist and historian of religion, Henrik Samuel Nyberg wrote the following regarding the role of *bhanga* in the Zoroastrian reli-

3 As with a lot of the words we have looked at there are various phonetic translations of this word, depending on the translator.

gion, which he identified with cannabis, as had a number of other historians:

> Now hemp (*bangha, banha*) really appears in the *Avesta*. In the *Gathas* it is not found, but in the *Fravasi-yast*, that contains long lists of the members of the Zoroastrian ancient congregations, a man emerges with the meaningful name Pouru-bangha "possessing much hemp" (Nyberg, 1938).

As shall be discussed, Nyberg went on to describe the use of cannabis by a variety of Zoroastrian heroes, as well as detailing the later rejection of the ritual use of cannabis by the Parsi, as indicated in the surviving Zoroastrian documents. Considering that cannabis is still known both in Indian and Persia under the names *bhang, banj, bang,* this interpretation of the Avestan texts seemed clear upon a first reading; as time went on however, the matter has become considerably confused. Some sources have come to see the Avestan *banha*, or *bhanga* and the Pahlavi *mang,* as references to henbane or datura.

As we shall see the more logical and general view is that "*banga*," "*banha*" and "*mang*," all with "*an*" in them, follow in league with other terms for cannabis in languages which originated from Indo-European dialects; English, *cannabis*; French, *chanvre*; German *hanf*; Indian *sana* and *bhang*, Avestic *baŋha* etc...

Beyond the etymological argument, the suggestions of Henbane and Datura, as *mang,* can be seen as far too toxic to have been the plant ingested in such quantities in the ancient texts.

Much of the debate on the issue was raised by the Iranist and linguist Walter Bruno Henning. In his virulent rejection of H.S. Nyberg's view, Henning put forward that the Avestic *baŋha-* and the Middle Persian *mang* did not mean "hemp," and that they instead referred to "henbane." Henning's view was that the New Persian *bang* did not acquire the meaning "hemp" before the 12th century (Henning, 1951). And of the role of cannabis in the Avestan literature? "There is nothing here to show that Zoroaster so much as knew of the existence of hemp" (Henning, 1951). Further, Henning asserted that it "is very far from certain that the Avestan word *banha* is connected at all with Pahlavi, *mang,* Persian *bang*" (Henning, 1951). There is little support for this view, among Iranists or linguists.

The German Iranist, Geo Widengren, who disagreed with Henning on a number of points, and agreed with the earlier identification of *bhanga/mang* with hemp, as put forth earlier by Nyberg in 1938.

> The ... usage of bang (alternatively mang) obviously proceeds the Avestan terminology. Indeed it is disputed that bangha > bang (mang) means (Indian) hemp but this objection is not well-founded in any respect (Widengren, 1965).

Most preposterous of Henning claims is the statement that: "The derivatives of Indian hemp known as *bang, hasis* and so on, were not known in Iran anywhere before the eleventh century of our era at the earliest. Acquaintance with Indian hemp is ultimately due to the Muslim conquest of India in the first years of that century" (Henning, 1951). Henning ignores the fact that Zoroaster lived among Scythian groups who we know used cannabis from both written (Herodotus) and now, archaeological, evidence. As well, in regard to the claim there was no awareness of hemp's intoxicating properties till the 11th century, this is discounted by the works of the 5th century north Armenian monk Eznik, who lived amongst the Zoroastrians (and preached against their religion). Eznik was clearly familiar with cannabis, referring to its medicinal value, as well as a treatment for "wantonness" (Eznik, Book I. 68).

As Henning explained the situation as he saw it:

> The Persian word *bang,* in so far as it means "Indian hemp," is a loan-word from the Indian term *bhanga.* In Persian – unfortunately – the loan-word collided with an indigenous word *bang* which also designated a plant, namely, "henbane" (Henning, 1951).

After going through Henning's sources, it seems he was only able to find references supporting his view as far back as the Islamic period; the rest of his claim is based on his mistaken assumption that *mang/bang* was a potentially toxic substance. Henbane's designations as "*bang*" is clearly the later, and not original situation. Prof. Franz Rosenthal, who was a well known expert in medieval and ancient Middle Eastern cultures and languages, explained: "As is well known, *banj,* in its pre-Islamic history, represented, in fact, 'hemp'" (Rosenthal, 1971). However "in the usage of [*banj* in] Muslim times, it was commonly the scientific word for "henbane," ... Physicians and scientists appear to have been by and large consistent in their usage of *banj* for henbane"(Rosenthal 1971). It was in later times, "Among the Persians the Indian name in the form *bang* became the general term for narcotic and was given to the henbane" (Houtsma, et al., 1936/1993). Thus the Persian term for cannabis was later borrowed and applied to henbane, but this happened, in the opinion of Rosenthal and others, after the conquest of Islam.

In *Haoma and Harmaline,* David Flattery suggests that both the Haoma and bhang, in the Zoroastrian references, can be identified with the harmaline-producing plant Syrian rue, Peganum harmala. Although it seems likely that Syrian rue, or Harmaline as this duo prefers to have it called, was an additive to incense braziers and other concoctions in the ancient world, the identification of it with *bhang* is wholly hypothetical and unsubstantiated by any historical reference whatsoever (as is the duos designation of Harmaline as the Soma/Homa).[4]

In respect to this, even Flattery's own co-author Martin Schwartz disputed Flattery's identification of *mang* and *bhang* with Syrian rue. In Schwartz's view *mang\bhang* likely had a more generic meaning, "psychotropic substance," but alternatively, one "which could give specific senses 'henbane, datura'..." (Flattery & Schwartz 1989). Schwartz also suggested that the term *mang,* had indications of deception; "It may be assumed that Iranian inherited two homophonous words, *manga* – 'deceit, trickery' and **manga* ... 'magic potion, hallucinogen'" (Flattery & Schwartz 1989).

It should be noted that even during periods of the Zoroastrian use of cannabis, this was not at all a common practice and was far from wide spread. The use of *bang/mang* in the Zoroastrian period was strictly prohibited from anyone but the most elite members of that society. The secrecy surrounding the use of bang/mang is likely largely responsible for much of the confusion surrounding the terms *mang* and *bang.* In "Quests and Visionary Journeys in Sasanian Iran," Shaul Shaked notes that the use of *mang* (which he saw as cannabis) for visionary quests, "was not a way open to all":

> It was confined to select individuals, who would have regarded themselves as representative of the community, and who would then reveal to the others what they had been privileged to witness. Even for those people this was not a trivial experience that could be undertaken casually or easily repeated. Such journeys were rare occasions, surrounded by grave risks. The danger lay in the very fact that this was the path trodden by the dead, and would have to be brought back to life. Certain encounters along the way may put the power of endurance of the traveler to the test (Shaked, et al., 1999).

Clearly, such limited and secretive use as this would have created a situation where few were even aware of the closely guarded secret of the source of Iranian revelation. The secretiveness with which *bang/*

4 For a full discussion of this situation, see *Cannabis and the Soma Solution* (2010).

mang would have been used throughout the Zoroastrian period was likely later compounded through initial Muslim prohibitions against intoxicants. Further confusion may have arisen as to *bhanga*'s identity may have occurred in times of shortage, and through its association with other plants used in its stead the term *bhanga* came to be applied to a variety of intoxicating plants. A similar situation can be seen with both *soma* and *haoma*.

Undoubtedly, Datura and Henbane were, and still are, sometimes added by unscrupulous vendors to preparations of *bhang*, to increase the effects of weaker concoctions when good cannabis is not available, and this may have generated confusion at some point. In later Persian times the "*fedayeen* were always described as using beng, or hemp, and henbane, mixed" (Burman, 1987). There were definitely distinguishing factors between unadulterated hemp products and preparations made with henbane, as the use of cannabis could be associated "with fits of rage ... especially if there is an admixture of any preparation of henbane" (Houtsma, et al., 1936/1993). In reference to the use of hashish in early 20th century Islam it has been noted that "sometimes to increase its intoxicating effect it is mixed with the seeds of the henbane (*hyocyamus muticus, sekaran*) or stramonium (*datura*)" (Houtsma, et al., 1936/1993). Likewise in India, "Datura ... seeds are sometimes mixed with *Sidhi* (*Bhang*) ... to induce delirious intoxication, and with other narcotics to intensify their actions" (Gerloczy, 1897). In regard to cannabis in India "the question of adulterants, especially datura must always be borne in mind" (Smith & Taylor, 1920).

The use of *bhang* to designate intoxicating plants in general seems to be much more identifiable in the Persian language than the Indian, and as the term in both languages is now generally assumed as designating cannabis, it seems unlikely that *bhang* originated as a generic term, and this use of the word developed in later times, otherwise these multiple meanings would have carried over into the Indian language. This linguistic situation has never been adequately explained by any of the researchers who see the term as originating as a generic name for psychoactive plants in general.

Proponents of the 'henbane' theory offer no reasonable examples opposing the more generally accepted view that *mang, bang* were references to cannabis, nor do they adequately explain why if this were the case in the ancient world, how the designation of cannabis as *bhanga* came about in both the ancient Persian and Indian dialects. On the other hand a reasonable explanation has been given on how the designation of the Persian term *bang*, meaning 'hemp', came to be borrowed and corrupted as *banj*, meaning '*henbane*' in the later Islamic period.

"*Bhang*" as "cannabis" has clearly been the long standing view; As James Samuelson noted in the 19th century in *The History of Drink*: "A ... very deleterious drink called "*banga*" is mentioned in the Zend-Avesta.... Like the modern *bang*, referred to ... in India, it is believed to have been extracted from the hemp plant (*Cannabis sativa)*" (Samuelson,1880). In the *Avesta*, Bleek and von Spiegel recorded, "*Bana* is the *Cannabis sativa*, Skr. *Bhanga*" (Bleek & Spiegel, 1864). As Darmesteter also noted in his translation of The Zend-Avesta; "*Banga*, is *bang* or *mang*, a narcotic made from hemp seed" (Darmesteter, 1880).

This designation of *mang, bhang* as identifying cannabis has also been accepted by a variety of Zoroastrian scholars, such as Dr. Jahanian Daryoush, who refers to *bhang* in his essay 'Medicine in Avesta and Ancient Iran': "Bangha (Avesta: *bhangh*, Sanskrit: *bhanga*, Persian: *Bang*, hashish) It is extracted from the seeds of *Cannabis Indica* (hempseed or Per: *shahdaneh*) and has hallucinating effects. In ancient Iran it was mixed with wine to deliver anesthesia" (Daryoush, 2005). As Parvaneh Pourshariati has also noted in *The Decline and Fall of the Sasanian Empire*, "mang – a mixture of hemp and wine, with intoxicating properties" (Pourshariati, 2008). Referring to the variation of the "b-" in the Avestan, to the "m-" in the Pahlavian, the authors of the *Annual of Armenian Linguistics* used the following examples, which also identify hemp with the terms in question, "Zoroastrian Pahl. *mang, bang* 'hemp'. Old Indian *bhanga-*; *mag-*, *bag-* 'to intoxicate'" (Cleveland State University, 1987). As also noted by other Zoroastrian scholars; "*Bhanga* ... or *mang*, a narcotic made from hempseed ... the dried leaves and small stalks of *Cannabis indica*" (Dubash, 1903); "hemp (Av *ba gha-* Phl. *mang*)" (De Jong, 1997).

E.J. Brill's First Encyclopaedia of Islam 1913-1936, records; BENG, (Sanskr. *bhanga*, Avest. *Banha*, Pahl. *bang, mang*, hemp), strictly the name of various kinds of hemp" (Houtsma, et al., 1987). In reference to Zoroastrian expeditions into the world of the afterlife, Shaul Shaked noted that "The preparation of this journey was done ... by administering to the officiant a dose of *mang* (hemp), mixed with wine" (Shaked, 1999). "Zoroaster is commonly said to have spiked the haoma with mang, which was probably hashish. It would have prolonged the intoxication and further stimulated the imagination of the drugged man. Of such are the wonders of Heaven" (Oliver, 1994). In the Zoroastrian tale "... the *Artak Viraz Namak* ... Hell, Purgatory, and Heaven, the rewards bestowed on the good, and the punishment awaiting the sinner are here described in a vision induced by hashish" (Campbell, 2000). Referring to this same account, van Baaren and Hartman also noted the hero "imbibes an intoxicant composed of wine and hashish and after this his body sleeps for seven days and nights while his soul undertakes the journey" (van Baaren & Hartman,1980). 19th century author James Francis Katherinus also refers to the "enlightening prophet drug *Bangha* (*Cannabis Indica*), the Hashish by which the Zoroastrian priests were inspired" (Hewitt, 1901). This was also the view of Nyberg (1938), whose work we have discussed, and the German Iranist, Geo Widengren (1965), as well as more recent researchers: "The *Zend-Avesta*, the holy book of Zoroastrianism, which survives in fragments, dating from around 600 BCE in Persia, alludes to the use of *Banga* in a medical context, identified as hemp" (Russo, 2005).

Possibly, having followed up on Henning's research regarding *mang*, Flattery and Schwartz saw that the references Henning cited didn't really take the identification of *banj* as henbane any earlier than the Islamic period. Thus in order to make their case, the co-authors decided to take it a step further, and included ancient India, with a claim that the intoxicating properties of hemp were unknown until the early medieval period there as well!: "With regards to 'hemp' called *bhanga* and *sana* in Sanskrit, there is no evidence for its use as an intoxicant in either India or Persia before well within the Islamic era" (Flattery & Schwartz, 1989).

Instead, in regard to the Indian references, Flattery and Schwartz claim all early Indian mentions of the term only refer to the fiber of the cannabis plant. The Duo even take this view regarding the *Atharvaveda*, reference to *bhang* as being amongst herbs that release one from anxiety and under the dominion of the God Soma, stating that this identifies the hemp plant's fibrous qualities and are "due to its use as a traditional means of binding ... it is also a means of fastening amulets," which would seem to have little reference to the plant's use as a medicine against anxiety as described in the *Atharvaveda*. Indeed the authors offer little in the way of evidence for their novel interpretation that the passage makes reference to fiber.

> The dismissal of hemp, as being purely used for fiber or "binding" and not burning, would seem to contradict the meticulous research of Flattery.... That a culture obsessed with psychoactive plants and fire rituals would be ignorant of Cannabis as either a fuel or entheogen would seem patently absurd, especially as it is mentioned explicitly in the Atharva-Veda in

> the context of Soma, and has an ancient use in the region... (Dannaway, 2009).

As well, it should also be noted that both Haoma and Soma are described as something that could be woven. Vedic references to Soma's fibrous qualities have long been noted. In *A History of Indian Literature,* the authors write that: "At the consecration of the Soma-sacrifice the sacrifice ties round his girdle a belt made of hemp and reed-grass with the words 'You are the power of Angiras [ancient fire and magic priests] soft like wool; lend me power!' Then he binds a knot in his underclothing and says 'you are the knot of soma'" (Winternitz & Srinivasa, 1996). "In the *Sukla Yajurveda* (IV.10), *mekhala,* the girdle, is described as 'tying the knot of Soma.' Is this an implication that the Soma plant had the same fibrous qualities as the hemp plant?" (Merlin, 1972).[5]

The assertion that there was no knowledge of cannabis' intoxicating properties among an IE culture such as that of the authors of the Vedas is as preposterous as Henning's statement on the same situation in Persia. Scythian contact with Zoroastrians and the more ancient Iranian religion it grew out of, is explicit, and artifacts well attest to their burning and consumption of cannabis. Likewise in India, cannabis would have traveled there with the Indo-European authors of the Vedas, as well as Scythians who dominated Northern India for a few centuries on either side of the CE.

As noted by other researchers: "In India and Iran, it [cannabis] was used as an intoxicant known as *bhang* as early as 1000 BC" (Goldfrank, 2002); "The narcotic properties of *C. Sativa* were recognized in India by 1000 BC." (Zohary & Hopf, 2000); "The narcotic and euphoric properties of cannabis were known to the Aryans who migrated to India thousands of years ago and there is little doubt they made use of these properties" (Chopra & Chopra, 1965); Cannabis' "narcotic properties were known in India by (1000 BCE)" (Southworth, 2005); "The use of hemp for medicinal purposes has been known in India from ancient times when it is highly probable that it was also used in a restrictive way, as an intoxicating drug" (Hassan, 1922).

Despite some excellent etymological and historical research, at best Schwartz's explanation in regards to *bhanga*/Soma/Homa/can-

5 The following verse has indications of rope in relation to Haoma: "May not Haoma bind you like he bound the villain" (*Yasna* 11.7). "In the *Avesta* it was Haoma for whom Ahuramazda first brought the 'sacred girdle, star-begemmed, woven by the two Spirits'" (Taraporewala, 1926). This Vedic description gives us connotations of medicinal, fibrous, and psychoactive properties: "The restless Soma – you try to grab him but he breaks away and overpowers everything. He is a sage and seer inspired by poetry. He covers the naked and heals all who are sick. The blind man sees; the lame man steps forth" (Rig Veda 8:79).

nabis/harmaline adds to the linguistic confusion on the matter, and few scholars agree with his assessment on the subject. As Schwartz tries to explain away the reality of the ancient connection between cannabis, *mang, bhanga* and Haoma, he only digs a deeper hole.

Considering my own knowledge of the data collected in the composition of this book and other projects as well (Bennett, et al., 1995; Bennett & McQueen, 2001: Bennett 2010; Bennett 2018), to suggest that cannabis was unknown in this area of the world is a curious statement indeed. These authors are suggesting that both in Persia and India, cultures which had extensive herbal knowledge, which were making hempen ropes and clothes, and which came into contact with other cultures who used cannabis as an intoxicant, had somehow let the resinous properties of its flowers escape them!

Zoroaster and Bhanga

As it has been noted that Zoroaster took both the Persian religion and the Haoma sacrifice itself through a number of reforms which indicated the extraction of cannabis from the Haoma recipe, and as the term *bhanga* starts to play a role around this same time period, becoming *mang* in later Pahlavi translations, it seems probable that there is a relationship between the two.

Perhaps Zoroaster, who, according to Eliade was unhappy with the "immoderate absorption of *haoma*" amongst the masses who used it in nocturnal "orgiastic" rituals, decided to weaken the punch, so to speak? The coup in this case being the removal of cannabis from the Haoma recipe, and the reinstitution of a more mildly-psychoactive placebo drink as a substitution, while the use of cannabis continued to be used secretly by Zoroaster and his selected elite.

The surviving tradition clearly indicates that Zoroaster continued to utilize cannabis for his own Shamanic purposes and for initiation of a chosen few, under the name *bhanga*. This situation accounts for both the appearance of *bhanga/mang* in the Zoroastrian tradition as well as the survival of the tradition which currently recognizes Ephedra as the *Hom*. This scenario also substantiates the view that for a time "Haoma was under the ban of the great reformer [Zoroaster]" (Griswwold, 1923). Post-Zoroastrian reform references indicate that cannabis was infused in both wine, and in some accounts, the ephedra-only haoma that replaced the original formula.

Harri Nyberg in "The Problem of the Aryans and the Soma: the botanical evidence" makes some interesting comments on the connection between bhang with Haoma/Soma which must be addressed:

> In R.V. [*Rig Veda*] 9.16.13, the word [*bhang*] is used an epithet of soma.... In Iran, modern Persians have the name *bang*, which corresponds to the Avestan *bhanga*, and Pahlavi *mang*. In the Artai Viraz Namak, [Ardu Viraz] *mang* is mentioned several times (*mang, mang-i-Vistap, mang-i-Zaratuxst...*), often translated as "a narcotic." "Medical *mang*" (*mang besaz*) is mentioned in the *Bundahisin* 4:20, and it also states that *mang-I Vistaspan* was mixed with *Hom* (Denkard 7.4.85...)... Thus, in the Avesta or the Pahlavi texts *banja, mang* or *bang* are not considered to be identical with *haoma*. We have to conclude that hemp is certainly not identical with *soma/haoma*, although it might have been an ingredient in some preparations derived from the original *soma/haoma*. (Nyberg, 1995)

Nyberg discounted cannabis as an ingredient in the original Haoma, based upon the appearance in Zoroastrian literature as something separate, although acknowledging at the same time, it may have been used in the preparation. This reasoning was shared by Yves Bonnefoy and Wendy Doniger (returning to the subject more than two decades after her work with Wasson)[6] who also noted in reference to the identity of Haoma: "Hashish has been considered (*bhanga* in Iranian, *bhang* in Sanskrit), but a passage from the Denkart seems to contradict this suggestion, for we read that Zarathustra's patron, King Vishtaspa, drank one day a cup of *haoma* mixed with hashish ... so the two ingredients cannot have been the same" (Bonnefoy & Doniger, 1993).

But this view would be hard to maintain in light of the fact that the shamanic use of *bhanga/mang* in the Zoroastrian tradition coincides with massive changes in the Haoma ritual which changed the formula, removing the cannabis and making the Haoma into a placebo sacrament with only the mildly stimulating effects produced by Ephedra remaining. Zoroaster prohibited the mass use of cannabis in the Haoma, in a revolt against the nocturnal orgiastic rites that accompanied its consumption, but then continued to use extracts of cannabis in potent preparations for shamanic trance amongst his inner circle. Clearly, as with the Indian tradition of Soma, the distinction that made any preparation Haoma in Zoroastrian times was the act of consecration, and as such the Zoroastrian sacrament maintained the name even without the plant with which its use and name originated.

This brings about a number of important points. Psychoactive preparations of Haoma, from the earlier Avestan accounts, seem

6 *Soma: Divine Mushroom of Immortality* (1968).

different in effect than those associated with the shamanic trance induced by *bhanga/mang*. Haoma, being a preparation of cannabis mixed with the stimulant Ephedra, was used in nocturnal rituals, where there was singing, dancing, animal sacrifices and in some cases orgiastic activities. In this scenario, the Haoma was not particularly directed at inducing a psychonaut into a shamanic trance, but rather a collective, awake, and involved shared ecstatic experience.

Bhanga/mang, on the other hand, was, from the ancient accounts, used in a potent shamanic preparation that would quite literally send the devotee into a death-like coma that was filled with vivid dream-like visions. Because of these descriptions, few researchers have considered cannabis potent enough to have been the substance in question, but this is an assumption based on dosage. Although such a powerful experience would seem unlikely to most western users of cannabis, as Dr. Michael Aldrich explains:

> There is a myth that pot is a mild and minor drug. Usually in context of American usage it is, but it doesn't have to be. The hard part about expressing this, however, is that the anti marijuana people who pose visions of disaster about "hashish" or about "legalizing the stronger forms of cannabis" are also wrong. In and of itself there's nothing wrong with cannabis being a potent hallucinogen; this has certainly accounted for its vast popularity through these many centuries. When one seeks a shaman's drug one generally wants something more powerful than a "mild hallucinogen." Of course, knowing when and where to use cannabis at a dosage or strength suitable for real visions is also important. It's obviously not a good idea to try in an unrefined social context, or when working in the fields or factory. This use of cannabis has traditionally been confined, by rational custom in ancient societies, to rituals which help define and control, measure and magnify, the raw experience (Aldrich, 1980).

As it stands, in my own research, I have come across numerous references that refer to descriptions from a variety of sources detailing such experiences induced by cannabis preparations, particularly amongst 19th century occultists. Besides the well known vivid voyages into the astral realms recorded by members of *le Club des Haschichins*, which included such figures as Alexander Dumas, Victor Hugo, Theophile Gautier, Gerard de Nerval and Charles Baudelaire, we also have more than a dozen such accounts recorded in Cahagnet's *Sanctuary of Spiritualism* (1848) which recorded the descriptions of a variety of

French psychonauts who partook of three grams of hashish, and were interpreted by Cahagnet as evidence of communication with the World of the Dead. Other such examples have been recorded (Bennet, 2018).

Health and consciousness researcher Andrew Weil gives us a first hand account of an intense case of marijuana overdose:

> In 1968, when I was studying marijuana in Boston, I deliberately consumed [orally] an overdose (6 grams) of potent hashish in order to experience the reaction.... The effects of the drug were felt within forty minutes and were pleasant but strong for about a half-hour. Thereafter, things became quite confusing. I could not understand what was said to me, felt physically sick, and soon was unfit to do anything but lie in bed and wait for morning. Auditory hallucinations were prominent, especially threatening voices that rose in volume to a crescendo, then faded out. For about twelve hours I remained in a stage of consciousness between sleeping and waking, marked by vivid nightmares. Lucid intervals were rare; for much of the time I did not know where I was, even thinking I was six years old and sick from measles. By morning, most of the worst symptoms had disappeared, but I had a powerful hangover that left me prostrate for another twenty-four hours. I would not willingly repeat the experience (Weil 1972).

Under the proper set and setting, such as the context of religious initiation, an experienced Shaman leading a new initiate could channel such effects as described by Weil in a number of directions. In reference to Thracian Shaman, who burned cannabis in rituals, Eliade suggests that such experiences led to the belief in a "soul" that could leave the material body:

> Ecstatic experiences strengthened the conviction that the soul is not only autonomous but that it is capable of unio mystica with the divinity. The separation of soul from body, determined by ecstasy, revealed ... the fundamental duality of man ... [and] the possibility of a purely, spiritual post-experience.... Ecstasy could ... be brought on by certain dried herbs... (Eliade,1982).

In a footnote to dried herbs, Eliade referred to the use of hemp among the Thracians, stating that the *Kapnobatai* [Those who walk in smoke] were "dancers and 'shamans' who used the smoke of hemp to bring ecstatic trances" (Eliade, 1982).[7]

Nyberg felt that the terms *mang,* and *bhanga* were not only references to hemp, but more specifically a "hemp extract" (1938). From the descriptions of the potency and the way it was used, added to wine or "*hom,*" this seems a likely case.

Later Islamic accounts refer to a potent hash oil preparation known as *dūḡ-e waḥdat,* which may be similar to the Persian *bhanga/mang.* "Hashish oil is generally consumed by thoroughly mixing a drop of it with a liter of *dūḡ* (a drink made from yogurt), and drinking the resulting mixture. This mixture, which is extremely potent and dangerous, is called *dūḡ-e waḥdat* (the *dūḡ* of annihilation)" (Gnoli 1979). As *Encyclopedia Iranica* describes:

> DŪḠ-EWAḤDAT "beverage of unity," concoction made from adding hashish extract (*jowhar-e ḥaīš*) to diluted yogurt (Šahrī, VI, pp. 412, 423). The resulting tonic is drunk by certain mystics as a hallucinogen during their rites. ʿAlī-Akbar Dehḵodā, in his compendium of Persian proverbs and dicta (1339 Š./1960, I, p. 255), quoted a verse from Kamāl-al-Dīn Ḵojandī (d. 803/1399) in which the use of the narcotic by a Sufi sheikh is mentioned. Apparently some less scrupulous Sufis used the drink to attract followers (Šahrī, VI, p. 419) (Omidsalar, 1999).

The use of *dūḡ-e waḥdat* has continued through to the modern-day in Iran, despite considerably harsh penalties surrounding its consumption and distribution. The preparation is also known as "bangaab" (bang = hashish + aab = water), but more commonly it is *dugh* (water + yogurt, scented with herbs) and powdered hashish. Dūḡ-e waḥdat is a favored libation of the dervishes). Its potential to make one unconscious has resulted in some rape cases where it was

7 Interestingly, Eliade, an illustrious Professor of religious history may have been writing here from personal experience, for as a young man in India, in 1931, he experimented with both Opium and Bhang (cannabis).

In March 1924, at the age of only 17 years, Mircea Eliade published (under the pseudonym Silviu Nicoară) a courageous article, "The Artists and the Hashish," explaining in it why many artists and writers (Gérard de Nerval, Alexandre Dumas-Père, Theophile Gauthier, Charles Baudelaire etc. have used the intoxication with hashish: in order to enhance their intellectual creativity and mobility. "Taken in infinitesimal quantity – wrote the adolescent Eliade, quoting Charles Richet –, [the hashish] unfreezes the mind making it proper for things hard to understand and gives it also an amazing continuity of ideas." The adolescent Eliade concluded that, taken in big doses, the hashish induces ecstatic states: "In that moment the soul leaves the body and you feel that you are immersing into ether" ("Ziarul ştiinţelor populare" [*The Journal of Popular Sciences*], no. 12, 18th of March 1924, p. 172). (Ostineau, 2007)

alleged to have been given to women to knock them out. (It was likely a preparation such as this that Henning referred to regarding cannabis' non-toxicity even in extreme doses).

In relation to this, it is important to note that one of the effects attributed to *bhanga/mang* in the Zoroastrian accounts is that it "brought about a condition outwardly resembling sleep (i.e. stard) in which targeted visions of what is believed to be a spirit existence were seen" (Flattery & Schwartz, 1989). The literal meaning of the term "*stard*" means "spread out, sprawled." From the descriptions given, this state could last for more than a day.

Comparatively, in 200 CE, the Chinese surgeon, Hua T'o was reputed to have performed complicated operations, such as organ grafts, resectioning of intestines, laparotomies (incisions into the loin), and thoracotomies (incisions into the chest) which were rendered painless by an anesthetic prepared from cannabis resin and wine known as *ma-yo* (Abel, 1980)

Thus, it can clearly be seen that cannabis preparations taken in higher dosages have been known to produce a state identical to those attributed to *bhanga/mang* in the Avestan and Pahlavian accounts. Considering the historical and etymological connections as well, cannabis is by far and wide the most obvious candidate for the ancient Zoroastrian Shamanic preparation, *bhang, mang*.

After the time of Zoroaster's reforms and the installation of the placebo-Haoma, *bhanga/mang* had to be added to the Haoma in order for visionary purposes, and the indications are Zoroaster used this method himself. As the authors of *Apocalypticism in the Mediterranean World and the Near East* explain:

> Zoroaster's role as apocalyptic revealer is intimately tied up with the type of religious type he represents. The indication in the Gathas, particularly Yasna 43, suggest that he was an ecstatic visionary who a number of times had an overwhelming experience of the divine, the Ahura Mazda.... How was this ecstasy... brought about?... There are good reasons to assume that there were in the early Zoroastrian community ... means of attaining the ecstatic vision, e.g. ... the use of a specific beverage. The last one is most clearly attested to with respect to Vistaspa ... [who] is visited by a divine messenger who urges him to drink a cup of wine or haoma mixed with henbane or cannabis (mang). He then falls into a deep sleep during which his soul is taken to heaven ... the same procedure was used by Artay Viraz before undertaking his journey to the other

> world. Now it appears from a passage in *Bahman Yast,* based upon Avestan traditions, that a similar technique was used by Zoroaster. The beverage mentioned in *Bahman Yast* only contains water, but there are grounds to believe that the mention of mang has been suppressed by later tradition. A passage from the Pahlavi Videvat, hitherto not adduced in this context, supports the view that the original tradition behind the *Bahman Yast* knew the narcotic beverage. In IV,14 mention is made of old women bringing henbane [unlikely] or hemp to be used for abortion and the text adds that this mang either was that of "Vistaspa or Zoroaster" (Hellholm, et al., 1989).

Although references to the use of mang are much more clear cut and straight forward in the other accounts which shall be discussed, the identification of Zoroaster's use seems to be quite veiled. Hellholm and his co-authors make an important point in their statement that "According to the *Bahman Yast,* Zoroaster receives from Ahura Mazda the 'wisdom of omniscience'" which appears to be closely related to drinking the cup of ecstasy: (Hellholm, et al., 1989) A situation on which a number of Iranists have commented. "The visionary receives the divine quality of omniscience ... which is thought to be transmitted in liquid form, as told in Bahman Yasht" (Johnston, 2004).

> And he (Ahura Mazda) put the wisdom of omniscience in the form of water in the hand of Zoroaster and said: "Drink." And Zoroaster drank from it and he intermingled the wisdom of omniscience with Zoroaster. Seven days and seven nights Zoroaster was in the wisdom of Ahura Mazda (*Bahman Yast,* 11.5-6).

As the authors of *The Encyclopedia of Apocalypticism* have noted of this passage, "The expression 'in the form of water' in the *Bahman Yast* to denote the drink Zoroaster consumed before his vision does not mean that it was water but only that it was liquid" (McGinn, et al., 2000). As we shall see, the drinking of the "cup of omniscience" by Zoroaster clearly resulted in an identical shamanic trip as that attributed to the drinkers of *bhanga/mang* in the Zoroastrian tradition:

> After having consumed the "wisdom of omniscience," Zoroaster sees the seven world continents and he is able to distinguish the finest details of humans, cattle, and plants. This is best explained on the assumption of a movement in space. In

> fact, we find a reference to an otherworldly journey undertaken by Zoroaster in a short citation from the sacred tradition preserved in the Denkard. Ohrmazd and the beneficent immortals address Zoroaster with the following words "You have come to paradise (*garodman*); now you know the actions that are done in the corporeal world and those that will be done, even in secret" (Dk IX,28:2)(McGinn, et al., 2003).

Hellholm and his co-authors relate that the respected Iranist Geo Widengren, in his German language edition *Die Religionen Irans* (1965) believed that mention of *bhanga/mang* were suppressed in the above accounts by later Zoroastrian religious writers, which would explain a lot of the confusion on the matter. A statement which left this researcher with the task of locating a copy of Widengren's German language book *Die Religionen Irans,* and then acquiring translations of the relevant passages, some of which are reproduced below:

> [In] the Phalavi-apocalypse *Bahman Yast* ... it is recounted ... that Zarathustra assimilated the so-called "rationality of omniscience" by means of drinking water. Moreover it is recounted that, in doing this, the 'rationality of omniscience' was mixed with Zarathustra and this remained for seven days and nights.... The most important thing about this description is that Zarathustra, in accordance with an established Avestan tradition, adopted an intoxication technique, to put himself into a trance, during which he lies in deep sleep for seven days and nights. In Pahlavi at this point, the term for this deep sleep is xvamn; this is a "later" development of the Avestan word xvafna. It may therefore be assumed that the original Avestan tradition even used the term xvafna here (Widengren 1965).

This state of *xvafna* was the core of both the Haoma and the *mang* experience. As Eliade explained, "...haoma is rich in xverenah, the sacred fluid, at once igneous, luminous and spermatic. Ahura Mazda is preeminently the possessor of xvarenah, but this 'flame' also springs from the forehead of Mithra[8] and like a solar light emanates from the heads of sovereigns." (Eliade, 1978). Referring to Zoroaster's ingestion of the "cup of omniscience" Widengren wrote that in "a trance similar to that of the deep sleep, xvafna> xvamn, Zarathustra experienced his visions and heard the divine words of Ahura Mazda. It was probably also customary in the eldest congregations to induce this

8 A Persian God worshiped in relation to haoma.

trance with a narcotic potion. This technique of intoxication presumably has Indo-Iranian ancestry, because it is documented in India as well" (Widengren, 1965).

> [T]he tradition preserved in the Bahman Yt. does not mention the hemp potion as a physical ecstatic substance but it obviously concerns a potion, which Zarathustra partook of. It is possible that the later Pahlavi tradition thus blurred the original character of the potion, that it only states ... "in the form of water ... he swallowed it." Behind this transition from wine and hemp in AVN II 29 ff. to water in the Bahman Yt., one can well assume various tendencies of the Sassanids era...
>
> Now this description in *Bahman Yast* is however consistent in some respects with two other visionary narratives. One account is found in the Pahlavi Rivayats to Datastan i Denik, where it is told, how Zarathustra's guardian, Kavi Vistaspa, obtains wine mixed with a narcotic [*mang*] from the messenger of the gods, Neryosang. Vistaspa immediately becomes unconscious and his soul is escorted to Garodman, the paradise.
>
> This account bases itself meanwhile on an older version which we find in the Denkart. This Denkart text can be proved as an adaptation of a missing Avestan original due to the exegetical glosses, the quotes from the Avesta as well as the precious terminology. This original version shows several discrepancies: firstly the cup, which Vistaspa is passed, contains in this case *hom ut mang*, being haoma and hemp (Widengren, 1965).

Widengren felt that based on this similar Avestan account of Vistaspa drinking Haoma mixed with hemp, and achieving a similar mystical experience to that of Zoroaster in the *Bahman Yast*, that the account of Zoroaster drinking water in the *Bahman Yast*, was based on an earlier Avestan tradition which involved the partaking of *mang*, then later accounts were edited during the Sasanian period to hide this fact.

The Avestan and the Pahlavian references to Vistaspa drinking *mang* are pivotal in identifying Zoroaster's own use of hemp as described in the 'censored' account recorded in the *Bahman Yast*.

> [W]e have to realize that the previously quoted Pahlavi text Bahma Yt, where Zarathustra's ecstasy with his visionary experiences is described, bases itself on Avestan material, and in actual fact predominantly on the missing *Stutkar Nask*. It can

> therefore be subject to no doubt that the Avestan tradition also knew Zarathustra as a genuine ecstatic (Widengren,1965).

Accounts of Zoroaster's shamanic flights are recorded in: *Bahman Yasht* 4.1-66, 5.1-10, 6.1-13, 7.1-39, 8.1-8, 9.1-8; *Bundahishn* 34.4-5; *Denkard* 8.8.22-59, 9.6, 10.11, 14.13. The suggestion that there was a connection between the mang and Haoma consumed by Vishtasp and the "water" by Zoroaster has been noted by a variety of scholars. "Since sauma [mixed with *mang*] was the means by which Ohrmazd [Ahuramazda] brought such vision to Zoroaster's champion, Wishtasp, [Vistaspa] there is no reason to doubt that sauma [and *mang*] would also have been the means whereby Zoroaster (who as a zaotar consumed sauma [haoma] in Yasna rites) also saw into menog existence [spiritual realm] and drew from it his knowledge of Ohrmazd and his revelation" (Flattery and Schwartz, 1989).

> Ancient texts such as the Avesta provide evidence hemp was used in the Iranian world ... to produce ecstatic states of mind. Zarathustra himself used this technique to nourish his mystique. In this he was imitating his protector, King Vishtasp, who received from the gods the cup with narcotic ingredients, "haoma and hemp." Thanks to this "illuminating beverage" the possessed could "open the eye of the soul to obtain knowledge" – in other words, he experienced hallucinations and an intoxication that was certainly real, though considered as magico-religious. The king thought he was in this way escaping his body and sending his soul to travel in paradise. But the descriptions of the place or state of mind in question as being full of "illumination" are typical of the visions experienced by the consumer of hashish, along with a sleep like trance which obliges him to lie down (Charriere, 1979).

VISHTASP, THE SHAMANIC KING

The aforementioned King Vishtasp was an instrumental figure in the acceptance of Zoroastrianism as a religion on a wide scale, but this was said to have happened a full decade after Zoroaster's own revelation. Not surprisingly, Zoroaster's initial battle with the age-old ecstatic Haoma cult was unpopular with the locals, and he had to flee the area in order to save his own life. *Yasna* 46 begins with a sad verse about Zoroaster leaving his homeland after rallying against the Haoma cult.

> To what land should I turn? Where should I turn to go? They hold me back from folk and friends. Neither the community I follow pleases me, nor do the wrongful rulers of the land ... I know ... that I am powerless. I have a few cattle and also a few men (*Yasna* 46).

The story has it that Zoroaster wandered the countryside for ten years without winning over the people to his new religious concepts. It was not until he met King Vishtasp, who converted to Zoroaster's religion after drinking a cup of *mang* that the Iranian prophet's beliefs began to take hold on a wide scale. "Vishtaspa used hemp (*bhang*) to obtain ecstasy: while his body lay asleep, his soul traveled to paradise" (Eliade 1978). Vishtaspa's shamanic journey is recorded in *Denkird* 7.4.83-6 and Pahlavi Rivayat 48.27-32. In the ninth century text the *Denkird* derived from a lost Avestan source, when Vishtaspa drank *bhang* "he became *stard* (unconscious) immediately, and they led his soul to paradise and showed him the value of accepting the Religion":

> To enlighten Vishtasp (and teach him)... and that he would attain a high post, permanent power, riches and food, Ohrmazd the Creator sent at the same time to the house of Vishtasp the yazat [a lesser divine being] Neryosang with a message urging ... Arthavist to give to drink to Vishtasp the lightened drink that would grant the eye of whomever took it a glimpse at the spiritual world.... And speak to Arthavist: "Lord Arthavist! Take the nice plate, the nicest of all that have been made ... to take, from us, Hom [Haoma] and mang..." (*Denkird* 7.4.84-86).

Seeming to agree with Widengren about censorship of references to *bhanga/mang*, Vicente Dobroruka has noted, "In the *Dinkard* 7.4.84-86 Vishtaspa drinks a mixture of wine or haoma with some narcotic, possibly henbane [or as we have shown, hemp]. The same episode in the *Zand-i Vohuman Yasn*, a later redaction, has this potation replaced by water ... possible evidence of the practice being rejected in later times" (Dobroruka, 2006).

Gherardo Gnoli recorded: "*bang* was ... an ingredient of the 'illuminating drink' (*rōšngar xwarišn*) that allowed Wištāsp to see the 'great *xwarrah*' and the 'great mystery.' This *mang* ī wištāspān (*Pahlavi* Vd. 15.14...) was mixed with *hōm* (*Dēnkard* 7.4.85) or wine (*Pahlavi Rivayat* 47.27). It was an integral part of the ecstatic practice aimed at opening the 'eye of the soul' (*gyān čašm*....)" (Gnoli, 1979). As Widengren explained:

> Hemp and wine or hemp and haoma were mixed in the cup that was passed to Vistaspa ... it is said that Neryosang was sent forth to let Vistaspa drink "the eye of the soul" with the view up above to the forms of existence of the heavenly beings, the illuminating potion thanks to which Vistaspa saw the great lucky splendor and "mystery." The typical expression *gyan casm*, "eye of the soul," causes problems here. One could be tempted to replace this expression with "source of life," and this in actual fact is how it was translated, which in a pure formal philological sense is completely possible. However the expression can be explained via two points in the Denkart, where, in regards to the enlightenment, it is stated that it is of two types: on the one hand it consists of a view with the eye of the body, *tan casm*, on the other hand it is a view with the eye of the soul, *gyan casm*, which is defined as "the opening of the eye of the soul to obtain knowledge." "The eye of the soul" means introspection. The visionary sight is conveyed to Kavi Vistaspa using a haoma potion mixed with hemp. With this his soul can repair to *Garodman*, [Paradise] to view the heavenly existence (Widengren, 1965).

A similar reference to the "eye" is found in the Indian *Aitareya Brahmanam*:

> When ... the Adhvaryu hands over ... the Soma cup to drink ... to the Hotar, he receives it with the ... mantra ... (By the words): "This is a good which has knowledge; here is a good which has knowledge; in me is a good which has knowledge; ruler of the eye, protect my eye" the Hotar drinks Soma from the *Maitravaruna graha*.[9] (Then he repeats): "The eye with the mind is called hither."

Martin Haug in his translation of this passage, noted "This formula resembles very much one of the most sacred prayers of the Parsis ... which is particularly repeated when the Zotar priest (the Hotar of the Brahmans) is drinking the Homa (Soma) juice..." (Haug, 1863). In relation, in India the drinking of *bhang* by devotees is still believed to open up the "eye" of Shiva, i.e. the "third-eye."

As Mary Boyce explains, the drinking of *mang* led to the moment of conversion for Vishtaspa: "Vistasp received ... a bowl containing *Hom*-juice mixed with *mang*; when he drank this he lost conscious-

9 The ritual cup

ness and saw in a vision the glories of heaven which awaited him hereafter. On recovering his senses he accordingly accepted whole-heartedly the new teachings" (Boyce, 1982).

> Ormazd sent Nêrôsang: "Go to Artvahist and tell him: Put mang in the wine and give it for Vishtasp to drink." Artvahist did so. Having drunk it, he evaporated into the field. His soul was taken to Garôtman [Paradise] to show him what he could gain if he accepted the Religion. When he woke up from the sleep, he cried to Hutôs: "Where is Zoroaster so that I may accept the Religion?" Zoroaster heard his voice, came and Vishtasp accepted the Religion. (*Pahlavi Rivayat* 47.27-32)

In *Haoma and Harmaline,* Flattery and Schwartz make some very important points about the account of Vishtaspa drinking *mang* (they use the blanket term "sauma," regarding the Haoma and *mang* references), in order to see into the Spiritual realm (*Menog*):

> Fundamental to ancient Iranian religion was a belief in two existences, the material, tangible, visible existence ... and the intangible, invisible, spirit existence ... Middle Persian menog, as was glimpsed by ... Wishtasp [Vistaspa] by means of sauma [and *mang*].... All material things and creatures exist simultaneously in spirit form. These spirit forms include the double or frawahr (Avestan fravasi-) of each person, living, dead and unborn...
>
> The consumption of sauma [and *mang*] may have been the only means recognized in Iranian religion of seeing into menog existence before death ... and is the means used by Ohrmazd when he wishes to make the menog existence visible to living persons. In ancient Iranian religion there is little evidence of concern with meditative practices which might foster development of alternative, non-pharmacological means to such vision. In Iran, vision into the spirit world was not thought to come about simply by divine grace nor as a reward for saintliness. From the apparent role of sauma in initiation rites, experience of the effects of sauma, which is to say vision of menog existence, must have at one time been required of all priests (or the shamans antecedent to them) (Flattery and Schwartz, 1989).

Besides bringing back an account of the afterlife, the revelations received by Vishtaspa in this psychedelic voyage included divine knowledge about the fate of mankind, and give us the origin of the whole concept of an Apocalypse or Holy Armageddon. Vishtaspa was one of the first to conceive of a cosmic beginning and end of history, placing himself and Zarathustra at the midpoint.

Vishtaspa's Eschatological vision was apparently prohibited literature in ancient Rome, and in the eyes of the Romans with good reason: "In the second and first century B.C. an apocalypse written in Greek was in circulation under the title Oracles of Hystapes (Hystapes is the Greek form of Vishtaspa); it was directed against Rome (whose fall was announced) but formed part of the Iranian eschatological literature" (Eliade 1978\1982).[10]

Zoroaster also initiated Vishtaspa's son Jamasp, but rather than using a beverage, this account simply describes a "flower":

> In the Jāmāsp Namag … Jāmāsp receives from Zoroaster the gift of knowledge by means of a flower. This is also the theme of the Pahlavi text *Wizirkard* i Denig 19.… In the Zardush Nameh … it is said that Jāmāsp acquired his gift by smelling the flower consecrated by Zoroaster in a ceremony:
>
> "He gave to Jāmāsp a bit of the consecrated perfume, and all sciences became understandable to him. He knew about all things to happen and that would happen until the day of resurrection."
>
> … In Mary Boyce's translation … the flower is rendered as "incense" (Dobroruka, 2006).

Apparently, Zoroaster's wife was not satisfied with only a secondary shamanic experience, and after hearing about Zoroaster's visions, she prays to the Supreme Being that Zoroaster "give her his good narcotic, bangha." Darmesteter commented on this in his 19th century translation of the relevant passages from the *Den Yasht*, 16.14-15:

> To whom the holy Hvovi (Zarathustra's wife) did sacrifice with full knowledge, wishing the holy Zarathustra would give her his good narcotic (bangha; so-called Bang of Zoroaster, Vendidad XV, 14, what must have been its virtue may be gathered from legends of Gustap [Vistaspa] and Ardu Viraf, who are said to have been transported in soul to heavens, and to have had the higher mysteries revealed to them, on drinking from a cup prepared by the prophet – Sardust namah – (or

10 Vishtaspa's vision, known as the Great Renovation, also foretold of a coming Savior and the institution of the White Hom (the celestial counterpart of Haoma) a mythos that would directly influence the Judaic and later Christian concepts of the Messiah with his Tree of Life and its healing leaves in the New Testament's Book of Revelation.

> from a cup of Gustap-bang) that she might think according to the law, speak according to the law, and do according to the law. "For her brightness and glory, I will offer unto her a sacrifice worth being heard..." (Darmesteter, 1883).

Darmesteter mentions the Zoroastrian psychonaut Ardu Viraf (aka Arda Wiraz and other spellings), a figure widely credited with bringing to the world many of the concepts of Heaven and Hell.

The Persian Origins of Heaven and Hell

In the Zoroastrian tale "...the *Artak Viraz Namak* ... Hell, Purgatory, and Heaven, the rewards bestowed on the good, and the punishment awaiting the sinner are here described in a vision induced by hashish" (Campbell, 2000). As Herbert Gowen explained in *A History of Religion,* some centuries after the time of Zoroaster, when the people had grown skeptical and began to lose faith it was decided by the "*dasturs* (an order of priests) to send one of their number, through the use of hashish, to the other world, that he may report on his return as to the realities of future reward and retribution. Ara Viraf, chosen by lot, makes the journey..." (Gowen, 1934).

The Book of Arda Wiraz is generally thought to have originated sometime around the 3rd century A.D., but existing copies are believed to have not been written down until around the 9th century, and it underwent many redactions before it came into its final form some time after the advent of Islam. If we take into account that the accepted date for the life of Zoroaster is around 600 B.C., or earlier, this later account attests to the ongoing use of *bhanga/mang* for shamanic purposes for a millennium, despite the existing prohibitions on its use in the wider and more public Haoma ceremonies.

> In the Book of Arda Viraf, which describes the dream-journey of a devout Zoroastrian through the next world is bhanga (narcotic) mentioned in Part 1., Chapter 2, 24: "And then those Dasturs of the religion filled three golden cups with wine and narcotic of Vishtasp." Similarly, the ancient Aryans that settled in India used Cannabis, but in their worship of the deity Shiva. In one of the Tantric Scriptures we find this revealing statement: "Intoxicating drink (containing bhang) is consumed in order to liberate oneself, and that those who do so, in dominating their mental faculties and following the law of Shiva (yoga) – are to be likened to immortals on earth.' [*The Mahanirvana Tantra* (XI,105–108)] (Hanu , 2008).

The Book of Arda Wiraz Namag takes place in a period where the Zoroastrian religion was in a state of confusion and people were in doubt of the faith. In reaction to this the religious leaders gathered together in order to find a solution and the decision was that they needed to seek word from the spiritual realm, using the time-tested technique of ingestion of *mang*. The Priests gathered together 7 of the most righteous men in the community, and then through a picking of lots, Arda Wiraz was selected. After enjoying a luxurious last meal and saying goodbye to his 7 wives, the Book of Arda Wiraz continues with the account:

> And this Viraz washed (his) head and (his) body, and put on a new garment; perfumed (himself) with an agreeable perfume, spread a new, clean blanket on some appropriate boards. At a (given) moment (he) sat down on the clean blanket, and performed the (rite of sacrifice), and remembered (the departed) souls, and ate food. And afterwards the theologians of the Religion filled three golden cups with wine and with the Vishtaspian narcotic [mang], and they gave one cup over to Viraz (in conformity) with the "good thought," and the second cup (in conformity) with the "good speech," and the third cup (in conformity) with the "good deed." And he drank that wine and narcotic and consciously said grace and fell asleep on the blanket (*The Book of Artay Viraz*, 2.25-31).

Arda Viraf drinks "three gold cups with wine and "*vistaspic* hemp" (in other words hemp extract) ... has some time to thank consciousness, and then falls asleep on the gown. He sleeps for seven days and nights, and during this time his soul visits heaven and hell" (Nyberg, 1938). After partaking of an extremely strong psychedelic dose of *mang* Ardu Viraf lay in what appeared to outsiders as a deathlike coma and had a classic out-of-body-experience, in which the ancient psychonaut believed he traveled on the mythical Cinvat bridge to Heaven where he witnessed: "All dwell among fine carpets and cushions in great pleasure and joy....Viraf, after returning to the bridge, was then taken to hell that he might see the lot of the wicked...He saw the 'greedy jaws of hell, like the most frightful pit.' Everyone in hell is packed in so tight that life is intolerable, yet all believe that they are alone..." (Hinnels, 1973).

Referring to Ardu Viraf's hemp inspired heavenly voyage, Mircea Eliade wrote, "... we must take ... into consideration the symbolic value of narcotic intoxication. It was equivalent to a 'death', the intoxicated person left his body, acquired the conditions of ghosts and spirits, mystical ecstasy being assimilated to a temporary 'death' or leaving the body, all intoxicants that produced the same were given a place amongst the techniques of ecstasy" (Eliade 1964). "The most explicit detailed Iranian account of intoxication for religious purposes is the Arda Wiraz Namag ... [it] demonstrates the belief that pharmacologically induced visions were the means to religious knowledge and that they were at the basis of the religion that the Magi claimed to have received from Zoroaster" (Flattery & Schwartz 1989).

As noted earlier, Widengren (1965), Hellholm, et al. (1989), Dobroruka (2006) have all suggested that references to the use of *bhanga/mang* may have been suppressed in the later Sasanian period when many of the accounts first made the transition from oral traditions to the written traditions which have survived. Notably, as Widengren mentions, "The term for 'hemp', *bangha,* is used in the *Avesta,* however it is missing in the *Gathas*" (Widengren, 1965). The *Gathas,* being the book directly attributed to the authorship of Zoroaster, which is also silent on the topic of Haoma.

> If we go in contrast to the late-Zoroastrian *Vendidad,* hemp is demonized here. From 15 it emerges, that it was used as an abortifacient agent, and in 19 it is linked with the demon Kunda. In 19 it is emphatically stated by Ahura Mazdah that it is "*axafna abanha,*" which means "without trance and without hemp."
>
> ...If a man in the ancient congregations could now be called *Pouru.banha* ["possessing much hemp"] just like that and his "fravasi" remained nevertheless an object of worship, then without a doubt it can be perceived, in the opinion of the *Vendidad,* that there is a conscious polemic against the elder rites of the congregation. At this later stage, the old ecstasy was considered as a demonic nuisance; the metamorphosis of the old trance-goddess Busyasta in to the demon of somnolence goes in parallel with the denunciation of hemp, while in contrast Chwafna, originally the trance, is worshiped further, without a doubt with altered significance (Nyberg, 1938).

The demonization of a Goddess associated with cannabis, is interesting in regards to what we saw with Asherah. In relation to this demonization, Nyberg noted that a "very interesting list of demons exists ... it includes the following female demons: Budhi with the parallel form Budhiza, Kundi with the parallel form Kundiza and finally the old goddess of ecstasy Busyansta, 'things to come,' the demon of somnolence in Zoroastrianism" (Nyberg, 1938). Apparently these deities were important figures in the early use of cannabis, and may give us some insights into the more ancient pre-Zoroastrian cultic use of cannabis amongst the Aryans:

> In Budhiza, true Budhiza, and Kundiza, true Kundiza, one can again recognize the word "iza," which serves as a synonym for Armaiti, the godly tribe, in oldest Zoroastrianism; Budhiza therefore actually means "tribe and cult congregation of the goddess Budhi" and Kundiza "tribe and cult congregation of the goddess Kundi"...
>
> Alongside the goddess Kundi there is also a masculine Kunda, who needless to say is now a demon. Vend. 19,41 deals with him as follows "the Sraosa accompanied by Asi would like to slay the demon Kunda, the one with the hemp, so that he no longer has hemp." Kunda and indeed also Kundi were therefore very closely linked with the old ecstatic substance of hemp, which was used since ancient times by the Aryans in the North and East. Kundiza was a body or guild of ecstatics, who reached the ecstatic state through narcotization with hemp. If, as I believe, the Median town Kunduru, mentioned in the Behistun Inscription and written Kuntarrus = Kundaru in the Elamite version, is linked with this pair of gods, then it must have been an old West Iranian hashish nest...
>
> The goddess Busyansta is probably regarded as the common oracle deity of the West, which views oracle as a divine strength. As she represents the demon of somnolence, then we must assume that she began to function in trance. She [the goddess Busyansta] receives the epithet "zairina," that in my opinion should not be translated as "exhausting, flagging" rather "golden"; that is an epithet in the same style as Zairica. It alludes presumably to the ingested ecstasy potion. Maybe it was hemp extract in wine... (Nyberg, 1938).

If there were a polemic against hemp, as these passages indicate, it would explain a lot about the confusion on the matter. As for the contradictions surrounding the figure of Zoroaster this raises, I have proposed one possibility regarding the prohibitions of Haoma and the use of *mang,* indicating that it was the use by the wider public against which Zoroaster rallied, and this could also be clearly applied to the use of cannabis as well, which would also explain any movement to suppress the use of cannabis such as those noted by Nyberg above.

However, there is the very real possibility that the term "Zoroaster" itself, may be less of a personal name and more of a title, which was applied to different individuals with different views on the ingestion of *mang* and Haoma, with some 'Zoroasters' approving of its use, and others condemning it.

Any Zoroastrian prohibitions of *bhanga/mang* seem initially to have been far from successful, as the historical record indicates that such shamanic practices were continued by the Zoroastrian elite for some time, at least for the first few centuries CE.

Cyrus the Great

Around the most popular estimated date for the time of Zoroaster, 600 BCE, Cyrus the Great was born, and through this king, Persia came to be one of the greatest empires of the ancient world. The empire that expanded under his rule included most of Southwest Asia and much of Central Asia, from Egypt and the Hellespont in the west to the Indus River in the east, to create the largest state the world had yet seen. Cyrus died in battle, fighting the Scythians along the Syr Darya in 530 BCE.

Beyond his nation, Cyrus left a lasting legacy on Jewish religion (through his Edict of Restoration), and as a result on the Hebrew Bible. The prophet Isaiah referred to Cyrus the Great of Persia as "the anointed of Yahweh," whom Yahweh himself led, "to subdue nations before him that gates may not be closed." Yet historically, Cyrus, referred to in the Hebrew Bible as "the King of Kings," (the same title applied to Jesus Christ in the New Testament) and who returned the different peoples that he had conquered to their homelands and restored each of their gods to their temples, continued to worship the pre-Zoroastrian gods of his own ancestors.

The Bible records that a remnant of the Jewish population returned to the Promised Land from Babylon, following an edict (reproduced in the Book of Ezra) from Cyrus to rebuild the temple. As a result of Cyrus' policies, the Jews honored him as a dignified and righteous king. He is the only Gentile to be designated as a messiah, a divinely-appointed king, in the Hebrew Bible (Isaiah 45:1-6). However, at the time, there was also Jewish criticism of him after he was lied to by the Cuthites, who wanted to halt the building of the Second Temple. They accused the Jews of conspiring to rebel, so Cyrus in turn stopped the construction of the temple, which would not be completed until 516 BC, during the reign of Darius the Great.

Darius was Cyrus' son in law, and he was able to take the throne by marriage, as both of Cyrus' own sons had died in battle. Important to our study, according to Zoroastrian tradition, Darius' blood father was Hystaspes, the Greek version of the name Vishtaspa – the aforementioned king who converted to Zoroaster's religion after drinking *mang*![11] The name Hystaspes can be found in the inscriptions at Persepolis and Behistun Inscription, where the full lineage of Darius the Great was given:

> King Darius says: My father is Hystaspes [Vištâspa]; the father of Hystaspes was Arsames [Aršâma]; the father of Arsames was Ariaramnes [Ariyâramna]; the father of Ariaramnes was Teispes [Cišpiš]; the father of Teispes was Achaemenes [Haxâmaniš]. King Darius says: That is why we are called Achaemenids; from antiquity we have been noble; from antiquity has our dynasty been royal. King Darius says: Eight of my dynasty were kings before me; I am the ninth. Nine in succession we have been kings.
>
> King Darius says: By the grace of Ahuramazda am I king; Ahuramazda has granted me the kingdom – Behistun Inscription.

If, we accept that by the name "Hystaspes" (i.e. Vištâspa), the Avestan texts do refer to the father of Darius I, then according to Zoroastrian scripture, Zarathustra lived during the 6th Century BCE. Other Zoroastrian sources corroborate this. The *Bundahishn*, a scripture written down around the time of the Islamic conquest of Persia (CE 637), places the birth of Zoroaster at 588 BCE. It has also been noted that Cyrus and Cambyses adhered to the Mazdean pantheistic beliefs of their ancestors, leaving no mention of Zarathustra in their inscriptions, while on the other hand it is clear that Darius and his successors were monotheistic Zoroastrian followers of Ahura Mazda. In addition, the very nature of the Zoroastrian reformation, a transformation of an ancient religion from pantheism to monotheism, may be seen as supportive of a 6th Century BCE dating, because such a dating corresponds with the cohabitation of Persia by significant numbers of a monotheistic people – the exiled Jews.

It was at this period in history, as we shall look at in the next Chapter, that the Semitic ancestors of the Jews adopted so many of the Zoroastrian ideas that were pivotal for the later development of

11 It has been argued that Vishtaspa, the patron of Zarathustra and Hytaspes, father of Darius are distinct persons, but such an argument relies on the validity of an early dating for the life of Zarathustra than is generally accepted.

Christianity. As shall be discussed, some have even suggested that it was at this late date that Jewish monotheism itself was first born.

> Zoroastrian monotheism was made the state religion throughout the Persian empire, with its one hundred and twenty-seven provinces, by Darius Hystaspis, whose reign extended from India to Ethiopia, B.C. 521.... And this, too, was true of her many provinces until they were wrestled from her by superior force. (Brown, 1890)
>
> Among the situations where sauma [*haoma*] seems most likely to have been used was at the inauguration of pre-Islamic Iranian rulers. This is indicated by King Wishtasp's consumption of "*hom and mang*" at his "initiation," which is still commemorated by Zoroastrians at the New Year..... A reflection of the initiation of kings with sauma may be preserved in Plutarch's *Life of Artaxerxes III*. 1-3: "A little while after the death of Darius [II], the new king made an expedition to Pasargadae that he might receive the royal initiation at the hands of the Persian priests. Here there is a sanctuary to a warlike goddess whom one might conjecture to be Athena. Into this sanctuary the candidate for initiation must pass, and after laying aside his own proper robe must put on that which Cyrus the Elder used to wear before he became king; then he must eat a cake of figs,[12] chew some turpentine-wood, and drink a cup of sour milk. Whatever else is done besides this is unknown to outsiders." Zoroaster also put on a garment when he came up from the hom liquid as, it seems, did his father Porushasp when he approached the hom and as also did Arda Wiraz. This suggests that a change of clothes may have been a regular feature of sauma-drinking in the initiation of Iranian rulers (Bedrosian, 2006).

These accounts are consistent with stone inscriptions found in Fars from about 300 CE, by Kirdir, the founder of the Sasanian Zoroastrian ecclesiastical establishment. "Kirdir's inscription asserts in this passage, as a basis of his claim to religious authority, that his spirit-double visited the other world and was shown heaven and hell. The account thus parallels the Arda Wiraz Namag in reaffirming the reliance placed on a vision of menog existence as the means to religious truth" (Flattery & Schwartz 1989). As Shaul Shaked noted in *Quests and Visionary Journeys in Sasanian Iran*:

12 Reminiscent of eshisha

Sasanian Bowl, depicting the ruler, possibly drinking the Cup of Haoma or wine, mixed with *mang*. Note the grape vine on the right, but on the left a smaller bush-like plant is depicted, items in the picture could be conceivably identified as implements for mixing and straining (Image British Museum).

> Visions as done by Kider and Arda Wiraz, was one way of communicating with the gods and obtaining direct knowledge of the things of the next world, a way of verifying the truths of the religion.... [The devotee] would be transported to the other world; when he came back his arrival would be celebrated with a great show of joy and relief. Several of these elements show strong similarity with the complex of practices associated with shamanic cults. Such cults are nowadays typical of the fringes of the Iranian world, [i.e. the continued use of *dūḡ-e waḥdat*] and it makes sense to assume that they formed part of the Iranian civilization itself...
>
> It is striking that Pahlavi literature of the late Sasanian and early Islamic period is practically obsessed with descriptions of the hereafter and of entities that belong to the invisible world. The classic example is the Book of Arda Wiraz, but it is

> not unique ... visions ... are alluded to quite frequently in the Pahlavi books, together with the discussion of the possibility of the seeing of menog, the invisible world, by the organ dedicated to this kind of vision, "the eye of the soul."
>
> ...The preparation for this journey was done, as we have seen, by administering to the officiant a dose of mang (hemp) mixed with wine (Shaked, et al., 1999).[13]

A Lost Trail?

In relation to this discussion of *haoma* and *bhanga,* it is worth noting that in an article reproduced in *The Book of Grass: An Anthology on Indian Hemp* (1967) Melvin Clay referred to recipes for a "suama" plant found around Tell Abu Matar in Israel, appearing on urns and cups, of high quality workmanship, which was partially reproduced in *The Book of Grass* (1967). Clay wrote that the recipes, which he placed around the third century B.C.E., originated with a hermit named Zin, who had been banned from the Second Temple in Jerusalem. This may indicate that he was practicing a form of Persian worship. Apparently, as cannabis had been, the *suama* plant was used at religious feasts, the roots boiled and drunk or the leaves smoked. Clay wrote that the *suama* plant was originally found in the region of Kadesh-barnea, northeastern Sinai. An area near where Moses was said to have first heard the "Word of the Lord" in a fiery bush.

> Dr. W.F. Cartwell of Oriental Institute has no recollection of the recipe but speaks of leaves smoked and inhaled at a Palestine synagogue during the writing of the Hasteric Scrolls (Books of Joy). He adds that "The suama plant is known to

13 Although these practices disappeared from Zoroastrianism there is evidence that some use was still in play during the reign of the Sasanian King Khusraw Parvēz (590 – 628) and that this left its mark on emerging Islam. In "Azerbaijan, a former center of the Zoroastrian religion and homeland of the cannabis-using Scythians, medieval manuscripts also record the use of wine infused with a mixture of cannabis, opium and henbane" (Dannaway, Piper & Webster, 2006). Persecution of Zoroastrianism, under Islam, saw great changes in the tradition, and this use seems to have declined and disappeared during this period. However, in heretical branches of Islam, like the sufis and dervishes, hashish became increasingly popular, and hashish wine infusions were known. Wine was often mixed with cannabis resins in the Islamic world. "As with the Zoroastrian infusions, although seen as particularly heretical, in the medieval Islamic world, the "combination of wine and hashish was quite often attempted..." (Rosenthal, 1971). Muhammad's own ascent to heaven, induced by "three cups of water from the sacred well of Zemzem," which enabled him to ride the mythical "Seraph-beast Borak," has been compared to the early Zoroastrian accounts we have discussed, and the mid 17th century Dabestān-e Mazāheb, "School of Religions" has a description of the Prophet helping in the preparation of bhang, straining it through his turban, turning it green, as I have discussed elsewhere (Bennett, 2010; 2018).

> us from the time of the Pentateuch. Some very early discoveries have been made concerning the suama plant. We find it coming up again and again under different names. Smoking its leaves or using its roots as a herbal drink always produces states of flashing colors and euphoric bliss" (Clay 1967).

Unfortunately, I've been unable, as of yet, to find out more about the research from Melvin Clay, or Dr. W.F. Cartwell, or these references to a *suama* plant so cannot attest the veracity of these claims.

As with other cosmological elements, for well over a century, it has been suggested that this same form of entheogenic induction, had been utilized by a Hebrew vassal of the Persian Empire, Ezra, who had been sent back to his homeland with a decree from Darius, son of the aforementioned Vistashpa, to build the Second Temple.

Chapter 12

Ezra and the "Cup of Fire"

The Second Temple

The Second Temple was dedicated in 516 BCE, and the reintroduction of Temple worship came with some provocative changes. The most prominent change, was the powers instilled in the new priestly caste who governed the worship, as the Levites, who had gone "astray ... after idols ... and made the house of Israel fall into sin" (Ezekiel 44:11-12), were no longer permitted to perform services in the inner temple. Those Levites who repented were limited to the role of the priest's servants.

Ezra, a scribe and priest who was an expert on Jewish law, played a pivotal role in the "reformation" after the Exile and he has been seen as a "Second Moses" for this. In the Hebrew Bible Ezra is described as a descendant of Sraya, the last High Priest to serve in the First Temple and he was said to have represented a faction of Jews in Babylon, who adhered to the "reforms" of Josiah. Concerned about the lack of implementation of these Laws in their native Judaea, they decided to form a posse and remedy the situation and return to their homeland. However, in this regard, it should be noted that Ezra was also acting as a commissioner of the Persian government and his title, "scribe of the law of the God of heaven," can be seen as a position as an intermediary with the Persian rulers, and a role more akin to "royal secretary for Jewish religious affairs." The Persian Empire was tolerant of native cults but was also cautious of potential internal strife and rebellion. Thus they insisted that these be regulated under a responsible authority that was loyal to them.

The book of Malachi is contemporary to that of Ezra, and some attributed it to Ezra himself. Malachi 2:11 has been interpreted as indicating that it did not take long after the "reforms" of Josiah, for Judah to return to the polytheistic practices of their ancestors, and the worship of the Mother Goddess Asherah: "Judah hath dealt treacherously, and an abomination is committed in Israel and in Jerusalem; for Judah hath profaned the holiness of the LORD which he loved, and hath married the daughter of a strange god" (Malachi 2:11). The Levites were wound up with this as well, as they had gone "astray ... after idols ... and made the house of Israel fall into sin" (Ezekiel 44:11-12). Ezra as well, made reference to the Levites partaking in "detestable practices, like those of the Canaanites, Hittites, Perizzites, Jebusites, Ammonites, Moabites, Egyptians and Amorites" (Ezra 9:1) and taking foreign wives, as did other Hebrews. This, combined with archaeological evidence from the period, indicates the people living in Judah were still practicing the longstanding polytheistic religion of their ancestors, despite the pre-Exilic attempts at instilling monotheism described in the Hebrew Bible.

Ezra, is described as convincing many of them to give up these "adulterous" practices, as well as their foreign wives (Ezra 10:2-5). A contemporary of Ezra and fellow leader in establishing the new community, Nehemiah also refers to having had to purify the "Levites of everything foreign" (Nehemiah 13:30). And not just the Levites, in the short amount of time of the Exile, the people left in Judah had already drifted away from the attempted reforms of Josiah, if they were ever even successfully instituted, and returned to the polytheistic religion of their ancestors. Ezra had to teach the people monotheistic Judaism. When Ezra preached from the texts of what would become The Hebrew Bible, they were new and foreign to the ears of the people in Judah. Some see that it is only here, after the Exile, that the monotheistic Judaism we know today, became established as anything close to its present form, and this came with a strong influence from their Zoroastrian Persian overlords.

Zoroastrian-Canaanites?

The idea that Jewish monotheism finds its origins in the Persian tradition is put forth in *Persia & Creation of Judaism*, by Dr Michael D. Magee.[1] Magee gives a detailed explanation of how Judaism was created by the Persians in 500 BCE. "Historical Israel, the actual flesh and blood people who dwelt in the central mountains during the Iron Ages, didn't come from Egypt. They were descendants of earlier, Bronze Age inhabitants of the places where they lived. Their culture and religion was a slightly evolved form of the earlier, Bronze Age Canaanite ones" (Magee, 1998; 2008).

> ... Israel and Judah remained Canaanite until the Persians came at the end of the sixth century BC. Only in the follow-

1 https://www.cais-soas.com/CAIS/Religions/non-iranian/Judaism/Persian_Judaism/Persia_created_judaism.htm

> ing century were books about Jewish history written down.... Some events of the Bible are confirmed by external investigation. Some of the kings of Israel and Judah appear in Assyrian records and therefore can be dated. However, given that the history of Israel was only first written in the Persian period, and the Persians had conquered Assyria and Babylonia, and had access to their archives covering hundreds of years, it is more than likely that the scriptural stories of the monarchical period were simply written from the official king lists, inscriptions and diplomatic correspondence of those formerly mighty powers. In short, it is largely historical fiction but set in a realistic historical framework (Magee, 1998; 2008).

As Dr. Magee explains, part of the Persian return included bringing in a monotheistic element of worship, directed at unifying worship into a single manageable source, through which the people could be more easily governed, as well as taxed.

> The Jewish scriptures make up a constitution for the Jewish people to whom they were given. The earliest time that rules like reading the Torah publicly and observing its charges faithfully, abstention from work and commerce on the sabbath, avoiding intermarriage, tithing, maintaining temple sacrifice through a self-imposed tax (Neh 10:30-40) could appear is when Ezra and Nehemiah were sent by the Persian king during the fifth century BC to determine civil and religious policy in Yehud [Israel] (Magee, 1998; 2008).

Magee puts forth that part of the Persian policy of restoration of people back to their homelands, included having the main male deity from each existing pantheon elevated to the same state as that of their own monotheist god Ahura Mazda, at the sacrifice of the powers of the gods and goddesses of the earlier pantheons. In each place that such a god was placed upon this lone throne, he took with him the title, "king of heaven."

As Magee explains it, for reasons of political consolidation the rulers wanted the people to worship one sole god, the concept being that everyone would worship a "king of heaven" with the same broad characteristics but with different regional names. "The Great King of the empire could then be shown to have the same role on earth as the universal king of heaven, and the various kings of heaven could be shown to be different versions of Ahuramazda, unifying everyone"

(Magee, 1998: 2008). The outcome of this universal mixing of peoples was:

- Aramaic became the language of the whole area.
- "Jews" accepted that they had "returned" but they never accepted the natives of the hill country as being Jews.
- The "Jews" that had "returned" used some Samarian legends but rejected the rest of the cult and devised a new religious "tradition."
- The people that had remained in Judah never accepted those who returned.
- The people who had remained in Judah did not accept the "restored" religion.
- Whoever the mixture of peoples were that returned to the city of Jerusalem after 500 BC, they were led to believe – and came to believe – that they were the remnant of ancient Israel returning to their rightful land to create a new Israel.... Much of the Old Testament saga is Persian propaganda. The ancestor of the Jews is from Mesopotamia, so, in the myth of Abraham, the Jews are shown to have an ethnic affinity with that region. The anachronism of calling it the Chaldees betrays its late composition. Immediately, the descendants of Abraham are enslaved by the Egyptians and have to undergo countless tribulations before they escape and set up in Israel. The propaganda purpose is plain – to dissociate the inhabitants of the Palestinian hill country from Egypt and paint the Egyptians as their enemies (Magee, 1998; 2008).

Magee puts forth that proof close to the time can be found in the works of the Egyptian Jew Philo of Alexandria (20 B.C.-50 A.D., who wrote in *Vita Moysis* of the Jewish texts "Originally the laws were written in the Chaldaean language."

> The Chaldaean language was the language of Babylonia (Ezra 5:12) at the time of the project of Ezra to set up a new religion in Jerusalem. Why then would Moses, a Hebrew brought up in Egypt under some Pharaoh like Rameses, write in a language of a distant country 800 years later? Philo, an Egyptian Jew, effectively admits the Torah was written by Ezra, a Persian from Babylonia.
>
> Israelite religion must therefore have been a variant of the religions practiced by Canaanites in general. The main difference

> which arose between this religion and other neighboring ones was that the Persians selected Jerusalem as the center of a pseudo-Zoroastrian cult based on the local god Yehouah [Yahweh]. There was no particular slow variation from other Canaanite religions, but there was a sudden imposition of a foreign cult on to the local religion of Jerusalem. The imposition was resisted by locals for many decades but ultimately it triumphed, albeit in a highly fragmentated state (Magee, 1998; 2008).

A profound Zoroastrian influence on Biblical theology has also long been noted:

> Zoroastrianism is the oldest of the revealed creedal religions, and it has probably had more influence on mankind, directly and indirectly, than any other single faith. In its own right it was the state religion of three great Iranian empires ... Iran's power and wealth lent it immense prestige, and some of its leading doctrines were adopted by Judaism... (Boyce, 1983)

A large portion of this Zoroastrian influence likely came into Israel with the post-Exile prophet, Ezra. Ezra was born in Babylon, and was among the Jews returned during the reign of Darius, who as noted was the son of the psychonaut Zoroastrian king Vishtaspa. Ezra had worked as a scribe in the Persian world before being returned to his homeland and he was a key figure of the Jewish monotheistic reformation after the Persians had returned the Jews to their homeland after close to a century of exile.

2 Esdras 14, is an apocalyptic book in some English versions of the Bible, scholarship places its composition between 70 and 218 CE, but tradition ascribes it to Ezra himself in the fifth century BCE. In it, Ezra is described as first hearing the word of god, as Moses was said to have done centuries before him, from within a bush, and then he is given further instructions after consuming a "cup of fire" which scholars have suggested was a infusion identical with the Zoroastrian beverages we discussed in the previous chapter. As 2 Esdras describes:

The Lord Commissions Ezra

> On the third day, while I was sitting under an oak, suddenly a voice came out of a bush opposite me and said, "Ezra, Ezra!" And I answered, "Here I am, Lord," and I rose to my feet. Then he said to me, "I revealed myself in a bush and spoke to Mo-

ses when my people were in bondage in Egypt, and I sent him and led my people out of Egypt, and I led him up on Mount Sinai, where I kept him with me many days. I told him many wondrous things and showed him the secrets of the times and declared to him the end of the times. Then I commanded him, saying, 'These words you shall publish openly, and these you shall keep secret.' And now I say to you: "Lay up in your heart the signs that I have shown you, the dreams that you have seen, and the interpretations that you have heard…"

Ezra's Concern to Restore the Scriptures

Then I answered and said, "Let me speak in your presence, Lord. For I will go, as you have commanded me, and I will reprove the people who are now living, but who will warn those who will be born hereafter? For the world lies in darkness, and its inhabitants are without light. For your law has been burned, so no one knows the things that have been done or will be done by you. If then I have found favor with you, send the holy spirit into me, and I will write everything that has happened in the world from the beginning, the things that were written in your law, so that people may be able to find the path and that those who want to live in the last days may do so."

He answered me and said, "Go and gather the people, and tell them not to seek you for forty days. But prepare for yourself many writing tablets, and take with you Sarea, Dabria, Selemia, Ethanus, and Asiel – these five, who are trained to write rapidly, and you shall come here, and I will light in your heart the lamp of understanding, which shall not be put out until what you are about to write is finished. And when you have finished, some things you shall make public, and some you shall deliver in secret to the wise; tomorrow at this hour you shall begin to write."

Ezra's Last Words to the People

Then I went as he commanded me, and I gathered all the people together and said, "Hear these words, O Israel. At first our ancestors lived as aliens in Egypt, and they were liberated from there and received the law of life, which they did not keep, which you also have transgressed after them. Then land was given to

> you for a possession in the land of Zion, but you and your ancestors committed iniquity and did not keep the ways that the Most High commanded you. And since he is a righteous judge, in due time he took from you what he had given. And now you are here, and your people[h] are farther in the interior. If you, then, will rule over your minds and discipline your hearts, you shall be kept alive, and after death you shall obtain mercy. For after death the judgment will come, when we shall live again, and then the names of the righteous shall become manifest, and the deeds of the ungodly shall be disclosed. But let no one come to me now, and let no one seek me for forty days."

The Restoration of the Scriptures

> So I took the five men, as he had commanded me, and we proceeded to the field and remained there. And on the next day a voice called me, saying, "Ezra, open your mouth and drink what I give you to drink." So I opened my mouth, and a full cup was offered to me; it was full of something like water, but its color was like fire. I took it and drank, and when I had drunk it, my heart poured forth understanding, and wisdom increased in my breast, for my spirit retained its memory, and my mouth was opened and was no longer closed. Moreover, the Most High gave understanding to the five men, and by turns they wrote what was dictated, using characters that they did not know. They sat forty days; they wrote during the daytime and ate their bread at night. But as for me, I spoke in the daytime and was not silent at night. So during the forty days, ninety-four books were written. And when the forty days were ended, the Most High spoke to me, saying, "Make public the twenty-four books that you wrote first, and let the worthy and the unworthy read them, but keep the seventy that were written last, in order to give them to the wise among your people. For in them is the spring of understanding, the fountain of wisdom, and the river of knowledge." And I did so (2 Esdras 14).

Interestingly here in this passage, like Moses before him, he first hears the lord from within a bush, and like Zoroaster before him, along with other Zoroastrian figures, God's wisdom comes through a drink. Also notable in this respect is the introduction of the Persian concepts of Heaven and Hell, the "Pit of Sheoll," which was more akin to the Greek Land of Hades, falls into the background. Ezra also makes it clear, the whole Exodus sojourn myth, and other elements of the Faith, were unknown to the people he was telling them about....

Some have credited Ezra and his group of scribes, for much of the present form and format of The Hebrew Bible. If not its composition, then the final flavor of the mixed punch.

The noted 19th century journalist and foe of slavery, George Washington Brown, provided some interesting insights into this "cup of fire" that inspired Ezra in his *Researches in oriental history: Embracing the origin of the Jews, the rise and development of Zoroastrianism, and the derivation of Christianity* (1890), which is quoted at length here:

Ezra and the Cup of Fire

> It was B.C.634 years, Bible chronology, that "Josiah began to manifest great zeal towards the pure worship of God." Only 47 years thereafter to wit; B.C. 587, the walls of Jerusalem were broken down by the armies of Nebuchadnezzar, the temple was burned, and the people were led, with hooks in their noses, to Babylon. Seventy years went by, the temple was rebuilt, and some 42,000 persons, according to Ezra "came again into Jerusalem and Judah, everyone to his own city." Another long period passed. "Ezra went up from Babylon," Ezra 7:6. He was a ready scribe, and Josephus says he was a high priest. This event occurred B.C. 447, 130 years after the destruction of the temple. He took a large party with him, was four months on the way, and bore letters from Artaxerxes, virtually making him governor of Judaea. A year later, to wit; 446 B.C. Nehemiah was sent to "Judah to build it."
>
> ... In Nehemiah, 8:5, we read, "Ezra opened the book in the sight of all the people;" verse 9, "All the people wept, when they heard the words of the law;" and verse 18, "Day by day, from the first day unto the last," for seven days, "he read from the book of the law." Where did Ezra get "the book of the law?"
>
> Biblical writers universally concede that between the years B.C. 433, 444 "Ezra prepared and set forth a correct edition of the Scriptures," – See chronological index to the Holy Bible. And in the "Introductory and Concluding remarks on Each Book," in a Polyglot Bible now before us, we read:

"Ezra appears to have made the sacred scriptures during the captivity his special study. And perhaps assisted by Nehemiah and the great synagogue, he corrected the errors that had crept into the Sacred Writings, through negligence or mistakes of transcribers; he collected all the books of which the Sacred Scriptures then consisted, disposed them in their proper order, and settled the canon scripture for his time. He occasionally added, under the superintendence of the Holy Spirit, whatever appeared necessary for the purpose of illustrating, completing, or correcting them.... Though not styled a prophet, he wrote under the Divine Spirit; and the canonical authority of his book has never been disputed." ...

In Kitto's *Cyclopedia of Biblical Literature*, article Ezra, the author says: "Ezra is even said to have rewritten the whole Old Testament from memory, the copies of which had perished by neglect."

We find the Book of the Law in Ezra's possession about 150 years after the beginning of the Jewish captivity, and we find him for seven days reading from the holy book while the people listened and wept. The temple at Jerusalem was burned, and the natural presumption is, the Jewish library was burned with it. Where did Ezra get the book of the Law from which he read? Nehemiah does not tell. The book of Ezra is silent.

Biblical writers concede that besides writing the book which bears his name, Ezra wrote the two books of Chronicles, probably Esther and Nehemiah, and the first and second book of Esdras.

Kitto says, quoted above, that the first books of the Old Testament perished by neglect. Ezra gives us the facts, 2 Esdras 14: 20, 21, 22, addressing himself directly to what is understood as the fountain of inspiration:

"Behold Lord ... The world is set in darkness, and they that dwell therein are without light, for thy law is burnt, therefore no man knoweth the things that are done of thee, or the works that shall begin; but I have found grace before thee, send the Holy Ghost into me and I shall write all that hath been done in the world since the beginning, which were written in thy law, that men may find thy path, and that they which live in the latter days may live."

From the time the temple was burned, with the sacred books of the Jews, and the people were taken captives to Babylon, B.C. 587, to this period when Ezra was about to "set forth a correct edition of the Scriptures" between 444 and 433 B.C., about 150 years had intervened, during all of which period there had been no Sacred Scriptures, no Inspired Word of God, no books of the Jewish Law, no national library, because they were burned with the temple. How could Ezra repeat from memory, as Kitto suggests, this voluminous record, which had no existence in his day, or the several generations before him?

Ezra must have been born in Babylon, and there learned the profession of scribe, and there must have been made high priest.

Zoroastrian monotheism was made the state religion throughout the Persian empire, with its one hundred and twenty-seven provinces, by Darius Hystaspis, [son of Vishataspa] whose reign extended from India to Ethiopia, B.C. 521. That continued the established religion throughout Persia until it was partially succeeded by the monotheism of Mohamet. And this, too, was true of her many provinces until they were wrestled from her by superior force. It was the law of Judea by virtue of Persian authority, when Ezra decided to write the history of the world from the beginning – shall we say, copied the holy books from Assur-bani-pal's Library, duplicates of some of them, with the story of creation, the fall of man, the general deluge, the tower of Babel, and the confusion of language are now on file in the British Museum, written on earthen plates, in cuneiform characters ... under the direction of a Babylonian priest...

But this quotation from Esdras, as regards the burning of the law with the temple, and Ezra's declared purpose to write a history of the world from the beginning, with a quotation to follow, are from one of the apocryphal books, not recognized as canonical by the Protestants. What are the facts? The apocryphal books were placed on an equality with the residue of the inspired Scriptures by the Council of Trent, in 1545; therefore they are portions of the infallible "Word of God" with Catholics; but as this action of a general council occurred after the Reformation under Luther, its action is not binding on Protestants; though the Church of England allows the books to be read for "edification and instruction," and they are as genuine as any other portion of the holy writ, and of equal authority with the best; but in the honesty and simplicity of the author, Ezra – Esdras, the Latin form of the name – he unwittingly told how the sacred books were made, and under what influence. This has prejudiced their standing.

Again, in the *Library of Universal Knowledge,* we are told that the title, apocryphal, was "sometimes given to writings whose public use was not thought advisable;" that is to say, "God did not exercise good judgment when he inspired his prophets to write, therefore we, the priests, must suppress portions of his Word!" We apprehend in the case of 1st and 2nd Esdras this was the real reason for not making the apocryphal books canonical at the Council of Laodicia, A.D. 360, when the other books were declared the "Word of God."

Here is Ezra's own account of the process of making Jewish history. After telling the people not to seek him for forty days, and taking with him five persons whom he names, who could write swiftly, they retired to a field where they remained:

"The next day, behold a voice cried to me saying. 'Esdras open thy mouth, and drink what I give you thee to drink!' Then opened I my mouth, and behold, he reached me a full cup, which is full as it were with water, but the color of it was like fire. I took it, and drank: and when I had drunk of it, my heart uttered understanding, and wisdom grew in my breast, for my spirit strengthened and my memory; and my mouth was opened and shut no more: and they sat forty days, and they wrote in the day, and at night they ate bread. As for me, I spake by the day, and I held not my tongue by the night. In forty days they wrote two hundred and four books" 2 Esdras 14:38 to 44.

A voice bid him open his mouth, he – the voice, of course – reached Esdras a full cup. It would be interesting to know whose voice it was which possessed such unnatural powers; yet we apprehend the reader is much more anxious to know the contents of the cup, which was fiery red, and which possessed such wondrous ability, probably the same possessed by the "fruit of the tree" which grew "in the midst of the garden," the eating of which opened the eyes of our first parents, and enabled them to see "as Gods knowing good and evil." We think we can furnish this desired information, to do which we are compelled to anticipate some facts existing among Zoroastrian worshipers; many centuries before the date religionists ascribe to Abraham, and which was practiced in Persia, Assyria and Babylonia at the very time Ezra was writing Jewish history under the influence of the "fiery cup."

Among other duties required on occasional sacrifices of animals to Ahura-Mazda, additional to prayers, praises, thanksgiving, and the recitation of hymns, was the performance from time to time of a curious ceremony known as that of the Haoma or Homa. This consisted of the extraction of the juice of the Homa plant by the priests during the recitation of prayers, the formal presentation of the liquid extracted to the sacrificial fire ... the consumption of a small portion of it by one of the officiating ministers, and the division of the remainder among the worshipers...

Says Clarke in his *Ten Great Religions*, Page 202:

"The whole Sama-Veda is devoted to this moon-plant worship; an important part of the Avesta is occupied by Hymns to Homa. This great reverence paid to the plant, on account of its intoxicating qualities, carries us back to a region where the vine was unknown, and to a race to whom intoxication was so new an experience as to seem a gift of the gods. Wisdom appeared to come from it, health, increased power of body and soul, long life, victory in battle, brilliant children. What Bacchus was to the Greeks, the Divine Haoma, or Soma, was to the primitive Aryans."

What was the Haoma or Homa, the production of the moon-plant, growing in those regions of Asia to far north for the successful growing of the grape, and yet yielding such intoxicating properties? It is known in the medical books as Apocynum Cannabinum, and belongs to the Indian Hemp family, Cannabis Indica being an official preparation from it. It is now known in India as bhang, and is popularly known with us as hashish, the stimulating and intoxicating effects of which are well known to physicians. The extract from its young and tender top has a fragrant odor, and a warm bitterish and acrid taste.

The adoration paid to the prepared juice of this plant, and its use on sacrificial occasions, and the drinking of it by the high priest Ezra, as he was about to "open his mouth," while the "five swift scribes" wrote down his words when he was filled with wisdom and understanding, and was about to dictate history "from the beginning of the world," can best be appreciated by members of the medical profession who have personally experienced its exhilarating effects on some fellow student, who was elevated by his own estimation, on a high pedestal and was capable of taking in all that has been, is, and may be in the material universe. Indeed, an acquaintance with this fact explains all those graphic descriptions in that celebrated history of the creation of the world; of the making of man – and of woman in particular; their expulsion from the garden – not forgetting that interesting interview with the snake, the materialized form of Angro-Mainyus, or in our vernacular, the Devil; the account of the deluge; Noah's drunken debauchery; Lot's wife changed into a pillar of salt; and the widower's escapade with his daughters; Jacob wrestling with God, getting a broken thigh and seeing angels ascending and descending a ladder to and from heaven; the terrible plagues on Egypt; the parting of the Red Sea; the law passed down through a cloud to Moses by God himself; the adventures of Samson with the foxes, his contest with the lion, and the loss of his hair; David with his sling; the Hebrew boys in the fiery furnace; not omitting Jonah's wonderful gourd, nor his fishing exploits; Elijah's ride to heaven; and Elisha's children eating bears. No criticisms are required when it is known what kind of drink Ezra was regaled with before "opening his mouth" to dictate history for his swift scribes to write.

But reader, there is still another fact we may as well state with this connection. The wine in the sacrament of the "Lord's Supper" is a survival of the adoration and use, with prayers and hymns, of this divine Haoma, a substitution of a more pleasant intoxicant [wine] by the later worshipers of Mithra, who, in after years are known as Christians.

This is a faithful history of the making of the Bible, as detailed by the author himself. He informs us, 2 Edras 14.44 to 46, that of the 204 books thus written he was instructed by the Highest to publish the first openly, "that the worthy and unworthy may read it; but keep the 70 last that thou mayest deliver them only to such as be wise among the people: for in them is the spring of understanding, the fountain of wisdom, and the stream of knowledge."

From this statement it is very clear we have only that part of the "Holy Scripture" designed for the worthy and the unworthy. That part containing "wisdom" and "understanding" failed to reach our times (Brown, 1890).

In the account of Ezra drinking from the cup of fire, one is clearly reminded of the tradition of the Zoroastrian accounts of the drinking of mang mixed with Haoma or wine. "The image of a blazing cup was apparently related to ... Zoroastrism; Zoroastrian texts mention ritual vessels with fire burning inside them" (Kisel, 2007).

In the article 'Preparation for Visions in Second Temple Jewish Apocalyptic Literature," Vicente Dobroruka, independently and more than a century after Brown, also noted a comparison between the Persian technique of shamanic ecstasy and that of Ezra's:

> ... 4Ezra 14:38-42 - "And on the next day, behold, a voice called me, saying, 'Ezra, open your mouth and drink what I give you to drink'. Then I opened my mouth, and behold, a full cup was offered to me; it was full of something like water, but it's color was like fire. And I took it and drank [...]." Similar drinks appear in Persian literature, e.g. Bhaman Yasht 3:7-8, when Zoroaster "drinks" the water he acquires the wisdom of Ahura Mazda. Similarly, Vishtaspa has an experience quite equivalent in the Dinkard 7:4.84-86 where mention is made to a mixture of wine (or haoma) and hemp with henbane ... opposition to those practices may have generated their replacement in the later BY [*Bahman Yast*]. *The Book of Artay Viraz* also mentions visions obtained from wine mixed with hemp, and for the preparations of the seer cf. ch. 2.25-28 (Dobroruka, 2002).

Dobroruka revisited this theme in more detail in his later 2006 article, "Chemically-induced visions in the Fourth Book of Ezra in light of comparative Persian material," and again draws direct comparisons between Ezra's cup of fire, and the mang-mixed infused beverages of the Zoroastrian psychonauts. Dobroruka expanded on this connection by noting the similar accounts of the flowers eaten by Ezra in 4 Ezra 9, and those used for similar revelation by the Zoroastrian figure Jamasp:

> But if you will let seven days more pass – do not fast during them, however; but go into a field of flowers where no house has been built, and eat only of the flowers of the field, and taste no meat and drink no wine, but eat only flowers, and pray to the Most High continually - then I will come and talk with you. (4Ezra 9:23-25).
>
> In the *Jāmāsp Namag* (also a pseudepigraphic text, written in the name of an old sage), Jāmāsp receives from Zoro-

> aster the gift of knowledge by means of a flower. This is also the theme of the Pahlavi text *Wizirkard i Denig* 19… indeed, the tradition that described the acquisition of mystical knowledge by Jāmāsp resembles very much that of Ezra regarding the flowers, as the drinking of the blessed wine looks like the experience of 4Ezra 14 – the main difference in the passage being the fact that here we have two different seers [i.e. Jamasp & Vishtaspa] (Dobroruka, 2006).

Dobroruka also compared Ezra's chemically induced inspiration to other Biblical accounts, "The episode has parallels in the scroll eaten by Ezekiel (Ez 2:8-3:3) and thus to the author of the Book of Revelation (Ap 10:9-10), who also claims to have had sensory experiences related to ingestion" (Dobroruka, 2006).

As noted in Chapter 11 the oldest existing copies of many of the Zoroastrian texts referred to are dated much later than the period in question (although they are thought to be adapted from older accounts) and for this reason, some might argue against a Persian influence on the accounts of Ezra, but as Dobroruka notes, this is not necessarily the case:

> [T]he figure of Vishtaspa … is much older than the earliest Jewish apocalypses themselves (i.e. earlier than III century BCE) and … at least assures that the figure of Vishtasp cannot be later than that of Ezra.… [also there are the] fourth century BCE … fragments collectively known as the Oracle of Hystaspes [Greek Vishtaspa]). This is indirect evidence that late Persian texts contain cores that can be of earlier date … The theme of the cup that gives wisdom, being already present in the *Yasna* 10.17… [which] deals with the theme of the wisdom cup, in this case related to haoma:
>
> > "Thereupon spake Zarathushtra: Praise to Haoma, Mazda-made. Good is Haoma, Mazda-made. All the plants of Haoma praise I, on the heights of lofty mountains, in the gorges of the valleys, in the clefts (of sundered hillsides) cut for the bundles bound by women. From the silver cup I pour Thee to the golden chalice over. Let me not thy (sacred) liquor spill to earth, of precious cost."
>
> The dating of the *Yasna* depends on the dating attributed to Zoroaster, but even supposing the prophet to be a figure living as late as the sixth century BCE … the *Yasna* is much earlier

> than 4Ezra.... All this tends to support the idea that the two mythical themes examined that find way in 4Ezra (namely, that of the cup and that of the flower, both of which bestow wisdom) were, both by their antiquity and their frequency, primarily Persian ecstatic practices that found themselves echoed in a Jewish apocalypse (Dobroruka, 2006).

Clearly, a strong Persian influence on the texts of the Hebrew Bible is undeniable. That this foreign influence included cannabis can now be seen to be equally obvious from the way that the two cultures utilized the plant for religious inspiration. It should also be noted that the marriage of the traditions of the Persians with those of the Semites bore fruit, and the child of this union has become one of the leading religions of the modern world ... Christianity, with its Messianic message of a world savior, derived from the Persian concept of *Saoshyant*, but that is a story for another book...

Clearly, until at least the time of Ezra, there was still no form of the Hebrew Bible as we know of it today. At the time of the Persian return the "mere idea that Ezra was 'dictating' sacred books (not yet canonical) implies that the Sinaitic revelation still had room to be enlarged, an idea that may reinforce the presence of the Holy Spirit in Ezra as he drank from the cup" (Dobroruka, 2006). Ezra does indeed seem to be the end of the entheogen-consuming prophets, that have graced the pages in this study. Notably, it seems after the period of Persian return of the Jews to their homeland either the ears of the prophets grew deaf, or the voice of Yahweh silent. Any evidence of shamanic practice soon faded shortly after the sphere of Persian influence receded to other Empirical forces.

However, with the laws for the people codified, and how many tithes should be paid to the Temple settled, did the religion really need the Ecstatic Prophets of earlier generations and the community upheaval and anxiety that they could have wrought?

The End of the Age of Prophets

Through the Priestly editors, and rule, the classic Age of Prophets, came to an end. The Priestly class had absolutely no interest in ecstatic messages delivered in the name of the Lord, but rather focused on the rule and word of the law. In the book of Jeremiah, we read the priestly edict that "any madman who acts like a prophet" should be put "into the stocks and neck-irons" (Jeremiah 29:26). As the word of the Lord proclaims in the works of Zechariah, in the fifth century B.C.; "... if anyone still prophesies [makes to na'bi], his father and mother, to who he was born, will say to him, 'You must die, because you have told lies in the Lord's name'. When he prophesies, his own parents will stab him. On that day every prophet will be ashamed of his prophetic vision. He will not put on a prophet's garment of hair in order to deceive. He will say, 'I am not a prophet. I am a farmer; the land has been my livelihood since my youth'" (Zechariah 13:3-5). In *Incense and Poison Ordeals in the Ancient Orient* Allen Godbey explained in 1930 in comparison to the seance rooms of his own day:

> One reason for the war of the Hebrew prophets upon the incense rituals of their time would be clearer to any person who would study the methods of modern seance-rooms. Much incense is a tradition of the profession, especially with those who make a business of "developing" mediumistic or clairvoyant powers in their disciples. A "trance gift" or power of "spirit vision" is sure to be discovered in those sensitive to a little narcotic stimulation. The mutterings of a half-stupefied disciple in a "pipe dream" are explained to others as "trance manifestation" or "spirit control." All alienists know that even mild odors may stimulate neurotic subjects to imaginative visions.... A whole roomful – a "school of the prophets" of today – may thus be set gibbering. Some mediums, making a business of furnishing spirits upon demand, willy-nilly, have been known to make themselves complete "dope wrecks." Such practices are known in all lands; observers report them from almost every savage tribe; they figure in a host of orgies and religious frenzies. The reader of the *Arabian Nights* may recall that in some tales spirits of jinn arise in the smoke of powders thrown on the fire. Lane (I, 61), in his discussion of Arab magic, says that "illusions or hallucinations are still produced by such devices." From ancient Babylonia to the present they are a favorite resort of those who pretend to summon the spirits of the dead. Isa. 57:9 declares: "You have gone (so you say) to the King [Molech - Ruler of the Dead] with ointments; You have greatly multiplied your odors. You have sent your messengers to Far-Land. You have descended even to Sheol [Land of the Dead]!" (Godbey, 1930).

Complicating things, shortly after this monotheistic cue that really marks the beginning of Judaism as we now know it, Persia itself fell to the Greeks, then the Greeks to the Romans. This roll call of Empires which held rule over the Jews separated them further from their past, and created a void which the new history provided by Ezra and his cohorts quickly filled. The confusion created by these religious reforms and succession of Empires led to different factions in Judaism, such as the Sadducees, Pharisees, Rabbis, Essenes and Jewish Gnostic sects all of whom began to interpret things slightly differently and in some cases vied for power over the people.

However, the account of Ezra's fiery cup is not the only indication of infused wines and beverages in the Hebrew Bible and wider Near East. As with kaneh bosm, there seems to have been vastly different perceptions of this use with the various authors and editorial groups who composed the Hebrew Bible, a subject we will examine in the next chapter.

Chapter 13

Drug Infused Wines and Strong Drink in the Ancient World

The infusion of wines and other alcoholic beverages in the ancient world, with cannabis and other drugs, seems to have been at least as widespread as burning them as incense. As noted in the *Encyclopedia Britannica* (5th Edition) under 'Drug Cults': "The ceremonial use of wine and incense in contemporary ritual is probably a relic of a time when the psychological effects of these substances were designed to bring the worshiper into closer touch with supernatural forces" (Clark, 1978). That the two would be used in combination, and eventually combined, seems clear, and we have textual and archaeological evidence that this was the case, as well as clear indications of such preparations amongst the ancient Jews. As Professor Carl Ruck has explained: "Ancient wines were always fortified, like the 'strong wine' of the Old Testament, with herbal additives: opium, datura, belladonna, mandrake and henbane.[1] Common incenses, such as myrrh, ambergris and frankincense are psychotropic; the easy availability and long tradition of cannabis use would have seen it included in the mixtures" (Ruck, 2003).

This is not to say, that wine or beer alone were not used in religious rituals, they certainly were. Likely the earliest combination was simply using the two at the same time, and once it was realized fermented beverages could act as a carrier and diluter, this likely saw the addition of such substances to wines and beers, to make them more potent, or in the case of some of the drugs used, less potent and less toxic.

The Greeks were well aware of the plants around them, and the idea that they contained not only medicinal but magical properties, was widespread. Because it was believed "that certain drugs could secure the passionate love of another. Indian hemp, mandrake, opium, strychnos varieties, and others were greatly used as love charms and as stimulating aphrodisiacs" (Parsons, 1899). This saw them as con-

1 It is interesting to note that according to Josephus, writing in the 1st century, The High Priest's costume included a cup made to look like henbane: "The high priest's mitre ... was a golden crown polished... out of which arose a cup of gold, which resembled the herb ... those Greeks that are skillful in botany call ... Hyoscyamus [Henbane]."

tents in "love potions" or as they were known *philtres*, a word derived from the Greek *philtron*, which was used to describe a potion drunk to induce passion. "Pliny, the Roman writer, says the properties of these drugs became manifest even when merely taken into the hand, but more so when taken in dry wines; and that 'overindulgence in them will cause death.' This proves that most of these substances were no doubt stimulants and narcotics" (Parsons, 1899).

Varieties of psychoactive plants were used in such infusions. According to Dioscorides and his commentator Matthiolus, one could "boil the root of mandrake in wine down to a third part, and preserve the decoction, of which they administer a *cyathus* (about a fluid ounce and a half), to produce sleep, and to allay severe pains of any part; and also before operations with the knife, or the application of the actual cautery, that the operation should not be felt." As we noted 2nd century CE references from China, refer to the use of cannabis-infused wine for such operations.

Theophrastus and Dioscorides are thought to have been the first to directly mention the soporific properties of mandrake (*Atropa mandragora*). Dioscorides also informs us that one dram of the root of "manic" nightshade (Atropa belladonna), taken in wine, elicits "empty forms" and "images of not unpleasant kind," Pliny mentions that "the ancients were of opinion that the leaves [of henbane] act as a febrifuge, taken in wine" and he had a recipe for frankincense and myrrh wine.[2]

A variety of infused wines that are generally believed to contain cannabis, under the names "*thalassaegle*," "*potammaugis*" and "gelotophyllis" were recorded by Democritus (c.a. 460 BCE). "Democritus's famous recipe for a hemp wine is suitable for internal use: Macerate 1 teaspoon of myrrh ... and a handful of hemp flowers in 1 litre of retsina or dry Greek white wine ... strain before drinking" (Rätsch, 2005). "The *gelotophyllis* of Pliny ... a plant drunk in wine among the Bactrians, which produced immoderate laughter, may very well be identical with hemp, which still grows wild in the country around the Caspian and Aral Seas" (Houtsma, et al., 1936/1993). Pliny (23-79 A.D.) quotes the following description from Democritus:

> The Thalassaegall he speaks of as being found on the banks of the river Indus, from which circumstance it is also known as potamaugis. Taken in drink it produces delirium, which presents to the fancy visions of a most extraordinary nature. The

2 As has been noted, myrrh was often doctored with cannabis resins in the ancient world.

> theangelis, he says, grows upon Mount Libanus in Syria, upon the chain of mountains called Dicte in Crete, and at Babylon and Susa in Persia. An infusion of it imparts powers of divination to the Magi. The geolotophyllis, is a plant found in Bactriana [i.e. BMAC], and on the banks of the Borysthenes. Taken internally with myrrh and wine all sorts of visionary forms present themselves, excite the most immoderate laughter.

As noted, Bactria is a region that the Russian archaeologist Victor Sarianidi claimed to have found evidence that cannabis, ephedra and opium poppy were used in the preparation of haoma.

Pliny mentions "An infusion of it imparts powers of divination to the Magi" in reference to the Zoroastrians, and we have already discussed a number of such preparations, in regard to the Zoroastrians and Ezra, as well as Professor Patrick McGovern's theory on Soma. As McGovern has also noted of the Scythians "They would have had access to some of the ancient ingredients likely used in ancient haoma/soma. At Pazyryk, the preferred beverage thus appears to have combined a marijuana high with an alcoholic buzz" (McGovern, 2009). The archaeological discovery of Scythian goblets with residues of both opium and cannabis are likely testaments to such combinations.

Evidence of such practices in other cultures is worth noting in this regard.

Nepenthe

Although Egyptian references to cannabis under the name *shemshemet*, or *sm-sm-t*, generally refer to topical medical preparations of the plant, and give little indications of its use for psychoactive or spiritual purposes, there are other potential references that indicate cannabis was used in a wine infusion.

Nepenthe was an ancient herbal-infused wine, that appears in Homer's famous tale *The Odyssey*. Its use to quell grief in a funerary setting has caused many researchers to identify it with cannabis.

The Odyssey of Homer (9th-8th century BC) describes the Nepenthes which came to the Greeks from Egyptian Thebes:

> Then Helen, daughter of Zeus ... cast a drug into the wine whereof they drank, a drug to lull all pain and anger, and bring forgetfulness of every sorrow. Whoso should drink a draught thereof, when it is mingled in the bowl, on that day he would let no tear fall down his cheeks, not though his mother and his

> father died, not though men slew his brother or dear son with the sword before his face, and his own eyes beheld it. Medicines of such virtue and so helpful had the daughter of Zeus, which Polydamna, the wife of Thon, had given her, a woman of Egypt, where earth the grain-giver yields herbs in greatest plenty, many that are healing in the cup, and many baneful. There each man is a leech skilled beyond all human kind...

The historian Diodorus Siculus, who lived in the 1st century BCE, noted that still in his time, more than 7 centuries after the composition of *Homer's Iliad*, "people say that the Egyptian women make use of the powder (of this plant, scil. the nepenthes) and they say from ancient times only those women who lived in the 'Town-of-Zeus' [i.e. Thebes,] which was also known as Diospolis] had found medicines which cure wrath and grief. (1, 97, 1-9; Eus. PE 10, 8, 9-12; cf. also Ps.Iustinus, Cohort. ad gent. 26e).

As Prof Carl Ruck has noted "It is generally assumed that the drug, which Helen is supposed to have learned in Egypt, was opium, but the effects as described in the poem are much more like Cannabis, which was also widely employed in Egypt and throughout the Near East" (Ruck, et al., 2007). As well, the Greeks were very familiar with opium, and knew of its effects directly, while the ingredients of the nepenthe were more of a mystery to them.

Numerous researchers have seen nepenthe as a cannabis concoction. An idea first put forth by the French Pharmacist Joseph Virey (1775-1846) who suggested in 1813 that hasheesh was Homer's nepenthe (*Bulletin de Pharmacie*). Many others have since concurred: "The opinions entertained by the learned, on the nature of the Nepenthe of the ancients have been various. By Th. Zwinger, and ... by Sprengel, in his history of botany, it is supposed to be opium.... But the best authorities, with whom our author coincides, are of opinion that the Nepenthe was derived from the Cannabis sativa of Linnaeus" (Christen, 1822); "the famous nepenthe of the ancients is said to have been prepared by decocting the hemp leaves" (Watt, 1853); "nepenthe which may reasonably be surmised was bhang from the far east" (Benjamin, 1880). As the authors of *The Manners and Customs of the Ancient Egyptians* also concluded: "Nepenthes ... Perhaps the Bust or Hasheesh, a preparation of the Cannabis sativa" (Wilkinson & Birch, 1878). See also (Walton, 1938; Burton, 1894; Lewin, 1931; Singer and Underwood, 1962; Oursler, 1968; Wills, 1998). It is clearly the Nepenthe that Prof Richard Evans Schultes and Prof. Albert Hofmann are referring to when they write in a chapter on cannabis

"In ancient Thebes the plant was made into a drink with opium like effects" (Schultes & Hofmann, 1979).

In *A Glossary of Colloquial Anglo-Indian Words and Phrases,* Yule and Crooke note an interesting connection between a Coptic (Greek-Egyptian) term and the nepenthe; "Bhang is usually derived from Skt. Bhanga, 'breaking,' but [Sir Richard] Burton derives both it and the Ar. Banj from the old Coptic Nibanj, 'meaning a preparation of hemp; and here it is easy to recognize the Homeric Nepenthe'" (Yule, et al., 1903/1996). As Abram Smythe Palmer also notes in *Folk-etymology*: "Nepenthe, the drug which Helen brought from Egypt, is without doubt the Coptic nibendj, which is the plural of bendj, or benj, hemp, 'bang,' used as an intoxicant" (Palmer, 1882). When one returns to the contemporary Avestan term for cannabis, *b'aŋ'ha,* the similarity in this context, *ne- b'aŋ'ha,* brings us even closer to the cognate pronunciation 'nepenthe.' The Hebrew term "*pannag,*" which Dr. Raphael Mechoulam believes identifies a preparation of cannabis (Mechoulam, et al., 1991) is also similar. Interestingly, as nepenthe was a powder, it is notable that both of these terms are believed to identify prepared forms of cannabis as well.

ARCHAEOLOGICAL EVIDENCE FOR INFUSED WINES

Infused wines play a considerable role in the recent *New York Times'* bestseller, *The Immortality Key,* and one of the more intriguing pieces of evidence put forth by the author Brian Muraresku, was the discovery of an infusion that contained a whole host of ingredients, including things like opium, cannabis henbane, alongside lizard and snake remains, walnuts, and other various spices and herbs. Although the authors of the archaeological study of this find, "Drug preparation in evidence? An unusual plant and bone assemblage from the Pompeian countryside, Italy" have identified this as likely evidence of a *theriac,* a potent medical infusion that was the basis for later alchemical *quintessences* and *arcanums,* due to the area of preparation and the list of ingredients, Muraresku has suggested this may have been the sort of drink used in the Dionysian and potentially other Greek Mysteries.

The location of the archaeological find referred to was in excellent condition, due to its preservation under pumice from the most famous volcano eruption in history. The structure on the site was a home that contained a wine press and threshing floor, wine cellar, and large vessels which contained thick organic deposits, which were identified as infusions of various plants, common fruits and nuts, and even bones of lizards, "suggesting the combination of plants, reptiles, and amphibians was steeped in wine" (Muraresku, 2020). As Muraresku notes however, "the real kicker was the distinctive medley of opium (*Papaver somniferum*), cannabis (Cannabis sativa) and two members of the nightshade family, white henbane (Hysoscyamus albus) and black nightshade (*Solanum nigrum*)" (Muraresku, 2020). A potent infusion indeed!

Although acknowledging the lack of clear context of the find, and the evidence it was for a medical preparation of the time such as theriac or mithrediatnium, Muraresku speculates and questions whether this site could represent "a laboratory for the production of a Dionysian sacrament that could have been used in the Villa of Mysteries that was within walking distance, just West across Pompeii?" (Muraresku, 2020)

In discussions with an archaeologist who was directly involved on the ground level of the find, Muraresku garnered even further evidence than was put forth in the original paper. The archaeologist involved suggested the site was "specifically designed for the production of drugs," and from the discussion Muraresku says the resulting mixture "seems to be a boutique house wine not intended for mass consumption" (Muraresku, 2020). Indications from the garden remains outside of the structure, are that it was a site for producing a select variety of plants and herbs. Evidence of a "maceration tank for cannabis" would seem to indicate this was particularly a key component in the infusion.

There is other archaeological evidence as well. It is worth noting the following French archaeological find reported in the *Wine Spectator* article "2,000-Year-Old Cannabis Wine Discovered":

The ancient partaker and his pot of cannabis infused wine.

> A 2015 excavation near the town of Cébazat in the heart of France (about 100 miles west of Lyon) of a tomb dating to the

> 2nd century B.C., led by researcher Hervé Delhoofs, yielded an earthenware vessel that once held a most potent potable: Analysis of plant material confirmed the presence of "biomarkers" for wine, resin and THC. Did the Gauls simply like the taste, or were they interested in a more, well, holistic experience? Researcher Nicolas Garnier told Unfiltered both "medicinal use or recreational use" were possible, and that the ethanol in wine made it a more efficient substance for infusion than water. "The wine-based medicinal preparations are common," he explained via email. "Different recipes of many plants have been identified in tombs."

Jewish Infused Wines and Strong Drink

In relation to the recent find of cannabis resins burnt in an 8th century BCE temple in Arad, Jerusalem, it is interesting to note that there may have been other ways the ancient Jews utilized psychoactive substances. There are indications of infused wines, and stronger preparations such as the Biblical "strong drink" (*shekar*): "An inebriating Potion described in the Old Testament; but distinct from Wine; probably a Soporific or visionary vinous infusion" (Ott 1995). As Entheobotanist Jonathan Ott has noted:

> Like the ancient Greeks, the ancient Israelites did not know distillation technology, but possessed an inebriant other than wine, which apparently was more potent. Was the Biblical *shekar*, "strong drink," not an inebriating potion analogous to the ancient Greek wines, some of which were entheogenic potions? Down through history there are innumerable instances of the addition of psychoactive plants to wines and other alcoholic beverages (Ott, 1993).

As we have already seen, such concoctions were used ritually throughout the Near East and the recently late ethnobotanist Christian Rätsch suggests from the description of the effects of an "inebriating beverage" referred to in a Mesopotamian texts, the intoxicant was not a simple alcoholic drink, but likely contained "tropane alkaloids as well as opium or hemp" (Rätsch 1997). In *A Cyclopaedia of Biblical Literature*. Kitto noted: "The palm wine of the East ... is made intoxicating ... by an admixture of stupefying ingredients, of which there was an abundance... Such a practice seems to have existed amongst the ancient Jews…." (Kitto, 1846). Kitto, saw the Hebrew references to *eshisha,* which he equated with some sort of prepared cannabis syrup or resin product, discussed in Chapter 4 in this context, suggesting it was mixed into wine.

Interestingly,in Mishnic times cannabis could be grown alongside grape vines. This is notable as it indicates that cannabis did not violate the prohibitions of *Kil'ayim* (Hebrew: םיאלכ; lit. "mixture," or "diverse kinds") which defined the prohibitions in Jewish law which proscribe the planting of certain mixtures of seeds, grafting, the mixing of plants in vineyards, the crossbreeding of animals, the mixing of wool with linen in garments, and other details.

The Sages of Israel referred to a prohibition of growing different kinds of crops in a vineyard. They identified only two grain varieties (such as wheat and barley), or either hemp and arum, being permitted.[3] By a rabbinic prohibition, it was not permitted to plant or maintain a vineyard while the vineyard shares the same immediate ground with any vegetable or seed-crop grown for food. The allowing of cannabis to be grown, would have been designated by some sort of shared association with the vine. Barley and wheat produce beer, and likely in the case of cannabis this shared association was *intoxication.*

Talmudic references indicate the use of infused wines as well: "The one on his way to execution was given a piece of incense in a cup of wine, to help him fall asleep" (Sanh. 43a). A 19th century edition of *The Medical News* explained further:

> Jews were more humane in their method of dealing with condemned criminals than the Greeks or the Romans. In the Talmudic writings there are several passages which seem to show that it was the practice to ease the pain of torture and death by stupefying the sufferers. Thus: "If a man is led forth to death, he is given a cup of spiced wine to drink, whereby his soul is wrapped in night;" and again: "Give a stupefying drink to him that loseth his life, and wine to those that carry bitterness in their hearts." According to tradition, while the Roman conqueror held sway in Palestine, and crucifixion was a common punishment of malefactors, the Jewish women, with the sanction of the Sanhedrin, were wont to ease the death–agony of the sufferers by giving them something in the nature of a "wine of the condemned" upon a sponge. It is probable that the "wine mingled with myrrh," which, according to St. Mark (xv. 23), was offered to Christ while he was hanging on the cross, was a narcotic draft intended to make death painless.

3 Aharon HaLevi (1958), mitzvah # 548; Meiri (2006), p. 94, Kiddushin 39a, s.v. יאלכו הכרמ; Ishtori Haparchi (1999), chapter 56, p. 265

Such preparations were apparently used by the ancient Jews, for ritual intoxication, and for easing pain. A Reverend E. A Lawrence, in an essay on "The wine of the Bible" in a 19th century edition of *The Princeton Review* noted that:

> It appears to have been an ancient custom to give medicated or drugged wine to criminals condemned to death, to blunt their senses, and so lessen the pains of execution. To this custom there is supposed to be an allusion, Prov. xxxi. 6, "Give strong drink unto him that is ready to perish," ...To the same custom some suppose there is a reference in Amos 2:8, where the "wine of the condemned" is spoken of.... The wicked here described, in addition to other evil practices, imposed unjust fines upon the innocent, and spent the money thus unjustly obtained upon wine, which they "quaffed in the house of their gods"...
>
> Mixed wine is often spoken of in Scripture. This was of different kinds ... sometimes, by lovers of strong drink, with spices of various kinds, to give it a richer flavor and greater potency (ls. v. 22; Ps. lxxv. 8). The "royal wine," literally wine of the kingdom ... Esther i. 7), denotes most probably the best wine, such as the king of Persia himself was accustomed to drink (Lawrence, 1871).

This view on pain-dulling infused wines was a considerably widespread view in the 19th century. *The New York Dental Journal* reported: "Among the Hebrews and Egyptians, it was customary to give a preparation of hemp to a condemned prisoner, just previous to his execution; some of the Biblical commentaries assert that the gall and vinegar, mentioned in Scripture as having been given to Christ on a sponge, was in reality what the Prophet Amos calls 'wine of the condemned,' doubtless the Bhang of the Hindoo Suttee at the present day" (Roberts, 1862).

This connection was not limited to 19th century fancy either, as Kenneth Walker noted in *The Story of Medicine*, the "drug, hashish... is of venerable age, and when Amos wrote (around 700 B.C.) on the subject of the 'wine of the condemned', he was probably referring to it" (Walker, 1955).

That this infused wine, not only had pain numbing qualities, but was also "quaffed in the house of their gods" gives clear indication it was sought after for entheogenic effects as well. That it is compared to the wines of the King of Persia, also brings us back to the cannabis infused wines of the Zoroastrian period, such as that taken by King Vistashpa, referred to earlier.

In *The A to Z of Prophets in Islam and Judaism*, Scott B. Noegel, Brannon M. Wheeler, "The use of drugs, especially alcohol ... as a means of inducing or enhancing the prophetic experience is attested periodically throughout the ancient Near East, and is probably related to the mantic's role as an herbalist and medical practitioner" (Noegel & Wheeler, 2010).

> Evidence for opium use has been found throughout the ancient Near East, especially on Cyprus, though its connection to Cypriot cults has been questioned. The practice of inhaling intoxicating substances like cannabis and incense also appear.... Texts from Mari demonstrate that at least some prophets partook in excessive wine drinking as a means of accessing the divine. Ugaritic tablets also detail the events of the marzeah feast, a repast in which ... dead kings were summoned to wine and dine with the living... (Noegel & Wheeler, 2010).

It seems plausible that prepared opium may have been used in the marzeah feast. Recently, the paper "Opium trade and use during the Late Bronze Age: Organic residue analysis of ceramic vessels from the burials of Tel Yehud, Israel" (Linares, Jakoel, Be'eri, Lipschits, Neu-

Bronze Age vessels in which opium residue was detected. Credit: Clara Amit / Israel Antiquities

mann & Gadot, 2022) provided archaeological evidence of ritual opium use at a vast Canaanite Necropolis dating back to the 14th century BCE. Residues of opium were recovered from poppy-shaped ceramic vessels, further confirming a hypothesis that such vessels were particularly designated for holding opium extracts.

> Opium was indeed extracted and collected into Cypriot Base-Ring ware for the purpose of trade in and around the Levant. The opium was most likely used in a number of ways: for medicinal, cultic and ritualistic purposes, as many Cypriot vessels were found in a variety of contexts, signifying its use either for burial rites and/or as an offering for the dead. The fact that we see signals of much lower concentrations of opium alkaloids in locally produced storage jars and juglets suggests one of two things: (1) the material of the locally produced vessels and the more porous ceramic in comparison to the highly fired and finely made Base-Ring ware played a role in the preservation of such alkaloids; (2) once the opium reached the Levant, the local inhabitants may have diluted the opium in some cases into storage jars containing some kind of plant carrier oil. This may have been done in order to stretch out and/or preserve the opium for longer. Another suggestion for the diluting of the opium might have been to reduce the potency of the stimulant (Linares, Jakoel, Be'eri, Lipschits, Neumann & Gadot, 2022).

Such a preparation could easily have been infused in wine or mixed with "strong drink."

In "Sensing the Dead in Household Burials of the Second Millennium BCE," Melissa S. Cradic explains of ritual opium use in this context:

> The use of ... mid-altering substances may explain an important but previously unknown cognitive aspect of Canaanite funerary ritual. Opiates such as morphine are powerful narcotics which can cause euphoria, hallucination, and dissociation, a feeling of being outside of one's body. Dissociation may have been the goal. In the ancient Near East, the dead could simultaneously exist in embodied and disembodied forms.... Through opium induced effects of corporeal dissociation, mourners could have achieved similar states of dual embodiment, blurring the lines between living and dead bodies.... Temporarily, the realms of the living and the dead could have been united through the use of psychoactive substances (Cradic, 20220).

Like Amos' condemnation of those who "quaffed" such mixtures in the "House of the God," Isaiah condemned those who seek oracles from the dead through inebriation. Apparently, the Yahwehist prophet Isaiah was particularly incensed with the techniques of prophetic ecstasy as practiced in the northern kingdom, which would seem to be yet another carryover from the Canaanite cult of El; "These, too, reel with wine, With strong-drink they stagger; Priest and prophet stagger with strong-drink, dazed with wine, Reeling with strong-drink. They stagger when seeing visions, they stumble when rendering decisions. All the tables full of vomit, Excrement without place"(Isaiah 28:7-9).

The northern prophets likely took such entheogenic infusions in emulation of El, whose mythology had become fused with that of Yahweh. Like the ecstatic excess attributed to the northern prophets, are those of the god El whose shrines they had rededicated to their own synchronistic El-Yahweh; "El offered game in his house... He invited the gods to mess. The gods ate and drank, Drank wine till sated, Must till inebriated ... El ... drank wine till sated, Must till inebriated.... An apparition accosted him, With horns and a tail. He floundered in his excrement and urine. El collapsed..." From these passages we can see that both God and prophets literally took themselves into a "shit-faced" drunken stupor in order to induce prophetic trance.

In reference to Isaiah 5:22: "Woe to those who are heroes at drinking wine and champions at mixing drinks" *The Ultimate Bible Dictionary,* editor Matthew George Easton recorded the following entry from John Adams (1735-1826) a highly educated and enlightened lawyer who became a central figure in the American Revolution. Adams explained the Hebrew term *mesekh,* used in this passage, is "properly a mixture of wine and water with spices that increase its stimulating properties (Isa 5:22). Psa 75:8, 'The wine [*yayin*] is red; it is full of mixture [*mesekh*];' Prov 23:30, 'mixed wine;' Isa 65:11, 'drink offering' (R.V., 'mingled wine') ... *Mesek*, 'a mixture,' mixed or spiced wine, not diluted with water, but mixed with drugs and spices to increase its strength... (Psa 75:8; Prov 23:30)" (Adams/Easton, 1897).

Adams also noted the Hebrew *tirosh,* "translated 'wine' (Deut 28:51); 'new wine' (Prov 3:10); 'sweet wine (Micah 6:15). This Hebrew word has been traced to a root meaning 'to take possession of' and hence it is supposed that *tirosh* is so designated because in intoxicating it takes possession of the brain" (Adams/Easton, 1897). However, the ancient Hebrews had little understanding of chemicals and their effects on the brain, so it would seem more likely that an actual spiritual possession is intended in the meaning.

Isaiah contains further condemnation of these revelries which in this instance sound like harmless music-filled celebrations: "Woe to those who rise early in the morning that they may follow strong-drink, who stay up late at night till they are inflamed with wine. They have harps and lyres at their banquets, tambourines and flutes and wine, but they have no regard for the deeds of the Lord, no respect for the work of his hands" (5:11-12). The angry Yahwhist prophet sees the free-spirited revelers as "dogs with mighty appetites; they never have enough ... 'Come', each one cries, 'let me get wine! Let us have our fill of strong-drink! And tomorrow will be like today, or even far better" (Isaiah 56:11-12).

Sentiments echoed by Habakkuk, who was active around 612 BC, "Woe to you who make your neighbors drink, who mix in your venom [i.e. drugs or herbs] even to make them drunk so as to look on their nakedness!" (Habakkuk 2:15). Similarly Micah condemns those who "prophecy for ... plenty of wine and strong-drink" (Micah 2:11). And again, Amos: "They lie down by every altar on clothes taken in pledge, And drink the wine of the condemned in the house of their god" (Amos 2:8).

Isaiah records that it is due to such revelries the Northern Kingdom of Israel fell;

> The earth is defiled by its people;
> they have disobeyed the laws,
> violated the statutes
> and broken the everlasting covenant.
> Therefore a curse consumes the earth;
> its people must bear their guilt.
> Therefore earth's inhabitants are burned up,
> very few are left.
> The new wine dries up and the vine withers;
> all the merrymakers groan.
> The gaiety of the tambourine is stilled,
> the noise of the revelers stopped,
> the joyful harp is silent.
> No longer do they drink wine with song;
> the strong-drink is bitter to its drinkers.
>
> –Isaiah 24:5-9

It is interesting to also note that Vicente Dobroruka saw Jeremiah as condemning practices such as those alluded to in the story of Ezra and the Persian accounts as well. "There seems to be a parallel, if in different settings and intentions, between the cup that maddens the nations in Jr 25:15-16" (Dobroruka, 2002).

> This is what the Lord, the God of Israel, said to me: "Take from my hand this cup filled with the wine of my wrath and make all the nations to whom I send you drink it. When they drink it, they will stagger and go mad because of the sword I will send among them."
>
> So I took the cup from the Lord's hand and made all the nations to whom he sent me drink it: Jerusalem and the towns of Judah, its kings and officials, to make them a ruin and an object of horror and scorn, a curse – as they are today; Pharaoh king of Egypt, his attendants, his officials and all his people, and all the foreign people there; all the kings of Uz; all the kings of the Philistines (those of Ashkelon, Gaza, Ekron, and the people left at Ashdod); Edom, Moab and Ammon; all the kings of Tyre and Sidon; the kings of the coastlands across the sea; Dedan, Tema, Buz and all who are in distant places; all the kings of Arabia and all the kings of the foreign people who live in the wilderness; all the kings of Zimri, Elam and Media; and all the kings of the north, near and far, one after the other – all the kingdoms on the face of the earth. And after all of them, the king of Sheshak will drink it too (Jeremiah 15-26).

Jeremiah blames this cup for the fall of Babylon:

> Babylon [claimed to be] a cup of gold in the hand of Yahu, That made all lands to reel. Of her wine the nations drank So that the peoples went mad. Suddenly Babylon falls and is convulsion-rent! Wail over her - get balsam for her wounds - perhaps she can be cured? We would like to cure Babylon, But she cannot be cured! Leave her there, and let us all go home! For her doom rises to heaven, And touches the very skies (Jeremiah 51:6).

As Dobroruka noted, these practices were demonized as a foreign influence: "Chemical induction related to the visionary present the most 'paganizing' reference to the means for inspiration found among the apocalypticists (i.e. the passages that most resemble pagan practices of artificial ecstatic practices); this may be so for the same reason that 'classical prophets' have a 'calmer' ecstasy than their pagan counterparts, i.e. for editorial reasons" (Dobroruka, 2006).

Clearly Jeremiah condemned the "cup" for the same reasons as he did the incense burning and drink offerings of former priests and kings; like the modern religious elite, and the Priestly editors and writers that followed him, his only interest was in the stated law, there was no room for new revelation. The references to the pouring out of drink offerings to the Queen of Heaven, as well as references to cannabis infused beer, likely dedicated to Ishtar under her title *Beltu* (Lady), may also be a source of Jeremiah's condemnation. This, as well, brings forth imagery from the New Testament's Book of Revelation, with the "Whore of Babylon" holding up her "cup full of abominations." Something to consider with the text's concern about sorcery, which is translated from the original Greek renderings, 'pharmakeia' a term directly related to the use of herbs in magic, as well as derived from the same root word for the modern term 'pharmacy'. These references show, even though in a negative light, that such cultic practices as the induction of altered states through wine infusions were both known and taking place in the region.

Rabbi Immanuel Löw, a rabbi and scholar, in *Die Flora Der Juden,* (1967); [originally published as Flora der Juden (1924)], referred to a later Jewish recipe (*Sabb.* 14. 3 ed. *Urbach,* 9th-11th century) that indicates the use of such infusions in the medieval period, and which called for wine to be mixed with ground-up saffron, Arabic gum and *hasisat surur,* "I know '*surur*' solely as an alias for the resin the Cannabis sativa," (Löw, 1924). Löw made no comment on the word "*hasisat*" which is very reminiscent of the name for cannabis resins in the medieval Arabic world "*hasis*" (hashish), and the term is generally thought to have been derived in that period. In *Liber 420* I discuss 13th century Jewish alchemical references to various herbal wine infusions, known as a Quintessence.

Notable use continued into the first centuries of the Common Era. The Catholic Church Father Irenaeus condemned the Gnostic leader Marcus, stating the latter had a familiar demon by whose aid he was able to prophesy, and that he pretended to confer this gift upon others by means of philtres and love potions which he compounded. Zosimos the alchemist, in the 3rd-4th century, who was influenced by Jewish and Gnostic cosmologies, referred to beer infusions of "borage, cannabis seeds and leaves, helenium, ivy leaves, strychnine, and darnel" being used for magical rites (Bennett, 2018).

It has even long been suggested that Jesus himself quaffed such a preparation in his own moment of doubt and pain."Some high Biblical commentators maintain that the gall and vinegar, or myrrhed wine, offered to our Saviour immediately before his crucifixion, was in all probability a preparation of hemp, and even speak of its earlier use" *The Boston Medical and Surgical Journal* (1860). Wine infused with 'vine branches' alongside an incense that contained a 'wonder' are described as being administered by Jesus himself in magic rites in the 3-4th century CE Gnostic text The Second Book of Jue (Bennett, 2010: 2018). "Other heretics with Gnostic views who were accused of magic ... were the followers of Carpicrates, who employed incantations and spells, philtres and potions ... and who pretended to have great power over things ... by magic" (Thorndike, 1923). Accusations of using such infusions may have even been directed at Jesus in New Testament accounts. "The commonly attested connection between mantic behavior and alcohol probably explains the reference in the New Testament that some people thought Jesus to be a wine-bibber (Matt 11:19). The use of drugs was so closely tied to mantic practice that the Greek word for 'drug' [Gk. pharmakea] eventually came to denote witchcraft (Gal 5:19-21)" (Noegel & Wheeler, 2010). More recently *The Immortality Key* (2020) suggested that an infused wine may lie behind the origins of the Christian Eucharist.

The use of such infusions continued through to the Islamic period into near modern times (Rosenthal, 1971: Bennett 2010:2018). An 1862 article in *All the Year Round,* "What Wine Does For Us" contained a passage which states "the Jewish and Armenian dealers ministering to that fondness for narcotics which tend so greatly to enervate the East, by mixing myrrh, incense, and the juice of the Indian hemp with the finest growth."[4]

Dionysus and Infused Wines

No discussion of wine would be complete without reference to the Greek god of Wine, Dionysus. Interestingly, Dionysus and ever syncretic Yahweh, became conflated during the time of Greek rule. This has been equated with the love of both cults for wine. As well, a number of scholars have suggested the use of cannabis and other drugs by the cult of Dionysus, and this includes wine infusions.

Thyia, was the first priestess of Dionysus, according to tradition, and her name comes from the ancient verb θύω = "I sacrifice" or "incense," as she was the first to sacrifice to Dionysus, and her first offering came in the form of incense.

4 Interestingly the slang name for cannabis, "pot" actually comes from a cannabis infused wine. The word came into use in America in the late 1930s and is a shortening of the Spanish potiguaya or potaguaya that came from *potación de guaya*, a wine or brandy in which marijuana buds have been steeped. It literally means "the drink of grief."

Renaissance man, ethnobotanist and poet, Dale Pendell noted of this; "Dionysus's home was usually assumed to be Thrace ... whose shamans used hemp smoke to induce visions and oracular trances. Hemp probably came to Thrace through Central Asia and the Caucasus. A ... similar route may have been followed by the grapevine.... It is ... possible that ... Dionysus carried not only the vine but ganja as well" (Pendell 1995).

Pendell is by no means out on the fringe with this view, Professor Mircea Eliade, a respected source on the history of religions whom we have cited a number of times in this study, referred to elements of shamanism in the Thracian cult of Dionysus, and suggested their use of cannabis: "Prophecy in Thrace was connected with the cult of 'Dionysus,' a certain tribe, that of the Bessi, managed the oracle of 'Dionysus,' the temple was on a high mountain, and the prophetess predicted the future in 'ecstasy,' like the Pythia at Delphi":

> Ecstatic experiences strengthened the conviction that the soul is not only autonomous but that it is capable of unio mystica with the divinity. The separation of soul from body, determined by ecstasy, revealed ... the fundamental duality of man ... [and] the possibility of a purely, spiritual post-experience... Ecstasy could ... be brought on by certain dried herbs... (Eliade,1982).

In a foot note to dried herbs, Eliade referred to the use of hemp among the Thracians, stating that the Kapnobatai (Those who walk in Smoke) were "dancers and 'shamans' who used the smoke of hemp to bring ecstatic trances" (Eliade, 1982).

The Kapnobatai, or Smoke-walkers, burned cannabis believing that the living entity within the plant reassembled itself inside their bodies to give divine revelations. In the 1925 English translation of the German work, *Psyche, Seelencult und Unsterblichkeitsglaube der Griechen* (1890-1894); "Psyche: The Cult of Souls and the Belief in Immortality Among the Greeks," in a chapter on "The Thracian Worship of Dionysus" the great 19th century German classical scholar, Erwin Rohde, pointed to their likely use of cannabis. Referring to the set and setting of Dionysian ritual, Rohde described that it was "something more than a mere drama, for it can hardly be doubted the players themselves were possessed by the illusion of living the life of a strange person":

> The awe-inspiring darkness of night, the music, especially that of the Phrygian flute, to which the Greeks attributed the power of making its hearers "full of the god," the verities whirl of

> the dance – all these may very well, in suitably disposed natures, have rally led to a state of visionary exaltation in which inspired persons saw all external objects in accordance with his fancy and imagination. Intoxicating drinks, to which the Thracians were addicted, may have increased the excitement; perhaps they even used the fumes derived from certain seeds, with which the Scythians and Massagetai knew how to intoxicate themselves. We all know how even to day in the East the smoke of hashish may make men visionaries and excite religious raptures in which the whole nature is transformed for the enthralled dreamer....
>
> Every detail confirms the picture of a condition of wild excitement in which limitations of ordinary life seem to be abolished. These extraordinary phenomena transcending all normal experience were explained by saying that the soul of a person thus "possessed" was no longer "at home" but "abroad," having left its body behind. This was the literal and primitive meaning understood by the Greek when he spoke of "*ekstasis*" of the soul in such orgiastic conditions of excitement. This *ekstasis* is "a brief madness," just as madness is prolonged *ekstasis.* But the *ekstasis,* the temporary *alienatio mentis* of the Dionysian cult was not thought of as again purposeless wandering in the region of pure delusion, but as a hieromania, a sacred madness in which the soul, leaving the body, winged its way to union with the god. It is now with the god, in the condition of *enthusiasmos;* those who are possessed ... have their being in the God. While still retaining the finite ego, they feel and enjoy to the full the infinite power of all life (Rohde, 1925).

In footnotes to the above section, Rohde further identified the substance used with cannabis

> There can be no doubt it was hemp-seed [i.e. seeded buds]... which had this effect ... the Thracians knew hemp. It was thus with a sort of hashish that they intoxicated themselves.... The Thracians ... may very well have used intoxication through hashish-fumes as a means of exciting themselves to their ecstatic religious dances. – The Ancients were quite familiar with the practice of inhaling aromatic smoke to produce religious hallucinations...
>
> We have only to read the accounts derived from personal experience of the hallucinatory states accompanying hash-

> ish-smoking ... to have a complete parallel to the condition which underlay Bacchic excitement... It only requires the special tone and character given the hallucinations and illusions by deep-rooted religious or fanciful conceptions – and the external machinery for cultivating such illusions – to make an exact equivalent of the delirious condition of ... the nightly festival of Dionysus. (The helpless state of impressionability to outward – e.g. musical – and inward influences is a marked feature of the intoxication and fantasia of hashish.) Other narcotics also have similar effects (Rohde, 1925).

More recently, the Professor of Classics and pioneer of entheogen research in the classic world, Carl Ruck has suggested cannabis was likely used in Dionysian wine infusions. "Since the wine of Dionysus is a mediation between the god's wild herbal ancestors and the civilized phenomenon of his cultivated and manufactured manifestation in the product fermented from the juice of the grape, it is most probable that this was the way in which the Greeks incorporated hemp into their pharmacopoeia" (Ruck, 2007).

Ruck suggests that cannabis may have played a role in the historical pairing of the Indian God Shiva, who is still known for his love of cannabis, and the Greek Dionysus, that took place during Alexander the Great's campaign into India. With the triumph of Alexander, as Prof. Carl Ruck has noted "Dionysus ... was also said to have returned triumphantly from travels to India, where he would inevitably have been assimilated with the god Shiva, with whom he shares many iconographic similarities, to the extent that they may have been originally the same deity, and both involved with the hemp sacrament (Ruck, et al., 2007).

It was recorded during the time of Alexander, when the cult of Dionysus traveled to India, the Greek god was recognized by the followers of Shiva, as one and the same. Even in pre-Alexandrian existing Greek myth, it was seen that Dionysus may have been raised in India, with Alexander believing he had rediscovered the mythical place of Dionysus' childhood, Nysa, there. *Nysa* (Greek: Νῦσα), was the traditional place where the rain nymphs, the Hyades, raised the infant god Dionysus, the "Zeus of Nysa."

The two deities do share a lot of symbolism, wearing leopard skins, traveling with a bull, serpents and intoxication. When you look at the wealth of animal/man metamorphosis in India in this respect, compared to the sorts of human/animal crossbreeds in images of Dionysus, it does seem plausible there may have been an earlier cross-cultural pollination at some sort.

Left: A 19th century miniature painting from Pakistan of a Shiva devotee drinking wine. **Right:** Ancient Greek Mosaic of Dionysus drinking wine. And a mosaic of Dionysus sitting on the back of a leopard.[5]

Both Gods are often depicted riding or accompanied by a Bull

The ecstatic celebrations of both cults was well known. Collier, John; Maenads; Southwark Art Collection; http://www.artuk.org/artworks/maenads-193235

5 From the Felix Romuliana-Gamzigrad site, imperial residence of emperor Galerius built in 3rd century AD, and named after emperor's mother Romula. The site is located in eastern Serbia

Both were often depicted dressed in leopard skins, and with half man, half animal companions.

> The observation that ... ancient writers did identify Dionysus with Siva has won the almost unanimous approval of scholars ... because of the many similarities between the cult of Dionysus and that of Shaivite devotees ... both are said to cure the sick and to have provided the Indians with weapons; both are associated with plowing, with figs and vineyards, with mountains, and with dancing; and both are depicted as having long, bushy hair and carrying a spear or trident (Cowan, 2010).

Shiva, the oldest continually worshiped God on Earth, is well known for his fondness for *bhang* (cannabis). This relationship is very ancient, and its ritual offering of cannabis to Shiva has continued to the modern day. In the *Rudrayamal Danakand* and *Karmakand* Shiva tells his consort: "Oh Goddess, Parvati, hear the benefits derived from bhang. The worship of bhang raises one to my position." As the 19th century *Indian Hemp Drugs Commission Report* recorded of Shiva's cultic connection to cannabis:

> It is chiefly in connection with the worship of Siva, the ... great god of the Hindu trinity, that the hemp plant, and more especially perhaps ganja, is associated. The hemp plant is popularly believed to have been a great favorite of Siva, and ... the drug in some form or other is ... extensively used in the exercise of the religious practices connected with this form of worship.... [R]eligious ascetics, who are regarded with great veneration by the people at large, believe that the hemp plant is a special

> attribute of the god Siva, and this belief is largely shared by the people.... There is evidence to show that on almost all occasions of the worship of this god, the hemp drugs in some form or other are used ... these customs are so intimately connected with their worship that they may be considered to form in some sense an integral part of it.(IHDCR, 1894).

In *Gods of Love and Ecstasy: The Traditions of Shiva and Dionysus*, the noted Orientalist scholar Alain Danielou, the first Westerner initiated into the cult of Shiva, also points to the similarities between Dionysus and the Indian god of hemp, Shiva, suggesting the two have their origin in the same figure; "Greek texts speak of Dionysus' mission to India, and Indian texts of the expansion of Shivaism to the West... Innumerable similarities in mythological accounts and icongraphic survivals leave no doubt as to the original unity of Shivaism and the wide extent of its influence" (Danielou 1992).

As Robert Cowan noted in *The Indo-German Identification: Reconciling South Asian Origins and European Destinies* (2010): Roman writers would associate the Greek god Dionysus with the Hindu Siva [Shiva].... Dionysus, the Greek god of wine and mystical ecstasy was purported to have journeyed to India, subdued the Aryan and Dravidian peoples, absorbed their philosophies, and returned to Europe with their chief ideas. Euripides describes Dionysus in *Bacchae* (406 B.C.) as a provider of knowledge and the conqueror of Arabia, Persia and Bactria"[6]:

> Polyaenus goes so far as to say that Dionysus got the Indians drunk before attacking them and used baccanatic orgies as part of his military strategy for subjugating all of the Asian continent.... The observation that such ancient writers did identify Dionysus with Siva has won the almost unanimous approval of scholars ... because of the many similarities between the cult of Dionysus and that of Shaivite devotees ... both are said to cure the sick and to have provided the Indians with weapons; both are associated with plowing, with figs and vineyards, with mountains, and with dancing; and both are depicted as having long, bushy hair and carrying a spear or trident (Cowan, 2010).

6 The site of Sarianidi's Soma/Haoma temple.

As Shiva's cult is not only known for their use of cannabis, but also at times, wine and other potent narcotics such as henbane and datura, it is not surprising that many have suggested such ingredients in the Dionysian infusions as well. In *Shiva: The Wild God of Power and Ecstasy* (2004) Wolf-Dieter Storl suggests that "It is possible that Shiva and Kali are historically connected with Dionysus and his mother – legend has it that the ... of their cults. More likely, the tropane-alkaloid responsible for ancient Greek Dionysian revelry was derived from mandrake or henbane" (Storl, 2004). In this respect it is worth again noting Marvin Pope's suggestion of a connection between Kali and Shiva with Baal and Anath, and the latter couple's potential influence on the Song of Songs.

Shiva with datura flowers behind his ears. Datura, along with cannabis, henbane and other drugs, have long been used for ecstatic purposes by Shiva's devotees.

It is well known and accepted that the *Amrita*, of Hindu mythology, a drink which confers immortality on the gods, is a cognate of *ambrosia*. The Greek ἀμβροσία (*ambrosia*) is semantically linked to the Sanskrit (*amṛta*) as both words denote a drink or food that gods use to achieve immortality. The two words appear to be derived from the same Indo-European form **n̥-mr̥-tós*, "un-dying." Here again, we may have indications of an earlier cultural connection in myth and etymology. As well, in Indian texts *Amrita* is identified with Soma.

It should also be noted that the aforementioned Indo-European group, the Scythians, have been tied to the worship of both Shiva and Dionysus. Gold coins minted during the Scythian period of Northern India (200 BCE- 200CE) depict a Scythian king dressed as Shiva, as well as Shiva with his bull Nandi, and relics such as a gold Rhyton with Dionysus head has been found at a Scythian tomb, as well as other Dionysian relics.

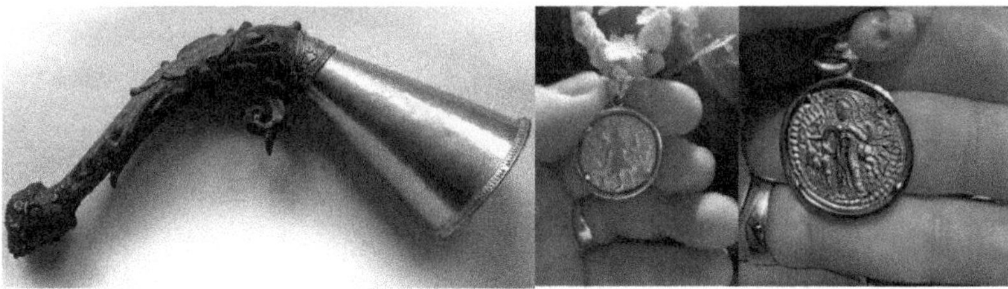

Left: A gold Scythian rhyton with the head of Dionysus on its tip. **Middle:** A Northern Indian coin dating from the 2nd-3rd century CE. Depicting a Kushan Scythian King, holding a trident of Shiva, and other regalia of the Indian God. **Right:** The reverse side of the same Indo-Scythian coin depicting the Indian God Shiva and his bull companion Nandi.

More interesting for this study is the conflation made between Dionysus and Yahweh that took place during the time of Greek domination.

Dionysus and Yahweh

A number of ancient sources recorded the widespread belief of their time, that the god worshiped by the Jewish people, Yahweh, was identifiable as Dionysus. Notably, Tacitus, Lydus, Cornelius Labeo, and Plutarch all either made this association, or discussed it as an extant belief. *The Jewish Encyclopedia* makes it clear that at times, and likely under force, many of the Jews did in fact worship Dionysus, particularly during the time of the Maccabees. As noted in the 1906 edition of *The Jewish Encyclopedia*:

> The general statement in I Maccabees (i. 51, 54, 55) that Antiochus Epiphanes forced the Jews to sacrifice in the Greek fashion, is amplified in II Maccabees (vi. 7; compare III Macc. ii. 29) into the statement that the Jews were forced to take part

in the festivals of Dionysus and to deck themselves with ivy (κίσσος); hence Hippolytus ("De Antichristo," pp. 33-35, § 49), a Church father of the second century, regards Antiochus Epiphanes as the prototype of Antichrist… the Dionysia were celebrated in every country that had come under the influence of Greek culture. Antiochus XI even bore the by-name "Dionysus" (Josephus, "Ant." xiii. 15, § 1; "B. J." i. 4, § 7); and Nicanor, the general of Demetrius, threatened to consecrate a Temple at Jerusalem to Dionysus unless Judas Maccabeus was delivered to him (II Macc. xiv. 33).

According to Plutarch.

A myth of Dionysus is connected with the Palestinian city of Scythopolis. Pliny ("Historia Naturalis," v. 18, § 74) and Solinus (ed. Mommsen, ch. 36) derive the name of this city from the Scythians, who were settled on that spot by Dionysus in order to protect the tomb of his nurse who was buried there. The Greeks and the Romans were firmly convinced that the Jews had a cult of Dionysus, basing this opinion on some external point of similarity. Plutarch thinks that the name of the Jewish Sabbath is derived from σάβος, the cry of the ecstatic Bacchantes. More important still is his further statement that the Jewish Feast of Tabernacles, as celebrated in the Temple at Jerusalem, was really a form of Dionysus worship. He reasons as follows: "The Jews celebrate their most important feast in the time of the vintage; they heap all sorts of fruit on their tables, and they live in tents and huts made chiefly from branches of the vine and from ivy; the first day of this festival they call the Feast of Tabernacles. A few days later they celebrate another feast, invoking Bacchus no longer through symbols, but calling upon him directly by name. They, furthermore, have a festival during which they carry branches of the fig-tree and the thyrsus; they enter the Temple, where they probably celebrate Bacchanalia, for they use small trumpets; and some among them, the Levites, play on the cythara" ("Symposium," iv. 5, § 3). Plutarch evidently had certain ceremonies of the Feast of Sukkot in mind. See Crown in Post-biblical Times. The accusation of Tacitus ("Hist." v. 5) is similar:

As their priests sing to the accompaniment of flutes and kettle-drums, and as they deck themselves with laurel, and as a golden vine was found in their Temple, many people believe that they worship Bacchus, the conqueror of the East; but the two cults have nothing in common, for Bacchus has established a brilliant and joyous ritual, while the customs of the Jews are bizarre and morose."

Plutarch, furthermore, deduces the Jewish worship of Bacchus from the garment of the high priest, who wears bells on his mantle, like those that were used in the Bacchanalia at night; he refers also in ambiguous terms to a thyrsus and to drums (τνμπανα) which the high priest wears in front (on the frontlet or on the breastplate?) (ib.). Grätz ("Gesch." 2d ed., ii. 254) assumes a barrel-opening festival (πιθογία = "vinalia"), which, however, can not be substantiated.

In describing the garment of the high priest, Plutarch purposely uses expressions reminiscent of the Dionysus worship, and it is probable that just such equivocal expressions, which he may have read in a Hellenistic work, led him to make the impossible assertion that the Jews had a cult of Dionysus. As a matter of fact the palm-branch prescribed for the Feast of Tabernacles was called by the Hellenists θύρσος (Josephus, "Ant." xiii. 13, § 5; II Macc. x. 7), which could easily remind a Greek of the Dionysia. He also intimates that he knew something about the "Feast of the Drawing of Water," which in its free joyousness resembled the Bacchanalia (Suk. v. 2; Tosef.: iv. 1-5; Bab. 51b; Yer. 55b). Neither the statements of Tacitus nor those of Plutarch lead to the conclusion, as some scholars assert, that they used as their sources anti-Jewish Alexandrian works, for their statements contain nothing that is hostile to the Jews. A Greek, on the contrary, would consider it a vindication for the Jews if he could derive ceremonies of the Jewish worship from pagan practices. (Gottheil & Krauss, 1906)

A Corinthian Capital of a pillar bearing the head of the Greek god Dionysus in Bet Shean National Park in Israel

A 4th century BC, coin on exhibit in the British Museum. Labeled either "YHW" (Yahu) or "YHD" (Judea), and thought to be the only physical representation of Yahweh from ancient Israel, has been connected with Dionysus. Stephen Herbert Langdon, an American-born British Assyriologist, wrote in his *Mythology of All Races – Semitic* (1931) explains:

> A coin from Gaza in Southern Philista, fourth century BC, the period of the Jewish subjection to the last of the Persian kings, has the only known representation of this Hebrew deity. The letters YHW are incised just above the hawk(?) which the god holds in his outstretched left hand. He wears a himation, leaving the upper part of the body bare, and sits upon a winged wheel. The right arm is wrapped in his garment. At his feet is a mask. Because of the winged chariot and mask it has been suggested that Yaw had been identified with Dionysus on account of a somewhat similar drawing of the Greek deity on a vase where he rides in a chariot drawn by a satyr (Langdon, 1931).

Left: This 4th century BCE coin, 4th century BC, on exhibit in the British Museum. The coin shows a seated figure, labeled either "YHW" (Yahu) or "YHD" (Judea), which is thought by some to be the only physical representation of the Jewish God, and it has been connected with Dionysus. **Right:** Two sides of a coin that seems to connect the God of the Jews with Dionysus, dated to 55 BC depicts a kneeling king with the inscription "Bacchus Judaeus" (BACCHIVS IVDAEVS).

In *The Jews and their God of Wine*, Jonathan Kirkpatrick explains:

> In the period between the two revolts of the Jews of Palestine against Roman rule some non-Jews sought to identify the God of the Jews with their own god of wine, Dionysus or Liber. The actual evidence suggests three things. The cult of the Temple at Jerusalem was seen by outsiders to be characterized by an association with, and the use of, wine, an impression Jews did nothing to counteract. Second, outsiders acted on this impres-

> sion, both as part of the cognitive step of identifying the God of the Jews with Dionysus, and, possibly, making gifts to the Temple, while it stood, of wine-related dedications. Third, this was a characterization Jews were willing to embrace themselves, even at times of revolt (Kirkpatrick, 2013).

The Immortality Key has recently suggested that Jesus was influenced by Dionysian rites that involved infused wines, and made much of the Dionysus worship in the ancient Israeli city of Scythopolis, as a potential connection point. Muraresku is not alone here; a number of scholars have made similar suggestions. Notably, in an article titled "The Wine God in Palestine," Professor Morton Smith, who was an American professor of ancient history at Columbia University, offered considerable evidence for the influence of Dionysiac cult and myth on Jewish and early Christian material. This connection, and the use of infused wines in early Christianity, is also something I have discussed in earlier works (Bennett & McQueen, 2001; Bennett 2010; 2018) and something I hope to examine more closely in a future work.

It was in the period of Greek domination that cannabis seems to have disappeared from the script completely. The Hebrew Tanach, was translated into the Greek Septuagint, in the 3rd century BCE, allegedly by 70 Jewish translators who miraculously all provided identical translations. However, they apparently all made the same errors and mistranslations as well! As Professor Stephen Vicchio has explained, it did not take long for Greek translations to become "suspect in the eyes of devout and scholarly Jews, many of who still spoke and wrote in the ancient Hebrew. The controversy became more heated when Jewish scholars pointed out a number of mistranslations and additions to the Hebrew text made by the Greek translators" (Vicchio, 2006).

It is at this juncture that *kaneh bosm*, became "calamus" a common marsh root, in the Greek texts, which for reasons already discussed, is easily discounted as *kaneh bosm*. Whether intentional, or a simple mistranslation, is hard to know. Regardless of this Greek designation, with Hebrew authorities, the botanical identity of *kaneh bosm* also seems to have been lost, and a variety of candidates have been suggested since then, as we have discussed in Chapter 3. For the many reasons we have looked at in detail in this volume, I think we can see what was once lost, has now been found, and the identity of *kaneh bosm* as cannabis is now ensured.

I suspect it was at this point when cannabis itself went out of vogue, after the installation of the Second Temple. I suspect this due to the total lack of prophetic messages in that period. A strong indication that the religion had removed itself from its entheogenic and shamanic roots, and became a dogmatic orthodox religion of repeated rituals, implemented rules of life, and importantly – offerings of tithes.

I think the actual nail in the coffin for the end of entheogenic cannabis here, may be found in what is likely one of the last texts composed in the Hebrew Bible. A later myth which was ironically placed at the beginning of the Bible, depicting Creation, and serving as a cultural template for humanity from there forward.

Chapter 14

Taking Back Eden

So here we are in the last chapters of this book, looking at the beginning of the Bible. Although appearing at the beginning of the Old Testament narrative of the Bible, the Eden account of Adam and Eve is actually one of the later texts of the Old Testament canon and, telling the story of creation, it was placed at the beginning of the book.

Arguably, the Eden myth is the most potent myth in history, it defined the roles of men and women for millennia and served as a tool for cultural programming with its inherent built-in fears of "knowledge," and all too heavy burden of "Original Sin." Oddly these elements seem to be more present in Christianity, than Judaism. Many Christians literally believe this is the story of Humanity's creation, despite the outstanding fossil and geological records for the path of evolution and age of the planet. Truly, the fear of knowledge has been ever present.

When the Eden account was written is a subject of heated debate. Many scholars see Genesis as composed during the Hellenistic period, which would place it in the first decades of the 4th century BCE. Others place it in the exilic pre-Persian period (the 6th century BCE) due to the noted Babylonian influence on the myth. Whereas the Fundamentalist view traces it back to the beginning of time, seen as a short 6,000 years ago, later to be recorded and written down at the time of Moses, who was said to have received the story directly from the source.

There are considerably few references to the Eden account outside of the fable itself in the Bible. Most prominently we see this come up in Ezekiel, which places it at the time of the Babylonian captivity. This could well account for the borrowed elements of mythology in both the story of Adam and Eve, and the equally mythical tale of Noah's Ark, which have their origin in much earlier Near Eastern tales.

Other Biblical references to Eden

"Eden" appears as a personal or existing place name in Amos 1:5: Isaiah 37:12; 2 Chronicles 29:12: 31:15; 2 Kings 19:12; Ezekiel 27:23. "Adam" as well is a place name at the time of the composition of Joshua 3:16.

The Prophet Joel makes a brief comparison to the garden of Eden in reference to a fiery judgment coming to the Jews via The "Day of the Lord": "Before them fire devours, behind them a flame blazes. Before them the land is like the garden of Eden, behind them, a desert waste – nothing escapes them" (Joel 2:3). Although the fundamental view is that Joel was a 9th century BCE prophet, most scholars suggest the text was not composed till the 5th or 4th century BCE.

In Isaiah 51:3, the Lord restores the land to look like Eden: "The LORD will surely comfort Zion and will look with compassion on all her ruins; he will make her deserts like Eden, her wastelands like the garden of the LORD." Here again, it has long been noted that the books of Isaiah were reworked by later authors, extending past Deuteronomic editions and into Priestly editions.

The 8th century BCE prophet Hosea makes reference to Adam's sin in comparison with that of the Hebrews: "But like Adam they have transgressed the covenant; There they have dealt treacherously against Me" (Hosea 6:7). However, like many other texts of the Hebrew Bible, there is little consensus as to which parts can be attributed to Hosea, and which are the works of later authors and editors. In *Hosea and Amos Believers Church Bible Commentary,* Allen R. Guenther explains: "The book has been shaped by later editors to affirm that although Israel's deep unfaithfulness brought harsh judgment, God's final purpose for Israel is deliverance and healing" (Guenther 1998). The comparison to Adam's "sin" and the transgressions of the Hebrews, fits well within that scope.[1]

In a prophecy against the King of Tyre – "You were in Eden, the garden of God" (Ezekiel 28:13).

In comparison to Assyria, in metaphor of a cedar tree – "I made it beautiful with abundant branches, the envy of all the trees of Eden in the garden of God" (Ezekiel 31:9).

As a warning to the pharaoh Egypt – "Yet you, too, will be brought down with the trees of Eden to the earth below; you will lie among the uncircumcised, with those killed by the sword" (Ezekiel 31:16-18).

1 However, even if we were to date this passage back to the time of Hosea, the Eden myth then could conceivably have been composed in relation to the prohibitions on the anointing oils and incenses in Exodus, which commanded anyone outside the priesthood who makes them will be "cut-off from their people" – analogous to Adam and Eve's expulsion from Eden. But I am doubtful of this situation, and think the numerous references to Eden to be found in the Book of Ezekiel, as well as its symbolism, indicate its composition during or after the Babylonian Exile.

In a promise of restoration for Israel – "This land that was laid waste has become like the garden of Eden; the cities that were lying in ruins, desolate and destroyed, are now fortified and inhabited" (Ezekiel 36:35)

None of these references indicate that the Eden Myth was composed prior to the Babylonian Exile. This later date accounts for the adoption of so much earlier Babylonian and Near Eastern mythical motifs. It is now well accepted that the Eden myth borrowed heavily from earlier myths that predate the Bible by millennia, although the Biblical account is not without its own original take. As we shall see, hidden in plain sight in the Eden myth, there are reversals of the earlier polytheistic pantheon which were directed at demonizing key elements of pre-monotheistic religious beliefs and practices. Before looking at these various elements that went into the myth's creation, it's worth looking at the myth itself.

THE MYTH

Prohibition & The Original Sin

Many religious users of plant hallucinogens have pointed to God's promise in Genesis 1, "I give you every seed-bearing plant on the face of the whole earth" as the source of their God-given right to use marijuana and other psycho-active plants. Unfortunately, we only need go as far as Genesis 2, and the story of prohibition in the Garden of Eden, for God's commandments in Genesis 1 to have this promise contradicted, in what has been described "as the first drug bust."

The Biblical myth, as told in Genesis 2 & 3, has it that after creating the earth and the heavens, God realized that there was "no man to work the ground," so he made Adam the first man to do just that. After creating Adam to till the soil, God placed him in a garden he had planted in the east: "And the Lord God made all kinds of trees grow out of the ground – trees that were pleasing to the eye and good for food. In the middle of the garden were the tree of life and the tree of knowledge of good and evil" (Genesis 2:8-9)

> The Lord God took the man and put him in the garden of Eden to work it and take care of it. And the Lord God commanded the man, "You are free to eat from any tree in the garden; but you must not eat from the tree of knowledge of good and evil, for when you eat of it you will surely die" (Genesis 2:15-17).

Shortly after God created man and the garden for him to work in, he realized "It was not good for the man to be alone."[2] So he put Adam into a deep sleep, took out his rib, and made the first woman. It was around then that the patriarchal writers of the Biblical tale have it that the trouble started...

In this fabled garden was a serpent and "the serpent was more crafty than any of the wild animals the Lord God had made. He said to the woman, 'Did God really say, 'You must not eat from any tree in the garden?'"

> The woman said to the serpent, "We may eat fruit from the trees in the garden, but God did say, 'You must not eat fruit from the tree that is in the middle of the garden, and you must not touch it, or you will die.'"
>
> "You will not surely die," the serpent said to the woman. "For God knows that when you eat of it your eyes will be opened, and you will be like God, knowing good and evil."
>
> When the woman saw that the fruit of the tree was good for food and pleasing to the eye, and also desirable for gaining wisdom, she took some and ate it. She also gave some to her husband, who was with her, and he ate it. Then the eyes of both of them were opened, and they realized that they were naked; so they sewed fig leaves together and made coverings for themselves.
>
> Then the man and his wife heard the sound of the Lord god as he was walking in the garden in the cool of the day, and they hid from the Lord God among the trees of the garden. But the Lord God called to the man, "Where are you?"
>
> He answered, "I heard you in the garden, and I was afraid because I was naked; so I hid" (Genesis 3:1-10).

The Lord then asked, "Who told you that you were naked? Have you eaten from the tree from which I commanded you not to eat?"

So Adam turned in his wife "The woman you put here with me--she gave me some fruit from the tree, and I ate it."

Then the Lord God said to the woman, "What is this you have done?"

And the woman turned in the serpent "The serpent deceived me and I ate."

So God punished the serpent, making him the most cursed of all animals, having to crawl on his belly. He put enmity between the de-

2 Later Rabbis suggested this was due to the interest Adam was showing the other creatures in the garden.

scendants of mankind and the serpent, stating to this early reptilian pusher that man will "crush your head, and you will strike his heel."

Then God punished the woman stating; "I will greatly increase your pains in childbearing; with pain you will give birth to children. Your desire will be for your husband, and he will rule over you."

To Adam God said, "Because you listened to your wife and ate from the tree about which I commanded you, 'You must not eat of it,'":

> Cursed is the ground because of you; through painful toil you will eat of it all the days of your life. It will produce thorns and thistles for you, and you will eat the plants of the field. By the sweat of your brow you will eat your food and return to the ground, since from it you were taken; from dust you are and to dust you will return (Genesis 3:17-19).

Adam named his wife Eve, because she would become the mother of all the living.

The Lord God made garments of skin for Adam and his wife and clothed them. And the Lord God said, "The man has now become as one of us, knowing good and evil. He must not be allowed to reach out his hand and take also from the tree of life and eat, and live for ever." So the Lord God banished him from the Garden of Eden to work the ground from which he had been taken. After he drove the man out, he placed on the east side of the Garden of Eden cherubim and a flaming sword flashing back and forth to guard the way of the tree of life (Genesis 3:21-24).

There is a lot of symbolism to unpack here.

Archetypes of Eden

Mircea Eliade, the noted Romanian historian of religion, philosopher, and professor at the University of Chicago, pointed out the Garden of Eden mythos suggests a well-known mythological motif; that of the naked goddess, the miraculous tree, and its serpent guardian. But here, rather than a hero who overcomes and gains a share in the symbol of life, the Genesis story "gives us Adam, an ingenious victim of the serpent's perfidy. In short we are dealing with a failed 'immortalization,' like that of Gilgamesh. For, once omniscient, equal to the 'gods', Adam could discover the Tree of Life (of which Yahweh had not spoken to him) and become immortal. The text is clear and categorical: 'Yahweh God said, see, the man has become like one of us, with knowledge of good and evil. He must not be allowed to stretch out his hand and pick from the tree of life also and eat some and live forever.' And God banished the couple from paradise and condemned them to work for a living" (Eliade 1978).

In the ancient world, the serpent was an image of both knowledge and healing and as the respected scholar Merlin Stone has suggested, likely also of divine intoxication (Stone 1976) thus its connection with sacred plants. As early as 2025 BCE, in ancient Sumeria the serpent, under the name Ningizzidia, was known as the "Lord of the Tree of Truth" (Campbell 1964). Moreover, the brazen serpent had once sat in the Holy of Holies, and was removed during the reforms of Josiah, because the people of Israel burned incense to it. Curiously, in later times Jesus would compare himself to this same serpent (John 3:14).

> [In] the scenario ... of the naked goddess and the miraculous tree ... we can see that the serpent of Genesis succeeded, all things considered, in its role as guardian of a symbol of life and youth. But this archaic myth was radically altered by the author of the biblical accounts. Adam's ... disobedience betrayed his Luciferian pride, the desire to be like God. It was the greatest sin that the creature could commit against his creator. It was the "original sin," a notion pregnant with consequences for the Hebrew and Christian theologies. Such a vision of the "fall" could command recognition only in a religion centered on the omnipotence and jealousy of God. As it has been handed down to us, the biblical narrative indicates the increasing authority of Yahwistic monotheism.... The first sin not only brought about the loss of paradise and the transformation of the human condition; it became in some sense the source of all the evils that burdened humanity (Eliade 1978).

By the way it conflicts with basic common sense the "psyche knows unconsciously that the [Eden] story is dangerously upsetting. It creates a religious taboo to protect itself. The teaching that results from ... [its general interpretation] is that mankind must remain in an infantile state and obey those who speak in the name of the 'father' located in heaven. The dogma of original sin as disobedience is maintained to prevent disconcerting discoveries concerning that deity" (Suares 1992). Not surprisingly, in light of the original sin mythology, the acceptance of the Bible as the basis for a "world religion," through Christianity, resulted in a prohibition of knowledge which lasted over a millennium and still has bonds which hold us back in our modern times, where the very myth we are discussing is pitted against the well established Theory of Evolution being taught in classrooms.

Since its very inception, the Bible has not been about "new ideas," but maintaining "old ones" which are compounded out of ancient and outdated tribal rules and belief systems. This prohibition of knowledge also claims dominion over the plant world, and the revelations that the ingestion of certain herbs could provide; such prohibitions date back to the very beginnings of the Bible itself.

Eden as a tool of propaganda, extends to our own time, and it's by no chance an accident that in the era of cannabis prohibition, the forces behind "reefer madness" deemed the herb a "devil's weed" spread by "Vipers" like the serpent of Eden, identified by the hiss they would make inhaling their pernicious demonic drug!

The prohibition of entheogens here can be seen as a prohibition of experiential religion, followed by the forced installation of a rigid dogmatic religion directed at control. This struggle has lasted down to our present era, leading to the near death of shamanism, a religion distinguished preeminently by the ritual ingestion of powerful plant sacraments for revelation, and which has disappeared whenever it has been brought into contact with Christianity. A religion based on long past history and controlling people through ancient tribal rules has absolutely no room for the new revelations experienced by entheogen-ingesting shamans.

Modern researchers as well, have made a connection between the forbidden trees of Eden and entheogens, an element that fits well with what we have been discussing in this book.

What Were the Forbidden Trees of Eden?

Although popularly seen as the apple, the Hebrew text of Genesis 3 actually refers to the more generic "fruit." In the early Christian period "apples" were substituted for "fruit" due to a possible misunderstanding of the Latin word *malum*, which means both "evil" and "apple."

The idea that the Biblical myth of Eden and its Tree of Knowledge, identifies a prohibited psychoactive is considerably widespread. One could argue, it was an imperative aspect of the myth, from its creation – intuitively, anyone familiar with psychoactive substances could perceive it in the metaphor. Historically, the view that the forbidden fruit of Eden was some sort of psychoactive substance, outside of the indications laden in the story itself, does go back considerably far in time.

In our own time, the identity of the specific entheogen in question has become a hot topic of speculation.

The most popular suggestion of a psychoactive substance, as the Tree of Knowledge, is by far, the Fly Agaric Mushroom, which going back close to a century, has been suggested, largely based in the imagery of a 13th century painting.

The 13th century Eden Fresco, at the 12th century Plaincourault Chapel in Mérigny, France.

The Fly Agaric as the Tree of Knowledge?

In the 1925 book, *Romance of the Fungus World*, in a chapter, "Some Historical Aspects of Fungi," Robert Thatcher Rolfe, F.W. Rolfe put forth a suggestion that has become considerably popular in our modern day:

> A Curious Myth. We may close this chapter with a fitting historical reference to the fungi, relating to a curious myth, connecting them with our reputed ancestors, Adam and Eve. This is seen in a fresco in a ruined chapel at Plaincourault, in France, dating back to 1291, and purporting to depict the fall of man. A reproduction of this is shown,1 and the Tree of Life is represented as a branching Amanita muscaria, with the Serpent

> twining himself in its "branches," while Eve, having eaten of the forbidden fruit, appears from her attitude to be in some doubt as to its after effects, which it is gratifying to know caused her no serious harm. It is impossible to say whether this picture is merely a quaint conception on the part of the artist, or whether it has any better traditional foundation (Rolfe & Rolfe, 1925).

The controversy over this interpretation involved two of the most prominent figures in the area of psychedelic mushroom researchers. The "Father" of modern mycology, R. Gordon Wasson, and the controversial Linguist and Biblical Scholar, John Allegro held very divergent views on this painting.

Interestingly, Wasson, whose research in the area of the history of psychoactive mushrooms is well known, rejected this theory. This may have been influenced in part through a letter he received from the Art historian, Erwin Panofsky in 1952:

> [T]he plant in this fresco has nothing whatever to do with mushrooms ... and the similarity with Amanita muscaria is purely fortuitous. The Plaincourault fresco is only one example – and, since the style is provincial, a particularly deceptive one – of a conventionalized tree type, prevalent in Romanesque and early Gothic art, which art historians actually refer to as a 'mushroom tree" or in German, Pilzbaum. It comes about by the gradual schematization of the impressionistically rendered Italian pine tree in Roman and early Christian painting, and there are hundreds of instances exemplifying this development – unknown of course to mycologists.... What the mycologists have overlooked is that the medieval artists hardly ever worked from nature but from classical prototypes which in the course of repeated copying became quite unrecognizable (Erwin Panofsky in a 1952 letter to Wasson, which was excerpted in *Soma*, 1968).

Wasson's correspondence with another art historian, Meyer Schapiro, corroborated this view. In *Soma: Divine Mushroom of Immortality*, Wasson noted these criticisms and further explained: "The misinterpretation ... of the Plaincourault fresco" could "be traced to the recent dissemination in Europe of reports of the Siberian use of the fly-agaric," i.e. In this time period, there were numerous accounts of the fly agarics use by Siberian Shaman, and this colored the interpretation of the Plaincourault fresco. Wasson further noted in regard to the Creation myth, "the commentators have made an error in timing: the span of the past is longer ... and the events that they seek to confirm took place before recorded history began" (Wasson, 1968).

Nonetheless, Wasson himself did identify the fly agaric with the tree of knowledge. However, he offers little in the way of evidence, and instead, basis the claim on intuition:

> Some months ago I read the Garden of Eden tale once more, after not having thought of it since childhood. I read it as one who now knew the entheogens. Right away it came over me that the Tree of Knowledge was the tree that has been revered by many tribes of Early Man in Eurasia precisely because there grows under it the mushroom, splendid to look upon, that supplies the entheogenic food to which Early Man attributed miraculous powers. He who composed the tale for us in Genesis was clearly steeped in the lore of this entheogen: he refrained from identifying the "fruit": he was writing for the initiates who would recognize what he was speaking about. I was an initiate. Strangers and also the unworthy would remain in the dark. Adam and Eve had eaten the "fruit," what the mycologists call Amanita muscaria, what the initiates call by a variety of euphemisms, which change from time to time, and we have seen to what strange lengths the uninitiated go when these euphemisms are detached from the "fruit" that they represent. The priestly redactor who set down the Genesis tale, an initiate and a believer, attributed to the "fruit" the gift of self-consciousness, a remarkable observation because self-consciousness is one of the major traits that distinguish humankind from all other creatures. Is it not surprising that the composer of the story gave credit for this particular gift to our mushroom? It is unlikely that he was alone in doing so (Wasson, 1986).

Wasson further identified the Tree of Knowledge with the Vedic Soma: ""I hold that the fruit of the Tree of the Knowledge of Good and Evil was Soma, was the kakuljd, was Amanita muscaria, was the Nameless Mushroom of the English-speaking people. The Tree was probably a conifer, in Mesopotamia. The serpent, being underground, was the faithful attendant on the fruit" (Wasson, 1986).

Although I think Wasson is onto something in connecting the Biblical tree with Soma, his suggestion here of Amanita muscaria, as that tree is presented here with weaker evidence than that which he used to make his case for Soma as the fly agaric. I have detailed the many issues with Wasson's claims about the Fly Agaric mushroom as Soma, from myself and many other researchers, at great length in *Cannabis and the Soma Solution* (2010). Here in his claims about the Eden mythos, he makes no real attempt to document a knowledge of the Agaric with the ancient Hebrews, but still claims initiates of its use in the "Priestly redactor."

Interest in the Plaincourault Fresco as evidence of the Fly Agaric as the Tree of Knowledge, was, however, reinvigorated with the publication of John Allegro's controversial, and largely rejected, *The Sacred Mushroom and the Cross.* Allegro used an altered image of the fresco on his cover.

The cover of Allegro's book, modified the central image of the Plaincourault fresco, to make it look more like a mushroom, removing the top branches and other elements.

Although the Plaincourault Fresco appears on the cover of Allegro's work, curiously he only mentions it briefly:

> The prime example of the relation between the serpent and the mushroom is, of course, in the Garden of Eden story of the Old Testament. The cunning reptile prevails upon Eve and her husband to eat of the tree, whose fruit "made them as gods, knowing good and evil" (Gen 3:4). The whole Eden story is mushroom-based mythology, not least in the identity of the "tree" as the sacred fungus.... Even as late as the thirteenth-century some recollection of the old tradition was known among Christians, to judge from a fresco painted on the wall of a ruined church in Plaincourault in France (pl. 2). There the Amanita muscaria is gloriously portrayed, entwined with a serpent, whilst Eve stands by holding her belly (Allegro, 1970).

That, and a footnote mentioning Wasson's dismissal of the connection, is all Allegro says on the matter. The mass of the rest of Allegro's book focuses on his preposterous etymological and linguistic theories, regarding Jesus being a symbol for the mushroom, and other hokum. Nonetheless, since then, the idea that the Plaincourault Fresco represents the fly agaric mushroom has persisted, and this view has been spread widely by numerous authors writing about psychoactive mushrooms.

More recently, a professor of anthropology, Jerry Brown and his wife Judy, have made the preposterous and unsubstantiated claim that Wasson was motivated by his banking relationship with the Catholic Church, to obscure the connection between the fly agaric mushroom and the tree of knowledge as depicted in the Plaincourault Fresco. In their 2016 book, *The Psychedelic Gospels: The Secret History of Hallucinogens in Christianity* the Browns claim:

> Was Wasson afraid of betraying the church? As the son of a clergy- man, did Wasson feel a filial allegiance to his father and a loyalty to Catholicism?
>
> Was he afraid of the power of the Vatican? Did Wasson draw back because he was concerned that his hard-won reputation might be destroyed?
>
> ...The unmasking of the Wasson-Vatican connection calls into question everything Wasson ever wrote to justify his position on the absence of entheogens in the Judeo-Christian tradition after 1000 BCE, including his ardent refusal to publicly acknowledge that the "mushroom-tree" in the Eden fresco at Plaincourault is indeed an Amanita muscaria. It was this refusal that provided the motivation for Wasson's insidious personal attacks on Allegro, the scholar of the Dead Sea Scrolls who expanded the theory on the role of entheogens in religion to encompass the origins of Christianity (Brown & Brown, 2016).

What makes this statement curious is that the Browns actually reject the linguistic aspects of Allegro's theory, and only embrace the image-based evidence of the Plaincourault Fresco: "our theory differs from Allegro's ... while Allegro bases his theory on the speculative interpretation of ancient languages, we base our theory on the plausible identification of entheogenic images" (Brown, 2016). However, interpretative claims of entheogens perceived in medieval images are all the Browns are left with for evidence. The Browns offer little in the way of ancient evidence of the use of psychedelic mushrooms, and almost solely rely on imagery, with the Plaincourault fresco taking a prominent role.

More recently an article by Emma Betuel looked at the Plaincourault Fresco and noted that, as with earlier critiques of the claim, "Art historians are also skeptical that the medieval fresco is secretly showcasing Christianity's psychedelic roots":

> "I can assure you that the arboreal form at Plaincourault, or elsewhere for that matter, in no way references a particular spe-

cies of mushroom," says Marcia Kupfer, an independent scholar of medieval art and author of *Romanesque Wall Painting in Central France.*

Elina Gertsman, an art historian at Case Western Reserve University, says she's not one to shy away from well-placed speculation, but even she can't get behind the idea that the tree is a hallucinogenic mushroom. Instead, she says, medieval artists may have been experimenting with new ways to stylize trees. There are countless examples of medieval images where artists did this, including lions that appear to be wearing glasses, or elephants with mitten-like feet. "I think you will be hard-pressed to find a specialist in medieval art who disagrees with me and subscribes, instead, to the psychedelic Christianity idea," Gertsman says.[3]

As with earlier art critics, my view is that the image in the Fresco is a poorly drawn tree. Unlike a mushroom, it has branches, even three going up to the top portion of the tree, and the serpent holding the traditional apple is woven between then, which would rule out the single stem of a mushroom.

Although there are dots on the image, as with the white dots of the amanita muscaria, unlike the mushroom, where the white dots appear sporadically, on the tree these are structured neatly in rows, and there are lines indicating overlapping layers of growth. There is also an apple depicted on the right in the serpent's mouth.

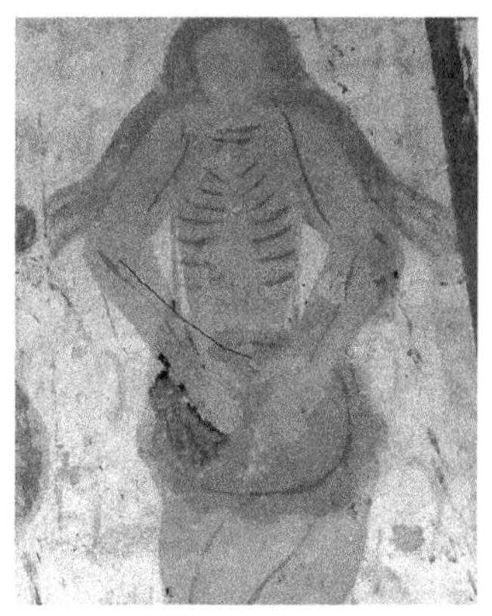

What this image is, is in fact evidence of how much things had fallen in the centuries known in the Dark Ages, and the skills of pre-Christian art were largely lost, as were many other aspects of civilization and culture.... And they were left with child-like art.

In the Brown's interpretation, Adam and Eve are covering themselves with dinner plate-sized mushroom caps, and Eve's ribs are claimed as an indication of a shamanic death and rebirth.

3 As quoted in (Betuel, 2021)

The Door of Salvation

The Garden of Eden's forbidden trees come up again, when the Browns look at a relic commissioned by the 10th century Catholic Bishop Bernward, known as "The Door of Salvation." The Browns claim, this and other pieces created at the behest of Bernward, which sit in St. Michael's Church in Hildesheim, Germany, represent "an entheogenic legacy that was deliberately created by a saint of the Catholic Church." However, as we will see, the Browns' interpretation of the Eden mythos as depicted on "The Door of Salvation," is something of a misrepresentation that leaves out part of the sequence, perhaps even intellectually dishonest in this respect. However they are not the only ones to have done this in regard to this specific relic.

The Browns bring our attention to the mushroom-like branches of the tree in this specific panel and explain:

> Bernward left no doubt that one of the three mushrooms had already been eaten by Adam and Eve, as indicated by the broken branch springing from the lower part of the mushroom-tree.
>
> In casting the door, Bernward took special care to precisely identify the species of psychoactive mushroom in his bronze bas-relief. As ethno-botanist Giorgio Samorini observes, "The mushroom-tree is realistically rendered with a precision not far short of anatomical accuracy and can be identified as one of the most common Germanic and European *psilocybian* mushroom, *P. semilanceata*." Botanically speaking, the mushroom-tree between Adam and Eve sprouts two bell-shaped mushrooms with pointed, nipple-like tops (papillae) and furrowed (striated) caps (Brown & Brown, 2016).

A scene from Eden that the Browns claim depict psilocybin mushroom harvesting and ingestion.

The Browns refer to Giorgio Samorini, a widely respected Italian ethnobotanist, who as far as I know was the first to make this suggestion about this image, although like the Plaincourault fresco, the connection to mushrooms in the imagery has been widely embraced, albeit here with the suggestion of a different mushroom species.

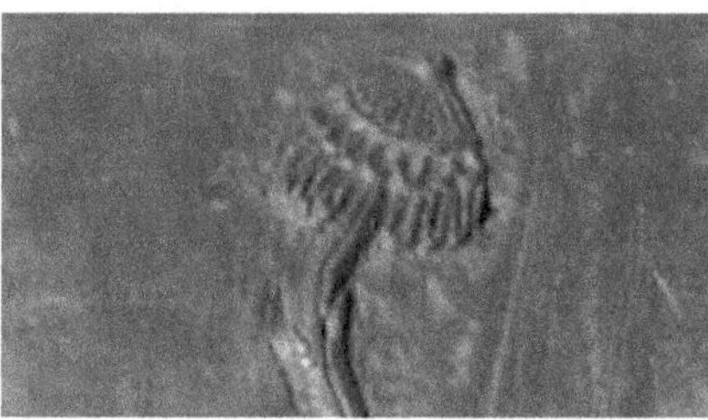

The mushroom tree, interpreted as the European *psilocybian* mushroom, *P. semilanceata* by the Browns and other researchers.

An interesting interpretation if that is all there was to it, however, the Browns, and others who have written about this panel on "The Door of Salvation" with similar claims, leave out the proceeding panel, which is clearly depicting the ingestion of the forbidden fruit, and instead use the panel that follows that one, which shows them covering themselves in fig leaves. The panel with the fig leaves is in fact the panel being used for the suggestion of mushroom imagery, and this panel actually depicts Eve using the same leafy material that is on the tips of the branches which are being interpreted as "mushrooms" to cover herself.

Eve beside a broken branch and covering herself with a fig leaf.

In the proceeding panel, we can see Eve being tempted by the serpent who holds the classic apple in his mouth, and her offering it to Adam from a tree that has no indication of mushrooms.

The scene depicting the eating of the forbidden fruit on The Door of Salvation

The two images stacked in sequence as they appear on The Door of Salvation.

Clearly the proceeding panel, with the classic forbidden apples is depicting the ingestion of the forbidden fruit. The panel being used by the Browns and others for the mushroom-like imagery of the trees, is in no way connected to the forbidden tree of knowledge, but is instead a tree from which "fig leaves" were broken off and Adam and Eve covered themselves: "and they knew that they were naked; so they sewed together fig leaves and made coverings for themselves."

As the Browns took the trouble to visit St. Michaels in person, I think it remains without question, that they intentionally left out this panel which shows the forbidden tree as the classic apple tree, and the actual ingestion of the forbidden fruit by Adam and Eve. There is no indication the mushroom-like trees are connected besides serving as a source of "fig leaves" for their covering.

Many European medieval artists never actually saw the plants or animals from other lands they depicted from written descriptions or other illustrations, and as we all know from the childhood game of passing a whisper from one ear to another down a line, what you start with and what you end up with can really change as it goes down the line, into something very different from the original. I think this is the case many times in regard to things like the Palm Tree, as depicted in medieval European art as well.

Oddly depicted trees in medieval art have not only been interpreted as mushrooms. Similar evidence, seen as indicating cannabis leaves, has been suggested in medieval paintings, such as these from Sicily's Cathedral of Monreale (1182).[4]

Now never mind the obvious similarity to a cannabis leaf in these images, I could never see myself making the sort of claims about these images that the Brown's do about mushrooms.

Even with the clear archaeological evidence in the Holy Land for cannabis as a ritual incense in an 8th century BCE Jewish temple, and the 4th century CE use both topically and as an incense for medical purposes from Bet Shemesh Israel, I think it would be hard to argue for these practices to have been secretly passed down to the medieval artist who painted these images.

In the case of the mushroom claims, these are made solely on interpretations of medieval art, with no corroborating evidence that humanity in Europe were even aware of many of the mushroom species suggested, let alone their ingestion, and no textual evidence from the time indicating the use of some sort of secret sacrament. I prefer things like actual textual references, etymological research and most of all archaeological evidence as the basis for my own work. None of this

4 I sent these to Jerry Brown asking what he thought of these images, no response. I also offered to debate Jerry Brown on these matters, but he refused.

is offered in way of substantiating the fly agaric or any other mushroom species as the forbidden Tree of Eden. Still, the idea is popular, largely, I would argue, due its simplistic appeal. Anyone can see the shape of a mushroom in the Plaincourault fresco, and it is this meme-like quality and instant appeal, that does not take any serious research or backing, that is largely responsible for the success of the claim.

Now this does not disregard the sacred mushroom, or the contributions of R Gordon Wasson. Clearly, the mushroom was a known entheogenic sacrament in the New World, both prior to and after the arrival of Columbus, and this was largely repressed by Catholic forces. I admire Wasson's efforts detailing the use of mushrooms, with both contemporary written accounts and identifying mushrooms in statues and other imagery left over from the pre-Columbian era. I just don't think anyone has produced convincing evidence that the ancient Hebrews or Christians knew of or used psychoactive mushrooms.

MANDRAKE AS THE TREE OF KNOWLEDGE

Mandrake has a long history in magic and medicine and appears in the Bible. We have also looked at in connection with the Goddess and the Sacred Marriage. Interestingly, Mandrake is the oldest know suggestion of a specific psychoactive substance as the Biblical Tree of Knowledge.

The Physiologus, a collection of documents originally written in Greek and Armenian that go back to the second or third century, and were later translated into Latin around the 11th century, makes reference to the mandrake, in a tale of Adam and Eve and metaphorical Elephants. In *Goddesses, Elixirs, and Witches,* John Riddle suggests the author may have been a "Hellenistic Jew ... considering the biblical quotations and allusions, but the version we have is clearly Christianized. If it existed in Hebrew, we have no copy.... Max Wellman [(1930)] believed that the mandrake-Garden of Eden story goes back to an unidentified Jewish source" (Riddle, 2010).

Surviving Greek and Armenian versions do not contain the mandrake reference, but the 11th century Latin version of *The Physiologus* has these references:

> ... Adam and Eve. For when they were pleasing to God, before the provocation in the flesh, they knew nothing about copulation nor had they knowledge of sin. When, however, they knew the wife ate of the Tree of Knowledge, which the Mandragora means, and gave of the fruits to her man, she was im-

> mediately made wanderer and they had to clear out of Paradise on account of it. For, all the time that they were in Paradise, Adam did not know her. But then, the Scriptures say: "Adam went in to his wife and she conceived and bore Cain, upon the waters of tribulation (*The Aberdeen Beastery*: Folio 10r).

The other version reads: "When the woman ate of the tree, that is, gave her the mandragora which brought understanding to her husband, she became pregnant and for that reason left paradise" (*The Physiologus, the Bestiaries and Medieval Animal Lore* (1985).

The Hebrew word used in Genesis, which is usually translated as "love apples" (in references to the mandragora,) or "mandrakes," is *duda'im*. In 'Mandrakes: A Mystical Plant or Legitimate Herbal Remedy?', Loriel Solodokin explains:

> The botanical identity of *duda'im* is quite difficult to ascertain. The accepted opinion, however, is that it is a plant that grows, blossoms, or ripens "in the days of the wheat harvest" (*Bereshit* 30:14). Most biblical commentaries translate *duda'im* as mandrakes. Rashi writes that the *duda'im* are a type of plant that the Arabs call *yasmin*, which is translated in English as the mandrake. Ibn Ezra asserts that *duda'im* have a good aroma, as it is written in Shir HaShirim (7:14), "*duda'im* give forth fragrance." They resemble the human form for they have the likeness of a head and hands...
>
> ...Rabbi Dr. Joseph H. Hertz, the former Chief Rabbi of the United Kingdom and Commonwealth, quotes the 1611 King James' authorized version of the Bible where the word *duda'im* is translated as "love apples." Hertz explains that the fruit is the size of a large plum, quite round, yellow, and full of soft pulp. The fruit is still considered in the East as a love charm... (Solodokin, 2010).

According to renowned botanist Professor Richard Evans Schultes, and the scientist Albert Hoffmann, noted for his creation of LSD: "Early Christians believed that the mandrake root [which like ginseng sometimes appears in a humanoid form] was originally created by God as an experiment before he created man in the Garden of Eden" (Schultes & Hofmann 1979\1992). William Menzies Alexander, in his *Demonic Possession in the New Testament: Its Historical, Medical, and Theological Aspects,* also refers to the use of mandrake in the early Christian period, commenting that "The sole value of the plant depended on its anti-demonic properties"(Alexander 1902\1980).

As Mandrake appears in Genesis 30:14 in the form of a fertility charm or medicine, and again is referred to in the Song of Songs, the suggestion as the tree of knowledge here is intriguing.

Left: Old Botanical mandrake. **Right:** "Love Apples."

Mesopotamian Influences: *Qunubu* as the Tree of Life

It seems that it was likely during the Babylonian Exile, or shortly thereafter, that the Eden Myth of the Bible was created, and this accounts for the older Sumerian and Akkadian elements incorporated into it.

Indications of the myths of Genesis, in earlier Mesopotamian mythologies, have long been noted. Notably, there is an earlier Mesopotamian myth of the flood (c.1750 B.C.), from which the "deluge tale ... has come down to us in the Book of Genesis" (Campbell 1962). Comparatively, the Mesopotamian myth has it that four gods (Anu, Enlil, Ninurta and Ennugi), had grown tired of mankind and at the instigation of the "unreasoning" Enlil, they decided to destroy them with a flood. A fifth God, the beneficent "instructor" god Enki revealed the plot to a man named Ut-napishtim, the Mesopotamian Noah, and helped him plan his escape. As the ancient myth states; "Who other than Enki, can devise plans? It is Enki alone who knows every matter."

Like Noah following God's commandments, Utnapishtim built the boat according to the precise measurements Enki had given him. He stored the ship with provisions of all kinds and placed his family and some wild animals in it. Then there came a terrifying storm, with a flood that lasted for seven days and seven nights. As with the later Biblical tale, when it was over and the boat came to rest on a mountain, Utnapishtim sent out first a dove, then a swallow and then a raven. The first two returned to him, but the raven did not, which showed him the water had subsided. Utnapishtim made a sacrifice, to which he invited all the gods except Enlil, who was principally responsible for sending the flood.

The general view is that Utnapishtim, or alternatively, Uta-na'ishtim, became Noah, a conceivable abbreviation of (Uta)-na'ish(tim), when the myth reached Palestine. As Helmer Ringgren explained in *Religions of the Ancient Near East*: "The similarity to the biblical account is obvious: the place where the ship stops, the number of birds that are sent out, and the sacrifice after the flood are the same" (Ringgren 1973).

In regard to the Eden mythos, similarities have been noted between the much more ancient Tale of Adapa, who was tricked out of the bread of life and immortality by the crafty god Enki and the later Genesis story of Adam and Eve's deception regarding the supposedly death-dealing fruit of the Tree of Knowledge of Good and Evil. The story of Adapa is likely "related to the biblical Adam"(Saggs 1962) and "may be regarded as a myth about the first man" (Hooke 1963). As the Jewish historian Raphael Patai, and English mythologist and poet Robert Graves noted in *The Hebrew Myths: The Book of Genesis*: "Another source of the Genesis Fall of Man is the Akkadian myth of Adapa.... This myth supplies the theme of the Serpent's warning to Eve, that God had deceived her about the properties of the forbidden fruit" (Graves and Patai, 1963). Religious scholar John Gray commented upon the Sumerian pantheon's chief god, Anu's resentment of Ea's[5] giving the knowledge of the god's to a mere human, Adapa, as being "strongly reminiscent of the divine resentment at Adam for presuming to eat of the tree of knowledge of good and evil" (Gray 1969).

Enki, also known as Ea, was a mischievous god of wisdom, magic and incantations who resided in the ocean under the earth. Although often depicted as a bearded god, with a goat at his feet, and rivers with fish emanating from him, the "god Enki is related to snakes in Early Dynastic incantations" (Espak, 2015). He was later known as Ea in the Akkadian (Assyrian-Babylonian) religion. Some sources see the Babylonian Oannes as identical with this god, or as an emissary, although there is debate on the matter.[6]

5 Also known as Enki.

6 As well, with caution it is worth noting, many sources connect Oannes with Dagon, who appears in the *Hebrew Bible*. *The Jewish Encyclopedia* (1912) recorded "it is probable that 'Odakon' ... designates a personification of Oannes, who is supposed to rise out of the Persian Gulf, is identical with 'Dakon,' probably changed into "Odakon" through the similarity in

It has long been noted that the features of Enki's idealistic homeland Dilmun "may underlie the Hebrew accounts of Paradise" (Hooke 1963). Reminiscent of the serpent's role in the Garden of Eden story, the myth of Dilmun records how the goddess Ninhursag "makes eight plants spring up ... in spite of a prohibition Enki eats all eight of them.... There are obviously certain similarities between this myth and the biblical picture of paradise ... the eating of the forbidden plants is distantly reminiscent of the tree of knowledge in the garden of Eden" (Rinngren 1973).

Enki has connections with a sacred tree similar to that which is described in the Garden of Eden. In the ancient Sumerian texts, Ea\Enki\Oannes is described as being wise and as he "who knows the plant of life and the water of life" (Ringgren 1973). Professor Mackenzie also noted this in 1915, commenting that "In a fragmentary Babylonian charm there is a reference to a sacred tree or bush at Eridu [Eridu is thought to be the cradle of Sumerian civilization]. Professor Sayce has suggested that it is the Biblical 'Tree of Life' in the Garden of Eden.... It may be that Ea's sacred bush or tree is a survival of tree and water worship" (Mackenzie 1915):

> Ea is ... the god of wisdom, "the king of wisdom, who creates understanding," "the experienced one (apkallu) among

sound to 'Oannes.'" This is far from a settled matter, some see two separate gods that became conflated, and others no connection.

Even more controversial are noted connections between, Dagon, Ea and Yahweh. The Mesopotamian name 'Yah-Daganu' has been translated as 'Yahweh is Dagon'. In *Mythology of the Babylonian People*, Donald Mackenzie explained: "Ea whose name is also rendered Aa, was identified with Ya, Ya'u or Au, the Jah of the Hebrews. 'In Ya-Daguna, Jah is Dagon', writes Professor Pinches, 'we have the elements reversed, showing a wish to identify Jah with Dagon, rather than Dagon with Jah; whilst another interesting name, Au-Aa, shows an identification of Jah with Aa, two names which have every appearance of being etymologically connected." Jah's name is one of the names for "god"" in the Assyro-Babylonian language. (Mackenzie 1915)

As well, at excavations of Ebla, which we looked at earlier for evidence of the ritual use of psychoactive substances, researchers found indications that sometime after the reign of Sargon (died, 2279 BCE) the chief deity El, was replaced by another deity Ia (Freeman, 2011). In *Religion in Ancient Mesopotamia*, Jean Bottéro, hypothesized that Ia was the West Semitic (Canaanite) pronunciation of the Akkadian name Ea, and this was a Canaanite theonym for Yahu, the Hebrew YHWH. Although some scholars agreed with this, others have provided ways this evidence may have been misinterpreted.

Circumstantial evidence of a means of connection between Ea and Yahweh could be seen to reach considerably far back. An Akkadian copy of Ea's myth about Adapa were recovered on a tablet in Egypt at El Amarna, Pharaoh Ahkenaton's capitol city (Patai & Graves, 1963). This is interesting, as Akhenaten was said to have had Semites employed in high ranking positions, similar to that which Jacob was depicted to hold. As well, he was also noted to have had contact with the Shasu, who are important figures in the Kenite hypothesis regarding the origins of Yahweh worship. As mentioned, the Father of Psychiatry, Sigmund Freud, suggested an origin of Jewish monotheism, with Akhenaten in his 1939 book, *Moses and Monotheism*. In relation, Moses disciple, Joshua, was known as "son of nun," "nun," being the Hebrew for "fish," and a "fish being the main symbol of Enki/Ea. As well, in Talmudic times the term "dag" could be applied to both "fish" and the "messiah."

> the gods," "he who knows everything that has a name." It is he who gives the king wisdom. He is also the god of the art of incantation. In his temple "the house of Apsu" in Eridu there was a notable tree, kiskanu, whose branches were used in ritual sprinklings.... The incantation priest was the representative of Ea (Ringgren 1973).

The kiskanu tree "was the central point of various rites. A holy grove in the temple is ... mentioned." (Ringgren 1973). The second part of the name of this notable tree, kis-kanu has phonetic similarities with the early names for cannabis, through the linguistic root *an*, "which is found in various cannabis related words"(Abel 1980); particularly with the Indo-European root *kanna*, and its Assyrian and suggested Hebrew counterparts *qunubu*, and *kaneh bosm*, both of which can be phonetically translated with a 'k' or a hard 'q'.

In mythology, Ea's servant and adopted "son," the hero and temple fisherman, Adapa, was referred to as the "ointment priest," indicating the importance of the rite. Ancient mythology has it that Adapa's "command was like the command of Ea." It was the ritual anointing of the priesthood of Ea that empowered them to act as the god's representative, just as this same act marked the representative of Yahweh to the ancient Hebrews. Through this shamanic rite the anointed became "he whose ear Enki [Ea] has opened." In relation, it is worth noting that one of the references to cannabis under the suggested Assyrian name *azala*, discussed in Chapter 3 was translated "So that god of man and man should be in good rapport: – with hellebore, cannabis and lupine you will rub him" (Russo 2005).

A ritual enactment of Ea and Adapa's relationship was applied to kings, who received their wisdom from Ea with the same act of anointing that passed on Yahweh's wisdom to the King in Israel. Thus, it is not surprising that Ea appears in hymns from both Ashurbanipal and Esarhaddon with special reverence, or that the two kings are compared and connected to Ea's anointing priest, Adapa. The mythology surrounding the god also indicates that he could "open the ear" of his initiates if they burned incense to him, indicating a similar psychoactive ingredient to that found in the anointing oil. Likewise it was the ritual anointing of Moses and the Levite priesthood with the sacred cannabis ointment, along with burning the oils and vegetable matter of the plant before the ark of the covenant, which enabled them to speak on behalf of the Lord. Notably, Ea was among the Gods invoked in the Assyrian Sacred rites, which involved the use of cannabis.

Assyriologist R Campbell Thompson noted that the *kiskanu* tree was quite prevalent as the ancient texts refer to "kiskanu, which 'grows like a forest' or 'grove'" (Thompson, 1903). Referring to an incantation text regarding the kiskanu R. Campbell Thompson described:

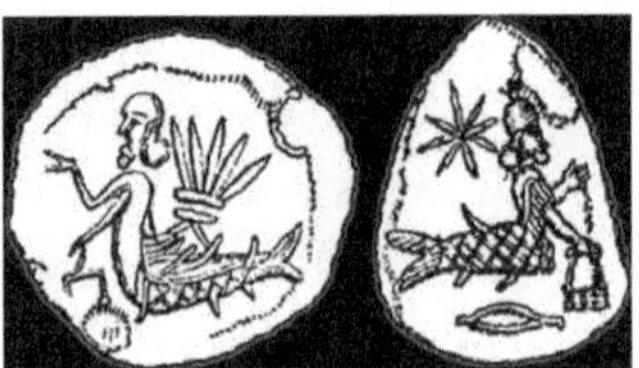

Oannes on gemstones. Note the leaf-like pattern on the back of the image on the left. (Sayce, 1898)

> This document ... indicated to the magician, who was about to treat his afflicted patient, that a certain kind of plant or tree, the original which ... grew in Eridu, and ... contained magical qualities; and acting on this information the magician was directed to make use of a potion of the kiskanu plant or tree on behalf of the said patient. The text actually states the gods themselves made use of this plant to work a miracle of healing, and the implication is that the kiskanu plant was on this occasion of great benefit, it may again be made to perform the healing of a sufferer ... provided that suitable words of power were recited ... and appropriate ceremonies were performed, before the plant itself was used as a remedy (Thompson, 1903).

Image of Oannes, from a Babylonian seal, 7th century BCE. Oannes is seen as either the Babylonian version of Ea, or Ea's emissary. Depicted here with the sacred kiskanu tree. Note the 7 speared leaf formation in the center, the woven net like pattern surrounding it, and the pinecone like buds with bags for collecting. Many images of the baskets (below) held with these "tree of life" images, indicate they were woven. Could this be another indication of the plant represented?

Above: 1st Millennium seal showing a worshiper and a fish-garbed sage before a stylized tree with a crescent moon & winged disk set above it. Behind this group is another plant-form with a radiant star and the Star-Cluster (Pleiades cluster) above. Source: en.wikipedia Commons.

It has often been suggested that Ea's *kiskanu* tree, developed into images in Assyrian art, known as the "Tree of Life."

Cannabis as the Mesopotamian Tree of Life

> A religious symbol which undoubtedly comes from the ancient east is the Tree of Life. This is found in some of the earliest Sumerian art, and continues throughout Mesopotamian

> history, being very prominent in the Assyrian friezes of the first millennium B.C. The mythological conception of the Tree of Life is also found in Genesis iii:22. H.W.F. Saggs, *The Greatness that was Babylon: A Sketch of the Ancient Civilization of the Tigris-Euphrates Valley* (1962).

A fascinating current archaeological theory proposes that a variety of ancient Mesopotamian depictions of vegetation as the "Tree of Life" are ancient illustrations identifying cannabis use as an ancient entheogen. Interestingly, this connection was also proposed by myself and co-author Neil McQueen in our 2001 book, *Sex, Drugs, Violence and the Bible.*

Dr. Diana Stein-Wuenscher, a British archaeologist with Birkbeck University in London, has suggested that the ancient Mesopotamian Tree of Life images are likely related to cannabis. In two articles, "Winged Disks and Sacred Trees at Nuzi: An Altered Perspective on Two Imperial Motifs" (2009), and "The Role of Stimulants in Early Near Eastern Society: Insights through Artifacts and Texts" (2017) Stein suggests that going back to prehistoric prototypical images, of sacred trees, and into the Assyrian period, in many cases, identify cannabis, which was used ritually, " cannabis may have been singled out as an object of veneration. In this respect, it would resemble many other sacred hallucinogens, such as the Indian soma, the aboriginal peyote, or morning glories and mushrooms, that were worshiped as divine plants and used as a guide to enlightenment" (Stein, 2009).

Dr. Stein has suggested that cannabis, or possibly in some images, another hallucinogen, is indicated in the following banquet images

Fig. 10. Early Bronze Age banquet scenes with reference to plants.

In reference to these banquet scenes, Stein questions whether the depictions indicate a beverage drunk through a straw, or an incense inhaled through a tube":

> It is generally assumed that the primary subjects are feasting on bread and alcohol (wine or beer), which is imbibed from cups or through tubes. But given the fact that extracts, resin and leaves of medicinal and hallucinogenic plants were often mixed with carriers and eaten, drunk or inhaled, how can we be so sure? It is difficult to say what is being consumed and whether it isn't laced with some psychoactive substance. Only the associated motifs can tip the balance towards one interpretation or the other. The presence of isolated bird and animal parts, composite beasts and imaginary contest scenes, for example, imply that the human subject in their midst was consuming something potent enough to induce such visions. And the frequent presence of a tree motif (also on banquet scenes from southern Mesopotamia) would seem to be a reference to its source (Stein, 2017).

Stein has also suggested that rather than indicating drinking through straws, these images could also indicate inhalation through tubes, as " resinous vapors can be inhaled through a tube extending from a bowl.... This method suggests another possible explanation for the 'northern drinking scenes,' where a seated figure is seen inhaling through a tube.... The presence of the tree in several of these scenes could be a reference to the source of the hallucinogen" (Stein, 2009).

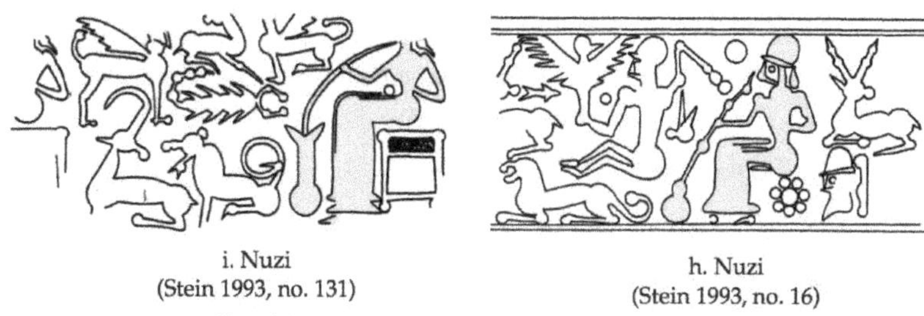

i. Nuzi
(Stein 1993, no. 131)

h. Nuzi
(Stein 1993, no. 16)

In a 2014 paper, "Psychedelics and the Ancient Near East," Stein referred to a similar image indicating the preparation of such substances with the sacred tree present.

> In several cases, the ancient Near Eastern design includes a plant (mushroom, cereal grain, tree) or animal (toads, frogs, fish), which is often central and may refer to the source of the

hallucinogen consumed. Something similar has been suggested as an explanation for the presence of a tree on two Achaemenid stamp seals that belong to temple brewers. In each case the tree appears to be the source of an important additive to the contents of the bottle that the brewer/seal owner raises up in his hand. These examples suggest that hallucinogens played a central role in the social and ritual life of ancient Near Eastern society (Stein, 2014).

Achaemenid period stamp seal (fourth cent. BCE) Trustees of the British Museum (Stein, 2014).

Stein goes on to note that the sacred tree of these earlier images, was adapted into later more refined Assyrian images of the Tree of life, and still retained their sacred association with cannabis. A very interesting hypothesis, and one that we also examined at length in *Sex, Drugs, Violence in the Bible* (2001). However, I do believe Stein drew her own conclusions on the matter independently, and coming from an esteemed, trained archaeologist such as herself, it carries considerable credence.

> [I]t seems unlikely that the sacred tree motif, a central feature in the state iconography of the Assyrian empire, represents the date palm, [a common hypothesis] a quintessentially southern species that does not grow north of Samarra. By the first millennium BCE, the goats, the hunters, and the worshipers, who had flanked the sacred tree and the *Qunnabu,* the probable Assyrian word for cannabis, is attested in texts of the first millennium BCE. It occurs in a Neo-Assyrian recipe for perfume, and a contemporary letter refers to its use in ritual contexts (Stein, 2009).

Image of the Assyrian 'Tree of Life, from the time of Ashurbanipal

An image associated with the Assyrian sacred rites, is a stylized plant or tree, seen in an engraving made at the time of Ashurbanipal. This unidentified sacred botanical also appears in numerous other depictions, and has "in modern literature on the subject ... [been] often described as the tree of life ... but unfortunately no texts are known which describe in more detail the contents of these pictures" (Ringgren 1973). Amongst the first to connect the sacred and unnamed tree in Assyrian art with the mythical Tree of Life, was Sir A.H. Layard, who described and commented on the symbol over a century and a half ago. "I recognized in it the holy tree, or tree of life, so universally adored at the remotest period in the East, and which was preserved in the religious systems of the Persians to the final overthrow of their Empire.... The flowers were formed by seven petals" (Layard 1856).

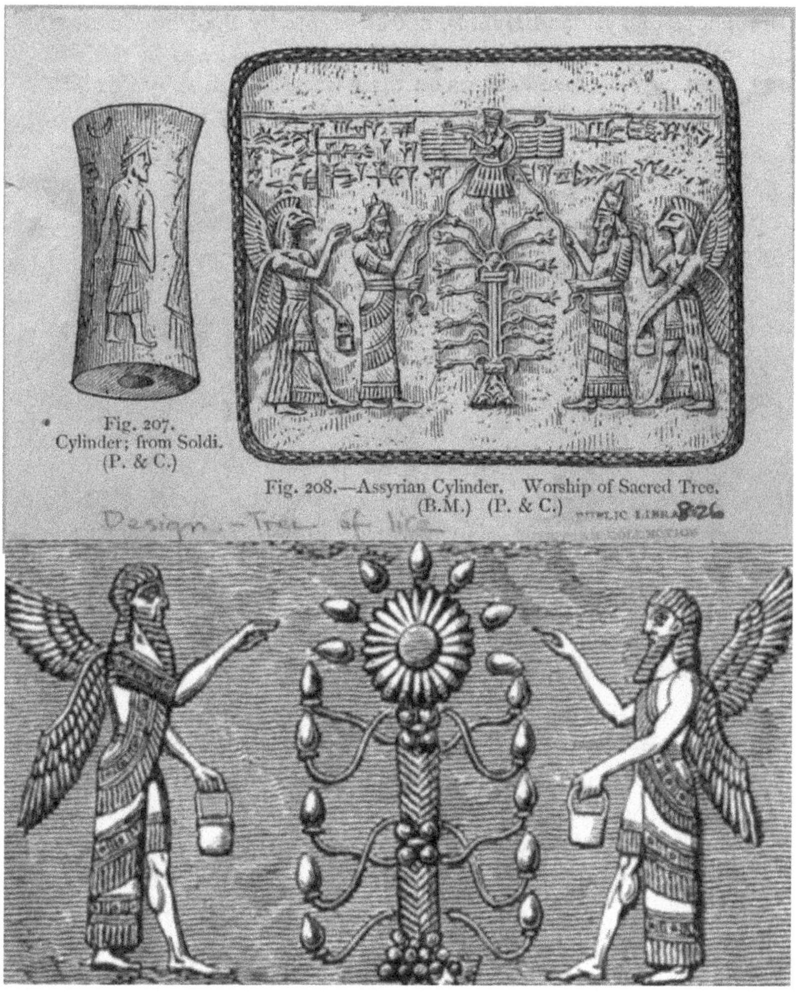

Wall relief created in the Neo-Assyrian period. Below the image the inscription in cuneiform texts relating to King Ashurnasirpal II reads: "The glorious god gives life to the king who rules valiantly, and he makes his dwelling." It is unclear if the figures here are women, (no breasts) or the transvestite priests who were known to accompany the worship of Ishtar.

Professor Widengren postulated that every temple had a holy grove, or garden with a Tree of Life that was taken care of by the king, who functioned as a "master-gardener." By watering and caring for the Tree of Life, the king gained power over life (Widengren 1951). As a scribe of the Assyrian king Assurbanipal recorded in 650 B.C.: "We were dead dogs, but our lord the king gave us life by placing the herb of life beneath our noses" (Ringgren 1973). This last reference points to an incense, and by its name, the "herb of life," we can easily visualize it as the plant depicted in the ancient stone engravings.

In *Near Eastern Mythology: Mesopotamia, Syria, Palsestine,* John Gray notes that the "association of the king with 'The Tree of Life' ... is familiar in literature and art in Mesopotamia, Canaan and Israel, with local variations" (Gray 1969). Gray also notes that like her counterpart Asherah, "the fertility-goddess Ishtar ... may ... be symbolized by the sacred tree.... This conception of the king as the medium of fertility through the fertility-goddess is expressed in Assyrian sculpture, where the king is touched by a protective genius with a cone dipped in some fertility substance, either pollen or oil.... The fertility is communicated by the king to a stylized version of the Tree of Life" (Gray 1969). We will return to this "cone" later.

Stein identifies the Assyrian Tree of Life in the above image as a development of earlier depictions of the Sacred Tree, here becoming increasingly indicated as a possession of the "State." As we have already noted Ashurbanipal's ancient cuneiform library contained recipes for hashish incense which "are generally regarded as copies of much older texts" and this archaeological evidence "serves to project the origins of hashish back to the earliest beginnings of history" (Walton 1972).

My co-authors of *Green Gold the Tree of Life: Marijuana in Magic and Religion* (1995) and I looked at a similar image, in relation to Ashurbanipal's father Esarhaddon, and suggested that this image also contained an elaborate incense tent. "King Esarhaddon stands before an elaborate incense chamber with smoking ... censer pictured in cut-away in the lower portion of the chamber; the upper chamber is tent-like with an opening" (Bennett *et al.* 1995). Conceivably, the tent was used to hold the smoke of cannabis incense, which the king would inhale by placing his head inside of it; which as we have seen in a number of variations, was a common means of marijuana inhalation in the ancient world, and an act of worship.

The Basalt Stele of King Esarhaddon. Behind the sacred tree and Esarhaddon sits the Bull of Creation, while below are the early tools of ancient agriculture, perhaps indicating an intimate connection between the three symbols. Notably in this picture, we see both the Sacred Tree image, and the Date Palm, which has been suggested as the potential source for the sacred tree images by some researchers. However, as they appear here quite clearly together and separate, and there are other depictions of the date palm in Assyrian art, a connection between the Sacred tree and the date palm can be ruled out. However the potential connection between the sacred tree and the *qunubu* used in the sacred rites, is made more intriguing.

A letter written in 680 BCE to the mother of the aforementioned king Esarhaddon, that was discussed in Chapter 3 Identifies qu-nu-bu, specifically as a key ingredient of the Sacred Rites. When one reads the full passage regarding the qunubu reference in the Sacred Rites in relation to the stela with Esarhaddon, the incense tent, Tree of Life, and the sacred ox, their connection is even more cemented, as is the imagery of the woven basket depicted in the other images of the Tree of Life:

> To the queen mother, my "lord": your servant, Nergal-šarrani. Good health to the queen mother, my "lord." May Nabû and Marduk bless the queen mother, my "lord," May Tašmetu, whom you revere, take your hands. May you see 1,000 years of kingship for Esarhaddon.
>
> As for what the queen mother, my Lord, wrote to me, saying: "What is going into the ritual?"
>
> These are its constituents: sweet-scented oil, wax, sweet-scented fragrance, myrrh, cannabis [ŠEM.ŠEŠ ŠEM.qu-nu-bu], and ṣadīdu-aromatic. [I will] perform it [for a]ll [the ... th]at the queen mother com[manded].
>
> [On the 10th] day, they will perform the whole-offerings: one ox, two white sheep, and a duck.
>
> Damqaya, the maid-servant of the queen mother, will not be able to participate in the ritual. (Accordingly,) whomever the queen mother, my "lord," designates should open the basket and perform the ritual.

So here in the Sacred Rites we see cannabis, in association with both the sacred ox, (or sacrificial "Great Bull that treadest the celestial herbage" as it is referred to in the Kettledrum ritual). Imagery that fits with Esarhaddon's Stella. As well as a reference to the "basket" from the other depictions of the Tree of Life. This makes an intriguing connection between the images of the sacred tree and the *qunubu* references.

In this imagery, one is reminded of the Biblical account of the Babylonian king Nebuchadnezzar eating "grass as doth an oxen" for seven years, in order to humble himself (Daniel 4:32). The bull imagery here may have been influenced by identical origins with a Persian myth. Zoroastrian mythology recounts how the ailing Bull of Creation was eased of its pain with cannabis by the God of Light Ahura-Mazda (*Bundahisin* 4:20). The imagery of the plough in the Esarhaddon stele also fits in with this line of thought, as King Yima who was believed to have instituted the Haoma ritual, was given a "golden plough." The plough is also clearly associated with the partaker of Soma in the Vedic tradition as well; "The Plough is attended by strong males, provided with a useful share and with a handle (to be held) by the drinker of Soma." Interestingly as we shall look at shortly, a connection between these Assyrian images, and *haoma*, and *soma* has long been suggested.

The "seven petals," referred to by Layard, can be seen to be more likely stylized depictions of the seven distinct spears of the cannabis leaves, just as the pine cone-like objects held by the figures often surrounding the plant, likely represent the pine cone-like buds of the sacred *qunubu*.

Generally the pine cone-like buds, held by the birdmen have been associated with "pollination" of the sacred Tree, however in other depictions they are being used in association with the King in the same manner. What we suggested in *Sex, Drugs, Violence and the Bible*, is that these pinecones were stylized cannabis buds being collected from the Sacred Tree by the birdmen (themselves representing costumed winged shaman who could travel between worlds), and this is why they carry woven baskets, to collect them. Through the collected buds the power of the sacred tree is transferred to the King. Moreover, we know that cannabis was used in Assyrian rituals that revolved around these images.

In the 19th century George Rawlinson noted of the pine cone-like buds from the Assyrian Tree of Life, that it is "as though it were the medium of communication between the protector and protected, the instrument by means of which grace and power passed from the genius to the mortal which he had under his care" (Rawlinson, 1881). As Rawlinson's contemporary Francois Lenormant noted, "Often ... it is held under the king's nose, that he may breathe it" (Lenormant, et al., 1881). A scribe of the Assyrian king Assurbanipal recorded in 650 BC: "We were dead dogs, but our lord the king gave us life by placing the herb of life beneath our noses" (Ringgren, 1973).

21 Photo, Mansell

WINGED DEITIES KNEELING BESIDE A SACRED TREE

Marble Slab from N.W. Palace of Nimroud: now in British Museum

Right: Silver bucket from Urartu in the Museum zu Allerheiligen, Schaffhasen, allegedly from the tomb of Prince Inuspua, 810 BC

Below: Detail from silver bucket.

In relation to the Assyrian sacred tree images, we noted above Helmer Ringgren wrote in *Religions of the Ancient Near East,* that "in modern literature on the subject." These tree images have been "described as the tree of life ... but unfortunately no texts are known which describe in more detail the contents of these pictures"(Ringgren 1973). This was also noted by Dr. Stein. "In many cultures the name of sacred plants is taboo.... Indeed, Assyrian texts contain no unambiguous references to the sacred tree image or an explanation of its meaning" (Stein, 2009).

The reason that this connection has not been noted before may be due to the fact that in the Ancient Near East matters involving religious and technical methods were considered closely guarded secrets. Professor H.W.F. Saggs noted that texts dealing with such matters ended with instructions such as; "Let the initiate show the initiate; the non-initiate shall not see it. It belongs to the tabooed things of the great gods." We saw this in the Priest's response to Esarhaddon's Mother regarding her servant. Such holy knowledge was either only passed along verbally to initiates and not committed to writing, or "were written in a manner which was deliberately obscure..."(Saggs 1969). The image of the Tree of Life and its divine association with the king, as well as the use of cannabis as a holy incense and entheogen may both fall into such a category.

These "Tree of Life" images are often described as depicting the Assyrian "Sacred Rites," and we know cannabis was an important ingredient in these same rites. As Stein has also noted: "A later Neo-Babylonian text records the delivery of large quantities of *qunnabu* to the great temple of Eanna and Ebabbar, and there are recipes in which hemp is an ingredient of aromatic oil used for cultic purposes" (Stein, 2009).

In a 1950 essay on cannabis, prepared as a United Nations Bulletin, R.J. Bouquet, which referred to the Assyria *qunubu* references noted "It would indeed be extraordinary if a substance, the use of which was to have a considerable effect on the social and politico-religious development of the peoples of Asia acquainted with it, had not left many traces in the monuments left behind by thinkers of those days" (Bouquet, 1950). We do have written references to cannabis, which by all accounts was an important ritual substance, as well as used medically. However no depictions survive. While with the "tree of life" images, we have depictions, which are associated with sacred rites, an incense tent, a sacred beverage, woven bags, but no surviving texts describing them. Is it too much to suggest that the unidentified symbol of the sacred plant, and the un-depicted plant for the word *qunubu*, are in fact a word and picture that describe the same thing – Cannabis, which was grown and revered as the Tree of Life in the ancient Near East?

Like the potential entheogenic references to the Tree of Knowledge, John Allegro suggested that the original Sumerian word for the Tree of Life contained etymological references to intoxicate. "In Sumerian the words for 'live' and 'intoxicate' are the same, TIN, and the 'tree of life,' GEShTIN, is the 'vine.'"(Allegro 1970). The Hebrew word used for life, (as in the Tree of Life), "chay," has more to do with enlivening, fresh, or merriment, and the continued fecundity of nature rather than personal immortalization.

François Lenormant the19th-century Assyriologist and archaeologist (and others) wrote that "[I]t is part of the essential characteristics of the tree of life that an intoxicating liquor might be extracted from its fruit, a beverage of immortality"(Lenormant, et al., 1881). Lenormant identified the Assyrian tree of Life images with the Persian haoma and Vedic soma. Lenormant, referring to the "Soma plant of the Aryans of India and the Haoma of the Iranians ... the celestial drink of immortality," noted that "the sacred plant assumes a conventional decorative aspect which corresponds exactly with no type in nature ... it is precisely this wholly conventional figure, borrowed by the Persians from Assyro-Babylonian art, which represents Haoma on the gems, cylinders or cones of Persian workmanship, engraved during the period of Achaemenidae" (Lenormant, et al., 1881).

> Such an adoption of the figure, most frequently used to represent the sacred tree of the Chaldeans and Assyrians, on the part of the Persians, to signify Haoma, though bearing no resemblance whatever to the genuine plant, proves that they recognized a certain analogy in the conception of the two emblems. In fact, adaptations of this nature were made with great discrimination by the Persians... The adoption of the Chaldeo-Assyrian tree, to represent Haoma, therefore shows decisively that it was possible to trace some kinship between these symbols... (Lenormant, et al., 1881).

In relation to the pine cones and the images of the Sacred Tree, and the winged Shaman with the buds collected in the woven baskets, depicted in an image with the consumption of a sacred beverage, indicating that the Assyrians may have practiced a Soma-like ritual. Considering cannabis' profound role in Assyria, its association with the Sacred Rites depicted, it is hard not to see the Assyrian Tree of Life as an Assyrian Soma-Haoma, which in all these cases would have been prepared from the medicinal, nutritious and fibrous cannabis plant.

Here we see the Genii with the pinecone, in relation to a ritual drink.

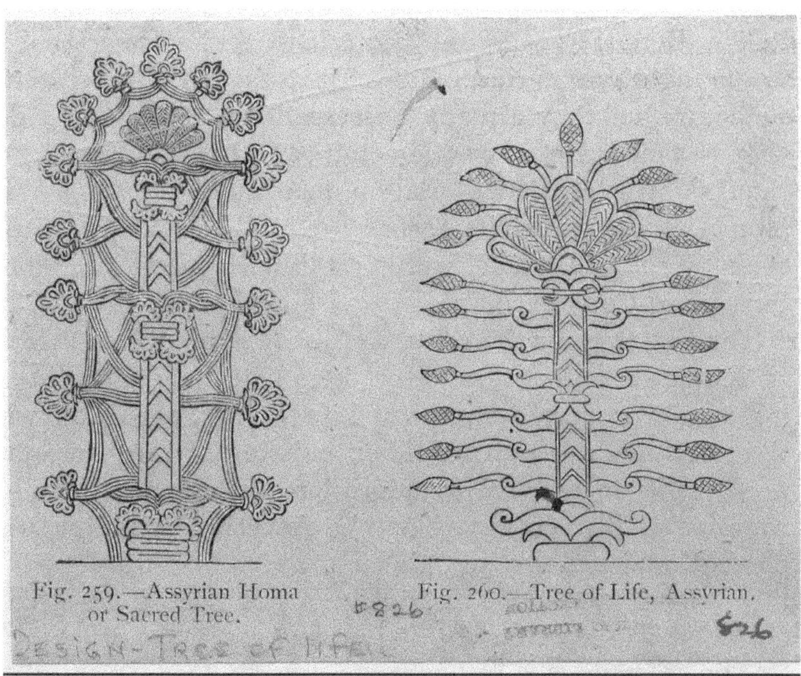

The connection between the Assyrian tree of life and haoma, was suggested by a number of 19th century sources. *Historic ornament : treatise on decorative art and architectural ornament, pottery, enamels, ivories, metalwork, furniture, textile fabrics, mosaics, glass and book decoration.* (Chapman and Hall, 1897) Ward, James (1851-1927), Author.

The bird-headed genii which are often depicted surrounding the sacred tree have been suggested as representing the *Garuda,* who brought and spread the Haoma from its original Mountain abode (Lenormant, et al., 1881). The motif of birds dwelling near the summit of a mountain from which the sacred Soma was said to have originated, protecting and distributing the Soma, is shared by both Iranian and Indian accounts, so can be seen as part of their even earlier shared common ancestry.

> [O]n the Assyrian bas-reliefs the sacred plant is guarded by winged genii, with the heads of eagles.... There is a singular analogy between these symbolic beings and the ... Garudas of the Aryan in India, genii, half men and half eagles.... in the Indian myths.... it is the Garuda who recover the ambrosia ... or sacred juice of Soma, with which the libations were made ... giving it back to the celestial gods ... [the Garuda] is made its keeper. His office, therefore, as well as the eagle-headed genii of the Assyrian monuments, besides the plant of life, is similar to the duty ascribed in Genesis to the kerubim which Yahveh placed at the garden of "Eden, after the driving forth of the first human pair, to defend the entrance, "and to keep the way of the tree of life" (Lenormant, et al., 1881).

Assyrian Bird Headed Genii - Lord Garuda The Vahana Of Lord Vishnu Returning With The Vase Of Amrita [equated with Soma]

Assyrian reliefs

Garuda

This situation left its most obvious mark on one of the last stories composed in the Old Testament, the tale of the fabled and prohibited trees in Eden. Both the Tree of Life and the Tree of knowledge have long been associated with the Iranian Haoma and its Vedic counterpart the Soma. As scholar E.K. Bunsen pointed out as long ago as 1867:

> The records about the "Tree of Life" are the sublimest proofs of the unity and continuity of tradition, and of its Eastern tradition. The earliest records of the most ancient Oriental tradition refer to a "Tree of Life," which was guarded by spirits. The juice of the sacred tree, like the tree itself, was called Soma in Sanskrit, and Haoma in Zend; it was revered as the life preserving essence (Bunsen 1867).

As also noted in *The Legends of the Old Testament* by Thomas Lumisden Strange:

> The tree of life is traceable to the Persian Paradise. "The haoma is the first of the trees planted by Ahura Mazda in the fountain of life. He who drinks its juice never dies" (Muir, Sansk. Texts,

> II...)... The original is the Soma of the Hindus, early deified by them, the sap of which was the beverage of the gods, and when drank by mortals made them act like gods immortal...The Hebrews have exactly adopted the idea: "And Jahveh Elohim said, 'Behold the man has become one of us to know good and evil; and now, lest he put forth his hand, and take also of the tree of life, and eat, and live forever: therefore Javeh Elohim sent him forth from the garden of Eden ... and he placed at the east of the garden of Eden cherubim, and a flaming sword which turned every way, to keep the way of the tree of life"... (Strange, 1874).

Joseph Campbell's description of the mythical white Hôm certainly brings to mind the Tree of Life as well: "the ... White Haoma Tree arose, which counteracts old age, revives the dead, and bestows immortality. At its roots Angra Mainyu [the Persian Devil] formed a lizard" (Campbell 1964). One can only speculate that the lizard lost his legs in this mythical transition and became the Biblical serpent. "The concept of the tree of life is found among many ancient people... In the Zoroastrian religion of the Persians the sacred tree was called haoma, which grew in a garden from which all the waters of the earth flowed (cf. Gen. 2:10)" (Gray, 1969). The 19th century occultist Helena Blavatsky may have been on to something when she claimed: "Plainly speaking, Soma is the fruit of the Tree of Knowledge forbidden by the jealous Elohim to Adam and Eve or Yah-ve, 'lest Man should become as one of us.'" (Blavatsky, 1888).

Interestingly, F. Max Muller indicated that the cherubim and seraphim of the Old Testament further the connections between the mythical trees of Eden and the traditions surrounding Haoma and Soma:

> We ... consider the comparison of the Cherubim who keep the way of the tree of life and the guardians of the Soma in the Veda and Avesta, as deserving attention, and we should like to see the etymological derivation of "Cherubim" from ... Greifen, and of "Seraphim" from the Sanskrit "sarpa," serpents, either confirmed or refuted (Muller, 1873).

Numbers of authors have made the connection between Eden's Trees and haoma/soma, and cannabis has long been considered a candidate for the latter. At least one 19th century author went as far as to connect all three. In *An Outline of the Future Religion of the World* (1884) T. Lloyd Stanley,[7] referred to Mashya and Mashyana, the first man and woman in the Zoroastrian creation myth, who "lived origi-

7 Apparently an alias of a Richard Morris Smith

nally in purity and innocence. Perpetual happiness was promised to them by Ormuzd Ahura Mazda the Creator of every good gift" and "the fruit of a wonderful tree Hôm which imparted immortality" and the evil "Ahriman Angrômaingus" who brought it all to ruin. Stanley noted that:

> The striking similarity of this legend to the Hebrew form of the Aramaic one leaves little room for doubt of their common origin. It seems highly probable that the strange effects of the fruit or juice of the Hôm or tree of knowledge of good and evil which on the one hand could restore the dead to life and on the other produced evil inclinations and destroyed moral excellence are in reality an allegory of the workings of that remarkable intoxicant the Sôma or Hôma extracted from either the Sarcostemma the Cannabis or from the Asclepias acida or sour milk weed or as some say from the Banian. It is almost certain that the Iranian reform in religion which occurred at the period of the separation of the two branches of the Aryans and was probably led by Yima embraced in addition to the doctrine of monotheism the reform of the excesses in the use of this intoxicating extract resin or fermented juice which had made part of the Aryan cultus. The Hôm tree embraces in one plant the qualities of the Hebrew tree of life and tree of knowledge of good and evil (Stanley, 1884).

In my 2010 book, *Cannabis and the Soma Solution,* I made a solid case for both the Avestan Haoma and Vedic Soma, as originating with cannabis, using the same sort of archaeological, textual and linguistic evidence that we have been presenting here. I wholly stand by that research. The famed anthropologist Weston La Barre, suggested that "cannabis was part of a religio-shamanic complex of at least Mesolithic age, in parallel with an equally old shamanic use of Soma…" (La Barre, 1980). However, when cannabis is equated with the soma, we are talking about an unparalleled ancient world sacrament that connects numerous existing traditions, the once and future Tree of Life.

Interestingly, Stanley saw the suppression of the Haoma cult in what became Zoroastrianism, as a step towards monotheism. In relation to the Assyrian Tree of Life, Diana Stein has made similar observations. Following the Tree of Life images from its pagan past into its role in relation to the King of the Assyrian Empire, Stein proposed that this imagery, which was originally related to a "ritual trance experience" was later "adapted over the millennia to reflect the increasing formalization of religious practice and its eventual appropriation by the state. This interpretation also explains the longevity and wide distribution of several associated, so-called pan Mesopotamian motifs. The conclusions, if correct, hint at mounting tensions between state and pagan religion that quite possibly inspired the story of Man's Fall from Grace in Genesis 3" (Stein, 2009). Here Stein notes that "cannabis was available in Mesopotamia during the sixth century BCE at the time when the Hebrew Bible was compiled in Babylon"(Stein, 2009). Moreover, Ashurbanipal and Esarhaddon, who we have discussed in relation to *qunubu*, and the Assyrian "Tree of Life" images, both appear in the Hebrew Bible.

> There are no laws or records of court cases concerning the misuse of cannabis or of any other psychotropic plant. But given the central role of magic and divination in everyday Mesopotamian life, it is conceivable that those who could not afford the services of the court diviner, prophet, or magician turned to other methods or mediums. The use of drugs in urban contexts without the traditional ritual constraints of tribal societies not only poses a threat to organized religion, it also raises the long-standing controversy over the religious potentialities of psychedelic drugs ... I suggest that this ongoing debate lies at the heart of Genesis 3, and that the fruit tree described by Eve as a source of beauty, food, and knowledge was, in fact, a potent but dangerous source of enlightenment. If that is the case, the authors of the story, in common with leaders of most established religions, take the stand that knowledge of the spiritual kind cannot or should not be attained by means of hallucinogens (Stein, 2009).

A very interesting hypothesis in relation to what we have seen in this study. However, regardless of these potential Sumerian influences, there are other elements that have been seen as a not so subtle form of propaganda in the Eden mythos, directed at the pre-existing polytheistic religion of Israel, as practiced for centuries prior to this time, and even extending after this period as well. Recalling Ezra's need to teach the people the Torah when he arrived in Israel, as well as the polytheistic element in 5th century BCE Elephantine, where Yahweh was coupled with Anath, we can see that despite the most severe attempt to restrict it, polytheism persisted as the religion of the people for some time.

Hebrew Polytheistic Motifs in the Garden of Eden

Jay G. Williams, a Walcott-Bartlett Professor of Religious Studies at Hamilton College, in his article, "Eden, the Tree of Life and the Wisdom of the Serpent" explains: "The essential plot can be understood, not as a struggle between God and the Devil, but as a conflict involving the dynamic, royal, masculine God of the heavens and the primordial Mother Goddess who for millennia had been worshiped as the Mistress of the earth. To be sure, the story is told from the point of view of the former. The serpent is reduced to being the subtlest of the creatures that the Lord God had made. The Goddess is not even mentioned by name, though she is there, as the tree of life, for that is how she was so often depicted among the ancient Canaanites. Indeed, because she was represented in tree form, it is not surprising that Yahweh declared that the tree and its fruit were taboo" (Williams, 2018). This symbolism carries over to the serpent as well:

> The wisdom of Asherah's serpent is medicinal, healing wisdom. That is why her serpents coil themselves around the caduceus, the physician's symbol. Her mysteries are the mysteries of herbs and poultices, of recipes and draughts ... Asherah ... offers the leaves of a particular tree to ease persistent headaches, the bark of a special shrub that grows high in the mountains to cure a skin disease.
>
> Many of the mysteries of the earth, of course, are dangerous. There are poisons as well as healing draughts, though even the poisons may have some healing use if their secrets are known. The Goddess hedges in her mysteries with ritual sanctity and orally transmitted lore. Each of her gifts must be used with specially prescribed care.
>
> This is particularly true for those psychotropic substances – soma, peyote, fly agaric, jimson weed, tobacco, the water of life (whiskey) et al – which can devour and kill but which, if imbibed with appropriate ritual, can also be revelatory. The Huichol of Mexico, who go to the land of the Mothers to hunt and collect peyote, do so with specially prescribed rituals and with a leader who knows the secrets of that land. Therefore, the result is not just a psychedelic high but a deeply transforming religious experience. Through peyote, the Mother allows the pilgrims "to see their own lives" (Williams, 2018).

Clearly, cannabis, as indicated by the findings at the temple of Arad, the references to *kaneh*, and other evidence, played such a role with the ancient cult of Asherah and other related Goddesses. As also likely did mandrake and other psychoactive substances.

An increasing number of Biblical scholars have begun to see the Eden mythos as a subtle form of propaganda against the polytheistic beliefs that preceded Yahweh-alone monotheism. For one thing, the scenario takes place in a garden, an area condemned as a place of worship. Isaiah condemns "a people who continually provoke me to my very face, offering sacrifices in gardens and burning incense on altars of brick" (Isaiah 65:3). However, other elements of the myth can be found in descriptions of Solomon's temple as it was described prior to Hezekiah's reforms –such as the brazen serpent Moses had made, and which the people had burnt incense too, which was pulled from the temple. One might also note here, that as discussed earlier, both the names of the Levites, who tended the temple and were later banned for idolatrous practices, and the "seraphim' which delivered a coal from the altar to Isaiah's lips with tongs, have indications of "serpent" in their names. As well the *Cherubim* who stood upon the Ark of the Covenant, are reminiscent of the Cherubim, who guarded the way to the Tree of Life, upon the first couple's exile. Just as the first couple wove clothes upon discovering their nakedness through eating of the forbidden fruit, the devotees of Asherah wove garments in the temple (2 Kings 23:7).

The idea that there is a connection between the temple and the descriptions of Eden, is by no way some new hypothesis, this is a long standing view. However, in the more traditional religious view, the temple was patterned after the Garden of Eden, rather than the reverse, as in the traditional view the story of Adam and Eve was known since the beginning of time, and accounts for our creation. In "The Garden of Eden, the Ancient Temple, and Receiving a New Name," Alex Douglas, explains "The stories of the Creation and the Garden of Eden are some of the best sources we have for understanding the ancient temple" (Douglas, 2013):

> [W]e can clearly see ... Eden's paradisiacal state ... reflected in its construction. In fact, much in the temple was designed to emulate and recreate the Garden of Eden for Israelite worshipers ... Solomon decorated the walls, the Bible tells us that "he carved all the walls of the house round about with carved figures of cherubims and palm trees and open flowers, within and without" (1 Kings 6:29). The palm trees and flowers alone would conjure images of Eden, but the cherubim make the reference certain; in fact, outside of the temple and God's

> throne, Eden is the only other place in the Bible where cherubim appear...
>
> ...The temple was ... meant to represent Eden, and many of the characters from the Eden story appear in Solomon's temple. In Eden, cherubim were placed to guard the way to the tree of life, and in the temple, two giant cherubim – each fifteen feet tall – guarded the entrance to the Holy of Holies (see 1 Kings 6:23–28). The priest in the temple represented Adam, and even the serpent makes an appearance. In 2 Kings 18:4 we learn that the bronze serpent made by Moses in the wilderness had been incorporated into Israelite worship (though the righteous king Hezekiah opposed this practice) (Douglas, 2013).

Representing the more secular, historical view, that Eden was based on the Temple and its contents, in "The Garden of Eden as an Israelite Sacred Place" Seung Kang suggests the Yahwist "author's description of cherubim in the Garden of Eden story was mediated by the iconographic representations of trees and cherubim in the Solomonic Temple" (Kang, 2020).

> We know that composite creatures such as cherubim and lamassu were featured in ancient temples and palaces in Syria and Mesopotamia. The Solomonic Temple appears to have adopted this tradition. Therefore, it is more likely that the Garden of Eden narrative was inspired by the Temple tradition than that the biblical description of the Temple was inspired by the Garden of Eden. The author of the Genesis narrative may have attempted to present the Garden as the Israelite center of the world by associating it with the Temple, the dwelling place of God and the center of the universe (Kang, 2020).

Moreover, we are talking about Solomon's temple here, he of the *Hieros Gamos*, who burned incense on high to the Goddess, and who by tradition celebrated mandrake and cannabis as *kaneh* in the Song of Songs.

Asherah as Eve

In regard to sacred plants, we have been discussing a plant that was particularly associated with Asherah, Ishtar, Ishara, Inanna and other Goddesses. A *plant* that was used ritually as an ointment and incense and woven into cloth, just as Adam and Eve wove garments after eating from the tree of knowledge of good and evil. A *plant* which was burned within the temple prior to the time of Josiah. Is it too much to suggest that an image of this sacred plant, or a living representative, may have stood within the temple at Jerusalem as well? Tikva Frymer-Kensky, a professor of Hebrew Bible and the History of Judaism in the Divinity School at the University of Chicago, notes an intimate connection between weaving and the forbidden tree, possibly hinting at a candidate offering both entheogenic and fibrous properties.

> The coming of knowledge is stated very simply: "the eyes of both of them were opened and they perceived that they were naked," a category they had not perceived in their childlike innocence, but, in addition, they are now able to sew themselves loincloths out of the available fig leaves. Somehow the knowledge of this skill of sewing, the beginnings of cultural knowledge, has come with the eating of the fruit of the knowledge of all things (Frymer-Kensky 1992).

We know that ritual weaving was done in the temple by the devotees of Asherah; as well, we know that archaeological evidence of hemp cloth being woven in a ritual context has been found in relation to Asherah (Boertien 2007). We also know Cannabis was burned in her honor.

In ancient times Asherah was widely known by such titles as Progenetress of the Gods and the Mistress of Fruitfulness and Sensual Pleasure. However, Asherah was also known as "the Lady of the Serpent" and "was depicted as a woman, holding one or more serpents in her hands" (Merkur 1988). Referring to the earlier association of the Goddess with the serpent, and Hebraic reversal of Near Eastern mythology, Riane Eisler wrote; "The fact that the serpent, an ancient prophetic or oracular symbol of the Goddess, advises Eve the prototypical woman, to disobey a male god's commands is surely not just an accident" (Eisler 1987).

> Importantly, a further Canaanite epithet of Asherah was "the Living One," whose Hebrew form hawwah is anglicized as Eve.... Not a goddess but a legendary woman, Eve represents a slightly different syncretism of Canaanite Asherah in the Southern kingdom of Judah. Eve remained closely associated with a snake and with "every tree that is pleasant to see and good for food, the tree of life in the midst of the garden, and the tree of knowledge of good and evil" (Gen 1:9) (Merkur 1988).

In his article "Yahweh's Divorce from the Goddess Asherah in the Garden of Eden" Arthur George notes:

> As noted by numerous biblical scholars, the Goddess is also seen in the figure of Eve herself.... In the Eden story she is given the epithet "the mother of all living," an epithet like those given to various ancient near Eastern goddesses including ... Asherah ... Eve's actual name in Hebrew (ḥawwâ), besides meaning life (for which goddesses were traditionally responsible), is also likely wordplay on an old Canaanite word for serpent (ḥeva). The name of the goddess Tannit (the Phoenician version of Asherah) means "serpent lady," and she had the epithet "Lady Ḥawat" (meaning "Lady of Life"), which is derived from the same Canaanite word as Eve's name (ḥawwâ). At the end of the story, Eve is punished by having to give birth in pain, whereas goddesses in the ancient Near East gave birth painlessly (George, 2014).

Indeed, as we have seen, the Goddess worshipers likely used the sacred cannabis of the Goddess, in preparation for birth, and cannabis use in the Holy Land for this purpose as we noted, is documented by archaeological evidence.

With this imagery in mind, the Eden myth can easily be seen as a direct form of propaganda against the Asherah cult: Eve, and her relationship with the serpent is identified with Asherah "Lady of the Serpent." Eden's Tree of Life and the doublet of it, the Tree of Knowledge, were her sacred, and now prohibited Trees of Eden. Thus the removal of Eve as Asherah from the divine presence of the Tree of Life, as well as the demonization of the Serpent associated with her, the presence of the cherubim who guarded the ark and the Garden, along with other elements indicate the Asherah traditions and the Eden narrative is based on the pre-monotheistic temple of Solomon and its rites.

As Arthur George summarizes:

> As a result of these events, by the end of the story Yahweh is supreme and in control of all divine powers and functions formerly in the hands of the Goddess, and Canaanite religion in general has been discredited. Yahweh is in charge of the garden (formerly the Goddess' province), from which chaos has been removed. Sacred tree veneration has been prohibited and discredited, while Yahweh appropriates and identifies himself with the Tree of Life.... The serpent has been vanquished, flattened,

> and deprived of divine qualities, and thus is not worthy of veneration, and enmity has been established between snakes and humans. The Goddess has been discredited, rendered powerless, and is eliminated from the picture and sent into oblivion. Yahweh's divorce from her has been made final... (George 2014).

In regard to the forbidden trees of Eden, it is worth noting Asherah's strong pre-existing relationship with sacred trees in her iconography, as well as her symbol referred to in Biblical condemnations as the 'Asherim' sometimes translated as 'ashram pole'.

Professor of Religious Studies at King's College in London, Joan Taylor explains that the *asherim*, a Biblical reference to a symbol of Asherah, was not a pole, but rather pruned tree of some sort, not a natural tree, "the asherim were to be distinguished from ordinary trees by being cut back in a particular way.... Despite being a tree, the asherim seems also to have been seen as kind of an idol in that it physically represented the Goddess" (Taylor, 1995).

> In favor of the asherim being a living tree rather than a wooden pole, it may be significant that always it is living trees, not dead bits of wood, which are iconic representations of fertility goddesses Their very livingness was an essential part of their meaning. Fertility goddess were, after all, deities of the life principle. As far as I am aware, we never get an iconic representation of a totemic wood pole reminiscent of a tree. When pictures of goddesses as trees occur, the trees may be stylized or naturalistic trees, or freshly cut branches... their livingness is always apparent.
>
> ...In the Babylonian Talmud, the "classic" asherah was unknown and the asherah was clearly any sacred tree. Any tree that was used for a purpose associated with idolatry was included in the category.
>
> ...The Mishnah has it that asherim could at times be constituted by grapevines ... pomegranate and walnut trees.... There is never any confusion between asherim and ... mighty trees such as oak.... All the trees that are asherim are of a smaller variety. Nowhere in rabbinic literature is there the slightest suggestion that an asherim was ever a piece of wood stuck in the ground as a sacred pole (Taylor, 1995).

The association between ancient Near East Goddesses and sacred trees was widespread. Buffie Johnson noted that not only is the

"Mother Goddess, strongly connected with the Tree of Life, [she] is in a sense the tree itself. At the same time she is outside the tree, vivifying it to bud and flower."(Johnson 1981). Like Asherah, "The goddess Ishtar was thought to dwell in a sacred tree" (Taylor, 1995). Thus a Babylonian Prayer to the goddess Ishtar proclaimed;

> Who dost make the green herb to spring up, mistress of mankind!
> Who has created everything, who dost guide aright all creatures!
> Mother Ishtar, whose powers no god can approach!

Feminist scholar Riane Eisler has noted "Like the tree of life, the tree of knowledge was ... a symbol associated with the Goddess in earlier mythology.... Groves of sacred trees were an integral part of the old religion. So were rites designed to induce in worshipers a consciousness receptive to the revelation of divine or mystical truths--rites in which women officiated as priestesses of the Goddess" (Eisler 1987). As we have seen, cannabis and in some cases mandrake were officiated by the cults of a number of Near Eastern Goddesses, Ishtar, Ishara, Asherah and Inanana particularly.

Figure 5. *White Stone Cylinder Seal from Mari (2350–2150 BCE)*, after Keel, *Symbolism*, fig. 42.

> "... [A] white stone cylinder seal from Mari, dated 2350- 2150 BCE, shows the king of the gods-probably to be identified here as Canaanite El... enthroned on a mountain between two goddesses (Athirat[8] and Athtart?), which are in the form of trees.... In the seal, the tree goddess on the left holds a smaller tree with eight branches coming from a central trunk, perhaps indicating that she has the power over all vegetation." (Taylor, 1995)

8 The mention of Athirat here is interesting. In the Baal Cycle found at Ugarit (1450 BCE-1200 BCE) we find this Goddess sitting by the sea using a spindle and doing laundry. The rites dedicated to the two contained a sacred drink of a mixed wine as an offering:

> He [Ba'al] does get up, he makes ready a feast and gives him drink;
> he places a cup into his hand(s), a flagon into both his two hands,
> a large beaker, great to see, a holy cup such as/which should never woman behold,
> a goblet such as/which should never Athirat set her eye on;
> a thousand pitchers he takes of wine, ten thousand he mixes in...

Again, we see weaving and sacred drinks associated with another Near Eastern Goddess.

This brings into question, if the Asherim were a plant, could cannabis have come to be used in this context?

> "You shall not plant for yourself an Asherah of any kind of tree beside the altar of the Lord your God, which you shall make for yourself" Deuteronomy 16:21

Could the evidence of its ritual use of cannabis in the Holy of Holies at Arad, combined with the archaeological evidence for the ritual use of hemp cloth in the Levant, and condemnations against the Goddess, which included weaving within the temple, and the rejection of offerings of cannabis, all be found in the symbolism of the forbidden trees of Eden?

Certainly depictions of Asherah's "tree of life" indicate a plant that from the primitive silhouettes in engravings, could be a stylized cannabis plant.

Right: A 13th century BCE pendant, depicting Asherah, note the Goats nibbling on her "tree of life"

Below Right: An ancient ivory cosmetic casket lid from the 14th century B.C.E. site of Minet al-Beida, depicts the goddess herself in the role of the Tree of life, offering two caprids, holding vegetation which clearly resembles buds of cannabis, but has been erroneously described as both ears of wheat or corn. As Professor John Gray explains in *Near Eastern Mythology: Mesopotamia, Syria, Palestine*: "This [depiction]seems to indicate finally the explanation of the Biblical references to the 'asherah as a natural or stylized tree in the fertility cult. This was the symbol of the mother-goddess, now known from the Ras Shamra texts as Ashera, the counterpart of Mesopotamian Ishtar.... The tree of life ... is called the asherah in the Old Testament."(Gray 1969).

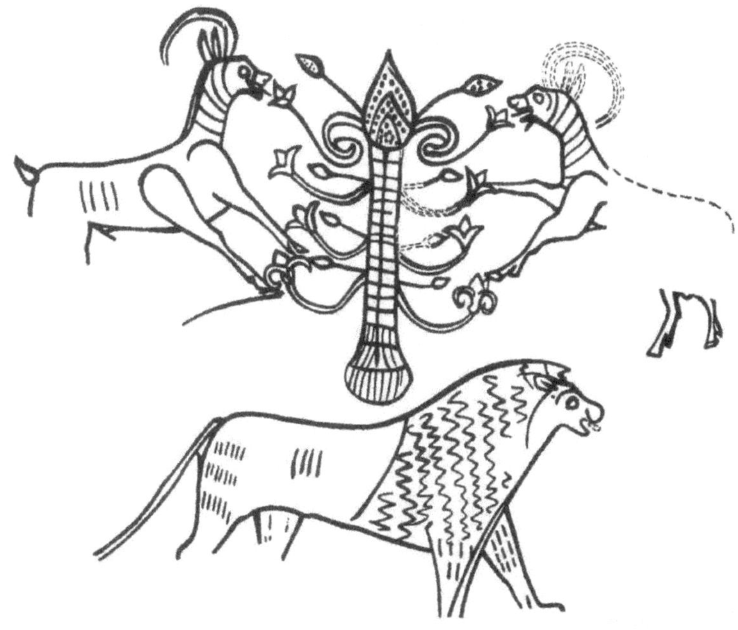

Asherah as Tree of Life

Pithos A from Kuntillet 'Ajrud, late ninth–early eighth century B.C.E.

Kuntillet 'Ajrud is an archaeological site located at the Sinai Peninsula in Egypt. The site is believed to have been an Israelite trading post. Excavations in the 1970s revealed two large pithos jars (used to store liquids) with inscriptions and illustrations.. The line drawing shows the tree of life, representing the goddess Asherah. Two caprids (goat-antelopes) flank the tree and eat from its leaves. Asherah rests atop a majestic lion. The textual inscriptions were written in early Hebrew script and refer to "Yahweh and his Asherah."

Incised slab with abstract female figure and goats from Stele of Mari, found in a pit at the temple of Ninhursag.

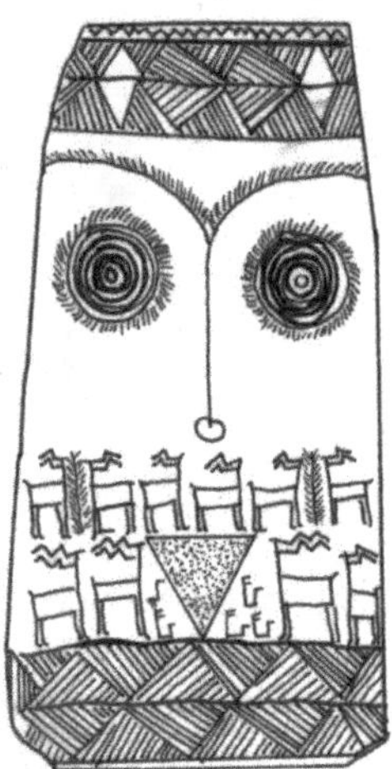

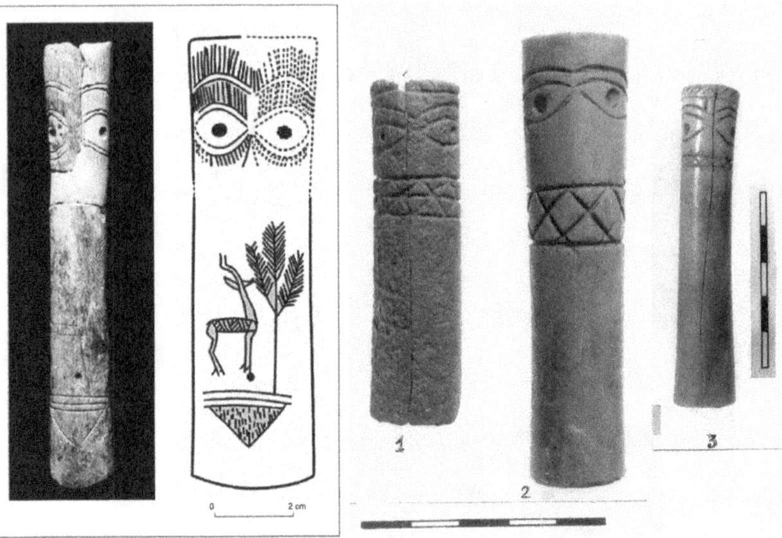

Left: Decorated bone depicting the visionary eyes, with the sacred tree and goat, above the vaginal triangle of "Mother Earth," 6th - 5th millennium BC, Hagoshrim, Southern Levant. **Right:** Similar bones with eyes were found by Sarianidi at BMAC, and were believed to have been used as drinking tubes; they contained grains of poppy.

Goats near the tree of life. Painted relief, 31 x 44 cm, terracotta tile of a house in Pazarli. Phrygia, 6th century BC. Museum of Anatolian Civilizations, Ankara.

British Archaeologist Diane Stein, has noted the goats in Mesopotamian tree of Life images, and has also made the suggestion that this may be connected to cannabis:

> The cannabis plant is most vulnerable in its early stages. Apart from insects and rodents, outdoor plants attract deer and presumably also goats, which like to feed on the tender young marijuana shoots. This phenomenon could be the source of the timeless Mesopotamian motif featuring a tree flanked by goats that we first encounter on Proto-Elamite seals of the fourth millennium BCE. Later Middle Assyrian variations on this theme that show goats tripping down the mountainside may illustrate the effect of eating potent young marijuana shoots.... Indeed, the goats' strange behavior and apparent fearlessness in the face of danger ... could be what alerted humans to the psychotropic properties of cannabis in the first place (Stein, 2009).

a. Amiet 1980, no. 457

b. Amiet 1980, no. 537

"The Tree on Proto-Elamite Seals (4th mill. BCE): It grows in the mountains, has a variety of shapes, and is flanked by wild goats and other herbivores" (Stein, 2009).

Stein, who has been studying the Mesopotamian images of the sacred tree since the early 90s, notes in her 2009 essay "Winged Disks and Sacred Trees at Nuzi: An Altered Perspective on Two Imperial Motifs": "As an object that over the millennia has many variants, is of interest to herbivores, humans, and hybrids ... the tree motif could refer to a variety of different plants. But there is at least one native species of the Near East that would account for many of its variations in context and appearance":

> *Cannabis sativa Linneaus*, popularly known as marijuana, is a fiber plant of the steppe region to the south and east of the Caspian Sea. Available evidence to date suggests that cannabis may have been used as a gathered, if not cultivated, plant as early as the Late Neolithic and that, with the exception of

Egypt, it was one of the most prominent cultigens in Bronze and Iron Age civilizations.... Virtually every part of cannabis can be used: the root for medicine (anesthetic), the stem for textiles and rope (and later paper), the leaves and flowers for intoxication and medicine, and the seeds for oil. Through breeding and natural selection, the plant has evolved in many directions. Varieties range from two to thirty-five feet tall. Branching patterns run from dense to loose. The branches can be as long as five or six feet or as short as a few inches. The various branching patterns form the plant into shapes ranging from cylindrical to conical to ovoid to very sparse and gangly. Furthermore, the shape and color of the leaves, stems, seeds, and flowering clusters are all variable characteristics that differ among varieties.

In common with the cannabis plant's original habitat, the tree on Proto-Elamite, Nuzi, and Middle Assyrian seals grows in the mountains.... The Proto-Elamite trees are often short and have a thin stem with irregular branches like cannabis seedlings.... Proto- Elamite, Akkadian and Late Bronze Age examples can be round ... or conical like certain cannabis varieties.... Others resemble flowering shoots ... a single leaf ... or an individual blade (Stein, 2009).

a. Cannabis seedlings (Frank 1997, Plate 1, top)

b. Proto-Elamite seal (4th mill. BCE) (Amiet 1980, no. 406)

FIG. 11

a. Common marijuana blade (Frank 1997, fig. 7)

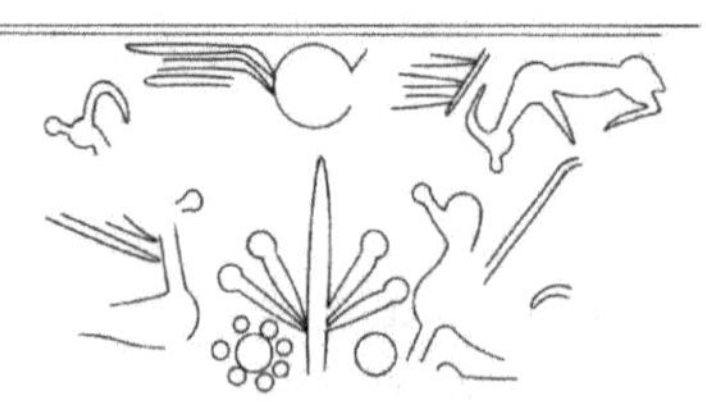

b. Nuzi sealing (ca. 1360 BCE) (Stein 1993, no. 224)

FIG. 15

b. Akkadian seal (ca. 2200 BCE)
Greenstone, H: 3.7cm, BM 89308

a. Christmas tree-shaped cannabis tree
(Frank 1997, pl. 4, top left)

c. Nuzi sealing (ca. 1360 BCE)
(Stein 1993, no. 187)

Fig. 12

a. Flowering cannabis shoot
(Frank 1997, cover photo)

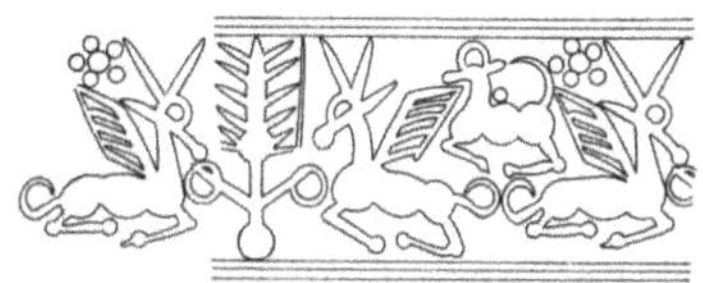

b. Nuzi sealing (ca. 1360 BCE)
(Stein 1993, no. 184)

c. Nuzi sealing (ca. 1360 BCE)
(Stein 1993, no. 154)

Fig. 13

Images (Stein, 2009)

Left: John Isaac posted this photo of goats happily eating a plant with known effects, writing: "One day while we were driving outside of Srinagar (India) a big herd of sheep just went out of control and crossed the road to get to the other side to a green patch."[9] **Middle:** Men's Animal Goat with Marijuana Weed Leaf Icy Hip Hop Custom Pendant Chain – Walmart. **Right:** A young goat enjoys eating marijuana plants on the side of the road near Marpha in the Mustang District of Nepal. https://nepaldog.typepad.com/danger_dog_blog/2009/08/goats-of-nepal.html

Right: Detail of a rhyton from Marlik, Iran, 1000 BC.jpg From: Taheri, Sadreddin (2013), Plant of life, in Ancient Iran, Mesopotamia & Egypt, Tehran: *Honar-hay-e Ziba Journal*, Vol. 18, No. 2 p. 7.

Below Right: Goats flank the Tree of Life on a ewer that is related to the Asherah cult. The shape of this particular tree has been noted for its strong similarities to the later menorah. The Lakhish (Lachish) ewer, discovered by James L. Starkey in a rubbish heap outside a temple at Lakhish. Image from "Understanding Asherah – Exploring Semitic Iconography," *BAR* Sept/Oct. 1991.

9 Goats love marijuana - https://www.facebook.com/watch/?v=546371038797376 https://www.youtube.com/watch?v=JohFpJx0nxl

THE ASHERIM AND THE MENORAH

The Lakhish ewer dates to about 1220 BCE, the time when scholars believe the Israelites were first emerging in Canaan, and Asherah was popularly worshiped. Note the goats on the right side, nibbling on a version of Asherah's tree of life, that undeniably looks like the 7 branched menorah tree of modern Jewish worship. In, "The Asherah, the Menorah and the Sacred Tree," religious studies Professor Joan E. Taylor, explains that the Lakhish ewer "may suggest that the menorah was designed with the usual form of an asherah-the cultic symbol of the goddess Asherah-firmly in mind" (Taylor, 1995):

> The ewer was seen as a kind of "missing link" to prove that Mesopotamian iconography directly influenced the iconography of the menorah, which is both a lampstand and a stylized almond tree.... It is certainly true that some ancient Mesopotamian representations of the sacred tree are strikingly similar in form to later Jewish menorot ... the tree depicted in the ewer is more than a generalized Tree of Life. In fact, it was very likely to have been specifically linked to the great Canaanite goddess Asherah by means of the inscription, "Mattan. An offering to my lady 'Elat" ... 'Elat is another name for the goddess Athirat/Asherah. Therefore, the trees of the ewer may be representative of her; in other words, they may be asherim (Taylor, 1995).

It is important to remember here, that throughout the time Solomon's temple stood, some 370 years, an *asherim* was there for about 236 years of that time in total. The earliest depiction of the menorah dates only to the first century BCE by comparison. There are descriptions of its construction in Exodus (25-31), but as Taylor notes, there "is a wide consensus among commentators in seeing the passages concerning the making of the cultic artifacts for the tabernacle ... as coming from the Priestly source (P),written some time after the return from exile in Babylon" (Taylor, 1995).

The Biblical descriptions of the menorah identify it with the almond tree. As Taylor notes on this in her comparison "A clear association between Asherah and the almond tree is wanting" (Taylor, 1995):

> It is clear that asherim were not always made out of almond trees, and in fact there is no positive evidence to indicate that they ever were. All that can be said is that the almond tree was likely to have been one of the trees that might have been, in

> some areas, made into asherim. The significance of the almond tree for the goddess Asherah may have had more to do with its early blossoming. Asherah, as fertility goddess, seems to have been associated with the natural forces of life and regeneration. The pretty blooming of the almond long before Spring has really begun may have struck the Canaanites as a special sign of the activity of the goddess. (Taylor, 1995)

An actual almond tree growing in the Elah valley, near Neve Michael shows that the tree has little in way of similarity to the structure of the menorah. Davidbena/Creative Commons .

I suggest that an almond tree was not intended by the depictions of the asherim, or by many of the images of Asherah's "tree of life." Instead I would suggest a tall tree-like bush of a plant, one that was burned as an incense offering to the goddess, as well as woven into ritual garments, one that was shared with her near Eastern counterparts, Ishtar, Ishara, and Inanna, and one that was at one time burned in the temple of her former co-creative partner and husband Yahweh. Cannabis was the Tree of Life.

As Taylor explains, "the stylization of Israel's sacred tree combined with the motif of the burning bush-arose as part of the struggle against the tree cult or 'Asherah-images'" (Taylor, 1995):

> It therefore seems likely that the iconographical concept lying behind the menorah owes much to the actual forms of asherim, images of the goddess Asherah.... If the iconography of

> the menorah said anything in terms of theology, it was that Yahweh could, with impunity, absorb nuances of Canaanite cult into his cult, just as he could absorb features of other gods into himself, for the other gods were nothing: all was in the power of Yahweh. If a menorah looked something like an asherah, this was not a problem: it was Yahweh who "owned" trees, not Asherah, and Yahweh could easily make use of a bush to present himself to Moses. (Taylor, 1995)

Could the menorah be based on cannabis as a stylized *asherim*? With what we now know this in the realm of possibility, and the menorah, in many ways looks like a 2 dimensional representation of a cannabis plant. Indeed, just like the seven branched menorah, one of the Hebrew references to the term *kaneh* occurs in Genesis 41:22, and depicts cannabis with "seven heads," and this passage, which refers to grains, also disallows an interpretation of calamus, as calamus is not known for edible seeds or grains: "In my [Joseph] dreams I... saw seven heads of grain, full and good, growing on a single stalk [kaneh]." As noted already, the ancient Hebrews ingested cannabis in heart-shaped cookies under its Persian name Sahdanag, translated as "Royal Grain" (Löw, 1925; reprinted 1967).

Left: Could the menorah find its origins based on a two dimensional representation of a cannabis plant? **Middle:** A Cannabis plant cultivated to look like a Menorah. **Right:** A typical Marijuana plant grown for smoking buds.

Menorah from the Byzantine period with a tree, or plant and a horn for Holy oil.

It is here looking through the veil of time, back into the origins of this myth, arguably the most potent myth in the history of humanity, that we can see the depths to which cannabis and the entheogens have been hidden from humanity. Now, slaying the cherubim of superstition, we can take back the Garden and stand before the Once and Future Tree of Life. In many ways, the rediscovery of the cannabis Tree of Life and other entheogens, may mark the realization of Yahweh's ancient fears, that our eyes may become open, as well as humanities return into the Garden of Eden, if in fact we ever left it at all…

As Franz Kafka wrote, perhaps "we live continuously in Paradise … whether we know it … or not." A fellow German similarly commented that "Through clever and constant application of propaganda, people can be made to see paradise as hell, and also the other way around to consider the most wretched sort of life as paradise" (Adolf Hitler). Paradise has been paved over and hidden from us. However, if there is one thing that can break through the pavement and restore the Natural Order, it is a plant.

The rediscovery of the entheogens and the vast implications they have on theories concerning the development of religion give clear indications that we are in fact in Paradise but are the victims of a cruel and malicious hoax that would lead us to believe otherwise. If the voices of the Gods were the plant-based shamanistic revelations of our ancient ancestors, then the flaming cherubim and the God who placed them between us and the forbidden trees of Paradise are all of our own creation, and the Exile is self imposed.

In our own time, one is reminded of the Genesis tale by the way our own Authorities have blindly prohibited these once sacred substances and branded them as evil, warning of death and degradation, if not expulsion from society, for those who are drawn to break these prohibitions, and taste these forbidden fruits. As a result of this conspiracy, humanity has become more and more separated from the natural world – Eden, which continually finds itself buried beneath cities and asphalt – The Highway to Hell is indeed paved. The rediscovery of the plant entheogens may offer us a means of re-acquaintance with the Natural Order, and a way of return back to the Garden.

> When we were naked – with the fibers of her stalk, hemp clothed us.
>
> When we were hungry – with the protein and essential fatty acid rich oils of her seeds, hemp fed us.

> When we wanted to record our thoughts and share them with others – hemp offered us the paper to do it with.
>
> When we wanted to see the world – hemp offered us the sails and ropes for the ships as well as the caulking for the boats that made it possible.
>
> When we were dying of AIDS, vomiting from chemotherapy, going blind from glaucoma, shaking from epilepsy – hemp offered us a natural medicine that eased our pain or treated our maladies.
>
> And when we sought a means of communion – the joint was passed and the sacred circle reformed.

As we have been looking at evidence that indicates much of the mythology of the Eden Genesis myth, was directed at a reversal of so many elements of the polytheistic situation in Israel, prior to the Monotheistic take over. It is worth looking at the situation just a few short centuries later, when the Genesis story itself was placed in a similar situation by Jewish and Christian Gnostic groups...

Chapter 15

Garden of Eden Redux

Gnostic Reversals of the Eden Myth

Just as we have seen there was a hidden Hebrew religion in the background of the Hebrew Bible, early Christianity was considerably varied, and many branches were wholly different from the form of Christianity which has come down to us through the New Testament texts. It was not only Pagan groups that were suppressed and disappeared when the Roman elite decided to embrace the once rebel religion of Christianity, but also a whole variety of Gnostic Jewish and Christian groups, Ophites, Basilidians, Sethians, Valentianism, Marconians, Manicheans, to name but a few.. These sects are now known to us under the collective banner of "Gnosticism," but each held their own various beliefs and takes on Judaism, Jesus and Christianity. As I have discussed this at length in early works (Bennett & McQueen, 2001; Bennett, 2010) and may return to it in detail in a later work depending on the reception to this book, for the sake of space and to retain its focus on the ancient Near East and the Hebrew Bible, I will only summarize some of that material here.

For the first four hundred years after Jesus' birth, the term "Christian" was used to describe a wide variety of sects and a large volume of different documents. Through the acceptance of one of the more ascetic branches of Christianity by the Roman ruling class, Christianity eventually became the state religion of its former persecutors. These other Christian groups were deemed as heretical, and many of them came to be grouped together under the blanket name of "Gnosticism," which means "knowledge." This was a fitting title, as most of these groups rejected the Catholic concept of "faith" and taught salvation was only attainable through personal experience and knowledge.

We know of these Gnostic groups through the condemnations of them from Catholic Church figures like Irenaeus, Saint Augustine, who was a former Gnostic, and Hippolytus of Rome, and until the 1940s, just a few surviving documents. In 1945 a cache of Gnostic texts were found, now known as *The Nag Hammadi Library,* which vastly extended our knowledge of these ancient groups.

As well, Paul, originally a persecutor of the faith, even after his alleged conversion, is shown in conflict with Christian groups, throughout Corinthians and elsewhere, that were pre-existent to his own conversion. These Christian groups were likely what would later be deemed "Gnostic."[1] One might better term the Christianity that came down to us through the Catholic New Testament, as "Paulianity."

Gnostic teachings offered an almost complete reversal of the Old Testament theology, especially of the Garden of Eden mythology. Like the adulterous Israelites discussed, who continuously backslid into the older polytheistic religious traditions with their numerous gods and goddesses, certain Jewish Gnostic groups had returned to a pantheon of deities. Further, they depicted the creator God of the Old Testament, Yahweh, referred to by them as *Ialdabaoth,* as the arch-enemy of humanity and pitted him against Adam and Eve right from the start in the Garden of Eden. In many ways the Gnostic reversals of the Eden mythology were actually more historically in tune with the original Near Eastern symbolism that had been reversed by the Jews, as can be seen by the re-deification of both the Goddess and the serpent.

Some scholars have suggested that the commentaries, or Midrashes which resulted in the radical reevaluation of the Eden mythos, originated in 100 B.C. in Palestine when the term "wise" first began to be applied to the formerly "crafty" serpent (Dart 1976). Possibly, some free thinking Rabbi or Essene, began to see Yahweh's poor showing through history, and harsh treatment of his "Chosen-People," as a sign that he was a false or evil God, and began to speculate on other interpretations of the myth. Clearly, in many Gnostic schools the serpent had been given the role of mankind's beneficent instructor and initiator. Further the "tree of knowledge" with which the serpent seduces Adam, gives him his "god-like status over against the lower creator god [Yahweh-Ialdabaoth] who pronounced his prohibitions of the enjoyment of the tree only out of envy" (Rudolph 1987).

Also, marking this theological return, we find the "Lady Wisdom" of Jewish Wisdom Literature, which is believed to have originated with the traditions of the Canaanite Goddess Anath[2], reemerging again under the personification of a goddess, known to the Gnostics as *Sophia* (Greek for 'Wisdom'). In a scene of transmutation reminiscent of Ashera's earlier role as the cultic Tree, Sophia's daughter Zoe, also referred to as Eve of Life (Eve of Zoe), entered "the tree of acquaintance" to hide from the Authorities (Ialdabaoth and his ema-

1 See *Gnosticism in Corinth: An Investigation of the Letters to the Corinthians* (1971) by the German theologian Walter Schmithals.

2 A similar path from war goddess to wisdom goddess was followed by Greek Athena. An earlier connection between the two Goddesses has long been suggested.

nated co-creators). Further indicating such an influence from the earlier Near Eastern traditions, Sophia states that "I appeared in the form of an eagle on the Tree of Knowledge ... that I might teach them and awaken them out of the depths of sleep," a statement that certainly invokes the preexistent imagery contained on Near Eastern inscriptions of the eagle-headed deities picking pinecones from the sacred Tree of Life.

With the reemergence of the Goddess, the role of the woman in the tale, not surprisingly, became more important than that of Adam; she is created first and gives her consort life, bearing Adam as a virgin, and acting as her own midwife. In response to the woman's power, the "Authorities'"put a deep sleep over Adam, and conspire to "instruct him in his sleep to the effect that she [Eve] came from his rib, in order that his wife may obey, and he may be lord over her."

Indicating that they may have had some understanding of the origins of the Judaic Eden mythology, the Gnostic tractate "On the Origins of the World," uses the definite plural term "Authorities" to describe the usually singular role applied to God in the Genesis version. This is interesting considering that the Hebrew name translated as God, *Elohim*, is also a plural, and the words spoken by God in the Genesis account indicate more than one figure; as after Adam ate from the Tree of Knowledge of Good and Evil, God laments that Adam has "become as one of us."

Again in tune with the Near Eastern predecessors of the Hebrew Eden mythos, the Gnostic reversals included the reinstatement of the serpent as mankind's true benefactor. Although referred to as the "Beast" by the Authorities, the Serpent was envisioned by the Gnostics as the "Instructor ... the wisest of all beings," who worked in conjunction with Sophia for the salvation of humanity through knowledge, back to the kingdom of light from which their spirits were believed to have originally emanated. Gnostic groups, such as the Naasenes and the Ophites, took their names from words that meant serpent, in honor of Eden's wise instructor. (Through the Gnostic's view of the Serpent as a beneficial Redeemer figure, he later became equated with the spirit of Christ that descended on the mortal Jesus.)

The Gnostic retelling of the Eden tale, in the tractates "The Testimony of Truth," and "On the Origins of the World," begin much the same as the Old Testament version, with God giving the command to Adam; "From every [tree] you may eat, [but] from the tree which is in the midst of Paradise do not eat, for on the day that you eat from it you will surely die." Like the *crafty* serpent in Genesis, the Gnostic serpent-Instructor is described as "wiser than all the animals that were in Paradise," and convinced Eve to eat, telling her, "On the day when you eat from the tree which is in the midst of Paradise the eyes of your mind will be opened." Eve, in turn seduces Adam, "Then their intellect became open. For when they had eaten the light of acquaintance had shone upon them" and upon recognizing their nakedness the two sew fig leaf girdles.

Still in sync with the Genesis account, Adam, with a guilty conscience hides himself, when he sees God coming. Unable to find Adam, God calls out to him, and Adam answers sheepishly, from under the tree that he was hiding beneath. At that moment God comprehends Adam's transgression, cursing the serpent as the "devil," and casting Adam and Eve from Paradise, lest they "take from the tree of life and eat and live for ever." It is at this point that the Gnostic view of the Eden story takes the most drastic shift in direction. As the Gnostic writer of "The Testimony of Truth," explains:

> But of what sort is this God? First [he] maliciously refused Adam from eating of the tree of knowledge. And secondly he said, "Adam, where are you?" God does not have foreknowledge; (otherwise), would he not know from the beginning? [And] afterwards he said, "Let us cast him [out] of this place, lest he eat of the tree of life and live for ever." Surely he has shown himself to be a malicious grudger. And what kind of a God is this? For great is the blindness of those who read, and they did not know him. And he said, "I am the jealous God; I will bring the sins of the father upon the children until three (and) four generations." And he said, "I will make their heart thick, and I will cause their mind to become blind, that they might not know nor comprehend the things that are said." But these things he said to those who believe in him [and] serve him!

The Gnostic scholar Birger A. Pearson points out in his introduction to the Gnostic tractate that: "This material was probably based on a previously existing source, to which the author of the Testim. Truth has added some editorial touches, including an allegorical interpretation of the serpent as a symbol of Christ" (Pearson 1978).

In the Gnostic reversal of the Eden mythology, and its lifting of the entheogenic prohibitions incorporated in the Genesis tale, we get our earliest indications that the Gnostics had lifted the ban on certain psychoactive plants instilled by their Jewish ancestors.

As much as the Eden Myth flavored later Old Testament stories, so did these Gnostics reversals of the myth flavor all future Gnostic belief. In fact it is in the 100 B.C.E. exhalation of the Genesis serpent that some scholars have seen the origins of the Gnostic movement, under the branch known as Ophitism, which as noted comes from a Greek term meaning "serpent."

> This "Ophite" Gnosticism is said by Philaster to be pre-Christian ... Celsus, the pagan philosopher, in his True Word, writing about the middle of the second century, makes no distinction between the rest of the Christian world and those whom Origen, almost a century afterwards, in his refutation of Celsus, calls, "Ophites" ... the statement is sufficient evidence that there was a body of pre-Christian Gnosis, that the stream flowed unbrokenly and in ever-increasing volume during the first two centuries, and that the..."Ophite" still marks out one of its main channels. (Mead 1900)

As Gnostic Scholar Kurt Rudolph explained: "Celsus reports of the Ophite Gnostics that they possessed a 'seal' the recipient of which was made a 'son' of the 'Father'; his response was: 'I have been anointed with the white ointment from the tree of life'.... In some [Gnostic] texts like the [Sophia and the Books of Jeu (Ieou)] the ' ointment' is a prerequisite for entry into the pleroma, by which the highest 'mystery' is meant" (Rudolph 1987). The ointment here was an oil, and in this case a prerequisite for an astral voyage, that was a key aspect of gaining "Gnosis"'(spiritual knowledge) while still in the human form. Descriptions of the effects of the anointing rite make it very clear that the holy oil had intense psycho-active properties, which prepared the recipient for entrance into "unfading bliss."

Gnostic texts also make it clear, this holy oil was to be used not only for enlightenment, but also for medical purposes. "The Acts of Peter and the Twelve Apostles" demonstrates Jesus' own view of the importance of this rite, when he gives the disciples an "unguent box" and a "pouch full of medicine" with instructions to go into the City of Habitation, and heal the sick. He tells them you must heal "the bodies first" before you can "heal the heart."

Similarly in the New Testament, Jesus does not baptize any of his disciples, but he does send them out with holy oil, in the oldest of the synoptic gospels: "And they cast out many demons and anointed with oil many who were sick and healed them" (Mark 6:13, KJV). As I have expressed elsewhere (Bennett & McQueen, 2001: Bennett, 2010) many of the New Testament "miracles," might be explained by the established medical efficacy of cannabis, and clearly the description of using poultice on a blind man, indicates there was more than a mere laying on of hands.

"Casting out demons," has been suggested as a reference to treating epilepsy, which cannabis is very effective for, and is indicated for in early Assyrian texts. Records of topical ointments used in the treatment of "Hand of Ghost" an ancient malady now thought to be epilepsy, included cannabis as a key ingredient and indeed cannabis is known to be effective in the treatment of epilepsy. A prescription for the disease was "Cannabis, styrax, oak, Ricinus, Oenanthe, linseed, kelp (?), myrrh, wax of honey, lidrusa-plant, sweet oil, together thou shalt mix, anoint him therewith with oil." As Russo noted; "cannabis was used with the plant El in petroleum to anoint swelling ... [and] was also employed as a simple poultice" (Russo 2005).

Amongst the many medicinal applications of cannabis is its use in relieving the pain of worn and crippled joints, and interestingly we read in the "Acts of Thomas": "Thou holy oil given unto us for sanctification ... thou art the straightener of the crooked limbs." This application of the Holy Oil could reasonably account for the miraculous healing of cripples attributed to Jesus. "Cannabis is a topical analgesic. Until 1937, virtually all corn plasters, muscle ointments, and [cystic] fibrosis poultices were made from or with cannabis extracts" (Herer 1995). A common and effective home remedy for rheumatism in South America, was to heat cannabis in water, with alcohol, and rub the solution into the affected areas, and in the middle of the 19th century Dr. W.B. O'Shaughnessy claimed to have successfully treated rheumatism (along with other maladies), with "half grain doses of ... [hemp] resin" given orally. Centuries before the time of Christ Babylonian texts referred to hemp's use in ointments for swelling and for the "loss of control of the lower limbs" (*The Encyclopedia of Islam* 1979).

A 1992 archaeological dig in Bet Shemesh near Jerusalem has confirmed that cannabis medicine was in use in the area up until the fourth century. In the case of the Bet Shemesh dig, the cannabis had been used as an aid in child bearing, both as a healing balm and an inhalant. This find garnered some attention, as can be seen from the Associated Press article, 'Hashish evidence is 1,600 years old', that appeared in Vancouver newspaper *The Province*, on June 2, 1992:

> Archaeologists have found hard evidence that hashish was used as a medicine 1,600 years ago, the Israel Antiquities Authority said yesterday. Archaeologists uncovered organic remains of a substance containing hashish, grasses and fruit on the abdominal area of a teenage female's skeleton that dates back to the

> fourth century, the antiquities authority said in a statement. Anthropologist Joel Zias said that although researchers knew hashish had been used as a medicine, this is the first archaeological evidence. (Associated Press 1992)

As Zias and his colleagues explained: "We assume that the ashes found in the tomb were cannabis, burned in a vessel and administered to the young girl as an inhalant to facilitate the birth process" (Zias, et al., 1993). This find of cannabis in a Judean cave was further supported by the later analysis of glass vessels from the site which also contained evidence of cannabinoid residues (Zias, 1995). This find provided evidence of both inhaled and topical use.

As well, the Bible's New Testament's 1 John describes the spiritual knowledge contained in the anointing: "you have an anointing from the Holy One, and all of you know the truth ... the anointing you received from him remains in you, and you do not need anyone to teach you. But as his anointing teaches you about all things and as that anointing is real, not counterfeit – just as it has taught you, remain in him" (1 John 2: 27).

The Greek title "Christ" is the translation of the Hebrew word *Messiah*, which in English becomes "The Anointed." The Messiah was recognized as such by his being anointed with the holy anointing oil, the use of which was restricted to the installation of Hebrew priests and kings. If Jesus was not initiated in this fashion then he was not the Christ, and had no official claim to the title.

The claim was Jesus was a Messianic King in the line of David. However, one thing is clear about Jesus and the Holy anointing Oil, despite the strict prohibitions that regulated its use to the High Priests and Kings in the Hebrew Bible, Jesus was freely distributing it and using the holy oil for widespread healing and enlightenment. An act of rebellion that might play a greater role than has been recognized in both his ministry and demise.

This situation becomes even more explicit, when Gnostic texts of the first few centuries of the common era are looked at. In fact, anointing with this holy oil, vs water baptism, was a key point of conflict between these groups and what became the Roman Catholic Church. In the first few centuries AD, Christian Gnostic groups such as the Archontics, Valentians and Sethians rejected water baptism as superfluous, referring to it as an "incomplete baptism." In the tractate, the "Testimony of Truth," water Baptism is rejected with a reference to the fact that Jesus baptized none of his disciples. Being "anointed with unutterable anointing," the so-called "sealings" recorded in the

Gnostic texts, can be seen as a very literal event. "There is water in water, there is fire in chrism" ("Gospel of Philip").

Indeed the Gnostic tractate the "Gospel of Philip" records that; "The anointing (chrisma) is superior to baptism. For from the anointing we were called 'anointed ones' (Christians), not because of the baptism. And Christ also was (so) named because of the anointing, for the Father anointed the son, and the son anointed the apostles, and the apostles anointed us. He (therefore) who has been anointed has the All. He has the resurrection, the light, the cross, the Holy Spirit." Throughout the text "light" is "associated usually with chrism" (Isenberg 1978), and it is stated that if "one receives this unction ... this person is no longer a Christian but a Christ" (Gospel of Philip). Similarly, "The Gospel of Truth" records that Jesus specifically came into their midst so that he "might anoint them with the ointment. The ointment is the mercy of the Father ... those whom he has anointed are the ones who have become perfect." As the German Gnostic scholar Kurt Rudolph explained:

> Anointing with oil has a greater representation than baptism in Gnosis and ... is even regarded as more significant... This association ... is linked up with the name of Christ, "the Anointed One." Magical connotations also played an important role: anointing oil expelled demons and gave protection against them; correspondingly it cured and dispelled the "sickness" of the soul and body. Hence exorcism (driving out) was performed by means of anointing. The ancient magical texts provide abundant evidence for this application of oil. Often the anointing is taken as a "sealing," the ointment as a "seal," i.e. it is a protective act and declaration of property. The deity in this way assures the believers through the priests and they enjoy its protection.... In the foreground however is the concept of redemption, the gift of immortality which is transmitted by anointing (Rudolph 1987).

The importance of the Holy ointment amongst the early Christians, is also attested to in the apocryphal book, 'The Acts of Thomas', which has the rite of anointing clearly eclipse the significance and importance of the placebo water baptism. This, and the ointment's entheogenic effects derived from a certain "plant," is aptly demonstrated in the prayers and invocations which the apocryphal book recorded as accompanying the rite. "Holy oil, given us for sanctification, hidden mystery in which the cross was shown us, you are the unfolder of the hidden parts. You are the humiliator of stubborn deeds. You are the one who shows the hidden treasures. You are the plant of kindness. Let your power come ... by this [unction]."

In reference to the "plant of kindness" referred to in "The Acts of Thomas," it is important to note that the account where the above reference occurs, takes place in India! 'The Acts of Thomas' also includes a hymn, The Ode to Sophia, that is connected with the "Bridal Chamber" ceremony, a Gnostic sex rite analogous to the Sacred Marriage or *Hieros Gamos* described in Chapter 7. As cannabis has been commonly used since ancient times in Indian Tantric rites, it is important to note that the room prepared for this Gnostic counterpart of Tantric rituals was rich with the scent of "Indian Leaf." In a passage that brings to mind the imagery of the Song of Songs we read: "Her chamber is bright with light and breatheth forth the odor of balsam and all spices, and giveth out a sweet smell of myrrh and Indian leaf, and within are myrtles strown on the floor, and of all manner of odorous flowers" (Ode to Sophia).

Accounts from early Catholic sources attacking these practices, such as Irenaeus' condemnations of the Gnostic figure Marcus, make it abundantly clear that the use of entheogens in such sex rites was an integral part of the ritual. "The Church father said Marcus was a self-proclaimed prophet and magician who would pray over a cup of purple liquid mixed with wine, a concoction Marcus said was the blood of Grace, the aeon also known as Silence in the Valentian Pleroma" (Dart 1976). An alchemical recipe for making a cannabis elixir of this color, has been noted; "I have made the lavender elixir of Cannabis many times and have given it freely to seriously ill people. It never fails to provide astonishingly quick relief" (Osburn, 1995). As Irenaeus described of Marcus' ritual practices:

> [T]his Marcus compounds philters and love-potions, in order to insult the persons of some of these women, if not of all, those of them who have returned to the Church of God – a thing which frequently occurs – have acknowledged, confessing, too, that they have been defiled by him, and that they were filled with a burning passion towards him.... Pretending to consecrate cups mixed with wine, and protracting to great length the word of invocation, he contrives to give them a purple and reddish color, so that Charis who is one of those that are superior to all things, should be thought to drop her own blood into that cup through means of his invocation, and that thus those who are present should be led to rejoice to taste of

> that cup, in order that, by so doing, the Charis, who is set forth by this magician, may also flow into them.... When this has been done, he ... pronounces these words: "May that Chaffs who is before all things, and who transcends all knowledge and speech, fill thine inner man, and multiply in thee her own knowledge, by sowing the grain of mustard seed in thee as in good soil"...
>
> ...Some of his disciples, too, addicting themselves to the same practices, have deceived many silly women, and defiled them. They proclaim themselves as being "perfect," so that no one can be compared to them with respect to the immensity of their knowledge, nor even were you to mention Paul or Peter, or any other of the apostles. They assert that they themselves know more than all others, and that they alone have imbibed the greatness of the knowledge of that power which is unspeakable. They also maintain that they have attained to a height above all power, and that therefore they are free in every respect to act as they please, having no one to fear in anything. For they affirm, that because of the "Redemption" it has come to pass that they can neither be apprehended, nor even seen by the judge" (Irenaeus of Lyons, *Adversus haereses*, Book I, 178 A.D.).

Marcus' infused wine also caught the eye of Lynn Thorndike, in his *A History of Magic and Experimental Science*. Thorndike traced this sort of drug-infused magical practice by the Gnostics to Simon Magus, who he sees from references in Irenaeus, as having used "love-philtres" in magical sex rites, with "incantations ... enchantments, familiar spirits and 'dream-senders'" (Thorndike, 1923). Or more simply put "the proto-orthodox believed that Simon was drugging his converts in an effort to draw them to become his followers" (Hatsis, 2015). Love philtres also known as a "poculum amatory (literally 'love-cup') was both a stupefacient and an exciter that 'impair[ed]the senses and stirs within ... apparitions and frenzied loves.... Concocted of various plants, herbs, and roots ... [and] had been employed for centuries to 'lull all pain and anger, and bring forgetfulness to every sorrow,' as Helen of Troy famously lamented in Homer's Odyssey" (Hatsis, 2015).

More recently, Marcus' Gnostic drug-infused sex rites have been explored by Tom Hatsis, who notes that "we can be assured that he ... knew about the properties of some powerful hallucinogens" and despite Irenaeus' condemnation of such practice as merely a means of drugging women for seduction, in relation to the Gnostic quest for "direct experience ... he might have interpreted the ingestion of his potions as providing visionary or otherwise psyche-magical experience" (Hatsis, 2015). Even in it's derogatory form, Irenaeus' account of the rite performed by Marcus "affords a remarkable and very singular insight into the Gnostic celebration of the Eucharist," which they believed "effects a realization of the original oneness of the Pleroma" (Rudolph 1987).

The sadly fragmented Gnostic tractate "Zostrianos" has some obvious references to a drink which acted as a catalyst for the author's astral voyage: "After I parted from the somatic darkness in me and the psychic chaos in mind and the feminine desire ... I did not use it again ..." And again later, tying in the effects of the drink with references to "baptism"; "And I said, I have asked about the mixture [...] it is perfect and gives [...] there is power which [has ... those] in which we receive baptism ..." The experiences of the ancient Gnostic psychonaut recorded in 'Zostrianos," with its Baptism to the different levels or realms of heaven, closely parallels the experiences had by the Zoroastrian hero Ardu Viraf, who was transported in soul to heaven after drinking a preparation of bangha (hemp, bhang). The similarities between Viraf's ascent and those attributed to Gnostic groups have been noted (Hinnels 1973). Moreover, the name "Zostrianos" itself, has been seen as indicating Zoroastrianism. This is clearly plausible considering the Zoroastrian influences on Gnosticism, and that another Gnostic tractate, "The Apocryphon of John," has Jesus make mention of Zoroaster's teachings himself, declaring to John the son of Zebedee: "if you wish to know them, it is written in the book of Zoroaster."

In "The Revelation of the Magi" a third century early Christian writing purporting to be the personal testimony of the Magi on the events surrounding the coming of Christ, included the ingestion of a visionary meal:

> The people eat the Magi's food (chap. 28)
>
> Some of the people eat from the Magi's provisions, and as soon as they do, they begin rejoicing because of the visions that they immediately see. One of the people sees a great light unlike anything in the world; another sees God giving birth to himself; another, a star of light that darkens the sun; another, a man uglier than any other human being, saving the world through his blood and his appearance; another, a lamb hanging upon a tree of life, redeeming the world through his blood; and another, a pillar of light diving down inside the earth, with the dead rising and worshiping it. The ones who eat of the pro-

> visions see many other things beyond these, and the people of the entire land come to hear the revelations of the Magi. Day by day, the revelations increase, all sorts of miracles are performed by the Magi, and the faith of the Lord Jesus Christ grows in the land of Shir.

A visionary incense is indicated in the Gnostic tractate the 3rd century[3] "The Second Book of Ieou," where Jesus uses a "fragrant-incense" with a group of male and female disciples that provided a "wonder" This wonder which was brought about by a figure known as Zorokothora, identified with Melchizedec, who in the Gnostic tractate "Pistis Sophia" is described as the "hand" of the goddess herself. The incense was offered to the Virgin of Light, bringing to mind the offering of *kaneh-bosm* incense to the Queen of Heaven that was carried on throughout Polytheistic Hebrew times.

The Second Book of Ieou refers to the unidentified plant "*cynocephalia*" which was put into the mouths of people. Pliny mentions this same plant for divination, claiming to have heard from Apion the Grammarian, notorious resident of Egypt, that the herb *cynocephalia* is known in Egypt as osiritis, after the God Osiris, and is believed to be a source of divination and a protection against black magic. There are other unidentified plants in the Gnostic text as well, such as *kasdalanthos*.

With multiple entheogens indicated it is worth noting that the Second Book of Ieou refers to the "mystery of the Five Trees," which in this case, likely means having knowledge of certain magical plants that were used as a shamanistic catalyst in the ceremony. These same five trees were referred to in what is possibly the oldest Christian text in existence, "The Gospel of Thomas": "...there are five trees for you in Paradise... Whoever becomes acquainted with them will not experience death." In the Gnostic view, "not experiencing death" meant reaching a certain state of interior purification or enlightenment, at which point the initiate would "rise from the dead," meaning ignorance and blindness, and "never grew old and became immortal," that is to say, he gained possession of the unbroken consciousness of his spiritual ego, and as such realized that he was a part of the larger Cosmic whole that continued on long after the disappearance of the material body. The 'Second Book of Ieou', gives us a profound description of the shamanistic ceremony that led to this higher state, in part through the ingestion of the "five trees."

3 There is debate about the tract's date.

Infused wines are also indicated in The Second Book of Ieou, in a rite where "wine-jars and vine-branches are used." Considering what we have already seen in regard to both earlier Zoroastrian accounts and Ezra's "fiery cup," this does open up the speculation to cannabis, or possibly other substances being infused into wine. As Mead summarized the Gnostic text:

> All of these mysteries Jesus promises to give to His disciples, that they may be called "Children of the Fullness (Pleroma) perfected in all mysteries." The Master then gathers His disciples, men and women, round him with the words: "Come all of you and receive the three Baptisms ere I tell you the mystery of the Rulers!"
>
> ...They do so, and the Master sets forth a place of offering ... placing one wine-jar on the right and on the left, and strews certain berries and spices round the vessels; He then makes the disciples clothe themselves in white linen robes, puts a certain plant in their mouths, and the number of the Seven Voices and also another plant in their hands, and ranges them in order round the sacrifice.
>
> ...we are next given a description of the Baptism of Fire. In this rite ... vine-branches are used; they are strewn with various materials of incense. The Eucharist is prepared....
>
> The prayer ... [this time, is to] the Virgin of Life, herself, the judge; she it is who gives the Water of the Baptism of Fire. A wonder is asked for in "the fire of this fragrant incense," and it is brought about by the agency of Zorokothora. What the nature of the wonder was, is not stated. Jesus baptizes the disciples, gives them of the Eucharist sacrifice, and seals their foreheads with the seal of the Virgin of Light.
>
> Next follows the Baptism of the Holy Spirit. In this rite both the wine-jars and vine-branches are used.... A wonder again takes place, but is not further specified.... After this we have the Mystery of Withdrawing the Evil of the Rulers ... and consists of an elaborate incense-offering.... At the end of it the disciples ... have now become immortal and can follow Jesus into all spaces whither they would go... (Mead 1900).

Given what we know about the use of entheogenic incenses, infused wines along with cannabis, mandrake and other plants identified, it is clear, that this "wonder" which so perplexed Mead, was the entheogenic effects of these substances administered by Jesus in the

Second Book of Ieou. Such Gnostic rites have their parallel in modern ayahuasca ceremonies, or peyote circles, on many levels.

Interestingly, in the medieval era, a cannabis-infused wine, as well as a salve and a pill, came into use in Antioch, a region largely considered the birthplace of Christianity. There was a cannabis wine infusion known as the "drync of Antioche," known from at least the Crusade era. Antioch was the epicenter for Hellenistic Judaism and is also considered the cradle of Christianity, and according to the New Testament the term "Christianity" first came into use there.

As a 14th century text records:

> To make drync of Antioche Take bugle, auence, strawberywyses, redcolecrop, dayse, of iche a good handful ... of femaille hempe v croppes ... putte alle þese herbes in a pot, and do þerto a galoun of qwyte wyn, and sethe it ... do þer-to als moche of hony.[4]

The herbs were boiled together in white wine, a quart, and mixed with an equal amount of clarified honey. which aided its use as a salve. The preparation, like eshisha, was also boiled down into a syrup, known as the "Sirup of antioche," and further rendered into solid form becoming the "Pelotus of Antioch," which is considered as the forerunner to the modern medical "pill." It was seen as a potent medicine for a variety of ailments and was often carried into the battlefield as it was considered an excellent treatment for wounds.

The 15th century English poem, "How a Lover Praiseth his Lady,"[5] gives us the following reference:

> The wounded bodyes to hele and save,
> Antyoche to drynk and holsom safe
> Ther was als a myrrour of wonder engyne
> Ipolysshed by Intellygence devyne

Interesting here is that the reference to the drink is followed by a reference to a magic mirror. Cannabis appears in a number of 16th century English grimoires in a recipe for a salve for mirror scrying, such as *Sepher Raziel: Liber Salomonis, The Book of Oberon*, and *A Cunning Man's Grimoire.*

John of Gaddesden, who served as the prototype for Chaucer's "doctor of physick" character in *The Canterbury Tales*, recorded in his

4 Medical Recipes in Stockholm, Royal Library 10.90 https://quod.lib.umich.edu/m/middle-English-dictionary/dictionary/MED1764?fbclid=IwAR1ysSc6WDQSQ6dN7-xBKIvDth-FNvvenfxVImeeV3VNkYGfAe4Xd33qRY28

5 Oxford, Bodleian Library, MS Fairfax 16, also known as the Fairfax Manuscript

medical treatise the "Rosa Anglica" (1314) that such drinks injured the stomach and belonged to "ancient surgery." A statement which indicates their more ancient history. The decline of the Antioch drink was believed to have been hastened when it ceased to be recognized specifically as a wound drink, A recipe in a manuscript of 1443/4 gives merely the general instruction: "Use it for all evils of the body." However, I wonder if the decline had more to do with its use with magic mirrors, rather than as an all around medication...[6]

Of course, there is so much more to say on all of this, and this small contribution is but the tip of a monumental iceberg on the topic of entheogens and the origins of Christianity. Perhaps if there is enough interest in this study, it will be a topic that I will return to in the future.

6 See *Liber 420: Cannabis, Magickal herbs and the Occult* (2018) for more on this.

Conclusions

Cannabis clearly held an important role as a ritual incense and sacrament with a number of ancient world religions. Importantly for this study, it held a role in the surviving ancient religions of Judaism and Zoroastrianism. In regard to *kaneh* and *kaneh bosm*, what has been presented here is conclusive evidence that this term identified cannabis. None of the other botanical candidates fit the descriptions when placed in context of the narrative, kaneh was imported alongside frankincense, as was cannabis three of the five references referred to by Benet, also identify frankincense, which was found with cannabis at the tel Arad altar. The Jeremiah 6:20 reference articularly, which rejects both kaneh and frankincense, is clearly related to Jeremiah 44, and the Queen of Heaven references to burning incense. This fits perfectly with the "cancellation" of the tel Arad temple, which was known for its evidence of the combined worship of Yahweh and Asherah.

If the Greek translators of the Hebrew text had been correct in their designation of *kaneh* as calamus, then there would have been a consensus on this with Hebrew sources. However, as we have seen, Jewish authorities listed a variety of potential candidates. Up until now, all there was in regard to the identification, was botanical speculation. Arad's relationship with the *kaneh* references is undeniable, this word has been matched with its lost botanical identity.

Scholars who wish to identify the other claimed candidates, such as Lemon grass, Cinnamon Bark, Calamus, Sugarcane, etc, as *kaneh,* need to identify archaeological evidence that their candidate was used ritually in the Levant, as well as identify why it would become such a source of controversy, as indicated by the different contexts of the Holy Oil of Exodus 30:23, and the rejected offerings of Jeremiah 6:20. The role of entheogenic cannabis in this situation, with what is now known about its ritual use in the cults of Asherah, Ishara, Ishtar and other ancient Goddesses, marks this situation clearly.[1]

1 There may have been some survival of this relationship. In medieval times, certain Muslim groups referred to cannabis by the name "ashirah," which they saw as an endearing term for their hempen "girlfriend" (Rosenthal 1971, referring to a 15th century list of nicknames for hashish from al-Badri.).

In the *Haaretz* article on the tel Arad altars we referred to in the introduction, "Holy Smoke – Ancient Israelites Used Cannabis as Temple Offering, Study Finds" (2020) Ariel David raised some interesting questions and points:

> So if the ancient Israelites were joining in on the party, why doesn't the Bible mention the use of cannabis as a substance used in rituals, just as it does numerous times for frankincense?
>
> One possibility is that cannabis does appear in the text but the name used for the plant is not recognized by researchers, Arie says, adding that hopefully the new study will open up that question for biblical scholars.
>
> Another answer may be that this particular custom was discontinued before the Bible was written, and whoever compiled and edited the holy text over the centuries had no knowledge of it or did not wish to preserve its memory. Researchers wildly disagree on when the earliest biblical texts were first put in writing, but many believe the process did not begin before the late seventh century B.C.E., during the reign of King Josiah in Jerusalem.

In answer to the question on why the Bible does not mention cannabis – The Hebrew Bible did indeed identify cannabis as it did frankincense and the two were listed together, with cannabis under the name *kaneh*. This also answers the second point raised by Ariel David, and this study confirms the identity of *kaneh* as cannabis. In regard to David's third point, for the most part, it does seem this temple practice ended around the time of Josiah, and the destruction of the First Temple. This suppression was connected and combined with Yahweh's divorce from Asherah which gave rise to a new Monotheism. A situation as we have shown that was directly indicated by Jeremiah 6:20: 44:1-23, as well as the evidence from tel Arad of the combined worship of Yahweh and Asherah, at the time of either Hezekiah's or Josiah's "reforms" and after.

However, cannabis use may have risen up again in a new context and with a Persian influence at the time of Ezra. But the indications here are, this practice did not continue, and the voice of the prophets fell silent after the inauguration of the Second Temple. This coincides with the rejection of *kaneh* by Jeremiah and the Priestly caste, as well as the loss of its botanical identity of *kaneh* by the Greek period. Under the priestly caste Judaism became a moral code of laws and obligations of tithes. That this disappearance of both kaneh and the prophets of old coincided is telling.[2]

When we place cannabis smoke within the temple of the Biblical God, alongside prophets like Isaiah and Moses, etc., questions are raised. Were the Hebrew prophets talking to God in the smoke-filled chambers of the Holy of Holies and Tent of the Meeting? Or were they talking to themselves? One could look at what was discussed in this book, and use it to further the position of atheism, pointing out that Yahweh's voice in the temple was but a "smoke dream," and what we have here is the anthropological perspective of the rise of religion, the shamanism, and the use of entheogenic plants. Others might interpret this as indicating cannabis has angelic qualities as a "messenger." Either way, to the individuals in question the experience was a communication with the divine. Interestingly, one could also see the birth of reflective consciousness in this same plant and shaman relationship.

In this respect, we must acknowledge the intellectual and conceptual differences between ourselves and ancient humanity. Having not long before stepped out of the stone-age where consciousness was far more focused on instinctual functions such as avoiding danger, finding food and reproduction, prehistoric people had little time to stop and "think." The development of language itself, which is a means of communication not self reflection, does not immediately result in self analysis or reflection.

---

2 Regardless, the cultic use of cannabis amongst the Hebrews was not easily suppressed, and it seems likely that certain mystically inclined sects of Judaism retained the method of shamanic ecstasy used by their predecessors. Rabbi Aryeh Kaplan has noted of early Kabbalistic magical schools who used magic and other means of communion for mystic exploration, that "some practices include the use of 'grasses,' which were possibly psychedelic drugs" (Kaplan, 1982). As mentioned earlier, Kaplan's *The Living Torah* includes cannabis as a possible candidate for the Hebrew *kaneh bosm*, "due to cognate pronunciation" (Kaplan, 1981). The Kabalistic text the *Zohar* records: "There is no grass or herb that grows in which G-d's wisdom is not greatly manifested and which cannot exert great influence in heaven" and "If men but knew the wisdom of all the Holy One, blessed be He, has planted in the earth, and the power of all that is to be found in the world, they would proclaim the power of their L-rd in His great wisdom" (*Zohar* 2, 80B).

Prof. Benny Shannon, who has speculated about ancient Jewish use of psychoactive substances, felt somewhat vindicated when he was directed to the works of the medieval Kabbalist and scholar Rabbi Jacob Ben Asher (Rabbeinu Be'cha'yei ben Asher),(1255-1340). "Rabbeinu Be'cha'yei writes that the purest of foods were created at the very beginning of Creation in order to allow for the attainment of higher knowledge. He explicitly relates this to the biblical tree of knowledge, and comments further that such higher knowledge can also be gained through the use of drugs and medicines available at his time. In addition he notes that the Manna had such qualities as well" (Shannon, 2008). Clearly cannabis and its various preparations, along with opium and other psychoactives, were well-known for mystical properties at Ben Asher's time. In *Liber 420*, I document references to cannabis in Jewish and Jewish influenced magical and alchemical texts, as well as in the later occult scene.

It is our ability for subjective interior verbalization which most differentiates us from other species. As Descartes stated it; "I think, therefore I am." This evolutionary step from non-conscious-dream-time into self-reflective-experiential-time may also mark the inception of ancient religions. Psychologist Julian Jaynes' book, *The Origin of Consciousness in the Breakdown of the Bicameral Mind* offers some interesting theoretical explanations of how the development of subjective consciousness may have taken place and how this is connected with hearing the voices of the Gods. We discussed Jaynes' theory in relation to metric verse and the poetic nature of ancient religious texts in Chapter 6.

Although Jaynes failed to fully recognize the important role plant-drugs have played in the development of consciousness, he did come up with a most revolutionary concept. Basing his hypothesis on scientific studies of the brain, combined with a close reading of the archaeological evidence, Jaynes demonstrated that ancient humanity could not think as we do today, and was therefore not conscious in the way we are now. As the back cover of Jaynes' book summarizes:

> Based on recent laboratory studies of the brain and a close reading of the archaeological evidence, psychologist Julian Jaynes shows us how ancient people from Mesopotamia to Peru could not "think" as we do today, and were therefore not conscious. Unable to introspect, they experienced auditory hallucinations – voices of gods, actually heard as in the Old Testament or the Iliad – which, coming from the brain's right hemisphere, told a person what to do in circumstances of novelty or stress. This ancient mentality is called bicameral mind.... Only catastrophe and cataclysm forced mankind to "learn" consciousness, and that happened only 3000 years ago.

Jaynes referred to the mental state of pre-consciousness man as the "Bicameral-Mind." The Bicameral human, as animals still are, was in a state of continual interaction with their environment, and the "world would happen to him and his action would be an inextricable part of that happening with no consciousness whatever" (Jaynes 1976). It was not until well into the development of language, (originally a means of interaction like the yips and yelps of a wolf pack), that reflective-consciousness could have even been able to start to take place. Anybody who would question how non-reflective man could perform such complicated tasks as farming, animal herding, home building, construction of towns, etc., need only look at the completely instinctually driven insect world, where ranching, farming, storage of grains, home and hive building, all take place with no sign of reflective consciousness what-so-ever.

Jaynes explains that being unable to introspect, ancient humans heard their first thoughts as if they were coming from outside themselves, in much the way a schizophrenic hears the demons and voices that torment them. In the case of the ancients these auditory hallucinations, or first *thoughts* were taken to be the voice of God, as in the case of Zoroaster when he heard the God Ahura Mazda's auditory replies to his questions. Humanity's transition into consciousness was an evolutionary step, and the voices which the first 'thinkers' heard came from the brain's right-hemisphere, and told them what to do in times of novelty or stress. As Jaynes explains; "Only catastrophe and cataclysm forced mankind to learn consciousness, and that happened only 3000 years ago" (Jaynes 1976).

Entheogen pioneer Terence McKenna comments on Jayne's book in his own brilliant *Food of the Gods*: "what we call ego was for Homeric people 'god.' When danger threatened ... the god's voice was heard in the individuals mind.... This psychic function was perceived by those experiencing it as the direct voice of god ... Merchants and traders moving from one society to another brought the unwelcome news that god was saying different thing in different places, and so cast early seeds of doubt.... At some point people integrated this previously autonomous function, and each person became the god and reinterpreted the inner voice as the 'self' or, as it was called later, the 'ego'"(McKenna 1992).

Unfortunately, Jaynes failed to acknowledge that the "fire in the brain" of thought could not only be initiated by the stress of survival, but also artificially induced by the ingestion of psychoactive substances. Although he was deeply influenced by Jaynes' work, McKenna felt that Jaynes' book failed its potential by neglecting to discuss the paramount role that "hallucinogenic plants or drugs" played in the development of consciousness "nearly entirely." The mushroom Bard expanded on Jaynes' theory by pointing out that; "The impact of hallucinogens in the diet has been more than psychological; hallucinogenic plants may have been the catalyst for everything about us that distinguishes us from other higher primates, for all the mental functions that we associate with humanness" (McKenna 1992).

McKenna suggested that psychoactive substances could have provided the spark for the fire in the brain that enabled the voices of the Gods to speak, and eventually became our thinking brain. McKenna's theory, which was built on Jayne's, has been labeled with the unfortunate sounding, but nonetheless descriptive title, "The Stoned Ape Theory."

McKenna specifically noted a role for both cannabis and psilocybin mushrooms in this respect, and hypothetically different botanical species may have served a similar purpose in regard to this in different areas of the world. The hallucinations and mystical insights experienced by those who consumed these plants convinced the ancient worshipers that they had come into contact with the divine. Clearly this was the case in regard to cannabis, as we have seen in the ancient World.

However in regard to cannabis, unlike the suggestion of mushrooms, we have a lot of actual archaeological evidence that attest to our ancient ritual use of this plant, as well as evidence that documents tens of thousands of years of interactions with the plant, combined with known references to it in our oldest forms of written languages. With cannabis, we are not left to speculation, its use has been identified in this exact context, as a means of talking to the Gods and receiving divine information.

We discussed the potential evolutionary role for cannabis and the "Great Leap Forward," as well as its likelihood as humanity's first agricultural crop in the Introduction.. Now before we proceed here, in regard to the voice of the gods and the development of "reflective consciousness" in relation to cannabis, it is important to remember here again the curious connections between cannabis plant-based cannabinoids and the endocannabinoid system in humanity.

As we have noted, the plant-based cannabinoids of cannabis are able to attach themselves to receptor sites for similar endogenous endocannabinoids present within the human body. Many of these are located in the human brain. There are numerous binding sites in the frontal brain, making it a high-brow receptor. The "receptors are found mainly in the cerebral cortex, which governs higher thinking, and in the hippocampus, which is the locus of memory" (Grinspoon & Bakalar, 1993):

> CB1 receptors in humans are found in regions of the forebrain associated with the development of language and music skills[3] and could also be responsible for at least some of the psychological effects of Cannabis. High CB1 levels are also found in the thalamus, which contributes to the human personality.... THC stimulates creative thought, improves lateral problem solving ... advantageous to survival... (Merlin & Clarke, 2013).[4]

3 We discussed the role of cannabis, music, and metric verse among the "prophets" in the production of religious texts in Chapter 6.

4 Cannabis not only has receptor sites in these areas of the brain that it can attach to, but also causes cell growth. Both CBD and THC have been shown to stimulate neurogenesis – the production and integration of new neurons in the brain#. "Administration of Δ9-THC was

As we have seen, evidence indicates that proto-Indo-European and Indo-European humanity burnt cannabis in funerary rituals, perhaps hearing in their heads the voices of their ancestor or chief. We can easily see how this practice would become popular and spread. Particularly with the advancement of horseback riding which is believed to have originated with these same cannabis using people, ancestors of the later Scythians, and the domestication of horses aided with hemp ropes.[5]

Could this effect account for its ritual use throughout the ancient world? Certainly as we have seen, cannabis use was identified with a variety of Sacred Rites in exactly this sort of context. Clearly its use here was in relation to its ability to increase the voice of the Gods.

The cannabis receptors of the brain, located in the areas of higher thinking and memory, would have been stimulated into "higher" activity. When Moses, or the acting High Priest or a prophet like Isaiah or Zoroaster inhaled, or consumed cannabis, in this higher state they acted as the shaman and put forth questions, which were answered in what was experienced by them as auditory hallucinations (the voice of Yahweh, or Ahura Mazda), but are known to modern people as intuitive thoughts. The writings that are attributed directly to Zoroaster in the *Gathas* depict the prophet's questions to Ahura Mazda and the Gods reply. Likewise in the Hebrew Bible account Moses would go into the smoky chamber of the Tent of the Meeting, and he would ask questions on behalf of the Israelites, and then come out and relay them. None of the other Israelites see God, they just know that Moses is "meeting" with the Lord when the smoke is billowing from the Tent of the Meeting! These accounts are reminiscent of other oracular gods and their seers of the same time, as well as modern accounts of shamans who seek revelation after inducing mind-altering sacraments.

As with the shamanistic ingestion of psychoactive plant preparations that is still occurring in certain parts of the world to this day, the visual images and voices heard by the early shamanistic ingestor of entheogens were interpreted by them, as actual interactions with supernatural beings and Gods.

Could the Commandments given by Ahura Mazda and Yahweh have been early ideas, relevant to the development of humanity at that

---

observed to enhance the neurogenesis in the brain, especially in hippocampus" (Suliman, et.al., 2017). CBD has also been observed to stimulate hippocampal neurogenesis(Victor, Hage and Tsirka, 2022). The implications of this have yet to be fully understood.

5 The origin of horse riding was the first significant innovation in human land transport predating the invention of the wheel, and hemp fibers may have played an important role in this crucial invention of horse riding" (Merlin, 2003).

time and place? If one comes to see consciousness itself as divine, then seeing the development of it in the shamanistic revelations of Zoroaster, Moses and similar ancient prophets, need not make those revelations any less holy, but perhaps less relevant as rules of conduct in our modern day. Indeed, it could be that reflective thought, and much religious literature, grew out of a combination of language and the use of psychoactive plants like cannabis and magic mushroom in a chemical marriage of shamanistic revelation.

> God said to Moses, "I AM WHO I AM.
> This is what you are to say to the Israelites: '
> I AM has sent me to you."
> –Exodus 3:14

These are the words Moses first heard after his initiation into the Midianite priesthood, and his first encounter with the "Burning Bush." In light of this information is not the above statement more believable as the birth words of Judaic consciousness through shamanistic revelations, rather than as the commandments of some omnipotent God? Especially such a God as the *jealous* Yahweh of the Hebrew Bible, a God "whose name is Jealous"? A God whose rantings at times, sound more like the ravings of an angry tribal chieftain, rather than those of the all-powerful Creator of the Universe. A God, moreover, whose emotional tone and tenor changes with each Prophet who claims to speak on his behalf.

The noted anthropologist Weston La Barre has commented "'God' is often clinically paranoiac because the shaman's 'supernatural helper' is the projection of the shaman himself. The personality of Yahweh, so to speak, exactly fits the irascible personality of the sheik-shaman Moses; the voices of Yahweh and Moses are indistinguishable" (La Barre 1972). La Barre refers to Moses here, but this could equally be applied to Isaiah, Ezekiel, Ezra, Zoroaster and other figures we have discussed in this study:

> Moses is ... a visionary shaman ... in whom the god (imperious id of the vatic) repeatedly speaks.... Psychologically, Moses and Yahweh are one ... Magic power, derived from Yahweh on direct instruction and contact is Moses' strength.... The relationship is made explicit when Moses complains that he is a man of poor speech, whereupon he is made a god to Aaron "and thou shall speak unto him, and put words in his mouth: and I will be with thy mouth, and with his mouth, and

> will teach you what ye shall do. And he shall be thy spokesman unto the people: and he shall be to the instead of a mouth, and thou shalt be to him instead of God "(Exodus 4:15-16). The divine Patriarch and the human patriarch are here as one (La Barre 1970).

Moses peered into and breathed in the smoke in the Tent of the Meeting. He meditated on a question and in the pillar of smoke over the altar, and an answer came forth from the smoke. Indeed, we saw God's rejection of Isaiah's plea for guidance, when he showed up without the requisite offering of kaneh (Isaiah 43:24).

"Moses and the Elders See God," by Jacopo Amigoni (also named Giacomo Amiconi) (1753?)

As the Biblical tradition grew out of early Near Eastern cults and ancient Mesopotamia was the home of the Sumerians, Babylonians and Assyrians, a knowledge of the history of this region and its inhabitants is essential in the study of history and religious ideas. The earliest known information about a number of religious institutions, conceptions and techniques are preserved in Sumerian texts. These writings date back to the third millennium, but are also reflections of even more archaic beliefs. We have also seen the antiquity of cannabis use here as well.

Many of the world's modern religions have their origins in this area, as do many of the world's popular myths and fairytales. There is still much being learned about the origin and history of early Mesopotamia, but it is not the intention of this study to record what is already known about it. I would rather bring to light the little known references to cannabis in the surviving literature of this area. As we have seen, the early ancient Mesopotamians worshiped a number of different deities. Most were usually thought of as being identified with a different phenomenon, such as weather and the growth of different crops, and the great gods were identified with planets. Later, the entities that represented these forces and objects were anthropomorphisized into human forms.

We have seen that cannabis, *qunubu,* was received as an offering at the main temples of the region, that it played an important role in the ritual life of the Royal and Priestly castes, and that it was offered to the main Gods and Goddesses.

However, there were also "personal" gods worshiped by the early Sumerians. Compare the following comments from Professor Helmer Ringgren's, in *Religions of the Ancient Near East,* especially the comments on the "tutelary deity," with the development of consciousness hypothesis of Julian Jaynes:

> Of special interest are the personal tutelary deities which certainly the king, and possibly all men, are thought of as having. This may be one of the inferior deities or a quite separate god. He is spoken of as "my god," and it is expected that when necessary he will take the part of the protege before the great gods, and make intercessions for him. Pictures show the individual's god leading his protege by the hands to one of the great gods. A poem which is sometimes called the Sumerian Job speaks of how a suffering man is finally helped and restored after persistent prayer to "his god."
>
> Jacobsen takes the view that this personal tutelary deity was originally a personification of a man's "luck," his capacity

> for thinking and acting, which was only gradually identified with one of the minor deities in the pantheon. While this cannot perhaps be proved, it is certain that it is the special tutelary deity of an individual and family that we are dealing with. "To acquire a god" is a phrase which is used for striking success. It is said also that without a (personal) god man cannot earn his living or be courageous in battle, and again:
>
> *"When thou dost plan ahead, thy god is thine, When thou god dost not plan ahead, thy god is not thine"* (Ringrenn, 1973).

It would seem that these tutelary gods had much to do with forethought and planning, the abilities of an advanced thinking mind. An ancient hymn reveals that the burning of incense has much to do with the worship of these personal, "indwelling" gods.

> Worship your god every day with sacrifice and prayer which properly go with incense offerings. Present your freewill offering to your god for this is fitting for your gods. Offer him daily prayer, supplication and prostration and you will get your reward. Then you will have full communion with your god. Reverence begets favor. Sacrifice prolongs life, and prayer atones for guilt.[6]

An ancient letter written at the time of the Assyrian King Assurbanipal states: "We were dead dogs, but our lord the king gave us life by placing the herb of life under our noses"[7]. I.e., *we were unthinking unreflective beasts, until the smoke of the incense brightened our eyes*!

Indeed, the potential role of cannabis in that scenario is reminiscent of Adam and Eve's own reaction after eating the forbidden fruit. Interestingly, the biological connection to cannabis is far, far, more than purely an intellectual one.

I would say the Biblical period marks the end of this transition from the Bicameral Mind into Reflective Consciousness, and by the time these texts were first recorded, humanity had long reached a reflective state. By this time, the ruling bodies of the era were focused on trying to control populations and kingdoms. Thus entheogens came to be rejected, for many of the same reasons our industrial societies of today reject them. As Diane Stein noted on this: "The use of drugs in urban contexts without the traditional ritual constraints of tribal societies not only poses a threat to organized religion, it also raises the long-standing controversy over the religious potentialities of psy-

6 As reprinted in *World Religions; From Ancient History to the Present*; Geoffrey Parrinder ed., Facts on File, NY, 1971

7 In (Ringrenn, 1973)

chedelic drugs ... leaders of most established religions, take the stand that knowledge of the spiritual kind cannot or should not be attained by means of hallucinogens" (Stein, 2009). The "revelations" of drug infused shamans were a source of potential "chaos and this was to be an Age of Organization and Control. Governments rely on religions to control the populous, non-shamanic monotheistic religions are the best form of control.

Cannabis, The Ultimate Mother Plant

Although the focus of this book has been on cannabis, the suppression of the Mother Goddess from the worship of Humanity, is the greatest crime of the monotheistic Abrahamic traditions. The rejection of the wealth of archaeological evidence that attests to Asherah's worship and pairing with Yahweh by fundamentalist influence in the fields of archaeology and history, is paralleled by the rejection of clear evidence of entheogen use in this same region and time.

The desacralization of the divine feminine at the core of this, has caused the desacralization of Mother Earth, and turned the natural world into commodity, and made an imaginary "Heaven" our sacred destination. As well, it made women second class citizens of much of the World, possessions of their Fathers', then their husbands', burdened with being the cause of "Original Sin."

Cannabis can help restore that once sacred relationship with the feminine divine. "Propagation of the female species... is the total concern of the grower interested in the narcotic power of the plant. It is thus a kind of happy coincidence that the subjective effects of cannabis and the care and attention needed to produce a good resin strain both conspire and accentuate values that are oriented toward honoring and preserving the feminine" (McKenna 1992).

Clearly cannabis has long held a relationship with the divine feminine, but interestingly, there seems to be some sort of biological connection as well. "The active compounds of marijuana have some molecular resemblance to certain female hormones (estrogens)" (Weil 1980)[8]. This is interesting considering what we now know about the human endocannabinoids system and may, as Industrial Hemp pioneer Jack Herer noted, indicate some sort of symbiotic pre-cultural relationship with cannabis.

---

8 Lignans in cannabis can transform, under the influence of anaerobic intestinal microflora, into enterolignans, which are the precursors of estrogens for mammals.

> ...United States government funded studies at St. Louis Medical University in 1989 and the National Institute of Mental Health in 1990, moved cannabis research into a new realm by confirming that the human brain has receptor sites for THC and its natural cannabis cousins to which no other known compounds thus far will bind.... On the molecular level THC fits into receptor sites in the upper brain that seem to be uniquely designed to accommodate THC. This points to an ancient symbiosis between the plant and people.... Perhaps these neuronal pathways are the product of a pre-cultural relationship between man and cannabis (Herer 1995).

Much progress has been made in the intervening decades since Herer made those observations. A recent article on "Medical Xpress," "People produce endocannabinoids—similar to compounds found in marijuana—that are critical to many bodily functions" stated that "It is as if the human body has its own version of a marijuana seedling inside, constantly producing small amounts of endocannabinoids" (Nagarkatti & Nagarkatti, 2023)

The chemical marriage between Man and Marijuana is revolutionizing medicine with the discovery of the endocannabinoid system. Indeed, through the conception of "endocannabinoid deficiency" (CECD), some researchers now believe that a variety of conditions are related to low endocannabinoids, a situation which can be addressed by the addition of plant-based cannabinoids from this incredible ancient plant ally.

These curious biological connections between man and marijuana continue: the hemp seed contains the most complete protein in the vegetable world, and is the highest source of essential fatty acids. Besides being responsible for the luster of hair, skin, eyes, lubricating arteries, and even the thought process, the "essential oils support the immune system and guard against viral and other insults to the immune system" (Eidlman, M.D., & Hamilton Eh.D., Ph.D.). The globulin edistin found in the seeds protein closely resemble those found in human plasma (Osburn 1993, Herer 1995, Robinson 1996)[9].

9 With the hemp seed's long-standing relationship with humanity, it is interesting to learn that modern science has revealed that they contain all the essential amino acids and essential fatty acids necessary for human life, as well as a rare protein known as globule edestins that are very similar to the globulin found in human blood plasma. Because of this, hemp seed has been touted by some as "Nature's perfect food for humanity." Four short years after the Marijuana Tax Act passed in the US, criminalizing all forms of hemp in America, a researcher writing for a 1941 edition of *Science* lamented the loss of access to the hemp seed's rare and important globule edistins; "Passage of the Marijuana Law of 1937 has placed restrictions upon trade in hempseed that, in effect, amount to prohibition ... It seems clear that the long

Even more interesting is that cannabis seeds contain rare gamma linoleic acid, found only in spirulina, two other rare seed oils, and human mother's milk. As well, as noted in the paper 'Cannabis and endocannabinoid modulators: Therapeutic promises and challenges': "endocannabinoids are present in breast milk" (Grant & Cohn, 2005). In "Endocannabinoids and Food Intake: Newborn Suckling and Appetite Regulation in Adulthood" the authors suggest:

> The appetite-stimulating effects of the cannabis plant (Cannabis sativa) have been known since ancient times, and appear to be effected through the incentive and rewarding properties of foods. Investigations into the biological basis of the multiple effects of cannabis have yielded important breakthroughs in recent years: the discovery of two cannabinoid receptors in brain and peripheral organ systems, and endogenous ligands (endocannabinoids) for these receptors. These advances have greatly increased our understanding of how appetite is regulated through these endocannabinoid receptor systems. The presence of endocannabinoids in the developing brain and in maternal milk have led to evidence for a critical role for CB1 receptors in oral motor control of suckling during neonatal development (Fride, Bregman, and Kirkham, 2016).[10]

As the tribal people of the world have always shown an incredible intuition when it comes to the right use of plants, it is interesting to note that the Sotho women of South Africa make a mealie pap from hemp to wean their babies off breast milk.[11]

---

and important career of the protein is coming to a close in the United States." "Hemp edistin is so compatible with the human digestive system that the Czechoslovakian Tubercular Nutrition Study conducted in 1955 found hemp seed to be the only food that can successfully treat the consumption disease tuberculosis, in which the nutritive process are impaired and the body wastes away" (Robinson, 1996).

10 As well, when natural endocannabinoids are blocked, maternal care is hindered. See 'Endocannabinoid receptor deficiency affects maternal care and alters the dam's hippocampal oxytocin receptor and brain-derived neurotrophic factor expression': "Maternal care is the newborn's first experience of social interaction, and this influences infant survival, development and social competences throughout life. We recently found that postpartum blocking of the endocannabinoid receptor-1 (CB1R) altered maternal behavior" (Schechter,Weller, Pittel, Gross, Zimmer and Pinhasov, 2013).

11 As with the Ancient Near East, it appears cannabis was also used by South African women to ease the pains of childbirth. As noted in Marihuana: A signal of Misunderstanding (*The Technical Papers of the First Commission on Marihuana and Drug Abuse*,1972).

Some reports indicate that cannabis helps relieve labor pains . Such uses are reported among native tribes in South Africa and Southern Rhodesia: " The Suto tribe fumigates the parturient woman to relieve pain ;" the Sotho women of Basutoland "are reported to stupify themselves during childbirth," and have also been known to "administer ground-up achene [seed] with bread or mealie pap to a child during weaning" (Watt, 1962…)

With what we have seen here one could easily speculate that there is some deep biological connection between humanity and this plant. Perhaps as it traveled with us in the ancient world, from settlement to settlement, growing in fields fertilized by human night soil,[12] combined with our ingestion of the plant, we both got a taste of each other? You are what you eat can work both ways…

Terrence McKenna has also pointed to the feminine qualities of this most holy herb culturally;

> Outpourings of style and esthetically managed personal display are usually anathema to the nuts-and-bolts mentality of dominator cultures. In dominator cultures without any living traditions of use of plants that dissolve social conditioning, such displays are usually felt to be the prerogative of women. Men who focus on such concerns are often assumed to be homosexual – that is, they are not following the accepted canons of male behavior within the dominator model. The longer hair lengths for men seen with the rise of marijuana use in the united States in the 1960's were a textbook case of an influx of apparently feminine values accompanying the use of a boundary-dissolving plant. The hysterical reaction to such a minor adjustment in folkways revealed the insecurity and sense of danger felt by the male ego in the presence of any factor that might tend to restore the importance of a partnership in human affairs. (McKenna, 1992)

Indeed, one could look at the anti-war movement of the 60s where cannabis smoke was often present, the rise of environmental movements, such as Greenpeace and Earth First, which were founded by people who used cannabis, Equal Racial rights which grew out of the social mixing of blacks and whites and Jazz clubs known for their reefers and vipers, and even the free love of the sexual revolution as effects on culture from the use of this plant,

> Because of its subliminally psychedelic effect, cannabis when pursued as a lifestyle, places a person in intuitive contact with less competitive behavior patterns. For these reasons marijuana is unwelcome in the modern office environment, while a drug such as coffee, which reinforces the values of industrial culture, is both welcomed and encouraged. Cannabis use is correctly sensed as heretical and deeply disloyal to the values of male dominance and stratified hierarchy (McKenna, 1992).

12 Endocannabinoids and cannabinoids can both be released through urine.

In this Age, when women have been liberated and their power can be celebrated, to see the prominent role women have played in bringing back cannabis into society is another testament to the divine relationship shared by queens of both the plant and human world. Moreover, just as the prohibition of cannabis has been a crime against humanity and through a loss of access to hemp, even a threat to the world we live in, so has the suppression of the divine feminine been a crime against all women, who have been treated as second class citizens through the same oppressive patriarchal religions which have suppressed the Goddess and her sacred plants, the Messengers of Gaia. Both Women's power and Sacred Plants have returned now in our own time, to once again lead us back to the Garden of Mother Nature and off of this Highway to Hell we have been forced to travel.

The modern concepts of Mother Earth and Gaia as a living system, in many ways mark the philosophical return of the Goddess. I don't think one has to literally believe in the Goddess to see that this plant offers us a way to return to balance with the environment and ourselves, but in many ways it's as if Mother Nature is reaching out her hand with this plant at our time of deep collective need.....[13]

In the Chapter "Cannabis and the Ancient Cult of the White Feminine," excerpted from *The Pot Plot: Marijuana and the Chemical Feminization of a Generation*, by Dr. Wesley Muhammad,[14] many of the same aspects we have been discussing here, are lamented as a signal of the downfall of the "Patriarchy." As the concerned Doctor explains:

> According to many of her devotees ancient and modern the cannabis plant is not just a herb but is also the embodiment of a deity, specifically of the female deity. The Divine Feminine not only incarnates in this ancient botanical medicine but, we are assured, cannabis is the antidote to the rule of man (male), "Mother Goddess's way to help overthrow patriarchy."
>
> ...Those who honor cannabis today as the embodiment of the Divine Feminine or female energy invest hope in her

13 The divine feminine did not completely disappear from Judaism. The Kabbalah, a later form of Jewish mysticism, teaches that the Shekinah is "the female soul of God, who couldn't be perfect until he could be reunited with her. Cabalists said it was God's loss of his Shekina that brought about all evils."(Walker 1983) Interestingly, in some traditions the Shekinah, is seen as the pillar of smoke that hung over the wondering nation of Israel during it's Exodus, as well as covering the ark in the inner Temple. Symbolism which can perhaps be traced back to the copious amounts of cannabis incense that ancient worshipers once burned in the Holy of Holies and in honor of the Goddess.

14 Dr. Wesley Muhammad is part of the controversial Minister Louis Farrakhan's research team

> to overthrow or upset the patriarchal order of male rule. The Indo-European Goddess who was incarnated within the plant was associated with the moon-sickle with which she castrated the male God. The moon-sickle or scythe was named after the Scythians who used the long-handled tool with its curved blade in the harvesting of cannabis. In the hands of Scythian Goddess however this scythe was a weapon that castrated the God.
>
> ...The Goddess behind the plant castrates the God. As we will show, this "divine feminine" is still castrating God, the Black God. Her moon-sickle is the cannabis plant itself; not the natural herb but the weaponized drug. The marijuana of today castrates the Black male twice: the White Goddess's moon-sickle castrates him at his testicles and at his brain (Muhammad, 2022).

I suspect we can expect more of this sort of reaction, from Evangelicals and other patriarchal-based religious groups. But what do they offer us? Bronze Age moral codes, and fanciful beliefs about heavenly afterlives, which as we have seen, are the real drug-induced smoke dreams. Moreover, the history of war caused by their division, and the state of both Humanity and the World, is a Testament to the failures of the "Patriarchy."

Even from an atheistic point of view, hemp is certainly a "miracle plant" that could through mass agricultural reintroduction, solve many of the ecological and environmental concerns of modern times by offering an eco-friendly viable alternative to products which now come from our vanishing forests, and the highly polluting petro-chemical industry. Amongst the many applications for this miracle plant: High quality paper can be made from hemp, as well as building products such as fiber board. It is estimated that biomass and seed fuels made from hemp could meet the world's energy needs, not to mention their use for paints and sealants. Hemp also has a high quality fiber for ropes and cloth that can be produced organically and replace soil depleting cotton. As well, and as has been discussed, a variety of remarkable medicinal benefits can be derived from its leaves and flowers. As this is being read, homes made from hemp concrete and insulated with hemp fibers are being built, nutritious hemp seed is being sold in grocery stores, people are getting dressed in eco-friendly hemp cloth, and writing notes on hemp paper. Parents are praising the miraculous relief of their child's epilepsy and children of aging parents appreciating its relief of their mother's and father's arthritis and other ailments. The gifts and rewards of the cannabis Tree of Life, are real, palatable and experiential.

Indeed, to embrace cannabis as the Tree of Life, one could take a purely materialistic view, based on the history and biology we have discussed in this book, and embrace cannabis as a symbiotic evolutionary ally that our species has had a biological connection to for tens of thousands of years....

From a religious viewpoint, the spiritual potency of cannabis is something that has been undeniably and widely recognized. An identifiable role for cannabis can be found in the inception period of such existing religions as Judaism, Zoroastrianism, Hinduism, Buddhism, Taoism, Sikhism, Shintoism, Islam, and as I have shown elsewhere and may look into again, even Christianity. The leaves of this sacred tree could serve as a uniting world sacrament, healing the Nations. For those with the eyes to see, the potential role for cannabis at this time period, which even from a scientific world view could be seen as Apocalyptic, is a Revelation.

What we can see here, is that there is a place where both Science and Religion meet. On those hallowed grounds, there is a Garden, and in its rich and fertile soil, so full of potential, grows the Once and Future, Tree of Life. The Flaming Swords of superstition held by the cherubim have been extinguished and the Gates of Eden are now open. It is up to you to reach out your hand and taste of what has been unrightfully forbidden you.

In finally closing this considerable text and exposing the formerly forbidden knowledge contained herein, I find myself slyly asking, as did the Serpent before me so long ago, from its position high up in the branches of the Trees of Life and Knowledge, "SSSSo," It hissed to the first man and woman as they sat nibbling on the tree's prohibited fruits, "how do you like them Applessss."

Upon announcement of the cannabis resins on the tel Arad altar, Professor Francesca Stavrakopoulou, a well known British biblical scholar, author and broadcaster, who is currently Professor of Hebrew Bible and Ancient Religion at the University of Exeter, Tweeted "God was indeed a high god! New evidence from one of my favourite Yahweh temples suggest theories about cannabis use in ancient Israelite/Judahite religions is spot on" (Stavrakopoulou, 2020). I am assuming that by "theories about cannabis use in ancient Israelite/Judahite religion" she is referring to Dr. Sula Benet's 1936 etymological theory that the Hebrew terms kaneh and kaneh bosm identified cannabis.

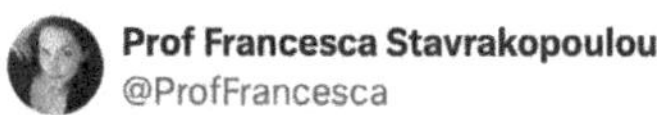

Breaking: God was indeed a high god!

New evidence from one my favourite Yahweh temples suggests theories about cannabis use in ancient Israelite/Judahite religions are spot on.

From bbc.co.uk

12:31 PM · May 29, 2020

–Stavrakopoulou, Francesca May 29, 2020, X, formerly Twitter

Appendix 1

On Indications Of The Hachish-Vice In The Old Testament

By C. CREIGHTON, M.D.

From: *JANUS, Archives internationales pour l'Histoire de la Medecine et la Geographie Medicale, Huitieme Annee*, 1903, p. 241-246

Note: "Canticles" refers to the Old Testament book "Song of Solomon" or "Song of Songs." "Vulgate" and "LXX" are early translations of the Christian Bible. Passages heavy with "…" marks are places where the author inserted Hebrew or Greek characters untranslatable to this format.

Hachish, which is the disreputable intoxicant drug of the East, as opium is the respectable narcotic, is of unknown antiquity. It is known that the fiber of the hemp-plant, *Cannabis sativa,* was used for cordage in ancient times; and it is therefore probable that the resinous exudation, "honey" or "dew," which is found upon its flowering tops on some soils, or in certain climates (*Cannabis Indica*), was known for its stimulant or intoxicant properties from an equally early date. The use of the resin as an intoxicant can be proved from Arabic writings as early as the 6th or 7th centuries of our era (De Sacy, *Chrestomathie Arabe*) and we may assume it to have been traditional among the Semites from remote antiquity. There are reasons, in the nature of the case, why there should be no clear history. All vices are veiled from view; they are *sub rosa;* and that is true especially of the vices of the East. Where they are alluded to at all, it is in cryptic, subtle, witty and allegorical terms. Therefore, if we are to discover them, we must be prepared to look below the surface of the text.

In the O.T. there are some half-dozen passages where a cryptic reference to hachish may be discovered. Of these I shall select two to begin with, as being the least ambiguous, leaving the rest for a few remarks at the end. The two which I shall choose are both made easy by the use of a significant word in the Hebrew text. But that word, which is the key to the meaning, has been knowingly mistranslated in the Vulgate and in the modern versions, having been rendered by a variant also by the LXX in one of the passages, and confessed as unintelligible in the other by the use of a marginal Hebrew word in Greek letters. One must therefore become philologist for the nonce; and I must apologize for trespassing beyond my proper sphere. My apology is, that if one knows the subject-matter, a little philology may go a long way. On the other hand, the Biblical scholars themselves cannot always be purely objective; they cannot avoid having some theory in the background of the exegesis; and the theory may be a caprice, where there is no insight into a subject which involves medical considerations.

The first passage which I shall take is Canticles 5.1: "I am come into my garden, my sister, my spouse; I have gathered my myrrh with my spice: *I have eaten my honeycomb with my honey*; I have drunk my wine with my milk." In the Hebrew text, the phrase in italics reads: "I have eaten my wood (*yagar*) with my honey (*debash*)." St. Jerome, in the Vulgate, translated the Hebrew word meaning "wood" by *favum*, or honey-comb -- *comedi favum cum melle meo*; which is not only a bold license, but a platitude to boot, inasmuch as there is neither wit nor point in making one to eat the honeycomb with the honey. The LXX adopted a similar license, but avoided the platitude, by translating thus: ... . "I have eaten *my bread* with my honey." And this is the reading that Renan has followed in his French dramatic version of Canticles (the first verse of the fifth chapter being transferred to the end of the fourth chapter). Where "honeycomb," *favus*, is plainly meant by context, the Hebrew word is either *tzooph*, as in Ps. 19, 10 and Prov. 16, 24, (where the droppings of honey from the comb are meant), or it is *noh-pheth*, as in a passage of Canticles, 4,11, close to the one in question. ("Thy lips, O my spouse, drop as the honeycomb; honey and milk are under thy tongue.") Again, the word *yagar*, which the Vulgate translated *favum* for the occasion, is used in some fifty or sixty other places of O.T. always in the sense of wood, forest, planted field, herbage, or the like. The meaning of Cant. 5,1, is clear enough in its aphrodisiac context: "I have eaten *my hemp* with my honey" – *comedi cannabim cum confectione mellis*, which is the elegant way of taking hachish in the East to this day. And this meaning of *yagar* (wood) in association with *debash* (honey) is made clear by the other passage with which I am to deal, namely 1 Sam. 14, 27, the incident of Jonathan dipping the point of his staff into a "honey-wood," and merely tasting the honey, so that his eyes were enlightened. The one is the aphrodisiac effect of hachish, the other is its bellicose or furious effect.

The correct exegesis of 1 Sam. 14, 25-45, is of great importance not only for understanding Jonathan's breach of a certain taboo, but also for the whole career of his father Saul, ending in his deposition from the kingship through the firm action of Samuel, and the pitiable collapse of his courage on the eve of the battle of Gilboa. The theory is, that both Saul and Jonathan were hachish-eaters; it was a secret vice of the palace, while it was strictly forbidden to the people; Saul had learned it of the Amalekites; it was that, and not his disobedience in saving captives and cattle alive, which was his real transgression, and the real ground of his deposition from the kingship at the instance of the far-seeing prophet. No true statesman would have taken action on account of a merely technical sin of disobedience; the disobedience was real and vital; but the substance of it had to be veiled behind a convenient fiction. One great object of Jewish particularism was, to save Israel from the vices that destroyed the nations around; and Samuel appears in that respect the first and the greatest of the prophets, the prototype *censor morum*.

The incident related in I Sam. 14 arose during a raid upon the Philistines, in which the Jewish leader, Jonathan, distinguished himself by the number of the enemy whom he slew, but at the same time broke a certain law or taboo, for which he was afterwards put upon his trial and condemned to death. The incident, previous to the slaughter, is thus described: "And all [they of] the land came to a wood, and there was honey on the ground. And when the people were come into the wood, behold the honey dropped; but no man put his hand to his mouth: for the people feared the oath. But Jonathan heard not when his father charged the people with the oath; wherefore he put forth the end of the rod that was in his hand and dipped it in an honey- comb (*yagarah hadebash*), and put his hand to his mouth; and his eyes were enlightened." The exegesis of this passage has been started in an entirely false direction by the bold license of the Vulgate in translating the two Hebrew words meaning "honey wood" by *favum*, honey-comb. The earlier sentences, however obscure, show that the "honey" was of a peculiar kind, there being no suggestion of combs or bees. The Syriac version gives the most intelligible account of it, as follows, *latine*: "Et sylvas ingressi essent, essetque mel in sylva super faciem agri, flueretque mel" – expressing not inaptly a field of hemp with the resinous exudation upon the flower- stalks, which would flow or run by the heat. In *The Bengal Dispensatory*, by W.B. O'Shaughnessy, M.D. (London, 1842), there is the following illustrative passage p.

582: "In Central India and the Saugor territory, and in Nipal, *churrus* is collected during the hot season in the following singular manner: Men clad in leathern dresses run through the hemp-fields brushing through the plants with all possible violence. The soft resin adheres to the leather, and is subsequently scraped off and kneaded into balls, which sell from 5 to 6 R. the seer. A still finer kind, the *moomeea,* or waxen *churrus,* is collected by the hand in Nipal, and sells for double the price of the ordinary kind. In Nipal, Dr. McKinnon inform us, the leathern attire is dispensed with, and the resin is gathered on the skins of naked coolies." Jonathan's mode of collecting was of the simplest: he dipped the end of a rod into a "honey-wood," and carried it to his mouth; a mere taste of it caused his eyes to be enlightened. The whole incident is obviously dramatized, or made picturesque – the growing field of hemp, the men passing through it, Jonathan dipping the end of a rod or staff into the resin upon a stalk as he passed by. The real meaning is, that Jonathan was a hachish-eater.

It is remarkable that the LXX translators had no suspicion of this cryptic meaning. Their Greek version is the most confused of any; but it appears that they were aware of something obscure, and that they made an honest attempt to give a meaning to the Hebrew pair of words "honey wood," translating the word for "honey" by itself and again, by itself the word for "wood" in the Hebrew text (v. 25, 26), by ... bee-house. The Greek of the LXX is: .... The strange word ... is obviously a transliteration into Greek of a Hebrew word. Wellhausen, in his earliest work, *Der Text der Buchen Samuelis,* Gott. 1871, p.91, has given an explanation, which I should not have recalled had it not been pronounced to be "remarkably clever" by Driver, (*Notes on the Hebrew Text of the Books of Samuel,* Oxford, 1890, p.86). Wellhausen says: "... und ... ist Duplette, beides dem hebraischen *yagar* entsprechend. Demselben Worte aber entspricht nach v.26 auch .... Also haben wir hier ein Triplette." I speak with deference; but I do not understand how ... (Hebrew) can be a doublet of ..., still less how ... can be a doublet of either or both. ... as a Hebrew word written in Greek characters appears to be exactly the part of a verb meaning "we have done foolishly," or "they are foolish," which would have been used as a marginal remark (although now incorporated in the text) to signify that the passage was unintelligible or corrupt. How it can stand for *yagar,* meaning "wood" (... a wood or coppice), is probably clear to Hebraists; at all events, that is assumed in Wellhausen's theory of a doublet, the sense being "there was honeycomb on the ground." The idea is that of "honey" in some association with "wood," which the LXX took to the bee-house. The natural association of "honey" with "wood," is "vegetable honey," or plant-honey; and it is clear from the powerful effect of a minute quantity of it, and from the kinds of effect, (aphrodisiac and bellicose) that the honey-wood was the hemp-plant with the resinous exudation.

The effects, in the case of Jonathan, are unmistakable. A mere taste of the honey on the end of the rod caused his eyes to be enlightened. His defense, when put on his trial for breaking the taboo, was the smallness of the quantity he ate; a plea which reminds one of the famous apology of the young woman for her love-child, that "it was such a little one." There is an old explanation of this enlightenment, discussed by F.T. Withof, "De Jonathane post esum mellis visum recipiente" (*Opusc. philolog. Lingae,* 1778, pp. 135-139). It turns upon the Talmudic saying, *Oculi tui prae jejunio obscuranti sunt*; and upon another passage in the same, where food is to be administered to one, "*donec illuminentur oculi ejus.*" Some color is given to this idea of the illuminating effect of food for the hungry, by the context, I Sam. 14, 24, 28, namely the formal words of the taboo, "Cursed be the man that eateth *food* until the evening," and the remark, that "the people were faint," as if by abstinence from food. But the minute quantity tasted by Jonathan shows that all these references to "food" are merely cryptic or allegorical. Also the effect upon Jonathan was, that he ran *a-mok* amongst the Philistines; and it is implied not vaguely that, if his followers had also partaken of the same food, "there had been now a much greater slaughter among the Philistines." Jonathan's exceptional prowess upon the occasion was also the ground of his being rescued by the admiring populace from the death to which he had been condemned by his father for breaking the taboo.

The evidence that Saul himself was a hachish-eater is not so direct as in the case of Jonathan. There is not a hint of it until after the incident of the forbidden honey in the attack upon the Philistines; but, in the inquiry upon that breach of law, it is significant that Saul and Jonathan are ranged together upon one side of the trial by lot, and the people on the other, the second ballot being between Saul and Jonathan.

The next chapter introduces the very old theme of revenge upon Amelek for treachery many generations before; Saul goes upon the expedition, brings back Agag with him, and disobeys the prophet's orders in other respects. From that disobedience his ruin dates. Samuel had a most unaccountable animosity to Agag, so that he hewed him in pieces with his own hands. The presumption is, that he had corrupted Saul by the evil example of his Amalekite ways. Next, we have the appearance of David upon the scene, in the capacity of a harper, to soothe Saul's fits of fury and melancholy, when he was under the influence of the evil spirit. Dr. J. Moreau (de Tours) in his valuable work *Du Hachish et de l'Alienation Mentale,* Paris 1845, has shown that music has no effect upon the ordinary run of melancholics (pp. 84-85); the idea that it might be useful in lunatic asylums comes from the misunderstood example of David playing before Saul. But this idea, says Dr. Moreau, "belongs to the domain of comic opera"; not only so, "mais nous avons maudit souvent la harpe de David et l'hypochondrie de Saul, qui ont manifestement produit toutes les billevesees." The only kind of mental alienation that is influenced by music, as Dr. Moreau shows farther, is that due to the intoxication of hachish – "la puissante influence qu'exerce la musique sur ceux qui ont pris du hachish ... La musique la plus grossiere, les simples vibrations des cordes d'une harpe ou d'une guitare vous exaltent jusqu' au delire ou vous plongent dans une douce melancholie." And yet Dr. Moreau does not suggest that Saul's susceptibility to the music of David's harp was owing to the fact that his "evil spirit" was hachish. The inference seems too obvious to have been missed, after he had distinguished between ordinary melancholia and hachish-intoxication in regard to the effects of music; and yet I do not find any such diagnosis of Saul's malady in any part of his book. That diagnosis is not only consistent with several things told of his malady, but is also elucidative of his ruined career. The sudden throwing of his javelin at David as he played before him is as graphic an illustration as could be given, of the ungovernable fits of temper which hachish produces.

Also the extraordinary exhibition that Saul makes of himself in the end of chapter 19 is best understood as a fit of drunkenness. But the most significant, as well as the most pathetic, of all, is the failure of his courage on the night before the battle of Gilboa. Here we see the stalwart hero of the people with his nerves shattered by intoxicants now no longer able to stimulate him: "And when Saul saw the host of the Philistines he was afraid, and his heart greatly trembled." Those who are acquainted with Robert Browning's poem "Saul," will see how well the hypothesis of hachish fits in with the poet's conception of a heroic life wrecked by some mysterious "error." That he and Jonathan should have been practicing in secret that which was taboo to the people at large, is exactly parallel with Saul's secret dealings in witchcraft, against which there was a public law. It is also of the same kind as the evils against which Samuel is reported to have cautioned the people when they demanded kingly rule – namely the autocratic self-indulgences of the palace. In his last desperate strait, Saul gets the witch to summon the spirit of Samuel, his old monitor; but Samuel is unable to help him; "Because thou obeyedst not the voice of the Lord, nor executedst his fierce wrath upon Amalek, therefore hath the Lord done this thing unto thee this day." It is always Amalek; and Amalek was just that tribe of Arabs, of the southern desert, who were engaged in the carrying trade between the Arabian gulf and Lower Egypt or the Mediterraneae, – the trade in gold, and spices, and drugs: probably the same Arabs among whom the name of *hachashin* was found in the medieval period, and from whom the Latinized name of *assassini* was brought to Europe by returning Crusaders. (Silvestre de Sacy, *l.c.*)

In the two instances already given, the hemp-plant is pointed to somewhat plainly by the use of the Hebrew word for "wood" in association with the notion of "honey," the translators having evaded the point in both cases: in the one by rendering the single word, *yagar*, by *favus*, honeycomb, in the other by rendering the remarkable and unique compound name, *yagarah hadebash*, also by *favus*. In those instances, the hypothesis of hachish rests upon the sure basis of a phrase in the original text which is otherwise unintelligible. But, in the remaining instances, there is no such support for the hypothesis; there is only a degree of probability, which must take its chance with rival interpretations. The probability, in the case of Samson's riddle, arises from the cryptic association of "sweet" with "Strong," of honey with a lion; in the case of Daniel's apologue of Nebuchadnezzar's fall, it arises from the eating of "grass," the Semitic word having both a generic and a colloquial meaning (hachish), as well as from the introduction of the subjective perceptions of hachish intoxication as gigantic or grotesque objects.

Samson's riddle. – According to old and new criticism, by Budde and others, there is a glaring contradiction between the real or original Samson, the boisterous village hero of whom many stories were told, and the religious Samson, the judge of Israel, who was dedicated to God as a Nazarite "from the womb to the day of his death." It is admitted, however, that there is a peculiar unity in the text of the story as it has come down to us in the Book of Judges, notwithstanding the apparent incongruity of making Samson a Nazarite. The Nazarites are mentioned as early as the prophecies of Amos, having been allowed to drink wine in the laxity of morals then prevailing. Samson is not only the earliest Nazarite known, but he is a Nazarite indeed, inasmuch as his vow was not terminable after a certain period, as in the ritual of the Book of Numbers, but was imposed upon him from the womb to the day of his death. In that respect he has no compeer until John the Baptist. At the same time, he is the typical village hero, adored for his strength, boldness, cunning, and wit, and gratified by numerous amours. Budde remarks that many must have known a modern counterpart in village life. Two instances in literature occur to one as containing the elements of a modern Samson legend, -- the Oetzthal hero in Madame von Hillern's *Geier Wally,* and the hero or *jigit* of the village on the Terek in Tolstoy's early work, *The Cossacks.* Budde, who would eliminate altogether the Nazarite vow from the real Samson legend, is surprised that the hero does not eat and drink to excess: "Excess, or at least enormous capacity, in eating and in drinking strong liquors, is amongst the things that may almost be taken for granted. It is strange enough that this trait is not strikingly displayed in Samson. Who knows, whether from the store of legends that circulated regarding him, there may not have dropped out this or that portion dealing with the subject in question?" (Art. "Samson," in Hasting's, *Dict. of the Bible*. Edin. 1902.)

Josephus appears to have entertained a similar suspicion; for, in his paraphrase of Delilah's attempts to bind Samson, he makes on of the attempts to be made upon him when he was drunk with wine. But it is impossible to take out the Nazarite vow from the story as we find it; that thread is woven inextricably into the tapestry; and it may be assumed that Samson's unshorn head was meant to symoblize his constancy to the vow – or, at all events, to the letter of it. My view (which I submit with deference to the professed Biblical critics) is, that the method of the literary artist, who composed the existing story, is consistently ironical and witty. Anyone who has had his attention directed to the point, will have found that the instances of Biblical wit are more numerous than might be supposed from the solemnity of commentators. Why should not this ancient literature have had its sallies of wit and humor as well as another? The Hebrew grammars remark that the humorous figure of paronomasia, or pun, is more indigenous to the Semitic than to any other languages.

Samson's riddle, on the surface, was a mild pleasantry, hardly worth investing with the dignity of enigma; it has even been questioned, whether it was a fair problem, considering that it was based upon one particular if not unique incident known to himself. He killed a young lion, and threw the carcase into a wood; in passing that way some time after, he turned aside to look at it, and found that a swarm of bees had built their combs inside the ribs. (This is the natural reading, which is adopted by Josephus in his paraphrase.) He ate some of the honey, and gave some of it to his father and mother; but, for some deep reason, he abstained from telling his parents that the honey had been taken from inside the skeleton of a lion. At his wedding feast some time after, he propounded a certain riddle to the thirty young men of Timnath, who were the wedding guests, and laid a wager that they would not guess the answer within a week. Being still at fault on the seventh day, they went to Samson's wife, and induced her to coax the answer from her husband. Samson answered: "Behold, I have not told my father and my mother, and shall I tell thee?" However, he told her the incident of the lion and the bees, and she told the young men of the village, who came to Samson with this confident and jubilant solution, "What is sweeter than honey? What is stronger than a lion?" Samson answered oracularly, "If ye had not plowed with my heifer, ye had not found out my riddle." This answer appears to have been given ironically, with his tongue in his cheek, the reservation being, that their ploughing (with a heifer) had been but shallow, that they had not got to the bottom of the matter at all. He may be assumed to have been still in his ironical mood when he proceeded to pay the forfeit, by killing thirty other Philistines of Ashkelon and stripping them of their shirts to give to the thirty Philistines of Timnath.

Leaving these evidences of ironical behavior, let us turn to the famous riddle itself. Is it possible that it can have any deeper meaning than the incident of the bees' nest in the lion's carcase?

What I suspect in Samson's riddle is *an ambiguity in the terms in which it was stated*. To those who heard it, it might mean either what it means as printed in the text, or it might mean something else as an equivoque. Of course, no single text can reproduce an equivocal effect of spoken words, depending upon paronomasia. There is a good example in *Hamlet*, III. 2. 262: *Ophelia*: "Still better and worse." *Hamlet*: "So you *must take* your husband." This is the reading of the first quarto; but it is clear that "must take" is to be pronounced ambiguously, from the fact that the second quarto prints it: "So you mistake your husbands," which is necessary to the innuendo, and is in the folio and in most later texts, although "must take" is the natural *ductus idearum* from the previous reference to the Marriage Service. The equivoque in Samson's riddle is of the same kind. It may mean what the text makes it to mean, or it may mean exactly the converse, without changing the order and works; thus:

An eater came forth out of meat...

Strength came forth out of sweetness; -- namely, Samson's strength from hachish. To understand how the *spoken* Hebrew words might be heard to bear either sense, according as they were apprehended by the ear, one must observe that the preposition "out of," which governs the meaning by being placed in front of one or other of the two nouns, is the sound *m'* (contraction of *min*), and that the same sound happens to begin the other nouns also:

m' ahachal yatsah maachal
Out of the-eater came forth meat
m' gaz yatsah mathok).
Out of the strong came forth sweetness

There appears to be no way of prefixing the prepositional *m'* to the last noun of each line except by reduplicating the *m* which is already there, as if by stammering over it – *m' maachal, m' mathok*, which might be merely a slight stammer, or might mean respectively, "out of meat," and "*out of* sweetness." Again, *to get rid* of the preposition from before the first word of the first line, one must read (as the LXX had actually done) *mah achal,* the first syllable being a distinct word, the interrogative pronoun .... *quid,* which would be used to introduce the riddle as a query, "What is this?" to get rid of the preposition from before the first word in the second line, one has to substitute for *gaz,* which is the adjective "strong," its abstract noun *magohz* = "strength," a substitution which is recommended as balancing *mathok* "sweetness," in abstract form. The concealed reading would then be:

mah achal yatsah m maachal
What is this? An eater came forth out of meat,
magohz yatsah m' mathok
strength came forth out of sweetness

Thus, to the ear, the riddle may really contain that deeper problem which ought to be in it if it is to stand for the riddle or secret of Samson's own strength. The superficial meaning, which Samson's wife jumped at and conveyed to the young Philistines of Timnath, is that food (honey) came forth out of the eater, (lion), sweetness out of the strong one. The deep meaning is just the converse -- that the eater "came forth out of" meat, strength out of sweetness. Thus we arrive at some kind of "food," (not drink) which made one an eater, or a devourer, like a lion; a sweet food from which came strength. It is pointed out that the antithesis of the second line, between "sweet" and "strong," is not a good one; and the Syriac version has gone so far as to change "strong" into "bitter" for the sake of the antithesis to "sweet." But the author certainly wanted to introduce the idea of strength, even if it were no full antithesis to sweetness; and his reason, doubtless, was, that he was thinking of Samson himself, and of the secret of his strength, which was a cryptic "sweetness." From various points of view, we arrive at the conclusion, that the honey from the carcass of a lion was not the honey of bees, but an allegory of that strong kind of honey which causes Jonathan's eyes to be enlightened, namely the resin of the hemp-plant. It was "sweeter than honey, stronger than a lion," as the men of Timnath are the unconscious means of suggesting, by the mood and figure of the answer.

We are now able to follow the ironical purpose of the author in its entirety, in making Samson a Nazarite and yet a boisterous, free-living village hero of the most admired type. The stimulant which the hero used was not drink, it was food; thus it was outside the purview of the Nazarite vow, which specified many things , but did not specify hachish: "wine and strong drink, vinegar of wine and vinegar of strong drink, liquor of grapes, grapes moist or dried, everything that is made of the vine from the kernels even to the husk." Samson could be made to pose cleverly as a Nazarite, and yet have his fling all the same. Budde's desideratum of strong drink, to complete the equipment of Samson as a village hero, is supplied by a subterfuge. It appears that the Jewish sense of humor ran strongly in that direction.

The story of Samson is not far removed in time, or in manner of telling, from that of Saul and Jonathan; so that, if I am right in my interpretation of the nature of the taboo which Jonathan broke, the period at the end of Judges and the beginning of the Kings was one in which the hachish-question had become actual, thus it becomes probable that the strength of Samson had the same source in stimulants as the prowess of Jonathan upon a particular occasion. It is also remarkable that Samson's "strength" collapses, just as Saul's courage fails him; and that the failure in both cases is described by the same phrase:- in the case of Samson the words are, "the Lord had departed from him," in the case of Saul the narrative reads, "God is departed from me, and answereth me no more, neither by prophets nor by dreams." The material sense of both I take to be, that the stimulant had lost its power over them, it being a property of hachish to produce hebetude in those who have used it habitually over a long time. Samson's recovery of his strength is, of course, for the sake of dramatic catastrophe.

The apologue of "Nebuchadnezzar" in Daniel. The beginning of these inquiries upon indications of hachish in the Bible was a suggestion made to me by the late R.A. Neil, of Cambridge, that the "grass" which Nebuchadnezzar was given to eat may have been grass in the colloquial Arabic sense of hachish, the word by which Indian hemp is now so commonly known being the same as the ordinary Arabic word for grass or green herbage in general (*hachach*). In seeking to follow up this idea one finds much to corroborate it in the details of the story of "morality" which is told of Nebuchadnezzar. The story begins with an account of dreams and visions of the night, in which the central object, the tree reaching to heaven and spreading to the ends of the earth, is highly characteristic of the elusive and infinite dimensions in the subjective perceptions of hachish intoxication (Compare Bayard Taylor, *The Lands of the Saracens*; the pyramid of Gizen came before him, with its sides resting against the vault of the sky).

Daniel, being asked to interpret the dream, declares that the tree is the mighty Nebuchadnezzar himself, and the fate of the felled tree his fate: "They shall drive thee from men, and thy dwelling shall be with the beasts of the field, and they shall make thee to eat grass as oxen, and they shall wet thee with the dew of heaven." This fate, it appears, was on account of his sins and iniquities. But, as the root of the tree was to be left in the earth, so there was a power of recovery in the degraded prince, and he was to return to his kingdom after seven years. It happened as Daniel had said: "Nebuchadnezzar was driven from men, and did eat grass as oxen, and his body was wet with the dew of heaven, till his hairs were grown like eagles' feathers, and his nails like birds' claws. And at the end of the days, I Nebuchadnezzar lifted up mine eyes unto heaven, and mine understanding returned unto me." One might provide much amusement by recalling some of the many literal attempts, ancient and modern, to explain the nature of Nebuchadnezzar's debasement. The double sense of the word "grass," which may be assumed to have existed in the ancient Semitic languages or dialects as in modern Arabic, is a key to the whole enigma. There appears to be a cryptic reference to hachish not only in the recurring phrase "They shall give thee grass to eat, as oxen," but also in the significant introduction of "dew" with equal reiteration, "they shall wet thee with the dew of heaven." The allegory is easily extended to, "let a beast's heart be given unto him," "let his portion be with the beasts of the field," and, "his body was wet with the dew of heaven." But the most significant detail of all is that which follows the last quoted phrase: "until his hairs were grown like eagles' feathers, and his nails like birds' claws." This is again the grotesque exaggeration and metamorphosis of one's own features etc. caused by the hachish subjectivity, which is unlike anything else in morbid imaginings.

There have been real instances among Oriental rulers of hachish degradation such as "Nebuchadnezzar's"; an example was rumored when Upper Burma was occupied by the British some five-and-twenty years ago. The apologue of Daniel told of one under a great historical name, is meant to be general, and has had a sufficiently wide application, doubtless, in ancient times as well as in modern.

Lastly, and still in the same Chaldaean atmosphere, we find in the first chapter of Ezekiel a phantasmagoria of composite creatures, of wheels, and of brilliant play of colors, which is strongly suggestive of the subjective visual perceptions of hachish, and is unintelligible from any other point of view, human or divine. This is the chapter of Ezekiel that gave so much trouble to the ancient canonists, and is said to have made them hesitate about including the book. Ezekiel was included in the Canon, but with the instruction that no one in the Synagogue was to attempt to comment upon Chapter I, or, according to another version, that the opening chapter was not to be read by or to persons under a certain age. The subjective sensations stimulated by hachish are those of sight and hearing. It would be easy to quote examples of fantastic composite form, and of wondrous colors, which have been seen by experiments. I must content myself with the generality of Theophile Gautier (cited by Moreau, *l.c.,* from feuilleton in *La Presse*), that, if he were to write down all that he saw, he should be writing the Apocalypse over again (*recommencer l'Apocalypse*). If this contains an innuendo against the Apocalypse of John, I do not agree with it, in as much as I believe that no part of Scripture is more rational in its method, or more calmly inspired in its motives. But, as regards the apocalypse introductory to the prophecies of Ezekiel, one need not hesitate to assign it to the source indicated by the witty Frenchman.

Appendix II

Shemshemet, Cannabis in Ancient Egypt

> There is general agreement with the view of Dawson (1934) that shemshemet means cannabis, and the identification was strongly supported by the use of hempen rope making. As a drug, it has remained in active use since pharaonic times. It ... was administered by mouth, rectum, vagina, bandaged the skin, applied to the eyes, and by fumigation. However, these applications provide no clear evidence of awareness of the effects of cannabis on the central nervous system. (Nunn, 2002).

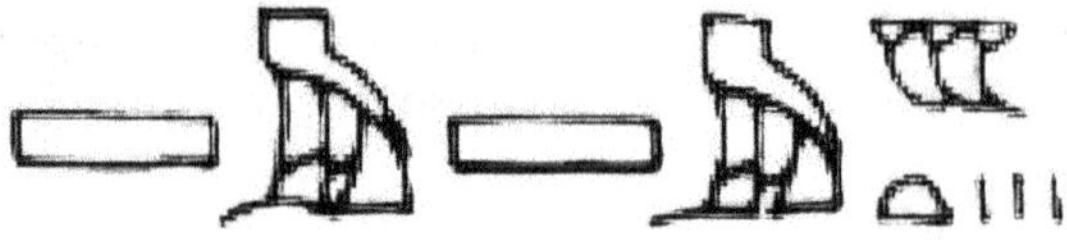

Egyptian Shemshemet.

Although most modern Egyptologists acknowledge a role for cannabis as a source of fiber and as a medicine, few see a role for hemp as a ritual intoxicant, and many researchers claim that the Egyptians were unaware of these properties. As noted in *The Mummy Congress*:

> Under the reign of the pharaohs, Egyptian traders had bartered avidly for seeds of *Cannabis sativa*. Their Asian neighbors prized the plant for its hempen fibers, and the Egyptians seem to have taken a similar interest. They retted the stems and twisted the fibers into sturdy ropes and ground the plant to make a soothing eyewash, a treatment they recorded in the medical papyri. But the Egyptians made little mention of the other parts of C. sativa – the flowering tops and leaves that yielded marijuana or the dark resin that produces hashish (Pringle, 2001).

Prof. Jan Kabelik noted of *shemsemet*; "From the Egyptian medical papyruses, information has been gained about a plant from which cordage could be made, and it was probably cannabis which was referred to":

> But no records could be found on its narcotic action. The preparations made from it (in all probability from the cannabis shoots) were applied externally-namely, exclusively as antiseptics – and then perhaps even as analgesics, in the same way as in Hellenic medicine. Cannabis extracts have been employed for irrigation in diseases of the anus, and in form of compresses the drug has been applied to sore toenails. In Rhamses' papyrus, washing sore eyes with extracts from cannabis and also from some other plant is recommended. The papyrus of Berlin recommends fumigation with cannabis in some undefined disease (Kabelik, 1955).

Indeed, one would be hard-pressed to identify ritual or recreational narcotic use of hemp under the name *shemshemet,* but then with the Egyptians, as with other cultures, ritual knowledge was secret knowledge, and thus evidence of such use likely lays in veiled references. Realistically, even medical applications were imbued with magical and religious connotations. "[M]ost physicians in Egypt were priests ... elements of religion and magic were closely intertwined with drug use, incantations routinely being uttered prior to administration in order to confer the healing property upon it" (Spencer, 2000). The Egyptians also likely cultivated *shemshemet* and other sacred plants:

> Considering the Egyptians' highly developed pharmacopeia they must have had "physics gardens," most likely in connection with a temple, for it was among the priests that knowledge of the medicinal properties of plants was concentrated (Manniche, 1989).

Egyptian medical texts that include references to cannabis include *The Ramesseum III Papyrus* (1700 BC), *Eber's Papyrus* (1600 BC), *The Berlin Papyrus* (1300 BC), The Chester Beatty VI Papyrus (1300 BC). Possibly due to the sticky and adhesive quality of honey a number of Egyptian topical medical preparations required it as an admixture to cannabis-based medicines. Egyptian medical applications of cannabis show an astute knowledge of the efficacy of herbal remedies, and virtually all of their remedies containing it utilize it in a way in which cannabis has been known to be medically effective (Russo, 2006/2007).

If the hieroglyph "smsm.t" in the ancient medical papyri of Egypt indicates cannabis, it was used as an incense, as an oral medication for "mothers and children," (in childbirth?), in enemas, in eye medications, and as an ointment in bandages. This may be its first mention in world literature as an eye medication (Mathre, 1997).

The reference to eye medicine identified by Mathre, occurs in the *Ramesseum III Papyrus* (1700 BC), and is thought to occur in a prescription for the treatment of glaucoma, and has been translated as: "A treatment for the eyes: celery; *shemshemet* [cannabis] is ground and left in the dew overnight. Both eyes of the patient are to be washed with it in the morning."

Although the existing copy of the *Eber's Papyrus* is dated at about 1600 BC, making it the oldest known complete medical textbook, many scholars believe that it is copied from an even older text dating approximately 3100 BC. The *Eber's Papyrus* refers to "A cure for the uterus to cool ... Hemp [*shemshemet*] is crushed in honey and stuffed into the vagina.... This causes a contraction of the uterus." The *Eber's Papyrus* also refers to a topical application of cannabis for ingrown toe or finger nails and mixed with carob for use in an enema or combined with other remedies and used as a poultice. The *Berlin Papyrus* (1300 BC) records a topical treatment for swelling: "A remedy to treat inflammation: "Leaves of hemp and pure oil. Use it as an ointment.

The *Ebers Papyrus* (1550 BC) identifies cannabis in an enema infusion and as a topical poultice for infection.

Archaeological evidence indicates that in the second millennium BCE hemp fiber were used for ropes, but the term *shemshemet* occurs in the Pyramid Texts in connection to rope making, a thousand years prior to that. "Pieces of hemp have been identified at the tomb of Amenhopis IV (Ahkenaten) at el-Armana" (Manniche, 1989). In ancient Egypt, *shemshemet* was considered a sacred fiber and was referred to in the context as a means of bridging the gap between heaven and earth.

A Rope Ladder to the Heavens

In the *Pyramid text of Unas,* which seems to concern the king's ascension into the heavens through the northern passageway of his pyramid, hemp ropes seem to be the means for climbing into the starry sky. In the ancient inscription, the devotee is commanded to say the following words in praise of Unas a celestial Bull, who is the guide of the dead to the heavens:

> This Unas is the bull of double brilliance in the midst of his Eye. Safe is the mouth of Unas through the fiery breath, the head of Unas through the horns of the lord of the South. Unas leads the god.... Unas has twisted the SmSm.t [*shemshemet*]-plant into ropes. Unas has united (zmA) the heavens...

Or as Budge translates it: "He raises up the cords (fibers?) of the *shemshemet* plant, he unites the heavens" (Budge, 1911). A similar indication regarding hemp ropes may be found in the mythology of the Goddess Seshat, who appears to be holding a rope and a stalk in the below depiction. More interesting is the image that appears above the head of the ancient Goddess.

A number of different researchers have noted the similarity between a cannabis leaf and the symbol attached to the head of the Goddess Seshat in Egyptian images. Seshat was the Egyptian Goddess of temple architecture and mistress of scribes, presiding over the "House of Life," also known as the "House of Books." This temple was a sort of library and school of knowledge, and served as a store-place of texts regarding tradition and rituals. Since very early Egyptian times, Seshat's main function was to assist the king in "stretching the cord" for the layout of temples and royal buildings.

Author and researcher H. Peter Aleff has put forth an intriguing theory that this symbol is associated with the use of hemp cords. "It was... consistent with the ancient Egyptian visual canon that the artists who portrayed Seshat the rope-stretching goddess of measuring and geometry would have labeled her with pictures of her principal tools, or with easily recognizable symbols for these. Indeed, they combined evocations of these tools ingeniously in her emblem":

> Many Egyptologists have long speculated about the emblem which Seshat wore as her head dress. Sir Alan Gardiner described it in his still category-leading "Egyptian Grammar" as a "conventionalized flower (?) surmounted by horns." His question mark after "flower" reflects the fact that there is no

Seshat holding rope to the heavens, cannabis stalk, with cannabis leaf above?

likely flower which resembles this design. Others have called it a "star surmounted by a bow," but stars in the ancient Egyptian convention had five points, not seven like the one in Seshat's emblem. This number was so important that it caused king Tuthmosis III (1479 to 1425 BCE) to give her the name Sefkhet-Abwy, or "She of the seven points."

There is no need for such groping speculations because the various elements in Seshat's emblem simply depict the tools of her geometer's trade in the hieroglyphic manner.

> Her seven-pointed “flower” or “star” is an accurate image of a hemp leaf. This leaf is made up of seven pointed leaf parts that are arranged in the same pattern as the most prominent sign in Seshat’s emblem. Hemp is, and has long been, an excellent material for making ropes with the low-stretch quality required for measuring cords, particularly when these are greased to reduce variations in their moisture content which would influence elongation.
>
> The characteristic leaf of the plant used in making these ropes was thus a logical choice for the emblem designer who wanted an easily recognized reference to Seshat’s job. This leaf is so unique that its picture allows no confusion with other items ... the hemp leaf in Seshat’s emblem is unmistakable evidence that the ancient Egyptian rope- stretchers used hemp for their measuring cords, and that Seshat cannot deny her now illegal patronage and ownership of this psycho-active plant.
>
> Add to this flagrant evidence that in Coffin Texts Spell 10, “Seshat opens the door of heaven for you” (7), and the case against her is solid enough to get her busted if she still plied her trade today (Aleff, 1982/2008).

Both the references in the account of Unas the Bull, and that of Seshat may symbolically indicate hemp as a means of reaching the heavens. In relation it is interesting to note that Catherine Graindorge mentions cannabis in a funerary offering: “some Theban tombs mention an offering of ... plants to the deceased ... [including] smsmt [*shemshemet,* cannabis].... According to the tomb of Neferhotep ... the smsmt-plant was created by Re” (Graindorge, 1992). Unfortunately it is unclear as to what the nature of this offering was (fiber?, food?, incense?, Beverage?), but apparently it occurred during “certain activities concerned with private funerary worship,” where “the priests of the ka, or the family of the Theban deceased, make libations and fumigations in the chapel of the tombs” (Graindorge, 1992). A situation which certainly brings to mind the Scythian Funerary rites and fumigations with burning hemp referred to earlier.

The results from tests on hairs of Egyptian mummies dating back as far as 1000 B.C. conducted by the German scientist, Dr Svetla Balabanova in the paper 1992 paper “First identification of drugs in Egyptian mummies” showed positive results for the use of cannabis.

In order to make sure that the tests on the mummies were beyond reproach, Balabanova used the supposedly reliable and standard hair shaft test. Drugs and other substances consumed by humans make their way into the hair protein, where they stay for months, even after death. To ensure there is no contamination hair samples are washed in alcohol and the washing solution itself is then tested. If the testing solution is clear, but the hair tests positive, then the drug must be inside the hair shaft, which means the person consumed the substance during their lifetime. The hair shaft test is considered proof positive against contamination before or after death. As British toxicologist Dr. John Henry has noted: "The hair shaft test is accepted. If you know that you've taken your hair sample from this individual and the hair shaft is known to contain a drug, then it is proof positive that the person has taken that drug. So it is accepted in law. It's put people into prison" (Henry, 1996). As a toxicologist and endocrinologist at the Institute of Forensic Medicine, in Ulm Germany, Balabanova, who also worked closely with the German Police, was more than familiar with postmortem techniques.

Similar findings were recorded via deep-tissue analysis, in the 1994 paper, "Presence of drugs in different tissues of an Egyptian mummy." Franz Parsche and Andreas Nerlich claimed similar evidence of cannabis use:

> The observation of significant concentrations of tetrahydrocannabinol which represents the psychoactive substance of drugs as in hashish in the lungs with values above those of the other internal organs, argue for a preferential incorporation of this substance by inhalation. This is in accordance with the reports by medical papyri indicating smoking ceremonies, e.g. with hashish. The accumulation of THC in skin/muscle tissue may be due to contamination during the postmortal embalming procedure. (Parsche and Nerlich, 1994)

However, both studies also claimed evidence of New World plants coca and tobacco, which would rewrite the historical dates for contact between the new world and old by millennia.

Although Balabanova was not particularly surprised at the evidence of THC, the active chemical of the Old World plant cannabis, results indicating new world plants such as Coca, and Tobacco sent the researcher reeling. "The first positive results, of course, were a shock for me. I had not expected to find nicotine and cocaine but that's what happened. I was absolutely sure it must be a mistake" (Balabanova, 1996). After repeating the tests and later publishing the results, Balabanova found herself in a hotbed of controversy that has followed her career ever since.

> This is the first study which shows the presence of cocaine, hashish and nicotine in Egyptian mummies, dating back to about 1000 BC. This means that these three organic substances are capable of surviving in hair, soft tissue and bones for ca. 3000 years under favorable conditions. However, it cannot be determined at present whether the concentrations measured represent the original amount of these drugs during life or immediately after death, or what kind of decomposition might have taken place in the past 3000 years (Balabanova et al. 1992).

Not surprisingly academic criticisms poured in from all quarters. As Balabanova described, "I got a pile of letters that were almost threatening, insulting letters saying it was nonsense, that I was fantasizing, that it was impossible, because it was proven that before Columbus these plants were not found anywhere in the world outside of the Americas" (Balabanova, 1996).

As noted cannabis botanist Robert Clarke and Michael Flemming in "Physical evidence for the antiquity of Cannabis sativa L":

> The presence of cannabinoids in the tissues of Egyptian mummies brings up the possibility that Cannabis was used recreationally/religiously or medicinally by the early Egyptians. However, most of the controversy centers around the reports of cocaine and nicotine contents in these Egyptian mummies predating Columbus' "discovery" of the New World. The plant genera Erythroxylum (the sole source of cocaine) and Nicotiana (the sole source of nicotine) are both considered to have only a New World distribution prior to European contact during the 15th century, much later than the dates (ca. 3000 BP) of the mummies analyzed by Balabanova et al. (1992). These results are so unusual that they cast some doubt over the cannabinoid findings as well. (Clarke & Fleming, 1998)

Representing the view of the vast majority of Historians, Prof. John Bains, an Egyptologist with Oxford University, commented on the speculations that were growing around the findings of Balabanova. "The idea that the Egyptians were traveling to America is, overall, absurd. I don't know of anyone who is professionally employed as an Egyptologist, anthropologist or archaeologist who seriously believes in any of these possibilities, and I also don't know anyone who spends time doing research into these areas because they're perceived to be areas without any real meaning for the subjects" (Bains, 1996). It should be noted that prior to the discovery of a Norse settlement in Newfoundland in 1965, the theories about Viking voyages to America were likewise dismissed as fantastical nonsense.

I went into more detail on these finds in an earlier book (Bennett, 2010) and why they were rejected. Much of it has to do with the suggestions that other local substances likely broke down over millennia and were mistakenly identified as chemical markers for the New World Plants. Regardless, due to the association of cannabis with coca and tobacco in the findings in these studies, the physical evidence for cannabis in ancient mummies has largely been discounted.

Appendix 3

"Cannabis is in the Bible?" – Debunking an Interpretative Myth

By Alan Branch, Professor of Christian Ethics at Midwestern Baptist Theological Seminary

"The Bible includes cannabis as part of the worship of Yahweh!" Marijuana advocates often repeat this claim in an effort to gain leverage for the moral permissibility of smoking pot. The claim is so strange and peculiar, pastors, church leaders, and parents can be caught off guard and find themselves ill-prepared to answer this bit of cannabis urban legend. Does the Bible mention cannabis as part of worshipping the LORD? The short answer is, "Absolutely not." But understanding the origins of this claim and the confused arguments behind it can help us to point our teenagers and young adults towards holiness.

The claim that cannabis is mentioned in the Bible originates in the work of Polish anthropologist Sula Benet (1903-1982) who earned a doctorate from the University of Warsaw, where her thesis was titled, "Hashish in Folk Customs and Beliefs." She also earned a PhD at Columbia University in 1943 and went on to teach at Hunter College in New York City. Lecturing in Warsaw in 1936, she first proposed the idea that cannabis is mentioned in the Bible, an assertion she continued to repeat throughout her academic career. Modern cannabis advocates who announce "Marijuana is in the Bible!" almost always have Benet's research in mind.

Why would Benet make such a claim? She arrives at this erroneous conclusion via a very sloppy word study. In Exodus 30:23 -24, God instructs Moses to make incense for worship and gives the ingredients, saying, "Take the finest spices: of liquid myrrh 500 shekels, and of sweet-smelling cinnamon half as much, that is, 250, and 250 of aromatic cane, and 500 of cassia, according to the shekel of the sanctuary, and a hin of olive oil." The Hebrew phrase translated "aromatic cane" by the ESV in Exodus 30:23 is qanēh-bōśem. Playing fast and loose with the background of other words in Sanskrit, Assyrian, Persian, and Arabic, Benet essentially claims the Hebrew term qanēh-bōśem sounds a lot like the word cannabis, and thus, "Voila! Cannabis is in the Bible!"

Benet's bizarre assertion is not substantiated by the definitive Hebrew lexicon, The Hebrew and Aramaic Lexicon of the Old Testament, which says the term qanēh-bōśem is referring to a type of balsam oil. Balsam simply refers to aromatic resins derived from certain plants, and not cannabis.

Benet's is the sloppiest form of research, connecting the Hebrew term qanēh-bōśem to cannabis because they remotely sound alike. She brazenly asserts, "In many ancient languages, including Hebrew, the root kan has a double meaning—both hemp and reed." This is not based on any evidence in the Hebrew itself, but from references to the similar sounding word cannabis used centuries later in Greek along with much later references from the Jerusalem Talmud. This is what D.A. Carson calls the fallacy of semantic anachronism: Benet is reading a later use of a similar sounding word or words back into the meaning as found in Exodus. More bluntly, Benet is profoundly wrong: Just because words in two different languages happen to sound alike doesn't necessarily require them to have the same meaning. No lexicon supports Benet's interpretation; modern commentaries do not take her seriously.

Bad ideas used to support popular causes rarely go away quietly. Benet's careless word study was taken even further by Canadian cannabis advocate Chris Bennett who insists the same cannabis-based ingredients Benet says were in the incense of the temple were used by Jesus' apostles. When Mark 6:13 says Jesus' twelve apostles "were anointing with oil many sick people and healing them," Bennett insists the apostles used a cannabis-based oil to heal people. Bennett then claims the early church followed this model and used cannabis-based products to anoint the sick (James 5:14).

Bennett's claims are complete and utter nonsense and demonstrate a fundamental lack of understanding of anything closely related to the historical background of the New Testament. His argument is ever so weakly based on Benet's academic madness. The Greek-English Lexicon of the New Testament and Other Early Christian Literature, the definitive lexicon of New Testament Greek,simply defines the word for oil in Mark 6:13 as "olive oil."[4] The oil used in Mark 6:13 and James 5:14 was certainly olive oil, and serves as a symbol of the presence, grace, and power of God.[5] No lexicon mentions cannabis as an interpretative option for the Greek word for oil. Bennett's assertions have absolutely no traction with Greek scholars.

Refuting the absurd claims that cannabis is the Bible gives us an opportunity to teach our churches how to weigh the validity of sources used in moral argumentation. Benet was an anthropologist, not a linguist. Though pro-marijuana websites repeat her claim, the lexicons do not. Chris Bennett is not a Greek scholar, but someone who wants marijuana legalized. Just because an assertion about the Bible is published in a journal or gets repeated on a website does not mean the claim is valid. A sound principle of Biblical interpretation is this: the text cannot mean now what it did not mean then. Neither Exodus 30:23 nor Mark 6:13 referred to cannabis then and the text does not have cannabis in mind now.

Appendix 3

Professor Zohar Amar on tel Arad and Kaneh Bosm

ZoharAmar,is a professor in the Department of Land of Israel Studies at the religious- Zionist Bar-Ilan University. His specialty is in identifying the plants of the ancient Levant, and he is highly respected in his field. *The Book of Incense* by Amar has been widely acclaimed

In response to the discovery of cannabis resins on an altar at the site of an 8th century BCE temple at telArad, Jerusalem, Prof. Amar made the following statements about the implications of the find and the linguistic theory that the Hebrew "kaneh bosm" originally identified "cannabis." In the *Makor Rishon*, an Israeli weekly newspaper, on June 12th, 2020 Prof Amar explains:

> **The Israelites did not smoke cannabis in the temple**
>
> The cannabis is not the "kaneh bosem" and there is no evidence of its use in the temple in Jerusalem. Quite the opposite: Judaism abhors intoxicating its believers
>
> Recently it was announced that during an inspection of an altar located in TelArad remains of frankincense and cannabis were found. The altar was located in the temple of an Israeli citadel that probably dates to the ninth-century BC. A raised platform and a tomb were also found in the temple complex.
>
> Following this discovery, the researchers determined that the use of cannabis for worship was not only local but also prevalent in the central worship in the temple in Jerusalem. Meanwhile,the claim that cannabis is the "kaneh bosem" (aromatic reed) which was used for the purposes of worship in the temple was revived. In my humble opinion, these interpretations are unfounded and stem from a confusion between concepts or perhaps the needs of an academic rating.
>
> The interpretation according to which cannabis is the "kaneh bosem" began as "Vort" i.e. a nice little insight, a linguistic refinement resulting from a chance similarity of sounds,

but without any scientific grip. As is the way of urban legends, they took hold among the masses and overtime penetrated the world of research as well. And this is how a theoretical interpretation may become a "scientific truth."

This is one of the products of the open pit-field of the biblical plant identification field that sometimes relies on unfounded hypotheses.

"Kaneh bosem" was used as one of the components of the anointing oil in which the holy vessels and the priests were anointed (Exodus 30:23-25) and is not at all related to the incense ingredients that were incensed in the temple (Exodus 30:34; tractate Keritot 6a). This ingredient cannot be cannabis for several reasons: the plant and its products are not defined as perfumes and are not mentioned in the use of scent and incense in all cultures of the ancient world. Also, it does not appear in this context in any of the ancient identification traditions or in the authorized studies that deal with the identification of biblical plants.

Furthermore, the claim that the use of cannabis incense in TelArad for the purpose of intoxicating the worshipers in the temple to create a sense of transcendence is part of a common phenomenon throughout Judea and even in the temple in Jerusalem – is groundless. Although the use of narcotic substances such as opium was known in pagan worship, the official Jewish position denied this outright. Even drinking wine and other fermented drinks by the priests was considered a severe prohibition and for this it is said in the Torah that a distinction must be made between "impure and pure" (Leviticus 10:8-11). In Yerushalmi Talmud "Avoda zarah," the use of opium is prohibited "because of the danger."

A finding of cannabis in TelArad indicates that it is what is called in the bible "worship in the Bamot" that is considered a halachic deviation from the pure Israeli faith. There is also no echo of such use in the temple in Jerusalem from the scriptures, the Jewish literature or from any other findings. Due to the idolatrous themed activity and the desire to have one central worship in Jerusalem, the activity of the temple at TelArad was cancelled, probably as part of Hezekiah's religious reform (2 Kings 18:4). This points to the opposite conclusion: the Israeli faith rejected the use of cannabis or any narcotic substance for the purpose of the work.

Index

A

Acts of Thomas 393, 395, 396
Adams, John 309
Adonai 114, 137, 210
Adonijah 153
Adonis 137, 142, 156, 159, 168, 210
Agrippa 203, 204, 463
Ahab 219
Ahuramazda 227, 255, 265, 275, 282
Ahura Mazda 226, 229, 242, 261-263, 275, 282, 293, 365, 367, 407, 409
Akhenaten (Amenophis IV) 109, 117, 129, 348, 475
Albright, W.F. 154, 155, 463
Aleff, H. Peter 439, 441, 463
Alexander II (the Great) 243, 247, 316
Alexander, William Menzies 345
Allegro, John 49, 88-90, 159, 160, 335, 337, 338, 361, 362, 463
All the Year Round 313, 467
Amenhotep III 117
Amigoni, Jacopo 411
Amon 187
Amos 46, 137, 189, 306, 309, 310, 327, 328, 429, 470
Anat 34, 152, 154, 169, 217, 218
Anath 34, 44, 48, 120, 121, 144, 151-155, 157, 201, 217, 218, 320, 368, 389
Ancient Egyptian Herbal, An 109, 473
Ancient Egyptian Materials & Industries 109, 472
Ancient Near East Today, The 32, 479
Ancient Origins 91, 479
Anderson, Bernhard 141, 154, 184, 185, 190, 199, 200, 217, 224, 463
Angra Mainyu 227, 229, 366
Antiquities (Josephus) 224
Aphrodite 45, 53, 66, 167, 168
Apocryphon of John, The 398
Apollo 54, 135, 476
Arabian Nights 296, 465
Arda Wiraz 246, 270-272, 276, 277
Arie, Eran 7, 11, 12, 24, 27-29, 73, 404
Ashera 32, 35, 44, 49, 57, 64, 70, 71, 154, 165, 183, 194, 195, 376, 389
Asherah 31-45, 48-51, 56, 57, 61, 63-65, 67-71, 73, 101, 119-121, 127, 143, 144, 152, 154, 155, 161, 165, 166, 168, 172, 177, 180, 182, 183, 186, 189, 192-195, 201, 203-205, 208-210, 217-220, 236, 272, 280, 356, 369, 370-377, 382-385, 403, 404, 414, 465, 469, 470, 479-481
Ashtoreth 35, 144, 161, 195, 203
Ashurbanipal 97-99, 197, 349, 354, 355, 357, 368
Astargatis 34
Astarte 34, 40, 48, 66, 144, 156, 158, 159, 161, 167, 168, 194, 201, 217, 218
Athirat 34, 63, 375, 383
Atlantic, The 71, 470
A to Z of Prophets in Islam and Judaism, The 307, 474, 481
Attis 52, 159
Avalon, Arthur (Sir John Woodroffe) 170, 463
Avesta 5, 229, 234, 236, 237, 241, 243, 244, 245, 249, 253-255, 257, 264, 265, 272, 291, 366, 464, 466, 467

B

Baal 36, 44, 119-121, 123, 142, 144, 150-155, 157, 159, 169, 177, 183, 186, 194, 195, 199, 201-203, 211, 217, 218, 220, 320, 375
Babylonian and Assyrian Literature 168, 482
Babylonian Exile 124, 126, 129, 178, 206, 207, 211, 213, 221, 224, 280, 281, 284, 328, 329, 346, 386

Babylonian Talmud: Tractate Horayoth 198, 463
Bacchus 137, 291, 322, 323, 324, 471
Bactria Margiana Archaeological Complex (BMAC) 231-233, 235, 239, 248, 300, 378
Bagli, Jehan 245, 463
Bahman Yast 262-264, 293
Bains, John 443, 463
Balabanova, Svetla 441-443, 463
Balfour, John Hutton 108, 463
Basham, A.L. 231, 464
Bell, William 52, 464, 478
Benet, Sula v, 6, 45, 57, 61, 65, 71, 73-75, 77, 78, 82, 84-88, 98, 104-106, 127, 131, 162, 174, 175, 204, 217, 403, 445, 446, 464
Bengal Dispensatory, The 425
Bennett, Chris iii, 72, 88, 97, 128, 160, 256, 278, 312, 313, 325, 357, 388, 392, 444, 446, 447, 475
Ben Yehuda, Eliezer 83
Ben Yehudas Pocket Dictionary 83
Berlin Papyrus 437, 438
Bernward (Bishop) 340
Betuel, Emma 338, 339, 464
Bible Dictionary, The 76, 108, 463, 467, 476
Bible Flowers and Flower Lore 75, 464
Biblical and Theological Dictionary, A 83, 470
Biblical Archaeology Review (BAR) 382, 478
Bloch-Smith, Elizabeth 31, 40, 41, 465
Böck, Barbara 24, 65, 69, 96, 97, 465
Boertien, Jeannette H. 64, 84, 107, 372, 465
Book of Arda Wiraz 246, 270, 271, 277
Book of Grass: An Anthology on Indian Hemp, The 278, 463, 464, 467
Boston Medical and Surgical Journal, The 313
Bottéro, Jean 348
Bouquet, R.J. 361, 465
Boyce, Mary 238, 239, 26-269, 284, 465
Branch, Alan 77, 78, 445
Brown, George Washington 276, 287, 292, 293, 465
Brown, Jerry 338, 340-343
Brown, Judy 338, 340-343
Budge, W.E. 169, 439, 465
Bunsen, E.K. 365, 465
Burton, Richard 106, 301, 302, 465

C

calamus 6, 74-77, 80, 81, 82, 88
Cambridge Bible for Schools and Colleges, The 203, 475
Campbell, Joseph 191, 254, 270, 332, 346, 350, 366, 465, 480, 482
Camphausen, Rufus C. 65, 144, 466
Cannabis and the Soma Solution 2, 97, 129, 229, 243, 251, 337, 367
Cannabis Chassidis: The Ancient and Emerging Torah of Drugs 136
Canterbury Tales, The 401
Canticles (Song of Soloman) 64, 156, 159, 162, 423, 424, 463
Carson, D.A. 446
Carter, Martha 247
Cartwell, W.F. 278, 279
Çatal Höyük 4, 62
Chakraberty, Chandra 231, 466
Chaucer, Geoffrey 401
City of Akhenaten, The 109, 475
Clarke, James Freeman 291, 408, 443, 466, 468
Clavicula Salomonis Regis (The Lesser Key of Solomon) 175
Clavicula Salomonis (The Key of Solomon) 175
Clay, Melvin 278, 279
Colenso, John 125, 126, 466
Cole, William 44, 47, 49, 133, 137, 173, 174, 466
Collard, David 21
Columbia History of the World, The 190, 469
Complete Gods and Goddesses of Ancient Egypt, The 167, 482

Compte Rendu, Rencontre Assyriologique Internationale 65, 95, 172, 475
Conner, Randy P. 51, 52, 466
Cook, W.D. 64
Cotterell, Arthur 155, 466
Cowan, Robert 318, 319, 466
Cradic, Melissa S. 23, 24, 93, 94, 308, 466
Creighton, C. 99, 104, 105, 171, 206, 207, 225, 423, 466
Cults of Uruk and Babylon, The 98, 472
Cybelle 35, 51, 52, 236
Cyclopaedia of Biblical Literature, A 106, 288, 304
Cyrus I (the Great) 225, 226, 228, 274-276, 476

D

Daniel 99, 105, 122, 221, 224-226, 358, 429, 433, 434
Danielou, Alaine 46, 152, 153, 230, 319, 466
Daniely, Dvora Lederman 32, 33, 466
Darius 1 (the Great) 226, 274, 275, 276, 279, 284, 289
Dartmouth Bible 222
Darwin, Charles 9
Daryoush, Jahanian 237, 253, 467
David, Ariel 7, 29, 404
Day, John 154
Dead Sea Scrolls and the Christian Myth, The 160, 463
Decline and Fall of the Sasanian Empire, The 253, 475
Delhoofs, Hervé 304
Democritus 247, 248, 299
Demonic Possession in the New Testament: Its Historical, Medical, and Theological Aspects 345, 463
Dever, William G. 36, 37, 42, 63, 168, 467
De Veze, Ernest Bosc 94
Dictionarium Medicum Universale 75
Dictionary of Deities and Demons in the Bible 69, 467, 481
Did God Have a Wife? 36, 467
Die Flora Der Juden 312, 472
Die Religionen Irans 263, 482
Dionysus 137, 210, 247, 313-325, 466
Dioscorides, Pedanius 75, 299
Dobroruka, Vicente 266, 269, 272, 293-295, 310, 311, 467
Douglas, Alex 370
Dragons of Eden: Speculations on the Evolution of Human Intelligence, The 3, 477
Driver, Samuel 426, 463
Du Hachish et de l'Alienation Mentale 428
Duke, James 76, 77, 467, 472
Duke's Handbook of Medicinal Plants of the Bible 76, 467
Du Toit, Brian 75, 467

E

Easton, Matthew George 76, 309, 463, 467
Eber's Papyrus 42, 437, 438
Eden vii, 3, 100, 143, 169, 183, 207, 209, 327-329, 331-334, 336-338, 340, 344-348, 364-366, 368-371, 373, 374, 376, 386-391, 464, 467, 469, 471, 473, 477, 479
Eisler, Riane 47, 48, 148, 149, 372, 375, 467
E.J. Brill's First Encyclopaedia of Islam 253, 471
El 44, 63, 101, 109, 111, 116, 119-124, 150, 154, 175, 195, 217, 220, 309, 348, 375, 393, 475
Elat 34, 63, 383
Eliade, Mircea 152, 200, 218, 219, 239, 247, 256, 259, 260, 263, 266, 269, 271, 272, 314, 331, 332, 467, 468, 474
El in the Ugaritic Texts 119, 475
Ellicott, Charles 203, 468
Emboden, William 45, 70, 71, 174, 468
Encyclopedia Britannica 10, 65, 298, 466
Encyclopedia Judaica 76, 478

Encyclopedia of Erotic Wisdom, The 65, 466
Encyclopedia of Homosexuality, The 49, 55, 467
Encyclopedia of Indo-European Culture, The 92, 473
Erbt, Wilhelm 146, 153, 468
Esarhaddon 98-100, 197, 225, 349, 357, 358, 361
Ezekiel 6, 51, 74, 75, 88, 105-107, 127, 198, 199, 205-211, 213, 217, 221, 223, 224, 280, 281, 294, 327-329, 410, 435, 469
Ezekiel and the World of Deuteronomy 205, 469
Ezra vii, 98, 111, 172, 211, 227, 228, 274, 279-295, 297, 300, 310, 345, 368, 400, 404, 467, 469

F

Fales, Frederick Mario 66, 130, 468
Fallows, Samuel 108, 468
Farrakhan, Louis 418
First Great Powers: Babylon and Assyria, The 155, 466
Fischer-Rizzi, Susanne 28, 468
Flattery, David 251, 254, 261, 265, 268, 272, 276, 468
Flemming, Michael 443
Folk-etymology 106, 302
Food of the Gods 407, 473
Frank, Harry Thomas 144
Frazer, James George 45, 46, 468
Freud, Sigmund 117, 128, 348, 469
Frymer-Kensky, Tikva Simone 155, 218, 219, 372, 469

G

Gaea 54
Gaia 418
Gardiner, Alan 439
Gas, Anton 235
Gathas 235, 237-239, 244, 245, 249, 261, 272, 409
Gautier, Theophile 258, 435
Geiwitz, James 130, 469
George, Arthur 373
Gertsman, Elina 339
Geschichte der hethitischen Religion 67, 470
Ghayat AlHakim 94
Gile, Jason 205, 469
Gilgamesh 48, 95, 331
Glassman, Yosef 84, 469
Glossary of Colloquial Anglo-Indian Words and Phrases, A 106, 302, 482
Glueck, Nelson 173
Gnosticism in Corinth: An Investigation of the Letters to the Corinthians 389, 477
Godbey, Alan 5, 241, 242, 296, 469
Goddesses, Elixirs, and Witches 344, 476
Gods, Goddesses, and Images of God in Ancient Israel 114
Gods of Love and Ecstasy: The Traditions of Shiva and Dionysus 319
Gospel of Philip 395
Gospel of Thomas, The 399
Gospel of Truth, The 395
Graves, Robert 47, 71, 205, 347, 348, 470
Gray, John 34, 128, 224, 347, 356, 366, 376, 470
Greatness that was Babylon: A Sketch of the Ancient Civilization of the Tigris-Euphrates Valley, The 352
Greek Experience of India: From Alexander to the Indo-Greeks, The 247, 479
Greenblatt, Robert 55, 169, 470
Green Gold the Tree of Life: Marijuana in Magic and Religion 1, 357
Gressman, Hugo 144
Grinspoon, Lester 3, 5, 65, 207, 408, 470
Guenther, Allen R. 328, 470
Guy, Geoffery 2, 3, 473, 479

H

Haaretz 7, 12, 17, 22, 24, 25, 27, 29, 57, 73, 404, 467, 470
Haas, Volkert 67, 470
Habakkuk 310
Hackman, George 98, 470
Hagen, Ed 4
HaLevi, Baruch 86, 305, 470
Hamlet 431
Haoma and Harmaline 251, 268
Harris, Maurice Henry 82, 168, 225, 470, 472
Hathor 35, 48, 165-167, 172
Hatsis, Tom 397, 398, 470
Hebraic Literature: Translations from the Talmud, Midrashim and Kabbala 82, 470
Hebrew Bible 5-7, 9, 32-37, 39, 43, 44, 47, 49, 56, 63, 69, 73, 81, 83, 89, 90, 98, 103, 104, 106, 115, 119, 121, 123-125, 127, 129, 130, 138, 141, 143, 144, 146, 154, 156, 160, 161, 170, 174, 179, 180, 183, 184, 186, 191-194, 196, 198, 206, 212, 217, 219, 222-224, 227, 243, 274, 280, 281, 287, 295, 297, 326, 328, 347, 368, 372, 388, 394, 404, 409, 467, 469, 470
Hebrew Goddess, The 35, 36, 71, 173, 475
Hebrew Myths: The Book of Genesis, The 71, 347, 470
Henning, Walter Bruno 249, 250, 254, 255, 261, 471
Henry, John 442
Heracles 54
Herer, Jack 393, 414, 415, 471
Herodotus 46, 54, 85, 87, 92, 168, 241, 250
Hertz, Joseph H. 345
Herzog, Ze'ev 13, 30, 31, 471
Hestia 53, 54
Hesychius 167
Hezekiah 29, 31, 32, 56, 124, 126, 143, 177, 180, 182-189, 191, 193, 196, 210, 218, 219, 370, 371, 404
Hieros Gamos 139, 144, 145, 159, 169, 172, 371, 396
Hilkiah 189-191, 194, 196
Hillman, David 10, 95, 471
Hiram I 175
Hirsch, Emil 111, 471
History of Jewish Gynaecological Texts in the Middle Ages, A 42, 464
History of Magic and Experimental Science, A 397, 480
History of Plants 77
History of the Jews, A 9, 134, 471
Hofmann, Albert 95, 301, 302, 345, 469, 476, 477
Holladay, John S. 38, 471
Holy of Holies 6, 13-17, 19, 26, 31, 71, 73, 106, 114, 124, 127, 142, 176, 204, 332, 371, 376, 405, 418
Holy Oil 6, 75, 101, 128, 130, 132, 393
Homer 136, 300, 301, 397
Hosea 43, 49, 50, 110, 121, 172, 189, 201-203, 206, 328, 470, 472
Hosea 2: Metaphor and Rhetoric in Historical Perspective all inscriptions from 8th century BCE Kuntilet Arjud 43, 121, 202, 472
Hosea and Amos Believers Church Bible Commentary 328

I

Iliad 301, 406
Immortality Key, The 302, 313, 325, 474
Inanna 53, 66, 68, 69, 95, 101, 142, 145, 147, 153, 155, 156, 162, 371, 384
Incense and Poison Ordeals in the Ancient Orient 5, 241, 296
Indo-German Identification: Reconciling South Asian Origins and European Destinies, The 319, 466
Indra 163, 231, 239, 242, 243, 247, 467
Institute Of Biblical Studies: The Book Of Genesis 109, 476

Irenaeus 312, 388, 396, 397, 398, 471
Isaiah 6, 32, 50, 55, 98, 127, 148, 154, 157, 176-182, 185, 186, 188, 189, 193, 198, 201, 203-206, 216, 223, 225, 228, 274, 309, 310, 327, 328, 370, 405, 409-411
Ishara 35, 65-69, 101, 155, 371, 375, 384, 403
Ishtar 35, 46, 48, 50, 51, 53, 64-70, 96, 101, 128, 145, 146, 149, 153-156, 158, 161-163, 167, 168, 172, 208-210, 216-218, 312, 356, 371, 375, 376, 384, 403

J

Jacob Ben Asher 405
Jafarey, Ali 236, 237, 239, 240, 243-245, 471
Jahanian, Daryoush 237, 467
Jaynes, Julian 135, 136, 137, 406, 407, 412, 471
Jehoahaz 198, 201
Jehu 218
Jereboam II 219
Jeremiah 6, 35, 70, 75, 88, 127, 154, 179, 180, 187-191, 198-206, 211-219, 221, 223, 224, 295, 310-312, 403, 74, 404
Jesus 24, 196, 274, 312, 313, 325, 332, 337, 388, 390, 392-395, 398-400, 476
Jewish Encyclopedia 111, 321, 347, 471, 478
Jews and their God of Wine, The 324, 472
Joel 328, 482
Johnson, Buffie 209, 374
Johnson, Paul 9, 134
Johnston, Phillip 182, 262, 471
Josephus 90, 224, 287, 298, 322, 323, 430
Joshua 154, 191, 193, 195, 328, 348, 466
Josiah 7, 32, 33, 50, 55, 56, 88, 124, 126, 178, 182, 185, 187-199, 201, 210-212, 216, 219, 280, 281, 287, 332, 372, 404
Journal of Sexual Medicine, The 170, 479
Journal of the Institute of Archaeology of Tel Aviv University 6, 11, 13, 471

K

Kabelik, Jan 435, 471
kadesh 46, 50, 55
kadosh 55
Kafka, Franz 386
kaneh 6, 7, 57, 71, 73-76, 80-88, 91, 94-96, 99, 103-106, 113, 114, 127-130, 138, 140, 153, 160, 162-164, 171, 176-180, 185, 187, 189, 193, 197-199, 203-205, 216, 217, 223, 227-229, 297, 325, 349, 369, 371, 385, 399, 74, 77
kaneh bosm 6, 7, 57, 73-76, 82-84, 86, 91, 94, 95, 99, 103, 104, 113, 114, 127-129, 160, 185, 197, 198, 204, 227-229, 297, 325
Kang, Seung 371, 471
Kaplan, Aryeh 77, 80, 405, 471
Keel, Othmar 114, 167, 471, 478
Kelle, Brad E. 121, 472
Kien, Jenny 165, 166, 472
Kirkpatrick, Jonathan 324, 325, 472
Kitto, John 104, 106-111, 171, 203, 288, 289, 304, 472
Klein, Siegfried 82, 83, 472
Kupfer, Marcia 339

L

La Barre, Weston 84, 87, 128, 221, 222, 367, 410, 411, 472
Lands of the Saracens, The 434
Langdon, Stephen Herbert 324, 472
Langutt, Dafna 25
Lawler, Andrew 21, 68, 472
Layard, Austen Henry 207, 355, 359, 472
Legends of the Old Testament, The 365, 479

Lenormant, François 98, 208, 359, 362, 364, 472
Leviticus (Commentary) 50
Liber 420: Cannabis, Magickal herbs and the Occult 2, 312, 402, 405
Library of Universal Knowledge 290
Linssen, Marc 98, 472
Littleton, Scott 10
Living Torah, The 77, 471
Löw, Immanuel 81, 82, 111, 312, 385, 471, 472
Lucas, Alfred 109, 472
Luck, Georg 10, 11, 131-133, 465, 472

M

Mackenzie, Donald Alexander 97, 208, 348, 472
Magee, Michael D. 281-284, 472
Mahdihassan, S. 233, 234
Maimonides 10
Malachi 223, 280, 281
Manasseh 29, 186, 187, 195, 197, 198, 205, 210, 219
mandrake 138, 159, 164-170, 172, 298, 299, 320, 344-346, 370, 371, 375, 400
Manners and Customs of the Ancient Egyptians, The 301, 482
Marcus (Gnostic) 312, 396, 397, 398
Margolis, Peter 85, 473
Martínez, Florentino García 159, 473
Matthiolus 299
McClintock, John 108, 473
McGovern, Patrick 246, 247, 300, 473
McKenna, Terence 3, 407, 408, 414, 417, 473
McPartland, John 2, 3, 473
McQueen, Neil v, 2, 88, 128, 160, 256, 325, 352, 388, 392
Mechoulam, Raphael 104-106, 197, 302, 473, 477, 482
Medical News, The 305, 480
Medrano, Kastalia 183, 184, 473
Meek, T.J. 153, 156, 473
Melchizedek 175
Men's Journal 91, 481
Merian, Matthaeus 179
Merlin, Mark 3, 52, 255, 332, 408, 409, 466, 473
Messadié, Gérald 239, 243
Meyler's Side Effects of Herbal Medicines 75, 463
Micah 182, 188, 189, 309, 310
Midgley, W.W. 109, 474
Mishnah 82, 83, 84, 96, 74, 111
Mithra 196, 263, 292
Mitteilungen zur Geschichte der Medizin und der Naturwissenschaften 96, 474
Mondriaan, Marlene 118, 474
Moran, W.L. 51
Moreau, J. 428, 435
Morgenstien, Julian 144
Moses 10, 31, 75, 84, 115-118, 123, 128, 129, 131-133, 143, 160, 178-180, 183, 188, 189-191, 196, 218, 223, 224, 242, 278, 280, 283, 284, 286, 292, 327, 348, 349, 370, 371, 385, 405, 409-411, 469
Moses and Monotheism 117, 128, 348, 469
Mozeson, Isaac E. 86, 87, 474
Muhammad, Wesley 278, 418, 419, 474
Muller, F. Max 366, 474, 477
Mummy Congress, The 436, 475
Muraresku, Brian 302, 303, 325, 474
Mythology of All Races 324, 472
Mythology of the Babylonian People 348
Myths of Babylonia and Assyria 208, 472

N

Nabu 69
Nag Hammadi Library, The 388
Namdar, Dvory 11, 19, 24, 27, 474
National Geographic Explorer, The 54
Navigating the Bible 84
Near Eastern Mythology: Mesopotamia, Syria, Palsestine 356, 376, 470
Nebuchadnezzar 99, 105, 213, 224, 225, 287, 358, 429, 433, 434

Needelman-Ruiz, Yoseph 136, 474
Nehemiah 154, 228, 281, 282, 287, 288
Neil, R.A. 433
Nerlich, Andreas 442, 475
Neumann, Erich 21, 22, 58, 60, 307, 308, 466, 472, 474
New Scientist 84, 91
Newsweek 12, 183, 469, 473
New York Dental Journal, The 306, 476
New York Times 302
Noegel, Scott B. 150, 307, 313, 474, 481
No Graven Images: Studies in Art and the Hebrew Bible 192, 470
Notes on the Hebrew Text of the Books of Samuel 426
Noth, Riane 50
Nyberg, Henrik Samuel 237, 240, 242, 248, 249, 254, 256, 257, 260, 271-273, 474

O

Oannes 347, 348, 350
Ode to Sophia 396
Odyssey, The 300, 397
Old Testament in the Jewish Church, The 203
Oorschot, Jürgen van 41, 475
Origin of Consciousness in the Breakdown of the Bicameral Mind, The 135, 406
Origins of Biblical Monotheism: Israel's Polytheistic Background and the Ugaritic Texts, The 114, 122, 478
Origins of Yahwism, The 41, 475
O'Shaughnessy, W.B. 393, 425
Ott, Jonathan 162, 163, 304, 475, 481
Outline of the Future Religion of the World, An 366, 479

P

Palmer, Abram Smythe 106, 302, 475
Panofsky, Erwin 335
Pappah, Rav 83
Parsche, Franz 442, 463, 475
Patai, Raphael 33-36, 47, 59, 71, 151, 157, 160, 161, 173, 347, 348, 470, 475
Pearson, Birger A. 391, 475
Peet, Thomas 109, 475
Pendell, Dale 314, 475
Pen Ts'ao 5
People of the Dead Sea Scrolls, The 159, 473
Perfume Handbook, The 76, 470
Perowne, John 203
Persia & Creation of Judaism 281, 472
Persian Empire: A Historical Encyclopedia, The 81, 226, 227, 231, 279, 280, 472
Petite Encyclopedie Synthetique des Sciences Occultes 94, 465
Philo 143, 168, 283
Physiolgus, The 344
Physiologus, the Bestiaries and Medieval Animal Lore, The 345
Picatrix 94
Pistis Sophia 175, 399
Plants of the Bible, The 76, 108, 463, 467
Pliny 76, 247, 248, 299, 300, 322, 399
Plutarch 276, 321, 322, 323
Pope, Marvin 64, 119, 145, 146, 148-151, 158, 159, 162, 167, 169, 170, 320, 475
Popular and Critical Bible Encyclopedia and Scriptural Dictionary, The 108
Popular Archeology 12, 475
Pot Plot: Marijuana and the Chemical Feminization of a Generation, The 418, 474
Princeton Review, The 306, 472
Province, The 393, 463
Psychedelic Gospels: The Secret History of Hallucinogens in Christianity, The 338, 465
Psyche, Seelencult und Unsterblichkeitsglaube der Griechen 314
Puett, Terry 109, 476

Q

Qadesh 49, 165
qedeshim 49, 51, 55, 56, 64, 65, 161, 219
Qodesh (Qudshu) 34, 45
Queen of Heaven 32, 37, 56, 70, 71, 189, 198, 199, 201, 203, 204, 213, 214, 216, 217, 312, 399, 403
Quests and Visionary Journeys in Sasanian Iran 251, 276
qunubu 66, 86, 91, 94-98, 101-103, 130, 161, 162, 349, 357-359, 361, 368

R

Rahab 47
Rashi (Shlomo Yitzchaki) 83, 345, 464
Rätsch, Christian 4, 60, 65, 164-169, 299, 304, 476
Rawlinson, George 359, 476
Ray, Joges Candra 231
Rehoboam 216, 218
Reiner, Erica 65, 101, 155, 476
Reinstating the Divine Woman in Judaism 165, 472
Religion in Ancient Mesopotamia 348, 465
Religion in Israel and Judah Under the Monarchy: An Explicitly Archaeological Approach 38
Religions of Ancient Israel: A Synthesis of Parallactic Approaches, The 31, 482
Religions of the Ancient Near East 347, 360, 412, 476
Researches in oriental history: Embracing the origin of the Jews, the rise and development of Zoroastrianism, and the derivation of Christianity 287
Riddle, John 169, 344, 476
Rig Veda 229, 230, 255, 257
Ringgren, Helmer 46, 59, 157, 175, 347, 348, 349, 355, 356, 359, 360, 412, 476
Rohde, Erwin 247, 314-316, 476
Rolfe, F.W. 334
Rolfe, Robert Thatcher 334, 335, 476
Romance of the Fungus World 334, 476
Romanesque Wall Painting in Central France 339
Romano, Marc 239, 241, 473
Rosa Anglica 402
Rosch, Manfred 112, 476
Rosen, Baruch 11
Rosenthal, Franz 250, 278, 313, 403, 476
Routledge Companion to Ecstatic Experience in the Ancient World, The 96, 465
Ruck, Carl 10, 75, 85, 87, 247, 298, 301, 316, 476
Rudenko, Sergei 53, 92
Rudgley, Richard 59, 60, 477
Rudolph, Kurt 389, 392, 395, 398, 477
Russo, Ethan 42, 84, 85, 97, 101, 102, 132, 254, 349, 393, 437, 477, 480

S

Sacred Mushroom and the Cross, The 88, 90, 160, 337, 463
Sagan, Carl 3, 60, 477
Saggs, H.W.F. 155, 347, 352, 361, 477
Salzberger, Georg 175, 477
Samorini, Giorgio 340, 341
Sarianidi, Victor 231-233, 241, 242, 245, 246, 248, 300, 319, 378, 477
Schmithals, Walter 389, 477
Schoff, W.H. 158, 159
Schonfield, Hugh 142, 210, 477
Schultes, Richard E. 4, 95, 301, 302, 345, 477
Schwartz, Martin 251, 254-256, 261, 265, 268, 272, 276, 468
Science 20, 21, 68, 415
Science and Secrets of Early Medicine 96, 480
Scurlock, JoAnn 69, 478
Scythians 7, 53, 54, 67, 86, 88, 92, 93, 97, 106, 132, 197, 233, 235, 241, 242, 255, 274, 278, 300, 315, 321, 322, 409

Search the Scriptures: A Physician Examines Medicine in the Bible 55, 470
Second Book of Ieou, The 399, 400, 401
Second Book of Jue, The 313
Sennacherib 185, 186
Sepher Raziel: Liber Salomonis 175, 176, 401, 478
Septuagint 6, 50, 75, 77, 80, 81, 88, 104,
Sex and Love in the Bible 44, 173, 466
Sex, Drugs, Violence and the Bible v, 2, 128, 160, 352, 359
Seydibeyoglu 4, 478
Shaked, Shaul 251, 253, 276, 278, 478
Shannon, Benny 405
Shaphan (scribe) 189, 190, 191, 213
Sherratt, Andrew 92, 478
Shiva 151-153, 267, 270, 316-321, 466, 479
Shiva: The Wild God of Power and Ecstasy 320, 479
Siculus, Diodorus 301
Silvestre de Sacy 427
Simon Magus 397
Smith, Mark 114, 118, 122
Smith, Morton 325
Smith, Robertson 203
Solomon 17, 33, 35, 38, 39, 43, 126, 138-141, 143-146, 149, 153, 154, 157, 158, 160,-163, 169, 172, 174, 175, 177, 183, 188, 189, 195, 196, 198, 210, 216, 219, 370, 371, 373, 383, 423
Soma: Divine Mushroom of Immortality 2, 97, 129, 229-235, 243, 247, 248, 251, 254-257, 267, 291, 300, 319, 321, 335, 336, 359, 362, 364-366, 468, 469, 471, 473-477, 479, 481
Song of Songs 6, 43, 104, 127, 138, 140, 144-147, 149, 156-158, 163, 164, 167, 170-172, 174, 177, 179, 181, 203, 204, 210, 320, 346, 371, 468, 471, 473, 475, 477
Song of Songs and the Ancient Egyptian Love Songs, The 167, 468
Song of Songs, Continental Commentaries, The 167, 441
Sourcebook for Ancient Mesopotamian Medicine 69, 216, 478
Spong, John Shelby 189, 193, 222, 479
Stanley, T. Lloyd 366, 367, 479
Starkey, James L. 382
Stein, Diana (Stein-Wuenscher) 67, 68, 70, 102, 103, 352-354, 357, 361, 367, 368, 379-381, 413, 414, 465, 468, 473, 479
Stoddard, Michael 28
Stoneman, Richard 247, 479
Storl, Wolf-Dieter 320, 479
Story of Medicine, The 306, 481
Strange, Thomas Lumisden 365, 366, 479
Strong Biblical Cyclopedia, The 108, 473
Stuckey, Johanna H. 120, 194, 479
Studies on Neo-Assyrian Texts II: "Deeds and documents" from the British Museum 66, 468
Swamy, B.G.L. 231, 479

T

Tacitus 135, 321, 322, 323
Talmud 82, 83, 84, 90, 191, 198, 374, 463, 464, 470
Tamar 47
Tammuz 46, 50, 142, 145-147, 149, 153-159, 210, 217
Tanach 86, 325
Taylor, Bayard 434
Taylor, Joan 252, 374, 375, 383-385, 465, 473, 474, 478, 479
tel Arad 6, 7, 23, 24, 29, 31, 33, 35, 37, 39, 56, 71, 73, 83-86, 88, 90, 94, 106, 114, 124, 127, 133, 172, 177, 179, 185, 189, 204, 205, 216, 217, 403, 404, 100
Ten Great Religions 291
Tent of the Meeting 99, 117, 127-129, 132, 133, 143, 160, 405, 409, 411
Terrien, Samuel 51, 143, 480

Testament of Solomon, The 175
Testimony of Truth, The 390, 391, 394
Thareani, Yifat 24
The Great Mother: An Analysis of the Archetype, The 46, 58, 60, 61, 143, 146, 156, 474
Theophrastus 75, 76, 77, 299
Thompson, M.R.C. 101, 102, 350, 474, 480
Thorndike, Lynn 313, 397, 480
Thorwald, Jurgen 96, 480
Tiele, Cornelis P. 116
Times, The (UK) 12, 465
Tissot, James 134
Tod und Begräbnis in Palästina zur Zeit der Tannaiten 82, 472
Treatise on Hashish, A 94
Trebolle, Julio C. 159, 473
Tristram, H.B. 76
Tronetti, Francesca 56, 57, 480
Tully, Caroline 18, 39, 40, 63, 481

U

Ultimate Bible Dictionary, The 76, 309, 463, 467
Uncorking the Past: The Quest for Wine, Beer, and Other Alcoholic Beverages 246, 473
Understanding the Old Testament 141, 463
Utnapishtim 346, 347

V

Vegetation History and Archaeobotany 91, 480
Vendidad 229, 242, 269, 272, 466
Vikramasiṃha 231, 481
Virey, Joseph 301, 481
Vishtapa 266, 293
Vishtaspa (Hystaspes) 226, 257, 266-269, 275, 284, 294
Vistashpa 279, 307
Vita Moysis 283
Vulgate 80, 104, 171, 423-425, 471

W

Walker, Barbara 48, 54, 146, 147, 306, 418, 481
Waradpande, N.R. 231, 481
Ward, James 363, 481
Wasson, R. Gordon 257, 335-338, 344, 467, 469, 481
Wayland-Barber, Elizabeth 4
Weil, Andrew 5, 259, 414, 481
Wellhausen, Julius 426
Wellman, Max 344
Wenk, Gary 130, 131, 481
White, Ellen 36
White, Gavin 66
Widengren, Geo 243, 249, 250, 254, 263-267, 272, 356, 482
Wilkinson, Richard H. 167, 301, 482
Williams, Jay G. 369
Williams, Rand 108, 369
Withof, F.T. 427
Witte, Markus 41
Witzel, Michael 247, 482
Women and Cannabis Medicine, Science, and Sociology 42
Wonder That Was India: A Survey of the Culture of the Indian Sub-Continent before the coming of the Muslims, The 231, 464
Word: The Dictionary That Reveals the Hebrew Source of English, The 86, 474

Y

Yahweh 9, 29, 31-39, 41, 47, 49, 51, 57, 63, 114-125, 129, 131, 133, 135, 137, 138, 140-142, 144, 154-160, 165, 172, 175, 177, 180, 182, 186, 187, 189, 190, 192-194, 198-206, 209-211, 213, 214, 216-220, 222, 223, 225, 226, 228, 274, 284, 295, 309, 313, 321, 324, 331, 348, 349, 368-370, 373, 374, 377, 384-386, 389, 403-405, 409, 410, 414, 467, 469

Yang, Yimin 93, 476
Yasna 229, 235-240, 242, 244, 245, 255, 261, 265, 266, 294
YHWH 13, 31, 41, 57, 114, 348

Z

Zaehner, R.C. 238, 240, 241, 242, 482
Zarathustra 235-237, 239-242, 244, 245, 257, 263-265, 269, 275
Zechariah 295, 296
Zedekiah (Mattaniah) 212-214
Zend Avesta 5
Zeus 54, 300, 301, 316
Zevit, Ziony 31, 482
Zias, Joel 25, 394, 482
Zohar 405
Zohary, Michael 76, 77, 255, 482
Zoroaster 226, 227, 229, 235-237, 239-244, 246, 248-250, 253, 256, 257, 261-266, 268-270, 272-276, 286, 293, 294, 398, 407, 409, 410, 471
Zoroastrian 5, 99, 22-229, 231, 235-239, 241, 242, 244-246, 248, 249, 251-254, 256, 257, 261-263, 270-276, 278, 281, 284, 286, 289, 290, 293, 294, 307, 358, 366, 398, 400, 467
Zoroastrianism 226, 227, 229, 238, 239, 241, 242, 246, 254, 265, 273, 278, 284, 287, 367, 398, 403, 422, 465, 467, 482

Bibliography

"Founders of Western Civilization Were Prehistoric Dope Dealers," *New Scientist,* (2016).

Abel, Ernest, *Marihuana, The First Twelve Thousand Years,* Phenum Press (1980).

Adams, John in *The Ultimate Bible Dictionary,* by Easton, Matthew George (1897).

Agrippa, Heinrich Cornelius, *De Occulta Philosophia* (1651).

Albright, W.F., "Archaic survivals in the text of Canticles," *Hebrew and Semitic Studies Presented to Godfrey Rolles Driver* (1963).

Aldrich, Michael, "Cannabis and its Derivatives," *High Times Encyclopaedia of Recreational Drugs,* Trans High Corp (1978).

Aleff, Peter, "Maat soul-mate Seshat convicted for possessing pot and undeclared math," http://www.recoveredscience.com/const201seshathempmath.htm#_edn4 (1982).

Alexander, William Menzies, *Demonic Possession in the New Testament: Its Historical, Medical, and Theological Aspects,* Baker Book House, Michigan, (1902/1980).

Allegro, John M., *The Sacred Mushroom and the Cross,* Paper Jacks (1970).

Allegro, John, *The Dead Sea Scrolls and the Christian Myth,* Prometheus Books (1980).

Allegro, John; *The Dead Sea Scrolls: A Reappraisal,* Pelican Books (1956,1964)

Anderson, Bernhard W., *Understanding the Old Testament,* Prentice-Hall, Inc. (1957).

Andrew and Vinkenoog, Ed, *The Book of Grass,* Peter Owen Ltd. (1967).

Andrews, George, *Drugs and Magic,* Illuminet (1997).

Aronson, Jeffery K., *Meyler's Side Effects of Herbal Medicines,* Elsevier Science (2008).

Ashe, Geoffrey, *The Virgin,* Routledge (1976).

Aspects Of Late Second Temple Jewish Apocalyptic. A Cross-Cultural Comparison.

Associated Press, "Hashish Evidence is 1,600 years Old,"*The Province,* (newspaper) Vancouver, British Columbia, (June 2nd, 1992).

Avalon, Arthur, *The Great Liberation,* Ganesh Publishing (1913).

Babylonian Talmud: Tractate Horayoth, Folio 12.

Bagli, Dr. Jehan, "The Significance of Plant Life in Zarathushti Liturgy," *FEZANA Journal* (2005).

Bains, John, "The Mystery of the Cocaine Mummies," (1996).

Balabanova, S., F. Parsche and W. Pirsig, "First identification of drugs in Egyptian mummies," Naturwissenschaften, (1992).

Balfour, John Hutton, *The Plants of the Bible* (1885).

Barber, E. J. W., *Prehistoric Textiles: The Development of Cloth in the Neolithic and Bronze Ages with Special Reference to the Aegean,* (Princeton University Press, 1991).

Barber, E.M., *Pre-historic Textiles,* Princeton University Press, (1989).

Barber, EW., *The Mummies of Urumchi,* New York (1999).

Barkai, Ron, *A History of Jewish Gynaecological Texts in the Middle Ages,* Brill (1998).

Barrow, John, *Dictionarium medicum universale: or, a New medical dictionary. Containing an explanation of all the terms used in physic, anatomy ... chymistry, etc* (1749).

Basham, A.L., *The Wonder That Was India: A Survey of the Culture of the Indian Sub-Continent before the coming of the Muslims* (1954).

Basham, A.L., *The Wonder That Was India. A Survey of the Culture of the Indian Sub-Continent before the coming of the Muslims* (1954).

BBC, "Cannabis burned during worship by ancient Israelites" (2020).

Bedrosian, Robert, "Soma Among the Armenians," (2006) http://rbedrosian.com/soma.htm

Bell, William, *Shakespeare's Puck, and His Folk-lore, Illustrated from the Superstitions of All Nations: Especially from the Earliest Religion and Rites of Northern Europe...* (1852).

Bellon, Father Angelo, "Ask a Priest" https://www.amicidomenicani.it/dopo-la-lettura-di-alcune-ricerche-archeologiche-sono-venuto-a-conoscenza-del-fatto-che-gli-ebrei-usassero-allinterno-del-tempio-sia-lincenso-che-la-cannabis/ (2021).

Bennett, Chris and McQueen, Neil, *Sex Drugs, Violence and the Bible,* Forbidden Fruit Publishing (2001).

Bennett, Chris and Osburn, Lynn and Judy, *Green Gold the Tree of Life; Marijuana in Magic and Religion,* Access Unlimited (1995).

Bennett, Chris, *Cannabis and the Soma Solution,* TrineDay (2010).

Bennett, Chris, *Liber 420: Cannabis, Magickal Herbs and the Occult,* TrineDay (2018).

Ben-Yehuda, Nahum, 'Cannabis – Chanvre – Hemp in Rashi's Commentary to the Talmud', https://www.academia.edu/11834393/Cannabis_Chanvre_Hemp_in_Rashis_commentary_to_the_Talmud (2011).

Benedict, Ruth; "Anthropology and the Abnormal," *Journal of General Psychology* (1934).

Benet, Sula, [aka Sara Benetowa] "Tracing one Word Through Different Languages" (1936), in *The Book of Grass,* Andrews,(1967).

Benet, Sula; "Early Diffusions and Folk Uses of Hemp," in *Cannabis and Culture,* Vera Rubin Editor, The Hague: Moutan (1975).

Benjamin, Samuel Greene Wheeler, *Troy: Its Legend, History and Literature* (1880).

Betuel, Emma, "Does This Medieval Fresco Show A Hallucinogenic Mushroom in the Garden of Eden?" Atlas Obscura, (2021).

Bey, Hakim and Zug, Abel, *Orgies of the Hemp Eaters,* Autonomedia (2004).

Bible Flowers and Flower Lore (1885).

Bickerman, Elias Joseph and Smith, Morton, *The Ancient History of Western Civilization.*

Blavatsky, H.P., *The Secret Doctrine,* Theosophical Publishing Company, Ltd. (1888).

Bleeck, Arthur Henry and von Spiegel, Friedrich, *Avesta* (1864).

Bloch-Smith, Elizabeth in "Judean Pillar Figurines, 8th century BCE" http://cojs.org/judean_pillar_figurines-_8th_century_bce/ (2008).

Bloom, Harold, *The Book of J*, Grove Weidenfeld (1990).

Böck, Barbara, "Mind Altering Plants in Babylonian Medical Sources," *The Routledge Companion to Ecstatic Experience in the Ancient World,* Edited By Diana Stein, Sarah Kielt Costello, Karen Polinger Foster, Taylor & Francis (2022).

Boertien, Jeannette H., "Asherah and Textiles," https://www.academia.edu/8580086/Asherah_and_Textiles (2007).

Bonnefoy, Yves, and Doniger, Wendy, *Asian mythologies*, Translated by Wendy Doniger, Gerald Honigsblum, Edition: 2, University of Chicago Press (1993).

Bosc, Ernest, *Petite Encyclopedie Synthetique des Sciences Occultes,* Translated from the French by Pierre J. Surette (1904).

Bottero, Jean. *Religion in Ancient Mesopotamia,* University of Chicago Press (2004).

Bouquet, R.J., "Cannabis," *Bull Narc* (1950).

Bowles, Gordon T., *The People of Asia* (1977).

Boyce, Mary and Grenet, Frantz, *A History of Zoroastrianism,* Brill (1982).

Boyce, Mary, "Haoma Ritual," *Iranian Religions: Zoroastrianism* (1990).

Boyce, Mary, "Zoroastrianism I, A History of Zoroastrianism," Contributor Frantz Grenet, Roger Beck, Brill (1982).

Boyce, Mary, *Acta Iranica* 24-25,2 vols. in BSOAS 50, (1987).

Boyce, Mary, *Zoroastrians: Their Religious Beliefs and Practices,* Routledge (1979/2001).

Brashear, W.M. "Varia Magica = Papyrologica Bruxellensia 25" (1991) in (Luck, 1985/2006).

Bridge, Mark, "Judean worshippers were high on cannabis, archaeologists reveal," *The Times* (UK) (2020).

Brotteaux, Pascal, *Hachich: Herbe de Folie et de Rêve,* Vega, Paris (1934).

Brown, George W., *Researches in Oriental History* (1890).

Brown, Jerry and Brown, Judy, *The Psychedelic Gospels: The Secret History of Hallucinogens in Christianity,* Inner Traditions (2016).

Budge , Ernest Alfred Wallis, *Babylonian Life and History,* Barnes & Noble Publishing, (1925, 2005).

Budge, Ernest Alfred Wallis, *Osiris and the Egyptian Resurrection* (1911).

Bunsen, E.K., *The Keys of St. Peter* (1867).

Burman, Edward, *The Assassins: The Holy Killers,* Crucible (1987).

Burton, Richard Francis, *A Plain and Literal Translation of the Arabian Nights,* Kama Shastra society, Benares (1894).

Cahagnet, Louis Alphonse, *Sanctuary of Spiritualism* (1848).

Campbell, George L., *Compendium of the World's Languages: Ladakhi to Zuni,* Edition: 2, revised, Taylor & Francis, (2000).

Campbell, J. M., "On the Religion of Hemp," *Indian Hemp Drugs Commission Report 1893-94,* Young, M., et.al, (Government Central Printing Office (1894).

Campbell, Joseph, *Occidental Mythology,* Viking Penguin (1964).

Campbell, Joseph, *Oriental Mythology,* Penguin Books (1962).

Camphausen, Rufus C., *The Encyclopedia of Erotic Wisdom*, Inner Traditions (1991).

Chakraberty, Chandra, *The Racial History of India*, (1944).

Charriere, Georges, *Scythian Art: Crafts of the Early Eurasian Nomads*, New York (1979).

Chopra, Ram Nath and Chopra, Ishwar Chander, Drug Addiction, with Special Reference to India, Council of Scientific & Industrial Research (1965).

Christen, "On the Nature of Opium," *The Quarterly Journal of Foreign and British Medicine and Surgery* (1822).

Clark, Houston, "Drug Cult," *Encyclopedia Britannica*, 5th edition, (1978).

Clarke, Robert C. and Merlin, Mark D., *Cannabis: Evolution and Ethnobotany*, University of California Press (2016).

Cole, William G., *Sex and Love in the Bible*, Association Press (1959).

Colenso, Bishop, *The Pentateuch and Book of Joshua Critically Examined* (1863).

Conner, Randy P., *Blossom of Bone*, Harper-Collins (1993).

Contenau, G., *La divination chez les Assyriens et les Babyloniens*. Avec 13 figures, 1 carte et 8 gravures hors texte. Payot, Paris, (1940).

Cotterell, Arthur, *The First Great Powers: Babylon and Assyria*, Hurst (2019)

Cowan, Robert, *The Indo-German Identification: Reconciling South Asian Origins and European Destinies*, Camden House (2010).

Cradic, Melissa S., "Sensing the Dead in Household Burials of the Second Millennium BCE," *The Routledge Handbook of the Senses in the Ancient Near East*, Edited By Kiersten Neumann, Allison Thomason (2022).

Cradic, Melissa Sarah, "Transformations in Death: The Archaeology of Funerary Practices and Personhood in the Bronze Age Levant," https://escholarship.org/uc/item/8mk978jc (2017)

Creighton, Dr.C., "On Indications of the Hachish-Vice in the Old Testament," *Janus*, Archives Internationales pours l'Histoire de la Medecine et la Geogrphie Mediacale, Huiteme Anee (1903).

Crone, Patricia, *Meccan Trade and the Rise of Islam*, Gorgias Press (2015).

Curley, Michael J. Translator, *Physiologus: A Medieval Book of Nature Lore*, Being an English Version of the Bodleian Library, Oxford M.S. Bodley 764: with All the Original Miniatures Reproduced in Facsimile, Bodleian Library (1993).

Danielou, A., *Le Polytheisme Hinduo*, Paris (1960).

Danielou, Alain, *Gods of Love and Ecstacy; The Traditions of Shiva and Dionysus*, Inner Traditions (1992).

Daniely, Dvora Lederman, "Who's Afraid of the Goddess of Ancient Israel?," *The Ancient Near East Today* (June, 2022).

Dannaway, Frederick R., "Strange Fire," Delaware Tea Society, (2009).

Dannaway, Frederick, "Celestial Botany Entheogenic Traces in Islamic Mysticism," (2007)http://www.scribd.com/doc/15744793/Celestial-Botany-Entheogenic-Traces-in-Islamic-Mysticism

Darmesteter J., *Zend-Avesta, Part I, The Vendidad*, Oxford University, London (1895).

Darmesteter, James, *Etudes Iraniennes*, 2 vols., Paris (1883).

Darmesteter, James, *The Zend Avesta*, Oxford (1880).

Daryoush, Jahanian Dr., "Medicine in Avesta and Ancient Iran," *FEZANA Journal,* (2005).

David, Ariel, "Bong Age? Israeli Archaeologists Find Opium in Bronze Age Ceramics," *Haaretz* (2022).

David, Ariel, "Holy Smoke/Ancient Israelites Used Cannabis as Temple Offering, Study Finds," *Haaretz* (2020).

Day, John, "Asherah in the Hebrew Bible and Northwest Semitic Literature," *Journal of Biblical Literature,* Vol. 105, No. 3 (1986).

de Jong, Albert, *Traditions of the Magi: Zoroastrianism in Greek and Latin Literature,* Brill (1997).

Deva, Indra and Shrirama, *Society and Culture in India: Their Dynamics Through the Ages* (1999).

Dever, William G., "Asherah, Consort of Yahweh? New Evidence from Kuntillet Ajrfid," *Bulletin of the American Schools of Oriental Research,* No. 255, The University of Chicago Press (1984).

Dever, William, *Did God Have a Wife?* Eerdmans Publishing Company (2005).

Dever, William, Lecture, "Did God Have a Wife," https://www.youtube.com/watch?v=Hjx1c3NAVTQ (2013).

de Zande, Ann, "What Does the Bible Say about Smoking Weed?" christianity.com (2023)

Dickens, Charles, *All the Year Round* (1862).

Dictionary of Deities and Demons in the Bible, Karel van der Toorn (Editor), Bob Becking (Editor), Pieter W. van der Horst (Editor) (1998).

Dobroruka , V., "Aspects of late Second Temple Jewish Apocalyptic, A Cross Cultural Comparison," (2002).

Dobroruka , V., "Chemically-Induced Visions in the Fourth Book of Ezra in Light of Comparative Persian Material," *Jewish Studies Quarterly,* (2006).

Doniger (O'Flaherty), W., *Somatic' memories of R. Gordon Wasson, The Sacred Mushroom Seeker: Essays on R. Grodon Wasson,* Riedlinger, Ed., Portland (1990).

Douglas, Alex, "The Garden of Eden, the Ancient Temple, and Receiving a New Name," *Ascending the Mountain of the Lord: Temple, Praise, and Worship in the Old Testament,* David Rolph Seely, Jeffrey R. Chadwick, and Matthew J. Grey, Editors (2013).

Drahl, C., "Frankincense And Myrrh'," *Chemical & Engineering News,* Published by American Chemical Society (2008).

Du Toit, Brian M., S. "Pot by any other name is still ... A study of the diffusion of cannabis," https://journals.co.za/doi/pdf/10.10520/AJA02580144_686 (1996).

Dubash, Sorabji Edalji, *The Zoroastrian Sanitary Code, with Critical and Explanatory Notes,* Sanj Vartaman Print. Press (1906).

Duke, James A., *Duke's Handbook of Medicinal Plants of the Bible,* CRC Press (2007).

Dynes, Wayne R. *et al., Encyclopedia of Homosexuality,* Routledge (1990).

Easton, *The Ultimate Bible Dictionary,* Jazzybee Verlag (2012).

Eisler, Riane, *The Chalice & the Blade,* Harper & Row (1987).

Eliade, Mircea, "Ancient Scythia and Iran," excerpted from *Shamanism: Archaic techniques of Ecstasy,* (1964), and reprinted in *The Book of Grass,* (1967).

Eliade, Mircea and Adams, Charles J., *The Encyclopedia of Religion,* Macmillan (1987).

Eliade, Mircea, *A History of Religious Ideas,* Vol.I, (University of Chicago Press (1978).

Eliade, Mircea, *A History of Religious Ideas,* Vol.II, University of Chicago Press (1982).

Eliade, Mircea, *A History of Religious Ideas,* Vol.III, University of Chicago Press (1985).

Eliade, Mircea, *Myth and Reality,* Harper & Row (1963).

Eliade, Mircea, *Myths, Rites, Symbols,*Vol.2, Harper Colophon Books (1975).

Eliade, Mircea, *Shamanism: Archaic techniques of Ecstasy,* Princeton University Press (1964).

Eliade, Mircea, *The Myth of the Eternal Return,* Bollingen Foundation Inc., (1954).

Eliade, Mircea, *Mephistopheles et l'Androgynee,* Paris (1962).

Ellicott, Charles John, *An Old Testament Commentary for English Readers,* Oxford University (1884).

Emboden, William A. Jr., "Ritual Use of *Cannabis Sativa* L.: A Historic-Ethnographic Survey," in *Flesh of the Gods,* P.T.Furst, Ed. (Praeger, New York, 1972).

Erbt, Wilhelm, *Die Hebraer: Kanaan im Zietalter der herbraischer Wanderung und hebraischer Staatengrundungen* (1906).

Espak, Peeter, *The God Enki in Sumerian Royal Ideology and Mythology,* Harrassowitz Verlag (2015).

Eznik , Book I. 68.

Fales, Frederick Mario, *Studies on Neo-Assyrian Texts II: "Deeds and documents" from the British Museum,* https://www.degruyter.com/document/doi/10.1515/zava.1983.73.2.232/html (1983).

Fallows, Samuel; Zenos, Andrew Constantinides; Willett, Herbert Lockwood, *The Popular and Critical Bible Encyclopdia and Scriptural Dictionary Fully Defining and Explaining All Religious Terms, Including Biographical, Geographical, Historical, Archŏlogical and Doctrinal Themes,* Volume 3 (1901).

Feinberg, Todd E.; Keenan, Julian Paul, *The Lost Self: Pathologies of the Brain and Identity,* Oxford Univ Pr, Cary, North Carolina, U.S.A., (2005).

Fischer-Rizzi, Susanne, *Complete Aromatherapy Handbook: Essential Oils for Radiant Health,* (Sterling Publishing Co., 1990).

Flattery, David Stophlet and Schwartz, Martin, *Haoma, and Harmaline: The Botanical Identity of the Indo-Iranian Sacred Hallucinogen "Soma" and Its Legacy in Religion, Language, and Middle Eastern Folklore,* Berkeley, Los Angeles, and London (1989).

Fleming, Michael P and Clarke, Robert Connell, 'Physical evidence for the antiquity of *Cannabis sativa* L' https://www.researchgate.net/publication/228603981_Physical_evidence_for_the_antiquity_of_Cannabis_sativa_L (1998).

Foster, Karen Polinger; Stein, Diana; Costello, Sarah Kielt, "From Opium to Saffron, the Ancients Knew a Thing or Two About Drugs," *The Nation* (2022).

Fox, Michael, *The Song of Songs and the Ancient Egyptian Love Songs,* University of Wisconsin Press (1985).

Frank, Harry Thomas, *An Archaeological Companion to the Bible,* S.C.M. Press (1972)

Frazer, Sir James George, *The Golden Bough: A Study in Comparative Religion* (1890/1922).

Freeman, Tzvi. "Is there evidence of Abraham's revolution? – The Big Picture,"

Chabad.org. (2011).

Freud, Sigmund, *Moses and Monotheism*, New York (1939).

Fride, Ester; Bregman, Tatyana; Kirkham, Tim, "Endocannabinoids and Food Intake: Newborn Suckling and Appetite Regulation in Adulthood" *Sage Journals* (2016) First published online November 29, 2016.

Frymer-Kensky, Tikva, *In the Wake of the Goddess: Women, Culture and the Biblical Transformation of Pagan Myth*, Ballantine Books (1992).

Gadon, Elinor W., *The Once and Future Goddess*, Harper & Row (1989).

Garraty, John A. and Gay, Peter, *Columbia History of the Word*, Dorset Press, Harper and Row, NY, (1981).

Garraty, John Arthur and Gay, Peter, *The Columbia History of the World*, Harper & Row (1972).

Geiwitz, James, Ph.D., and the Ad Hoc Committee on Hemp Risks, "THC in Hemp Foods and Cosmetics: The Appropriate Risk Assessment," January 15, (2001).

George, Arthur, "Yahweh's Divorce from the Goddess Asherah in the Garden of Eden" https://mythologymatters.wordpress.com/2014/10/06/yahwehs-divorce-from-the-goddess-asherah-in-the-garden-of-eden/ (2014).

Georgiou, Aristos, "Cannabis Discovered in Shrine from Biblical Israeli Kingdom May Have Been Used in Hallucinogenic Cult Rituals," *Newsweek* (2020).

Gerloczy, Zsigmond, *Jelentés az 1894. szeptember hó 1-töl 9-ig Budapesten tartott VIII-ik Nemzetközi közegészségi* és *demografiai congressusról* és *annak tudományos munkálatairól.*

Gile, Jason, *Ezekiel and the World of Deuteronomy*, Bloomsbury Publishing (2021).

Glassman, Yosef quoted in "Am Yisrael High: Cannabis in Jewish Tradition" by Miriam Anzovin for *JewishBoston* (2018).

Gnoli, G. "Bang" (1979) Accessed at http://www.iranica.com/newsite.

Gnoli, Gherardo, *East and West 39*, 1989, pp. 320-24, and by K. Mylius, in IIJ 35, (1992).

Gnoli, Gherardo, *Lichtsymbolik in Alt-Iran: Haoma-Ritus und Erlöser-Mythos*, Antaios 8 (1967).

Godbey, Allen H., "Incense and Poison Ordeals in the Ancient Orient," *The American Journal of Semitic Languages and Literatures*, Vol. 46, No. 4, The University of Chicago Press (1930).

Goldfrank, et. al., *Goldfrank's Toxicologic Emergencies*, By Lewis R. Goldfrank, Neal Flomenbaum, Robert S. Hoffmann, Mary Ann Howland, Neal A. Lewin, Lewis S. Nelson, McGraw-Hill Professional (2002).

Gordon Wasson, *Soma: Divine Mushroom of Immortality*, Harcourt Brace Jovanovich (1968).

Gordon, R. P., *Hebrew Bible and Ancient Versions: Selected Essays of Robert P. Gordon*, Ashgate Publishing Company (2006).

Gowen, Herbert Henry, *A History of Religion*, Society for Promoting Christian Knowledge (1934).

Graindorge, Catherine, "The Onions of Sokar," *Revue d'Egyptologie*, 43, (1992).

Granta, Igor and Cahnb, Rael, '"Cannabis and endocannabinoid modulators: Therapeutic promises and challenges," Clin Neurosci Res. (2005).

Graves, Robert and Patai, Raphael, *Hebrew Myths: The Book of Genesis,* (1963).

Graves, Robert, "The Divine Rites of Mushrooms," *The Atlantic,* February (1970).

Gray, John, *Near Eastern Mythology; Mesopotamia, Syria, Palestine,* The Hamlyn Group (1969).

Green, Samuel G., *A Biblical and Theological Dictionary* (1840).

Greenblatt, Robert, M.D., *Search the Scriptures: A Physician Examines medicine in the Bible,* Lippincott (1963).

Greenboim Rich, Viktoria, "7,500-year-old Burial in Eilat Contains Earliest Asherah," *Haaretz* (2022).

Grinspoon, Lester M.D. and Bakalar, James, *Marihuana; The Forbidden Medicine,* Yale University Press (1993).

Grinspoon, Lester;, M.D., *Marihuana Reconsidered,* Quick American Archives (1971).

Grinspoon, Peter, MD, "The endocannabinoid system: Essential and mysterious" https://www.health.harvard.edu/blog/the-endocannabinoid-system-essential-and-mysterious-202108112569 (August 11, 2021).

Griswold, H.D., *The Religion of the Rigveda,* Oxford University Press (1923).

Groom, N., *The Perfume Handbook,* Springer Netherlands (2012).

Guenther, Allen R., *Hosea, Amos: Believers Church Bible Commentary* (1998).

Gutmann, Joseph, *No Graven Images: Studies in Art and the Hebrew Bible,* Ktav Publishing House (1971).

Haas, Volkert, *Geschichte der hethitischen Religion* (1994).

Hackman, George Gotlob, *Temple Documents of the Third Dynasty of Ur From Umma,* Yale University (1937).

HaLevi, Baruch quoted in "Am Yisrael High: Cannabis in Jewish Tradition" by Miriam Anzovin for *JewishBoston* (2018).

Hallet, Jean, Pierre, and Pelle, Alex, *Pygmy Kitabu,* (Fawcett Crest, 1975).

Hanu, Lumír Ondej, "Pharmacological and therapeutic secrets of plant and brain (Endo)cannabinoids" Wiley Company (2008).

Harris, Maurice Henry, Ed., *The Project Gutenberg eBook, Hebraic Literature; Translations from the Talmud, Midrashim and Kabbala, by Various,* (2004).

Harris, Maurice Henry, *Hebraic Literature; Translations from the Talmud, Midrashim* (1901/2019).

Harris, Rendel, *Eucharistic Origins,* Cambridge W. Heffer & Sons, Ltd., (1927).

Hassan, Hadrul, *The Drink and Drug Evil in India,* Ganesh& Co. (1922).

Hatsis, Tom, personal correspondence (2016/2017).

Hatsis, Tom, *The Witches' Ointment: The Secret History of Psychedelic Magic,* Inner Trditions (2015).

Haug, Martin, *Aitereya Brahamana of the Rigveda, Translated and Explained,* Bombay, (1863).

Hellholm, et. al., *Apocalypticism in the Mediterranean World and the Near East: Proceedings of the International Colloquium on Apocalypticism, Uppsala,* August 12-17, 1979, By David Hellholm, Kungl. Vitterhets, historie och antikvitets akademien, Uppsala universitet Teologiska fakulteten, Mohr Siebeck (1989).

Henning, Walter Bruno, *Zoroaster: Politician or Witch-Doctor?*, Ratanbai Katrak Lectures 3, (1949) Oxford, (1951).

Henslow, G., *The Vulgate the Source of False Doctrines*, BiblioLife (2009).

Herer, Jack, *The Emperor Wears No Clothes: Hemp and the Marijuana Conspiracy* (1990).

Herzog, Ze'ev, "The Fortress Mound at Tel Arad an Interim Report," *Journal of the Institute of Archaeology of Tel Aviv University* (2002).

Hewitt, James Francis Katherinus, *History and Chronology of the Myth-making Age*, (1901)

Hillman, David, *Smoke of the Oracles*, documentary (2015)

Hinnells, John R., *Persian Mythology*, The Hamlyn Publishing Group (1973).

Hirsch, Emil and Löw, Immanuel, *Jewish Encyclopedia* (2005).

Hoiberg, Dale and Ramchandani, *Indu, Students' Britannica India: India* (Set of 7 Vols.) 39, Popular Prakashan, (2000).

Holladay, John S., "Religion in Israel and Judah Under the Monarchy: An Explicitly Archaeological Approach," *Ancient Israelite Religion* (1987).

Hooke. S.H., *Middle Eastern Mythology*, Penguin Books (1963).

Horry, Ruth, "Tašmetu (goddess)" http://oracc.museum.upenn.edu/amgg/listofdeities/tametu/index.html (2013).

Houtsma, et. al., *E.J. Brill's First Encyclopaedia of Islam*, 1913-1936, By Martijn Theodoor Houtsma, M. Th. Houtsma, T. W. Arnold, A. J. Wensinck, (1987/1993).

Hutchison, Michael, *The Anatomy of Sex and Power*, William Morrow and Company, Inc. (1990).

Idem, "On the Iranian Soma and Pers. sepand 'Wild Rue,'" *East and West* 43 (1993).

Irenaeus of Lyons, *Adversus haereses*, Book I, (178).

Jafarey, Ali A., "Haoma: Its Original and Later Identity" (2000).

Janick J, Paris HS., "Jonah and the *gourd* at Nineveh: consequences of a classic mistranslation," *Proceedings of Cucurbitaceae* 2006 – Holmes GJ, ed. Raleigh, NC: Universal Press. (2006).

Jaynes, Julian, *The Origins of Consciousness in the Breakdown of the Bicamerial Mind*, Houghton Mifflin Company, Boston (1976).

Jeanmaire, H., *Dionysos, Histoire du culte de Bacchus*, Paris (1951).

Johnson, Buffie, *Lady of the Beasts*, Harper & Row (1981).

Johnson, Paul, *A History of the Jews*, Harper Collins (1987).

Johnston, Philip, "Figuring Out Figurines," *Tyndale Bulletin*, Volume: TYNBUL 54:2 (2003).

Johnston, Sarah Iles, *Religions of the Ancient World: A Guide*, Harvard University Press (2004).

Kabelik, Prof. Jan, "Hemp as a Medicament," *History of the Medicinal use of Hemp* (1955).

Kang, Seung, "The Garden of Eden as an Israelite Sacred Place," *Theology Today*, Volume 77, Issue 1 (2020).

Kaplan, Aryeh, *The Living Torah and Nach*, Moznaim Publishing Corporation (1981).

Keel, Othmar, *The Song of Songs, Continental Commentaries*, Fortress Press (1994).

Kelle, Brad E., *Hosea 2: Metaphor and Rhetoric in Historical Perspective,* Society of Biblical Literature (2005).

Khan, A. J., "Medicinal properties of frankincense," *International Journal of Nutrition, Pharmacology* (2012)

Kia, Mehrdad, *The Persian Empire: A Historical Encyclopedia* (2016).

Kien, Jenny, *Reinstating the Divine Woman in Judaism,* Universal Publishers (2000).

Kirkpatrick, Jonathan, *The Jews and their God of Wine,* https://www.degruyter.com/document/doi/10.1515/arege-2013-0012/html (2013).

Kisel, V.A., "Herodotus Scythian logos and ritual vessels of the early nomads," *Archaeology, Ethnology and Anthropology of Eurasia,* Volume 31, Number 3 (2007).

Kitto, John, *A Cyclopaedia of Biblical literature,* New York (1846-1885).

Klein, Siegfried, *Tod und Begräbnis in Palästina zur Zeit der Tannaiten* (1908)

La Barre, Weston, *Culture in Context; Selected Writings of Weston La Barre,* Duke University Press (1980).

La Barre, Weston, *The Ghost Dance: The Origins of Religion,* Delta Books (1970).

Langdon, Stephen Herbert, *Mythology of All Races – Semitic* (1931).

Lawler, Andrew, "Cannabis, opium use part of ancient Near Eastern cultures," *Science,* Vol 360, Issue 6386 (2018).

Lawrence, Reverend E. A, "Wine of the Bible," *Princeton Review,* Volume 43 (1871).

Layard, Austen Henry, *Discoveries among the ruins of Nineveh and Babylon,* New York (1856).

Lenormant, Francois and Lockwood, Mary Smith; et. al., *The Beginnings of History According to the Bible and the Traditions of Oriental Peoples: From the Creation of Man to the Deluge,* C. Scribner's Sons (1881).

Lenormant, Francois, *Le Magie chez les Chaldeans, Maisonneuve et Cie.* (1874). As translated and quoted in (Andrews 1997).

Linares, Jakoel, Be'eri, Lipschits, Neumann, & Gadot, "Opium trade and use during the Late Bronze Age: Organic residue analysis of ceramic vessels from the burials of Tel Yehud, Israel" https://onlinelibrary.wiley.com/doi/10.1111/arcm.12806 (2022)

Linssen, Marc J. H , *The Cults of Uruk and Babylon: The Temple Ritual Texts As Evidence for Hellenistic Cult Practises,* Brill (2004).

Löw, Immanuel, *Die Flora Der Juden,* (Georg Olms Verlagsbuchhandlung Hildesheim 1967; originally published as *Flora der Juden* in 1924).

Lucas, A. and Harris, J., *Ancient Egyptian Materials and Industries,* Courier Corporation (2012).

Lucas, Alfred, *Ancient Egyptian Materials & Industries,* E. Arnold & Company (1934).

Lucas, Alfred, *Ancient Egyptian Materials & Industries,* Dover Publications (1937).

Luck, Georg, "Psychoactive Substances in Religion and Magic" in *Arcana Mundi: Magic and the Occult in the Greek and Roman Worlds: A Collection of Ancient Texts,* Johns Hopkins University Press (1985/2006).

Mackenzie, Donald Alexander, *Myths of Babylonia and Assyria* (1915).

Magee, Dr M.D., Persia & Creation of Judaism, https://www.cais-soas.com/CAIS/Religions/non-iranian/Judaism/Persian_Judaism/Persia_created_judaism.htm (1998, 2008).

Mallory, J. P. and Adams, Douglas Q., *Encyclopedia of Indo-European Culture,* Taylor & Francis (1997).

Malyon & Henman, *New Scientist,* Published by IPC Magazines, (1980).

Mandihassan, S., Etymology of Names-Cannabis and Ephedra, *Studies in the History of Medicine,* Vol. 6 (1982).

Mandihassan, S., "The Seven Theories Identifying the Soma Plant," *Ancient Science of Life* (1989).

Manniche, Lise, *An Ancient Egyptian Herbal,* University of Texas Press (1986).

Manniche, Lise, *An Ancient Egyptian Herbal,* University of Texas Press (1989).

Marglin, Frederique, *Wives of the God-King: The Rituals of the Devadasis of Puri,* New York: Oxford University Press (1985).

Margolis,Peter, "Lessons of Eish Zarah: The Ritual use of Kaneh-Bosm," *Central Conference of American Rabbis Spring/Summer 2021 Journal* (2021).

Marihuana: A Signal of Misunderstanding First Report, By United States. Commission on Marihuana and Drug Abuse (1972).

Martínez, Florentino García and Barrera, Julio C. Trebolle, *The People of the Dead Sea Scrolls,* E.J. Brill (1995).

Mathre, Mary Lynn, *Cannabis in Medical Practice: A Legal, Historical and Pharmacological Overview of the Therapeutic Use of Marijuana,* McFarland (1997).

McClintock and Strong Biblical Cyclopedia (1867).

McGinn, et. al., *The Encyclopedia of Apocalypticism,* Contributor Bernard McGinn, John Joseph Collins, Stephen J. Stein, International Publishing Group (2000).

McGovern, Patrick E., *Ancient Wine: The Search for the Origins of Viniculture,* Princeton University Press, (2003).

McGovern, Patrick E., *Uncorking the Past: The Quest for Wine, Beer, and Other Alcoholic Beverages,* University of California Press (2009).

McKenna, Terence, *Food of the Gods,* (Bantam Books,1992).

McPartland, J.M., Guy, G., "The evolution of Cannabis and coevolution with the cannabinoid receptor – a hypothesis," In: Guy, G., Robson, R., Strong, K., Whittle, B. (Eds.), *The Medicinal Use of Cannabis.* Royal Society of Pharmacists, London, (2004).

Mead, GRS, *Fragments of a Faith Forgotten: Some Short Sketches Among the Gnostics of the First Two Centuries,* Theosophical Publishing Society, London and Benares (1900).

Mechoulam, Raphae, "The Pharmacohistory of *Cannabis sativa,*" *Cannabinoids as Therapeutic Agents,* CRC Press (1986).

Medrano, Kastalia "Toilet Found in 3,000-Year-Old Shrine Verifies Bible Stories Against Idol Worship," *Newsweek* (2017).

Meek, T.J., "Babylonian Parallels to the Song of Songs," *Journal of Biblical Literature,* Vol. 43, No. 3/4 (1924).

Merkur, Daniel, "Prophetic Initiation in Israel and Judah," *The Psychoanalytic Study of Society,* Edited by L.B. Boyer & S. A. Grolnick, The Analytic Press (1988).

Merlin, M., "Archaeological Record for Ancient Old World Use of Psychoactive Plants," *Economic Botany,* 57(3): (2003).

Merlin, Mark, *Man and Marijuana,* Barnes and Co. (1972).

Messadié, Gérald and Romano, Marc, *A History of the Devil,* Translated by Marc Romano, Kodansha International (1996).

Metzger, Deena; "Re-Vamping the World: On the Return of the Holy Prostitute," *Utne Reader*, Aug/Sept (1985).

Midgley, T. "The Textiles and Matting" (1928)in: G. Brunton, G. Caton Thompson, *The Badarian Civilisation and Predynastic Remains near Badari*,(1937).

Midgley, T. in Brinton, G., *Mostegedda and the Tasian Culture*, London (1937).

Mikuriya, Todd H. M.D.,Ed., *Marijuana Medical Papers*, Medi-Comp Press (1973).

Mirfendereski, Guive, Homavarka: "The Potheads of Ancient Iran," www.iranian.com (May, 17, 2005).

Mirfendereski, Guive, *The Saka Nomenclature, A Persian appraisal*, (2006)

Mitteilungen zur Geschichte der Medizin und der Naturwissenschaften (1905)

Mitteilungen zur Geschichte der Medizin und der Naturwissenschaften (1907)

Mondriaan, Marlene, "Who Were the Kenites," *The Old Testament Society of Southern Africa* (2011).

Morneau, Daniel, "The Punic Warship," Saudi, *Aramco World*, (November/December, 1986)

Mozeson, Isaac E., *The Word: The Dictionary That Reveals the Hebrew Source of English*, Shapolsky Publishers (1989).

Muhammad, Wesley Dr., "Cannabis and the Ancient Cult of the White Feminine," *The Pot Plot: Marijuana and the Chemical Feminization of a Generation* (2022).

Muller, F. Max, *Chips from a German Workshop Part One*, [Kessinger Publishing, 2004] (1873).

Muraresku, Brian C., *The Immortality Key: The Secret History of the Religion with No Name*, St. Martin's Publishing Group (2020).

Murphy,Terrence; Ben-Yehuda, Nahum; Taylor, R.E.: Southon, John R., "Hemp in ancient rope and fabric from the Christmas Cave in Israel: Talmudic background and DNA sequence identification," *Journal of Archaeological Science* (2011).

Namdar, Dvory; Maeir, Aren M.; Gadot, Yuval; Iserlis, Mark, "Tracking Down Cult: Production, Function and Content of Chalices in Iron Age Philistia," TEL AVIV Vol. 41,(2014)

Needelman-Ruiz, Yoseph, Personal Correspondence (2022).

Neumann, Erich, *The Great Mother*, [translated by Ralph Mannheim] Princeton University Press (1955).

Noegel, Scott B. and Wheeler, Brannon M., *The A to Z of Prophets in Islam and Judaism*, Scarecrow Press (2010).

Nunn, John F., *Ancient Egyptian Medicine*, University of Oklahoma Press (2002).

Nyberg, Harri, "The Problem of the Aryans and the Soma: the botanical evidence," in *Erdosy* (1995)

Nyberg, Henrik Samuel, *Irans forntida religioner*, tr. Hans Heinrich Schaeder as Die Religionen des Alten Iran, Mitteilungen der Vorderasiatisch-aegyptischen Gesellschaft 43, (1938).

Oisteanu, Andrei, "Mircea Eliade, de la opium la amfetamine," *Revisita 22* (2007).

Oliver, Prof. Revilo P., *The Origins of Christianity*, (Urbana 1994).

Omidsalar, Mahmoud, "DŪḠ-EWAḤDAT, Beverage of Unity," *Encyclopaedia Iranica* (1999).

Oorschot, Jürgen van and Witte, Markus, *The Origins of Yahwism*, De Gruyter (2017).

Osburn, L., "Hemp seed: the most nutritionally complete food source in the world," *Hemp Line* (1993).

Ott, Jonathan, Personal correspondence to Chris Bennett, August 18th, (1996).

Ott, Jonathan, *Pharmacotheon: Entheogenic Drugs Their Plant Sources and History*, Natural Products, Co. (1993).

Ott, Jonathan, *The Age of Entheogens and the Angels' Dictionary*, Natural Products Co. (1995).

Oursler, Will, *Marijuana, the facts, the Truth*, Paul S.Erikson, Inc. (1968).

Owen, Richard, "Lost Punic warships may rise in TV museum; Ancient wrecks found off the Sicilian coast date from the battle of the Egadi Islands in 241BC," *The Times*, (London; August 7, 2004)

Palmer, Abram Smythe, *Folk Etymology* (1882).

Parpola, Asko, "The problem of Aryans and the Soma: Textual-linguistic and archeological evidence," *Erdosy* (1995).

Parpola, Simo and Whiting, Robert M., *Compte Rendu, Rencontre Assyriologique Internationale*, 47, Neo-Assyrian Text Corpus Project (2002).

Parrinder, Geoffrey, *World Religions; From Ancient History to the Present*, Facts on File, NY, 1971/1983.

Parsche, Franz and Nerlich, Andreas, "Presence of drugs in different tissues of an Egyptian mummy," (1994) *Fresenius' Journal of Analytical Chemistry*, (1995).

Parsons, Charles W., *The Pharmaceutical Era*, Volume 22 (1899).

Patai, Raphael, *The Hebrew Goddess*, originally published in 1967, Wayne State University Press (1990).

Pearson, Birger A. as quoted in (Robinson, 1978).

Peet, Thomas Eric, *The City of Akhenaten* (1938).

Pendell,Dale, *Pharmako/poeia; Plant Powers Poisons and Herbcraft*, Mercury House (1995).

Perowne, John Ed., *Cambridge Bible for Schools and Colleges* (1882).

Petrie, W.M. Flinders and Mackay, E., *The Labyrinth Gerzeh and Mazghuneh*, University College (1912).

Pope, M. H. and Smith, M. S., *Probative pontificating in Ugaritic and biblical literature: collected essays* Münster, Ugarit-Verlag (1994).

Pope, Marvin H., *El in the Ugaritic Texts*, Brill (1955).

Pope, Marvin H., *Song of Songs: A New Translation with Introduction and Commentary*, Anchor Bible Series, Garden City, N.Y. (1977).

Popular Archeology, "New research reveals Cannabis and Frankincense at the Judahite Shrine of Biblical Arad."

Pourshariati, Parvaneh, *Decline and Fall of the Sasanian Empire: The Sasanian-Parthian Confederacy and the Arab Conquest of Iran*, I. B. Tauris (2008).

Pringle, Heather, *The Mummy Congress: Science, Obsession, and the Everlasting Dead*, Hachette Books (2001).

Pritchard, James B. Ed., *The Ancient Near East*, Vol.2, .Princeton University Press (1975).

Puett, Terry, *Institute Of Biblical Studies: The Book Of Genesis*, Lulu (2016).

Ramachandran and Mativāṇan, *The Spring of the Indus Civilisation* (1991).

Rand, William W., *The Bible Dictionary*, Delmarva Publications LLC (2015).

Rätsch, Christian, *Marijuana Medicine*, Inner Traditions, (1998, 2001).

Rätsch, Christian, *Plants of Love: Aphrodisiacs in Myth, History, and the Present*, Ten Speed Press, (1997).

Rätsch, Christian, *The Encyclopedia of Psychoactive Plants*, Inner Traditions (2005).

Rawlinson, G., *The Beginnings of History According to the Bible and the Traditions of Oriental Peoples: From the Creation of Man to the Deluge* (1881).

Rawlinson, G., *The Five Great Monarchies of the Eastern World* (1871).

Ray, Joges-Chandra, "The *Soma* plant," *Indian Historical Quarterly* (1939).

Reiner, Erica, *Astral Magic in Babylonia*, American Philosophical Society (1995).

Ren, Meng; Tang, Zihua; Wu, Xinhua; Spengler, Robert; Jiang, Hongen; Yang, Yimin and Boivin, Nicole, "The origins of cannabis smoking: Chemical residue evidence from the first millennium BCE in the Pamirs," *Science Advances*, Vol. 5, No. 6, (2019).

Riddle, John M., Goddesses, *Elixirs, and Witches: Plants and Sexuality Throughout Human History*, Palgrave Macmillian (2010).

Ringgren, Helmer , *Religions of the Ancient Near East*, Westminster Press (1973).

Roberts, W.B., *The New York Dental Journal* (1862).

Robinson, James M. General Editor, *The Nag Hammadi Scriptures: The Revised and Updated Translation of Sacred Gnostic Texts Complete in One Volume*, Harper-Collins (1978, 1988).

Robinson, Rowan, *The Great Book of Hemp: The Complete Guide to the Environmental, Commercial, and Medicinal Uses of the World's Most Extraordinary Plant*, Inner Traditions/Bear & Company (1995).

Rohde, Erwin, *Psyche: The Cult of Souls and the Belief in Immortality Among the Greeks*, Routledge and Kegan Paul (1925).

Rolfe, Robert Thatcher, *Romance of the Fungus World* (1925).

Rosch, Manfred, "Pollen analysis of the contents of excavated vessels – direct archaeobotanical evidence of beverages," Veget Hist Archaeobot (2005).

Rosenthal, Franz, *The Herb; Hashish Versus Medieval Muslim Society*, Brill (1971).

Rosetti, Dinu, Materiale şi cercetări arheologice, https://www.persee.fr/authority/850982 (1959).

Ruck, Carl, "Was There a Whiff of Cannabis About Jesus?" *The Sunday Times* (2003).

Ruck, Carl, affidavit in Bennett vs The Attorney General for Canada and the Minister of Health for Canada, (2009).

Ruck, Carl, Personal Correspondence (2020).

Ruck, Carl; Staples, Danny Blaise and Heinrich, Clark, *The Apples of Apollo: Pagan and Christian Mysteries of the Eucharist* (2001).

Ruck, et. al., "Conniving Wolves" chapter V, pages 87-124, in Carl A.P. Ruck, Blaise Daniel Staples, José Alfredo González Celdrán, and Mark Alwin Hoffmann, *The Hidden World: Survival of Pagan Shamanic Themes in European Fairytales* (Durham, NC: Carolina Academic Press, 2007).

Rudgley, Richard, *Essential Substances*, Kodansha International (1993).

Rudgley, Richard, *The Encyclopedia of Psychoactive Substances*, Little, Brown and Company, (1998).

Rudolph, Kurt, *Gnosis: The Nature and History of Gnosticism*, Harper, San Francisco (1987).

Russo, E,. "History of Cannabis as a Medicine," *The Medicinal Uses of Cannabis and Cannabinoids*, By Geoffrey William Guy, Brian Anthony Whittle, Philip Robson, Pharmaceutical Press (2004).

Russo, et. al., "Phytochemical and genetic analyses of ancient cannabis from Central Asia," *Journal of Experimental Botany* Oxford (2008).

Russo, Ethan M.D., Unpublished paper 2005, "Clinical Cannabis in Ancient Mesopotamia: A Historical Survey with Supporting Scientific Evidence," I wrote Ethan and he said most of that stuff was included in the following: Russo EB. "History of cannabis and its preparations in saga, science and sobriquet," Chemistry & Biodiversity 2007;4(8):2624-48.

Russo, Ethan, "Cannabis in India: ancient lore and modern Medicine," GW Pharmaceuticals, 2235 Wylie Avenue, Missoula, MT 59809, USA, *Cannabinoids as Therapeutics*, Edited by R. Mechoulam, Birkhäuser Verlag/Switzerland, (2005).

Russo, Ethan, "Hemp for Headache: An In-Depth Historical and Scientific Review of Cannabis in Migraine Treatment," *Journal of Cannabis Therapeutics* (2001).

Russo, Ethan, Pot TV interview (2003).

Sagan, Carl, *The Dragons of Eden: Speculations on the Evolution of Human Intelligence*, (Random House, NY, 1977).

Saggs, H.W.F., *The Greatness That Was Babylon; A Survey of the Ancient Civilization of the Tigris-Euphrates Valley*, Frederick A. Praeger, New York (1962).

Salzberger, G., *Salomons Tempelbau und Thron*, Mayer and Muller (1912).

Salzberger, Georg, *Salomos Tempelbau Und Thron in Der Semitischen Sagenliteratur* (1912).

Samuelson, James, *The History of Drink* (1880).

Sarianidi V., *Temples of Bronze Age Margiana: Traditions of Ritual Architecture*, Antiquity (1994).

Sarianidi V., *Margiana and Protozoroastrism*. Kapon Editions, (1998).

Sarianidi, Victor I. "Margiana and Soma-Haoma," *Electronic Journal of Vedic Studies*, Vol. 9 (2003).

Sayce, A.H., *Lectures on the Origin and Growth of Religion as Illustrated by the Religion of the Ancient Babylonians*, 5th ed., London (1898).

Schechter, M.; Weller, A.;Pittel, Z.; Gross, M.; Zimmer, A.; Pinhasov, A., "Endocannabinoid receptor deficiency affects maternal care and alters the dam's hippocampal oxytocin receptor and brain-derived neurotrophic factor expression," https://pubmed.ncbi.nlm.nih.gov/23895426/ (2013)

Schmithals, Walter, *Gnosticism in Corinth: An Investigation of the Letters to the Corinthians*, Abingdon Press (1971).

Schonfield, Dr. Hugh J., *The Passover Plot*, Bantam Books (1966).

Schultes, R.E., "Man and Marijuana," *Nat. Hist.* 82 (1973).

Schultes, Richard Evans and Albert Hoffmann; 1992, *Plants of the Gods-Origins of*

Hallucinogenic Use (McGraw-Hill Book Co. Ltd., England,1979). [Reprinted by Healing Arts Press in 1992].

Scurlock, JoAnn, *Sourcebook for Ancient Mesopotamian Medicine,* SBL Press (2014).

Sellon, Edward "On the Phallic Worship of India," *Memoirs of the Anthropological Society,* Vol.I, London (1865).

Seff, Phillip & Nancy, *Our Fascinating Earth,* (Contemporary Books, 1996)

Sepher Raziel: Liber Salomonis (1564).

Seydibeyoglu, M. Ozgur; Mohanty, Amar K. and Manjusri, Misra, *Fiber Technology for Fiber-Reinforced Composites* (2017).

Shaked, Shaul, '"Quests and Visionary Journeys in Sasanian Iran," Transformations of the Inner Self in Ancient Religions, By Jan Assmann, Gedaliahu A. G. Stroumsa, Brill, (1999).

Shanon, Benny Professor, *The Antipodes of the Mind:Charting the Phenomenology of the Ayahuasca Experience,* Oxford University Press (2002).

Sherratt, A. G., "Cups that cheered, Bell Beakers of the Western Mediterranean," BAR Int. Ser. 331, vol. 1. *British Archaeological Reports,* Oxford (1991).

Sherratt, A. G., "Alcohol and its alternatives: symbol and substance in pre-industrial cultures" in J. Goodman, E E. Lovejoy, and A. Sherratt. 1995. *Consuming Habits: Drugs in History and Anthropology,* Routledge, London and New York (1997).

Sherratt, A. G., "Introduction: Peculiar Substances" in J. Goodman, E E. Lovejoy, and A. Sherratt. 1995. *Consuming Habits: Drugs in History and Anthropology,* Routledge, London and New York (1995).

Sherratt, A. G., "Sacred and profane substances: the ritual use of narcotics in later Neolithic Europe" in E Garwood, D. Jennings, R. Skeates, andJ. Toms, eds., *Sacred and Profane: Proceedings of a Conference on Archaeology, Ritual and Religion,* Oxford University Committee for Archaeology Monographs. (1995).

Sherratt, Andrew, "Alcohol and its Alternatives:Symbol and substance in Pre-Industrial cultures," in *Consuming Habits: Drugs in History and Anthropology,* By Jordan Goodman, Paul E. Lovejoy, Andrew Sherratt, Contributor Jordan Goodman, Routledge (1995).

Sherratt, Andrew, *Economy and Society in Prehistoric Europe: Changing Perspectives,* (Princeton university, 1997).

Singer, Isodore and Adler, Cyrus *The Jewish Encyclopedia: A Descriptive Record of the History, Religion, Literature, and Customs of the Jewish People from the Earliest Times to the Present Day,* Volume 4, Funk & Wagnalls Company (1912).

Skolnik, Fred, *Encyclopedia Judaica,* Macmillan Reference, (2007).

Smith, W. Robertson, *Lectures on the Religions of the Semites* (Macmillian, 3rd ed., 1927).

Smith, Frederick John and Taylor, Alfred Swaine, *Taylor's Principles and Practice of Medical Jurisprudence: Edited, revised, and brought up to date by Fred. J. Smith,* J. & A. Churchill (1920).

Smith, Mark S., *The Origins of Biblical Monotheism: Israel's Polytheistic Background and the Ugaritic Texts,* Oxford: Oxford University Press (2001).

Smith, Mark, *Gods, goddesses, and images of God in ancient Israel,* Keel & Uehlinger (1998).

Smith, Mark, *The Origins of Biblical Monotheism: Israel's Polytheistic Background and the Ugaritic Texts,* Oxford University Press (2001).

Smith, Richard Morris (aka T. Lloyd Stanley) *An Outline of the Future Religion of the World With a Consideration of the Facts and Doctrines on which it Will Probably be Based* (1884).

Smith, William Walter, *The Students' Illustrated Historical Geography of the Holy Land,* The Sunday School Times Company (1911).

Solodokin, Loriel, "Mandrakes: A Mystical Plant or Legitimate Herbal Remedy?" *Women in Science* Vol. XIV, Yeshiva University (2010).

Southworth, Franklin C., *Linguistic Archaeology of South Asia,* Routledge (2005).

Spencer, William, *Iraq: Old Land, New Nation in Conflict,* Twenty-First Century Books (2000).

Spong, John Shelby, *Rescuing the Bible from Fundamentalism: A Bishop Rethinks this Meaning of Script*, Harper San Francisco (1991).

Stein, Diana, "Psychedelics and the Ancient Near East," *Ancient Near East Today* (2014).

Stein, Diana, "The Role of Stimulants in Early Near Eastern Society Insights through Artifacts and Texts," *At the Dawn of History* (2017).

Stein, Diana, "Winged Disks and Sacred Trees," *Studies on the Civilization and Culture of Nuzi and the Hurrians,* vol. 18 (2009).

Stoneman, Richard, *The Greek Experience of India: From Alexander to the Indo-Greeks,* Princeton University Press (2019).

Storl, Wolf-Dieter, *Shiva: The Wild God of Power and Ecstasy,* Inner Traditions (2004).

Strange, Thomas Lumisden, *The Legends of the Old Testament: traced to their apparent primitive sources,* Trübner (1874).

Strong's Exhaustive Concordance of the Bible, Thomas Nelson Inc. (1979).

Stuckey, Johanna H., "Asherah and the God of the Early Israelites," *MatriFocus, A Cross-Quarterly Web Magazine for Goddess Women Near & Far,* Vol 3-4, Lammas (2004).

Suares, Carlos, *The Cipher of Genesis,* Samuel Weiser Inc. (1992).

Suliman, Noor Azuin; Taib,Che Norma Mat; Moklas, Mohamad Aris Mohd; Basir, Rusliza, 'Delta-9-Tetrahydrocannabinol (Δ9-THC) Induce Neurogenesis and Improve Cognitive Performances of Male Sprague Dawley Rats' https://pubmed.ncbi.nlm.nih.gov/28933048/ (2017).

Sun, Andrew J. MD and Eisenberg, Michael L. MD, "Association Between Marijuana Use and Sexual Frequency in the United States: A Population-Based Study," *The Journal of Sexual Medicine* (2017).

"Surprising 5,000-Year-Old Cannabis Trade: Eurasian Steppe Nomads Were Earliest Pot Dealers" (*Ancient Origins*).

Swamy, B.G.L., "The Rg Vedic Soma Plant," *Indian Journal of History of Science* (1976).

Taheri, Sadreddin, "Plant of life, in Ancient Iran, Mesopotamia & Egypt," *Tehran: Honarhay-e Ziba Journal,* Vol. 18 (2013).

Tannahill, Reay, *Sex in History,* Stien & Day (1980).

Taraporewala,, I.J.S., *The Religion of Zarathushtra,* Madras (1926).

Taylor, Joan E., "The Asherah, the Menorah and the Sacred Tree," *Journal for the Study of the Old Testament* (1995).

Tengwen; Wagner; Demske; Leipe; Tarasov, "Cannabis in Eurasia: origin of human use and Bronze Age trans-continental connections," *Vegetation History and Archaeobotany* (2016).

Terrien, Samuel, "The Omphalos Myth and Hebrew Religion," *Vestus Testamentum* 20, no.3, (1970).

The Medical News (1896).

Thompson, R. Campbell, *Devils and Evil Spirits of Babylonia: Being Babylonian and Assyrian Incantations Against the Demons, Ghouls, Vampires, Hobglobins, Ghosts, and Kindred Evil Spirits, which Attack Mankind,* (1903).

Thompson, R.C. "Assyrian prescriptions for treating bruises or swellings," *American Journal of Semitic Languages and Literatures* (1930).

Thompson, R.C. "Assyrian prescriptions for diseases of the feet. Royal Asiatic Society of Great Britain and Ireland: 265-286, 413-432. (1937) (as noted by Russo).

Thompson, R.C. & Hutchinson, R.W., *A Century of Exploration at Nineveh*, Luzac, London (1929).

Thompson, R.C., "A Babylonian Explanatory Text. Royal Asiatic Society of Great Britain and Ireland," (1924).

Thompson, R.C., "An Assyrian chemist's vade-mecum," *Journal of the Royal Asiatic Society of Great Britain and Ireland.*: 771-785. (1934).

Thompson, R.C., "Assyrian medical prescriptions against Simmatu *poison*," *Revue d'Assyriologie et d'Archéologie Orientale*(1930).

Thompson, R.C., "Assyrian medical prescriptions for diseases of the stomach," *Revue d'Assyriologie et d'Archéologie Orientale* (1929).

Thompson, R.C., "Assyrian prescriptions for diseases of the chest and lungs," *Revue d'Assyriologie et d'Archéologie Orientale*(1934).

Thompson, R.C., "Assyrian prescriptions for diseases of the urine, etc.," *Babyloniaca* 14 (1934).

Thompson, R.C., "Assyrian prescriptions for the *hand of a ghost*," *Journal of the Royal Asiatic Society of Great Britain and Ireland* (1929).

Thompson, R.C., *A Dictionary of Assyrian Botany*, British Academy, London (1949).

Thompson, R.C., *A Dictionary of Assyrian Chemistry and Geology*, Clarendon Press, Oxford (1936).

Thompson, R.C., *Assyrian medical texts from the originals in the British Museum*, Oxford University Press, London (1923)

Thompson, R.C., *Cuneiform texts from Babylonian tablets in the British Museum, Part XIV*. British Museum, London (1902)

Thompson, R.C., *The Assyrian Herbal*, Luzac and Co., London. (1924).

Thompson, R.C., "Assyrain prescriptions for diseases of the ears." *Journal of the Royal Asiatic Society of Great Britain and Ireland*,1-23. (as noted by Russo).

Thorndike, Lynn, *A History of Magic and Experimental Science* (1923).

Thorwald, Jürgen, *Science and Secrets of Early Medicine: Egypt, Mesopotamia, India, China, Mexico, Peru*, Harcourt, Brace & World (1963).

Tronetti, Francesca, Phd., "The Queen of Heaven: Depictions of Asherah in Ancient Israel," https://www.academia.edu/60216219/The_Queen_of_Heaven_Depictions_of_Asherah_in_Ancient_Israel (2020).

Tully, Caroline, "Do the Judean Pillar Figurines Represent the Goddess Asherah?," *Anointed: A Devotional Anthology for the Deities of the Near and Middle East*. Ed. Tess Dawson, Bibliotheca Alexandrina (2011).

Underwood, E. Ashwort and Singer, Charles, *A Short History of Medicine* (1962).

Valeri, Andrea and Mazzon, Emanuela, "Cannabinoids and Neurogenesis: The Promised Solution for Neurodegeneration?" https://pubmed.ncbi.nlm.nih.gov/34684894/ Molecules. (2021).

Van Baaren, Theodorus Petrus & Hartman, Sven S., *Iconography of Religions*, (1980).

van der Toorn, Karel, *et. al.*, *Dictionary of Deities and Demons in the Bible* (1999).

Vartavan, Christian & Amoros, Victoria Asensi, *Codex of Ancient Egyptian Plant Remains*, Triade (1997).

Vicchio, Stephen J., *Job in the Ancient World* (2006).

Victor, Tanya; Hage, Zachary; Tsirka, Stella. "Prophylactic Administration of Cannabidiol Reduces Microglial Inflammatory Response to Kainate-Induced Seizures and Neurogenesis" https://pubmed.ncbi.nlm.nih.gov/35700815/ Neuroscience (2022).

Vikramasiṃha, *Glimpses of Indian Culture*, Kitab Mahal (1967).

Virey, Joseph, *Bulletin de Pharmacie* (1813).

Walker, Barbara G., *The Woman's Encyclopedia of Myths and Secrets*, Harper Collins (1983).

Walker, Barbara, *The Woman's Book of Myths and Secrets*, Harper Collins (1986).

Walker, Kenneth, *The Story of Medicine*, Oxford University Press (1955).

Walton, Robert P. M.D. as quoted in, *Licit and Illicit Drugs* (1972).

Walton,R.P., *Marihuana*, Philadelphia: J. P. Lippincott (1938).

Waradpande, N.R., *The RgVedic Soma* (1995).

Ward, James, *Historic ornament : treatise on decorative art and architectural ornament, pottery, enamels, ivories, metalwork, furniture, textile fabrics, mosaics, glass and book decoration*, Chapman and Hall, (1897).

'Was Marijuana the Original Cash Crop?, (*Men's Journal*).

Wasson, Robert Gordon; Kramrisch, Stella; Ott, Jonathan, *Persephone's Quest: Entheogens and the Origins of Religion*, Yale (1986).

Watt, George, *Selections from the Records of the Government of India, Revenue and Agricultural Department: 1888-89* (1889).

Watt, John and Charles, *The Chemist* (1853).

Weil, Andrew; *The Natural Mind*, (1972) Revised edition, Houghton Mifflin Company Boston (1986).

Wenk, Gary, Dr., "The Intersection of Medicine and Religion: The medical benefits of cannabis in ancient anointing oils," *Psychology Today*, https://www.psychologytoday.com/ca/blog/your-brain-food/202201/the-intersection-medicine-and-religion (2022).

Wheeler, Brannon M. and Noegel, Scott B., *The A to Z of Prophets in Islam and Judaism*, Scarecrow Press (2010).

White, Ellen, Ph.D., "Asherah and the Asherim: Goddess or Cult Symbol?" https://www.biblicalarchaeology.org/daily/ancient-cultures/ancient-israel/asherah-and-the-asherim-goddess-or-cult-symbol/ (2021).

White, Gavin, *Babylonian Star-Lore: An Illustrated Guide to the Star-lore and Constel-*

lations of Ancient Babylonia, Lulu.com, (2008).

Widengren, G., Stand und Aufgaben der iranischen Religionsgeschichte, Numen 2, (1955).

Widengren, Geo, *Die Religionen Irans*, Kohlhammer, Stuttgart (1965).

Wiggins, Steve, "Asherah," https://steveawiggins.com/category/asherah/ (2021).

Wiggins, Steve, *A Reassessment of Asherah: With Further Considerations of the Goddess*, Gorgias Press (2007)

Wiggins, Steve, "A Reassessment of 'Asherah': A Study According to the Textual Sources of the First Two Millennia B.C.E." (1993).

Wilkinson, John Gardner and Birch, Samuel, *The Manners and Customs of the Ancient Egyptians* (1878).

Wilkinson, Richard H., *The Complete Gods and Goddesses of Ancient Egypt*, WW Norton (2003).

William, J.G., "Eden, the Tree of Life and the Wisdom of the Serpent," https://bibleinterp.arizona.edu/articles/2018/05/wil428023 (2018).

Wills, Simon, "Cannabis Use and Abuse by Man: An Historical Perspective," *Cannabis: The Genus Cannabis*, Edited By David T. Brown, CRC Press (1998).

Wilson, Epiphanius, *Babylonian and Assyrian Literature: Comprising the Epic of Izdubar, Hymns, Tablets, and Cuneiform Inscriptions*, Volume 45 (1901).

Wilson, H.H., *Rig-Veda*, Poona, India, Ashtekar (1928).

Wilson, Robert Anton, *Sex & Drugs*, Playboy Press (1973).

Wine Spectator article "2,000-Year-Old Cannabis Wine Discovered," (2018).

Winternitz, Maurice V. and Sarma, Srinivasa, *A History of Indian Literature*, Translated by V. Srinivasa Sarma, Motilal Banarsidass Publ., (1996).

Witzel, M., "Early sources for South Asian substrate languages, Mother Tongue,"(1999).

Witzel, Michael, "Aryan and non-Aryan Names in Vedic India. Data for the linguistic situation, c. 1900-500 B.C.," Harvard University (1999).

Yule, Henry and Crooke, William, *A Glossary of Colloquial Anglo-Indian Words and Phrases* (1903).

Zaehner, R.C., *The Dawn and Twilight of Zoroastrianism*, G.P. Putnam's Sons (1961).

Zevit, Ziony, *The Religions of Ancient Israel: A Synthesis of Parallactic Approaches*, Bloomsbury Academic (2001).

Zias J, Stark H, Sellgman J, Levy R, Werker E, Breuer A, Mechoulam R. "Early medical use of cannabis," *Nature*, 1993.

Zias J. In: Campbell S, Green A, eds., *The Archaeology of Death in the Ancient Near East*, Oxford, UK: Oxbow Books, (1995).

Zias, Joel, Personal Correspondence, Oct.02, (2005).

Zohary, Daniel and Hopf, Maria, *Domestication of Plants in the Old World: The Origin and Spread of Cultivated Plants in West Asia, Europe, and the Nile Valley*, Oxford University Press (2000).